Samurai Armour

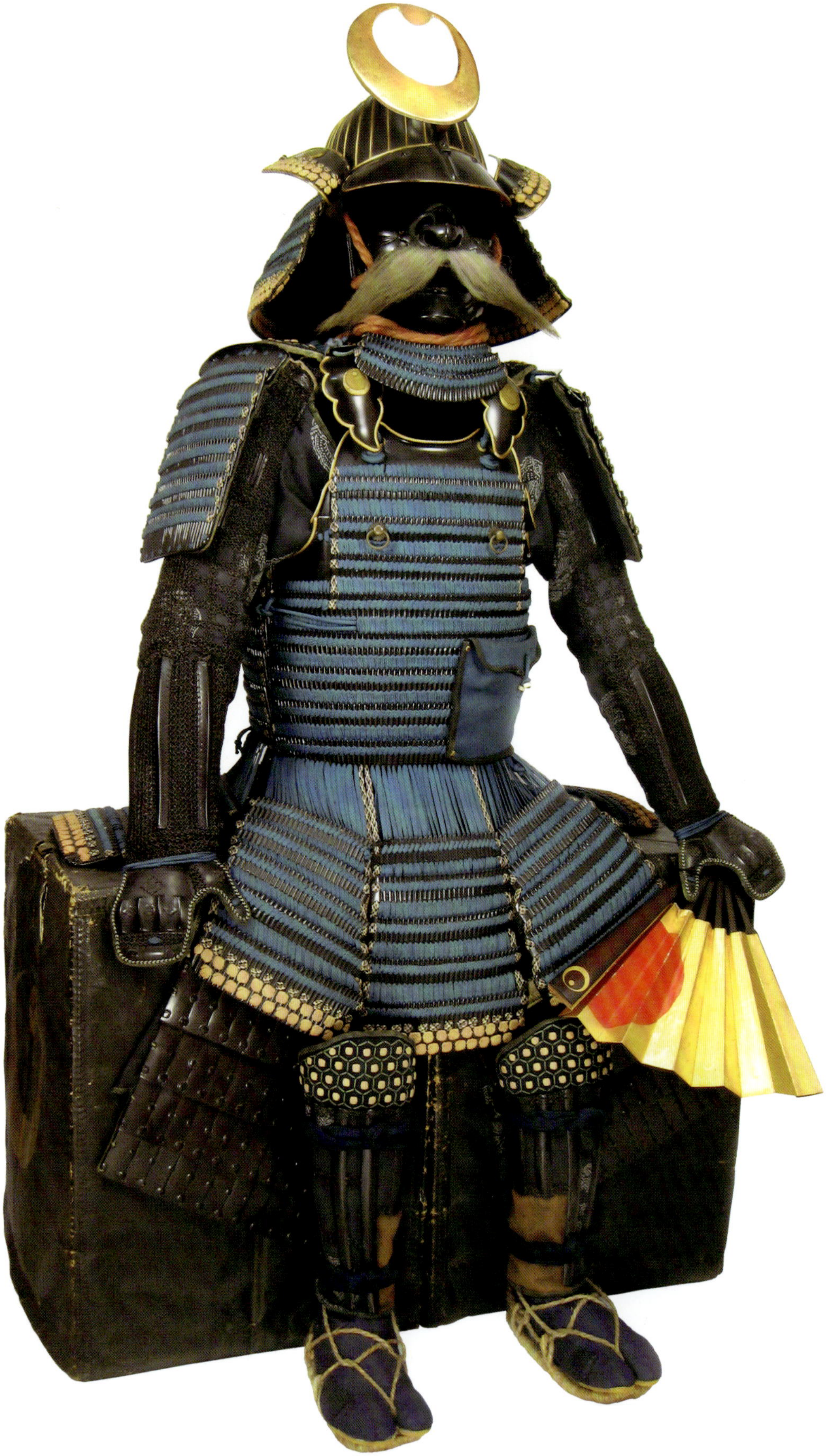

Samurai Armour

VOLUME I: THE JAPANESE CUIRASS

TREVOR ABSOLON

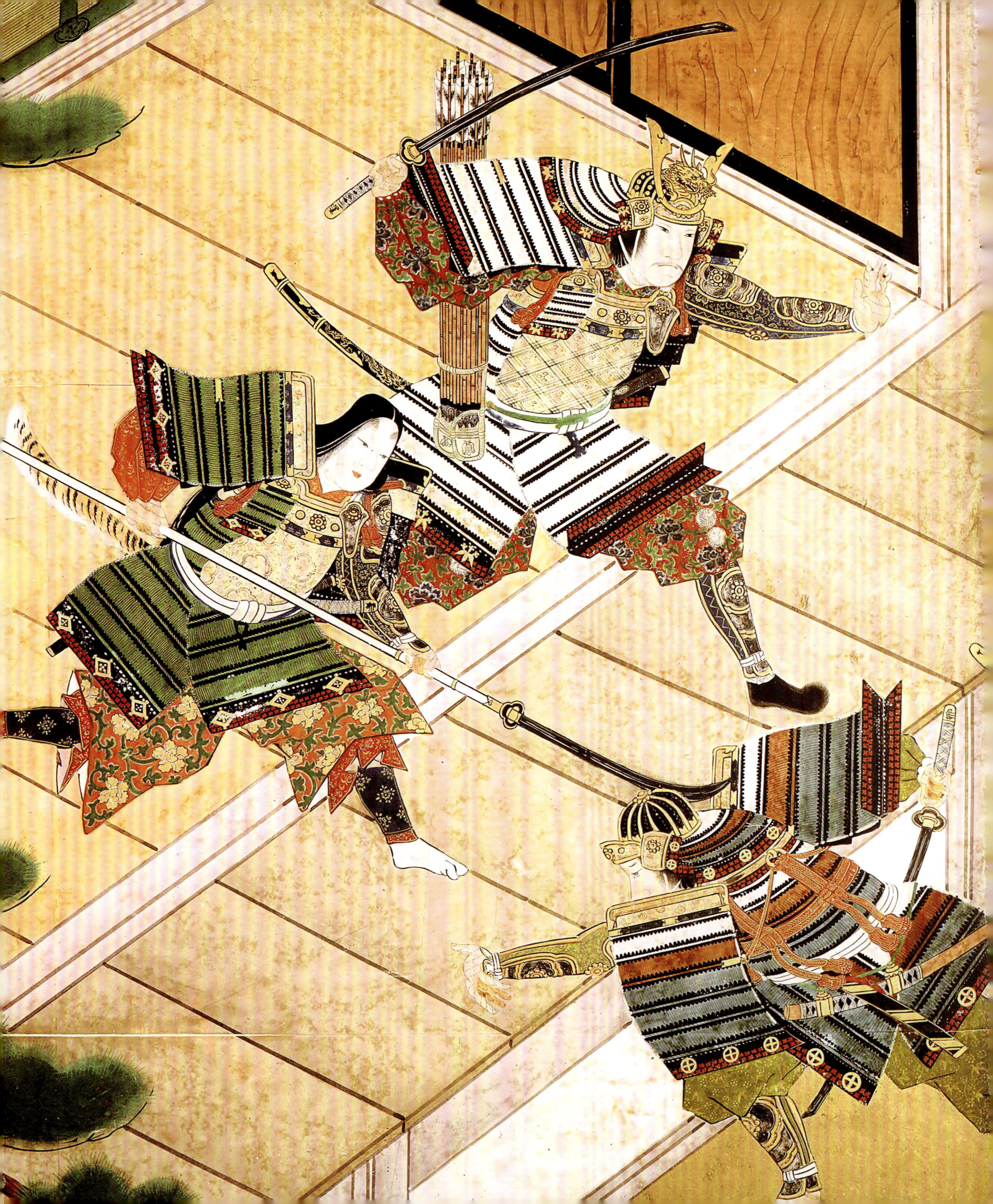

To my loving wife and children, who patiently missed out on so much without complaint while they supported me through the writing of this book.

&

In memory of Anthony Bryant, 1961–2013, with whom this book was originally to have been co-written. I'm sure this book is lacking for your absence, Anthony.

Osprey Publishing
c/o Bloomsbury Publishing Plc
PO Box 883, Oxford, OX1 9PL, UK
or
c/o Bloomsbury Publishing Plc
1385 Broadway, 5th Floor, New York, NY 10018, USA

E-mail: info@ospreypublishing.com

www.ospreypublishing.com

OSPREY is a trademark of Osprey Publishing, a division of Bloomsbury Publishing Plc.

First published in Great Britain in 2017

© 2017 (Trevor Absolon)

All rights reserved. No part of this publication may be used or reproduced in any form without the prior written permission except in the case of brief quotations embodied in critical articles and reviews. Enquiries should be addressed to the Publisher.

Every attempt has been made by the Publisher to secure the appropriate permissions for material reproduced in this book. If there has been any oversight we will be happy to rectify the situation and written submission should be made to the Publisher.

A CIP catalogue record for this book is available from the British Library.

Trevor Absolon has asserted his right under the Copyright, Designs and Patents Act, 1988, to be identified as the Author of this Work.

ISBN: HB: 9781472807960
ePub: 9781472822253
ePDF: 9781472822246
XML: 9781472822239

17 18 19 20 21   10 9 8 7 6 5 4 3 2 1

Index by Zoe Ross
Typeset in Adobe Garamond and Myriad Pro
Page layout by Myriam Bell Design, UK
Originated by PDQ Digital Media Solutions, Bungay, UK
Printed in China through C&C Offset Ltd

EDITOR'S NOTE
All quotations from Japanese language source material are translated into English by Trevor Absolon.

IMAGE ACKNOWLEDGEMENTS
All line drawings and artwork unless otherwise accredited were commissioned from and produced by Brian Snoddy, an exceptional artist and valued friend.

All images and photographs are from the author's personal archive unless otherwise accredited.

Front cover: A cuirass made in the *yokohagi-okegawa-dō* style.

Back cover: An outstanding 18th century set of armour assembled around a cuirass constructed in the style of a 14th century *yoroi*. (New York Metropolitan Museum of Art/CC0 1.0)

Half-title page: A historically accurate reproduction of the Japanese National Treasure *aka odoshi ō-yoroi*. The original armour is said to have belonged to the famous 12th century Genpei War samurai Hatakeyama Shigetada. (Ōme Municipal Museum of Provincial History)

Title page: An outstanding example of a mid-18th century *kebiki odoshi*-laced *kiritsuke kozane ni-mai-dō gusoku*.

Dedication page: *Legend of Muge Hoju no Tama*. Detail of a Japanese folding screen of the 18th century, at the Museum of Eastern Art in Venice, Italy. (Photo by Roger Viollet/Getty Images)

Osprey Publishing supports the Woodland Trust, the UK's leading woodland conservation charity. Between 2014 and 2018 our donations are being spent on their Centenary Woods project in the UK.

To find out more about our authors and books visit **www.ospreypublishing.com**. Here you will find extracts, author interviews, details of forthcoming events and the option to sign up for our newsletter.

CONTENTS

	FOREWORD	8
	PREFACE	10
	INTRODUCTION	22
CHAPTER 1:	JAPANESE HISTORY AND THE SAMURAI Prehistoric era to the early 17th century	32
CHAPTER 2:	THE *DŌ* (CUIRASS) The foundation of Japanese armour	52
CHAPTER 3:	ANCIENT ARMOUR *Tankō, keikō, uchikake-keikō* and *men'ōchū*, 2nd century BC–9th century AD	76
CHAPTER 4:	EARLY FORMS OF SAMURAI ARMOUR *Yoroi, dō-maru, maru-dō, haramaki* and *hara-ate*, 10th–15th centuries	102
CHAPTER 5:	PRE-MODERN *DŌ* DESIGNS The *Mōgami, nuinobe* and *tatami* methods, late 15th–16th centuries	182
CHAPTER 6:	*TOSEI-DŌ* MODERN CUIRASS DESIGNS, PART I *Yokohagi-okegawa* and related styles of *dō*, 16th century onward	208
CHAPTER 7:	*TOSEI-DŌ* MODERN CUIRASS DESIGNS, PART II *Tatehagi-okegawa* and related styles of *dō*, 16th century onward	248
CHAPTER 8:	*TOSEI-DŌ* MODERN CUIRASS DESIGNS, PART III *Ashigaru, tatami* and variations	274
CHAPTER 9:	COMING FULL CIRCLE The revival of ancient armour styles, 17th–19th centuries	310
CHAPTER 10:	THE WESTERNIZATION OF JAPANESE ARMOUR 19th–early 20th centuries	324
	NOTES	344
	BIBLIOGRAPHY	346
	IMAGE SOURCES	348
	GLOSSARY	349
	INDEX	366

A very high quality mid-17th century *kebiki odoshi hon kozane ni-mai-dō gusoku* that was made for a senior member of the powerful Matsudaira clan, who were closely related with the ruling Tokugawa Shōguns.

FOREWORD

It is indeed an honour and pleasure to be asked by Trevor Absolon to write a foreword for his new publication. I have known Trevor for nearly ten years and during that time he collaborated with me on an exhibition in 2010 which focused on samurai arms and armour at the Art Gallery of Greater Victoria in British Columbia, Canada. He generously loaned many examples from his own collection and kindly offered his expertise for making the exhibition a major success with the public. Trevor has also donated some important samurai paraphernalia to our art museum including a magnificent helmet (*kabuto*), a face protector (*menpo*), sections of armour and four important samurai banners/standards (*sashimono*).

Trevor Absolon's book provides a new and refreshing look at the military history of Japan and the improvement of samurai armour through the ages. His absorbing examination of a complex theme provides us not only with a wealth of knowledge but also much new and interesting research material. The book makes a serious attempt to trace the development, influences, exchanges and the perfection of early Japan's protective armour, and is vital to understanding the subject. Trevor's new perspectives and spontaneous writing style provide us with a fascinating read. It will no doubt become an important reference book in the future for all those who love the subject matter of Japan's great warriors, the samurai.

Trevor's wonderful historical narrative is accompanied by a brilliant array of works of art and detailed illustrations of samurai armour. He has chosen the images well, not only for their beauty and story-telling but also in the case of armour for its practical usage in battle and for its symbolism and pageantry. Connoisseurs of the military arts will no doubt be satisfied with this marvellous presentation. I warmly and enthusiastically recommend this book.

Barry Till
Curator of Asian Art (1981–2017)
Art Gallery of Greater Victoria,
British Columbia, Canada

A superb *kinpaku nuri hon kozane ni-mai-dō* from the late 16th century.

PREFACE

Military items have interested me for as long as I can remember. How far this interest would have carried, however, is hard to say, had I not become childhood friends with a boy from England. As it turned out my friend had also lived in Belgium for a number of years near the town of Waterloo, where the last great climactic battle of the Napoleonic Wars had been fought in 1815. Naturally he was quite fascinated by this fact, as most boys would be if they grew up in a town where they were daily exposed to pictures, postcards and places that heralded the deeds and deaths of brightly uniformed soldiers and famous historical personalities.

Needless to say, I was suitably impressed with his collection of historical picture-books, toy soldiers and other novelty items associated with Napoleon's final battle when he first showed them to me. So much so, that I soon found myself reading every book I could lay my hands on that had anything to do with Napoleon and the Napoleonic Wars. My friend's collection turned out to be the catalyst that sparked my lifelong fascination for history and passion for the collecting of historical items.

Over time my interests have broadened, to the point that I would like to think I am fairly well versed in a broad range of historical topics, time periods, and personalities, though clearly my knowledge is significantly stronger in some areas than in others.

One of the by-products of my deep interest in historical subjects was that I also became an avid collector of antiques, which I found to be an immensely satisfying pastime. In fact, my passion for history and the collecting of antiques, which has seen me amass sizeable collections of everything from Prussian pickelhaubes to regimental Scottish sporrans, ultimately metamorphosed into a successful full-time business, through which over the years I have bought and sold everything from the personal effects of Eva Braun to documents signed by Napoleon I. This is why it is somewhat ironic that my ultimate area of expertise has ended up being in the rather obscure and unrelated field of the study of Japanese samurai armour.

Irrespective of this strange twist of fate, antiques to me have always been an invaluable tool in furthering my understanding of history. For the greater the physical interaction one can have with historical items from a certain period or genre, the greater one's comprehension of that period or genre will be, assuming that one is already well versed in that particular era and subject matter.

For example, a person who has seen a late-18th century British Brown Bess musket is going to have a better level of comprehension when reading about the battlefield experiences of a British soldier of the Napoleonic Wars than someone who has not. Their level of comprehension will be further elevated if they have had a chance to hold a Brown Bess. For in doing so they can now better relate to the Napoleonic soldier's experience and appreciate what it would have been like to have to carry a heavy, unwieldy weapon like the Brown Bess around as a soldier. Have that person load and fire the musket and their comprehension will again be significantly more intimate than that of a person who has only held one.

In this regard I have been exceptionally lucky, particularly when it has come to authentic items of Japanese samurai armour, as I have had the opportunity to hold many tens of thousands of individual pieces in my hands and closely examine them over the years. While my experience did not simply come about as the result of good luck, I'm aware of just how lucky I have been. For while I'm not alone in this regard, I'm conscious of how few people have had the opportunity that I have had to be so up close and intimate with such a huge number of authentic pieces of samurai armour and how this experience has honed my understanding of this complex subject matter in a way that could never be achieved simply by reading or viewing these items via visual reference material.

I'm also well aware of just how bare the cupboards are when it comes to quality reference material on Japanese armour. While a considerable number of books on this subject exists, I know from experience that the majority of them are at best little more than alternative presentations of any number of previously published books, and while my personal library consists of well over 200 such titles, I could probably whittle this number down to fewer than twenty books and feel that I was not depriving myself of a significant amount of important information. Sadly, of the books that would remain, the majority would be texts that are only available in Japanese, due to the simple fact that only a handful of truly authoritative books on this subject matter have ever been produced in languages other than Japanese.

There are several reasons why this is the case, the most obvious of which is that it is extremely challenging to write about another culture's history, particularly when the culture in question is as distinct and unique as is Japanese culture. Compounding any such efforts are the considerable complexities associated with the Japanese language, which is widely recognized as being one of the most difficult languages in the world to learn to speak, let alone read and write. Thus even before one can start, there are a multitude of substantial barriers to overcome before the non-native-speaker student of Japanese armour can begin to access the information that exists on this subject in Japan.

For this reason alone, it is easy to appreciate why so few good books on the subject of Japanese armour have been released outside Japan. Furthermore, while there may be a large number of people with a passion to learn about these items, the number of non-native Japanese individuals who actually become proficient enough to study this subject in Japanese is extremely limited in number; of these, the number who can or will take the time and effort to document in English the knowledge they have gained in a book is even smaller still.

While proficiency in the Japanese language allows one access to a much greater level of knowledge than is available in any other pool of source material on the subject of Japanese armour, it is surprisingly not quite the informational utopia that one would expect.

While many aspects of the history of Japan and the samurai were meticulously documented, surprisingly little has survived of original period documents and information directly related to how Japanese armour was constructed. Considering that samurai armour was produced in its various forms by the Japanese for over a millennium, the scarcity of such material is something of an enigma.

It would be easy to understand the lack of information if its absence was proportional to the passage of time, with there being relatively little historical documentation about the items that were produced in the 10th century, while volumes of information were available in regards to the pieces that were produced at the start of the 19th century. Strangely, however, this is not the case, which is rather unfortunate. And while volumes of original period documents are

Preface

What was it about the making of samurai armour that caused it to be so poorly documented? After all, the Japanese were still producing samurai armour at the start of the 19th century just as they had done for almost a millennium, unhindered by and for the most part totally unaware of the sweeping changes that would turn their world upside down half a century later.

While I'm painting with large strokes, the answer to this mystery most likely lies in the fact that the production of Japanese armour began and ended largely as a cottage industry, with a few minor exceptions. And while certain clans at certain points in Japanese history dictated that their warriors would wear armour that conformed with a certain finished look, such as the red lacquer armours that were favoured by the samurai of Hikone, or the five-piece sectional cuirasses that were utilized by the warriors of the powerful Date clan fiefdom, or *han*, these items were never produced by a centralized source on an industrial scale.

As such the Japanese armour maker was very much an independent artisan who had a vested interest in limiting the amount of information that he shared with other craftsmen about his trade. And while there were guilds, and Japanese armour makers did work with each other on various levels, such as the buying of prefabricated parts from other smiths who specialized in the production of certain pieces, in general the production of samurai armour never evolved beyond the level of a relatively small cottage industry in Japan, where knowledge of the trade was passed directly from one generation to the next via a teacher–apprentice relationship.

While this practice ensured the livelihood of many generations of armour makers and their supporting artisans, from a historical perspective it was a flawed process that lacked foresight. For when Japan's feudal period came to its sudden and arguably unforeseen end in the late 1860s with the warrior class inadvertently toppling itself from power after a millennium of control over the country, the need for samurai armour evaporated

A period illustration of a typical armour maker's shop. The production of samurai armour was at best a cottage industry in feudal Japan. Much of the knowledge of the craft was limited to a relatively small number of craftsmen working in various associated guilds. The skills required were not written down but were passed on via master–apprentice relationships. This continuous link was broken when Japan began to modernize in the 1870s, as the number of young men wanting to apprentice in what was quickly coming to be seen as an archaic and dying trade rapidly began to dwindle. A considerable amount of important information about samurai armour was therefore lost to history at the end of the 19th century as most of the former armour makers from Japan's feudal period passed away un-apprenticed, and largely unappreciated as the last practitioners of a bygone trade.

available on the various details of the uniforms that were worn by French soldiers during the Napoleonic Wars for example, extremely little exists when it comes to contemporary-period items of Japanese armour.

almost overnight. Suddenly the carefully hoarded knowledge that the armour makers had relied on for several centuries to sustain themselves had become a worthless commodity.

This spectacular reversal of events, which had seen Japan turned upside down and inside out in little more than a decade, left the armour makers scrambling to make ends meet, which most did by using their existing skill sets to make other items. Naturally only the most marketable and relevant of their former armour-making abilities were passed on to their post-feudal period apprentices, which meant that a large percentage of the knowledge related to the making of samurai armour was lost during the waning years of the 19th century as the last generation of smiths who had actually produced armour for the warrior class faded into history.

Sadly, very few people saw any point in bothering to ask the surviving armour makers to document what they knew about Japanese armour in the decades following the demise of the samurai. For most people could see no value in recording information about obsolete items as archaic as samurai armour was considered to be during Japan's hectic post-feudal period rush to catch up to the industrialized Western nations.

Ironically, the groups who did the most to preserve samurai armour were the two groups that most samurai found the most offensive, entrepreneurial merchants and foreigners, the latter of whom were fascinated by the idea that a class of noble hereditary warriors had existed in Japan until the modern age. Partially through a lack of reliable information and largely as a result of wilful ignorance, Westerners created a

A posed image of late 19th century Japanese curio shop. Though staged, this image clearly illustrates how a considerable portion of the armour and equipment of the abolished warrior classes ended up being pawned off by their former owners in order to make ends meet. This photograph also demonstrates the interest Westerners, for whom these images were produced, had in both this sort of shop and the merchandise available. (Photo by T. Enami / Wikimedia Commons / Public Domain)

persona for the samurai that equated them with the highly romanticized 19th century concept of the chivalrous medieval European knight.

The ever-astute Japanese curio dealers were quick to capitalize on the influx of Western tourists and their fascination with the former warrior class and did all they could to accommodate them with suitable souvenirs, one of the most popular of which was a full set of samurai armour. These they acquired for a fraction of their original value from financially desperate former members of the defunct warrior class, large numbers of whom were forced to sell off the trappings of their lost social status to make ends meet.

As with businessmen anywhere, the Japanese merchants did what they had to do to close a sale. If spinning the truth or fabricating the facts was what it took to keep their customers satisfied, then that is what they did. The foreigners who acquired these items were for the most part both willing and ignorant enough about the facts in relation to Japanese armour not to feel the need to challenge or doubt what they were being told. And as the former samurai and armour makers had almost no involvement with these transactions, very little in the way of accurate information accompanied the sets of armour that worked their way abroad to join the curio cabinet collections of the wealthy of Western society.

Again, while painting in broad strokes, the point is that while samurai armour had existed in various forms for over a millennium, it was never a particularly well-documented subject or a topic that was well understood by more than a small percentage of Japanese society. Those with knowledge on this subject found themselves the trustees of what was almost universally thought to be a worthless commodity in post-feudal period Japan, and as such, mostly severed their connections with samurai armour, a void that was filled by astute entrepreneurs. To the entrepreneurs, armour was a commodity that didn't require more than a cursory understanding to market to foreigners. From the perspective of the Western tourists, the vendors would have appeared extremely knowledgeable, for they would have known most of the key words and terminology related to samurai armour simply because they were Japanese. And as native Japanese, it was assumed by their foreign clientele that by default the vendors were somehow experts on those items, a mistake that is still commonly made today. Thus almost from the beginning misinformation, unintentional or not, has distorted a significant part of the Western understanding of the subject of Japanese armour.

Unfortunately, as with most subjects, the earliest reference sources play a significant role in the future perspective on a specific topic, and as earlier sources are referenced and re-referenced by scholars of later generations the information in the early sources becomes increasingly difficult to refute.

This situation has been compounded when it comes to the study of Japanese armour by the fact that very few Westerners have specialized in the study of samurai armour. And of these only

Dr Bashford Dean (1867–1928), an American zoological professor, photographed wearing a set of samurai armour from his personal collection. Dean became deeply immersed in the study of Japanese armour while visiting Japan in the 1890s on scientific trips, and by 1900 had collected over 125 samurai-related items. His collection was the largest of its kind in the US at that time and became the foundation of the New York Metropolitan Museum's Japanese Arms and Armour Collection in 1904. Additional contributions by Dean made the Metropolitan's collection of samurai items the most comprehensive one in the world outside Japan by 1927. (Image © and courtesy of the New York Metropolitan Museum of Art: Image source: Art Resource, NY)

a handful have been able to speak the Japanese language or had experience living in that culture. Many Western scholars have thus been forced to rely on the existing works of other Western scholars to supply the reference material for their texts on samurai armour and, as a result, very few Western texts have been able to take the study of Japanese armour to higher levels.

Though I'm conscious of the fact that I'm not alone in possessing these skill sets, I am one of the few non-Japanese with a deep interest in Japanese armour who both speaks the Japanese language and has lived in Japan for a large part of my life. Where my experience becomes increasingly specialized, however, is that my chosen profession for many years provided me with an almost unrivalled opportunity to study a huge number of authentic pieces of Japanese samurai armour first hand. And while the theoretical study of samurai armour in both English and Japanese had formed an essential part of my fundamental understanding of this topic, it was my regular access to a huge number of authentic items of armour made in different styles and from various periods that helped to crystallize my understanding of this subject matter.

Rounding out my understanding of Japanese armour was one other unique experience, which was my participation in the Soma Noma-oi, the last authentic samurai festival still held in Japan. One of Japan's best-kept secrets, the soon to be 1,100-year-old Soma Noma-oi Festival is largely unknown even to most Japanese, even though it is designated as one of that country's Important Cultural Heritage Events. Said to have been started by the famous samurai Taira no Masakado in the 10th century, the Soma Noma-oi was originally a rigorous training event that Masakado used to hone the equestrian skills of his warriors. This event eventually morphed into a full-scale mobilization drill that helped ensure the samurai of Soma (part of present-day Fukushima Prefecture) could quickly rally to the defence of their domain.

The rural isolation of the Soma *han* allowed the clan to disregard many of the official state dictates that originated from the new post-feudal period Meiji government prohibiting the continued observance of feudal practices such as those that were at the very heart of the Soma *han*'s traditions. The Soma *han* was not in a time lock, but they did manage to protect this ancient tradition, which they continue to observe annually to this day, and while the modern-day event has metamorphosed into a festival, it is the single most historically accurate samurai training event still conducted anywhere in the world.

For this reason, I was immensely proud when I was allowed to join the festival, which I participated in for several years. Other non-Japanese have participated in the Soma Noma-oi over the years, but I am the only one of these to have earned an official rank in this event, that of *tsukai-ban*, or messenger, and while humble, it was a significant honour all the same. It was made that much better by the fact that I was acting in the service of the

The author wearing a *kiritsuke-kozane kebiki odoshi ni-mai-dō gusoku* during the prestigious Soma Noma-oi Festival. Designated an Important Cultural Heritage Event, the Soma Noma-oi, or 'Wild Horse Chase' festival is one of the last authentic samurai events still held in Japan. Dating back to the 10th century, this incredible event has been held annually for more than a millennium. The descendants of the founder of the festival, the famous Taira no Masakado, now in their thirty-fifth generation, still preside over this amazing historical event each year. The author was the first non-Japanese person to earn a formal position in this ancient event, where he served in the *daimyō*'s entourage as a *tsukai-ban*, or messenger to the *hatamoto*, who was the personal bodyguard of the Soma clan lord. Correctly wearing armour and riding horses using traditional horse furnishings is an essential part of this gruelling three-day event.

Left: Soma Michitane, the thirty-fourth Lord of Soma, a direct bloodline descendant of the famous 10th century warrior Taira no Masakado, who was a key figure in the evolution of the samurai class. Masakado also established the traditions that evolved into the modern Soma Noma-oi Festival, the last authentic samurai festival still held in Japan. (Image © and courtesy of the photographer Everett Kennedy Brown)

Right: Soma Yoritane, the younger brother of Michitane, wearing one of the Soma family's heirloom *gusoku*, which includes a 15th century *kabuto*. The Soma family continue to preside over and paricipate annually in the Soma Noma-oi Festival as they have done for several centuries, in their ancestral domain in Fukushima.

hatamoto, or bodyguard, to the *daimyō*, who was the 36th unbroken bloodline descendant of Taira no Masakado and thus descended from all former generations of Soma *han* feudal lords.

It is almost impossible to explain the Soma Noma-oi to someone who has not experienced or seen it. But it will suffice to say that for those interested in Japanese armour, there is no better experience available. For not only is the wearing of historically accurate or original items of armour a prerequisite, such armour must also be worn properly and almost continuously throughout the day, much of which is spent galloping around on horseback surrounded by several hundred other armour-clad men, most of them descendants of the region's former samurai class.

Wearing armour and utilizing it in this manner is about as close as one can possibly hope to come to understanding something of what it must have been like to be a samurai. And while the wearing of armour would have been just one very small and rather narrow aspect of their worldly experiences, from the standpoint of those interested in the topic of Japanese armour, I can think of no other experience that is as enlightening as that of participating in the Soma Noma-oi. For it allowed me an understanding of Japanese armour that could only be gained by using it in this manner. Wearing it clarified many aspects of its design and functionality and the limitations it placed on the wearer's freedom of

SAMURAI ARMOUR

movement and overall dexterity, which one could never hope to achieve simply through the theoretical study of samurai armour or the physical study of existing pieces.

For all my knowledge on the subject of Japanese armour, the fact remains that I am not a historian – or at least not a formally educated one. I don't feel any less qualified to write on this fascinating subject matter due to my lack of institutional affiliations or official qualifications, however; on the contrary I consider this to be something of a blessing, since it allows me to present theories and opinions that are often avoided because of their political sensitivity. Free of concerns for how such opinions might affect my academic standing or potential for future funding, I'm able to shed light on theories that many consider to be taboo, particularly in Japan.

Even so, to truly understand the subject of Japanese armour, these delicate topics must be discussed, the most controversial of which surrounds the origin of the samurai. And while this book is not about the samurai, it is impossible to truly comprehend samurai armour without understanding something about the Japanese warrior class, for the two are intrinsically intertwined.

Having said this, it is important to note that my objective is not to create controversy, but to put it to rest. So much myth and misunderstanding surrounds the subject of Japanese armour that it is often difficult to discern fact from fiction. Surprisingly, a considerable degree of the blame for this dilemma, as later chapters will show, lies squarely at the feet of the former warrior class, who not only fabricated, but rather bizarrely

A beautiful 17th century *gin-paku oshi hon kozane kebiki-odoshi ni-mai-dō gusoku*. This armour typifies the 'aesthetic ideals' that the Japanese academic Ikegami Eiko observed were invariably incorporated into the items produced by the Japanese, irrespective of the utilitarian purpose for which the item was being created. While visually impressive and highly artistic, this fine *gusoku* is in fact by design a very functional, battleworthy set of armour.

18

Preface

also believed in many of the fantastical fables that they created about the armour they wore. Having said this, I am cognizant of the fact that the Japanese people during the periods being discussed lived life in a different reality from ours, which does much to justify their acceptance of many of the fables in regards to armour that will be discussed in the course of this text. In some cases, however, it is difficult to believe that people were ever capable of accepting some of the more ridiculous myths that were developed to justify and explain the existence of certain features found on items of samurai armour. And though such tales are an interesting and integral part of the history and study of the subject, it is important that anecdotal explanations be identified as such so as to prevent them from overshadowing the facts.

And while the facts are not stranger than fiction in the case of Japanese armour, they are far more fascinating. For when one stops seeing Japanese armour for what it is perceived to be, one is finally able to see it for what it really is: a brilliantly conceived and intricately crafted functional work of art. And while this is not to say that artistic considerations dictated the design and evolution of samurai armour, virtually every aspect of traditional Japanese culture was endowed with what Japanese academic Ikegami Eiko refers to as 'aesthetic ideals'.[1] As such it was almost impossible for the Japanese to produce a purely utilitarian item, irrespective of the implement's purpose, armour included. For aesthetic considerations were by default incorporated to some degree into virtually every item's finished design.

An impressive *tetsu kuro urushi nuri tsure-yamamichi hishi-toji koshi-tori ni-mai-dō gusoku*. This armour embodies many of the characteristics that were typical of fighting armours at the end of the 16th century. It is both functional and serviceable, with additional protective mail-faced panels fitted behind the connective bands of lacing around the waist of the sturdy cuirass. It was also made with a removable, and thus washable, cloth liner. Though not visible in this photograph, it also features a shot-proof tested 62-plate helmet. And while visually attractive, it is also psychologically intimidating.

Herein lies one of the least celebrated aspects of Japanese armour: the brilliantly balanced merger of the aesthetic ideal with utilitarian necessity that defined its construction and design. No other item produced by the Japanese involved the contribution of such a wide variety of craftsmen as did samurai armour, which is why I refer to Japanese armour as being the all-encompassing canvas of the traditional Japanese artisan. Its construction incorporated the combined talent of carpenters, lacquerers and leatherworkers, who laboured in conjunction with metalworkers, weavers and a number of other highly specialized artisans to produce the complex array of component parts and materials that went into the assembly of a set of armour. And as each of these craftsmen was endowed with the 'aesthetic ideal', the art in Japanese armour is not simply obvious in the sum total of their efforts, but can also be found discreetly incorporated into almost every level of a set of armour's construction. It is this point that I feel is often overlooked. The art in Japanese armour could be as subtle as a floral-shaped rivet head on a shot-proof cuirass or hinges made in the realistic form of a butterfly. And while the level of detail, ornamentation and quality obviously varied in accordance with the standing of the warrior for whom the armour was produced, the aesthetic ideal was never absent from the finished product, regardless of the warrior's rank or status.

This is why I find Japanese armour so fascinating. While subtle beauty can be found at almost every level of its fabrication, it doesn't dilute the effectiveness of the end product. On the contrary, Japanese armour was incredibly well suited to the role it was designed to serve. At the height of its evolutionary development it was a form-fitting amalgamation of parts that provided suitable protection without impeding a warrior's range of dexterity. It was likewise capable of stopping a shot from a matchlock or defeating a cutting blow from some of the sharpest edged weaponry ever produced. It was a resilient, easily repaired visual statement about the warrior within. Japanese armour was also designed to psychologically intimidate a foe while it simultaneously emboldened the warrior who wore it. In short it was a phenomenal, multifaceted military implement that was as beautiful and refined as it was effective and functional.

As already noted, it is essential that students of this subject begin with a broad grasp of Japanese history in order to develop a well-rounded understanding of the development and evolution of the forms of armour that were utilized in Japan over the course of two millennia. I have therefore attempted to incorporate as much relevant history into the text as possible, particularly in the foundation-laying early chapters. These efforts have by necessity been kept relatively brief, and as such are often, at best, broad overviews of what are more often than not highly complex subjects. As a result, some of the terminology employed to discuss certain subjects is almost certainly not up to the standards of scholarly papers. Even something as simple as using the word 'Japan' to refer to the 6,852 islands in the archipelago that we now identify as that nation state when discussing the samurai is technically incorrect. For Japan as we know it did not exist until 1868, 1871, or 1889 depending on how you interpret the different historical events that led to its creation. Ironically 11 February is 'National Foundation Day' in Japan, a national holiday that commemorates the birth of the nation, which the Japanese Government officially states occurred in 660 BC.

The term 'Japan' is also skewed in that the land masses that we now associate with this term do not correspond with the areas that the so-called 'Japanese' peoples of the archipelago would have considered to have been part of their collective independent *kuni*, or 'countries' within the same archipelago. For large land masses such as Hokkaidō and the Ryūkyū Islands were not even seen as being 'Japanese' territories until well into the 1870s.

As this one term alone demonstrates, there are multiple ongoing high-level scholarly debates about whether terms like 'Japan' should even be used when discussing the archipelago prior to the Meiji period. To do justice to such debates in this text would only add to the difficulties of mastering the already complex subject matter at hand, and so I have chosen to utilize existing generic terminology, rather than to attempt to address the numerous difficult debates that exist around this subject in the narrow confines of this text.

In closing, I need to pay my respects to those that have preceded me down this path towards publication. For every new author on this subject matter has to some degree only become so by standing on the shoulders of those that have gone before us. As such I have the greatest degree of respect for those individuals, particularly when one realizes how hard it must have been to gather information on this highly complex and confusing subject matter prior to the modern-day conveniences of the internet and digital photography.

Thus I realize that this book is also their book. And like their publications, I expect in time that someone will use my book to take our understanding of this subject matter to an even higher level, for I openly admit that I do not have all the answers, just as those who published in the centuries and decades before me did not.

I also accept that by publishing a book one becomes the target of criticism, which is fine, if it helps to move the discussion forward. For I know this debate is far from finished. Each year, new discoveries and information come forward that reshape many of the fundamentals of this subject matter that were considered to be established fact only a generation or two earlier. Thus I'm comfortable saying that what I have written here is what I know now, to the best of my ability. That said, I believe the vast majority of the enclosed information will stand the test of time and find itself passed on in the texts of other authors to future generations. That which is proved wrong will, I trust, help to empower others to find out what is right for the benefit of us all. I accept this. For I have seen this occur with most of the leading authorities of our time, some of whom I've had the pleasure to know. I respect the courage that it took for them to put into print information that is as difficult and complex to vet and verify as is the case with most of the details that are associated with this difficult and unusual subject matter. For my goal in publishing this book, as I believe was true for those whom came before me, is not to gain laurels for myself, but to share as much information as I possibly can to help ensure the future preservation of these unique and fabulous tangible pieces of feudal Japanese history.

An example of a unique late Edo period *gusoku* that features a hybrid form of *yoroi*-like cuirass. This *gusoku* is indicative of the growing revivalist movement that occurred throughout the 18th century in Japanese armour designs and that saw many now-obsolete features, formerly used between the 10th and 14th centuries, revisited, largely for aesthetic reasons.

INTRODUCTION

As with any subject matter, it is essential that one masters the basics of Japanese armour before attempting to delve too far into this interesting but highly complex subject matter. Ideally this process should begin by learning to identify each of the most common components of a conventional set of armour, or *gusoku*, which means 'one set' or a 'grouping'.

Although Japanese armour changed considerably between the 4th century and the latter part of the 19th century when Japan's feudal period came to an end, most of the terminology that is now used to describe even the most ancient forms of armour are generally terms that originated in the 18th and 19th centuries. Thus the best way to learn the key terminology associated with this subject matter is to begin with the items that were common to the composition of most conventional full sets of samurai armour as they existed during the latter part of the Japanese feudal period.

In general, a set of samurai armour is broken down into component parts that provide protection for the head, the body and the extremities. Traditionally the head protection was limited to some form of helmet or *kabuto*, which was later joined by the appearance of items of facial armour, or *mengu*. The body, or more specifically the torso, was protected by a form of cuirass, or *dō*, while the extremities, namely the arms and legs, were protected by individual items of armour that were collectively referred to as the *sangu*, or 'set of three'. A conventional *sangu* includes a matched though mirrored pair of armoured sleeves referred to as the *kote*. The thighs were protected by a single bifurcate apron-like panel called a *haidate*, while the shins were protected by a matched pair of shin guards, or *suneate*.

Most armours also featured a matched pair of shoulder guards, or *sode*. The *sode* are something of an anomaly in that while they are not technically part of the *dō*, they were almost always made in conjunction with the cuirass. That said, there were periods of time in the history of Japanese armour when warriors preferred not to wear *sode*. In fact, some forms of armour were even fabricated without shoulder guards between the late 16th and early 17th centuries, as will be explained in later chapters. However, for those new to the study of Japanese armour it is best to start by assuming that a complete *gusoku* will always be accompanied by a pair of *sode*.

While learning to identify the various component parts of a set of armour is essential, it is equally important to learn the correct terminology associated with these items. For this reason this text makes extensive use of Japanese words wherever possible. As such once a new item has been introduced and explained the use of English-based equivalent terms gradually declines. This has been done to help the reader develop and retain an effective command of the correct Japanese terminology.

Part and parcel of mastering the required vocabulary is ensuring proper pronunciation of the terms. Ideally this is something that serious students will take upon themselves to practise

SAMURAI ARMOUR

and study outside the limited confines of what can be presented in this text. Having said this, however, a basic overview of how Japanese words are structured and pronounced is in order.

Japanese is at its most basic a syllable-based language comprising five vowels and fourteen consonants, which in their various combinations create a list of one hundred distinct syllable sounds. The five vowels as they appear in Japanese order are a, i, u, e and o. These are pronounced as follows:

'a' as in the 'a' in 'father'; 'i' as in the double 'ee' of 'meet'; 'u' as in the 'u' of 'rude'; 'e' as in the 'a' of 'say'; and 'o' as in the 'o' of 'old'.

JAPANESE ARMOUR NOMENCLATURE

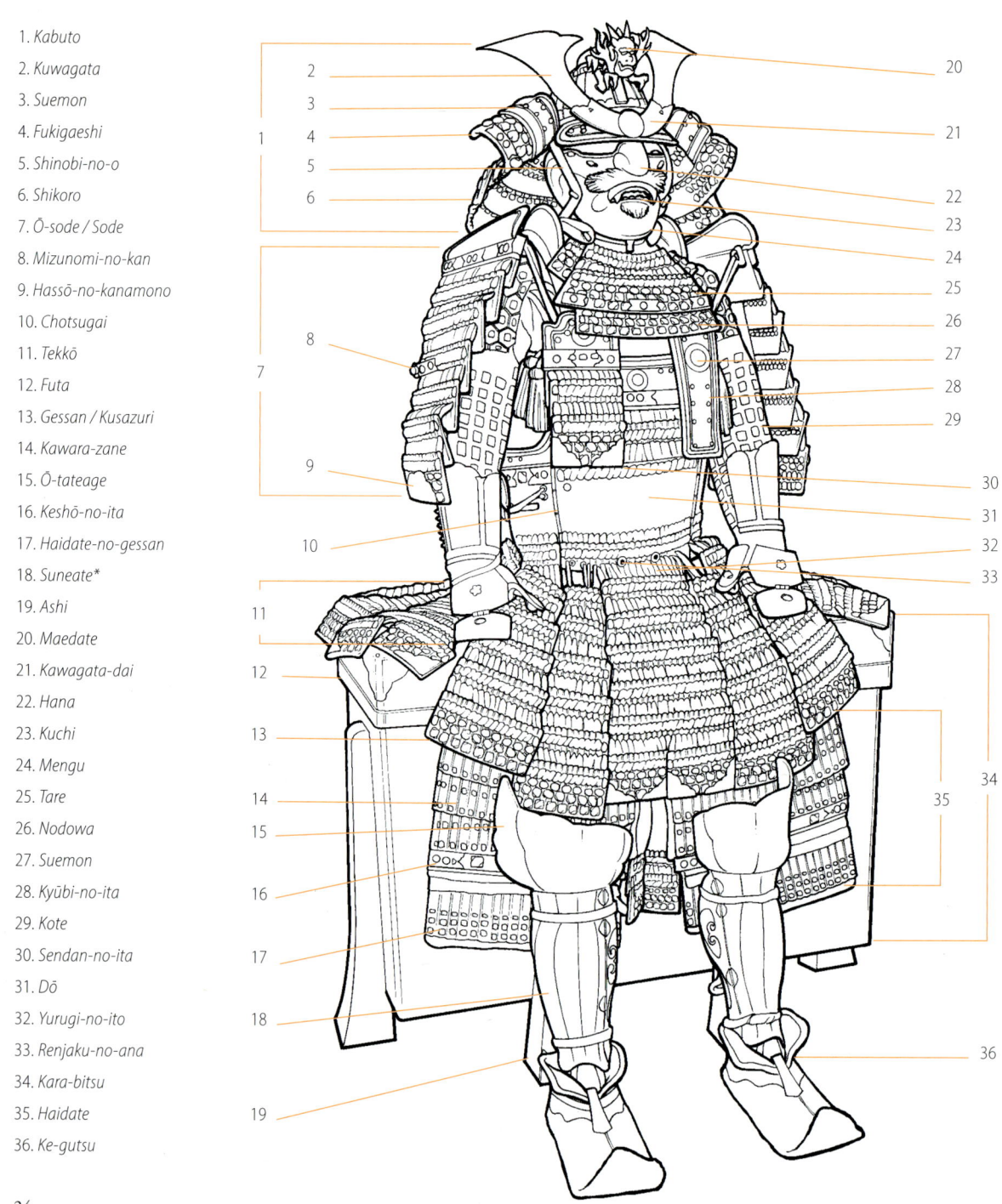

1. *Kabuto*
2. *Kuwagata*
3. *Suemon*
4. *Fukigaeshi*
5. *Shinobi-no-o*
6. *Shikoro*
7. *Ō-sode / Sode*
8. *Mizunomi-no-kan*
9. *Hassō-no-kanamono*
10. *Chotsugai*
11. *Tekkō*
12. *Futa*
13. *Gessan / Kusazuri*
14. *Kawara-zane*
15. *Ō-tateage*
16. *Keshō-no-ita*
17. *Haidate-no-gessan*
18. *Suneate**
19. *Ashi*
20. *Maedate*
21. *Kawagata-dai*
22. *Hana*
23. *Kuchi*
24. *Mengu*
25. *Tare*
26. *Nodowa*
27. *Suemon*
28. *Kyūbi-no-ita*
29. *Kote*
30. *Sendan-no-ita*
31. *Dō*
32. *Yurugi-no-ito*
33. *Renjaku-no-ana*
34. *Kara-bitsu*
35. *Haidate*
36. *Ke-gutsu*

24

In most cases each vowel can be joined with one of the following consonants to create a syllable: b, d, h, k, g, m, n, p, r, s, t, w, y and z. Japanese consonants for the most part are pronounced like those in English with the exception of 'g', which is always pronounced with a hard 'g' sound as in the word 'get'. Thus the vowel 'i' in conjunction with the consonant 'k' becomes 'ki', which would be pronounced like 'key'. Note also that when two vowels appear in a word in succession, as in *tateage*, they are each pronounced separately: 'tah-tay-ah-gay'.

The one exception to the rule that every syllable ends in a vowel is the sound 'n', for example in *han* and Genpei War. This is often seen written in English as 'm' where it appears before another consonant; as such 'Gempei' is a commonly encountered variant.

Japanese is missing a number of consonants found in English, namely c, f, l, q, v, and x, thus native Japanese often find it very difficult to pronounce words containing the associated sounds. Thus 'France' would be pronounced as 'Huransu' in Japanese, which would represent the closest syllabized pronunciation.

Note that Japanese stress on the syllables when arranged in groups to form words remain consistent and equal for all syllables throughout the pronunciation of the word. This cadence is called a mora. This means that a two-syllable word should sound exactly twice as long as a single syllable word. Thus a word like 'green' or *midori* in Japanese would be pronounced 'mi-do-ri' in three equal parts, all of which would be flat, with no added emphasis on any one syllable.

When a vowel is diacritically marked, such as 'ā', 'ō' and 'ū', the pronunciation remains the same but the sound is held twice as long. Thus a word like *shōgun* would be pronounced 'sho-o-gun'.

Rendaku, or Japanese morphophonology, is another unique characteristic of the Japanese language that it is important to have an understanding of in order to comprehend a considerable portion of the terminology associated with samurai armour. *Rendaku* is a pattern of sequential voicing that occurs with compound or prefixed words. In such cases the first syllable of the second word of the compound is 'voiced' or pronounced using an alternative, though associated, consonant sound. For example, *hito* or 'person' in compound with *hito* again would not be pronounced 'hitohito' but

An outstanding example of a high quality *tetsu-sabiji muna-koshi-tori go-mai-dō gusoku* from the early 18th century. This fabulous armour was originally produced for a family member of the ruling Tokugawa Shōgunate.

SAMURAI ARMOUR

would instead be sequentially voiced as 'hito**bi**to' (emphasis added for clarity), to create the word 'people'. Likewise, the word *ori*, which means 'fold' in compound with the word *kami*, for paper, becomes 'ori**ga**mi'.

Sequentially voiced words commonly appear amongst the terminology associated with the study of Japanese armour. For example, a *shikoro*, or 'neck guard', when in compound with a descriptor such as *Hineno*, becomes *Hineno-jikoro*, which is a unique style of neck guard. Without an understanding of the principles of *rendaku* as were outlined by the famous 19th century linguist Benjamin Lyman in 'Lyman's Law', it is not uncommon for those new to this subject matter to fail to recognize the association that exists between related terms. For example, without an understanding of the principles of *rendaku* it is difficult to recognize the relationship between the term *kote*, or armour sleeve, and the morphed descriptive variation of the word, *shino-gote*, which is a distinctive form of armoured sleeve.

Another practice that will serve serious students of Japanese armour well is to develop the habit of identifying and referring to sets of Japanese armour by the style of the *dō*, or cuirass, that the set of armour is formed around. This long-established practice dates back to the 10th century when the samurai were first beginning to emerge as a distinct social class. This event occurred simultaneously with and in part due to the appearance of a revolutionary new form of cuirass known as the *yoroi*, the ownership of which quickly became synonymous with an individual's affiliation with the emerging warrior class.

The trademark status of the *yoroi* established an early precedence amongst the evolving traditions of the developing samurai class, who viewed the cuirass as being the centrepiece of a *gusoku*. As such, sets of armour are always identified and referred to by the style of the *dō* at the centre of the *gusoku*, irrespective of the complexity or detail found on any of the other accompanying component pieces.

This fabulous mid-Edo period *tetsu kuro urushi nuri byō-toji tatehagi-okegawa muna-tori go-mai-dō gusoku* clearly demonstrates the aesthetic and fabricational consistencies that are indicative of matched sets of armour. And while less obvious in a photograph, numerous identical aesthetic features and fine details can be seen in each of the various individual parts of the armour, which confirm the originality of these parts to each other and that this armour is a true *gusoku*.

INTRODUCTION

This long-established precedent, however, is increasingly being disregarded in favour of the practice of identifying sets of armour by the style of *kabuto*, or the helmet that the set features. This has largely evolved out of the practice amongst modern-day collectors, particularly in Japan, to collect only *kabuto* due to the limitations of display and storage space in most Japanese homes. As a result, the traditional importance of the *dō* has been overshadowed by the collector's attraction to *kabuto*.

Furthermore, while the *kabuto* or other parts of a *gusoku* can often be quite spectacular pieces on their own, their finished form was always determined by and reflective of the aesthetic appearance of the cuirass. This was due to the fact that the *dō* was traditionally the focal point of a *gusoku*. Aesthetic detail found on the *dō* will also be found on the other parts of a set of armour. For example, if a *dō* is fitted with a twisted braid-like gilded metal moulding around the open upper edges of the cuirass, then an identical form of decorative edge trim will also be found fitted to specific parts on the *kabuto* and *sode*. In short, the *dō* sets the standard by which the other component parts are fabricated and finished. Significant difference between the finished aesthetic features of the cuirass and the various component parts that form a set of armour generally indicate that the armour has been compiled from various unrelated pieces and as such is not a true *gusoku*.

As this text will demonstrate, no other part of a *gusoku* does more to determine and confirm the composition and finished form of the various component parts of a set of armour than the *dō*. For this reason serious students of this subject need to learn to identify the main components of a conventional cuirass. Likewise, they must also learn to recognize the numerous different forms of *dō* and the key characteristics that differentiate each of the various makes of cuirass from each other.

For the purposes of this book the term *gusoku* not only refers to a complete set of armour with all its necessary component parts, but specifically to a matched set of armour. This means that all the components were by design fabricated in a similar manner to create a specific set of armour. As such, when the set is an actual *gusoku* it should be possible to visually trace several consistent features between each of the various components of a set of armour. For example, the colouration and texture of the lacquer work applied to each part of a *gusoku* should be exactly the same, irrespective of the part being examined. Thus to find a set of armour with black-lacquered *kote*, but brown lacquered shin guards, or *suneate*, would be highly unusual. Such a combination would generally tend to suggest that the parts were originally from different sets of armour that were later amalgamated to create what looks like a *gusoku*, but is in fact a composite set of armour.

This impressive-looking set of armour is an excellent example of how easy it is for composite groupings of armour parts to be compiled to create what appears to be a matched *gusoku*. The mixed use of different lacing styles and the unmatched colours of the fabrics of the *sangu* are the most obvious visual indicators that the parts are not original to each other. Note how the *kabuto* and *menpo* have been laced in the *kebiki odoshi* style while the *gessan* of the *dō* have been laced in the open *sugake odoshi* style. Also note how the *gessan* feature *mimi-ito*, which are absent on the *kabuto* and *menpo*. The fabric that has been used to create the sleeve bags of the *kote* appears to differ from the material used for the *haidate*. The light-coloured fabric affixed to the *suneate* is also different. And while difficult to ascertain from photographs, the *suneate* are in fact modern reproductions.

Samurai Armour

Having said this, it is important to note that it would be insufficient to simply rely on a comparative examination of the lacquered finish to judge whether the various components of a set of armour were original to each other or not. *Kuro urushi,* or black lacquer, was commonly used to finish many items of armour. Thus further comparisons must also be made to confirm this, and are generally quite easy to do. For example, the colour, pattern and style of any fabrics affixed to or associated with the various parts can be compared. As with lacquer work, such materials must also be identical to one another. This will also be true of lacing, leathers, edge trims and generally all other visible materials. For example, if all three *sangu* items utilize mail in their fabrication, but the style of mail used is different on one of the items, then the part with the different mail will more than likely not originally have belonged to the armour that it presently accompanies.

These important details, however, are not always obvious to the untrained eye, which is why this text places considerable emphasis on the minute details associated with the materials and fabrication techniques used in the construction of Japanese armour. For the old idiom that 'the devil is in the detail' is especially apropos when it comes to the subject of antique sets of samurai armour.

Another subject that needs to be broached early on in the discussion of Japanese armour is the age-old question of what it was made from, or more specifically, what material was used to produce the base component of the protective parts of these items. The simple answer to this question is either rawhide or metal, if one is talking about samurai armour, but the full answer is obviously much more complex. Some of the oldest forms of armour used in Japan were originally made from wood. Such items, however, preceded the appearance of the samurai by several centuries and wood was never utilized as the primary form of protective material to produce armour after the 4th century.

Irrespective of this fact, many sources continue to suggest that samurai armour was made from materials such as bamboo. This persistent misconception most likely stems from the existence of numerous simple breastplate-like forms of cuirass that in appearance resemble the forms of armour worn by the samurai. And while these items were in fact based on a generic form of post-16th century design of *dō*, the samurai never used bamboo-made items of armour in battle. For bamboo lacks the resilience necessary to adequately protect a warrior from the cutting and stabbing effects of edged and pointed weaponry. It is also incapable of stopping missiles like arrows or defeating high-velocity projectiles, such as shots fired from a matchlock.

An impressive *kuro urushi nuri nerigawa hishi-toji yokohagi-okegawa ni-mai-dō gusoku*. Visually it is often impossible to tell if an armour was made from rawhide or metal in the case of high quality examples of *nerigawa*-based *gusoku* such as this. In the absence of more complex tests, the substantial difference in weight is the most obvious indicator that an item has been made from rawhide.

INTRODUCTION

Commonly made from a series of vertically arranged bamboo-splints, these rudimentary breastplates, which first appeared in the early 19th century, were specifically made to protect the torso from the bamboo and wooden training swords that were used in sparring matches. Such items were used in the various swordsmanship schools that continued to exist long after the demise of the samurai in the early 1870s. In fact, bamboo-made cuirasses are still used by some modern-day practitioners of the *kenjutsu*-related martial art of *kendo*.

The armour that the samurai wore in battle between the 4th and 19th centuries was made almost exclusively from just two primary types of protective material: rawhide, referred to as *nerigawa*, or metal, commonly referred to as *tetsu* (iron). In fact, the vast majority of sets of armour utilized by the samurai over the centuries were generally assembled from a skilful combination of both materials. For example, it was common for the helmet bowl of a *kabuto* to be fabricated from *tetsu*, while the neck guard would commonly be assembled from lames constructed from hundreds of rawhide scales. The proportion of metal to rawhide that was utilized in the construction of an item of armour or a *gusoku* could vary considerably from armour to armour for any number of reasons, such as the budget of the original owner, the period in which the armour was fabricated or even the style in which the armour was made. While *gusoku* were sometimes assembled entirely from *nerigawa*, it was extremely rare for a set of armour to be made exclusively from metal, primarily due to the impracticality of the weight that was involved.

While *nerigawa* as a material speaks for itself, the term *tetsu* requires additional explanation. This is due to the fact that the Japanese also utilized steel, or *kōtetsu*, to make armour. It should also be said, however, when the primary material is metal, exactly what ferrous metal was used is almost never specified when it comes to items of samurai armour, all of which are generically referred to as being '*tetsu*'-based.

Exactly why this practice came about is impossible to say, though it may simply be a reflection of the fact that the overwhelming majority of ferrous-metal-made items of armour were fabricated from iron. Steel when it was utilized appears to have been used in relatively limited quantities. This was in part due to the extra time and cost that was involved in the production of steel as well as the fact that an item made from *kōtetsu* was significantly heavier than an identical piece fabricated using iron.

An outstanding shot-proof *tetsu-sabiji byō-toji tatehagi-okegawa go-mai-dō gusoku*. The cuirass features a *hatomune*, or 'pigeon breast' medial ridge down the middle of the breastplate. This feature, which was copied from the peascod style of cuirass worn by the first Europeans to arrive in Japan in the early 1540s, significantly improved the ability of a *dō* to defeat and even deflect a shot fired from a matchlock.

SAMURAI ARMOUR

Prior to the 16th century, steel, if it was utilized at all in the construction of a cuirass, would have represented a mere fraction of the overall number of scales that were used to make a lamellar cuirass. These would have been mixed with *nerigawa* scales within the lamellar boards, or lames, that were used to construct a cuirass, with the *kōtetsu* scales being strategically placed to enhance the protective abilities of the armour where it covered a particularly exposed or vital area of the torso. It is far more likely, however, that when metal scales were used in this manner, the majority of these would have been made from iron.

Steel began to be somewhat more common in the construction of the cuirass after a reliable design of firearms was introduced into Japan in the early 1540s. Driven by a demand from their clientele to produce armour that could provide protection from firearms, the *katchū-shi*, or Japanese armour makers, began to tap into the long-established wealth of metallurgical knowledge that Japanese sword makers had developed over the centuries. For the Japanese are known to have produced steel swords as early as the 5th century, and over time they also learned how to create swords from lamellar combinations of iron and steel that took advantage of the different metallurgical characteristics of these two ferrous metals to produce incredibly strong and resilient blades.

Armour makers were able to adopt this knowledge to produce laminate metal plates that featured steel façades backed by a layer of iron. Composite construction of this kind allowed the *katchū-shi* to combine the superior tensile strength of steel with the impact-absorbing flexibility of iron. Incredibly, examples of ferrous metal plate laminate examined by the Royal Armoury in the United Kingdom show that in some cases the *katchū-shi* were able to produce laminate plate armour that was a mere 1 mm in thickness, a fact that attests to the phenomenal metal-working skills of the feudal-period Japanese smiths. Having said this, armour made from steel or laminate ferrous metal plate appears

An aesthetically simple, yet very high quality, battleworthy 17th century example of a *tetsu kuro urushi nuri yokohagi-okegawa go-mai-dō gusoku*. Note the orange cord that secures the *saihai* baton to the *saihai-no-kan* that is affixed to the right breast of the cuirass. As only commanders carried *saihai*, these swivel-ring-like fixtures were originally only affixed to *dō* worn by high-ranking samurai. Over time, however, *saihai-no-kan* became a decorative accoutrement common to most armours.

to have been relatively scarce, and almost certainly never accounted for more than a small fraction of the overall number of items of armour that were produced from the mid-16th century onward.

That steel or laminate plate was utilized, however, fails to explain why the Japanese do not differentiate between these materials when they identify items of armour. Whether this was always the case or a trend that took over at a certain point in time is unknown; as the preceding paragraphs demonstrate, the Japanese had a well-developed understanding of the metallurgical differences between iron and steel.

Irrespective of this fact, this text follows the existing Japanese practice of only identifying whether the primary protective material used in the fabrication of the armour is rawhide or metal. As such all metal-made items of armour will be referred to as being *tetsu*, which in turn should be understood to mean iron, unless otherwise noted.

While this book is about Japanese armour, I have made an effort to incorporate as much relevant history as possible. I have done so to establish an understanding of some of the circumstances that ultimately led to the design and evolution of the many items of armour that are discussed in this text. This, however, has often required that I paint with rather broad strokes. As such, by necessity I have only been able to include the most relevant historical events and personalities in this text where and when the inclusion of such information is pertinent to the evolving story of Japanese armour.

In this regard I have also decided to avoid usage of some of the many other historically correct terms that were used to refer to the evolving warrior class in Japan over the centuries, such as *bushi*, *mononofu*, and *tsuwamono*. For the sake of simplicity, I make consistent use of the term samurai, irrespective of the terminology that may have actually been used to refer to these warriors during a specific period from the 10th century onward. To do otherwise would only further complicate an already complex subject matter.

Finally, please note that while this book is about samurai armour, it is impossible to cover every aspect of this fascinating subject matter in the level of detail that is required in a single text. Therefore this book focuses primarily on the evolution and history of the various forms of cuirass that were made and utilized in Japan from the earliest known examples until the end of the Japanese feudal period and the samurai in the later half of the 19th century.

The helmets, face masks and other items of armour that were worn to protect the extremities, which are a subject unto themselves, are discussed in detail in Volume II, a separate companion text, along with the other related items of supporting equipment, such as armour storage cases and a number of less well-documented forms of auxiliary armour that were commonly utilized by the samurai.

A superb set of armour from the late 18th century assembled around a cuirass constructed in the style of a 14th century *yoroi*. (New York Metropolitan Museum of Art/ CC0 1.0)

CHAPTER 1

JAPANESE HISTORY AND THE SAMURAI

Prehistoric era to the early 17th century

As most people with more than a passing interest in history know, history as it is presented is very rarely an accurate reflection of historical facts. In other words, much of what is referred to as history is actually more often than not a rather one-sided reflection of a victor's perspective on a preferred version of events. Naturally this is also true of Japanese history, which, in the opinion of the author, tends to be often even more edited, unreliable and one-sided than much of the historical information that has been passed down to us over the centuries from various cultures.

Contrary to what is often perceived, much of the historical record regarding the origin and evolution of Japan and its people is still open to debate. What is known, however, is that the ancient chronicles produced by the Japanese to document their history were fundamentally little more than fables that were written with the specific intent of trying to disassociate the Japanese from their actual past, as will be explained later in this chapter.

While this book is about armour, it is impossible to talk about Japanese armour without some understanding of the samurai

A reproduction of a unique Jōmon period *dogū* (earthenware figurine). The original piece in the Tōkyō National Museum is dated to around 3000 BC. (Courtesy of J.L. Badgley)

Samurai Armour

themselves. Therefore, to understand how Japanese armour evolved into the unique equipment that it became, it is necessary to look backwards in time to the factors that influenced its development, factors which of course also played upon and influenced the evolution of the Japanese warrior class.

While most histories of the samurai begin with their appearance around the middle of the 9th century, the truth is that the origin of the samurai began long before the 9th century. In fact, to truly understand the samurai we need to go much further back in the historical record, back to the time when people first started to inhabit Japan, which is believed to have been around 40,000 years ago according to the stone (or lithic) tools that have been found by archaeologists.

It is unclear if these first peoples stayed or if they were transient. What is known, however, is that over the course of many tens of thousands of years several separate waves of a post-Mongoloid-like people with south-east Asian genetic characteristics migrated into the chain of islands that we now refer to as the Japanese archipelago. And though these peoples were genetically similar, each migration occurred independently of those that had preceded it, with some groups entering the archipelago from the north, via the land bridge that the Kuril Islands then formed, while others entered Japan from the south through the Ryūkyū chain of islands.

Collectively these people came to be known as the Jōmon, a name that is derived from the distinctive style of pottery that they made, which featured decorative impressed patterns around their façades that were made using ropes. The Jōmon period, likewise named after the pottery produced by these early inhabitants of Japan, is presently considered to have started around 14,500 BC and to have ended around the middle of the first millennium BC. That said, these dates have changed a number of times in the past few decades, as have many other historical dates, as new archaeological finds continue to reveal hitherto unknown facts about the Jōmon people and their culture.

Primarily hunter-gatherers, the Jōmon people slowly became semi-sedentary as they learned to cultivate plants, possibly around 7,000 BC. Over the millennia their understanding and mastery of agricultural techniques improved to the point at which it is believed that they learned to cultivate rice, possibly as early as 4,000 BC according to recent archaeological discoveries.

The Jōmon population appears to have peaked around 3,000–2,000 BC before falling into sharp decline. Climatic changes may have accounted for the initial decline in the

A representation of a Yayoi period military commander from the early 3rd century AD, wearing a lacquered *mokusei katchū* (wooden cuirass). (Artwork by Angus McBride, from *Early Samurai AD 200–1500* © Osprey Publishing)

population as it upset the fragile balance of the Jōmon's semi-sedentary lifestyle. Devastating as these changes may have been, it was the arrival of a new race of peoples, with north-east Asian characteristics, in Japan via the southern Japanese island of Kyūshū from the Korean peninsula around the middle of the first millennium BC that proved to be the biggest threat to Jōmon survival.

These new peoples and their culture are now known to history as the Yayoi, a name which was derived from a district in Tōkyō where archaeologists first discovered the distinctive hybrid style of Jōmon and peninsular pottery that these new peoples to the archipelago produced. Their superior levels of knowledge in agriculture and metallurgy allowed the Yayoi to establish themselves quickly and prosper in their new territories. For unlike the Jōmon, the Yayoi were well versed in the continental practice of wet-rice farming, which allowed them to establish strong permanent communities. Their knowledge of metallurgy was instrumental in this endeavour, for it allowed them to fabricate strong tools and weapons from bronze, and in later centuries iron, to develop and defend their lands.

The Jōmon appear to have managed to co-exist with the Yayoi during the first half of the Yayoi period, which dates from around the middle of the first millennium until approximately 250 BC. However, as the Yayoi population grew, both naturally and as the result of further waves of migration, tensions and then conflict erupted between the two cultures as the Yayoi pushed ever further into the traditional territories of the Jōmon in an effort to secure additional areas of land suitable for their agricultural needs.

Though the various Yayoi tribes collectively controlled a considerable portion of the main southern island areas of the Japanese archipelago by the time the first references to them began to appear in Chinese historical records in the 1st century AD, they were far from a unified society. The fragmented nature of Yayoi culture was documented in the *Book of Han*, from the *Twenty-Four Histories*, in which the 'Wa', as the Chinese texts referred to the Yayoi, were described as the people who lived in the land that was divided 'into one hundred tribes'.[1]

The huge number of small independent tribes noted by the Chinese was gradually reduced between the 1st and 2nd centuries AD, a period of intense inter-tribal conflict. For even

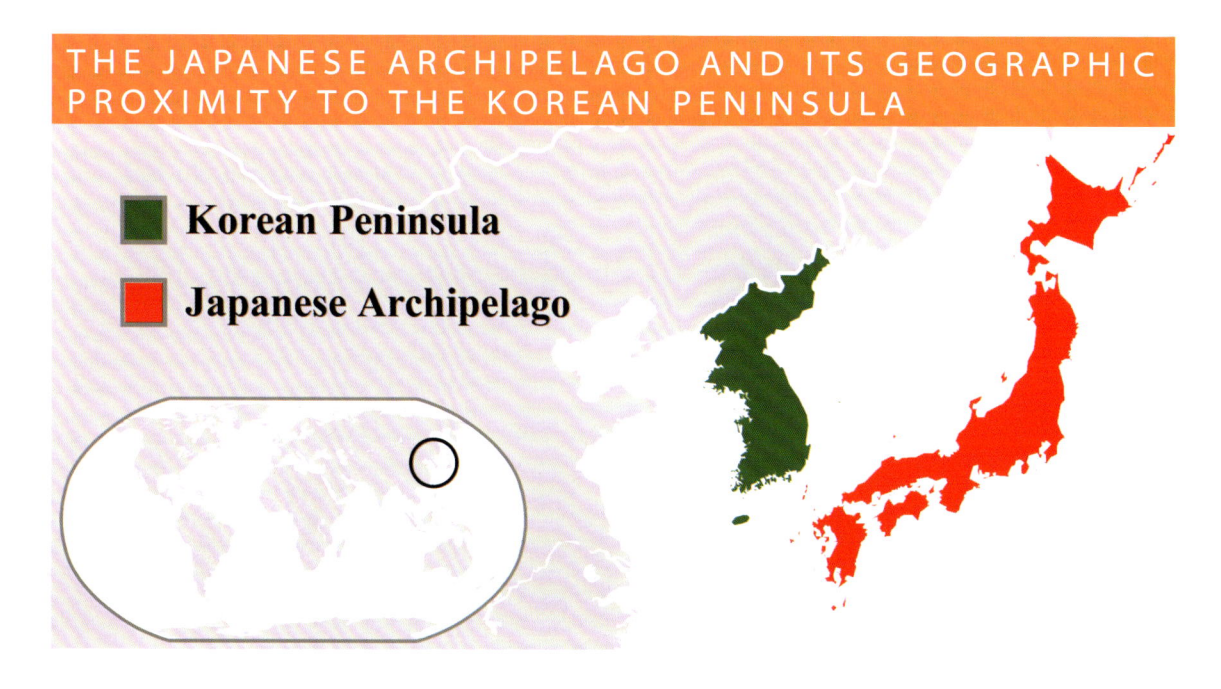

THE JAPANESE ARCHIPELAGO AND ITS GEOGRAPHIC PROXIMITY TO THE KOREAN PENINSULA

■ **Korean Peninsula**

■ **Japanese Archipelago**

as the Yayoi fought amongst themselves, the most powerful clans merging in alliance or absorbing those they defeated, the Yayoi continued to harass the Jōmon peoples that they encountered along their continually expanding frontiers. It was not until Queen Himiko of Yamatai-koku, a shaman priestess, came to power in the late 2nd century that the level of inter-tribal warfare among the Yayoi began to wane and the concept of a common identity began to emerge. The still embryonic Japanese imperial household would eventually be able to trace its lineage back to the leaders amongst the most powerful of these unifying clans.

Many of the details about Himiko and her life remain the subject of a considerable degree of scholarly debate, including the actual length of her reign, which does appear to have been close to half a century and is in some sources stated to have lasted an astonishing 68 years. Irrespective of the precise number of years, Himiko reigned for an unusually long time, the duration of which clearly played a significant role in the evolution and development of the first 'proto-Japan' form of a centralized government.[2] The catalyst for this pivotal event was Himiko's death at some time towards the latter part of the 250s AD. This created a massive power vacuum amongst the Yayoi clans that caused the tribes to fall out with each other in a dispute over her successor. After a short, sharp period of conflict, the tribes bridged over their differences and came together to create a government in the form of a loose confederacy that was dominated by the powerful Yamatai to form the Yamato state.

Another significant event that may have arisen as a result of Himiko's death was the sudden appearance of huge, keyhole-shaped burial mounds in Japan, called kofun, the oldest of which dates to the middle of the 3rd century AD. The fact that the first kofun appeared around the time of Himiko's death has led some scholars to speculate that the first one may have been built as her tomb. While this remains unclear, the influence of this first massive kofun was immediate and set the standard by which the Yamato peoples constructed the burial mounds for all other important personalities until the arrival of Buddhism in the 7th century. Until that time, however, the kofun were so

A speculative representation of the Yayoi period Queen Himiko, who ruled over the powerful Yamatai-koku clan throughout the first half of the 3rd century AD. The numerous independent Yayoi clans united after Himiko's death to form the first quasi-centralized state in the Japanese archipelago. (Image © and courtesy of the Kyōto Costume Museum)

central to Japanese cultural development that the period in Japan between the 3rd and 7th centuries is now referred to as the Kofun period.

While the appearance of kofun was a pivotal event in Japanese history for several reasons, one of the most important aspects of these tombs was that several different Yayoi tribal burial mound designs were incorporated into the construction and design of the kofun. The amalgamation of these different tribal practices into the tombs of the elite was a physical expression of the individual Yayoi tribe's membership within the confederacy that came to be known as Yamato.

A hugely significant event in the evolutionary path towards the development of the samurai class occurred during the latter part of the 4th century when Yamato began to establish cultural and economic relationships with the various kingdoms on the Korean peninsula, with whom they seem to have shared some ancestral links.

Many older reference sources have described the Yamato peoples' relationship with the kingdoms on the Korean peninsula as one of reverse colonization or even as an invasion of the peninsula by the Yamato. This view though has largely been based on two 7th century legitimatory Japanese texts, the *Kojiki* (Records of Ancient Matters) and the *Nihon Shoki* (Chronicles of Japan). Both of these texts were compiled several centuries after the majority of the events that they purport to document. They were also written at a time when the Japanese were desperate to distance themselves from their former continental connections and as such were far from balanced or accurate reflections of the actual historical events that had taken place in Japan and between Japan and her neighbours prior to the 8th century.

If the Yamato people invaded Korea, it was with an army of craftsmen, students and traders who were eager to benefit from the advanced levels of knowledge and technology of the kingdoms on the peninsula, whose various experts they eagerly invited to Yamato. And while there is some evidence to support the claim that the Japanese did establish a settlement on the Korean peninsula, called Mimana, this was most likely a trading community as opposed to a bridgehead from which the Yamato

An illustration based on events described in the 8th century Japanese legitimatory texts, the *Kojiki* and *Nihon Shoki*, which accurately captures the unreliable nature of these materials as historical reference sources. In this scene, the fictional early 3rd century Empress Regent Jingū is depicted receiving tribute from Korean emissaries after her successful invasion of the Korean peninsula. As with the existence of Jingū herself, there is no evidence to support the idea that the peoples from the Japanese archipelago conducted a large scale military invasion of the Korean peninsula during the 3rd century.

launched military operations into the heartland of the peninsula.

While the Korean kingdoms may have benefited from the import of some raw materials and foodstuffs from Yamato, the latter in reality had little to offer their more advanced neighbours other than their support as allies. And while Yamato had initially interacted closely with the Kingdom of Kaya (also sometimes written as Gaya), by the end of the 4th century the majority of the interactions had shifted to the Kingdom of Paekche. The Paekche welcomed this relationship as they were eager to have Yamato as an ally, for the kingdom was almost continuously at war with one or more of the other major states on the Korean peninsula during that time, namely the Silla and Goyuryo (also sometimes written as Koguryo) and their extremely powerful, though on-again, off-again allies, the Tang Dynasty Chinese.

The benefits of the relationship with Paekche were immediate and obvious for Yamato. Huge cultural and technological advances swept across Yamato from the end of the 4th century as skilled Paekche craftsmen and other specialist immigrants poured in at the request of the Yamato court. These included artists and engineers, metalworkers, potters, priests and scholars. Paekche princes and princesses began to appear within the Yamato court, which resulted in the introduction of the Chinese writing system, Confucian studies and in later centuries even the introduction of the Buddhist faith into the fledgling Japanese court and lands of Yamato. The cultural flowering that occurred as result of these influences marked the beginning of a new era that came to be known as the Asuka period (c. AD 552–645), which is synonymous in Japanese history with advanced architectural designs and the development of the fine arts.

From the standpoint of the future evolution of the Japanese warrior class, the relationship with the Korean peninsula was a critical one, for it introduced the Yamato people to the concept of the mounted warrior, which had existed on the continental mainland for several centuries. Yamato learned a considerable amount about equestrianism and horse furnishings from Kaya. This knowledge was further expanded upon via their close relationship with the Paekche, who also appear to have introduced their allies to lamellar armour, or armour that was assembled from a series of small rectangular plates that were laced or otherwise secured together to form a protective garment. This new continental form of armour differed significantly from the rigid styles of cuirass that were used by the Yamato people, which, while effective, were not as well suited as lamellar armour to the needs of a mounted warrior.

While Yamato's alliance with Paekche remained strong, it continued to court the development of diplomatic and economic relationships with the other kingdoms on the peninsula. These efforts may have been kept somewhat in check, however, by the growing presence of expatriate Paekche nobility within the Yamato court, who maintained a strong sense of allegiance to their homeland. The increasingly contradictory position towards the kingdoms on the peninsula was reflected in the fact that while Yamato periodically sent troops to assist their Paekche allies throughout the course of the 6th and 7th centuries, they were also dispatching embassies to China and the other Korean kingdom enemies of their ally.

One of the most successful of these missions spent twenty years in the Tang court before returning to Yamato. The vast array of information and ideas that returned to Japan with this embassy, particularly in the area of socio-economic reforms, would go on to play a significant role in the evolving identity of Japan, the imperial court and the future rise of the samurai class.

Many of these ideas were eventually codified in the Taika Reforms that were introduced by Emperor Kōtoku in AD 645. One of the more significant edicts among the Taika Reforms was the creation of a national army that mirrored the formations and organizational structure of the Tang Dynasty Chinese armies. This new force was to be sustained by a national draft and was to be equipped and trained in the style of the Tang Chinese forces.

This appears to have been a fight-fire-with-fire approach by Yamato, which seems to have seen the writing on the wall and realized that it was only a matter of time before their Paekche ally would be defeated by the Tang Dynasty-backed Silla armies. Yamato realized that when that day came, they were almost certainly going to have to answer for having taken up arms over the centuries alongside the Paekche. This epiphany on the part of Yamato may have contributed to the slow and ultimately failed effort by the court to send troops to help save the embattled Paekche kingdom, which ultimately fell to a united force of Silla and Tang Dynasty troops in AD 660.

While Yamato may have suspected that Paekche would be defeated, the kingdom's demise appears still to have come as a shock in Yamato, which suddenly rallied to fight for their fallen ally. For between AD 661 and 662 Yamato sent a massive force of their new model army troops, said to have numbered 37,000 strong, to the Korean peninsula in an effort to liberate and resurrect the fallen Paekche kingdom.

Yamato's knee-jerk decision to invade the peninsula was almost certainly influenced by the nobility of the fallen kingdom who had poured into the Yamato court ahead of the tidal wave of refugees that had fled Paekche for the Japanese archipelago. The new model Yamato army, spurred on by ancestral and political loyalties as well as by a desire for revenge was, however, no match for the combined force of Tang Dynasty Chinese and Silla troops, who virtually annihilated the force from Yamato at the battle of Hakusukinoe in AD 663 (also sometimes referred to by the Korean name Baekgang).

The defeat at Hakusukinoe was a game changer for Yamato and another of the pivotal moments in the future evolution of the samurai. For Yamato was now on its own and weak from its recent defeat, which had left it exposed to invasion by a huge and irritated enemy force that was only a couple of days' sea journey away from their coast. Adding to this burden was the huge number of Paekche refugees, the majority of whom were no longer bringing with them skills or knowledge that did not already exist in

The influence of Tang China on Japan is evident in this representation of a 7th century Japanese court official. (Image © and courtesy of the Kyōto Costume Museum)

Yamato. This undermined their ability to take care of themselves, while it also damaged the economies of the communities that they huddled around.

The stress on Yamato society caused by the refugees became a source of considerable concern for the court, which recognized the substantial potential for civil unrest that this large number of displaced and largely unwanted people represented. The court's answer to this problem was to push the majority of the refugees towards the frontier regions along the eastern outskirts of the domain that is now referred to as the Kantō plain. The modern-day prefectures of Chiba, Gunma, Kanagawa, Saitama, Tochigi and the Tōkyō Metropolis are all within the boundaries of this massive 17,000 square kilometre plateau.

While this subtly enforced exodus was important for the future expansion of the frontiers of Yamato, it also contributed to the development of the samurai. For a large number of former mounted Paekche warriors are thought to have been amongst the groups of refugees that were directed towards the east, an area that by happenstance was also ideally suited to horses and that in later centuries would give rise to several households of equestrian warriors who would feature prominently in Japanese history.

Having failed to liberate their homeland, the quasi-Paekche–Yamato court scrambled to build a series of defensive forts along the coast of Kyūshū to fend off a retaliatory Tang Chinese and Silla invasion. The Japanese were so certain that they were next on the chopping block that the court in Yamato began a concerted effort to disassociate themselves from their fallen ally. They did this by commissioning a history of the archipelago and its people that expunged the past and nullified any connection or influence from the continent. Through plausible deniability they hoped that they could stave off the aggressive attentions of the Silla and their powerful Tang allies.

This effort can clearly be observed in the *Kojiki* and *Nihon Shoki* texts, which saw the key families amongst the Yamato court rebranded with spotless new domestic lineages that could be traced back to the first emperor of what was to become Japan, the mythical 8th century Jimmu, who himself was proclaimed to be a direct descendant of one of the main Japanese creation myth deities, Amaterasu. These same fables were also used to establish the Japanese as a distinct and unique people whose achievements and knowledge were entirely homogeneous and devoid of outside influence. The huge and bewildering gaps that were left in the expunged historical record were patched over with a series of carefully conceived legends and mythical creation stories that conveniently ignored the vast contributions that China and Korea had made towards the advancement of society in the hitherto state of Yamato, with the newly emerged 'Japanese' peoples reassigning credit for every cultural, social and technological achievement that had occurred within Japan to themselves.

It is ironic to note, however, that while the Yamato people laboured to officially disassociate themselves from their past and any signs of foreign cultural influences, the evolving Japanese state became increasingly more Tang Dynasty-like in form and organization. For the rebranded Japanese court was anxious to strengthen the country, which they did in part by uniting it under the control of a strong central government with an emperor at its head. This marked a significant change in Japan, for the authority of the emperors and empresses who had ruled over the Yamato confederacy had not been precisely defined, nor had their authority been absolute.[3]

In AD 702 the Taihō Code was introduced, which divided the government into an administrative section and a religious section, the latter still heavily influenced by the indigenous Shintō religion even though Buddhism was already well established and highly popular across Japan.

The administrative body of the government was itself an almost exact copy of the system

JAPANESE HISTORY AND THE SAMURAI

utilized by the Tang Dynasty Chinese, with governmental responsibilities being divided between two controllers, each of whom was responsible for overseeing four separate ministries. More important, however, to the ultimate rise of the samurai was the court's programme of land redistribution, which made all lands the property of the imperial household. Thus even the domains of some of the oldest and strongest Yamato clans were forfeited to the state and redistributed as provinces, or *kuni*, each of which was under the control of a governor, or *kami*.

To compensate some of the powerful families who were affected by this reorganization, as well as to provide the nobility and the temples with a means of income, the court established *shōen*, or private landholdings. These were distributed among the aforementioned groups as well as to those who earned favour with the court through military or political service. Everything within the boundaries of a *shōen* became the property of the governor to whom the landholding was assigned, and whose control over the landholding was absolute.

Fundamentally tax-free havens, the *shōen* were also entirely independent of the court and were under the exclusive jurisdiction of the entity who controlled the land grant, which made them the ideal incubators for the seeds of the Japanese warrior class.

For the most part, the majority of the *kami* were junior members of the imperial lineage who were officially disinherited from imperial prerogatives and who took up the surnames Minamoto or Taira, which identified them as descended from the imperial family. As the third, fourth and fifth sons of nobility they

A 19th century *ukiyo-e* impression by Utagawa Kuniyoshi of the mythical figure of Susanoo no Mikoto, the brother of one of the founding deities of Japan, Amaterasu. According to the *Kojiki* and *Nihon Shoki*, Mikoto discovered a sword in the tail of an eight-headed serpent called Yamato no Orochi after killing it. The sword is now said to be part of the three items in the imperial Regalia of the present-day Imperial Household in Japan. (Wikimedia Commons/Public Domain)

often found themselves without duties and as such devoid of opportunities for advancement within the court.

In an effort to disperse and diffuse the growing numbers of these frustrated and superfluous young nobles, the court dispatched them to the fringes of the imperial domain to govern *shōen* in the frontier provinces. Overseeing this seemingly benevolent act was the powerful Fujiwara family, who through a series of carefully arranged political marriages and subtle intrigues had managed to fill the majority of imperial posts and secure the best *shōen* with members of their clan. As such the Fujiwara wielded a huge degree of political power. To ensure their hold on the control levers of the state, they were only too happy to banish troublesome members of the nobility to frontier *shōen* in the guise of doing them a favour.

While many young nobles floundered in their posts for lack of experience or interest, preferring to rely on local authorities to administer their domains, others prospered. Free from the restrictive trappings of court life they took an avid and sincere interest in the development of the *shōen* they controlled. Irrespective of whether they were led by a minor noble or by a local magistrate, the *shōen* for the most part tended to prosper, secluded and undisturbed as they were by the increasingly irrelevant edicts that were being conceived in the far-off court, which by the start of the 8th century had been relocated to Nara.

One of the byproducts of the court's policy of sending its young and superfluous nobles to the frontier regions was that it forced the expansion of the frontier, primarily further into the northern Tohoku area of Honshū, because new *shōen* were needed to accommodate the seemingly endless number of displaced members of the nobility and their followers. This sparked a renewed and vicious series of conflicts with the indigenous Jōmon inhabitants. But things had changed during the intervening centuries since the Yamato, or Japanese, had last made major pushes into Jōmon territories. For the people that the Japanese encountered along the frontier at the end of the 7th and in the early 8th century were far more capable of resisting their intrusions and did so with considerable success.

Several factors had empowered the rise of these post-Jōmon-like peoples, but none more so than the introduction of the horse and equestrian knowledge from the continent. For

A representation of a late 7th century member of the Japanese court. The extremely high status of this individual is attested to by the use of gold leaf to finish the helmet and *keikō* style of lamellar armour that he wears. (Artwork by Angus McBride, from *Early Samurai AD 200–1500* © Osprey Publishing)

A retouched image of an Ainu man in armour. Until the end of the 19th century the Ainu, now generally considered to be the descendants of the post-Kofun era Jōmon peoples, continued to utilize a form of lamellar armour which closely resembled the *keikō*, which was introduced into the Japanese archipelago from Korea in the mid-4th century AD. While the armour worn by the Ainu took on some unique characteristics over the centuries, their 8th century Emishi forefathers more than likely wore forms of cuirass similar to that seen in this image whilst resisting the Japanese national army's forces and forebears of the emerging samurai class. (Reproduction from an album of historical photographs of Hokkaidō, 1868–1926, in the Hokkaidō University Library)

the horse was ideally suited to their needs as quasi-nomadic hunter-gatherers. And though a breed of small horse appears to have been indigenous to the Japanese archipelago, there is debate as to whether these animals were still available by the beginning of the Yayoi period. Irrespective of this, there is no evidence to suggest that the Jōmon or Yayoi ever made use of domesticated horses for any purpose until the larger and stronger Mongolian breeds of horses that were utilized by their Korean counterparts were introduced into Japan.

Equestrian knowledge gradually reached the Jōmon peoples who lived along the fringes of the frontier regions of Yamato. For the majority of Yamato communities would have included a considerable number of Jōmon people who had willingly merged with Yamato society. Such individuals would have been conduits for interaction with their families and former communities. In their general isolation, trade would also have occurred to the mutual benefit of these two cultural groups. The passing of equestrian knowledge to the Jōmon, however, would ultimately prove to have been a bad deal for the future Japanese. For the Jōmon were quick to embrace and master the art of equestrianism. Their skill in this area was in large part due to their much greater reliance on the horse to sustain themselves than was generally the case with their more sophisticated neighbours.

Thus by the time Yamato's nearly three-century-long period of interaction with the Korean peninsula began to come to an end, the post-Jōmon peoples along the frontier were a far more advanced and capable people than they had been just a few centuries earlier. They had been able to achieve these changes in part from having absorbed the technological advancements within Yamato that were useful to them and by the fact that they had generally been left in peace throughout Yamato's long period of infatuation with the Korean peninsula. And while the Yamato peoples along the frontier were more than likely well aware of the abilities of their post-Jōmon neighbours, the distant court and the rest of population in Yamato, or Japan as it shall be referred to from here on, remained ignorant and unaware of the transition that had taken place.

Thus the court was shocked when their vastly larger, new model Chinese-style army of conscript troops were routed again and again and forced onto the defensive by the post-Jōmon forces they had been sent to suppress along the frontier. For the Japanese troops were wholly unprepared for the foe they were confronting, who relied heavily on ambushes and hit-and-run tactics to pick off and wear down their opponents. Having 'gathered together like ants' and just as quickly 'dispersed like birds', the post-Jōmon were able to take on and defeat forces that were much larger than themselves.[4] The ability of the post-Jōmon to successfully repeat these tactics was in large part due to the fact that most of them fought as mounted archers, who could race in and dispatch their mostly spear-carrying, foot-borne Japanese opponents at a safe distance before reeling away and vanishing into the

SAMURAI ARMOUR

surrounding forests. So effective were these Jōmon warriors that even official court documents from the 7th century recorded how a single mounted archer was capable of defeating ten Japanese conscript troops.

The exceptional ability of the post-Jōmon as mounted archers was a by-product of their hunter-gatherer lifestyle, which by necessity had honed their skills with a bow. Their talent in this regard appears to have been reflected in a new word that the Japanese began to use for these post-Jōmon peoples around this time period, 'Emishi'. While this term is commonly translated to mean 'barbarian peoples', it is also possible that its actual origin may have stemmed from the Japanese word *yumi-shi*, or 'bowman'.

Whatever the origin of the word, the Emishi were formidable and deadly opponents. Their mounted archery skills, which as hunter-gatherers were highly efficient, in combination with their intimate knowledge of their territories allowed them to attack and then quickly disperse into the dark recesses of the countryside, where unlike their antagonists they were able to find comfort, shelter and sustenance.

While the fighting skill and tenacity of the Emishi helped them resist the Japanese, they were also significantly assisted in their endeavours by a number of major flaws within the concept of the Chinese-style conscript army that the court in Yamato had introduced in the 7th century. One of the key issues with the conscript army was that it had primarily been established to counter an invasion from the continent. As such it had been modelled along the same lines as the enemy forces that the Japanese had assumed they would have to confront. While this army may initially have been quite professional, its potential as a fighting force had dwindled over time. This was in part due to the fact that it saw little or no action, and thus very few men amongst its ranks had any actual battlefield experience.

The conscript force had, however, also been established as a way to strip military power from the various Yayoi tribal leaders in an effort to amalgamate it under the central authority of the court. While this move strengthened the court's position immensely, it greatly weakened the nation as a whole, and communities quickly became entirely reliant on the state for their protection. This precarious situation was made

Rear view of a speculative representation of a conscripted Japanese national army soldier wearing the mandated 8th century *menōchū* form of armour. National service was a huge burden on conscripts, who were expected to supply their own armour and equipment and to sustain themselves for the duration of their national service. Front view shown in Chapter 3. (Image © and courtesy of the Kyōto Costume Museum)

even worse with the introduction of the Taihō Code in AD 702, which placed harsh restrictions on the ownership of weapons.

While a huge conscript army may have been justified after the fall of Paekche, when a massive domestic force appeared to be the only way to stave off invasion and subjugation, the huge force that was created placed an enormous burden on the populace. For as with most conscript armies, the lower classes, the majority of whom were farmers, bore the brunt of this burden, and their national service obligations denied farms access to the manpower that they needed to work the land. Compounding this difficult situation was the fact that the conscript was obligated by the state to provide his own armour and equipment in accordance with established government edicts, the cost of which could only be paid for by working the land.

Conscripts were selected from a rotating draft that chose from one-third of all able-bodied men between twenty and sixty years of age. The draftee was required to serve the state for four years, three of which would include duty in the dangerous frontier regions. Almost unbelievably, the conscripts were not only responsible for the expense of fielding their own armour and equipment, but were also expected to cover the cost of procuring their own provisions while in the service of the state.

While many might have been willing to suffer these devastating expenses while the survival of the country was at stake, it was a burden that could not be sustained for long. Yet long after the threat of invasion from the continent had passed, national service remained in place. For many, the only way to fulfil their obligations to the state was to sell or grant their properties to the local *shōen*, a practice that greatly increased the wealth and power of the virtually autonomous private estates, whose owners were able to buy their way out of national service.[5]

The burden for sustaining the cavalry, which on paper was supposed to form a major component of the new model Taika Reform army, was another cost that the conscript was obligated to finance. While it was expected that wealthier members of society would field these units, it was not uncommon for the cost of maintaining a mount and its equipment to be assigned to a group of six men to subsidize. Economic considerations aside, the Japanese should in theory have been able to field a sizeable number of cavalry units, skilled in the use of spears and crossbows. However, training a conscript to be a competent cavalryman took a considerable degree of time and effort, and this investment was continually undermined by the rotational organization of the conscript army, which prevented cavalry elements from attaining and maintaining a level of competency comparable to that of their Emishi opponents.

For the majority of the populace, maintaining the conscript army was a financial burden that over the long term few could afford to sustain. The economic hardship they suffered as a consequence of these obligations made support of the army highly unpopular. Dissatisfaction with national service manifested itself in many ways, from poor quality equipment to disgruntled troops who had little interest in their duties. This poor state of morale was particularly evident along the frontiers. For unlike their Yayoi or Yamato forefathers, the conscripts were not fighting to gain and hold land that they needed for their own survival. Instead most felt little or no connection to the rural frontier regions. Their priority was to get through their service so they could go back to their small plots of land and help their families survive.

This combination of factors gave the Emishi a significant advantage over the Japanese forces. For the Emishi were everything the imperial conscript troops were not: effective, well-trained fighters with a strong determination to defend their territories. It was factors such as these that allowed the Emishi to defeat numerically superior enemy forces, the most famous example of which was the destruction in AD 789 at the battle of Subuse (sometimes written Sufuse) of a large part of what historical chronicles claim was a 52,000-strong Japanese expeditionary force led by Shōgun Ki no Kosami against the Emishi, though this figure is somewhat dubious.

Shōgun Ki no Kosami's crushing defeat was nonetheless a pivotal moment in Japanese history. For it forced the court in Nara, where the capital had been moved in AD 710, to concede the fact that the conscripted national army was no longer capable of performing its primary duty. Nearly a century of defeats and setbacks at the hands of the Emishi, whom the national army vastly outnumbered, attested to the ineffectiveness of the costly conscript force.

Yet it was not simply the defeats suffered by the conscript army that made the court revisit its policy of a national force, for the state required some form of armed force to deal with its enemies. What brought the idea of a national army into question was why its troops were so ineffective when, as the court was becoming increasingly aware, the privately employed warriors from the frontier *shōen* estates, particularly those from the Kantō plain region, were reportedly able to take on and defeat the Emishi on a regular basis. What was it that these isolated frontier *shōen* fighters did that made them such an effective fighting force, even in comparison to the fighters who served *shōen* elsewhere across Japan?

While the answer is multifaceted, there was one factor seemingly unique to the Kantō plain region *shōen* fighters that may have influenced their ability to fight the Emishi, and that was the influx of former Paekche mounted warriors that had flooded into the region as refugees after the fall of the Korean kingdom during the latter part of the mid-7th century. And though there is little direct evidence to support such a claim, it is interesting to note that the region these warriors are believed to have taken refuge in is the same that would within a few generations produce some of the finest mounted archers and capable warriors in the entire Japanese archipelago.

In saying this it is important not to overlook the multitude of other factors that contributed to the superior fighting abilities of the *shōen* warriors, particularly those near the frontiers, in comparison to the conscript troops of the national army. Key amongst the factors that motivated the *shōen* warriors was money. For at heart they were fundamentally mercenaries in the service of the local *kami*, who was legally entitled to employ men to police and protect his autonomous domain as he saw fit. They were technically not allowed to have armies, but that is what these quasi-police forces slowly metamorphosed into over time. Irrespective of this fact, the experience of the conscript soldiers contrasted sharply with that of the *shōen* warriors, considering that the former were expected to shoulder the cost of the privilege of being placed in harm's way.

Unlike the conscripted national force, the *shōen kami* could pick and choose the men who served them, which meant that only the most capable and talented of fighters earned and held positions with an estate. This motivated the fighters to maintain their weapons and equipment and to develop their proficiency in the martial arts, skills that could only be maintained if a man was free from other responsibilities. This meant that a fighter needed to be paid a sufficient and motivating wage, something that only the wealthy *shōen kami* were capable or willing to offer.

Adding to the *esprit de corps* that was emerging amongst the *shōen* warriors was the fact these fighters were primarily individuals who had been born and raised along the frontier. They were used to living a hard, Spartan lifestyle. They were comfortable on the land and, like their opponents, felt a connection with it that made them willing to fight for it, unlike the conscript national army troops to whom the frontier was to all intents a foreign land.

Finally, it would be unrealistic to rule out any benefit to the fringe elements of Yamato society from the presence of Emishi who had been drawn into and merged with it over the centuries. Mixed relationships and interaction would naturally have been greatest along the frontier and may very well have been even more common in the Kantō region, where the local Yayoi shared a passion for horses that was far more in keeping with that of the Emishi than in other places across the archipelago. This form of interaction and cultural understanding would have given the warriors from this region an advantage when engaging the Emishi. For they would have had an intimate understanding of their opponents' mindset, tactics and lifestyle, knowledge that would have allowed them to take the fight to the Emishi in the same way that the latter preferred to engage the conscript troops of the imperial army, through ambush and hit-and-run tactics.

While the imperial court had eyed with concern the growing size of many of the frontier *shōen*'s domestic police forces, which were clearly far larger than was realistically necessary to maintain local control, they were willing to turn a blind eye to the size and strength of these paramilitary groups due to the simple fact that it was becoming increasingly evident that the presence of these warriors was the only thing preventing the eastern frontiers of Japan from collapsing.

Thus when a large part of Shōgun Ki no Kosami's huge expeditionary force was annihilated by the Emishi in AD 789, the imperial court knew that they were going to have to find an alternative to the inept conscript army and that this needed to be done in a timely manner if they wished to hold the state together. The impressive and proven exploits of the Kantō plain area *shōen* warriors made them the logical choice to take over from the national army, which was thoroughly disheartened, poorly led and bankrupting the nation to the benefit of the private *shōen* estates, whose warriors were everything that the imperial troops were not: well equipped, well trained, highly motivated and more importantly capable of bring the Emishi to heel. In short they were exactly what the court needed. They were the right people, in the right place, at the right time. They were also primarily led by men who, as the cast-off descendants of imperial court nobility, bore the honorific family names of Taira and Minamoto that identified their connection to the imperial lineage.

A representation of the famous early 10th century *shōen kami* or lord of an autonomous estate, Taira no Masakado. While the major border conflicts with the Emishi had largely been resolved by the time of Masakado, it was the powerful and wealthy *shōen* leaders such as he, with their connections to the imperial family, who became the hired enforcers of state will. Many of these state-hired warriors came from the Kantō plain area estates, whose warriors were renowned for their equestrian abilities. (Artwork by Angus McBride, from *Early Samurai AD 200–1500* © Osprey Publishing)

SAMURAI ARMOUR

This was a hugely significant factor in the eyes of the court. For just as the names and imperial pedigrees of the *shōen* leaders had impressed and carried considerable clout amongst their rural countrymen and paid retainers, it also helped to legitimize the court's decision to commission the *shōen* leaders and their warriors to fight its battles for it along the frontier. For this allowed the court to maintain what outwardly appeared to be control over the military forces operating within the state. It was also hoped that these distant connections would help to bind the *shōen* leaders to the court.

Initially this move was an almost ideal scenario for the imperial court, for it allowed them to slowly phase out the costly and ineffective conscript army which had devastated the economy and to do so without incurring further debts or jeopardizing national security. They could now subcontract responsibility for national security out to existing elements within the state who by lineage were extensions of the state. The court conveniently avoided paying for the services of these agents by agreeing to compensate them for their efforts with land grants, including portions of any new territories gained through the conquest of the state's enemies, which was an excellent deal for the *shōen* holders. For land meant agricultural land, and this equated to an increase in the production of foodstuffs, namely rice, which was and remained the basis for currency in Japan until the very end of the Japanese feudal period in 1868.

If a historical date could ever be associated with the emergence of the samurai, it would be the year AD 792. For it was in this year that the imperial court announced the discontinuation of conscription. This act, in conjunction with the commissioning of internal agencies to fight on behalf of the state, signified the end of the court's monopoly over domestic military affairs and in turn created a market for professional military men for hire, and the results were almost immediate. After nearly a century of continuous conflict along the frontier regions, the Japanese began to drive the Emishi back as they experienced their first real battlefield successes against their ancient domestic foe. This success culminated in AD 802 when Shōgun Sakanoue no Tamuramaro led his expeditionary forces in a crushing campaign against the Emishi which ended with the capture of over 500 enemy warriors in a single engagement.

The devastating psychological impact that the defeat and capture of over 500 of their warriors had on the Emishi peoples and their willingness to continue to resist was, however,

A representation of a Heian period warrior from the imperial Guard. Free from the highly intricate etiquette and elaborate trappings of court, the rural *shōen* fighters were better able to focus their time and attention on improving their martial skills than their brethren closer to the capital. (Image © and courtesy of the Kyōto Costume Museum)

unfortunately squandered when the imperial court had the entire contingent of prisoners that Tamuramaro had sent to the capital executed. This had been done contrary to Tamuramaro's advice and reversed the standing imperial practice of dispersing Emishi prisoners, particularly women and children, throughout the western provinces of Yamato in an effort to entice their menfolk to lay down their arms and merge with Japanese society.

A late 19th century depiction of a samurai of around the 14th century by an unknown artist. (Library of Congress, Prints & Photographs Division, LC-DIG-jpd-01046)

The court's decision to execute the Emishi prisoners reignited tensions all along the frontier and caused the Emishi to fight with a renewed vigour. Feeling that they had no option left open to them but to fight and die, the Emishi continued to resist throughout most of the 9th century, as they were slowly driven northward by a series of expeditionary campaigns commanded by various *shōen* lords who were granted the temporary title of *shōgun* for the duration of these operations.

The title *shōgun*, which roughly equated to the rank of commander-in-chief of an expeditionary force, was first used in AD 710 and was based on the dramatic style of rank titles that were at that time common to the armies of the Tang Dynasty Chinese. Effectively a temporary court-backed military commission, the term *shōgun* was an abbreviation of the formal court title of *Jeisetsu Sei-I-Shōgun* or 'barbarian-quelling general', in reference to the Emishi peoples that the holder of this rank was intended to have to deal with, even though it would eventually evolve to be a term synonymous with a military dictator.

From the standpoint of this book, the evolution of the samurai ends at the point where most histories of the samurai begin. It is for this reason that my account of the history of the samurai ends here. For there is a large number of excellent books on the history of the samurai that cover the period from the early 9th century onward in the most minute detail. My goal has been to introduce readers to the major historical events and players who contributed to the early evolution of the Japanese warrior and in turn the forms of armour that these forces and the future samurai class would utilize. For the Jōmon, Yayoi and Paekche all contributed to how armour in Japan evolved, as did the Tang Dynasty Chinese and other Korean peninsula kingdoms to various degrees. Without an understanding of these groups and how they fit into and contributed to the historical timeline of Japanese history, the evolution of Japanese armour cannot be fully understood.

It is important to note that I have intentionally used very broad brush strokes to create my portrait of early Japanese history for the simple reason that again this is not a book about the samurai or Japanese history as such. Therefore, out of necessity a great deal of important detail, such as names, places and other historical events, has been passed over in the interests of moving the discussion towards the main topic of this text, Japanese armour. Having said this, a brief summary of the growth of the warrior class from the 9th century onward is in order.

While the imperial court's decision to commission the wealthy and independent *shōen* landholders to act as the military arm of the state did help to turn the tide in the ongoing conflict with the Emishi in favour of the Japanese, it was a foolish and shortsighted act. For the court was effectively empowering domestic rivals to their long-held hegemony over state power. As the power, prestige and wealth of the *shōen* continued to grow throughout the 10th and 11th centuries, the court's influence over them began to wane until the most powerful *shōen* families began to act unilaterally when their interests were affected, which included going to war against other landholding families.

Ultimately the court found its authority being challenged by two of the most powerful landholding families, the Minamoto and Taira, who were fighting each other to gain supremacy over the state. The Minamoto eventually prevailed and established Japan's first military dictatorship in Kamakura under the governance of a shōgunate.

A scene from the 16th century *Illustrated Story of the Night Attack on Yoshitsune's Residence at Horikawa*, depicting the raid that occurred in 1185. Yoshitsune is depicted wearing *yoroi*, while his mistress Tomoe Gozen, who is standing beside him, and the two other retainers, wear the more practical *dō-maru* styles of cuirass. (Wikimedia Commons/ Public Domain)

An Edo period image now housed in Ōsaka Castle Museum depicting Tokugawa Ieyasu, the 'Great Unifier', who gained control following the battle of Sekigahara in 1600 over the hundreds of small independent countries, or *kuni* that made up the Japanese archipelago at the end of the 16th century. Ieyasu was the father of the Tokugawa Shōgunate that was to control Japan for over 250 years. The Tokugawa Shōgunate ended in 1868 with the resignation of the fifteenth Tokugawa Shōgun, Tokugawa Yoshinobu, who died in 1913. (Wikimedia Commons/Public Domain)

The Kamakura Shōgunate lasted until the first half of the 14th century. Its grip on power was, however, severely weakened by two separate invasion attempts by Mongol forces during the 13th century. For the shōgunate was unable to compensate the various warrior families who expended their personal wealth in their efforts to defend the nation. Traditionally, warriors had been compensated for their efforts by receiving a portion of the spoils of war, which generally included a distribution of land, but as the fighting had been in defence of the homeland, there were no conquered lands to divide up amongst the various concerned factions, which led in turn to conflict.

The imperial court used this as an opportunity to briefly regain control over the country but was quickly ousted again after only three years at the helm and replaced by a new shōgunate. This second military dictatorship's grip on power, however, never matched that of the first shōgunate, a fact that many of the powerful regional governors, or *shugo daimyō* as they came to be referred to, gradually became aware of over the course of the late 14th and 15th centuries.

These men, who were the forerunners of the feudal warlord *daimyō*, began to prey on each other, attacking and seizing the territory of their neighbours, irrespective of the wishes of the shōgunate. These small local wars gradually flared in scale and intensity until eventually the majority of Japanese provinces were at war with each other on a more or less permanent basis from the late 15th through until the latter part of the 16th century, an era that subsequently came to be known as the Sengoku Jidai, or 'Country at War' period.

By the 1560s, the famous Japanese warlord Oda Nobunaga had emerged from the fray and begun the first serious drive towards national unification. Nobunaga, however, after gaining control over a sizeable portion of the country, was assassinated by one of his subordinates in 1582 before he could complete unification. The task fell to another of his subordinates, Toyotomi Hideyoshi, but Hideyoshi was a commoner by birth and was therefore according to established precedent unable to assume the unifying rank of Shōgun.

When Hideyoshi died in 1598 a joint regency was established to govern the nation until his five-year-old son could come of age and take the helm. Not surprisingly the regency quickly dissolved into a disagreement that split the country into two opposing armed camps that ultimately met on the battlefield of Sekigahara in 1600 to determine who would control the nation, ostensibly on behalf of the regent. This colossal battle, which saw some 160,000 samurai take to the field, ended in victory for the eastern army, which was commanded by Tokugawa Ieyasu.

Ieyasu, who had initially been a foe and then an ally of Nobunaga, went on to serve his successor Hideyoshi before finally becoming Shōgun in 1603 and establishing the Tokugawa Shōgunate, which ruled over Japan under the descendants of Ieyasu and the Tokugawa clan.

A high-quality *gusoku* from the early 19th century that combines components and features indicative of armours from several different periods. (New York Metropolitan Museum of Art/CC0 1.0)

CHAPTER 2

THE *DŌ* (CUIRASS)

The foundation of Japanese armour

Ask any truly knowledgeable collector, curator or dealer of samurai armour to describe a specific set of armour and they will, according to long-established precedent, begin by identifying the style of cuirass around which the other components of the grouping are assembled.

It is impossible to say exactly when the Japanese began to identify the forms of armour that they produced by the style of the cuirass, or *dō*, though it seems reasonable to assume that this practice began very early on in the evolutionary history of Japanese armour, perhaps as far back as the 5th century, when the rigid *tankō* and the lamellar *keikō*, the first two consistently reproduced forms of *dō*, began to appear.

By the end of the 10th century, however, the unique forms of cuirass, or *yoroi*, as the *dō* of that period are referred to, were clearly viewed as the dominant element amongst the various component parts that came to be commonly associated with a complete and matching set of armour, or *gusoku*. Note, however, that the term *gusoku* only came into use in relation to Japanese armour in the early part of the 16th century. For this reason, it is never used by the Japanese to refer to sets of armour that existed prior to the end of the 9th century or for those that were developed between the 10th and late 15th centuries. As such, the four main types of armour that existed during these periods are identified based solely upon the style of cuirass irrespective of the fact that this was generally accompanied by other items of armour, such as matching helmet and shoulder guards. The one exception to this rule is the *yoroi* style of cuirass, which is referred to as an *ō-yoroi* when accompanied by other pieces.

The prominence of the *yoroi* over the other armoured component parts of its period may to some extent have been the result of the incredibly complex nature of its construction, which made it an extremely expensive item to procure and thus by default the centrepiece of the ensemble. This unpleasant reality was in part offset by the *yoroi*'s proven ability to protect its wearer from missiles, such as arrows, which were the primary weapons that warriors encountered in battle in the centuries leading up to and immediately after the turn of the first millennium.

Equally important to the Japanese, however, was the aesthetic beauty of the *yoroi*, which seems to have come about in part from the

A late Edo period reproduction of a yoroi. *The lamellar* ichi-mai-dō yoroi *was the only form of cuirass utilized from the early 10th century until the latter part of the 13th century. Note the box-like shape of the suspended* kusazuri *thigh armour.*

seemingly happenstance evolutionary twists of cuirass designs in Japan over several centuries. And while it would be unrealistic to assume that the unique Japanese sense of aesthetics did not influence some aspects of the *yoroi*'s overall shape and design, for clearly it did, it was also the unique nature of the method by which the *yoroi* was constructed that endeared it to the Japanese. For every aspect of its assembly easily lent itself to the incorporation of a substantial degree of artistic embellishment, the presence of which did not undermine the military effectiveness or practicality of this make of cuirass.

The *yoroi* also came into use just as the concept of a warrior class was beginning to take shape in Japan and it remained the most common form of cuirass for a number of centuries. As such the *yoroi* was virtually synonymous with the idea of the warrior, to the point that it continued to be worn by the elite of the Japanese military caste for several centuries even after it had become obsolete. For the *yoroi* had become a symbolic icon of the core principles by which the samurai identified themselves. These principles were primarily based on the 'benchmarks for samurai excellence' that were established during the 12th-century Genpei War between the Minamoto and Taira clans, and immortalized in artworks and tales depicting that conflict.[1]

This is not to suggest that Japanese armour-making techniques had reached their zenith by the end of the 12th century, as this was not the case. The precedent, however, had been set. When referring to a set of armour the *yoroi* was the defining or central element within a grouping of armoured items. And as the martial culture of Japan was built upon an adherence to tradition, it became the established practice to identify all sets of armour by the style of the cuirass that the set was assembled around, irrespective of the importance, cost or grandeur of some of the other accompanying pieces.

This is why the *dō* in its various forms is the first thing that students new to the subject of Japanese armour should learn about. Unfortunately it is an area of study that is not particularly well defined in the majority of existing Western literature that is available on this subject. Adding to the complexity of the topic is the 'bewildering variety of styles and types of armour' that were utilized by the Japanese between the 4th and 19th centuries.[2]

In *Japanese Armor: The Galeno Collection* Ian Bottomley simplifies his introduction to this confusing subject matter by breaking the 'profusion of styles of armour that were made and worn throughout this long period of time' into three distinct categories.[3] These are based on the developmental changes or phases that occurred in the evolution of Japanese cuirass designs. This approach is also utilized by Japanese scholars, who likewise divide the history of the *dō* into three separate categories that are

The *Dō* (cuirass)

A 5th century sankaku-ita byō-toji variety of tankō. The tankō was one of the first regularly reproduced forms of cuirass utilized in the Japanese archipelago. (Image courtesy of J.L. Badgley)

differentiated from each other based on how cuirasses were constructed during different time periods. Bottomley's breakdown differs from the conventional Japanese perspective, however, in that he intentionally avoids discussing the forms of armour that are generally lumped together within the first historical category of cuirass designs, which include the oldest, or proto-historical examples of Japanese *dō*. Bottomley

The mae-dō portion of a hon kozane ni-mai-dō. Armour made in Japan between the early 10th and late 15th centuries was constructed from sane-ita assembled from dozens of individual leather or iron scales called kozane.

makes it clear that he has done so due to the fact that such items are almost unknown outside Japan and are therefore generally of less interest and little relevance to non-Japanese students of this subject matter.

Thus Bottomley's first category corresponds with what most other reference sources generally regard as the second categorization or major evolutionary stage in Japanese armour design, which was a universal transition to forms of cuirass that were assembled using lamellar construction. While lamellar armour is known to have existed in Japan as far back as the 4th century, this second evolutionary stage is generally regarded as having lasted from the early 10th century until the early 16th century. Commonly referred to as the early to high medieval era in Japanese history, this period saw four main distinctive designs of cuirass utilized: the *yoroi*, the *dō-maru*, the *haramaki* and the *hara-ate*.

Bottomley's second category again corresponds with what is generally viewed as being the third major evolutionary stage and categorization of Japanese cuirass designs, which was the development and introduction of the so-called *tosei* or 'modern' forms of cuirass. These differed from the cuirasses of earlier centuries in that they were primarily assembled from various arrangements of solid metal plates, referred to as *ita-mono*, that were generally riveted together.

This new method of fabrication and assembly led to the creation of a huge number of unique designs of cuirass. These are generally distinguished from each other based upon the manner in which they were assembled and the number of sectional pieces that were utilized to create the cuirass. While there was a short transitional period prior to the development of the first true forms of *tosei-dō*, these new forms of cuirass, which began to appear in the decade prior to the middle of the 16th century, continued to be utilized until the very end of the Japanese feudal period in the late 1860s. As such *tosei-dō* are commonly portrayed as having represented the final evolutionary stage in the development of Japanese cuirass designs.

According to Bottomley, however, another, less easily defined, form of cuirass evolved out of the *tosei-dō* styles, one that originated in the 'more relaxed social atmosphere' that was synonymous with the predominately peaceful Edo period, the years of the Tokugawa Shōgunate, which lasted from the early 17th century until the latter half of the 19th century.[4] Though Japanese scholars have not yet formally recognized this fact, this author is in complete agreement with Bottomley in this regard, and likewise believes that a separate post-*tosei* categorization of armours clearly did begin to take form sometime around the latter part of the 17th century. These cuirasses differed from conventional *tosei-dō,* which had grown progressively more practical in design over the course of the 16th century, in that the post-*tosei* examples of cuirass were increasingly fabricated in ways that actually reversed most of the practical and technological advances that had been made over the course of the preceding centuries until the cuirass that resulted would have had no practical benefit in battle.

Though not defined by Bottomley, this author refers to such items, or cuirasses, as revivalist *dō*. For the revivalist items of armour that were produced primarily between the early 18th and mid-19th century were fundamentally hybrid makes of cuirass that amalgamated pre-*tosei-dō* features with *tosei-dō* construction techniques. While this trend resulted in the creation of some of the most visually impressive examples of armour ever produced in Japan, the usefulness of these items was often severely undermined by the fact that many of them incorporated highly impractical and often long obsolete pre-*tosei* features into their method of construction and finished designs.

While Bottomley's insightful theories have been instrumental in helping to challenge some of the rather dated status quo perspectives on Japanese armour, this author believes that another evolutionary stage in the development of Japanese armour designs still needs to be added to the historical timeline. For while armour continued to be fabricated from plate and scale in various forms throughout the Edo period, a new style of mail- or *kusari*-based armour also began to emerge. Overshadowed by their more elaborate plate or scale counterparts, items of armour made from mail were extremely common through the latter half of the Edo period. In fact, by this time the wearing of conventional armour was largely limited to that of a dress uniform for ceremonial purposes. The primary form of armour worn by most samurai, for actual protective purposes, through the latter half of the Edo period was made of mail in combination with plate.

The *mae-dō* portion of *kuro urushi nuri yokohagi-okegawa ni-mai-dō*. The Japanese began to use solid plates to assemble armour in the late 15th century. By the 1540s, 'modern cuirasses', or *tosei-dō*, assembled from horizontally arranged solid plates riveted together began to appear.

The Dō (Cuirass)

These largely overlooked items represented the last and in many ways the logical final evolution in the long history of Japanese armour. That said, they are rarely discussed in depth or given their place in the historical timeline of Japanese history. This is primarily due to the fact that these items fail to conform to the preconceived notion of what Japanese armour was supposed to have been, the most commonly held image of which is generally also incorrect. For most people when they think of samurai armour envision items that are more closely associated with the 18th and 19th century revisionist forms than any of the actual forms of armour that had been utilized for close to a millennium prior to that time.

As noted, certain forms of armour are synonymous with certain periods. That said, it is important to keep in mind a number of factors when considering the timelines involved. Firstly, these are for the most part only guidelines and are not meant to indicate well-defined dates. It would be unrealistic to discount the considerable degree of overlap that existed between time periods as the transitional shift took place and saw one form of cuirass slowly fade out as the next evolutionary stage of *dō* fabrication technique and style began to take hold.

Secondly, while many forms of cuirass are unique to specific periods, as already noted, many old and otherwise obsolete styles were

Left: An 18th century hybrid form of *dō* that is a combination of construction techniques and designs from various time periods.

Right: *A kinpaku oshi,* or applied gold leaf, finished *karuta-gane kusari katabira*. Folding, lightweight items of armour such as this that made extensive use of chainmail were what the majority of the samurai actually utilized for protection from the mid-18th century onward. Conventional lamellar or plate armour was primarily reserved for ceremonial purposes.

revisited in later eras. As such it is quite possible to find a cuirass, such as a *yoroi*, that in form looks as though it dates to the 12th century when it was actually produced in the mid-19th century. Attempts to date armour based on physical features alone should therefore be avoided, especially if one is not exceptionally well versed in the numerous small idiosyncrasies that will actually differentiate 12th century items from extremely well-made 19th century reproductions.

All forms of cuirass, irrespective of the period in which they were produced, can be further organized into seven important subcategories. These are based on the number of independent sections, or *mai*, that were utilized to construct the main body of the *dō*. While the term *mai* technically translates as a 'flat thing' or 'plate' in Japanese, when it is used with regard to *dō* it refers to a single segment of armour, irrespective of how that segment was constructed. In other words a *mai* can be assembled from several stacked rows of *sane-ita*. It could also be made from a number of either horizontally or vertically arranged solid plates. Alternatively a *mai* can be constructed from a single solid piece of plate armour, or from a combination of both solid plate and *sane-ita*, as long as the two materials form at least one vertical segment of the portion of the *dō* that is referred to as the *nagakawa*. The *nagakawa* is the portion of the cuirass that surrounds the torso from the base of the sternum downward to a line about 1.5 cm below the navel.

One of the best ways to comprehend the *mai* method of categorization is to study the *go-mai*, or 'five-section', a design of cuirass that was introduced in the 16th century and is one of the seven major subcategories of cuirass. The *go-mai* style derives its name from the fact that the *nagakawa* of the cuirass is composed of five separate pieces of armour that when joined together by an arrangement of hinges are able to enclose the torso. The most common form of *go-mai-dō* usually consists of a portion of armour that covers the area of the belly, called the *mae-dō-no-ita*. This will generally have a section of armour called the *hidari-dō-no-ita* hinged to its left edge to provide protection for the left side of the torso. This segment will in turn have a back plate, called an *ushiro-dō-no-ita*, hinged to its rear edge. A narrow segment, referred to as the *ushiro-migi-dō-no-ita*, or 'rear right-hand cuirass plate', which is usually about

A *go-mai-dō,* or five-section cuirass, disassembled to show the five individual armour plate segments that are used to create the Yukinoshita variety of *go-mai-dō*. The pieces from left to right are referred to as: *mae-migi-dō-no-ita*, *mae-dō-no-ita*, *hidari-dō-no-ita*, *ushiro-dō-no-ita*, and the *ushiro migi-dō-no-ita*. Note that the *wadagami* have been removed.

The *Dō* (Cuirass)

three-fifths of the width of the *hidari-dō-no-ita*, will then be hinged to the right-hand edge of the back plate portion to cover the rear right side of the torso. An almost identical, though mirror-image segment called the *mae-migi-dō-no-ita* (or front right-hand cuirass plate) will be affixed by a hinge to the right edge of the front portion of armour to cover the front right side of the torso. The front and rear *migi-dō-no-ita* and *hidari-dō-no-ita* segments were designed to close over each other like a pair of overlapping saloon doors, with the rear *ushiro-migi-dō-no-ita* closing over the top of the *mae-migi-dō-no-ita*. This arrangement of five conjoined sectional portions of armour forms a *nagakawa* that can fully enclose the torso with no gaps in the protective covering.

The seven subcategories of *dō* are as follows: *ichi-mai-dō* (one-section cuirass), *ni-mai-dō* (two-section cuirass), *san-mai-dō* (three-section cuirass), *yon-mai-dō* (four-section cuirass), the aforementioned *go-mai-dō*, and, though relatively rare, also the *roku-mai-dō* (six-section cuirass) and *isei-dō* (unusual cuirass), rare examples of *dō* that have been assembled from an unusually large number of separate pieces.

While it is essential that students of Japanese armour learn to recognize and categorize cuirasses based on the number of sectional pieces that they are assembled from, it is important not to fall into the habit of equating the number of *mai* in the *nagakawa* of a *dō* with the overall age of a cuirass, as is often done. For contrary to popular belief, the oldest Japanese cuirass designs were not by default the simplest. In fact, the earliest extant examples of *dō* were primarily examples of *ni-mai* and *san-mai-dō*. The popular belief originates from the fact that most histories of Japanese armour and the samurai start around the beginning of the 10th century when the trend was towards the construction of cuirasses that featured a continuous single-piece *nagakawa*, which meant that these early forms of lamellar cuirass were *ichi-mai-dō*.

Even if this often cited rule-of-thumb is applied to *dō* created after the 10th century it is still a highly inaccurate way of determining the age of a cuirass, for a number of reasons. For even though the *yoroi*, which was a form of *ichi-mai-dō*, was over the course of time superseded by the reintroduction of multi-

Overview profiles of the most common forms of the seven sub-categories of cuirass, as determined by the number of sections utilized in their construction. The seventh category – *isei-dō* – is not shown, owing to their rarity and irregular methods of assembly. Note that only the most commonly encountered forms of sectional assembly have been shown. Circles are used to represent hinges between separate sections. Overlapping sections of armour devoid of hinges would be tied together using lengths of cord anchored to the individual sections of the *dō*.

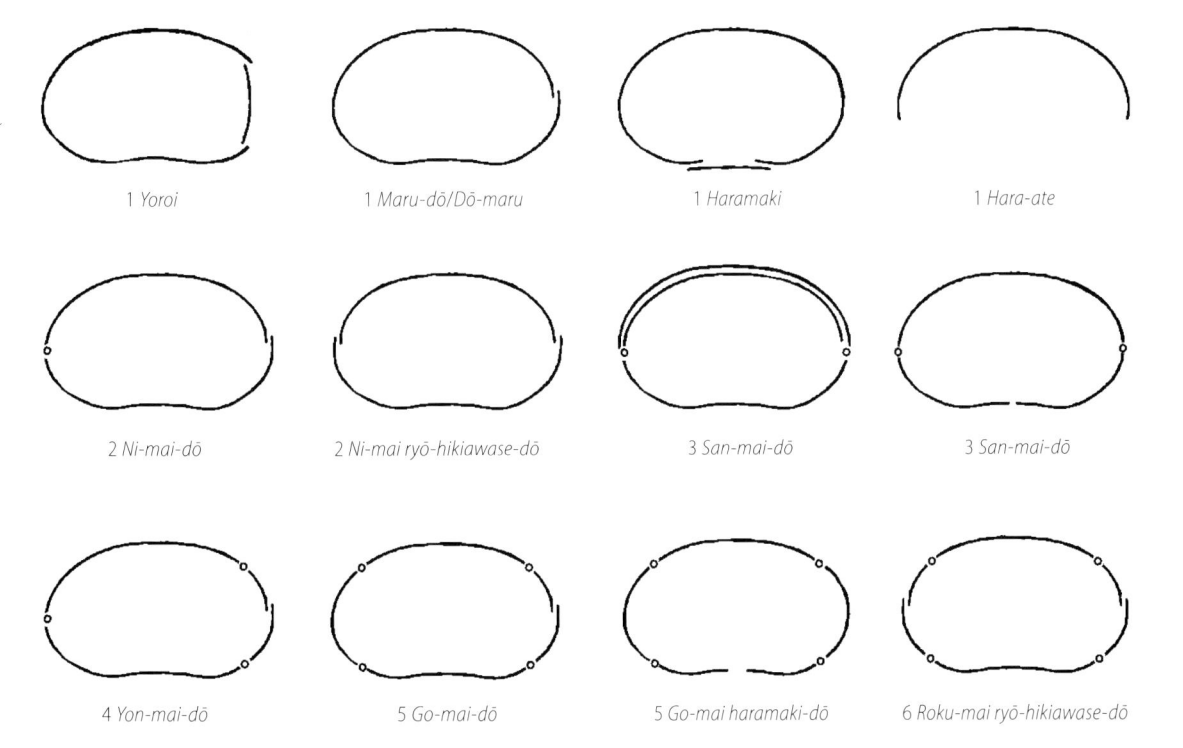

1 *Yoroi*

1 *Maru-dō/Dō-maru*

1 *Haramaki*

1 *Hara-ate*

2 *Ni-mai-dō*

2 *Ni-mai ryō-hikiawase-dō*

3 *San-mai-dō*

3 *San-mai-dō*

4 *Yon-mai-dō*

5 *Go-mai-dō*

5 *Go-mai haramaki-dō*

6 *Roku-mai ryō-hikiawase-dō*

sectional cuirass designs, their development did not occur in order of the number of sectional pieces that were used to construct a cuirass. In other words, the *ichi-mai-dō* was not followed in its development by the appearance of cuirasses made in two sections, in turn followed by the appearance of a *dō* that was made in three sections and so on. In fact an early forerunner of the *go-mai-dō* was being utilized long before the first reintroduced designs of *ni-mai-dō* began to appear prior to the middle of the 16th century.

Furthermore, as noted earlier in this chapter, revivalist *dō* represented one of the last developmental stages in the evolutionary history of Japanese cuirass designs. Yet these cuirasses by design intentionally mimicked many of the forms of *dō* that had been utilized several centuries before they were fabricated. As such, a large number of 18th and 19th century *ichi-mai-dō* also exist. In fact, far more historical reproductions of 10th through 15th century forms of cuirass exist than the original period items that they were fabricated to replicate.

There is also the fact that it was quite common for the Japanese to recycle or re-mount items of armour. Thus it is not uncommon to find a mid-19th century *gusoku* assembled around a refurbished cuirass from the late 16th century. Thus unless one is extremely well versed in the subtle historical details and facts that for example distinguish a late 16th century *go-mai-dō* from a five-section cuirass made in the mid-19th century, one should refrain from dating pieces based simply on the number of sectional pieces that were utilized to assemble a cuirass.

An important factor to keep in mind when attempting to associate a cuirass with one of the above subcategories is that the number of sections is not affected by the way the sections are arranged. For example, a *san-mai-dō* could be composed of a section of armour that protects the belly with two mirror-image sections

A high-quality late Edo period revisionist version of a *yoroi*-style cuirass. The single continuous piece construction that is indicative of an *ichi-mai-dō* is apparent when the *yoroi* is laid flat and expanded. Note that a *yoroi* only covered the front, left and back of the torso and that the right-hand side was protected by a separate piece of armour called a *waidate*, not shown in this image. Also note the hundreds of individual *kozane*, or scales, that have been used to assemble the lames, or *sane-ita*. A thick cord, called a *dō-jime*, that is used to tighten the cuirass around the waist is secured to the *yoroi*.

The Dō (cuirass)

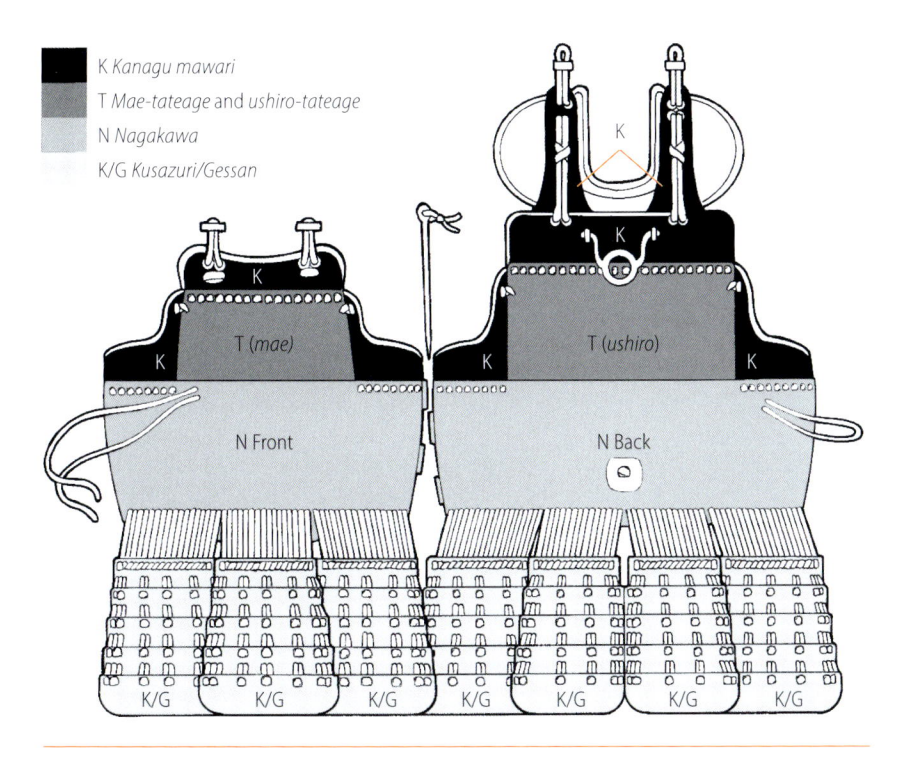

K *Kanagu mawari*
T *Mae-tateage* and *ushiro-tateage*
N *Nagakawa*
K/G *Kusazuri/Gessan*

An exploded view of a *tosei ni-mai-dō* with the main sectional portions of the cuirass construction highlighted. It is important to note that while there were major structural differences in how a *kodai-dō*, or pre-16th century cuirass, and post-16th century *tosei-dō* were assembled, the sectional portions of most conventional cuirasses, namely the *kanagu mawari*, *mae-* and *ushiro-tateage*, the *nagakawa* and the *kusazuri*, or *gessan*, remained largely consistent in form over the centuries. In some cases the words used to refer to certain components of a section of a cuirass differ depending on whether the cuirass was *kodai-dō* or *tosei-dō*.

attached to its outside edges that close clamshell-like around the sides and back of the torso. Alternatively, this arrangement could be reversed, with a large *ushiro-dō-no-ita*, or single solid back plate, fitted with two side plates that close around the sides and front of the torso. Or the cuirass could be constructed from an *ushiro-dō-no-ita* that has two full-size *mae-dō-no-ita* or solid frontal plates secured to its left and right edges that close over each other across the chest, which would double the thickness of the armour covering the front of the torso.

The upper body portion of cuirass, or the solid-plate portions above the *nagakawa*, is collectively referred to as the *kanagu mawari*, or literally 'metal pieces all around'. Originally the *kanagu mawari* were always fabricated from solid pieces of metal plate, even when the rest of a cuirass was assembled from lames, and hence their name. That said, it is possible for these plates also to be constructed from pieces of *nerigawa* or rawhide as well, particularly on *dō* that were made from the 18th century onward, though in such cases the entire cuirass will also usually be made from *nerigawa*.

The *kanagu mawari* on most conventional *dō* include the following key components: a breast-board, or *muna-ita*, a back or upper shoulder board called an *oshitsuke-no-ita*, armpit plates that are referred to as *waki-ita* and a pair of *wadagami* (which literally translates as 'shoulder above') shoulder straps. Depending on the design of the cuirass it is possible for there to be two, three or even four of any of the aforementioned plates in some cases.

The areas on the front and back of a cuirass above the *nagakawa* and between the *waki-ita* are referred to as the *mae-tateage* and the *ushiro-tateage* respectively. These two sections can be made en suite with the *nagakawa* or may be different in finished appearance from the latter. Irrespective of this fact, neither the *mae-tateage* nor *ushiro-tateage* are considered to be part of the *kanagu mawari*.

While it is important to understand the five evolutionary categories of cuirass development, students of this subject matter should also be able to correctly identify and assign *dō* to the correct subcategories. For all formal references to a *dō* or *gusoku* should always include the number of *mai* that were utilized in the assembly of a particular form of cuirass.

As only a handful of unique forms of cuirass designs were utilized in Japan prior to the late 15th century, the aesthetic characteristics of the materials that were utilized to fabricate a cuirass represented the majority of the information that was incorporated into the formal title of a cuirass. This was largely due to the fact that all makes of cuirass utilized during this period were variations of *ichi-mai-dō*. Thus it was unnecessary to reiterate this fact, for the *yoroi*, *dō-maru*, *hara-ate* and *haramaki* were all synonymous with the concept of an *ichi-mai-dō*. In fact, as no alternative method of *dō* construction technique existed through this period, there was

SAMURAI ARMOUR

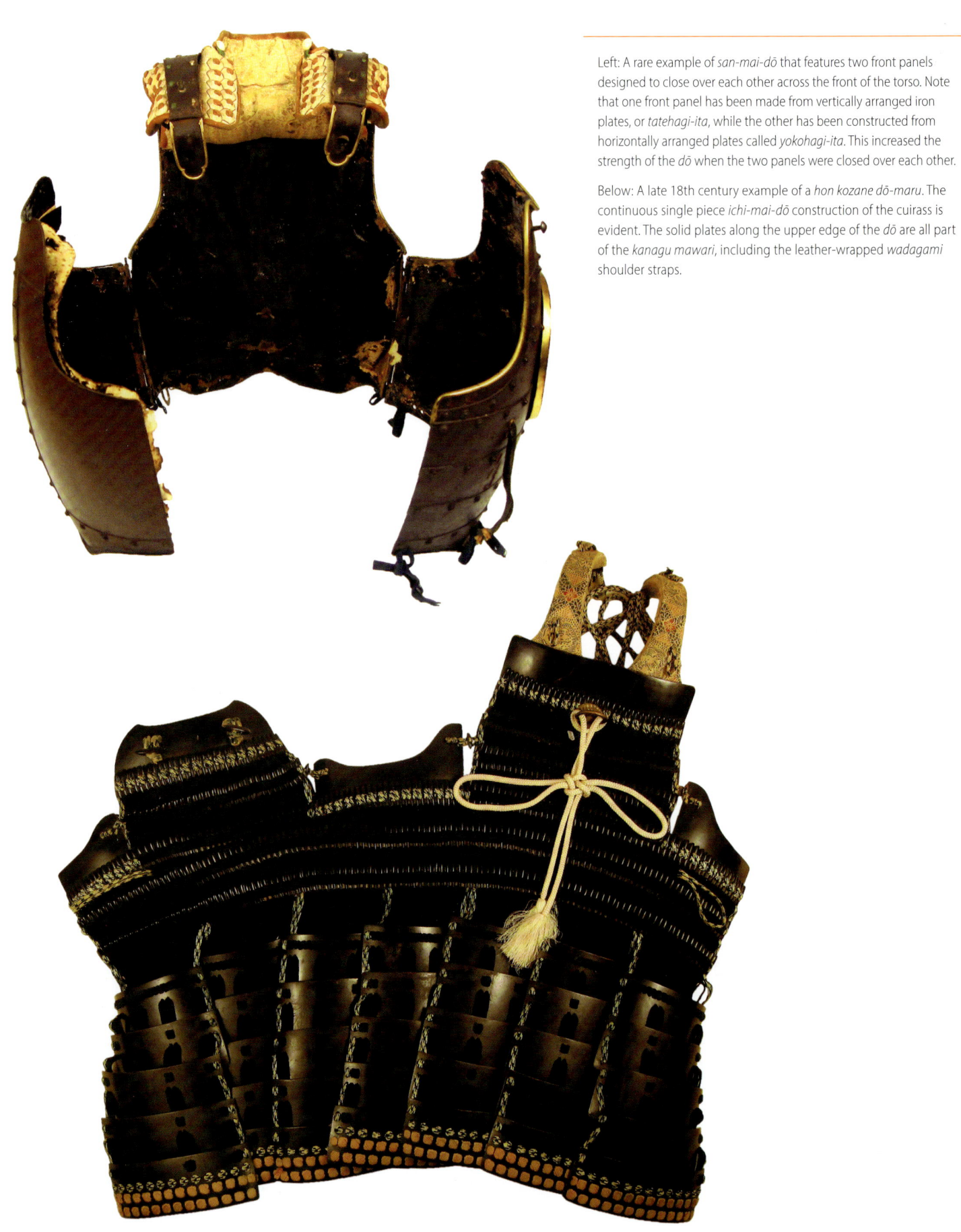

Left: A rare example of *san-mai-dō* that features two front panels designed to close over each other across the front of the torso. Note that one front panel has been made from vertically arranged iron plates, or *tatehagi-ita*, while the other has been constructed from horizontally arranged plates called *yokohagi-ita*. This increased the strength of the *dō* when the two panels were closed over each other.

Below: A late 18th century example of a *hon kozane dō-maru*. The continuous single piece *ichi-mai-dō* construction of the cuirass is evident. The solid plates along the upper edge of the *dō* are all part of the *kanagu mawari*, including the leather-wrapped *wadagami* shoulder straps.

The Dō (Cuirass)

probably no need for a term like *ichi-mai-dō* at that time either.

Initially the aesthetic descriptors used were fairly rudimentary. For example a *yoroi* that was assembled using red lacing or *aka-ito odoshi* would be referred to as an *aka-ito odoshi yoroi*. As the aesthetic detailing that was utilized grew over time, it became common to incorporate additional descriptors into the identifying title of the piece. For example a cuirass might be described as being a *fusebe-gawa odoshi wada koshi kurenai moegi dō-maru*, which translates as a 'smoked-leather laced *dō-maru* style cuirass with the upper rows of lamellae laced in (separate) bands of crimson and light green'.

When the huge number of alternative forms of *tosei-dō* designs of cuirass began to be introduced in the 16th century, the form in which a *dō* was constructed could no longer be assumed, as many of the *tosei* forms were assembled from multiple independent segments or *mai*. Thus formal titles for cuirasses and the *gusoku* that were formed around them also began to include information about the number of segments used to assemble the cuirass, as was demonstrated with the *go-mai-dō*.

Learning to identify the bewildering array of different forms of *tosei-dō* that were created can prove to be quite challenging, as this type of cuirass was the foundation of a huge variety of armour styles. Mastering an understanding of the different forms of *tosei-dō* is, however, not as difficult to achieve as it might appear, for the *tosei-dō* was simply a foundation upon which different styles of cuirass were established. In other words, for all their aesthetic differences,

Above: The horizontal plate construction that is indicative of a cuirass made in the *yokohagi-okegawa-dō* style is clearly visible in this image. Seven *gessan*, three suspended from the front of the *dō* and four from the back, is a typical arrangement for a *tosei-dō*.

Left: An example of a two-section cuirass assembled using vertically arranged plates in the *tatehagi-okegawa-dō* style. Note the arrangement of eight detachable *gessan*, with four each of these tassets suspended from the front and rear sections of the armour. Also note the *gattari* on the back of the *dō*.

the vast majority of *tosei-dō* are fundamentally similar when broken down to their core elements.

Strictly speaking, only four new subcategories or designs of cuirass were established with the introduction of the *tosei-dō*, namely the *yon-mai-dō*, the *go-mai-dō*, the *roku-mai-dō* and certain rare examples of *isei-dō*, for the *ni-mai-dō* and *san-mai-dō* had been invented during the proto-historical period. That said, the reintroduction of these latter two styles almost certainly came about devoid of any historical influences. As such they should be viewed as having occurred without knowledge of the earlier-period items and were therefore separate evolutionary events.

The point to note here is that irrespective of the fact that there are numerous different finished forms of *tosei-dō*, all of them can be subcategorized even further as being one of just three base forms of construction technique: *yokohagi-ita* (horizontally arranged board), *tatehagi-ita* (vertically arranged board), and *ichi-mai-ita* (one solid board). Thus the five-section cuirass used in previous examples might, depending on its actual method of construction, be described as being a *yokohagi-okegawa go-mai-dō*. Note that when multiple *ita* or 'boards' are being discussed, the term *okegawa* is utilized. Thus, including *ichi-mai-dō*, which by the nature of its design cannot be assembled from solid plates, nineteen different combinations of *tosei-dō* are possible. However, it was the manner in which the nineteen combinations of cuirass were assembled and finished that created the huge number of varied forms of *tosei-dō*.

For example, *go-mai-dō* constructed from horizontal plates that were fastened together with countersunk and thus largely invisible rivets would simply be referred to as a *yokohagi-okegawa go-mai-dō*. If, however, prominent external rivets with protruding dome-like heads were used, then the latter would become the first aesthetic feature to be mentioned, which would make the cuirass a *byō-toji* (fastened by externally visible rivets) *yokohagi-okegawa go-mai-dō*. If, however, the exterior façade of a *yokohagi-okegawa go-mai-dō* were covered with a thick application of lacquer that hid the horizontal or vertical bands of the plate construction under a smooth exterior finish, then the cuirass would be identified as being *nuri-gome hotoke go-mai-dō* (heavily lacquered smooth-finished five-section cuirass). Note that reference to the *yokohagi-okegawa* method of assembly is dropped from the formal title of the cuirass when as a feature it is no longer visibly apparent on the façade of the *dō*, even though as the base method of construction the feature continues, unobserved, to exist.

As the above examples demonstrate, a simple *go-mai-dō* could metamorphose into a number of seemingly different forms of cuirass depending on which aesthetic features were incorporated into the construction of the *dō* and how it was finished. The resulting cuirasses were identified by or named after their most prominent feature or combination of features, which superseded the pre-*tosei-dō* practice of identifying cuirasses based upon the materials that were used to assemble the *dō*.

For the most part the formal identifiers that differentiate between and define the various styles of *tosei-dō* are fairly straightforward, for they are derived from an ordered explanation of the physical features of a cuirass. However, except for the description of the cuirass being concluded

A fine example of a rawhide, or *nerigawa* example of *ni-mai-dō* that has been constructed using *ichi-mai-ita*, or single-plate pieces. Note the prominent *hatomune* (pigeon breast) medial ridge running down the front of the *mae-dō*.

The Dō (Cuirass)

Three examples of *go-mai-dō* that have been constructed in the *yokohagi-okegawa* style. While fundamentally identical in overall construction, the three cuirasses are surprisingly different in appearance. This was one of the factors that made the *tosei-dō* method of cuirass construction so popular. For the use of solid plates riveted together freed armour makers from the limitations peculiar to *dō* that were assembled from lamellae which had to be laced together. Note how subtle aesthetic differences could significantly alter the finished appearance of a cuirass, such as the colour or use of a lacquer finish. The colour of the *odoshi-ge* and the manner in which it was strung could also significantly alter the appearance of a *dō*.

by mention of how many sections it is assembled from, there are no rules that define exactly what must be included in the formal title of a cuirass or in what order the features or materials must be mentioned. The best practice, however, is to include as much information about a cuirass as is possible, beginning with external aesthetic features and working backwards or inwards towards the base method of construction.

The first feature that should be identified if possible is whether the armour has been assembled from *tetsu* (iron) or *nerigawa* (rawhide). This should generally be followed by the finish applied to these materials. For example a *tatehagi okegawa go-mai-dō* that has been assembled from iron plates might feature a black lacquer, or *kuro urushi nuri* finish. In this case the cuirass would be referred to as a *tetsu kuro urushi nuri tatehagi okegawa go-mai-dō*. Alternatively a red lacquer finish referred to as *shu urushi* may have been applied, in which case the cuirass would be referred to as a *shu urushi nuri tatehagi okegawa go-mai-dō*. Or the iron could be devoid of a thick lacquer covering and feature a treated surface that produces a rich russet iron patina that is referred to as *tetsu-sabiji*. It was also common for plates to be wrapped in leather or faced with cloth. A multitude of variables are possible when it comes to external finishes, which is why such features should be identified in the formal title if possible.

SAMURAI ARMOUR

When dealing with *tosei-dō* that have been assembled from sections of *sane-ita* or *ita-mono* that feature a replicated scale façade, the observer begins by identifying the finish applied to the scales and then identify the type of scale, or *sane*, the various styles of which will be discussed in detail in the following chapters.

The next feature to be identified differs depending on whether a cuirass is assembled from lamellar or solid-plate sections. If *sane-ita* or *ita-mono* are used with a replicated lamellar façade, the colour and then the method of lacing utilized is generally the next feature to be described. For example, if a solid-plate constructed two-section cuirass was made with a façade that gives it the appearance of being assembled from thousands of individual small scales, or *kozane*, the cuirass will then usually be laced in the tightly spaced vertically strung *kebiki odoshi* style. If the lacing is a dark blue tone then the cuirass will be referred to as a *kiritsuke kozane kon kebiki odoshi ni-mai-dō* or a 'replicated small scale navy blue closely spaced lacing two-section cuirass'.

If, however, a cuirass is constructed in a manner that incorporates a certain number of features that can collectively be identified or referred to by a brand-like

Three examples of *tatehagi-okegawa go-mai-dō*. As with the *yokohagi-okegawa* examples, these three cuirasses appear to share few similarities when in fact they are fundamentally identical to one another in overall form. The huge difference that the colouration of the *urushi* used can make to the finished appearance of a cuirass is clearly visible in the top and lower left cuirasses. The lower right example again looks completely different due to the fact that it has been faced in red and gold lacquered leather with prominent external rivets.

name, then the name used for that particular style is always used in the formal title in lieu of describing that particular combination of physical features. For example, if a two-section cuirass is constructed with a façade where the style of the replicated scale exterior and method of lacing corresponding to that portion of the façade abruptly changes from one form of replicated scale and lacing style to another, creating two visually different horizontal bands around the exterior of the *dō*, then the cuirass is referred to as a *dangae ni-mai-dō*, or literally a 'step changing two-section cuirass'. If the stylistic name reference was not used, then the same cuirass might be described as being a *kiritsuke kozane kebiki odoshi muna-tori iyozane sugake odoshi koshi-tori ni-mai dō,* or a 'replicated small scale closely spaced lacing upper torso band with a replicated large scale widely spaced lacing lower torso banded two-section cuirass'. Thus it is easy to appreciate why it is generally much less confusing to utilize style-specific brand-like names to refer to certain commonly recurring forms of aesthetic finish or styles of cuirass.

While it is much easier to use a single name to refer to complex finished forms or styles, as the above example demonstrates, a considerable degree of important information is often not transmitted when names are utilized in lieu of descriptive references. For a cuirass could be assembled in the reverse order of the *dō* described in the previous example and still be considered to be made in the *dangae* style, as could several other alternative finished variations of this make of cuirass. And this is where many students of Japanese armour begin to run into trouble. For they learn to associate the aesthetic characteristics of a cuirass finished in a certain way with one specific example of *dō* made in that particular style. In other words they mistakenly assume that a cuirass must correspond almost exactly to the example version of a particular style of *dō* to be that form of cuirass. Thus if the cuirass that was described in the above paragraph is again used as an example, the student might assume that for a cuirass to be a *dangae* style of *dō,* the upper torso portion would always have to feature replicated small scales laced in the *kebiki odoshi* style while the lower portion of the *nagakawa* would have to feature *iyozane* laced in the *sugake odoshi* style, when in fact the order of construction could be inverted and the *dō* would still be a cuirass made in the *dangae* style.

This sort of thinking for the most part originates from the fact that it is rare for a reference source to present more than a couple of visually different examples of a particular style of cuirass when introducing a certain form of *dō*. This has a narrowing effect on what students will associate with a certain style. This situation is often compounded by the generic explanation of what features must be present for a cuirass to be considered a specific style of *dō*.

A classic example of a *dangae ni-mai-dō*. The *mae-tateage* and uppermost band of the *nakagawa* have been finished in the replicated small scale *kiritsuke kozane* style with *murasaki iro* (purple, now faded) lacing strung in the closely spaced *kebiki odoshi* style. The remaining bands of the *nakagawa* have been finished in the replicated large scale *iyozane* style with *kon iro* (dark blue) *sugake odoshi*.

For example, if every *dangae* cuirass that a student studies is a two-section *dō* then there will be a tendency to assume that for a cuirass to be made in the *dangae* style, it must be a *ni-mai-dō* in base construction, which is not the case.

While style-specific names are extremely important identifiers, they should not be allowed to supersede other important information. For example it is common for a cuirass made in the *dangae* style to be referred to as being a *dangae-dō*. While it may be convenient to identify a cuirass in this manner, the number of sections that were utilized to assemble the cuirass should still be included in the formal title. For there are very few styles of cuirass where one of the essential elements of that style is a *dō* assembled from a set number of sectional pieces. In other words, unless it is stated, there is no way to automatically identify a *dangae-dō*, for example, as being a two-section cuirass due to the fact that there is no correlation between base construction and the finished façade in the case of the *dangae* style.

One of the few examples of cuirass style where the number of sectional pieces is considered to be an essential element of the finished style is the famous *Yukinoshita-dō*, which is a unique variation of the *go-mai-dō*. Because a *dō* must be made from five sectional pieces constructed in a prescribed manner to be a *Yukinoshita-dō* it is superfluous to state how many sections the cuirass has been assembled from in the formal title. This, however, can cause confusion. For as the single most famous example of a *go-mai-dō*, the *Yukinoshita-dō* generally features quite prominently in most literature on Japanese armour to the point that it is easy to understand why those who are not well versed in this subject matter could come to think that the two terms are synonymous with each other, which is not the case. For even though all *Yukinoshita-dō* are *go-mai-dō*, not all *go-mai-dō* are by default *Yukinoshita-dō*. This point once again highlights the need for a

Two examples of *kebiki odoshi* laced *ni-mai-dō*. While the upper *maru-dō* is made from *hon kozane* and the lower from *kiritsuke kozane ita-mono*, the main visual differences between these two *dō* are due to the colours of *odoshi-ge* that were used and the manner in which they were laced. Note the bear fur trims applied to the *gessan* of the second cuirass.

thorough understanding of the fundamentals of cuirass construction and design, which dictates that irrespective of the façade, cuirasses should also be studied from their base construction forward.

The order in which features are introduced changes somewhat when a *tosei-dō* is obviously not of *sane-ita* construction or lamellar in appearance. In such cases the base material that the armour has been fabricated from, *tetsu* or *nerigawa*, is again the first item to be identified. The next feature to be identified is generally the feature that is the most unusual or rare, knowledge of which can usually only be gained through time and experience. For example, in the case of a *tetsu kuro urushi nuri byō-toji tatehagi okegawa go-mai-dō* or an 'iron black lacquer finished external rivet horizontal plate construction five-section cuirass', the external rivets are the most obvious and unusual feature on the façade of the cuirass. However, if the same cuirass was constructed with a prominent medial ridge running vertically down the front face of the *dō*, then the medial ridge, referred to as a *hatomune* or literally 'pigeon breast', would become the rarest or most unusual of all the visible external features. This again would simply be due to the fact that the *hatomune* feature is relatively uncommon and certainly encountered far less often than external rivets on a cuirass. In such a case the cuirass would be identified as a *tetsu kuro urushi nuri hatomune byō-toji tatehagi okegawa go-mai-dō*.

While the general rule-of-thumb as outlined above is to add features to the base form of a cuirass in order of their visual presence and importance, there are a couple of exceptions when this practice is not always observed and the feature is mentioned after the base form of cuirass is introduced. This anomaly generally occurs in three different cases, all of which are based on styles of cuirass that feature bands of decorative vertical lacing around portions of the *dō*. If the vertical lacing is across the upper chest *mae-tateage* portion of a cuirass it is referred to as *muna-tori*, or literally 'chest around'. If it is around the lower portion of the *nagakawa*, it is called *koshi-tori*, or 'around lower back'. When both the *mae-tateage* and lower *nagakawa* are laced then the style is referred to as *muna-koshi-tori*. When any of these features are present, it is not uncommon for them to be mentioned after the base form of the cuirass has been introduced when a *dō* is being described as part of the formal title of a full *gusoku*. For example, a set of armour could be described as a *shu urushi nerigawa byō-toji tatehagi okegawa muna-koshi ni-mai-dō gusoku*. However, the same set could also correctly be referred to as a *shu urushi nerigawa byō-toji tatehagi okegawa ni-mai-dō muna-koshi gusoku*.

Almost all makes of *dō*, with a limited number of exceptions, were produced with a series of pendant-like sections of protective armour suspended from the lower-edge circumference of the cuirass. These free-moving tasset-like portions

A typical example of a cuirass made in the distinctive *Yukinoshita* style. A unique variety of *go-mai-dō*, the *Yukinoshita* was perhaps the most advanced form of cuirass produced during the feudal period in Japan. Incredibly resilient, easy to produce and repair, the *Yukinoshita* design evolved in response to the battlefield realities of almost a century of continuous conflict, now commonly referred to as the Sengoku Jidai, or 'Country at War' period.

SAMURAI ARMOUR

of armour provided protection for the groin, buttocks and upper thighs. What these portions of a *dō* were originally called on the oldest forms of cuirass is unknown, though they are now universally referred to as the *kusazuri* on all makes of pre-*tosei* forms of cuirass. The name *kusazuri*, which literally means 'rubbing the grass', most likely came about as a reference to their low-hanging reach.

Contrary to what is sometimes written, the term *kusazuri* should not be considered synonymous with the hip armour made from lames. For many proto-historical examples of *kusazuri* were assembled from suspended pieces of solid plate, as were the tassets on some transition-period examples of pre-*tosei* makes of cuirass that were made in the *Mōgami* style.

At some point after the introduction of the first variations of *tosei-dō* the word *kusazuri* began to fade from use and a new term, *gessan*, was introduced. While the *gessan* served exactly the same function as the *kusazuri*, the term *gessan* initially denoted the latter form of hip armour as being made from solid plates. Over

An example of a *tetsu kuro urushi nuri hatomune byō-toji tatehagi-okegawa go-mai-dō*. Note the detachable *koshi-kawa-tsuke gessan*, which are secured to the base of the cuirass by *kohaze* toggles. The padded shoulder yoke *eri-dai* that is an integral part of the *eri-mawashi* brigandine armoured collar and *kobire* is visible on the interior of the cuirass.

An interesting example of a *tetsu kuro urushi nuri byō-toji yokohagi-okegawa muna-koshi-tori go-mai-dō*. Note the hinged *wadagami* with *chotsugai*-affixed *gyōyō*, and the *gattari* bracket and *machi-uke* cup on the *ushiro-dō* portion of the cuirass that are used to secure the holder for the warrior's heraldic *sashimono* battle flag.

THE DŌ (CUIRASS)

Below: A detached portion of 'hip armour'. The *hon kozane koshi-kawa-tsuke gessan* are laced in the *kebiki odoshi* style. The detachable hip armour is made to be fitted to the *ushiro-dō* section of a *ni-mai-dō*. Note the grommet-lined holes in the lacquered leather waist belt. These would correspond with the placement of toggles with swivel heads fitted around the base of the cuirass.

Bottom: The liner, or *urabari*, of a *tetsu kuro urushi nuri yokohagi-okegawa ni-mai-dō*. The lacquered leather liner conforms perfectly to the interior contours of the cuirass. The liner covers the combined areas of the *mae-* and *ushiro-tateage* and the lower torso *nagakawa*. Note the padded shoulder yoke *eri-dai* and the *shu urushi nuri*-finished *sugake odoshi*-laced *ita-mono gessan*.

time, however, the term *gessan* simply became synonymous with hip armour in general, with no distinction made between tassets that were assembled from *sane-ita* or *ita-mono*. As such, the term *kusazuri* should never be used to refer to the hip armour pendants on a *tosei-dō* even if the latter are assembled from lames, as is sometimes the case on cuirasses made during the latter half of the Edo period. How many *kusazuri* or *gessan* that a particular form of cuirass was fitted with and how they were attached along with other details about their style and design will be expanded upon further in the following chapters.

One final aspect of the construction and design of most makes of *dō* that is seldom discussed is how they were finished on their interior surfaces. The oldest form of cuirass that may have featured an internal liner was the 4th century solid-plate *tankō*. While no example has survived to prove their existence it is possible that in some cases panels of leather were stretched across the inner surfaces of the cuirass to create a liner, or *urabari*. The *urabari*, which literally translates as 'back applied', may have been secured in place by having its outer edges folded over onto the exterior surface of the cuirass along the entire outer-edge length of the *dō*. The leather panels would then be bound in place with leather thongs that would be threaded through a series of holes punched at regular intervals around the outer edges of the cuirass. Fastening the leather sections in this manner created a liner while it also simultaneously capped the rough outer edges of the cuirass.

Early *sane-ita* forms of cuirass such as the *keikō* were almost certainly made without *urabari*, primarily due to the fact that the individual scales and lames needed to be bound together and a liner would hinder the upkeep and replacement of these essential bindings. Liners were also somewhat unnecessary on cuirasses assembled from *sane-ita* since there were very few rough or uncomfortable surfaces created when a cuirass was constructed from

SAMURAI ARMOUR

scales that were bound together by lacing or thongs. Furthermore, the smooth lacquer finishes that the individual scales and lamellar sections featured as result of the way that they were produced resulted in their reverse faces having a fairly presentable appearance, which further diminished the need for cuirasses assembled from lames to be fitted with *urabari*.

Liners are primarily associated with the various makes of *tosei-dō*, the majority of which were assembled from sections of plating that were riveted together. *Urabari*, while not essential to the construction or design of *tosei-dō*, served two primary functions, the first of which was to protect the wearer and his garments from the rough interior surfaces of a cuirass. The second function was related to the first in that an *urabari* hid the unfinished inner from view. While smiths, or *katchū-shi*, were clearly more than capable of refining the finished appearance on the interior of a cuirass, it was not worth their time and effort to do so. Instead it was much cheaper and easier to simply cover over the rough finishes on the interior surface so they could not be seen. This allowed *katchū-shi* to move on to other projects as soon as possible, which was essential, particularly during the Sengoku period, when the demand for armour was at its zenith.

In most cases panels of horse hide, or *uma-gawa*, were fitted over the interior surfaces of the section of cuirass to be covered. The panel was then glued with an adhesive to the exterior

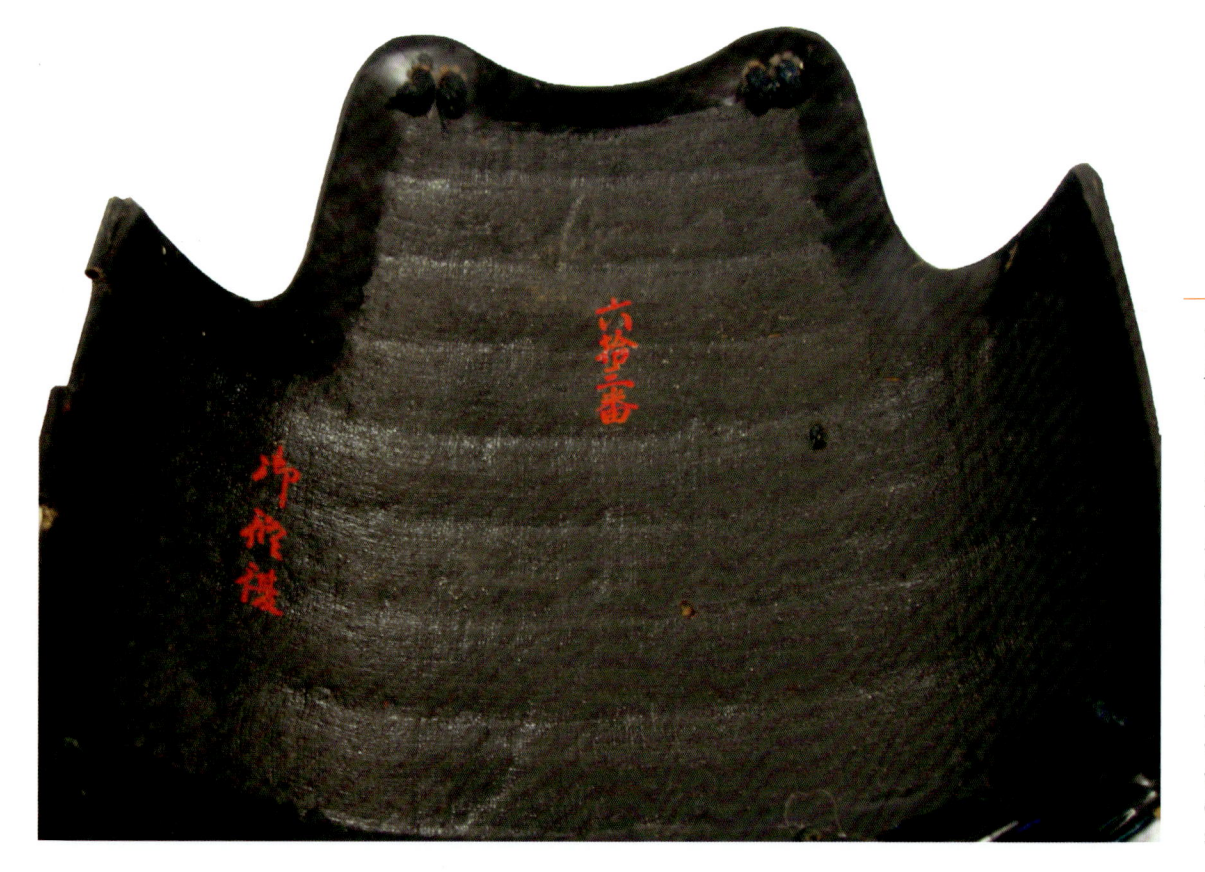

Sheets of *washi* (rice paper) under a leather *urabari*. Paper was sometimes used to line and smooth over the inner surfaces of a cuirass before the liner was fitted. Note how materials and man-hours have not been wasted lacquering the unseen interior surface of the cuirass. Only a thin base coat of *urushi* has been applied to the metal plates to help prevent corrosion.

The *jika-bari*-style liner of a *yokohagi-okegawa okashi ni-mai-dō*. The arsenal number of this cuirass is recorded in red lacquer in the middle of the *mae-dō*. The four kanji read '*roku-jū san-ban*', which identify this *dō* as 'Number 63'. The same number would be written in the *ushiro-dō* portion of the cuirass to ensure the correct two sections were lent out when the *dō* was issued. This was done because cuirasses were generally stored broken down into sections to save space inside the arsenal.

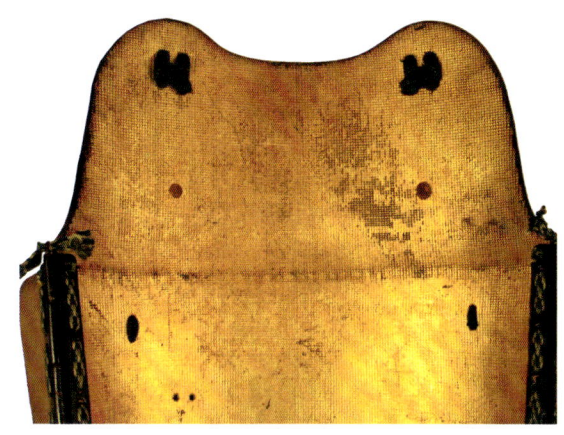

THE DŌ (CUIRASS)

Left: A protective religious sutra to the Buddhist war god Hachiman that has been engraved onto the interior surface of a cuirass. Note the framed lacquer window and the rich *byakudan* finish that is created by the application of clear *tome* lacquer over *kinpaku*, or gold leaf.

Right: An example of a *jika-bari*, or a liner, that is created by adhering fabric directly to the interior surface of a cuirass by laying it over the lacquer finish before the *urushi* has dried. This example is typical of the *jika-bari* that were applied to interiors of cuirasses made by the Maeda *han* smiths of Kaga, who tended to use a fine mesh-like weave of the fabric for this purpose. Note the use of a gold dust-infused lacquer.

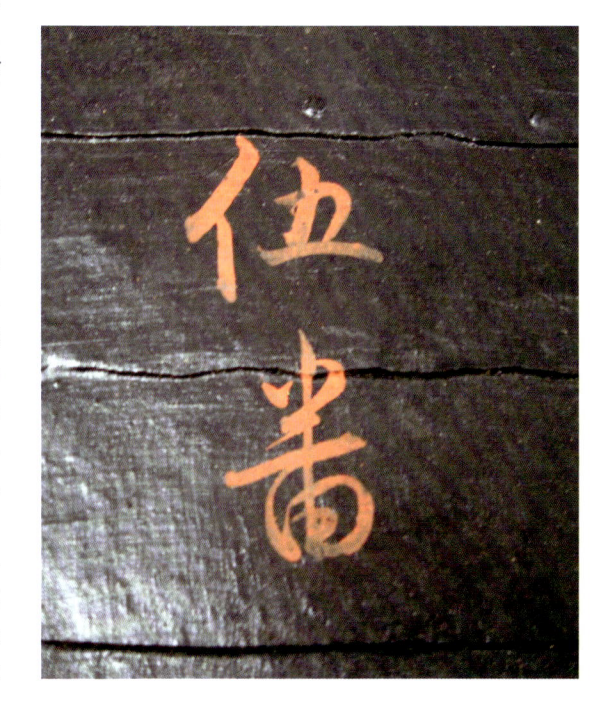

The *jika-bari* of a *yokohagi-okegawa okashi ni-mai-dō*. The roughly finished edges of the metal plates and heads of the rivets that secure the *ita-mono* together are clearly visible under the lacquered-over layer of hemp cloth that has been adhered to the interior face of the *dō*. Note the *shu urushi* arsenal marking of *go-ban* or 'Number 5'.

edge circumference of the cuirass section. When the glue had dried, the excess material was trimmed around the hide so the panel conformed to the contours of the edge of the *dō*. Thick applications of lacquer were then built up over the edge of the *uma-gawa* panel to further anchor it to the edges of the section of cuirass. If the *dō* sections were generally flat in form, like the pieces used to assemble a conventional *go-mai-dō*, the *uma-gawa* sections would usually be moistened before they were applied. This would allow the material to soften and stretch. The central portion of the panel would be kept moist until the glue and applications of lacquer had securely set. The leather would then be allowed to dry. This would cause it to be drawn taut like a drum skin across the interior surface of the section of cuirass as the leather shrank.

In some cases, cotton wadding was packed behind the liner to help make a *dō* more comfortable to wear and to fill in any voids that were created by various aspects of the finished design of the cuirass, such as behind embossed features. Strips or sheets of old rice paper, or *washi*, were also sometimes used to smooth over and fill any voids between the inner surface of a cuirass and the liner. Several sheets of paper were also sometimes layered together to create padded areas.

The *urabari* were generally lightly lacquered and often finished in a colour tone that contrasted with the exterior finish of the cuirass. In the case of high-quality pieces, it was not uncommon for the liner to be covered with an application of gold-dust coloured lacquer or to be faced with gold leaf, or *kinpaku*, which literally means 'gold pressed'. In some cases, particularly on cuirasses that were made during the mid to late Edo period, it was not uncommon for the name of the *katchū-shi* who produced the *dō* to be written in lacquer on the liner. *Shu urushi*, or red lacquer, was commonly employed for this purpose. Likewise, it was also not uncommon for the cuirass to have the name of one of its original owners written on the liner along with a date, the latter often corresponding with the date of fabrication of the cuirass or the completion of a significant refurbishment of the piece. Munitions grades on *okashi-dō* were also commonly marked on their interior surfaces. The markings on cuirasses of this calibre were used to document when and to whom a cuirass was issued or where it was kept when it was returned to the arsenal.

In some cases, particularly when a *dō* was engraved on its inner face with the working name of a famous smith, a small *mei-mi-no-ana*, or 'signature viewing hole', would be formed in the liner that allowed the signature to be seen. In such cases it was common for the surface area around the signature to be highlighted with an application of gold leaf, or *kinpaku*.

While leather was by far the most common material used to make liners, fabrics such as cotton, hemp and silk were also sometimes utilized. That said, it is important to note that fabric liners are only considered to be *urabari* if the materials are affixed in a manner that covers the inner surfaces of a cuirass without significantly altering the finished appearance or feel of the material. When fabrics adhered directly to the inner surfaces of a *dō* are then covered in layers of lacquer, the liner is no longer referred to as an *urabari*, but is instead called a *jika-bari*, which literally means 'directly applied'. This is because *urabari* are technically supposed to be suspended over, without adhering directly to, the interior surfaces of a cuirass.

In general, it is unusual for better-quality cuirasses to feature interior surfaces finished in the *jika-bari* style. Among the few exceptions to this rule were the *dō* produced by the *katchū-shi* employed by the powerful Maeda clan of Kaga during the early to mid Edo period. Cuirasses produced by the Maeda were commonly finished on their interior surfaces with a fine grid-like pattern that was created by lacquering an open mesh-like fabric to the inner surfaces of the *dō*.

An unusual example of a removable *urabari*. Lengths of *odoshi-ge* are used to tie the stiffened hemp cloth liner in place. Though the liner is made from cloth, it is not considered to be a *jika-bari*, as it is not adhered to the interior surface of a cuirass. This liner is suspended over the interior surface of the cuirass and as such, is still considered to be a form of *ura-bari*. As the liner is removable, the *katchū-shi* who made this cuirass made sure to fully lacquer and finish the interior surfaces of the *dō*. These areas would normally be left unfinished, hidden under the permanently affixed liner. Note the knuckled *chotsugai* hinge to the left of the image that secures the front and back sections of the cuirass together.

THE DŌ (CUIRASS)

For the most part, however, *jika-bari* finishes are generally indicative of cuirasses of rather rudimentary or poor-quality construction, such as those that were virtually mass-produced for issue to the low-ranking *ashigaru* (literally 'fast-feet') grade retainers who made up the rank and file of the warrior class. Munitions-grade cuirasses such these, referred to as *okashi-dō*, literally 'lent cuirass', often had a layer or two of coarse-weave hemp cloth lacquered over the interior faces of the *dō*. While this rudimentary form of liner often did little to hide the outlines of the method of construction of the cuirass, it was sufficient to blunt any rough and unfinished edges.

It is important to remember that anomalies and exceptions to the rule are to be expected when dealing with Japanese armour, even when it comes to a subject as mundane as liners. This author has seen high-quality cuirasses with *nuri-gome*, or smooth, thick lacquer finishes on their interior surfaces. I have also seen *dō* that were made with removable persimmon-juice-stiffened cloth *urabari* and a *dō* with highly detailed *maki-e* images of birds made from gold and silver powders sprinkled on lacquer that were applied to the unseen interior surfaces of the cuirass. Thus unusual features should never be ruled out or overlooked just because they seem out of place.

Two views of highly detailed and ornate *maki-e* images that were applied to the hidden interior surface of a high-quality *go-mai-dō*. The images were produced through the careful application of lacquer to create raised-in-relief designs. Fine flecks or the dust of various precious metals are sprinkled on *urushi* before it dries to produce colours.

An early 20th century reproduction of a *keikō* from the late 5th century produced by Dr Suenaga Masao. The *keikō* was the first widely utilized form of cuirass assembled from scales to have been made and utilized in the Japanese archipelago. (Kansai University Museum)

CHAPTER 3

ANCIENT ARMOUR

Tankō, keikō, uchikake-keikō and *men'ōchū*, 2nd century BC–9th century AD

The early inhabitants of the Japanese archipelago, like many Palaeolithic peoples, almost certainly utilized animal hides and leathers to create various kinds of protective garments. What forms of protective equipment may have existed, however, is unknown due to an absence of historical evidence such as surviving pieces, written records, sculptures or paintings that could attest to the existence of such items.

By the latter half of the first millennium BC some inhabitants of the archipelago began to use wooden panels to produce rudimentary items of armour, the oldest known example of which dates to the 2nd century BC. Though it is impossible to know exactly where wooden armour, or *mokusei katchū*, first began to be utilized or just how common these items were, by the end of the 2nd century AD, archaeological evidence shows that numerous variations of *mokusei katchū* were being utilized throughout the Japanese archipelago.

Though very little is known about the earliest forms of *mokusei katchū* due to the limited number of extant examples, at least two varieties are known to have been utilized. One consisted of little more than crudely shaped panels of wood that were often formed from a hollowed log. These were fitted with shoulder straps and lengths of cord or leather that allowed the panel to be tied in place around the torso. A second variety consisted of several wooden slates bound together. These rudimentary cuirasses were probably worn over jackets or vests made from animal hides that had the fur left on them to help make the armour more comfortable to wear.

It should be noted that much of what is known about these items is actually based on the remnants of the lacquer shells that early inhabitants of the Japanese archipelago applied to these items to help protect them from the acidic nature of that region's soil and its extremely high levels of humidity.

While it is impossible to track the evolutionary development of *mokusei katchū* over the centuries given the scant and fragmentary surviving evidence, it would seem reasonable to conclude that the existing designs and fabrication techniques gradually improved over time. Wood panels were carved or steamed to create curves that were better contoured to the shape of the torso. Cuirasses also began to be assembled from several sectional pieces that were bound together using lengths of cord or leather thongs, called *kawa-toji*, and some examples of these were strikingly similar in shape to the so-called 'modern' forms of *tosei-dō* that started to appear around the end of the 15th century.

By the 1st century AD, most examples of cuirass were being made from three to five shaped wooden panels. These were fastened together by bindings that allowed the panels to articulate so they could close around the torso. The front panels were designed to come together like a pair of saloon doors in the middle of the chest where they could be tied together to close the cuirass.

Why the large number of unique forms of *mokusei katchū* that appear to have existed prior to the 1st century AD suddenly faded out in favour of this style is unclear. It may simply have been the result of the next obvious evolutionary step in cuirass designs having being reached. It is far more probable, however, that these changes came about as the result of external influences, namely the continued large influx of migrants from the Korean peninsula who brought with them knowledge of armour designs from the continent that were more advanced than the domestic designs of cuirass that existed within the archipelago during that period.

If the forms of cuirass that began to appear were based on imported types of armour, these apparently merged with some aspects of the indigenous armour designs, which seem to have favoured large, shield-like back panels that stood well above the wearer's shoulders. The shape and style of these back panels varied considerably between regions, as did some aspects of the decorative designs that were engraved or lacquered onto them. An example of *mokusei katchū* discovered in Iba, in Shizuoka Prefecture, for example, featured round wing-like panels fitted to the rear of the cuirass. This design contrasts sharply with an example of wooden cuirass discovered at an excavation site near Souri, in Fukuoka Prefecture, which featured a large flat shield-like form of back board affixed to the cuirass. Because the back board on the *mokusei katchū* from Souri stood well above the shoulder, the middle portion of the back-panel between the shoulder blades had a U-shape indentation cut in it that enabled the person wearing the cuirass to tilt their head backwards.

At some time during the first half of the 4th century AD these regional forms of cuirass faded out as a new design of cuirass from the Korean peninsula gained popularity in the Japanese archipelago. This new form of cuirass was unique in that it was assembled from a

A conjectural reconstruction of a 2nd century example of a wooden cuirass, or *mokusei katchū*, on display in National Museum of Japanese History. The armour is based on artifacts recovered during an archaeological excavation in Okayama Prefecture. (Courtesy of J.L. Badgley)

series of vertical plates, or *tatehagi-ita*, that were bound together by leather thongs, called *kawa-toji*, which allowed the armour to be wrapped around the torso like a corset.

The *tatehagi-kawa-toji* cuirass, as this style of armour came to be known, is presently considered to be the oldest known iron-made form of body amour made and used in the Japanese archipelago. It is probable that the first iron examples of this make of cuirass were imported and then copied domestically, for metal armour of this kind was already being utilized on the Korean peninsula during this period. The fabrication of armour from organic materials, such as wood, appears to have fallen off at this time. This does not seem to have been the case with rawhide, however, which may have been utilized well into the early 5th century. According to a 2014 publication, 'Armor in Japan and Korea' by Joseph Ryan and Gina Barnes, there is also evidence to suggest that some cuirasses were assembled from hybrid combinations of organic materials and iron during this transitional period.[1]

The *tatehagi-kawa-toji* cuirass was designed to cover the back of the torso from the top of the shoulders downward, while the chest was covered from the base of the clavicle to the top of the hips. This design of cuirass was also unique in that the *tatehagi-ita* were forged with a subtle top-down taper which gave the armour a more form-fitting hourglass-like shape. This unique example of cuirass was to be the first in a series of related evolutionary designs of body amour that would be developed between the early 4th and mid-5th centuries that are now, outside of the archaeological world, collectively referred to as *tankō*, which literally means 'short shell'.

During the latter half of the 4th century the Yamato armour makers started to produce a variation of the *tatehagi-kawa-toji* design of cuirass that utilized large, generally rectangular plates, called *hōkei-ita*, in lieu of the long, vertical *tatehagi-ita*. The resulting armours were in many ways fundamentally 'copies in iron' of the wooden cuirasses that the Yamato *katchū-shi* had previously produced from arranged horizontal rows of leather-thong-connected wooden slates.[2] While the use of this indigenous construction technique significantly altered the visual appearance of the cuirass, the overall form of the original *tatehagi-ita* design was retained. As leather thongs continued to be used to assemble the cuirass made in this manner, they came to be known as *hōkei-ita-kawa-toji*, or literally 'rectangle plate leather bound', cuirass.

By the beginning of the 5th century, the practice of assembling cuirasses from vertically

A modern reconstruction of a variety of *mokusei katchū*, with wing-like boards affixed to the rear of the cuirass, based on artifacts recovered from the archaeological excavations conducted at Iba in Shizuoka Prefecture.

Scholars are unsure if items such as this were utilized in battle or if they were worn for ceremonial purposes. Note the sectional construction and leather thong bindings. (Courtesy of J.L. Badgley)

arranged iron plates had already been superseded on the Korean peninsula by the use of lamellae, or scales, to construct armour. While this transition was taking place on the continent, the armour makers in Yamato, who appear to have worked from a largely centralized location, continued to focus on the development of the *tankō* form of cuirass.[3] The changes they introduced at this time were perhaps the most significant in regards to the overall form of the *tankō*, which from the early 5th century onward became a truly distinctive form of uniquely 'Japanese' cuirass.

Why the Yamato chose to embrace the *tankō* at a time when they were clearly aware of the developments that were occurring on the Korean peninsula in regards to lamellar armour is unclear. It may, possibly, have been a matter of pride, with the Yamato leaders preferring to retain the *tankō* as an outward emblem of their independence as a quasi-national state. For as noted the *tankō* was increasingly becoming unique to them during this period.

The key innovation that was introduced in Yamato to the *tankō* design was the addition of a skeletal frame of sturdy, spaced vertical bands around the body of the cuirass that substantially improved the overall rigidity of the armour. In fact, many experts are of the opinion that cuirasses only became *tankō* after the skeletal frame was added to the design. As such the term *tankō* is not used by archaeologists to refer to the early, primarily vertical-plate-assembled Korean forms of cuirass that are devoid of this distinctive feature.

The skeletal frame consisted of a wide, slightly inward-angled base band that was several centimetres wide. An intermediate band of protective plating that was also several centimetres in overall height filled the space between the base band and the next rib, which was a long, narrow horizontal band that wrapped around the lower abdomen area of the armour. This was followed by another intermediate section of plating that was itself capped by another horizontal band that wrapped around the upper chest area of the cuirass. This band was divided into two short portions that covered either side of the breast area of the torso before terminating near the armpits. This band continued as a single long piece around the rear of the cuirass in the area of the shoulder blades. It was then capped by yet another intermediate band of plating that was followed by a wide cap band, which extended around the full upper circumference of the armour. The cap band was generally about the same width as the base band around the frontage of a cuirass, but was fabricated so

A 4th century example of a *tatehagi-ita kawa-toji* cuirass. This form of armour, which was based on similar designs of cuirass worn on the Korean peninsula, is believed to have been the first type of metal body armour utilized in the Japanese archipelago. (Courtesy of J.L. Badgley)

that it swelled to nearly double its frontal width around the rear upper portion of the cuirass. This allowed the six lower tiers to maintain a fairly universal appearance around the exterior circumference of the *tankō*, while it simultaneously extended upward far enough to cover most of the upper back.

Along with the structural framing, the Yamato *katchū-shi* also introduced two diffcrent forms of intermediate protective plating. The first form was fundamentally little more than horizontal rectangular pieces of plate called *yoko-ita* that were cut and shaped as required to conform to the horizontal gaps between the bands of the external skeletal framing. The second form of intermediate plate was made in the form of a triangle, or *sankaku*. These triangular *sankaku-ita* were arranged with their wide bases secured to the upper edge of a lower framing band. The inverted triangular gaps that were left between these plates were filled by other *sankaku-ita* that would be affixed tip down to the lower edge of the frame band immediately above the latter. As leather thongs continued to be utilized to assemble the individual component pieces, these cuirasses came to be identified respectively as *yoko-ita-kawa-toji* and *sankaku-ita-kawa-toji tankō*.

Much of the work shaping the rounded curvatures that were indicative of the various makes of *tankō* appears to have been accomplished using wooden dies. These were cut from logs that were then shaped to create dressmaker-like models of the cuirass. These significantly simplified the process of producing the various curved plates that were require to fabricate a *tankō*.

At some time before the middle of the 5th century the *katchū-shi* in Yamato began to utilize *byō*, or rivets, to assemble *tankō*. This method of construction was again more than likely borrowed from the Koreans, who had developed the practice of using flat rivets to assemble items of armour, although, for reasons unknown, the Yamato armour makers chose to make use of rivets with round heads. The cuirasses produced were substantially stronger and much more resilient than their leather-thong-bound counterparts. Even so, it appears that *kawa-toji*-assembled examples of *tankō* continued to be made for a couple of decades alongside riveted cuirasses before the practice was finally abandoned in favour of the *byō-dome* or 'rivet-stopped' method of fabrication. When rivets were utilized to construct a cuirass, the forms of cuirass discussed above are referred to as *yoko-ita-byō-dome* and *sankaku-ita-byō-dome*.

An early 5th century example of a *sankaku-ita kawa-toji* variety of *tankō*, the first truly unique Japanese make of cuirass. The *tankō* is identified by the skeleton-like arrangement of prominent horizontal bands that frame the body and outline of the cuirass. Note the leather bindings utilized to assemble the individual iron pieces. (Courtesy of J.L. Badgley)

One of the issues that armour makers had to overcome when they began to use rivets to fabricate *tankō* was that the armour lost most of the flexibility that had hitherto been an integral characteristic of a cuirass assembled using leather thongs. As it was a variety of *ichi-mai-dō* this flexibility was necessary for warriors to don this armour, made of a single continuous piece. When rivets were used for assembly, it became extremely difficult to spring the left- and right-hand sides of the cuirass far enough apart where they came together down the centre of the chest for a warrior to enter the *tankō* without the assistance of others.

The solution to this dilemma was to construct the main body of the *tankō* in two pieces, with the front right quadrant of the cuirass being made of a separate removable panel. This section was originally designed to marry up with the main body of the armour, and cords were used to secure it in place. An alternative version had both the front left- and right-hand quadrants of the cuirass constructed as separate removable panels, which greatly simplified the effort that was required to don the cuirass. As such, depending on how they were constructed, *tankō* can be *ichi-*, *ni-* or even *san-mai-dō*.

As cords proved unreliable at holding the heavy, sectional pieces of armour in place, the *katchū-shi* began to affix various rudimentary forms of hinges to the sides of the cuirass and separate sectional pieces. And while these seem often to have taken the form of simple hook-and-eye-like appendages, they also appear to have worked well to hold the separate pieces of the cuirass together.

The exposed leading edges of the cap and base plates were almost always finished with a band of leather thong that was carefully braided through a series of closely spaced holes punched around the outer edge of these plates. Alternatively, a narrow band of leather was sometimes also bound to the rims of these plates.

The *tankō* was devoid of integral shoulder straps, or *wadagami*, and instead utilized a series of closed leather loops that were knotted through the front and back plates of the cuirass to provide anchoring points through which a length of cloth or leather cord could be strung. It appears that the closed leather loops were originally arranged to protrude from the exterior surface of the cuirass, though in later examples this arrangement was reversed so they were hidden on the protected interior surface of the *tankō*. The length of fabric or cord that formed the shoulder straps would be pulled through the open loops and drawn tight until it began to lift the weight of the cuirass off the hips, at which point the ends would be knotted together.

Like the *tosei-dō* that were introduced in the mid-16th century, the *tankō* was designed to have its weight load rest on the hips of the wearer, hence its stylish though practical hourglass design. As the rigid construction of the *tankō* did not allow for a significant degree of adjustment, it is evident that the majority of these items were custom-made for specific individuals, as this would have been the only way to ensure that a cuirass sat comfortably on the wearer's hips. This was important, as a weight load that is properly balanced on the hips can be comfortably sustained for much longer periods of time than is possible with an identical weight load suspended from the shoulders. As such, the *tankō* needed to be tightly bound at the waist to ensure it stayed properly positioned, seated on top of the hips.

Supporting the idea that these items were custom-made for specific individuals is the fact that the *tankō* that have been recovered from kofun appear not to have been random offerings: archaeological studies of the items recovered suggest they were instead the personal items of the individuals entombed in the burial mounds. Likewise, contrary to the impression created by many historical images, *tankō* were, even at their peak of production towards the end of the 6th century, still exceedingly rare items that appear primarily to

ANCIENT ARMOUR

have been owned and worn only by the most affluent and important members of Yamato society. This would have been in keeping with their status, which was intrinsically linked with a powerful martial element.

Other than a metal helmet, which appears to have been adopted around the same time that the first *tatehagi-ita-kawa-toji* examples of cuirass began to be utilized in Japan, the earliest armour was more than likely worn without additional fixtures or equipment. Gradually, however, other protective items of armour were introduced and worn in conjunction with the *tankō*. These included protective coverings for the upper chest area and shoulders. Armour for the forearms and shins was also produced, all of which will be discussed separately and in detail in the companion book, Volume II.

The one additional item of armour that is often portrayed as though it were an integral part of the *tankō* was hip armour, or *kusazuri*, which provided protection for the groin, buttocks and most of the upper legs; but this might not have been case. In fact, of the six hundred and some *tankō* that have been recovered to date, fewer than ten examples of iron-made *kusazuri* have been found in conjunction with these cuirasses. This could, however, be a result of organic materials, such as rawhide, or very thin metal plate having been utilized to fabricate the *kusazuri*. Evidence to support this theory can be found on the many terracotta warrior statues called *bushi-haniwa* that were produced in large numbers between the 4th and 6th centuries. For most of the *bushi-haniwa* which show *tankō* depict them being worn in conjunction with *kusazuri*. Whether these statues accurately portrayed how warriors actually appeared or if a degree of artistic license was involved in their creation is difficult to say. It is equally possible that they are depictions of very high-ranking warriors, and as such are actually atypical examples.

Kusazuri first began to appear on *tankō* sometime in the 5th century. As with many of the items of armour utilized in Yamato, the inspiration for hip armour attachments may have come from the long, low-hanging coats of lamellar armour that were worn by warriors on the Korean peninsula. That said, the form of *kusazuri* that the Yamato armour makers developed appears to have been a domestic design that was unique to the archipelago. Fauld-like, the *kusazuri* formed a large skirt-like profile in the shape of a bell, coming down to the knees. This was achieved by constructing two mirrored segments, each of which comprised several flat crescent-moon-shaped bands. The bands were forged so that each one was slightly larger in diameter than the band that preceded it in the top-to-bottom suspended arrangement of the bell-like skirt, which was held together by several long, vertically arranged bands of leather. This allowed the skirt to collapse or telescope over itself as was required to accommodate the movement of the legs.

While the majority of *kusazuri* appear to have been made from horizontal lames, the

Wooden dies such as this were employed by the armour makers of Yamato to help them mould the complex array of curved iron plates that were required to create a *tankō*. The plates were positioned over the die in the corresponding position of the piece that was needed and then hammered into the required shape. (Courtesy of J.L. Badgley)

SAMURAI ARMOUR

An impressive collection of various forms of iron *tankō*, including *yoko-ita kawa-toji* and *sankaku-ita kawa-toji* varieties of this distinctive form of cuirass. A number of auxiliary items of armour such as *akabe-yoroi* neck guards and *kata-yoroi* shoulder guards that were commonly worn in conjunction with the *tankō* are also displayed along with a collection a various helmets. (Image © and courtesy of the Ōsaka University Department of Archaeology)

ANCIENT ARMOUR

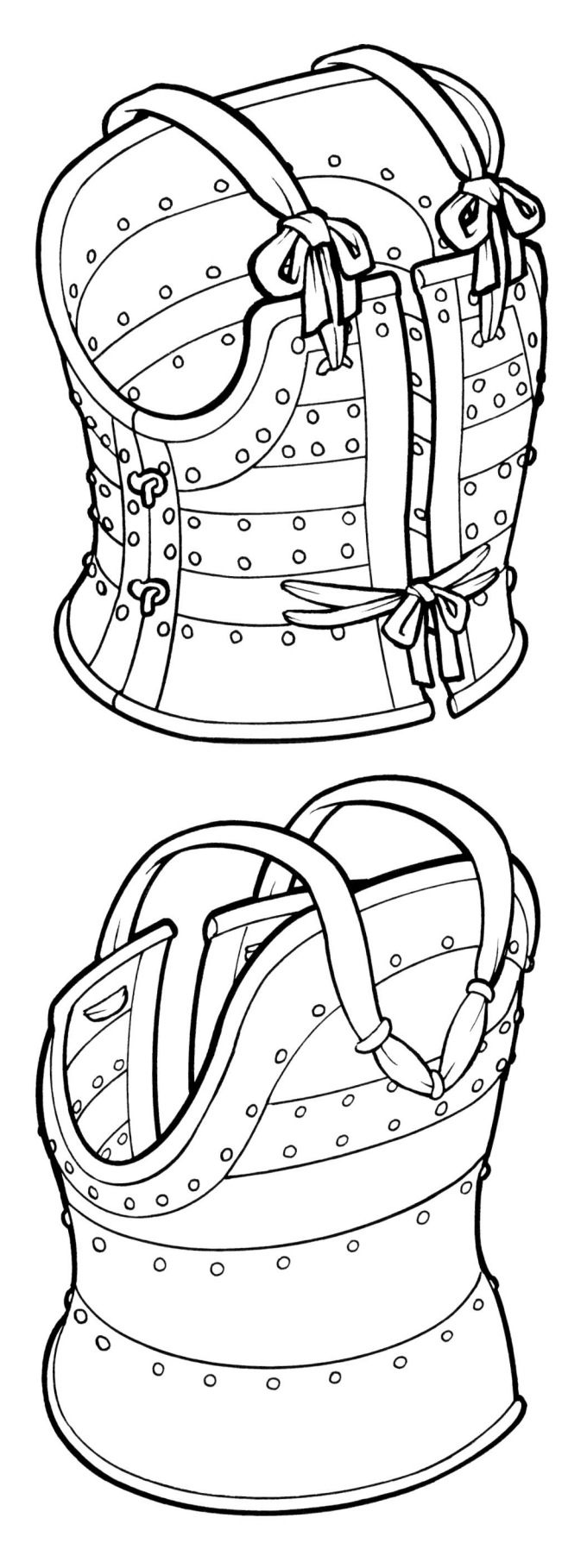

number of which could vary from as few as four to more than a dozen, depending on the width of each plate, other alternative forms of hip armour may have also been utilized. And while archaeologically this is not supported by the evidence of the items that have been recovered to date, the *bushi-haniwa* appear to show that several seemingly different forms of *kusazuri* were utilized. The *bushi-haniwa* are generally accepted as being fairly accurate historical representations of the equipment that they were created to depict, but it is quite possible that many of their portrayals contain errors. This may have occurred as the result of artistic license or the original artists having lacked actual first-hand experience with these items.

One unique design of *kusazuri* that is depicted on some examples of *bushi-haniwa* features a tapered skirt that appears to have been made from several trapezoidal plates. Efforts by Dr Sasama Yoshihiko, a renowned Japanese scholar and former president of the Association for the Research and Preservation of Japanese Helmets and Armour, to demonstrate how a *kusazuri* made in this form may have looked and been constructed resulted in a number of detailed drawings.[4] While these showed how an arrangement of trapezoidal plates bound together with leather thongs could have been arranged to produce a functional form of *kusazuri*, in the absence of extant examples such works must remain purely conjectural.

Most examples of *kusazuri* appear to have been assembled using several wide strips of leather. These vertically arranged strips were positioned at regularly spaced intervals around the inside surfaces of the skirt hoops. The strips were made long enough to let the majority of the surface area of each band show as it hung over and past the plate immediately above it in the descending order of the telescoping skirt. The bands appear to have been initially secured to the support straps by leather thongs, though in the case of some later examples they may have been riveted in position.

Another speculative method of securing the bands of the *kusazuri* together is based on designs seen on some examples of *bushi-haniwa* that appear to show the horizontal lames of the skirt being secured together by large triangular panels of leather that were affixed to the façade of the *kusazuri*. Conjectural drawings produced by Dr Sasama show how such an arrangement may have been organized, with one row of shorter downward-pointing

Front and rear perspectives of a *tatehagi-ita byō-dome tankō* that show how the *wadagami* shoulder straps may have been secured. While leather was utilized, unless buckled, cloth straps might have been preferred as they could be tied as required to ensure the weight of the armour sat properly on the hips and not just the shoulders.

SAMURAI ARMOUR

triangles being secured around the top portion of the skirt so as to join the uppermost lames of the *kusazuri* together. A row of larger, upward-pointing triangles are shown fitted around the base of the skirt, joining several of the lower bands of the *kusazuri* together. Depending on the size, colour and arrangement of the triangular pieces of leather being used for this purpose, a number of attractive diamond, hourglass and saw-tooth-shaped patterns could have been created around the façade of the *kusazuri* if this method of fastening the bands of the hip armour together was actually utilized.

Hip armour assembled from three or four suspended pendant-like lamellar sections was also introduced, but only after lamellar armour started to become common in Japan around the middle of the 5th century.

Based on the limited number of *kusazuri* that have been recovered, it appears that they were designed to be worn over the top of the cuirass. Exactly how the kusazuri were secured to the cuirass, however, is unclear. Sturdy waist-belt-like cords were more than likely used for this purpose but buckles and other methods may have also been employed.

The appearance of lamellar *kusazuri* was a harbinger of the coming demise of the *tankō*, which reached a zenith in both design and production around the end of the 5th century. In fact, fabrication of the *tankō* form of cuirass appears to have come to an abrupt end at the very beginning of the 6th century when it was replaced by lamellar armour. Why the elite in Yamato, who almost certainly had knowledge of lamellar armour designs as far back as the mid-3rd century AD, suddenly chose to make this transition is also unclear.

The most commonly accepted reason for the change that occurred in the form of cuirass that was utilized suggests that the *tankō* was poorly suited to the needs of a mounted warrior. While sound and more than likely generally accurate, this theory is not as black and white as it appears. For numerous *tankō*

A representation of a 5th century warrior wearing a *yoko-ita byō-dome* example of *tankō* in conjunction with *kusazuri* (hip armour). Several recovered items of armour confirm that gold leaf was sometimes applied to the façades of the armour worn by elite members of Yamato society. Note the *akabe-yoroi* (neck guard), *kata-yoroi* (shoulder guards) *kote* (gauntlets), and helmet, which are discussed in Volume II. (Image © and courtesy of the Kyōto Costume Museum)

86

ANCIENT ARMOUR

A *yoko-ita kawa-toji* iron plate *tankō* from the early 5th century with *kusazuri* hip armour. Note the construction of the *kusazuri*, which were assembled from loose lamellar bands of tombstone-shaped iron scales, or *tetsu-zane*. One of the hinges that secured the right front quadrant of the *tankō* in place is visible protruding on the right of the cuirass. This *tankō* was recovered from the archaeological excavations in Ukiha City, Fukuoka Prefecture. (Courtesy of J.L. Badgley)

have been found in conjunction with horse furnishings amongst the tumuli of various kofun. This suggest that the elite of Yamato society, who were the first to own horses and master the art of equestrianism, wore the *tankō* as a symbol of their status while mounted. Having said this, it is probable that as such persons may not have been required to be as physically involved in martial matters as lower-ranking individuals, the rigid form of the *tankō* had little effect on their ability to ride. This viewpoint is supported by the fact that *tankō* have been found with horse furnishings in eighty-three of the 114 known 5th century kofun. While sets of lamellar armour were found in thirty-one tombs alongside horse furnishings, these items primarily dated from the late 5th century, at a time when they may still have been very rare even amongst the elite.

The transition when it came, as noted, was almost overnight, and thus it appears to have been something of a collective decision, perhaps inspired by or directed from above. Evidence of *tankō* being produced after this period does not exist, which further supports the theory that armour production was fairly centralized. For if these items were being fabricated throughout the archipelago, their production more than likely would have come to an end in a more piecemeal manner over the course of the 7th century.

The decision by the elite of Yamato to transition to lamellar armour was almost certainly influenced by their knowledge of the growing use and effectiveness of mounted forces on the Korean peninsula. Given that a martial element was intrinsically linked with their elite status, this would have been a prudent and a logical choice for them to make. For it would have been a visual statement to both their friends and their foes that they understood the evolving nature of the warrior and were capable of utilizing these new techniques and technology. Having said this, it may also have been an effort by the elite to rebrand themselves, as the Japanese scholar Hashimoto Tatsuya has suggested, in order to reassert their dominant status within and over Yamato society.[5]

This theory was given added credence in 2013 by a discovery made during the archaeological excavations at the Kanai Higashiura site in Gunma Prefecture, where a small rectangular panel of lamellar armour assembled from *sane* carved from animal bones was unearthed. The smooth, polished appearance of the bone scales, which are believed to date from the late 5th or

An illustration of one of the more common forms of hip armour, or *kusazuri*. Exactly how hip armour was worn is unknown. It is probable that the two sectional halves of the *kusazuri* were worn cinched tight around the waist by cords (although this is conjectural), though buckles and other arrangements may have been utilized. It is also unclear whether the *kusazuri* were designed to be worn over or under the cuirass.

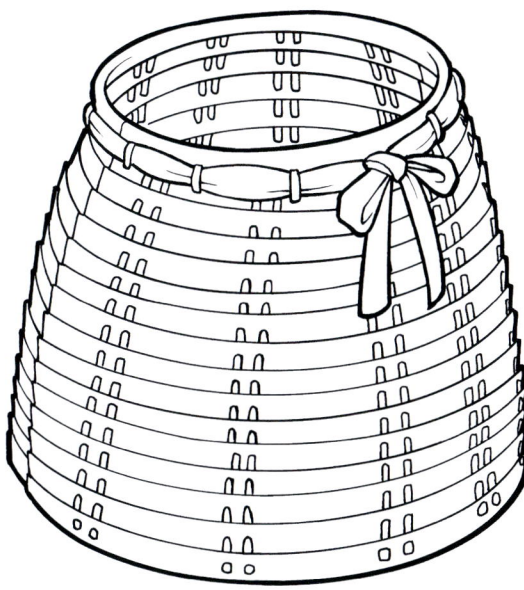

Samurai Armour

early 6th century, suggests that they were worn for aesthetic or ceremonial purposes and that they were not intended to be used as protective armour. This would be in keeping with the idea that lamellar armour was associated with the elevated status of the elite within Yamato society.

The bone scales from the Kanai Higashiura site were discovered inside armour that was found near a *keikō*, the name that is used to refer to the most common form of lamellar armour that was first produced in Yamato, the earliest examples of which date to the middle of the 5th century. This particular *keikō*, however, was unique, for it is the only set amongst the 200 or so examples of ancient lamellar armour found in Japan to date to have been recovered with the skeletal remains of the individual who was wearing it when he died still inside it. This individual is believed to have been an important local leader, which is in keeping with the idea that lamellar armour was indicative of the elite.

While the *tankō* could be used in a mounted role, as the rigid designs of the riveted iron-plate examples of cuirasses produced and utilized in the 16th century attest, lamellar armour was generally better suited to the needs of the mounted warriors of that period. This was in part due to the fact that it was generally lighter, and as such was less taxing for a warrior to wear. The flexible nature of its design also greatly enhanced the range of uninhibited upper body movements that a warrior was capable of making. Ironically these same characteristics reduced the effectiveness of lamellar armour outside an equestrian role, which again may have been one of the reasons why the *tankō* was retained as long as it was. For the Jōmon and Yayoi, along with the latter's Yamato descendants, always fought on foot, utilizing bladed weaponry such as spears and swords, against which plate armour provided better protection.

While the earliest examples of lamellar armour used by the elite

An illustrated representation of a late 6th century Yamato warrior. The warrior is depicted wearing a *yoko-ita byō-dome* iron plate *tankō* with lamellar *kusazuri* similar to the excavated cuirass with hip armour seen on the previous page. By this time the *tankō* was generally worn in conjunction with other items of armour for the extremities such as neck, shoulder and forearm protection. Shin guards were also sometimes worn. (Artwork by Angus McBride, from *Early Samurai AD 200–1500* © Osprey Publishing)

ANCIENT ARMOUR

of Yamato may have been Korean-made cuirasses, the armour makers in the archipelago appear to have quickly mastered the technique associated with fabricating armour from *sane*. The size and shape of these appear to have been almost identical to those scales that were utilized on the Korean peninsula, with the *sane* measuring about 6 cm in height, 3 cm in width and about 3 mm in thickness.

Bottomley and Hopson describe the *keikō*, or 'hanging shell', as this form of lamellar cuirass came to be known, as 'a sleeve-less coat' with a flared lower skirt that terminated mid-thigh, in silhouette somewhat resembling a *tankō*.[6] Like the *tankō*, the *keikō* wrapped around the body of the wearer and was fastened vertically down the middle of the chest by a number cords or leather thongs attached for this purpose. Unlike the *tankō*, however, all *keikō* were *ichi-mai-dō* by the nature of their construction.

The majority of *keikō* appear to have been assembled from approximately 800 elongated tombstone-shaped lacquered iron scales, or *sane*, which is why the *keikō* is also sometimes referred to as the *kozane-kō*. The *keikō*, unlike the forms of lamellar cuirass that the Japanese produced in later centuries, was a more complex armour, assembled from six or more varying types and sizes of scale. In general, however, the *sane* averaged about 7 cm in height and about 2–4 cm in width, which varied depending on where the scale was to be used in the overall construction of the cuirass. The *sane* would be arranged in loosely thonged horizontal bands to create 'steps' that were then laced together by vertically strung lengths of cord or lacing.

A typical *keikō* featured a *nagakawa* that, based on surviving examples, was commonly assembled from two steps, each of which was composed of seventy-four *sane*. The number of *sane* was different between the left- and right-hand portions of the divided *mae-tateage*, which itself was assembled from three steps. The right three steps were usually each made from eleven *sane*, while the top band of the left three steps would be made from thirteen *sane* and the lower two each from fourteen *sane*. This created a degree of overlap when the two halves were tied together and also tapered the shape of the *mae-tateage* so that it did not interfere with the movement of the arms.

An illustration of a *sankaku-ita kawa-toji* version of *tankō* presented with a flat hoop-like arrangement of *kusazuri*. The use of triangular sections of leather to secure the individual lames of the hip armour together is based on designs found on contemporary ceramic models of cuirass and *bushi-haniwa*. This image is based on the conjectural drawings that were produced by Dr Sasama Yoshihiko to show how leather panels such as these could have been arranged to assemble the *kusazuri*.

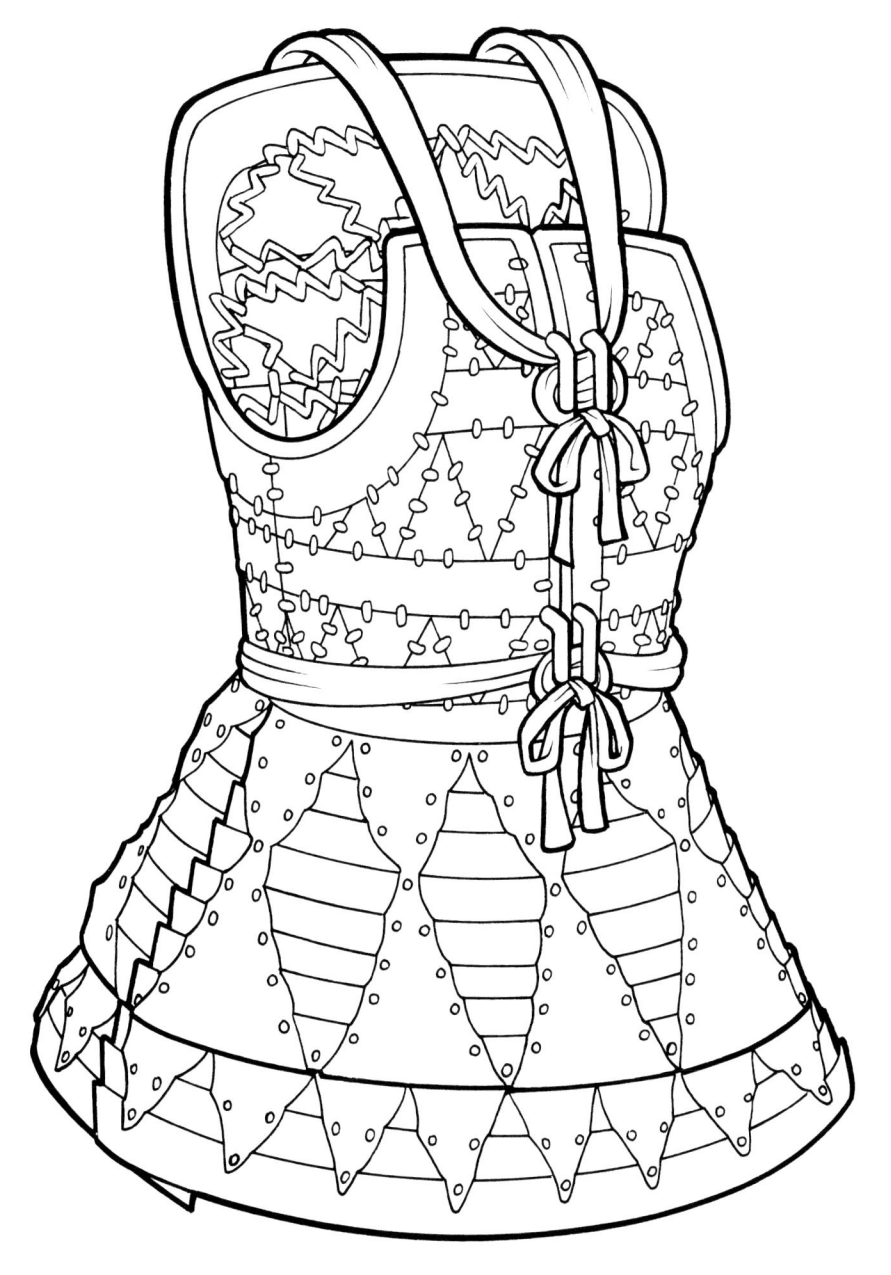

The *ushiro-tateage* also tapered from top to bottom. It was assembled from four steps, with the top two usually constructed of twenty-six *sane*, while the third step would be made from twenty-eight and the bottom one from twenty-nine *sane*.

It appears that a large, flat-bottomed U-shaped panel of leather was bound by leather thongs to the top of the *ushiro-tateage*. The arms of this U-shaped piece would be arched over and secured to the tops of the two *mae-tateage* sections to create shoulder straps, or *wadagami*. There is some evidence to suggest that in some cases the *wadagami* were cut and fitted with buckles that allowed them to be secured together near the top of the chest just below the collar bone. While buckles would have helped the wearer adjust the vertical fit of the cuirass to a degree, the open-front design of the *keikō* also made it extremely easy to wear. Thus it seems likely that buckled *wadagami* were limited to relatively wealthy warriors and were as such far from a common feature.

One of the most unique features of the *keikō* was that a special elongated form of *sane* was utilized in its construction to connect the *kusazuri* to the cuirass proper. These specialized scales, called *koshi-zane*, or literally 'waist scales', were flat at either end but had a mid-section which curved inward towards the body. Often measuring between 16 and 30 cm in length, the upper end of the *koshi-zane* would be placed over and laced to the exterior surface of the lower half portion of the bottom lame of the *nagakawa*. The uppermost lame of the *kusazuri* would then be laced to the flat lower end surface of the *koshi-zane*. While a greater percentage of the weight load of the *keikō* was by design intended to be borne by the shoulders via the *wadagami*, it is also clear from the inward-curving arch of the *koshi-zane* that the *keikō* was also intended to rest on the hips, contrary to the 'hanging shell' image that is conjured up by its modern name.

The concave recess created by the inward arch of the *koshi-zane* allowed the *keikō* to be drawn tight at the waist without impacting on the diaphragm. It also created a hollow that helped the waist-belt and equipment that was worn stay in place, as these items once tied were

A representation of a warrior from the 6th century wearing a lamellar *keikō* form of cuirass. Approximately 800 individual tombstone-shaped scales, or *sane,* were required to produce a *keikō*. The *kata-yoroi* shoulder guards were independent pieces of auxiliary armour that were generally worn in conjunction with the *keikō*. (Image © and courtesy of the Kyōto Costume Museum)

ANCIENT ARMOUR

unable to slide down past the outward-flaring arch of the *koshi-zane* and suspended *kusazuri*.

The *kusazuri* portion of a *keikō*, like the upper portion of the cuirass, was again constructed from horizontally arranged rows of *sane*. The uppermost step or *ichi-no-ita* of the hip armour was generally composed of around sixty *sane* that were wider than those used to assemble the upper-body portion of the cuirass, which produced a lamellar band that was just slightly longer than the bottom band of the *nagakawa*. The next band in the descending order of the overlapping and telescoping arrangement of the *kusazuri* was the *ni-no-ita* or second board, which was generally assembled from approximately ninety-two slightly narrower *sane* than those used in the *ichi-no-ita* band. The third band, or *san-no-ita*, would be assembled from ninety-six *sane* and the bottom or lowermost step, called the *suso-no-ita*, from as many as 114 special miniaturized *koshi-zane*-like scales that were the same height as the *sane* used in the other lamellar bands of the *kusazuri* but with a concave midsection. Why the *suso-no-ita sane* were made in this way is unclear, though it was more than likely a purely aesthetic feature.

Narrow bands of leather, called *kawa-fukurin*, were folded over the *sane-gashira*, or rounded upper heads of the scales and the lower edges of the lamellar bands in some cases. *Kawa-fukurin* were applied for a number of reasons which varied depending on where they were utilized. For example, the *sane-gashira* along the uppermost band of the *nagakawa* between the *mae-tateage* and *ushiro-tateage* that covered the sides of the torso under the armpits were often capped with *kawa-fukurin*. In this case the *kawa-fukurin* were applied to prevent the heads of the *sane* from

An illustrated representation of a 6th century Yamato warrior wearing a *keikō*, the first commonly reproduced form of lamellar armour that was made and utilized in the Japanese archipelago. The neck and shoulder guards were independent items of armour. (Artwork by Angus McBride, from *Early Samurai AD 200–1500* © Osprey Publishing)

SAMURAI ARMOUR

damaging the wearer's garments and to stop the *sane* from pinching the warrior. The leather bands also helped to further bind the rows of lamellae together in these areas.

The *sane-gashira* of the *koshi-zane* and the scales in the uppermost band of the *kusazuri* were also capped by a *kawa-fukurin*, as were both the upper and lower edges of the *sane* used to assemble the *suso-no-ita*. In the case of the *suso-no-ita* the leather edge caps also helped to protect the knotted ends of the lengths of cord or leather thong that bound the lamellar steps of the cuirass together, which originated from the heads of the *suso-no-ita*. Likewise, the *kawa-fukurin* along the lower edge of the *suso-no-ita* protected the horizontal or lateral bindings, called *karage*, that bound the individual *sane* together to form the row of lamellae.

While archaeologists and scholars were able to understand the overall form of the *keikō* based on studies of extant examples and *bushi-haniwa* recovered through archaeological excavations, they were uncertain as to exactly how the *keikō* was assembled. This was due to the complete absence of any surviving portions of the connective bindings, which having been primarily made of cord and leather were prone to rapid and total decomposition. It was not until the early 1940s that a fairly reliable, though still conjectural, explanation of the method of assembly was presented by Dr Suenaga Masao, who carefully reconstructed examples of every known form of ancient cuirass including the *keikō*, which he documented in his authoritative work, *Nihon Jōdai no Katchū*.

Each row of scales in the upper-body portion of the cuirass proper was bound together by two lengths of lateral binding called *karage* that were strung through holes punched in the mid- and lower sections of each *sane*. In the case of the *sane* used to assemble the *kusazuri*, one *karage* only was strung through the lower edge of each scale. The lacquered iron *sane* would be arranged from left to right with each *sane* overlaying about one-quarter of the face width of the right-hand edge of its neighbouring scale. This would

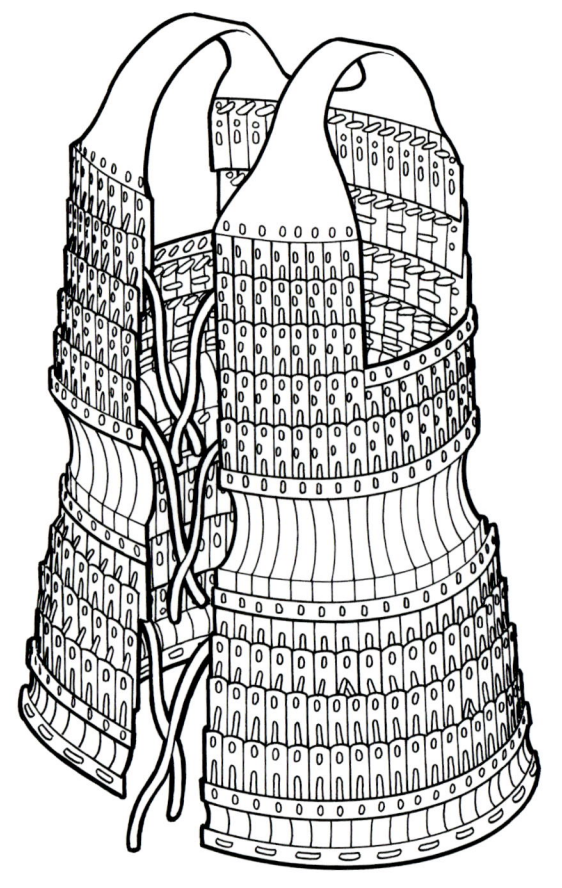

An illustration of the sleeveless coat-like *keikō* form of lamellar cuirass. Several unique forms of scale were used to assemble the *keikō*, with the size and shape of the scales varying depending on where they were utilized in the construction of the cuirass. Several hundred individually lacquered scales were required to construct a *keikō*. Note that the while the *wadagami* are depicted as continuous pieces, there is evidence to suggest that they were sometimes made from two pieces that buckled or tied together in the area of the clavicles.

A modern reconstruction of a *keikō* made by Suenaga Masao some time prior to 1942. Some of the several varieties of specifically shaped scales required to fabricate the *keikō* are visible in this image. Note the distinctive external method of vertical connective lacing. Small thongs of leather were threaded through the lacing itself, and corresponding holes pierced in the head of each scale to allow the thongs to be passed through the scales and knotted closed on their reverse. This method of lacing was eventually replaced by more durable and practical methods of vertically connecting the loosely bound horizontal bands of *sane* together. (Image © and courtesy of the Gunma Prefectural Museum of History, Gunma Prefecture, Japan)

92

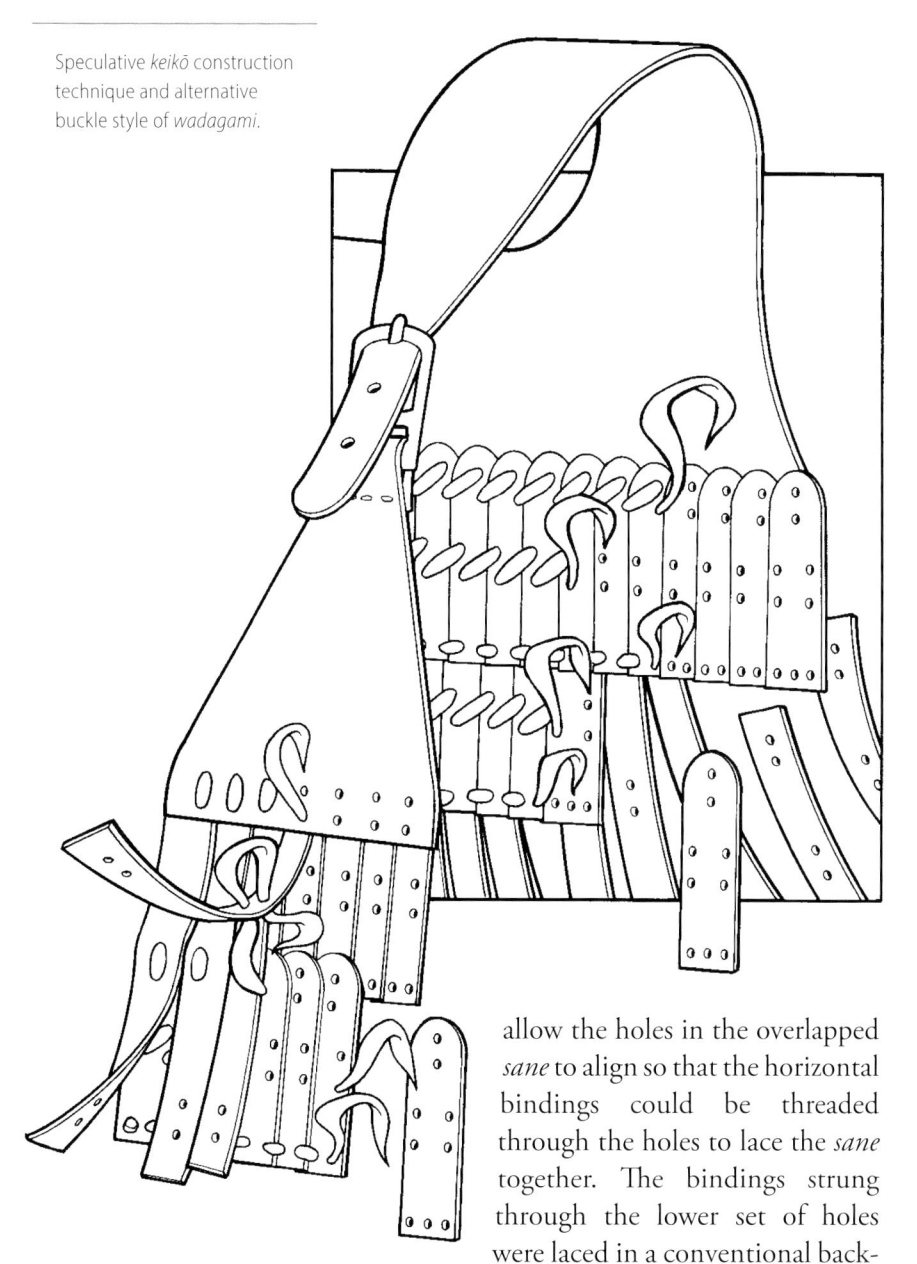

Speculative keikō construction technique and alternative buckle style of wadagami.

allow the holes in the overlapped *sane* to align so that the horizontal bindings could be threaded through the holes to lace the *sane* together. The bindings strung through the lower set of holes were laced in a conventional back-to front quilt-like thread pattern, while the midsection bindings were threaded through the overlapping scales from front to back. The *karage* thong was then pulled straight down and inserted back through the overlapped scales. It was next pulled upwards to the left and pushed back through to the exterior surface of the next pair of adjacent overlapping scales and the pattern repeated.

The assembled lamellar boards were then attached together by lengths of vertically strung cord, *odoshi-ito*, or long narrow lengths of leather called *kumi-himo*. There appear to have been a number of different methods of vertical lacing, not all of which are fully understood. According to the reconstructions produced by Dr Suenaga, however, two highly plausible and apparently common methods of lacing were used, based on the various examples of *bushi-haniwa* that have been discovered wearing *keikō*. The older of the two methods had the connective vertical bands of *kumi-himo* applied to the exterior surfaces of the lames. These were strung up the middle of the arranged lames, with the lacing itself secured to the upper head portion of each consecutive *sane* by a small leather thong that would be pushed through from the rear of the scale and then drawn through the middle of the connective *kumi-himo* lacing. The small thong would then be drawn over the surface of the connective lacing and reinserted back through the lacing and scale where it would be extracted through the back side of the *sane* and knotted together. In other words, the *kumi-himo* was laced to the *sane* and was not itself strung through the scale.[7]

Though only one non-excavated, rather fragmentary example of *keikō* is known to exist, it appears that the *kumi-himo* strips were, by the early 8th century at least, being made from dyed strips of leather. This is based on the portions of cuirass and connective laces that were found on a *keikō* recovered from the treasure house located on the grounds of the Shōsōin temple compound in Nara Prefecture.

The vertical lacing that bound the lames of the *kusazuri* together terminated at the *koshi-zane* and began again from the lower band of the *nagakawa*. To accommodate the widening design of the *kusazuri*, additional connective thongs had to be added periodically, which resulted in some bands of connective lacing being strung diagonally between upper and lower bands due to the difference in the number of *sane* used in the construction of the ascending lames.

The second, more conventional, under-over lacing technique of vertical binding was also introduced, in which the connective bindings were drawn through the lower edge of a *sane*, up along its reverse face and then out to the front face near the head of the scale. The lacing was then drawn back through another hole to the reverse of the scale and then inserted through to the reverse of the bottom of the *sane* immediately above it, where the pattern was repeated.

Unlike the *tankō*, which in its earliest forms had been worn by itself, the *keikō* was clearly designed to be accompanied by a complement of other items of protective armour, such as the *akabe-yoroi*, which was a form of gorget with attached shoulder guards, which is discussed in Volume II. As it was also primarily intended for utilization by mounted warriors it was common for it to be worn with a *haidate*, which was a new form of armour that was designed to protect the lower thighs. Along with a helmet, forearm protection and shin guards, it appears that the *keikō* may also have been worn with crescent-moon-shaped metal plates, called *waki-biki*, that were designed to be suspended from the shoulders to cover the area on the torso that was exposed when the arms were lifted.

The next major evolutionary development in armour designs within Japan did not occur until the latter half of the 7th century, when an alternative version of *keikō* was introduced. This also happened to be the last form of armour that was included in the kofun before the practice of tumuli burial mounds was discontinued. The new design, which has come to be known in recent centuries as the *uchikake-keikō*, or literally the 'long garment hanging shell', differed from the original version of *keikō* in that it was constructed as an *ichi-mai* or in some case *ni-mai-dō* consisting of separate front and back panels that were worn poncho-like in conjunction with two independent side panels. Other than for shifting the vulnerable closure point away from the middle of the chest, where it had been in the existing design of *keikō*, it is hard to understand why the Japanese armour makers considered the *uchikake* form of *keikō* to be an improvement over the original version of this style of cuirass. For the quartered construction of this make of *dō* did little to simplify the method of assembly, nor did it make the armour easier to wear. In fact, if anything, the sectional design appears only to have complicated matters.

There were other changes to the manner in which the *uchikake-keikō* was constructed besides its sectional design. The most significant amongst these was that the front and back panels of the cuirass were assembled without an intermediary band of *koshi-zane*. These were replaced by two or three rows of conventional *sane* which were secured in place in the usual manner. The *wadagami* were also designed to be buckled together just below the area of the clavicle.

As separate pieces, the side panel portions of the armour became independent items of armour referred to as *waidate*. Besides being separate pieces, the *waidate* were fundamentally unchanged in their design and overall method of construction, being composed of a two-step *nagakawa* with an intermediary band of *koshi-zane* from which a *kusazuri* composed of four lames was suspended.

While the significance of this bizarre design was almost certainly not appreciated at the time, after the introduction of lamellar armour

A 6th century *bushi-haniwa* recovered during the excavations at Iizuka-machi in Ota City, in Gunma Prefecture. The terracotta figure depicts a warrior wearing a *keikō*, a form of lamellar armour that was introduced into Japan around the middle of the 5th century. A National Treasure, this *haniwa* is displayed in the Tōkyō National Museum. (Courtesy of J.L. Badgley)

ANCIENT ARMOUR

construction techniques into Japan, the appearance of the *uchikake-keikō* was perhaps the second most important evolutionary development on the path towards the appearance of the forms of armour that would go on to be synonymous with the samurai. Exactly what route this process took, however, after the creation of the *uchikake-keikō*, is unclear. For just as the Japanese were on the threshold of developing their own truly unique forms of armour, a number of important geopolitical factors came into play, which significantly derailed and then redirected the developmental process of armour construction techniques and design within Japan, sending them off on an entirely new tangent.

Derailment came in the form of the fall of the Paekche Kingdom in AD 660. One of the

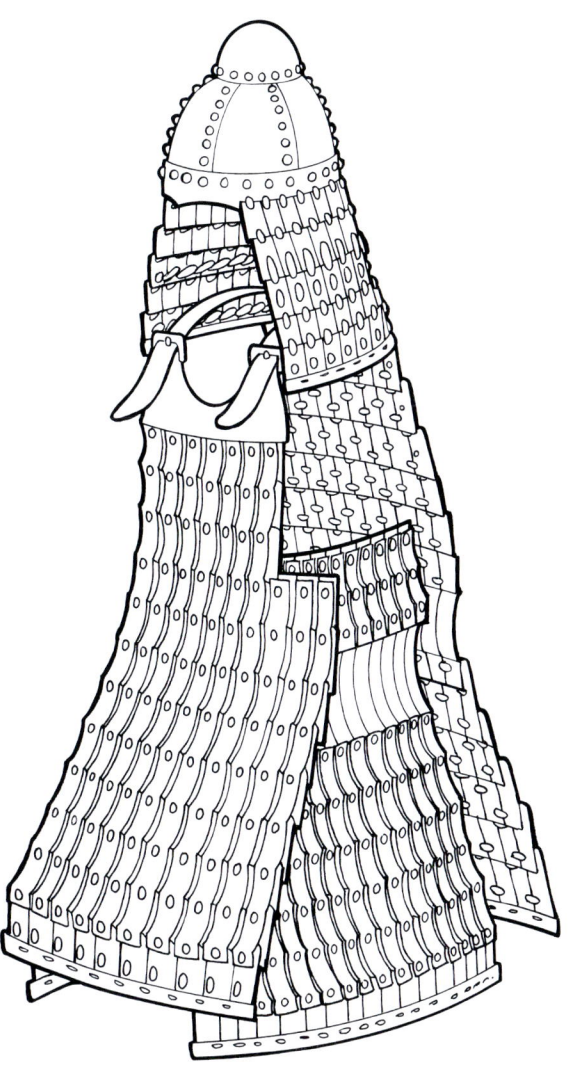

Left: An illustration of an 8th or 9th century warrior wearing an *uchikake-keikō*. Poncho-like, the *uchikake-keikō* had to be worn with two independent side panels of lamellar armour called *waidate*, which cover the sides of the torso. (Artwork by Angus McBride, from *Early Samurai AD 200–1500* © Osprey Publishing)

Above: An illustration of the *ni-mai-dō* variety of *uchikake-keikō*. Note the concave *koshi-zane* on the *waidate*.

95

major side-effects of the collapse of Yamato's Korean allies was that it cut the archipelago off from one of its major sources of iron, which they had imported in the form of ingots. Though Yamato had possessed the ability to smelt iron since the latter part of the 6th century, a century later it appears to have remained heavily reliant on the import of iron ingots to satisfy the demand for this base material. This forced the Japanese to reconsider the use of other materials for the making of armour, the most readily available and practical substitute being rawhide, or *nerigawa*, which would go on to play a continuous and significant role in the construction of Japanese armour for the next twelve centuries.

Fear of retribution in the form of an invasion by the Tang and their cohorts for having allied with the Paekche caused the Yamato state to hurriedly reinvent itself. Ironically many of the changes that were implemented were based on the socio-economic practices of Tang Dynasty China, whose influence had started to creep into Yamato culture in the decades prior to the fall of Paekche.

From the standpoint of the evolution of lamellar armour in Japan, the Taihō Code that was drafted in AD 701 was a pivotal event, for it called for the creation of a national army that was to be manned by conscripts. While conscription had existed at various levels in Japan since the Taika Reforms of AD 645, the number of men serving in such a capacity had been relatively limited. How long conscripts served, what equipment they used and what was expected of them could vary considerably from region to region. The haphazard nature of mandatory military service came to an end with the introduction of the Taihō Code, which clearly and exactly stipulated through a series of regulations the conscript soldier's obligations to the state as a member of the national army. Included amongst these regulations were rules that stipulated in detail the form of armour that the conscript was obligated to procure for himself. While these rules helped to ensure more of a uniform appearance for the national army, a need for uniformity was not the only driving factor behind the issuing of such regulations.

Throughout the 7th and 8th centuries, iron continued to be a relatively scarce commodity in Japan. As such it needed to be reserved for the creation of other articles, namely weaponry, since rawhide could be substituted for metal when it came to the production of armour. Furthermore, in keeping with the fight-fire-with-fire approach, the new national army was established along the lines of those fielded by the Tang Dynasty Chinese. This was not limited to its organizational structure, but also mimicked the forms of weaponry and equipment that were used by the Tang forces.

The implementation of the Taihō Code national army abruptly redirected the evolutionary path of armour development in Japan, sending it down an entirely new track. Surprisingly, very little is known about this new form of armour due to an almost complete absence of extant examples, except for a handful of rectangular iron plates that are thought possibly to have been used in the construction of a *men'ōchū*, or 'cotton coat' as this new Chinese style of armour came to be referred to in later centuries.

The few surviving contemporary images and references of *men'ōchū* suggest that most examples resembled an overcoat-like garment with short sleeves, but how they were made remains unclear. Some scholars believe that they were made of metal or leather plates that were attached directly, by rivets or sewing, to the outer surface of the fabric coat and accompanying hood-like cloth cap. Alternatively, the *men'ōchū* may have been a form of brigandine, with the armour plating sandwiched between two cloth layers.[8] It is equally possible that *men'ōchū* were fabricated in both manners, for similar examples of Chinese armour made of brigandine and jazerant are known to exist.

It is also possible that the *men'ōchū*, in at least some cases, was made entirely of fabric, particularly those items that were made for very low-ranking warriors. In lieu of armour plating, the *men'ōchū* could have simply been an extremely thick coat made from multiple layers of cloth that were sewn in a grid-like pattern that helped keep the overlapping fabrics evenly layered and in position. Support for this theory comes from the fact that padded-cloth *men'ōchū*-like forms of protective garment are known to have existed in China. Alternatively, quilted areas stuffed with cotton, or more commonly typha (bulrush) cotton may have also been used to create the layer of protective padding.

Based on contemporary images, the majority of *men'ōchū* appear to have been made from materials that were dyed either orange or red in colour. It is possible, however, that these colours were chosen by the period chroniclers more for the quality of the visual presentation than because they accurately reflected the actual colours of the items that were being depicted. Light brown is another likely colour of these items, which were more than likely tailored from hemp cloth. For hemp, or *asa*, would have been by far the cheapest, most readily available and most durable form of fabric available for such purposes, and as such ideal for the fabrication of mass-produced items of armour for conscript soldiers.

The absence of a single surviving example of *men'ōchū* adds some credence to the 'all cloth' construction theory. However, the large number of surviving examples of similar forms of brigandine and jazerant *men'ōchū*-like items of armour in China does not support this belief. A more plausible explanation for the absence of surviving examples of *men'ōchū*, which as the only recognized form of armour for the national army must have been produced in huge numbers during the 8th century, is that these items were broken down and salvaged for their useful materials in later centuries.

While a considerable number of these items were almost certainly lost to history through decomposition and other events, it is highly unlikely that these items would simply have been allowed to rot away en masse in a country as poor in natural resources as Japan has been throughout almost all of its recorded

A representation of an 8th century Japanese soldier wearing a speculative example of the elusive *men'ōchū* form of armour. The exact appearance and make-up of this form of armour is unclear due to an absence of extant examples. The red scale-like outlines printed on the garment are meant to replicate the individual outline-stitched fabric-stuffed or brigandine compartments that this form of armour is thought to have relied on as protection. (Image © and courtesy of the Kyōto Costume Museum)

SAMURAI ARMOUR

history. Instead, the vast majority of the iron or leather plates that were more than likely utilized in the construction of *men'ōchū* were probably salvaged from these items in later centuries for incorporation into other forms of armour after Emperor Kanmu ended conscription in AD 792.

Adding to the absence of extant examples of the forms of armour made between the 8th and 11th centuries was the discontinuation of the kofun burial mounds that had been a significant part of the cultural practices of the people of Yamato in previous centuries. This practice started to fade out over the course of the 7th century as Buddhist funerary practices were adopted in conjunction with the rapidly expanding influence of this imported continental faith. From a historical perspective this was an unfortunate turn of events, for the kofun have turned out to be one of the greatest single sources of information about the forms of armour that were utilized in Japan between the 4th and 8th centuries.

The production of lamellar armour, while severely curtailed, clearly did not stop when conscription and the national army were introduced. Scholars debate, however, whether lamellar armour continued to be used by the elite or officer class of the new national army. While there is no way to be sure, this may have been the case, due to the fact that lamellar armour continued to be used through the 8th century by the military elite of the Tang Dynasty Chinese, whose military organization and

An illustration depicting what the *men'ōchū* form of armour is generally thought to have looked like. The image also depicts the shift that was occurring in lamellar armour designed between the 8th and 9th centuries. This was primarily because lamellar armour continued to be worn by the elite in Japanese society and the private protection forces that they employed, unlike the rank-and-file of the national army conscripts, who were obligated to wear the *men'ōchū*. (Artwork by Angus McBride, from *Early Samurai AD 200–1500* © Osprey Publishing)

structure were the model after which the Japanese had developed their own national army.

The private *shōen* estates and frontier regions more than likely continued to produce and utilize lamellar armour, for they were under no obligation to adopt the new Chinese-style *men'ōchū* forms of armour. And while there is again no proof to support such a theory, the fact that the mounted warriors from the frontier *shōen* estates were able to engage and defeat the Emishi in battle well before the end of the 8th century, at a time when national army troops were regularly being defeated by the latter, suggest that if any one group was responsible for the continued evolution of lamellar armour designs in Japan during the 8th century, it was the private mercenaries whom the powerful frontier *shōen* estates employed as fighters.

Supporting this theory is the fact that the Emishi are known to have continued to utilize lamellar armour, most examples of which were similar in form to the late 5th century design of *keikō*, which they had no doubt copied from the forms of lamellar armour that had originally been utilized in Yamato.

While it is presently impossible to say with any certainty exactly what developments occurred with the design of the *uchikake-keikō* between the 8th and the early 10th centuries that caused it to metamorphose into what Bryant referred to as a 'proto-*ō-yoroi*' form of cuirass, the evolutionary path was a logical one.[9] Key amongst the various changes that were implemented was the eventual discontinuation of the practice of producing the cuirass from four separate pieces. At some point the left *waidate* was merged back into the cuirass proper. In what order this occurred is unknown, but gradually armour makers chose to construct the cuirass as a form of *ichi-mai-dō* that in cross-section had the appearance of a flattened C. The open right-hand side of the torso that was not covered by the cuirass was covered by a separate *waidate* panel. This arrangement greatly simplified the process of

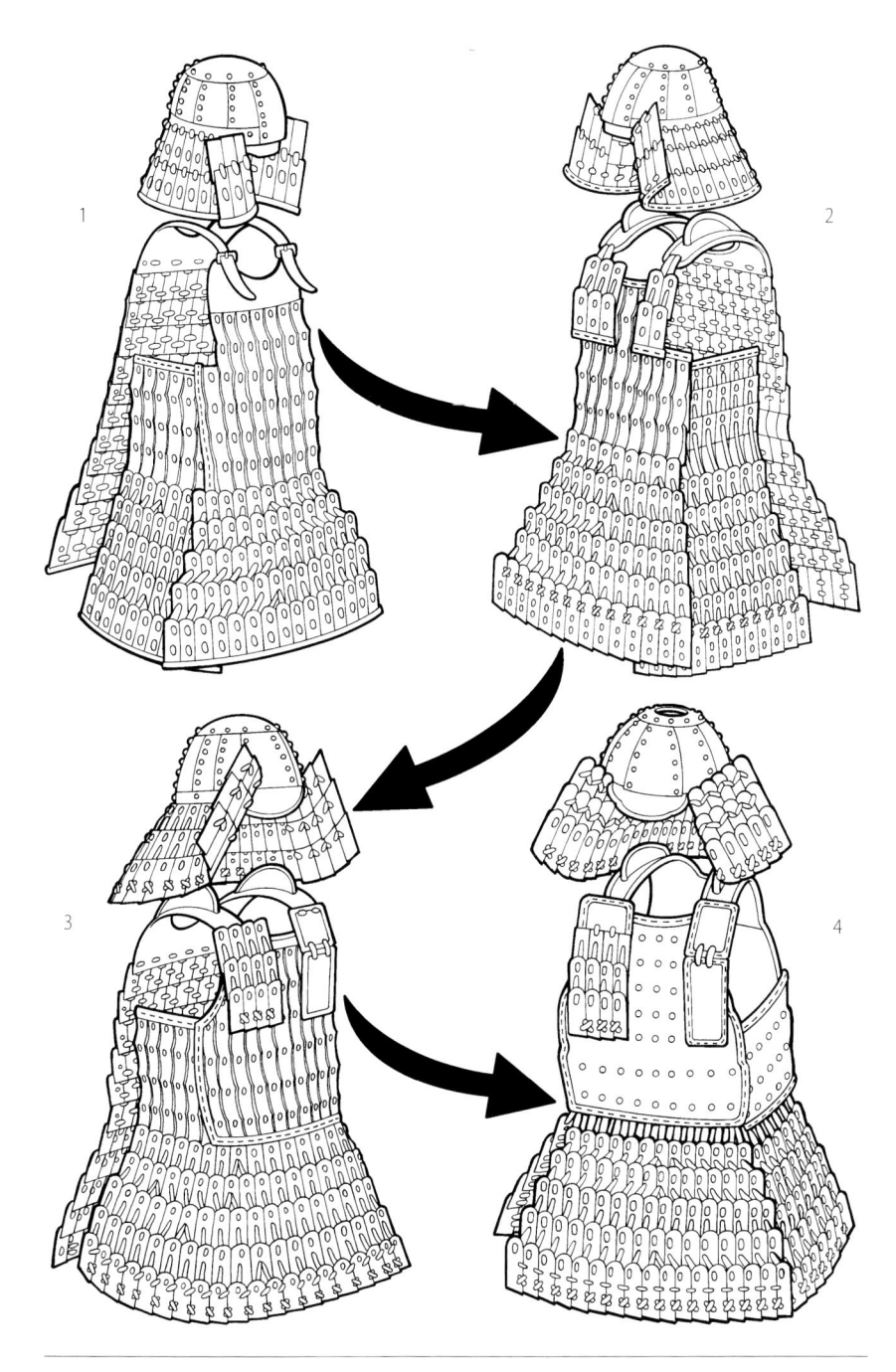

How cuirass design evolved from the *uchikake-keikō* of the mid 7th century into the *yoroi* of the early 10th century is unknown owing to an absence of extant examples of these items. While speculative, many scholars believe that the *uchikake-keikō* gradually became more box-like in form (figure 1). Over time, small lamellar pendants began to be suspended from the ends of the *wadagami* to protect the connective cords (figure 2). At some point the separate side panels of the *uchikake-keikō* design were reunited with the main front panel of the cuirass, while the back panel continued to hang free (figure 3). The lamellar sections that were suspended from the *wadagami* gradually grew in width and length during this same period and began to take on the form and roles of the *kyūbi* and *sendan-no-ita*. At some point the opening down the rear edge on the left side of the cuirass was closed together (figure 4). To compensate for this, the right side of the armour was separated and again made into a separate section of armour, as it had been on the original *uchikake-keikō*. This created the C-shaped form that became the *yoroi*.

donning the armour as the various straps and cords that would have been required to hold four separate sections together were done away with. The open right side of the cuirass meant that it was still easy to put on. This design also ended the problem that warriors had often encountered with the multi-piece designs of *keikō*, the various sections of which had a tendency to slip or be jarred out of alignment with each other while a warrior was riding, resulting in both discomfort and the exposure of various areas.

Japanese legend says that this design of the *uchikake-keikō* came about after the pregnant Empress-Regent Jingū who was on campaign and fighting in Korea asked to have the side of her cuirass cut away so that it could better accommodate her enlarged abdomen. This colourful story is somewhat undermined by the fact that Jingū was a mythological figure. The logic behind the choice of leaving the right-hand side of the armour open was almost certainly influenced by the mounted warrior's growing reliance on the bow, which they were trained to draw with their right hands. This meant that when mounted, the most practical direction for a warrior to fire an arrow was to his immediate left. As most warriors were engaging other mounted archers, the left side of the body was the side most commonly exposed to an enemy, and thus armour makers designed the *uchikake-keikō* with the idea of restricting any opening in the cuirass to the less exposed right side of the torso.

Warriors therefore took every opportunity they had to target their opponent's more vulnerable right flank, which was particularly exposed when a warrior was attempting to launch an arrow or lifting his sword to defend himself from a close-quarter attack. Thus over time, armour makers attempted to offset some of the vulnerabilities that existed on the right side of the cuirass by fabricating the separate suspended side panel from a single solid piece of iron plate rather than from lamellae. A large *kusazuri* assembled from *sane-ita* was suspended from the lower edge of the *waidate* to complete the protective coverage down the right side of the torso.

The use of *koshi-zane* was discounted, as was the use of sections of cloth or leather, from forming the *wadagami*. The shoulder straps were instead made from solid, arched pieces of iron or rawhide that were bound to the rear upper edge of the cuirass. Toggles suspended from cords hung from the forward ends of the *wadagami* replaced the system of buckles that had previously been used to secure the frontal portion of the cuirass to the shoulder straps.

The *wadagami* were also mounted with rounded fin-like flanges called *shōji-no-ita* that stood erect on the shoulder straps to provide protection for the sides of the neck. At some

A superb reconstruction by Dr Suenaga Masao of the poncho-like *ni-mai-dō* variety of *uchikake-keikō* used during the 8th and 9th centuries. One of the two independent *waidate* side armour panels is clearly visible. (Kansai University Museum)

ANCIENT ARMOUR

Another reconstruction by Dr Suenaga, of a *sankaku-ita kawa-toji* example of the *tankō* variety of cuirass from the latter half of the 6th century. Note the large, flared skirt-like independent *kusazuri*, which are shown fastened in place around the lower edge of the cuirass. Also note the unique combination of auxiliary items of armour worn that were commonly worn in conjunction with the *tankō* and *kusazuri*. (Kansai University Museum)

point it became common to suspend a couple of narrow pendants, composed of two or three rows of lamellae, from the *taka-himo* or connective cords that held the toggles that connected the front of the cuirass to the *wadagami*. Why these pendant-like lamellar sections were initially added is unclear, though they may have been designed to protect the connective *taka-himo* cords. Gradually the two pendants developed into distinct pieces, with the left-hand pendant, called the *kyūbi-no-ita*, taking on the shape of a long, narrow plate of solid iron that was designed to swing out in front of the armpit when the left arm was raised, to protect the armpit area.

The right-hand side pendant, which was designed to protect the right armpit, was called the *sendan-no-ita*. It continued to be made from two or three narrow rows of suspended lamellae. This allowed the *sendan-no-ita* to collapse back on and telescope over itself if required so that it would not impede the movements of the warrior's right arm when he drew his bow.

The bow, or *yumi*, directly influenced the addition of another major transitional feature, the *tsurubashiri-gawa*, or 'bowstring running leather', which was a broad panel of leather that was fitted over the entire front face of a cuirass to prevent the bowstring of a *yumi* from snagging on the *sane-gashira* of the lamellae. This feature attests to the fact that the bow had become the Japanese warrior's primary weapon by the end of the 9th century and mounted archery the most important martial skill.

While each of the aforementioned features would go on to become an integral part of the finished design of the *yoroi* style of cuirass, along with a multitude of other unique features and aesthetic details, the factor that ultimately ended up distinguishing the *yoroi* from its ancient predecessor, the *uchikake-keikō*, was the introduction of a new method of lamellar construction, which first began to be used sometime around the beginning of the 10th century.

An outstanding example of an *ō-yoroi* from the early 14th or early 15th century. Donated by one of the Ashikaga shōguns to the Kurama Temple, near Kyōto, the armour later became the property of the military governor of Kyōto, the *daimyō* Sakai of Wakasa, during the later part of the Edo period. (New York Metropolitan Museum of Art/CC0 1.0)

CHAPTER 4

EARLY FORMS OF SAMURAI ARMOUR

Yoroi, dō-maru, maru-dō, haramaki and *hara-ate*, 10–15th centuries

Emperor Kanmu's decision to commission the private fighting forces employed by the *shōen* landholders to prosecute the state's ongoing campaigns against the Emishi and to end conscription in AD 792 created the group of warriors that history came to know as the samurai.

While the imperial court may initially have felt that it had simply reorganized the military apparatus of the state, what it had actually done was massively undermine the court's monopoly on power that it had striven to build since the time of Himiko. Like an hourglass that had been turned on end, the court's power, authority and prestige gradually trickled away over the years and slowly accumulated in the hands of these hired, third-party interests, who gradually became aware of the shifting dynamics of their relationship with the court. Powerful clans such as the Fujiwara, Minamoto and Taira blossomed around the Emperor as the latter's all-encompassing dominance over state affairs wilted away and the court grew increasingly reliant on these external agencies to enforce its will.

The Fujiwara emasculated the court from within through centuries of skilful intrigues that saw their offspring married off and then descendents born into the very highest positions within the imperial family, while relatives staffed virtually every important governmental office associated with the court. The Minamoto earned power, prestige and wealth fighting brigands and pirates in the west of the country while the Taira similarly established themselves in the east of the country subduing the Emishi.

One of the first significant signs that the balance of power was shifting in favour of the *shōen* landholders came in AD 939 when Taira no Masakado, a powerful provincial official and *shōen* leader from the Kantō region with close connections to the imperial family, led an attack on government offices in Hitachi.

SAMURAI ARMOUR

Masakado, whose actions were initially in retaliation for events that had occurred during a prolonged family feud, believed that he was both legally and morally justified in doing what he did. The court, however, had grounds to feel otherwise and labelled Masakado a rebel. Taira no Masakado responded by invading eight other provinces and declaring himself Emperor. The speed and relative ease with which Masakado established himself in his new domains spoke for itself and testified to a growing sense of dissatisfaction and indifference that was felt towards the authority of the imperial court throughout much of Japan.

This caused the court to quickly commission and dispatch warriors from other provincial landholders to suppress Taira no Masakado, whose short-lived rebellion ended a few months later in AD 940, when he and many of his followers were killed in battle. The court's victory was a hollow one, however, for Taira no Masakado had clearly demonstrated just how powerful the regional warrior families had become over the course of a couple of centuries. That one of these men could rise against the state and declare himself Emperor rocked the imperial court onto its heels. This uncomfortable reality was further amplified by the fact that the court's salvation rested in the hands of warriors from other provincial landholders, on whom the court had been obligated to rely in order to suppress Masakado and his followers.

While Taira no Masakado's failed rebellion represented the frustrated adolescent-like stirrings of the samurai, the latter was not the only group that was beginning to flex its muscles and challenge the authority of the court. For along with the samurai, the first recorded reference to whom is believed to have appeared in the late Heian period collection of poems called the *Kokin Wakashū* (Ancient and Modern Japanese Poems), published in AD 920, there were also the large private armies of mercenaries called *sōhei* that were employed by many of the powerful monastic orders of Japan's various

An outstanding late Edo period example of an *ō-yoroi* made for a senior administrator within the Tokugawa Shōgunate. With the exception of the bifurcated *haidate* thigh guard panels and the *menpo* facial armour, this *ō-yoroi* accurately portrays the style of armour that was worn by mounted warriors in Japan until well into the 14th century.

Early Forms of Samurai Armour

An illustration of a samurai from around the late 11th century, with his retainer. The ability of the court to control the warrior families across Japan who it relied on to enforce its will had slowly eroded over the course of the 10th to 11th centuries as the samurai became increasingly conscious of the substantial degree of power that they held and as such, their ability to influence domestic political events. (Artwork by Angus McBride, from *Early Samurai AD 200–1500* © Osprey Publishing)

Buddhist sects. These monk armies, dressed in religious robes that concealed the armour they wore underneath, several times marched on the capital from their temple compounds in Kyōto and Nara to ensure through intimidation that the court enacted certain policies that benefited and empowered their religious orders.

The samurai came of age in the late 11th century when Minamoto Yoshiie fought a successful campaign against the forces of the Kiyohara in the northern provinces. Famed for his military abilities and leadership, Yoshiie had established his reputation in the Zenkunen War when he had been commissioned by the court to conduct a punitive campaign against the Abe, a powerful provincial warrior family in the northern provinces that had shown contempt for the imperial court's authority. However, the Gosannen Kassen, or 'Late Three Years War' that Yoshiie waged against the Kiyohara, which came to an end in 1089, had not been sanctioned by the court. As such, even though the court welcomed the war's outcome, it refused to compensate Yoshiie for his efforts. This placed Yoshiie in a very difficult position, for samurai service was fundamentally based on the principle that warriors who fought for a lord would in return benefit from the division and redistribution of the properties and wealth of the vanquished. Snubbed, Yoshiie proved his mettle by dividing his own lands amongst his retainers to compensate them for their loyal service.

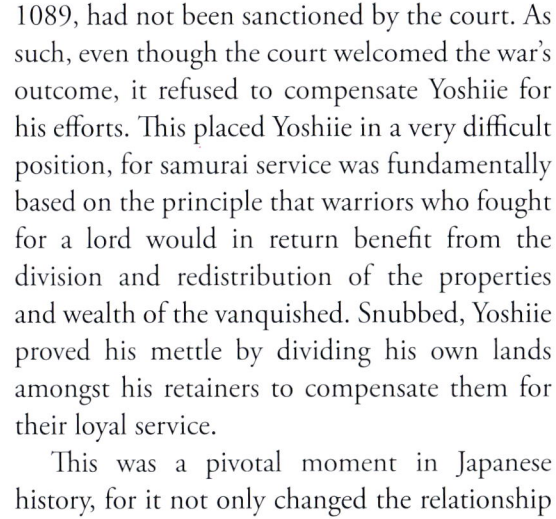

This was a pivotal moment in Japanese history, for it not only changed the relationship between the imperial court and the regional military families upon whom the court was so reliant, but it also dramatically altered the alliance or bond between the powerful military families and the warriors who served them. For Yoshiie had demonstrated that with or without the court, the warrior families were capable of rewarding those who served them. His action also demonstrated the ability of the powerful regional families to act unilaterally, without imperial sanction, when it was in their best interests to do so. Yoshiie's selfless act effectively nullified the relevance of the imperial court, whose importance on the political stage dwindled rapidly over the next several decades as the increasingly self-aware and powerful warrior families wrested the final few levers of state control from the court's weak and delicate hands.

Events ultimately came to a head during the latter half of the 12th century, when the Minamoto and Taira clans along with their respective allies fought each other for ultimate control over the state in the epic Genpei War, lasting from 1180 to 1185. The Minamoto clan ultimately prevailed and went on to establish the first military dictatorship, or Shōgunate, in 1192 in Kamakura under Minamoto no Yoritomo. Thus from the late 12th century onwards, with a few brief exceptions, the imperial court had been effectively removed from control over the state and became little more than a figurehead, with no real authority.

SAMURAI ARMOUR

Above: The C-shape of the *yoroi* is easy to appreciate when the cuirass is laid on its side. The continuous one-piece *ichi-mai-dō* construction of the *nagakawa* is visible as are the hundreds of individual *kozane* scales that were used to assemble the *kusazuri*.

Right: A view of an Edo period example of a cuirass made in the *yoroi* style. The open right side of the *yoroi* is clearly visible.

The style of armour that had been worn throughout this entire tumultuous period was the *yoroi*, which, like the warriors who wore it, also came of age between the 10th and 12th centuries. For this reason, the *yoroi* style of cuirass is intrinsically linked with the quintessential image of the samurai. For all the legendary figures of early samurai history, from Taira no Masakado to Minamoto no Yoritomo, had worn cuirasses made in the *yoroi* style. And since much of the central ethos of the samurai ideal was based upon the actions, deeds and events, legendary or factual, in which these important historical personalities had participated, it is easy to understand why the *yoroi* continued to be utilized by the elite of the Japanese warrior class until the very end of Japan's feudal period in the latter part of the 19th century, several hundred years after changes in the manner of warfare and weaponry had made the *yoroi* obsolete as an effective form of body armour.

THE DESIGN AND CONSTRUCTION OF *YOROI*

While the overall form of the *yoroi*, which consisted of a C-shaped *ichi-mai-dō* with a separate *waidate* side panel to cover the right-hand side of the torso, had more than likely been invented sometime during the latter half of the 9th century, these early versions were still more like *uchikake-keikō* until armour makers began assembling them using new construction techniques that were introduced during the first few decades of the 10th century. In fact, the oldest known example of a *yoroi*, which is now held in the prestigious Ōyamazumi Jinja Museum collection, is believed to have been made sometime between AD 900 and 920.

The most significant change that was introduced to the way that lamellar armour was constructed was that *katchū-shi* stopped assembling the horizontal rows of *sane* from individually finished scales bound together in the *yurugi-zane* or 'loose scale' style. While this method of construction gave a lamellar cuirass a degree of flexibility, it also meant that when a missile like an arrow struck the armour, the majority of the impact was absorbed by a single *sane* and perhaps a few of the surrounding scales. Even if the *sane* defeated the arrow, the warrior could still be injured as the flexible nature of the lamellar construction transmitted the majority of the missile's kinetic energy through the *sane* into the warrior's body as a powerful blunt-force impact.

At some point armour makers realized that lamellar armour could be made significantly more resilient if the individual *sane* were arranged in horizontal rows that were bound together and then lacquered, creating rigid boards. Lames made of *sane* assembled in the *nurigatame-zane* style, or literally the 'lacquer-stiffened scale' manner, transferred the energy of an impact through the entire length of the board, which significantly dissipated the amount of force that was transmitted through to the body of the warrior.

SCALES (*SANE*)

Somewhat strangely, the term *sane* appears to have metamorphosed into the word *kozane*, or literally 'small scale', around this time, even though the size of the scales changed very little until well into the 13th century, when they did in fact get smaller. Some scholars believe this change in terminology took place to differentiate clearly between the words *sane* and *sane-ita*, or 'scale board', which was itself a new term that referred to the rigid lames assembled in the *nurigatame-zane* style.

The process of making a set of armour in the *yoroi* style began long before the cuirass could begin to be assembled, for up to two thousand individual *kozane* were often required to make such armour during the Heian period, each one of which was by itself an individually labour-intensive item to produce.

Late Heian period *kozane* were large. Fabricated from both iron and rawhide, they generally measured between 3.0 and 4.7 cm in width and stood about 6.7–8.0 cm in height. The vast majority of scales used to assemble a *yoroi* were *kawa-zane*, or rawhide scales. This was primarily due to economic considerations, since iron scales, or *tetsu-zane*, were significantly more costly to produce than their rawhide counterparts due to the continued scarcity of iron in Japan at that time. *Tetsu-zane*, however, while more resilient than rawhide, were also proportionally much heavier and as such significantly increased the overall weight of a cuirass when they were used in large numbers. The greater strength of *tetsu-zane* was reflected in the fact that they were generally about 1.5 mm thick, while most examples of *kawa-zane* were about 3 mm thick.

It should also be noted that during the latter part of the Edo period, scales were also sometimes produced from *washi*, or Japanese rice paper. *Kami-zane*, or paper scales, were constructed from dozens of layers of *washi* that were glued together to produce a laminate that

SANE NOMENCLATURE

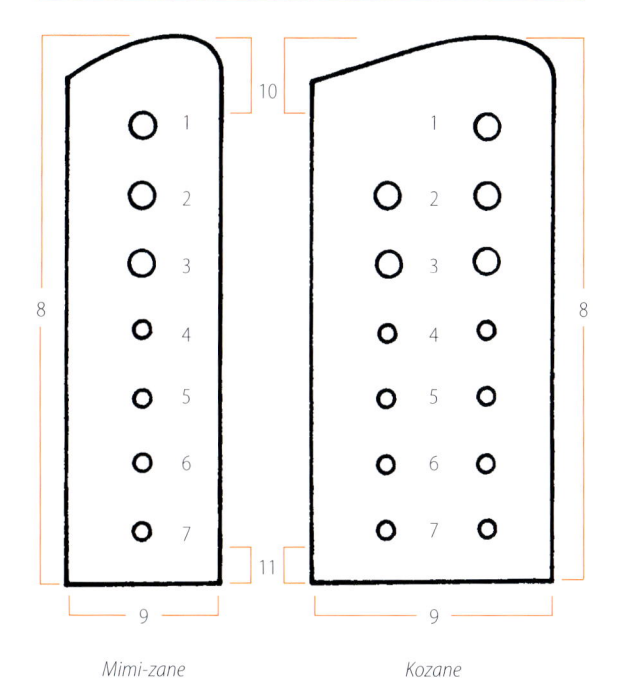

Mimi-zane   *Kozane*

1., 2. *Karami-no-ana*
3. *Kedate-no-ana*
4.,5.,6.,7. *Shita-garami-no-ana*
8. *Sane-ashi*
9. *Sane-haba*
10. *Sane-gashira*
11. *Sane-jiri*

when lacquered was surprisingly strong and durable. Many display and novelty armour sets that were produced during the Meiji and Taisho periods were assembled using *kami-zane*.

Kawa-zane were usually fashioned from the hides of cattle and horses, both of which were also relatively scarce in Japan before the 10th century. This fact is evident from most early examples of *yoroi* where the fluctuating thickness of the individual scales suggests that *katchū-shi* utilized every available piece of rawhide to make *kozane* due to the limited availability of *nerigawa* of a consistent quality.

This fact is contradicted, however, by one often-cited 12th century Japanese folktale that claims that a *yoroi* made for a member of the famous Minamoto clan was assembled exclusively from *kawa-zane* that were made from pieces of hide cut from the knees of cattle. According to the legend, this was done because it was assumed that *kozane* made from the knee areas of cattle hides would be thicker and thus more durable as result of the tendency of these animals to kneel. This, it was claimed, created a cuirass that was significantly more resilient than other examples of *yoroi* that were assembled from *kozane* that had been cut from less stressed sections of the hide.

Irrespective of what part of the hide was used, the Japanese made *nerigawa* by soaking hides in water that was mixed with a measured amount of wood ash. The alkali in the ash stalled the natural decomposition process of the hides and stimulated a form of fermentation that caused the hairs and other fatty tissue to loosen after the skins had soaked for several days. The hides were then scraped to remove any remaining surface materials before they were washed in a second alkali mixture that prevented further fermentation. The skins were then stretched and left to dry for several days, which caused the hides to harden into rigid, semi-translucent rawhide sheets that were generally around 3 mm in overall thickness.

Dies were used to cut identically shaped *kozane* from the dried sheets of *nerigawa*.

A pile of *nerigawa kozane* (rawhide scales). The edges have been filed and necessary apertures punched in the *kozane*. By the 14th century, often over 3000 individual *kozane* were being utilized in the fabrication of a single *gusoku*. Even at this early stage, *kozane* were labour-intensive to fabricate. For each scale had to be individually chiselled from a sheet of *nerigawa*, punched and filed. (Courtesy of Robert Soanes. © Katchushi Armour Studio)

Rectangular in overall shape, early *kozane* were flat, with the exception of the top left corner section of each scale, which was bent slightly backwards, since this made it easier for the connective lacing to be strung between individual scales that had been assembled into sections. The upper edge of each scale also featured a subtle left-to-right incline that generally extended about three-quarters of the distance across the *sane-gashira*, or head of a scale, before it abruptly declined to the right-hand side of the scale, usually terminating at a point that was lower than the left-hand edge of the *kozane*. This feature, along with the rearward-folded corner of the *kozane*, differentiated the top of the scale from the bottom and clearly distinguished a left and right side, which was important when a group of *kozane* were being arranged in a row to create a lame.

Each *kozane* was then drilled or punched as required with thirteen evenly spaced holes that were inset from the outer edges of the scale. The holes were arranged in two vertically aligned rows, with six holes being punched on the left side of the *kozane* and seven on the taller right-hand side of the scale with the row generally being aligned under the apex of the left-to-right incline of the *sane-gashira*. The bottom four holes of each row are collectively referred to as *shita-garami-no-ana* and were pierced with smaller holes that were just big enough to accommodate the leather-thong bindings called the *shita-garami* that were used to bind the

Early Forms of Samurai Armour

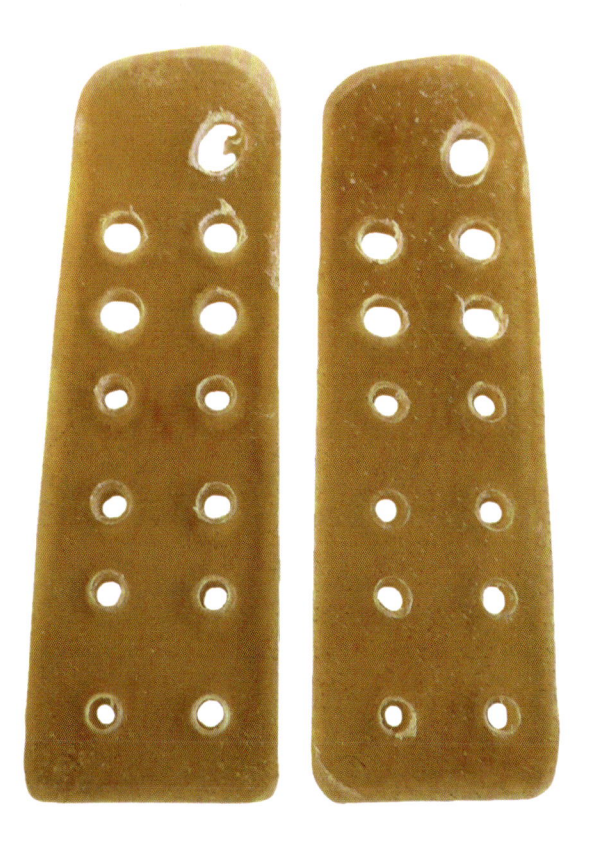

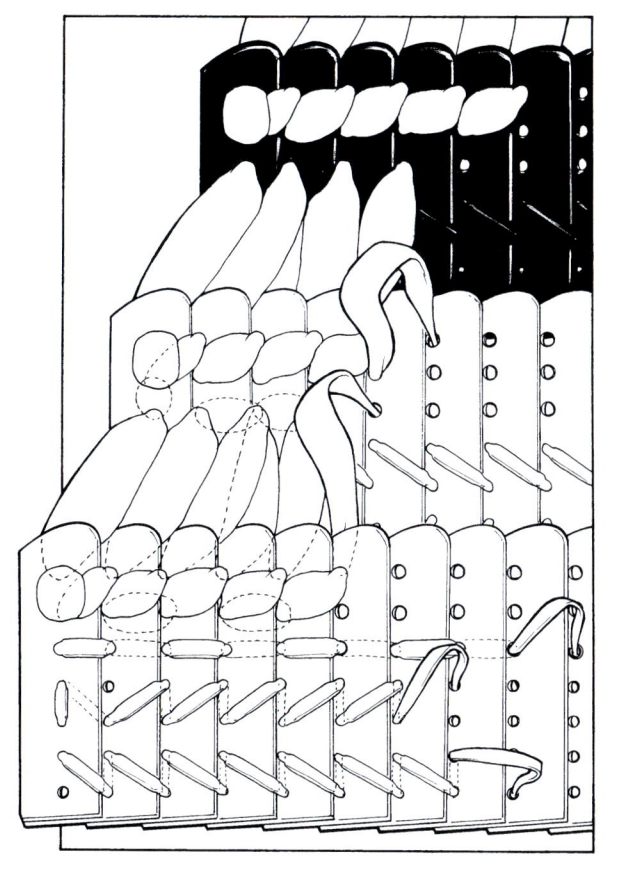

individual *kozane* horizontally together to form lames. While similar in overall form and function, the *shita-garami* were bound differently from the leather-thong *karage-ito* bindings that had been used to assemble the pre-*yoroi* forms of lamellar cuirass designs.

The connective lengths of lacing that vertically fastened one row of scales to another in suspended rows originated from the *karami-no-ana*, which includes the top hole in the left-hand row of apertures and the top two holes in the right. The lacing would be inserted into the *kedate-no-ana* apertures of the *kozane* in the lame immediately above them, which comprised the second from the top left-hand hole and the third hole from the top in the right-hand row of apertures. These two holes are collectively referred to as the *kedate-no-ana*, which translates as 'cord standing holes' in reference to how the connective lacing stood, or more accurately, hung vertically between the two separate lames that the lacing physically secured together. To accommodate the thicker nature of the connective lacing, or *odoshi-ge*, the *karami-no-ana* and *kedate-no-ana* were punched using a die that was approximately double the diameter of the lower *shita-garami-no-ana*.

In size and overall physical appearance, *kozane* made from iron were fundamentally identical to those made from rawhide, though as already mentioned they were not as thick. Unlike *kawa-zane*, iron scales had to be individually chiselled from the edges of small hammered sheets of iron plate. *Tetsu-zane* were naturally stronger and more resilient than rawhide scales and so provided a superior degree of protection. The main drawback to the use of iron scales, as previously noted, was that they significantly increased the overall weight of an item of armour when they were utilized in large numbers, which made the already heavy *yoroi* style of cuirass even more burdensome and uncomfortable to wear. The added weight of a large number of *tetsu-zane* also placed a much greater degree of strain on the bindings and segments of lacing that held the lamellar sections of the cuirass together. Thus when *tetsu-zane* were utilized, they had to be used sparingly, which forced armour makers to conceive ways that they could maximize the protective qualities of *tetsu-zane* while using as few as possible.

Top: Two conventional *kozane* made from *nerigawa*. Note the larger diameter of the upper *karami-no-ana* and *kedate-no-ana* apertures compared with the smaller *shita-garami-no-ana*. Also note the downward slope of the scale's head, or the *sane-gashira*. (Courtesy of Robert Soanes. © Katchushi Armour Studio).

Left: An illustration that shows how the *kedate* portion of the connective *odoshi-ge* was strung between *sane-ita*. Note how the laces closest to the edges were initially strung on a sharp angle to account for the longer length of the lower *sane-ita*. This process was repeated two or three times before the lacing reverted to the proper angle. This sharp angle was achieved by threading the *odoshi-ge* through the same aperture twice. Note the *shita-garami* and *uname* bindings.

Samurai Armour

The most common approach to this problem was to stagger *tetsu-zane* with *kawa-zane* in an alternating one-for-one arrangement referred to as *ichi-mai-maze*, or literally 'single piece mix'. Armour pieces assembled from *ichi-mai-maze* were primarily reserved for incorporation into the sections of the cuirass that covered the abdomen and chest areas, thus ensuring that these vulnerable and important parts of the body were duly, though not overly, protected, since the right side of the torso was the area of the body that was most commonly targeted by an opponent due to the mounted archery tactics of that period. This was because a warrior had a significant advantage over his opponent if he could attack the right side, for it was almost impossible for a mounted samurai to seat and fire an arrow with any effect at an attacker engaging him on his right flank. This was primarily due to the size of the Japanese *yumi*, which prevented the bow from easily being transitioned from the left to right flank of the warrior's mount. It was also, however, due in large part to how the warriors were trained to use their bows. For according to traditional practices, which were rigidly adhered to before modern times, the bow was held with the left hand while the right hand was used to extract, seat and release arrows. As such all movements developed around the practice of seating and launching of arrows at angles perpendicular to the left side of the body. Thus an attacker who was able to gain his opponent's right flank was relatively safe from countermeasures as long as he stayed outside the arc of his enemy's sword arm.

Tetsu-zane were also sometimes strategically positioned to reinforce and strengthen areas of the *yoroi* that were prone to additional strain or wear, such as along the lower left-hand side of the armour where the warrior's sword was hung and would rub against the *sane-ita*. In such cases, several *tetsu-zane* would be arranged together in a small group referred to as *kane-maze*, or 'metal mix'.

The uppermost section of the *mae-no-kusazuri*, or front hip-armour pendant, was also often made in the *ichi-mai-maze* style to protect the groin, as was the left-hand half of the uppermost *sane-ita* of the rear *kusazuri*, or *hitsushiki-no-kusazuri*, which required reinforcing to protect it from the scabbard of the warrior's sword, which would also wear on the hip armour in this area.

The differing thicknesses of the rawhide that a *kozane* was cut from could create weak points in an item of armour. To compensate for the thinner nature of some scales, armour makers created a new form of *kozane* called the *mitsume-zane* or 'three eyed scale', which was about one-third wider than a standard scale. This made each *mitsume-zane* wide enough to overlap or be overlapped by a portion of the two scales to its immediate left or right when arranged in layered rows. This meant that sections assembled using these scales were effectively three layers thick at any given point across the entire length of the *sane-ita*. After lacquering, this equated to armour that was approximately 2 cm in overall thickness, which

Detail of how *odoshi-ge* was strung to create the connective *kedate* portions of lacing between separate *sane-ita*. The illustration also depicts the *ichi-mae-maze* method of constructing a *sane-ita*, which consisted of an alternating mix of lightweight *kawa* or rawhide scales with stronger and more resilient, though also heavier, metal *tetsu-zane*. Note the *mimi-ito* and structural *shita-garami* leather bindings.

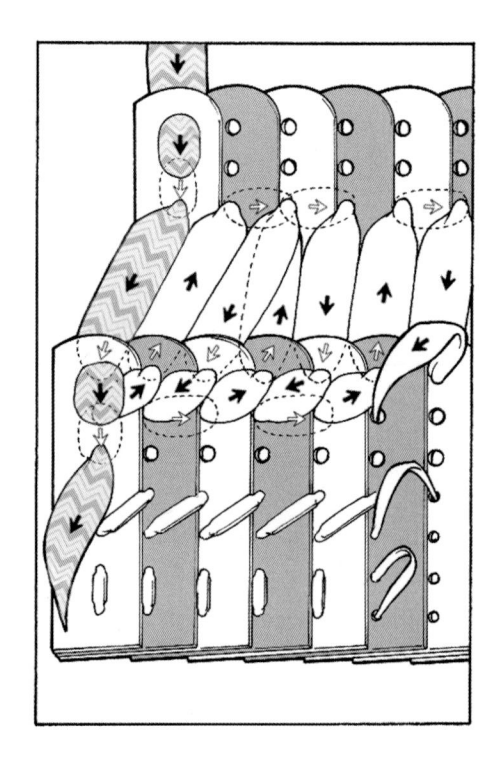

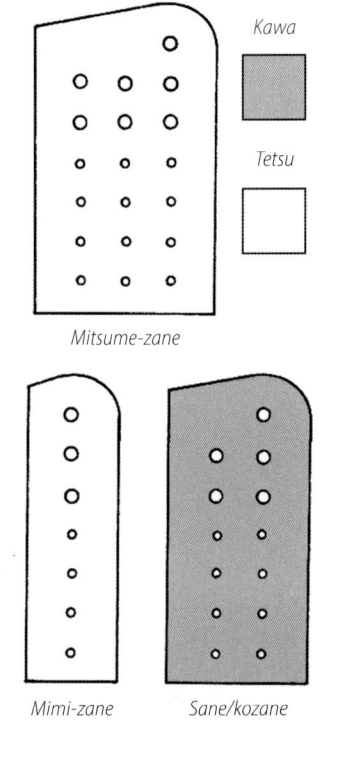

Kawa

Tetsu

Mitsume-zane

Mimi-zane

Sane/kozane

meant that pieces assembled using *mitsume-zane* had the same basic stopping power as a 3 mm thick sheet of iron plate, which was more than capable of stopping an arrow released at a relatively close range.

This was important as the bow was the primary weapon on the battlefield until the latter part of the 14th century. For as Thomas Conlan noted in *War and State Building in Medieval Japan*, 99% of all projectile wounds during the 1300s were caused by arrows.[1] Rocks apparently accounted for the remain percentage of injuries inflicted by projectiles. While this statistic may seem to contradict earlier statements about the protective power of the scale armour, it is important to keep in mind that the majority of these wounds more than likely represented injuries that were sustained by areas of the body that were not well protected, such as the forearms, lower legs and face.

The greater width of the *mitsume-zane* required that each scale be pierced with a third column of six holes down the extended left side of the scale, which allow the *kozane* to be bound to a third scale when overlapped. Some scholars believe that the increased number of binding points between rows of lamellae assembled from *mitsume-zane* was actually what the *katchū-shi* were trying to achieve when they created this wider form of scale. For some items of protective armour continued to be produced using rows of lamellae assembled in the *yurugi-zane* style even after the *nurigatame-zane* style of construction used for the *yoroi* had been introduced. The increased number of *shita-garami* bindings between *mitsume-zane* helped to make the lamellar boards more rigid, which prevented the sagging effect that often occurred with lames assembled using conventional *kozane* bound together in the *yurugi-zane* style.

There were, however, drawbacks to using *mitsume-zane* to construct items of armour. Primary amongst these was the fact that the triple thickness significantly increased the overall weight of the armour. Items of armour

A Meiji period *ukiyo-e* by Utagawa Hiroshige III that depicts the labour-intensive processes that were required to collect *urushi* from the bark and branches of 'varnish trees'. (Courtesy of The Lavenberg Collection of Japanese Prints)

assembled from *mitsume-zane* were also much more costly to produce. This was due to the fact that the lames made in this style consumed one-third more rawhide and lacquer than a *sane-ita* made from conventional *kozane*, which in turn meant that a lame assembled from *mitsume-zane* also took about one-third more man-hours to produce.

Some armour makers clearly took the *mitsume-zane* concept even further by creating even larger forms of *kozane*, the most extreme examples of which were nearly double the width of a conventional scale. Referred to as *ō-arame-zane*, or literally 'big rough scale', this form of *kozane*, examples of which are known to have measured up to 8.7 cm in width, must have been highly impractical due to the fact that so few examples of *ō-zane*, as this form of scale was also sometimes referred to, are known to have existed. In fact, most scholars discounted the existence of *ō-arame-zane* until some extant examples of this form of *kozane* were discovered during an excavation in 1978 at the Hōjū-ji Temple in Kyōto. Thus it is possible that Japanese folklore tales were accurate when they claimed that the famous 12th century warrior Minamoto Tatetomo wore a *yoroi* assembled from *ō-arame-zane*.

Along with the alternative styles of *kozane* mentioned above, other specialized forms of scales had also been introduced by the start of the 10th century, such as the *mimi-zane*, or 'ear scale'. These were *kozane* that were half the usual width of a conventional scale and were cut and shaped the same as the taller right-hand half of a standard *kozane* with the usual arrangement of seven vertical holes punched in them. *Mimi-zane* were finishing scales that were placed at both ends of a length of lamellar assembled from *kozane*. Because conventional *kozane* overlapped each other, they effectively doubled the thickness of the armour section. However, because the end scales were not followed by another *kozane*, the section abruptly tapered to the thickness of a single scale at its edges. As the outside edges of these single *kozane* were exposed and unsupported, they were prone to damage. To counter this, the half-width *mimi-zane* were added so as to continue the doubled thickness to the outer edges of the *sane-ita*. While the *mimi-zane* helped to strengthen the *kozane* at the ends of a lame, they also helped to improve the overall appearance of the *sane-ita* by maintaining a consistent thickness across its entire length.

When *sane-ita* were assembled from *mitsume-zane*, two *mimi-zane* had to be added to both ends to account for the triple-layered thickness of the armour. One of these was fundamentally no more than a conventional *kozane* punched with the usual arrangement of holes while the second would be the narrower variety of *mimi-zane* with a single row of holes. The conventional *kozane* would be applied to the outer edge of the *mitsume-zane* first and then have the *mimi-zane* bound in place to continue the triple thickness of the lame to its outer edge.

LACQUER (*URUSHI*)

The Yayoi peoples appear to have had a rudimentary understanding of the preservational benefits of lacquer and a working knowledge of its application well before the start of the first millennium AD. That said, lacquering techniques appear to have remained fairly primitive in the Japanese archipelago until Chinese lacquering techniques were introduced in the 6th century, which the Yayoi immediately recognized as being superior. While the Chinese method of lacquering was extremely labour intensive, the Yayoi quickly mastered the process, for they understood that it represented one of the only ways to protect items from the highly destructive effects of Japan's exceptionally humid climate.

Urushi, the Japanese term for lacquer, was made from the sap of a small tree known as *Rhus vernicifera* that is indigenous to the Asian mainland. Cultivated in Japan since the 6th century, the 'varnish tree', as it is commonly referred to, was cut with a series of lateral incisions during the summer months. The milk-like sap that wept from these incisions was collected and then filtered to remove debris and other contaminating materials. The sap was then heated to evaporate unwanted viscous liquids and concentrate the *urushi* into a paste. Even in this most basic form, *urushi* produced a durable dark-brown waterproof finish when it was applied to items, and when dried it was impervious to acids, alkalis and alcohol. *Urushi* is also capable of withstanding temperatures up to 300°C. Like most natural materials, however, *urushi* deteriorates when it is exposed to ultraviolet rays for a prolonged period of time.

The *urushi* that was applied to *kozane* was usually mixed with various mineral-based pigments or powders ground from filings of base metals that significantly enhanced the natural colour of the lacquer. By far the most common modifying colour combination was black, or *kuro*. This was created by mixing carbon dust or compounds of iron with the *urushi*. Bold red or vermilion tones could be achieved by mixing *urushi* with cinnabar, while combinations of carbon dust and cinnabar produced a wide range of brown-coloured lacquer tones.

Prior to the start of the 10th century, *kozane* were lacquered individually and then bound together to create lamellar boards. This process began with each scale being covered with several thick applications of an inferior-grade *seshime urushi* that created an adhesive base layer that helped the later applications of *urushi* to adhere to the surface of the *kozane*. These initial coats of lacquer were applied as soon as was possible after a scale was fabricated as they helped to protect the *kozane* from moisture. This was particularly important because *kawa-zane* will expand and warp over time if they are exposed to high levels of humidity prior to being lacquered. Even a small degree of expansion can cause hairline cracks to appear in the lacquer finish of a *kozane*, and even fine cracks can be sufficient to allow additional moisture to be absorbed by the internal *nerigawa* scale. Even a slight degree of rehydration can be detrimental, for as cracks expand, the process of rehydration is accelerated, which in turn causes the lacquer covering to fragment even more. For this reason, the production of *kawa-zane* and process of lacquering were both limited to certain times of the year when the levels of humidity were low.

To help ensure that the initial applications of lacquer adhered to the scales, smiths sanded the surfaces of *kawa-zane* and scored the surfaces of *tetsu-zane* with a coarse whetstone. Each application of *urushi* was then allowed to dry before the next coating of lacquer was applied. The *kozane* were then polished smooth and covered with a special mix of *urushi* called *kokusa*, or *sabitsuke*, which was thickened with a powder made from burnt clay that was in some cases also mixed with fibres of finely chopped hemp. The *kokusa* layers of *urushi* acted as a form of filler that was used to smooth over and fill in any discrepancies that existed on the surfaces of the *kozane*.

Once the *kokusa* layer of lacquer had dried, three or four more separate applications of a finer-quality *urushi* were applied using brushes made from women's hair. Each of these applications of lacquer was individually polished to a smooth finish in charcoal powder before the final two coats of the best-quality

The transformation of a bound row of rawhide scales into a rigid lacquer-covered *sane-ita* as the various layers of *urushi* are added and finished. While in reality the entire length of a *sane-ita* would be lacquered the same at each stage of the lacquering process, the image illustrates the progressional changes as multiple applications of lacquer were applied, from the first coarse layers to the final polished applications of *urushi*.

Kawa-zane being threaded together by a leather thong *shita-garami* to form a *sane-ita*. Note the *mimi-zane* and the substantial amount of overlap between adjacent scales that was typical of conventional *kozane*.

urushi were applied and left to dry. The scale was then polished for a final time in a special mixture of ash made from deer antler mixed with charcoal dust and a small amount of vegetable oil, which gave the finished layer of *urushi* a deep black satin-like appearance.

When *katchū-shi* began constructing rigid lengths of lamellar board early in the 10th century the lacquering process changed. The practice of fully lacquering each individual *kozane* and then binding them together in the *yurugi-zane* style was gradually discontinued. Instead, individual *kozane* were covered only with a few base coats of *urushi* to waterproof them. They were then arranged in overlapping right-to-left rows that resulted in the left-hand side of each scale being overlapped by half when conventional *kozane* were utilized. Leather thongs were then strung through the aligned *shita-garami-no-ana* of the overlapping scales and drawn tight to create predetermined lengths of *sane-ita*. The arranged rows of bound *kozane* were then covered with up to eight applications of *urushi* which were allowed to dry before they were polished. This produced rigid, board-like lames that were far more resilient than identical lengths of *yurugi-zane*-assembled pieces.

Nurigatame-zane, as these lacquered, rigid lames were called, were not only more resilient, they also helped the *yoroi* to maintain its form much better than had been possible when they were assembled using the *yurugi-zane* method of construction that had been utilized in previous centuries. This was important as it prevented gaps from appearing between the sections of a cuirass as it shifted and settled during vigorous activity, which also made the armour uncomfortable to wear after a prolonged period of time. This fact, along with the superior level of protection offered by solid sections, more than compensated for the way the rigid *yoroi* style of cuirass restricted some upper-body movements. As these limitations did not interfere with the mobility of the arms and thus the warrior's ability to use a bow, the impeding aspects of a cuirass assembled from rigid lengths of *sane-ita* were deemed negligible.

Before the *nurigatame-zane* process of creating a solid lamellar board could begin, the lightly lacquered *kozane* had to be bound together in rows. This was achieved by threading two separate lengths of *shita-garami*, a leather thong about 5 mm in thickness, through the lower *shita-garami-no-ana* of the overlapping scales. Sakakibara Kōzan, a late 18th-century researcher and authority on Japanese armour, noted his highly influential book *Chūko Katchū Seisakuben* (The Manufacture of Armour and Helmets in 16th Century Japan), first published in 1800, that the preferred choice of material for this leather was the skin of a wild dog, owing to the low salt content of the hides of these animals, which, he says, do not eat salt. Using *inu-gawa*, or 'dog-leather', for this purpose was supposed to reduce the risk of the *tetsu-zane* developing rust blooms around the *shita-garami-no-ana* after they were threaded with the bindings.

ARMOUR LACING METHODS AND MATERIALS (*ODOSHI ZAIRYŌ TO YARIKATA*)

There were a few different methods of stringing the *shita-garami*, or 'lower stitches', the method of which sometimes varied depending on the type of *kozane* being utilized. In most cases, however, the thongs were strung from left to right, with one length of binding being threaded through the lower two *shita-garami-no-ana* while the second length was strung through the third and fourth holes from the bottom of the *kozane*. The actual method of lacing was the same for both lengths of thong, but one was strung in the reverse manner to the other. For example, the lower *shita-garami* thong was generally threaded through the lowermost *shita-garami-no-ana* so that it exited from the back, out through the inner face of a pair of overlapping scales. The thong was then pulled vertically up and over the exterior face of the *kozane* between the bottom and the second-from-the-bottom *shita-garami-no-ana*. It would then be inserted back through the scale and pulled out on the reverse side of the overlapping *kozane* and be drawn tight. This would leave a small vertical dash on the face of the *kozane* where the thong had tracked between the two *shita-garami-no-ana*. The thong would then be pulled downward to the right across the reverse face of the *sane-ita* and inserted back through the lowermost *shita-garami-no-ana* of the next scale to the immediate right of the first *kozane*, and drawn tight. The thong would be drawn through to the exterior surface of the next scale and the process repeated, which would create a repetitive pattern of vertical dashes along the lower edge of the lame.

The upper length of thong would first be threaded from the exterior face of the overlapping *kozane* through the fourth *shita-garami-no-ana* from the bottom of the scale. The *shita-garami* would be pulled out to the reverse of the *kozane* and would then be pulled vertically downward and inserted through the third hole from the bottom of the same. It would then be pulled back through to the exterior surface and drawn tight. From there it would be pulled upward and to the right and inserted into the top *shita-garami-no-ana* of the neighbouring scale. Before the thong was drawn tight, the end piece of the thong that hung from the fourth *shita-garami-no-ana* where the lacing process had begun would be pulled downward and to the right. The end piece would then be tucked under the length of *shita-garami* that was being pulled upward to the right before the latter was drawn tight, which would anchor the end of the *shita-garami* in place. The loose portion of the thong would then be pulled out through the back of the *kozane* and pulled vertically downward. It would be inserted back through to the outer face of the *sane-ita* via the third *shita-garami-no-ana* and then the entire process would be repeated with the exception of having to anchor the tail end of the thong. This would create a repetitive series of left-to-right upward-angled diagonal dashes along the lower half of the *sane-ita*, bridging the overlap between adjacent scales.

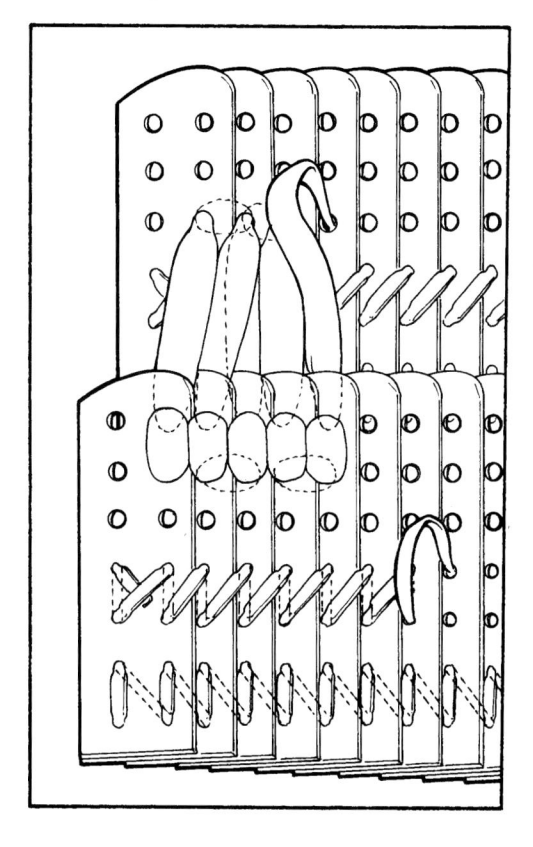

Detail of how the leather thong *shita-garami* bindings were strung. Note the reverse order of the lacing pattern between the upper and lower rows of bindings. Also note the use of *mimi-zane* and how the *kedate* portions of *odoshi-ge* were strung. The apertures in the *kozane* down the outside edges of the *sane-ita* would be threaded with *mimi-ito*.

SAMURAI ARMOUR

Left: Detail of the stringing pattern used to thread the shita-garami thongs when they were bound in the decorative hishinui style across a sane-ita where the lower half of the sane-ita was left exposed to view. Note how the upper and lower lengths of thong were threaded to mirror each other, and how the cross-knots bridge the overlaps between adjacent scales. Also note the length of thong that is threaded horizontally along the length of the sane-ita above the shita-garami, referred to in this case as the uname.

more than half of the visible façade of a section, armour makers used a decorative cross-knot-like method of binding called *hishinui*, or 'diamond lacing', when they assembled the lengths of *sane-ita* that were to be used as the lowermost suspended sections on an item of armour. When the leather thongs are strung in this manner they are no longer referred to as *shita-garami*, but are instead known as *hishinui*.

Like the *shita-garami*, the *hishinui* comprised two independent lengths of leather thong. These were laced in a manner similar to how shoes are commonly tied, with both ends of a single length of thong being inserted through an adjacent vertical pair of holes at the same time. The common practice was for the lower of the two separate rows of *hishinui* to have the cords protrude through from the rear left-hand edge of the lame to the front and then cross over each other, with the lower cord always passing over the length of thong that exited the upper

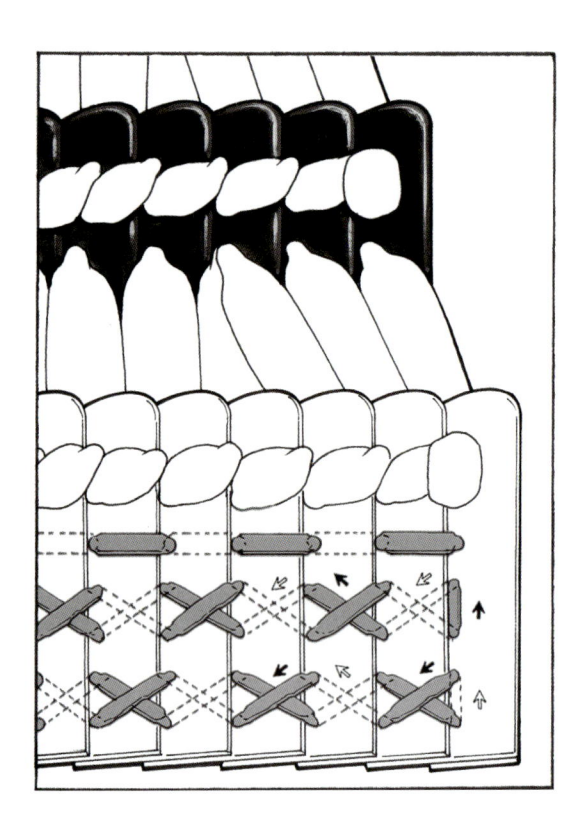

This process would be repeated until the end of the assembled lame. The tail ends of the *shita-garami* would then be reversed and tucked under the last diagonal length of the binding to prevent the thong from coming undone until the multiple layers of *urushi* that were characteristic of the *nurigatame-zane* lacquering process could be applied.

At some point prior to the development of the *yoroi*, *katchū-shi* introduced an alternative method of stringing the *shita-garami* that was reserved for binding together sections of *sane-ita* that would not have another lamellar section suspended from them. While the usual *shita-garami* method of binding was effective, it was also aesthetically unattractive. This was generally not an issue, as the *shita-garami* were hidden under the lengths of suspensory lacing or intermediary bands of leather that connected a lower suspended portion to the *sane-ita* immediately above it. However, as the lowermost *sane-ita* were not followed by another suspended lamellar section, the *shita-garami* were exposed. To compensate for the unfinished appearance of conventional *shita-garami*, which accounted for

Kusazuri with hishinui that have been strung using lengths of red leather thong. Note the offset arrangement of the hishinui on the upper and lower rows. Also note how the same odoshi-ge that was used to string the mimi-ito portions of lacing has also been threaded horizontally above the hishinui to form the uname. Note that while the leather thong bindings are red, they are kaki-bishi, or 'brushed diamond', a term referring to hishinui that have been covered with urushi, and then had their raised-in-relief profiles 'picked-out' in red lacquer. Note the convex shape of the kusazuri and staggered appearance of the sane-ita due to their hon kozane construction.

Early Forms of Samurai Armour

hole. The ends of the thong would be inserted back through to the back side of the *sane-ita* where the top length would then be passed downward to the right over the lower length, which would be passed upward. The ends would be inserted back through to the front and the process repeated so that the overlap between every other scale was covered by a left-to-right, bottom-over-top cross-knot.

The upper, or second row of *hishinui* would be strung in the same overall manner with the exception that the bindings would begin with the two ends of the leather thong being threaded through the upper pair of *shita-garami-no-ana* from front to back to create a short vertical band or *tate* of lacing on the exterior face of the lame above the left side of the lower rows of *hishinui*. Starting the upper row of bindings in this manner offset the first cross-knot, which had the effect of creating a staggered checkerboard-like pattern between the upper and lower rows of *hishinui*. The upper band of cross-knots were also strung with the length of thong exiting the uppermost *shita-garami-no-ana* passing over the length that exited from the lower hole, opposite to how the lower row of *hishinui* were bound.

With an ever-present eye for symmetry, Japanese armour makers were careful to count the number of *kozane* that were used when they constructed and bound a *sane-ita* in the *hishinui* style. For the number of *kozane* used determined how many full 'X'-like *hishinui* cross-knots could be tied. Whenever possible *katchū-shi* endeavoured to string a length of *kozane* so that the lower row of bindings started and ended with full cross-knots. The upper row of *hishinui* in such cases was then intentionally strung so the binding began with a vertical *tate* band and ended with a *tate*, and thus the two rows were offset and visually different in appearance. If the lower row of *hishinui* started or ended with a vertical band then the upper row was always bound so the vertical *tate* band appeared at the opposite end of the lame from where it was located in the lower row of *hishinui*.

Unlike the *shita-garami*, the *hishinui* bindings were not strung until after the assembled *sane-ita* was fully lacquered. To enhance the visual presentation of the bindings, red-dyed lengths of leather lacing or *kawa-odoshi* were then strung through the apertures of the *shita-garami-no-ana* and the row of open *kedate-no-ana* apertures that were left unused on the *hishinui-no-ita* between the uppermost rows of *shita-garami* bindings and the apertures that the lengths of connective lacing were drawn through, with the leather thong threaded through these holes being referred to as *uname-garami* (see below). When the cross-knots were bound using lengths of dyed leather the individual cross-knots are referred to as being *kawa-bishi*, or 'leather diamonds', even though the style of lacing is still referred to as *hishinui*. The bold contrast between the *kawa-bishi* and dark lacquer finish of the *sane-ita* that the cross-knots decorated resulted in any *hishinui*-bound length of suspended lamellar board being referred to as a *hishinui-no-ita*, or 'diamond sewn board'.

An example of *ito-bishi*, or 'sewn diamond' *hishinui* cross-knots formed through the use of silk *odoshi-ge*. Note how *ito-bishi* tend to have a somewhat square appearance compared to the rather evident X-like form of the *hishinui* that are strung using leather thongs. The lacing used to string the *mimi-ito* has been used to lace the *uname*. Note the highly detailed gilded copper *sukashi kaza domari-no-kanamono* fitted to the corners of the *hishinui-no-ita*.

It should be noted that the *hishinui-no-ita* was often further decorated with the addition of large raised-in-relief decorative chrysanthemum-shaped gilded copper rivets called *suso-no-kanamono*. The split-shank *suso-no-kanamono*, which often measured 3–4 cm in diameter, were generally fitted to the left, centre and right-hand edge of a *hishinui-no-ita*.

At some time during the 13th century, silk *odoshi-ge* also began to be used to string the *hishinui*. When silk lacing was used to bind the cross-knots, the latter were referred to as *ito-bishi*, or 'cord diamonds'.

While aesthetically attractive, lames that had the *hishinui* strung after they were lacquered were not as strong as conventional *sane-ita* where the *shita-garami* were bound and then covered with *urushi*. Furthermore, *hishinui* that were strung after the *sane-ita* was lacquered were vulnerable to the effects of edged weapons, a weakness that was increasingly exposed by the ferocity and prolonged nature of the military campaigns that occurred throughout the volatile Nanbokuchō period.

To rectify this problem, *katchū-shi* began stringing the *hishinui* first and then lacquering over them in the same way as was done with the *shita-garami* on a conventional *sane-ita*. While this helped to protect the bindings and made the lamellar boards stronger, it greatly detracted from the visual appearance of the *hishinui*. Armour makers overcame this problem by applying red lacquer, or *shu urushi*, to the raised surfaces of the covered *hishinui*. These were carefully picked out to ensure that their decorative cross-knot form stood out in sharp contrast against the deep-black lacquer finish of the *sane-ita*. This form of *hishinui* is referred to as *kaki-bishi*, which literally translates as 'brushed diamond'.

The practice of lacquering the *hishinui* in the *kaki-bishi* style gradually faded out towards the end of the 14th century and was replaced by a return to the use of silk lacing to bind the *hishinui*. This transition was promoted by the fact that *kaki-bishi* were labour intensive to create as it took a considerable degree of time, effort, patience and money to carefully copy the outline of each binding in *shu urushi*. Attesting to this was the fact that within a few short decades of *kaki-bishi* being introduced, most armour makers had already discontinued the practice of lacquering the *hishinui* on both faces of a *hishinui-no-ita*, as had originally been done, in favour of only lacquering the bindings that were visible on the façade.

Another factor that contributed to a return to the use of *odoshi-ge* to lace the *hishinui* was the introduction of narrow reinforcing strips of rawhide, called *shiki*. These were fitted to the reverse face to help the *sane-ita* maintain its shape. This was achieved by laying the *shiki* horizontally between the *shita-garami-no-ana* where it would be fixed in place by applications of lacquer. The *hishinui* were then strung so the bindings crossed over the *shiki*, which further increased the structural integrity of the armour piece.

The appearance of *hishinui* that have been bound using *odoshi-ge* is quite different from their *kawa-bishi* or *kaki-bishi* counterparts. This is due to the fact that when woven lacing, particularly silk, is not drawn taut under a load

A rare view of the reverse of a *kusazuri*. Note the small *nawame-odoshi* portions of lacing that show where the *kedate* portions of *odoshi-ge* have been strung. Also note how the *hishinui* have been knotted over the *shiki-gane* strip along the lower edge of the *hishinui-no-ita*. The *shita-garami* bindings anchoring the *shiki-gane* in place are also visible along the lower edges of some of the upper *sane-ita* under the thick applications of lacquer.

A superbly executed painting of the famous 12th century Japanese National Treasure *aka-ito odoshi dō-maru gusoku* (red laced *dō-maru* style armour) housed in the Oyamatsumi Shrine in Ehime Prefecture, Japan. This armour is said to have been worn by the famous samurai general Minamoto Yoshitsune. The powerful visual and, in turn, psychological impression that a cuirass laced in bold colours such as this, would have made on friend and foe alike cannot be underestimated.

it tends to expand slightly, which causes *ito-bishi* cross-knots to look somewhat square in appearance.

When all the necessary lengths of *sane-ita* that were required to assemble a section of armour were ready, the individual lames were strung together using lengths of connective *odoshi-ge* lacing, which literally translates as 'lacing hair'. This term appears to have been derived from the verb *odosu*, which means to 'make armour'. The bureaucrat-scholar and advisor to the Tokugawa family, Arai Hakuseki, states in the 'Armour Book' volume from his 12-book *Honchō Gunkikō* (General History of Military Discipline) series, in which he wrote about the forms of armour used in Japan between the 10th and 16th centuries, that the term '*odosu*' was first used in the creation tales of the sun goddess Amaterasu that were written between the late 7th and early 8th centuries. As the main forms of armour utilized by the Japanese from the late 8th century onward were items assembled from scales, it is easy to see how the long, vertically strung strands of tightly spaced lacing materials came to be referred to by a term for hair, particularly when one considers the incredibly long, straight lengths of hair that the women of elevated Japanese society wore during those periods.

It is interesting to note, however, that the kanji character that is used to write *odosu* (to make armour) and *odoshi* is also the same character that is used to write the homophonous Japanese verb *odosu*, which means to intimidate, menace or threaten. The awe-inspiring appearance of items of armour assembled from boldly coloured lengths of lacing may have been the origin of the connection between these words. For the visual impact of a warrior in a brightly laced set of armour would have been quite intimidating, especially at a time in history when the majority of society lived life in a world composed of largely drab colours due to the simple fact that colourful dyes were costly to obtain and as such were a luxury that few could afford or justify. Over time, the sense of *odusu* as intimidating or menacing in reference to the appearance of armour may simply have become synonymous with the idea of armour in general, especially after the *yoroi* style of cuirass was introduced and became the only form of armour that was made. The large, flat and regular surfaces of the *yoroi* were also the ideal canvas for pursuing artistic presentations through the utilization of lacing and one of the reasons why the art of lacing, both the physical act of stringing the *odoshi-ge* and the large variety of lacing materials available, developed to the extent it did between the 10th and 13th centuries. Having said this, it is important to note that other words and kanji were also utilized over the centuries to refer to what most students of Japanese armour now refer to as *odoshi-ge*.

The earliest examples of Heian period *yoroi*, like many of the various forms of armour that had existed in previous centuries, were laced together using narrow strips of leather called *kawa-odoshi-ge*, or 'leather lacing hair'. *Shikka-gawa*, or deer hide, prepared from a small indigenous species of spotted deer, was the primary variety of leather for the making of *kawa-odoshi-ge*. This was largely due to the fact that the highly durable hides of these animals remained soft and pliable even after they had been tanned, which made the leather easy to utilize as lacing.

Lacing made from smoked leather, or *fusebegawa*, was slowly replaced as dyed varieties of *kawa-odoshi-ge*, called *some-gawa*, were introduced. By the turn of the first millennium AD *kawa-odoshi-ge* was being produced in a multitude of colours, the visual presentation of which was often further enhanced by the addition of repetitive floral or geometric decorative patterns that were reverse-stencilled onto the hides before they were cut into strips.

Though *kawa-odoshi* had been the mainstay of lacing materials for most of the evolutionary history of Japanese armour, fragmentary evidence of lamellar sections recovered from kofun show that *odoshi-ge* fabricated from lengths of braided cord made from cotton and hemp were also being used as far back as the 5th century. *Ito-odoshi-ge* or 'cord lacing hair', was for many centuries almost as labour intensive to produce as *kawa-odoshi-ge*, and was often inferior to the latter in durability and even suitability when used to lace lamellar items of armour together. This was because most weaves of cord lacked the unique combination of tensile strength and ability to stretch that was typical of *kawa-odoshi-ge*, which, depending on the portion of leather used, could bear a load of 170–350 kg and stretch an additional 20–60 per cent of its original length without tearing.

The introduction of sericulture (the cultivation of silkworms) into Japan between the 5th and 6th centuries AD was the origin of a reliable alternative to *kawa-odoshi-ge*. For silk, or *kinu*, had even better load-bearing and tensile-strength qualities than leather. And while this was almost certainly appreciated, the limited domestic supply of silk was reflected in its cost, which prohibited it from being a viable alternative to leather lacing until after the end of the first millennium. While silk would eventually go on to become the primary material used to fabricate *odoshi-ge* by the 13th century, the production and use of *kawa-odoshi* as a form of lacing material was never entirely discontinued.

A number of factors helped to promote the shift towards silk lacing, including the fact that *kawa-odoshi-ge* could only be produced in relatively short lengths of no more than 1.5 metres due to the small size of the deer hides. Silk-made *ito-odoshi-ge*, however, could be made in consistent 3-metre lengths. This alone greatly simplified the process of lacing, for it largely removed the time-consuming and difficult task of joining separate sections of *odoshi-ge* together when the lengths of lacing were too short to complete one continuous horizontal band of suspensory lacing. The twill weave of silk *ito-odoshi-ge* also allowed it to be pulled and stretched far beyond the stresses that leather lacing was able to tolerate before the leather was no longer able to return to its original length or width, having been stressed beyond the natural limitations of its elasticity.

Kinu-ito-odoshi-ge was also better suited to lacing the smaller, more closely spaced arrangement of scales that started to be used during the 13th century. And unlike leather lacing, which began to look distressed after it was drawn through too many small holes, a

An example of *kawa-odoshi*. This particular pattern of deer-hide lacing is referred to as *ko-zakura-gawa*, or literally 'small flower leather'. Also note the red leather *hishi-toji* bindings along the *sane-gashira* of the uppermost *sane-ita* of the *nagakawa* that anchor it to the *e-gawa*-faced *kanagu mawari* plate.

EARLY FORMS OF SAMURAI ARMOUR

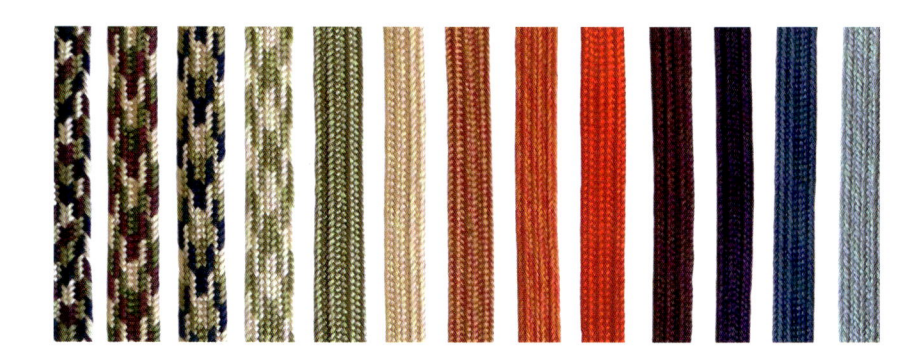

Various examples of *odoshi-ge*. All of these are woven from silk and as such are technically *kinu-odoshi-ge*. Note the pliable, twill-like weave of the lacing and multitude of colour variations. The four laces on the left are examples of *mimi-ito*, which generally differ from conventional *odoshi-ge* in that the lacing is slightly wider and commonly features a distinctive *chidori*, or 'plover', chevron-like pattern in the weave. (Courtesy of Robert Soanes. © Katchushi Armour Studio)

single length of silk lacing could be drawn through multiple holes consecutively without looking worn. The pliable twill weave of *kinu-ito-odoshi-ge* also allowed more than one strand of lacing to be drawn through a single hole in a *kozane*, as was sometimes required, which was something that was extremely difficult to achieve using *kawa-odoshi*.

These factors aside, the attribute that attracted most warriors to silk lacing was the fact that it could be produced in almost any colour. It was also capable of being produced in different widths and could have patterns incorporated directly into the weave of the material. The lacing was woven on a special loom, a *takadai*, or 'high stand', that used lead-weighted bobbins to regulate the tension of the pre-dyed strands of silk as they were 'passed over and under pairs of other threads to produce a characteristically ribbed braid' of the flat, eight-ridge single-layer twill lace.[2]

As *kinu* became the primary material used to weave *ito-odoshi-ge*, from here on, unless otherwise noted, the term *odoshi-ge* should be considered to be synonymous with the concept of silk lacing as is common practice in Japanese works.

The process of assembling a *yoroi* began with the *sane-ita* required to create a specific section of the armour being arranged in ascending order on a flat surface. Cords were then strung through the extreme left- and right-hand edge *kedate-no-ana* holes of the individual lames to secure them together in ascending order. A third band of *odoshi-ge* was often strung horizontally through the open *kedate-no-ana* of the *hishinui-*

An early Meiji period *ukiyo-e* that depicts women sorting through trays of silkworm cocoons. The cocoon of one silkworm larva when unravelled can commonly yield a single thread of silk 500–600 metres long. Silk became one of post-feudal period Japan's largest export commodities, and this continued until well into the 20th century. (From the Dai Nippon Bussan Zue Series by Utagawa Hiroshige III. Courtesy of The Lavenberg Collection of Japanese Prints.)

121

no-ita if the latter had not already been laced using the same material and in the same manner as the *hishinui*.

The lengths of *odoshi-ge* that were used to fasten the sections of *sane-ita* together before they were laced were originally the same material as was used to lace the entire section of armour. At some point during the 11th century, however, armour makers started to string the *sane-ita* together using lacing that was intentionally chosen to contrast with the colour of the *odoshi-ge* that was to be used to lace the section of armour. This was done purely for aesthetic purposes, as the contrasting colour of the edge lacing not only clearly delineated edges, it also greatly enhanced the overall visual appearance of a section or item of armour. Eventually this lacing came to be referred to as *mimi-ito*, or literally 'ear cord', probably because, like the ears, the *mimi-ito* strands flanked the body of a piece of armour. While similar, *mimi-ito* differed from conventional *odoshi-ge* in that a decorative design was almost always incorporated into the weave of the lacing. *Mimi-ito* was also generally a stronger and slightly wider cut or weave of lacing due to the fact that it was utilized as the connective lacing when sections of armour were first being assembled. When the *mimi-ito* was made from *shikka-gawa* the decorative pattern on the lace was stencilled on and could take a number of forms. When the lacing was made from cord, the pattern was generally limited to a herringbone chevron-like design called *chidori*, or 'plover', a name that was almost certainly derived from the similarity between the pattern and the plumage on a species of Japanese plover.

Aesthetic detailing aside, *mimi-ito* was fundamentally the same as conventional *odoshi-ge*, except when it came to the manner in which it was strung. For unlike regular *odoshi-ge*, which connected one suspended lamellar section to another horizontally, *mimi-ito* was strung to connect a number of independent sections together vertically, whether two lames or five. Thus *mimi-ito* always primarily appears as *tate*, or 'standing' lengths of lacing along the exterior edges of a section of armour, except when it is used to lace the intermediary band on a length of *sane-ita* that is referred to as the *uname-garami*, which is discussed in greater detail below.

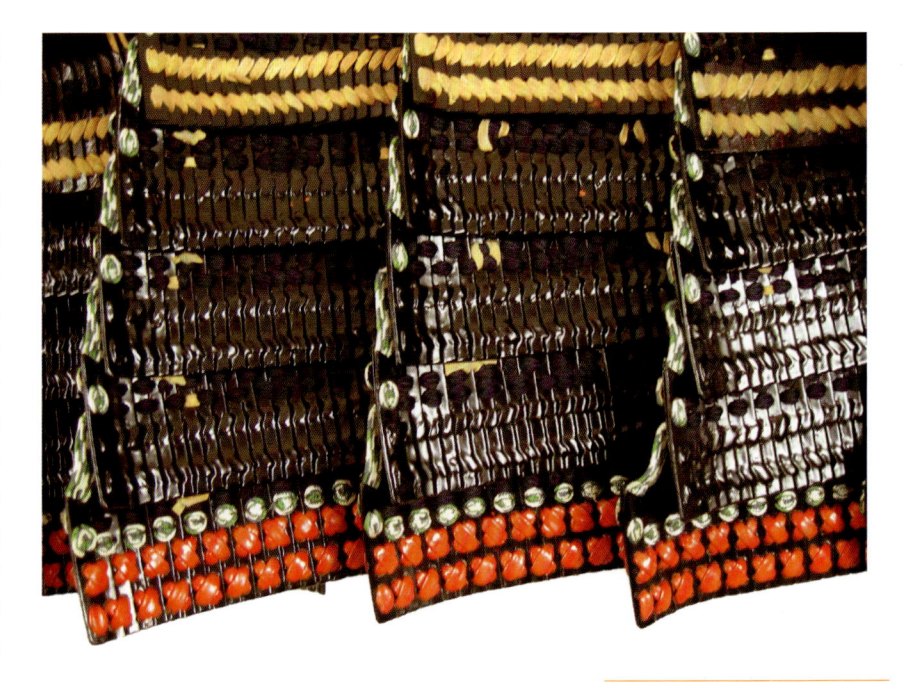

Arai Hakuseki records that weaves of *mimi-ito* made from only two different colours of thread were avoided because the word *ni-ke*, for 'two colours', sounded like the Japanese word for retreat, '*nige*'. While a good story, this, like most Edo era theories that retroactively attempted to justify how armour had become what it was, tended towards overly dramatized fictional philosophical answers that had little to do with the facts. For ironically one of the oldest and most popular examples of *mimi-ito* featured a repetitive pattern that consisted entirely of alternating white and dark blue chevrons. The pattern's similarity in appearance to the features of a species of Japanese hawk resulted in this particular weave of *mimi-ito* being referred to as *takanoha-uchi*, or 'hawk feather braid'. This pattern was gradually enhanced, first with the addition of a transitional light blue chevron and in later centuries with a navy blue chevron, the

The use of *mimi-ito* to connect multiple *sane-ita* together can be observed in this image. The *tate*, or 'standing' nature of *mimi-ito* is clear as the green and white lacing highlights the edges of the *kusazuri*. Note the use of the same *mimi-ito* to lace the *uname*, and the red leather *hishinui*.

addition of which created another highly popular pattern of lacing called *takuboku-uchi*, or 'woodpecker braid', which was commonly used on later-period sets of armour.

By the Kamakura period *mimi-ito* was being produced using a wide range of colours, including red, green, purple and orange, and in a wide array of unique colour combinations and patterns. Some texts claim that the colours used in a weave of *mimi-ito* were specifically selected to ensure that they did not clash with the colours associated with the five elements that defined a warrior's character according to the ancient Chinese philosophical principles of *go-gyo-setsu*. While such considerations may have been factored into the colours selected to weave custom lengths of *mimi-ito* for incorporation into a set of armour made for an exceptionally high-ranking and wealthy warrior, in general most examples of *mimi-ito* were generic in nature and produced in bulk. The colours and patterns selected were chosen to ensure that the *mimi-ito* would complement the widest possible range of different *odoshi-ge* colour schemes so as to ensure the marketability of the lacing.

From the 12th century onward it became common to lace the *kedate-no-ana* with the same *mimi-ito* that had been used to string the vertical edges of a section of armour. This broke with the original practice of using the same material to lace the *kedate-no-ana* as had been used to bind the *hishinui*. Some sources claim that the *mimi-ito* that was used to edge a section of armour, such as a *kusazuri* for example, was strung using one long continuous piece of lacing that would run from one vertical edge, across the horizontal frontage of the piece and then be laced up the vertical edge on the opposite side of the piece. While this may have been the case in some instances, surviving armours suggest it was more common for three separate lengths of *mimi-ito* to be utilized for this process.[3] Irrespective of this fact, the portion of *mimi-ito* that is strung in a series of short horizontal bands across the midsection of a suspended *sane-ita* between the *hishinui* and the upper portions of connective lacing should always be referred to as the *uname-garami*, or more commonly simply as the *uname*, which means 'path between rice fields'. This is true even if the *mimi-ito* is a single continuous piece of material, or has been strung using separate pieces of lacing.

An Edo period print of a *katchū-shi* lacing a *sode* that has been suspended from a rack by cords which allowed the shoulder guard to be rotated back and forth. This greatly simplified the lacing process for the *katchū-shi* as it allowed them to quickly transition from one face of the item to the other as the lacing was strung. Note the flat-nosed tongs that were used to grip and pull the lacing.

After the laid-out armour pieces were strung together with *mimi-ito*, the section of suspended *sane-ita* was hung from a swivel ring mounted in the centre of a large open rack. This allowed the *katchū-shi* to rotate the section of armour back and forth between the front and back surfaces of the suspended section as the remainder of the lacing was put in. The lacing was always strung from left to right and from the uppermost section downward as each intermediate band of connective lacing was completed between connected lames, so as not to put unnecessary strain on the primary *mimi-ito* suspensory lacing.

This method of lacing differed from how armour had been assembled prior to the introduction of the *yoroi*, and was another one of the features that set this make of cuirass apart from its forefathers. The *uchikake-keikō* and other earlier versions of lamellar cuirass were laced vertically, with a length of lacing running continuously from top to bottom between aligned columns of scales. Due to a lack of extant examples with the suspensory lacing still intact, however, scholars are still unsure as to exactly how the lacing was strung on items of armour made before the early 10th century, which included some of the earliest examples of *yoroi*. A number of possible vertical or *tate-dori-odoshi* methods of lacing appear to have existed based on the highly detailed reconstructions of proto-historical items of lamellar armour that were made by Dr Suenaga Masao in the late 1930s and early 1940s, though to date none of the methods that Dr Suenaga thought may have been used to lace items has been confirmed.

By the mid-10th century, however, surviving examples confirm that an improved method of lateral lacing was being used. This method was better suited to the ridged board construction of the *yoroi*, and would, with minor changes, continue to be utilized in the assembly of items of armour for close to a millennium. Known as *kebiki odoshi*, or 'hair spread over lacing', this method of stringing *odoshi-ge* began with the lacing being inserted from the rear through the second-from-the-top *kedate-no-ana* hole in the right-hand row of leftmost *kozane*. The *odoshi-ge* was then pulled vertically upward and inserted through the top *kedate-no-ana* in the same row and pulled back through to the rear of the scale. It was then pulled upward and over the face of the upper length of *sane-ita* and inserted into the third-from-the-top *kedate-no-ana* of the upper board. The lacing was pulled through to the reverse face and then drawn to the right and passed back through the third *kedate-no-ana* from the top of the neighbouring *kozane* to the immediate right. It was then drawn vertically downward over the face of the upper *sane-ita* and inserted from the rear through to the front of the top *kedate-no-ana* on the lower suspended lame. It was then pulled downward again and inserted in the second-from-the-top *kedate-no-ana* and drawn out towards the rear and to the right, at which point the process would repeat itself. This created a closely spaced continuous horizontal band of vertically strung laces that slightly overlapped each other between the upper and suspended lower *sane-ita*, which is why *kebiki odoshi* is often referred to as 'full lacing'. The intermediate lengths of lacing that connected the upper *sane-ita* to the lower one and in the process covered the lower half portion of the upper *sane-ita* are referred to as the *kedate*, or 'standing hairs' for their resemblance to the appearance of a thick, closely space section of erect hairs.

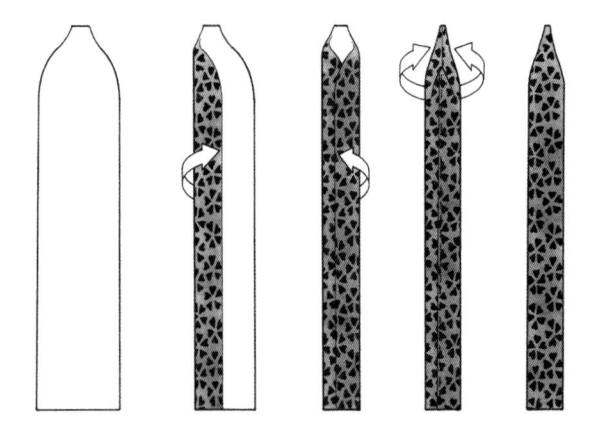

An illustration of how strips of silk twill, or *aya*, were folded and sewn together along the reverse side of the material to produce a lacing. This practice was on occasion also sometimes utilized to produce *kawa-odoshi*. Due to the nature of its weave, *aya* needed to be folded to improve its ability to endure the strain and day-to-day wear and tear that lacing was subject to.

An illustration of the diagonal *nawame-odoshi* (highlighted in grey) portions of the *kedate*. The *nawame* method of threading the connective *odoshi-ge* prevented the lacing from being able to slip and retract backwards if it was cut. Note that the *sane-ita* transition from *kozane* to *iyozane*. Lamellar made from a mix of different types of scales were sometimes utilized in the late 15th century.

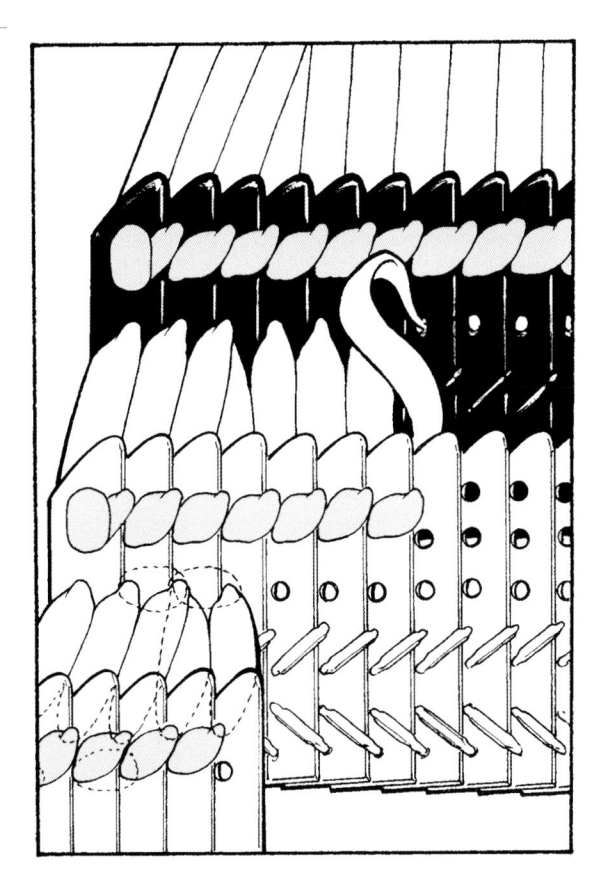

This particular early form of *kebiki odoshi* is also referred to as *tate-odoshi*, or 'standing cord', in reference to the fact that the lacing was strung vertically between adjoining lames, including the short vertical lengths of the lacing that were visible on the façade of a *sane-ita* – called *tate-dori* – that were strung through the *karami-no-ana* apertures. While effective, the *tate-odoshi* method of lacing was quickly improved on by *katchū-shi* and was largely discontinued by the start of the 11th century as the much stronger *nawame-odoshi* method of lacing was introduced.

Nawame-odoshi, or 'wave eye lacing', was so named after the fact that the lower *tate-dori* portion of the lacing was strung so that the laces no longer went straight up and down, but angled diagonally upward and to the right. This was done for more than just aesthetic reasons. *Katchū-shi* realized they could make the lacing more secure and even strengthen the board further if they pulled the *odoshi-ge* upward and to the right when it came through the second-from-the-bottom *kedate-no-ana* of a scale. The lacing could then be inserted into the top *kedate-no-ana* of the neighbouring scale to the immediate right of the scale where the lacing originated. The connective *kedate* portion of the lacing process was then strung as normal with the exception that as it returned downward from the upper *sane-ita* and was inserted through the *kedate-no-ana* from the rear to the front of the lower *kozane* in the lower lame, it was then pulled downward and to the left. It was then inserted into the second-from-the-top *kedate-no-ana* of the scale to the immediate left of where it had originated. The lacing was then drawn horizontally to the right across the back face, bridging the two neighbouring scales before it was inserted back out to the front of the *sane-ita* through the second-from-the-top *kedate-no-ana* so that the lacing process could be repeated.

Because the *nawame-garami*, or 'wave-eye stitches', crossed between neighbouring scales they helped further strengthen the structural integrity of the lame. The diagonal binding also helped prevent cut sections of lacing from threading backwards and coming undone. As this method of lacing became the standard for almost 800 years, the need to distinguish it from the obsolete *tate-odoshi* method of lacing was largely nullified; as virtually all existing examples of 'full lacing' are by default examples of *nawame-odoshi*, the latter can therefore simply be referred to as *kebiki odoshi*.

To assist with the process of lacing it was common for the armour makers to cover the leading end of the *odoshi-ge* with lacquer. The *odoshi-ge* was trimmed first to create a narrow point. The long tapered end was then covered with *urushi* to create a narrow needle-like tip that when dried could easily be inserted and drawn through the narrow holes in the overlapping *kozane* using a pair of flat-nosed tongs. Knots were tied in lengths of *kawa-odoshi* to prevent the lacing from being pulled backwards through a hole when it was being strung. When *ito-odoshi-ge* was used, the end of the lace was pinched open to form a hollow tube and then dipped in glue. The frayed ends of the *odoshi-ge* were then tucked backwards on themselves into the centre of the tube to create a tulip-bulb-like knob at the end of the lace, which when dried was of sufficient diameter and hard enough to prevent the *odoshi-ge* from being pulled backwards through the hole in the *kozane* when tension was applied.

In later centuries *katchū-shi* developed a method of locking the lengths of *odoshi-ge* in the *kedate-no-ana* to prevent them from being pulled through when under pressure. This was achieved by placing small tapered plugs of chewed or rolled paper or leather under the lacing. These would be pushed through from the front of the *sane-ita* underneath the length of lacing so their ends protruded slightly on the reverse side. This would be sufficient to prevent the *odoshi-ge* from being pulled further through the *kedate-no-ana*.

By the latter part of the 11th century a third form of *odoshi-ge* known as *aya-odoshi-ge* was introduced. An attractive cross-weave variety of silk twill, or *aya*, was by itself both too thin and fragile to be utilized as *odoshi-ge*. Armour makers compensated for these defects by wrapping cotton or hemp cloth lengths of lacing with an outer sheath of *aya* silk. While aesthetically attractive, *aya-odoshi-ge* and its counterpart, *kara-aya-odoshi*, which was made from imported Chinese twill, both had a number of drawbacks, beginning with the complexity of production. The inner core of each lace was laid centrally over a matched length of *aya* silk that was cut to be slightly less than three times as wide as the inner lace. The *aya* was then folded over and behind the reverse side of the inner lace and tacked closed with a light running stitch. While this gave the *aya* the vertical strength and thickness to support a suspended lamellar section, the silk sheath was easily damaged if it was strung through too many holes, which would distort the appearance of the weave and cause it to wrinkle. This meant that *aya-odoshi-ge* could only be strung in short lengths, which added considerably to the amount of time and effort that was required to lace each section and in turn to the overall cost of the armour.

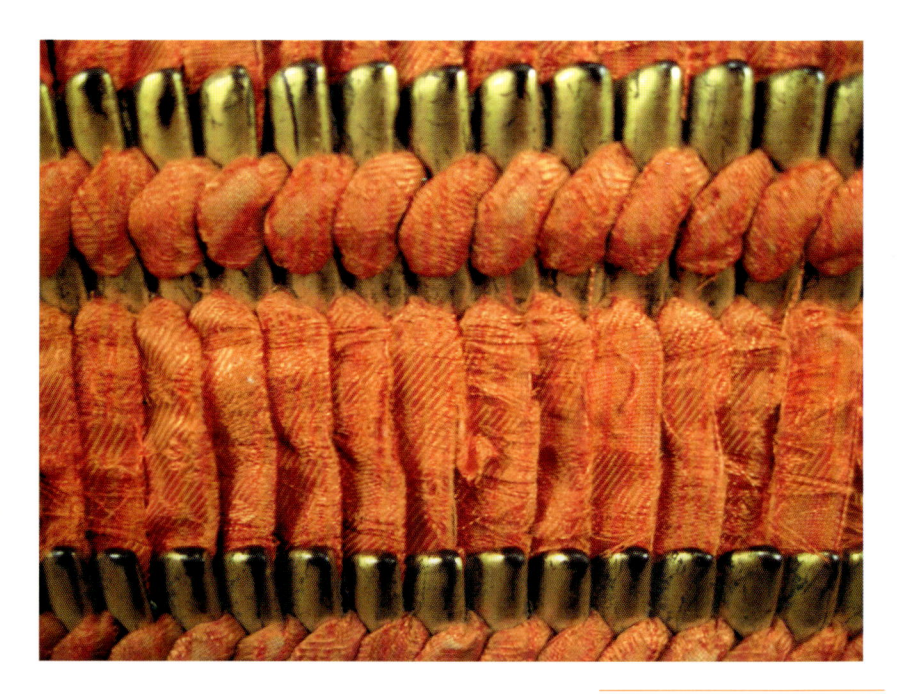

Factors such as these bring into question just how common *aya-odoshi-ge* was as a lacing material. And while historical records such as the *Genpei Jōsuiki*, the famous 14th-century account of the 12th-century Genpei War, recorded that renowned warriors like Minamoto Yoshitsune owned at least one *kara-aya-odoshi-ge* laced set of armour, there is little evidence to suggest that there was much demand for *aya-odoshi-ge* amongst the rank-and-file members of the fledging warrior class. Based on the cost and overall impracticality of *aya-odoshi-ge* it is far more probable that it was never utilized on a wide scale like *kawa-* or *ito-odoshi*.

Aya-odoshi, however, like *kawa-odoshi*, was never entirely abandoned as a lacing material, although unlike leather lacing, its usage appears to have dropped off rapidly from the 13th century onward as the duration and intensity of the military campaigns that the samurai were called upon to participate in gradually escalated. And whereas *kawa-odoshi*-laced items became increasing uncommon,

A rare view of *aya-odoshi-ge*, or silk twill lacing. Though worn, the twill pattern weave is still visible. Hidden within the folds of the *aya-odoshi-ge* were narrow strips of a fine weave, and much more durable fabric. This was done not only to reinforce the silk twill lacing but also to help to maintain a more regular appearance and form.

A superb painted rendering of the famous 12th century *aka-ito-odoshi yoroi* that is said to have belonged to the famous warrior Hatakeyama Shigetada. One of Japan's National Treasures, this beautiful *ō-yoroi* is housed in the Mikate Shrine in the Tōkyō Metropolis. It is interesting to note that the *yoroi* features a loosely connected *waki-ita*, a feature that was not introduced until the 13th century. The presence of this plate may represent a later period upgrade of the cuirass. Note the connective *kōmori-tsuke* panel that secures the *imuke-no-kusazuri* to the cuirass.

aya-odoshi laced pieces became extraordinarily rare, until this form of lacing was only seen on extremely high-quality sets of armour, and even then, only occasionally until the very end of Japan's feudal period.

The *ito-odoshi-ge*, which for the purpose of this book shall always be considered to be silk unless otherwise stated, was almost always produced as a single solid colour if it was made to be used to lace the main body of a lamellar section. Conventional *ito-odoshi-ge* was also devoid of incorporated patterns other than the naturally occurring ribbed appearance of the weave. *Ito-odoshi-ge* could be produced in a huge array of colours, including blue, green, purple, red and yellow, as well as various shades of those colours.

Kon, or indigo blue, is often cited as having been one of the most popular colours used to lace items of armour. The popularity of *kon-ito-odoshi* may in part have stemmed from the greater availability and as such the lower cost of indigo compared with other dye colours, indigo having been introduced to Japan sometime in the 10th century. Adding to indigo's popularity may have been the fact that the dye's dark colouration was able to hide soiled and stained sections of lacing. This would have helped to maintain the aesthetic appearance of an item of armour for longer, which would have reduced the need to replace sections of lacing when they were still physically sound.

The seemingly strong preference for *kon-ito-odoshi*-laced items of armour by the samurai may to some degree also be a mistaken historical assumption based on the fact that the vast majority of surviving examples of *yoroi* were laced using indigo *odoshi-ge*. For contemporary illustrations tend to suggest that many warriors preferred items of armour that were laced in bold colour tones such as red, or *aka*. Such representations, however, were often made long after the events that they were meant to record and as such were often distorted representations of the facts, heavily embellished for artistic effect. Thus there is no way to be entirely sure just how common certain colours were during those periods.

The lack of surviving examples of items of armour that were originally laced using bold colours of *odoshi-ge* in comparison with the rather large number of original *kon-ito-odoshi*-laced sets that are known to exist can, however, be explained by the fact that indigo-dyed lacing is better able to resist the damaging effects of ultraviolet rays. For ultraviolet rays affect the structural integrity of the silk when they are able to pass through the material. Unlike light and bright colours, *kon*-coloured *odoshi-ge* is able to absorb, and thus better resist the damaging effects of, ultraviolet rays. Thus while light or brighter colours of lacing may have been equally or even more popular, the molecular make-up of the dyes used to create those colours does not protect the lacing in the same way as dark coloured dyes. As a result, light or bright coloured materials tend to disintegrate faster, the situation compounding with the passage of time and additional exposure. Thus *kon-ito-odoshi* may not have the most popular colour of lacing, but simply the one that has best survived over the centuries, which in turn has created the impression that *kon-ito-odoshi* was one of the most popular colours for lacing.

While ultraviolet light can significantly accelerate the molecular decomposition of silk, the deterioration of the silk fabric is inevitable. For silk, like most organic materials, will naturally begin to break down after about one hundred years irrespective of exposure to damaging effects of ultraviolet light. While it is possible for silk to last several decades more under careful preservation, the naturally occurring levels of decomposition within its molecular structure will eventually cause woven silk to disintegrate into a fine powder at the slightest touch.

While it is highly unlikely that the Japanese fully understood why indigo-coloured *ito-odoshi-ge* retained its structural integrity for significantly longer periods of time than other colours of lacing, they may have been cognizant of this reality and recommended *kon-ito-odoshi-ge* to their customers.

Accelerating the decomposition of *aka-* and purple-, *murasaki*, dyed *odoshi-ge* were the dyes themselves, which were made from extracts of madder and gromwell respectively. The natural acidity of these dyes would damage the molecular structure of the silk fibres, hastening the decomposition of the lacing.

The colour of lacing that a warrior utilized, contrary to what is often written, was not regulated. And while there was a hierarchy of colours within the imperial court, where a colour was reflective of one's rank and status, such considerations were largely ignored by the samurai, whose use of colour tended to be based on personal choice rather than being indicative of rank or family.[4] Likewise, the samurai never associated colours with virtues in the same way that the Victorians and early students of heraldry argued that Western heraldic colours did. While both Japanese and Western historians in the past tried to ascribe meaning to patterns and colours of lacing, this was simply not the case and would, as Anthony Bryant notes, have been 'laughable' to the 'Japanese warrior of the historic age'.[5] This is not to say that individually or in small groups warriors did not establish such beliefs, but rather that such concepts were never codified or even close to universally recognized or applied when it came to determining the colour of lacing that could be utilized to assemble a set of armour.

Attesting to this was the fact that it was not uncommon for sections of armour to be laced together using between three and six different colours of lacing arranged in separate horizontal or vertical bands, though never a combination of the two. That multiple colours, often contradictory according to the *go-gyo-setsu*, could appear together further undermines theories that certain colours of *odoshi-ge* were visual representations of certain moralistic virtues. If there was a factor that dictated the colour or colours of *odoshi-ge* that a warrior could or would utilize, and if the lacing was to be arranged in a certain pattern, it was the warrior's financial situation that determined this and nothing else.

It is also important to note that the Japanese never used the colour of *odoshi-ge* to differentiate one force of warriors from another in the way that was often seen with European armies of the 17th, 18th and 19th centuries, for example, the French troops of the Napoleonic Wars commonly wearing blue tunics, and British soldiers commonly wearing red. The closest the Japanese came to use of colours as a means of identification prior to the 16th century were periodic examples of dynastic warrior families demonstrating a preference for certain colours, such as the Taira clan's penchant for purple lacing while their enemy, the Fujiwara, were said to have favoured green. Beyond the immediate family unit, though, there is no historical evidence to support the suggestion that it was possible to identify the warriors fighting for either clan strictly by the colouration of their armour.

Evidence in this regard can be found in two incidents recorded in a 14th century *gunchūjō*, or petition for military reward document that Professor Thomas Conlan discusses in his article 'The Nature of Warfare in Fourteenth Century Japan: The Record of Nomoto Tomoyuki'.[6] In one incident he reports, a warrior questions whether other samurai arriving on the field were allies or enemies, while in another Conlan

A painting of the 13th century white-laced, or *shiro-odoshi*, *ō-yoroi* that is housed in the Hinomisaki Shrine in Shimane Prefecture. The armour, also one of Japan's National Treasures, was restored in 1805 by the order of the seventh *daimyō* of the Matsue *han*, Matsudaira Fumi, and as such has some post-13th century features.

documents how samurai mistook enemies for allies. If, as is often suggested, groups of warriors were clad in armour that was laced in the same general identifying colour, then incidents such as these should not have occurred. That they did further supports the idea that forced uniformity simply did not exist amongst the samurai when it came to the colouration of the items of armour that they wore prior to the 16th century.

In fact, there was little need for warriors to wear any form of identifying feature between the 11th and latter part of the 13th centuries, for warfare seldom escalated beyond small-scale skirmishes where the majority of the fighting was restricted to one-on-one engagements. In accordance with the practices of those periods a samurai was expected to announce his name and lineage prior to engaging an opponent. While this is not to say that this practice was as rigidly and formally observed as is often suggested, this fact too undermines the idea that the samurai observed a practice whereby colour, or more specifically the colour of *odoshi-ge*, could be relied on to distinguish unknown warriors as being a member of an allied or enemy force.

Nevertheless, it is important to understand that amongst local allies the individualistic nature of the colour of lacing in which a warrior had his armour laced and the pattern in which the *odoshi-ge* was strung was often used to identify counterparts in battle. It could also have been used to identify a foe in smaller engagements if the opposing warriors were familiar with each other and were therefore already aware of such details.

As the military campaigns that the samurai engaged in grew larger and longer, and the number of combatants participating in those conflicts grew in number, distinguishing friend from foe, even those known personally to a warrior, was significantly complicated. This was due to the fact that while samurai were free to choose the colour and pattern of lacing that was used in the assembly of the sets of armour that they wore, there were only a limited number of colour choices and possible lacing patterns available, thirty-two known variations of which are documented in Dr Sasama Yoshihiko's massive *Nihon Dai Katchū Zu-Kan* (Large Illustrated Book of Japanese Armour). Thus it did not require many samurai on a battlefield before warriors clad in almost identical sets of armour could be seen amongst the ranks of the combatants on both sides of the field. As the larger, more complex engagements fundamentally nullified the opportunity for warriors to individually identify themselves in battle, alternative ways for warriors to identify themselves were improvised. An example of the sort of changes that were implemented was also documented by Conlan, who cites an incident in which a retainer named Nobutsune kills an enemy horseman. Conlan records that Nobutsune was able to distinguish that the horseman was an enemy because the opposing forces had developed the practice of attaching 'special badges or emblems' to their armour to help identify them to both friend and foe on the battlefield.[7]

The badges and emblems referred to are known as *kamon*, family crests, and *jirushi*, which translates as 'mark'. Family crests began to be fitted to armour in various ways, as will be discussed later in this chapter and in further detail in the companion book, Volume II. *Jirushi* appeared in a number of forms, but were in general small cloth banners that were often attached to the rear of the helmet and to the left *sode* shoulder guard of a set of armour. The *jirushi* were often made from lengths of coloured cloth and emblazoned with crests or other patterns that made it easy for warriors to recognize their allies, even when mixed amongst an opposing force.

The colour of a *jirushi*, it should be noted, was often more important than the crest emblazoned on it, for warriors from related families who shared the same *kamon* frequently found themselves opponents. As such, the colour of the *jirushi* was a key identifying factor that distinguished between opposing forces.[8]

SAMURAI ARMOUR

ARMOUR LACING PATTERNS (*ODOSHI NO MOYŌ*)

Lacing patterns, like the colour of *odoshi-ge* used, were a matter of individual taste, with the only governing factor being the financial limitations of the warrior who commissioned the armour. While the number of patterns available increased over time, the vast majority of them appear to have come into existence within a fairly short period once *katchū-shi* began to experiment with the idea of using multiple colours of lacing to assemble a section of armour. This appears to have gradually evolved into more complex patterns and arrangements, as also noted, which in some cases saw two sections of lamellar board laced together with up to six different colours of *odoshi-ge*.

One of the most common patterns was referred to as *iro-iro odoshi*, which literally means 'many colour cord'. *Iro-iro odoshi*-laced items of armour could feature between three and six different colours of *odoshi-ge* arranged in separate horizontal bands with no set order in regards to which colour was at the top or bottom of the section of armour or which colours appeared next to each other in the overall order.

An alternative to this arrangement was for multiple similar colours of lacing to be arranged so they faded or gained in intensity depending on the top-to-bottom horizontal arrangement of the various shades of *odoshi-ge* that were utilized. When the colours went from dark to light, starting from the top lame in a section of armour, the style was referred to as *nioi odoshi*. Lacing that began with the darkest colour at the bottom of the piece and lightened towards the top was referred to as *susogu odoshi*. It should be noted that with *nioi-* or *susogu*-laced items the darkest colour band of lacing is usually mentioned in the formal title of the lacing style. Thus a *nioi odoshi*-laced item of armour that begins with a dark blue band of lacing would be referred to as *kon-nioi odoshi*, while a green-laced top band would be referred to as *moegi-nioi odoshi*. A vertically arranged section of lacing that fades from dark to light from the outside edges towards the centre of a section of armour is referred to as

Various examples of common lacing patterns. Note that the colours shown here are only examples and not indicative of a specific pattern. Thus other colour combinations are equally possible. 1) *Aka* (red) *odoshi*. 2) *Murasaki* (purple) *susogu odoshi*. 3) *Aoi* (blue) *shiro* (white) *dan odoshi*. 4) *Moegi* (light green) *koshi-dori shiro*. 5) *Moegi-nioi odoshi*. 6) *Murasaki kata-iro kawari*. 7) *Aka hata-susogu odoshi*. 8) *Moegi hata-nioi odoshi*. (Courtesy of Kyōto Yoroinoya Usagijuk armour artists Nagatoshi and Ako Uzuki)

hata-susogu odoshi. An even rarer version of this style of lacing is arranged so that the laces come from the edges inward and transition from light to dark and then back to light by the middle of the laced section before the pattern is repeated towards the opposite side of the piece being laced. This style is referred to as *hata-nioi odoshi*.

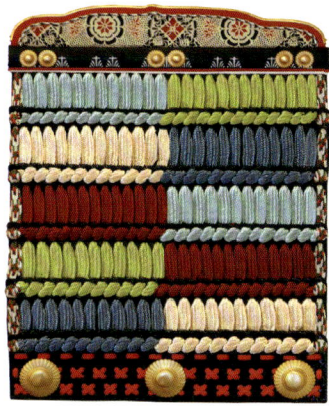

When a section of armour is all one colour with the exception of the topmost band or two of lacing then the style is referred to by using the colour of the main body of the lacing followed by the term *wada* and then the colour of the top band of *odoshi-ge*. Thus a black *odoshi-ge*-strung section of armour with a red-laced band across the top is referred to as *kuro-odoshi wada aka*. If the uppermost band or two of lacing is the same colour as the lower bands with a band or two of different coloured lacing between them, then the style is referred to as *katadori*. Thus if a red-laced section of armour has a dark blue band of *odoshi-ge* running through the middle, then the style of lacing is referred to as *aka-odoshi-katadori-kon*. If the contrasting band of lacing is running vertically and appears in the middle of the section of armour, then the term *naka* is used to describe the style. For example, a red-laced section with a dark blue intermediate vertical band of lacing is described as *aka-odoshi naka kon*.

If the contrasting band appears at the bottom of a section of armour laced in a single colour, then the style is referred to as *koshi-tori*. Using the same red base colour with a dark blue band, for example, the lacing pattern is described as *aka-odoshi koshi-tori kon*.

Various examples of common lacing patterns.
1) *Moegi hata-nioi odoshi*. 2) *San shokū* (three colour) *iro-iro odoshi*. 3) *Go shokū* (five colour) *iro-iro odoshi*. 4) *Aoi-odoshi naka aka*. (Courtesy of Kyōto Yoroinoya Usagijuk armour artists Nagatoshi and Ako Uzuki)

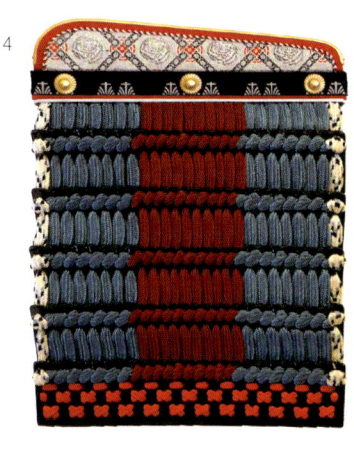

When two different colours of *odoshi-ge* are laced in alternating rows, the style is referred to as *dan odoshi*, or literally 'stepped cord'. This style should not be confused with *iro-iro odoshi*, for unlike *iro-iro odoshi*, which often features multiple colours of lacing, *dan odoshi* utilizes only two colours of *odoshi-ge* that will always appear in a repetitive horizontally arranged strip-like pattern. If red and dark blue are used, the pattern is referred to as *aka-kon dan odoshi*. When only one colour is mentioned in the description of a lacing pattern done in the *dan odoshi* style then the unmentioned colour is by default always white, or *shiro*. Thus an *aka-dan odoshi*-laced item features a repetitive red and white striped horizontal pattern over its surface.

One of the most exotic patterns of lacing was the style referred to as *omodaka odoshi*, which is said to have derived its name from its resemblance to the leaves of a Japanese variety of alisma or water plantain. The design features a pyramid-like shape centred in the middle of the laced section of armour. The pyramid often terminates one lame down from the top row in a suspended section of *sane-ita*, but is sometimes also extended into the uppermost row of lacing as well. The outside edges of the pyramid will generally comprise two or three parallel strands of white *odoshi-ge* that stagger inwards towards a central apex. The interior of the pyramid will generally be framed by one or two more rows of *odoshi-ge* of a different colour with a final, generally darker colour being used to fill the central void. More elaborate examples of *omodaka odoshi*-laced sections of armour may feature as many as five colours within the pyramid, while simpler examples may utilize as few as two different colours of *odoshi-ge* including the lacing that is used to create the white exterior frame. The main colour of the surrounding lacing is always included when describing items laced in this manner. Thus a section of armour laced in purple with this pattern is described as *murasaki-omodaka odoshi*.

SAMURAI ARMOUR

When the pyramid is inverted and originates from the top of a section of armour and tapers downward towards its tip, the lacing pattern is described as *saga*. Thus the purple laced section would be described as *murasaki-saga omodaka odoshi*.

Lacing strung using contrasting colours laced to form a horizontal series of narrow pyramids is referred to as *fuji odoshi*, or literally 'wisteria lacing', since the pattern is meant to represent the hanging floral blooms of the wisteria.

A close relation of the *omodaka odoshi* style is the *tsumadori* arrangement of lacing. This unique style of lacing usually features a wedge-shaped section of lacing along one edge of a section of armour that tapers to a point from top to bottom. While the wedge of lacing resembles the pyramid of the *omodaka* method of lacing, white was rarely used to frame the outer edges of the wedge-like section of lacing strung in the *tsumadori* style. The wedges could consist of multiple staggered parallel bands of different coloured *odoshi-ge* or be a solid colour. As with other lacing styles, the main lacing colour is usually mentioned when describing items laced in the *tsumadori* style. For example, if a section of white *odoshi-ge* laced armour features this pattern, the style of lacing is referred to as *shiro-tsumadori odoshi*.

When the pattern is inverted so the wedge tapers upward to a point then the style is referred to as *kata-tsumadori*. It should be noted that it is not uncommon for some items of armour to feature a combination of lacing patterns. For example a section can feature both a coloured upper band and an edge wedge, in which case both features would need to be included in the description of the lacing style. If the main *odoshi-ge* is dark blue with a white upper band and red wedge down the leading edge of the section of armour, then the lacing pattern is referred to as *aka-tsumadori-kon-odoshi wada shiro*.

A number of less common but attractive lacing patterns included the *murago odoshi* style, which was made up of various combinations of rectangular blocks of lacing of contrasting colours. The rectangular blocks would be strung to reach midway across a lame, with the remaining half portion being laced in an alternative colour. As few as two colours could be used, with just a couple of brick-like block sections of contrasting colours of lacing covering the surface

1) *Aka saga omodaka odoshi*. 2) *Murasaki saga omodaka odoshi*. 3) *Aoi tsumadori odoshi*. 4) *Shiro-tsumadori odoshi*. 5) *Murasaki-tsumadori odoshi*. 6) *Shiro kata-tsumadori odoshi*. 7) *Murasaki fuji odoshi*. 8) *Asagi omodaka odoshi*. (Courtesy of Kyōto Yoroinoya Usagijuk armour artists Nagatoshi and Ako Uzuki)

area of a section of armour. Alternatively, the entire surface area of a section of armour could be composed of blocks of lacing of different colours, in which case the style would be referred to as *murago iro-iro odoshi*, where it was not uncommon for five or six different colours of *odoshi-ge* to be utilized to lace a single section of armour, such as a *sode* or the facing surfaces of a cuirass. As with most patterned styles of lacing the predominant colour of *odoshi-ge* is always mentioned when describing items of armour strung in the *murago odoshi* style. Thus if a section of armour features rectangular blocks of white lacing set within a navy blue field the style is referred to as *kon murago odoshi*.

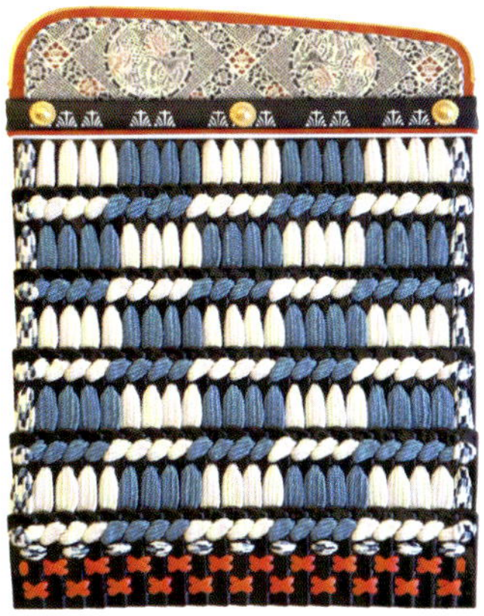

The *shikime odoshi* style of lacing features two different colours of *odoshi-ge* strung in short sections that alternate back and forth between the two colours. The order in which the colours are arranged will alternate between ascending lames to create a checkerboard-like pattern. In some cases, the pattern was limited to a small section of the lacing so that when several sections of laced lamellae were arranged together a small pattern like a Swiss cross was created in the centre of the laced portion of armour. When the colours are arranged in a checkerboard pattern, the brighter colour is usually mentioned first, followed by the duller of the two colours. Thus a red with black checkerboard lacing pattern is referred to as *aka-kuro shikime odoshi*. If one colour of lacing appears more than the other, then the main colour is mentioned first.

Lacing that was strung to create rudimentary images or shapes on items of armour is referred to as *mongara odoshi*. Two of the most common examples of *mongara odoshi* were sections of armour centrally emblazoned with a bold *hinomaru*, or 'sun circle', and the ancient Sanskrit *manjū* swastika symbol of Buddhist theology.

While images in some period texts appear to suggest that a number of other exotic lacing patterns existed, no examples of items laced in such a way have survived to confirm the existence of such patterns, which may have been based more on artistic license than factual observation on the part of the chronicler. Of these one of the few confirmed patterns was the unique *tateawe odoshi* style, which generally featured two or three different colours of *odoshi-ge* arranged in wavy vertical bands. Because the laces were strung in the conventional manner, the side-to-side wave of the vertical bands had something of a stepped or staggered appearance due to natural flow of the *odoshi-ge*. In later centuries the harsh left-to-right transition of the lacing as it rose vertically up a section of armour was softened in appearance by the addition of extra lengths of connective *kedate* lacing, which were strung so that they ran diagonally between an upper and lower board instead of straight up and down. This had the effect of smoothing or rounding off the transition between the snaking columns of vertically arranged bands of lacing.

When *kawa-odoshi-ge* was utilized, the pattern was generally printed on the lacing itself; thus decorative lacing patterns were both uncommon and unnecessary. As such the style of the lacing was referred to based on the pattern that was printed on the *odoshi-ge*. Thus if a section of armour was strung together using the popular *kozakura-gawa* pattern, which featured a pattern of small cherry blossoms of a contrasting colour to the main field, such as white on blue, or green on yellow, then the type of lacing would be described as being *kozakura-gawa-odoshi*. It is common for the colours of the lacing to be mentioned in the formal title in such cases. Thus a cuirass

1) *Shiro-aoi shikime odoshi*. 2) *Murasaki murago odoshi*. 3) *Aoi murago odoshi*. 4) *Asagi* (light blue) *mongara odoshi*. (Courtesy of Kyōto Yoroinoya Usagijuk armour artists Nagatoshi and Ako Uzuki)

strung using green leather lacing stencilled with yellow cherry blossoms would be referred to as being a *midori-ji ni kiro nuki kozakura-gawa odoshi yoroi*. It should be noted that the term *nuki* means 'take out'. This is in reference to the fact that the cherry blossom motifs were actually the void portion of the press blocks where no image was transferred. In other words, if the *kozakura-gawa odoshi* was dark blue with white cherry blossoms, the colour of the cherry blossom was the original or dyed colour of the hide, which in this case would have been white. The blue would have been applied via the overlaid stencil. This is contrary to what is often assumed, which is that the lacing was dyed the base colour first and then had a floral pattern applied by stencil.

One of the few examples of *kawa-odoshi* where a pattern was incorporated into the lacing process occurred when the highly popular *shina-gawa* pattern of *kawa-odoshi-ge* was used. This pattern of lacing featured a regularly spaced repetitive design of two fern leaves pointing in opposite directions with their stems crossed. As the pattern was wider than the width of several laces, the complete appearance of the pattern was generally obscured when items were laced using this material. It was possible, however, with considerable effort, to lace a section of armour so that the pattern was recreated when the vertically arranged lengths of *kawa-odoshi-ge* were strung.

It should be noted that when patterns were incorporated into the lacing of an item of armour, such as a *yoroi*, that the pattern that appeared on the front of a cuirass would be mirrored on the back piece of the cuirass. The *kusazuri* would generally also be laced to feature the same patterns, as would the neck guard, or *shikoro*, of the helmet and the *sode* shoulder guards, which were considered to be part of the *mitsu-mono*, or 'three things' that along with the cuirass made up what was originally seen as a full armour grouping around a classic period *yoroi*. The thigh armour, however, was sometimes simply laced in the base colour of the armour or the colour of lacing closest to the base of the cuirass. In other words, if a cuirass was laced in the *susogu odoshi* style with the lacing transitioning from dark blue at the bottom of the cuirass to white at the top, then it would not be uncommon for the *kusazuri* to be laced entirely in dark blue *odoshi-ge*.

Patterns that involved triangles or wedge-like shapes, such as the *omodaka* or *tsumadori odoshi* styles of lacing, often had the *kusazuri* laced so that the direction of the triangle or wedge was rotated at 180 degrees to how it appeared on the main body of the cuirass, *shikoro* and *sode*. This, however, was a matter of choice and not a rule. The only restricting factors in such matters were the personal tastes of the samurai commissioning the armour, his budget and obvious aesthetic considerations.

TORSO ARMOUR SECTIONS: *NAGAKAWA, USHIRO-TATEAGE* AND *MUNA-ITA*

The *nagakawa* of the *yoroi* style of cuirass was composed of four long C-shaped *sane-ita* that were long enough to extend from the front right-hand edge of the body, around to the left side and then back to the rear right-hand edge of the torso. These four *sane-ita* that covered the abdomen area were generally *ichi-mai-maze* in construction as were the two short lames that formed the *mae-tateage*, which protected the mid-chest area of the torso between the outer edges of the pectoral muscles.

It is interesting to note how the number of *kozane* that were required to construct a lame

YOROI NOMENCLATURE

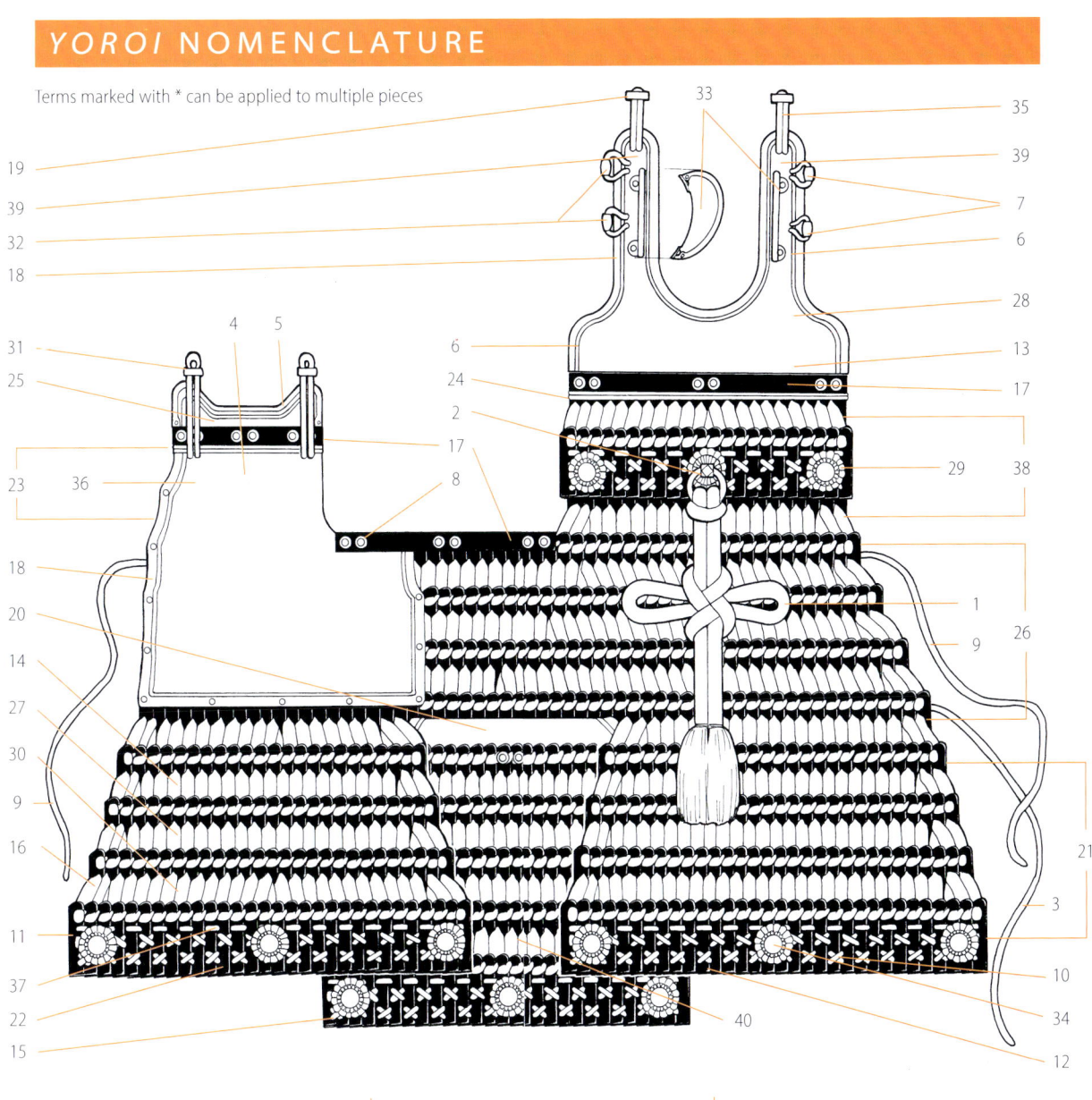

Terms marked with * can be applied to multiple pieces

1. *Agemaki*
2. *Agemaki-no-kan*
3. *Dōsaki-no-o*
4. *E-gawa**
5. *Fukurin**
6. *Fusegumi**
7. *Gumi kanamono**
8. *Hassō-no-byō**
9. *Hikiawase-no-o**
10. *Hishinui**
11. *Hishinui-no-ita*
12. *Hitsushiki-no-kusazuri*
13. *Ichimonji*
14. *Ichi-no-ita**
15. *Imuke-no-kusazuri*
16. *Kedate**
17. *Keshō-no-ita**
18. *Koberi-gawa**
19. *Kohaze**
20. *Kōmori-tsuke**
21. *Kusazuri**
22. *Mae-no-kusazuri*
23. *Mae-tateage*
24. *Mizu-hiki**
25. *Muna-ita*
26. *Nagakawa*
27. *Ni-no-ita**
28. *Oshitsuke-no-ita*
29. *Saka-ita*
30. *San-no-ita**
31. *Seme-kohaze**
32. *Sode-tsuke-no-gumi-wa*
33. *Shoji-no-ita**
34. *Suso-no-kanamono**
35. *Takahimo**
36. *Tsurubashiri-gawa*
37. *Uname**
38. *Ushiro-tateage*
39. *Wadagami**
40. *Yon-no-ita**

of the *nagakawa* increased between the 10th and 15th centuries with the change in the size of the scales utilized. While the number of *kozane* also varied between each of the four lames of the *nagakawa*, if only the top *sane-ita* is compared between sets of armour made in the *yoroi* style between those periods, a clear increase in the number of scales can be noted as the *kozane* themselves grew smaller in size. This is well documented in the book by Miyazaki Masumi and Yamagishi Motō, *Nihon no Katchū Kiso Chishiki* (Japanese Armour Basic Knowledge), where they record that fifty-seven *kozane* were used to assemble the *ichi-no-ita* of a Heian period *yoroi*. By the middle of the Kamakura period (13th century), eighty-three scales were utilized in the armour examined. By the early 14th century the number had increased to 108 and then it decreased slightly to 103 by the middle part of the same century. By the end of the 14th century, 117 *kozane* were utilized to construct the *ichi-no-ita* of a set of armour. This increased to 134 in an example of *yoroi* that was made in the mid-15th century.

The *ushiro-tateage* consisted of three *sane-ita* assembled from *kawa-zane*. The *ushiro-tateage* was unique, however, in that the middle-length section of the three *sane-ita*, called the *saka-ita*, was intentionally positioned and laced so that its lower edge overlapped the outside *sane-gashira* of the lowermost *sane-ita* of the *ushiro-tateage*, which is known as the *ushiro-tateage san-no-ita*. This was done to allow the upper portions of the cuirass, namely the *wadagami* shoulder straps, to be tilted backwards to make it easier for a warrior to get into or take off the cuirass. To maximize the ability of the rear of a *yoroi* to flex backwards, the connective lacing that ran from the *ushiro-tateage san-no-ita* to the *saka-ita* was laced in reverse. This was achieved by stringing the *kedate* portion of the lacing to the underside, or back face of the *saka-ita*. There it was drawn through the *kedate-no-ana* and then laced in the usual manner to the uppermost *sane-ita* of the *ushiro-tateage*, referred to as the *ushiro-tateage ichi-no-ita*. As the connective *kedate* strands of lacing do not cover the face of the *saka-ita*, the constructional *shita-garami* are replaced by *uname* and *hishinui* across the exposed lower half portion of the *sane-ita*, which makes the *saka-ita* look like a *hishinui-no-ita* fitted to the upper back of the cuirass.

Smiths compensated for the austere appearance of the *saka-ita* by fitting a large and generally ornate gilded copper swivel-ring fixture known as an *agemaki-no-kan* to its centre. A large, ornately tied and heavy silk bow called an *agemaki* was suspended from the swivel ring. The *agemaki* performed the dual purpose of holding the *saka-ita* down against the pull of the lacing while it also provided a place to attach the shoulder guards. These were themselves also secured to the cuirass via a series of cords, which are discussed in detail in Volume II. It was also common for *suso-no-kanamono* to be fitted to the left- and right-hand edges of the *saka-ita* if the *hishinui-no-ita* portions of the armour were mounted with these decorative floral fixtures, in which case the identical form of *suso-no-kanamono* would be utilized.

The upper chest was covered by the *muna-ita*, which was made from a single moulded piece of thick rawhide that featured an inward stepped lower edge that allowed it to sit on top of the *sane-gashira* of the upper lame of the *mae-tateage* and then drop down and behind the *sane-ita* to provide a surface to connect the *muna-ita* to the *mae-tateage*. The same width as the *mae-tateage*, the *muna-ita* was generally rectangular in shape with short raised tabs along the outside upper edges of the plate. The raised tabs on the *muna-ita* were positioned to correspond to the downward curve of the arched shoulder straps so as to provide anchoring points for the arrangement of cords and toggles that were used to connect these two portions of the cuirass together.

THE USE OF DECORATIVE LEATHER, BRAIDS AND EDGE TRIM: *EGAWA*, *FUSEGUMI* AND *FUKURIN*

'Picture leather', or *e-gawa*, the oldest examples of which date to the 10th century, was produced from the tanned hides of a small indigenous species of spotted Japanese deer. Decorative designs were stencilled or pressed onto the tanned hides, which when devoid of applied imagery are referred to as *shikka-gawa*, or deer leather. Note the holes around the exterior of the hide from the tanning process.

The *muna-ita* was almost invariably covered with a variety of decorative 'picture leather', or *e-gawa*, as were all of the other solid-plate portions of a set of armour, including the *oshitsuke-no-ita* on the rear of a *yoroi*, the upper plate *kanmuri-no-ita* portion of the *sode* shoulder guards, the *waidate* side panel, the peak of the *kabuto* helmet and several other portions of the various components that created a *gusoku*, the individual parts of which will be introduced later on in this chapter and those that follow. It is important to note that the same pattern of *e-gawa* was always used to cover all of the solid-plate portions of a single set of armour.

The only time an alternative pattern or type of leather would be utilized on a single set of armour was when it was used to cover the interior or reverse surfaces of the aforementioned parts, such as the *oshitsuke-no-ita* and the undersides of the *wadagami* shoulder straps.

One of the earliest known examples of *e-gawa* from the late 10th century featured an arrangement of tightly spaced, blue, medallion-sized floral roundels, each of which featured an internal six-point honeycomb-like design that was framed by a herringbone-like border around the interior edges of the circles. The majority of the arched, triangular intermediate spaces between the circular medallions were filled with blue- and red-dyed leaf-like patterns. This pattern appears to have been something of an anomaly, however, as the majority of surviving examples of *e-gawa* from the 10th and 11th centuries tended to be based on geometric grid-like designs that favoured stylized floral motifs set centrally within the framed diamond-shaped spaces that were produced by the diagonal boundaries of the grid.

The background field of these patterns was inevitably the off-white or pale yellow colouration of the tanned deer hides that were used, which were overlaid with blue and red inked stencils. This in itself was a time-consuming and labour-intensive process, for the stencils, which were hand-cut from sheets of copper, were relatively small, and so each stencil had to be applied and inked several times to cover the entire surface area of an individual hide. And as most designs featured at least two colours, the entire process had to be performed at least two times, with the secondary stencils being carefully positioned to ensure correct alignment with the blanked-out spaces that had not been inked when the first stencil had been applied. The process was often further prolonged by the need to allow the inked areas time to dry before the next stencil could be applied. Even after the stencilling process was complete, the hides were often allowed to dry for a further few months before they were utilized.

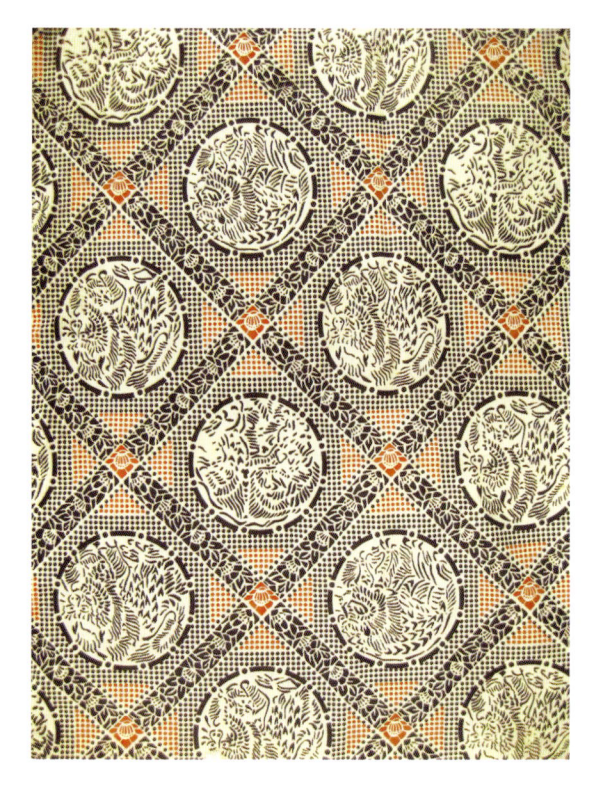

In later centuries many patterns were created using a combination of both stencils and resist-dyeing, or *rōketetsu-zome*, in which wax was applied or infused into surfaces to prevent dyes from permeating certain portions of the material.

Towards the latter part of the 11th century, stylized images of mythical dog-like Chinese lions, called *shishi*, began to replace the central floral motifs within the framed diamond areas of the diagonal grid-pattern designs that continued to be produced. Some patterns featured only the head of the *shishi* while others incorporated the whole body of the lion in the designs, which were almost always circular in overall form.

By the late 12th century, examples of *e-gawa* devoid of the diagonal grid-like overlays that had been a mainstay of most patterns of stencilled leathers in previous centuries began to appear. Initially the designs were often quite simple, little more than an open-spaced pattern of small chrysanthemum blooms on arching stems. This pattern, known as *eda-giku*, or 'chrysanthemum

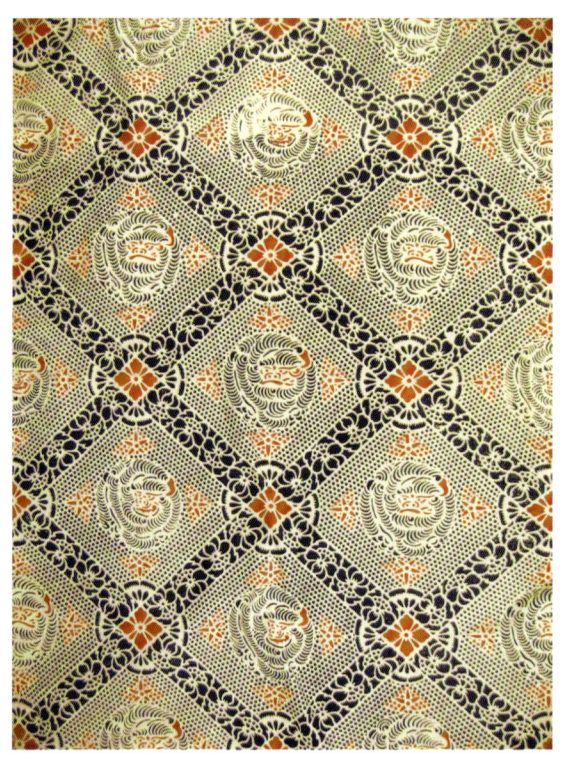

Three examples of *e-gawa* designs. The majority of *e-gawa* patterns produced prior to the 12th century were based on repetitive geometric designs. Most patterns were created utilizing only two colours offset against the background colour of the hide.

branch', also sometimes referred to as 'autumn flowers', was used to cover the front of the famous 12th century national treasure, the transitional-design *aka-ito dō-maru yoroi* version of cuirass that is now housed in the Ōyamazumi Jinja Museum collection.

Shishi continued to be a popular decorative motif and appeared in various forms 'gamboling among rather indifferently drawn foliage' that was interspersed with a random arrangement of small red flowers.[9] Ironically this pattern is referred to as *shishi-no-sakura-gawa*, or 'lion and cherry blossom', irrespective of the fact that the flowers as actually represent peonies.

Gradually the stencilled images became more pictorial. These large, often non-repetitive single-image designs greatly enhanced the visual presentation of a cuirass, especially when they were used to make the *tsurubashiri-gawa*, or 'bow-string running leather', which covered most of the front portion of a *yoroi* and some later-period transitional versions of cuirass. One of the most famous of these large pictorial patterns of *e-gawa* is the early 14th century *fudo-no-e-gawa*, which depicts the fierce, warlike Buddhist deity Fudo Myō-ō flanked by his two loyal attendants standing with his sword in hand on a pillar of broken land surrounded by a swirling conflagration of bright red flames. As the introduction of large, often non-repetitive patterns limited how armour makers could cut the leathers they acquired, the *e-gawa* producers started to stencil the hides with the generic shapes of the various parts that would generally be covered in *e-gawa* already shaped out on the hide, to ensure that the pattern was properly depicted wherever it was applied.

The increasing need for armour during the latter half of the 14th century appears to have had a streamlining effect on *e-gawa* designs. This was in large part due to the decline in the need for large pattern prints as other forms of cuirass began to be introduced that did not feature *tsurubashiri-gawa*. As a result, patterns tended to become smaller, which in turn meant that almost any portion of the hide could be used, as the need to utilize selected portions of the pattern had been removed. The patterns themselves also became increasingly stereotypical, with *shishi*

Top: An example of the impressive *fudo-no-e-gawa* pattern of stencilled leather. (Image from the *Sengoku Daimyō* website, courtesy of J.L. Badgley)

Bottom: An example of the famous and highly popular *shōhei-gawa* pattern of *e-gawa*. This sample clearly shows how the leather maker applied the pattern to the hide in a way that made the best use of the material. The designs were also laid out so as to correspond with the overall forms of the various *kanagu mawari* plates that were generally faced with *e-gawa*. (Image from the *Sengoku Daimyō* website, courtesy of J.L. Badgley)

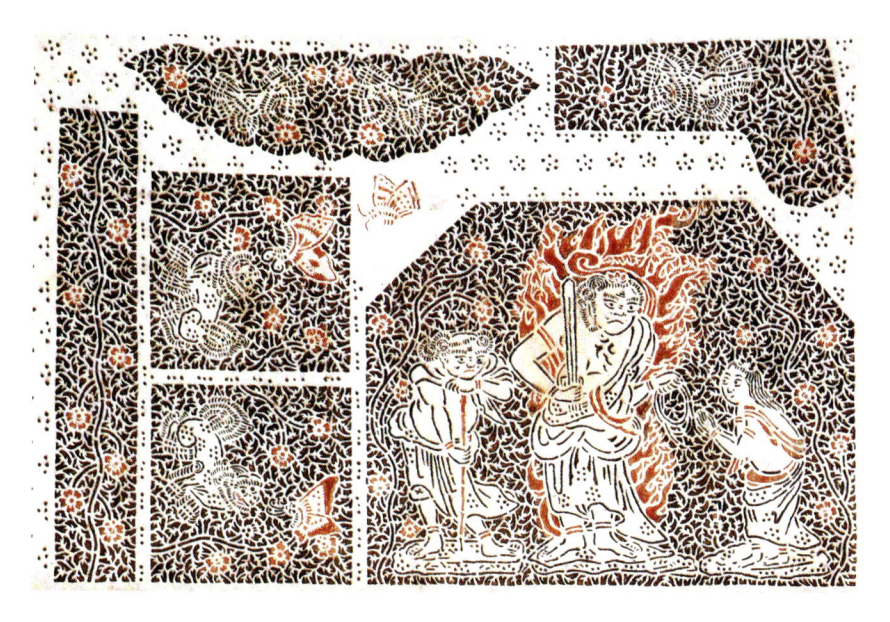

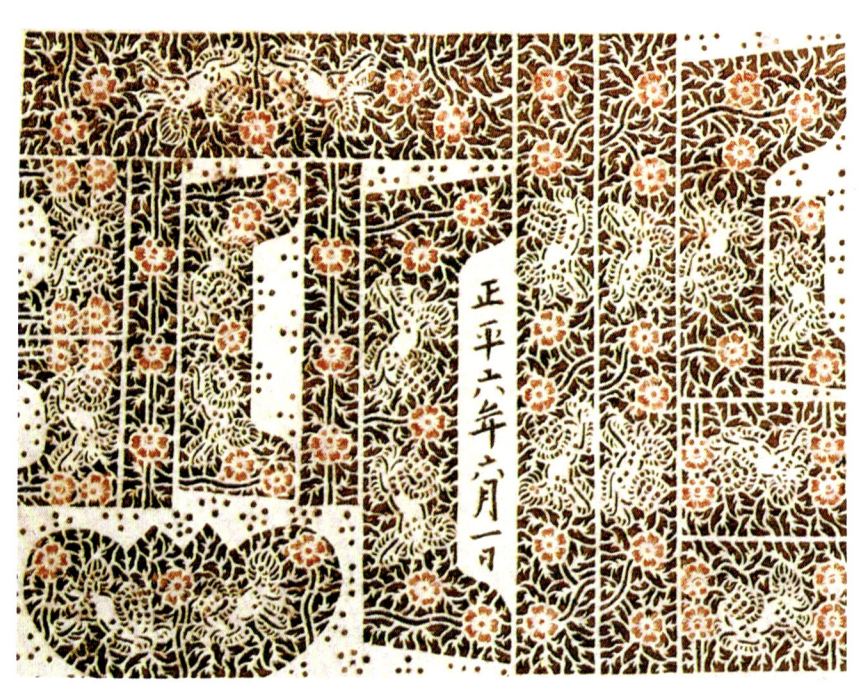

SAMURAI ARMOUR

featuring prominently in most designs. The latter were generally presented in various poses set amongst a background field of thick, stylized foliage interspersed with bright red *botan*, or peony blooms.

The most famous *e-gawa* pattern to emerge from the trend towards more standardized designs of printed leathers in the 14th century was the highly popular *shōhei-gawa*, which featured a series of *shishi* in various poses set on a background field of waterweed and *botan*. One of the unique features of the *shōhei-gawa* design was that a commemorative kanji character date-block set in an open rectangular space was included in the pattern's repetitive design. The date stamp reads '*Shōhei Roku Nen, Roku-Gatsu Tsui-tachi*', which translates as 'June 1st, the Sixth Year of Shōhei (1352)', that being the year the pattern received an imperial patent that licensed it for production.

Attesting to the huge popularity of the *shōhei-gawa* design is the fact that the pattern continued to be produced and utilized in the production of armour until the very end of Japan's feudal period, several centuries after it was first introduced. Even today, it is one of the few traditional patterns of *e-gawa* that continues to be commonly reproduced in Japan. The date stamp on the pattern, however, is often a source of confusion and misinformation for collectors of Japanese armour, who mistakenly misinterpret the year on the leather that faces the armour as being representative of the year that the armour was made. This is also true of a later Edo-period pattern of *e-gawa* called *tenpyō-gawa*, which was made to closely mimic the *shōhei-gawa* design. Like the latter, *tenpyō-gawa* features a commemorative year-stamp as part of its overall design. The date, '*Tenpyō Jū-ni Nen Hachi-Gatsu*', or 'August of the Twelfth Year of Tenpyō (AD 740)', was clearly created to make it appear as though *tenpyō-gawa* was an even older officially sanctioned pattern of *e-gawa*, which presumably was intended to add to the desirability and prestige of the pattern. In

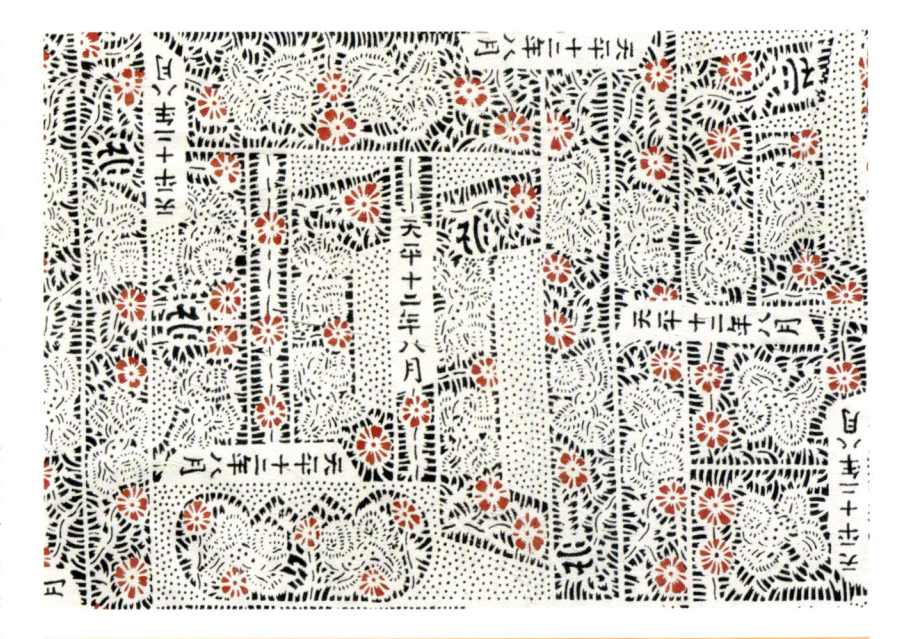

A view of the popular Edo-era *tenpyō-gawa* pattern of *e-gawa* which was an imitator of the famous 14th century *shōhei-gawa* design of stencilled leather. The year AD 740 was intentionally incorporated into the pattern to make it look as though this design was older and thus more prestigious than *shōhei-gawa*, which received an imperial patent in 1352. (Image from the *Sengoku Daimyō* website, courtesy of J.L. Badgley)

reality, however, the date stamp is bogus and has no reflection upon the era in which the pattern was first created, which was close to a millennium later than is represented.

Whenever a section of armour was covered by *e-gawa*, the picture leather was always framed by a narrow band of doe-skin that was usually dyed or smoked, called *koberi-gawa*. These bands were applied around the exterior edges of the solid-plate pieces of armour where the leather coverings were most likely to be rubbed or touched as a way of helping to

A typical example of one of the most common patterns of *shobū-gawa*. Note the highly simplified crucifix-like form of the central floral device that made this pattern of *koberi-gawa* highly popular with Christian converts amongst the warrior class.

protect and preserve the more costly and ornate *e-gawa* panels. For unlike the latter, *koberi-gawa* were generally rather plain and were therefore relatively cheap and easy to replace if they became damaged or worn.

Generally about 1.4 cm in width, the *koberi-gawa* on early-period armour was almost always red in colour. In some cases, it was decorated with a repetitive cross-like pattern of five white dots that was referred to as *go-sei aka-gawa*, or literally 'five-star red leather'. In later centuries a number of dark blue stencilled examples of *koberi-gawa* that left voided designs in white became common. The majority of these patterns featured a crucifix-like floral stem with a rudimentary form of bloom on top set between four to eight outward-arching blades of grass or leaves that progressively decreased in height from the centre outward. The names of these patterns differed depending on the plant or item that was being depicted, though collectively they came to be referred to as *shobū-gawa* due to the similarity in overall appearance between these various designs. Iris flowers, cedar trees and even nails flanked by blades of grass were common themes. The *koberi-gawa* featuring a crucifix-like design would become particularly popular amongst the Christian-convert samurai of Kyūshū during the latter half of the 16th century.

Over time the relatively realistic appearance of the central devices and surrounding leaves became increasingly abstract in form, with the designs metamorphosing into art-deco-like truncated triangular shapes. These forms inadvertently gave rise to new patterns of *shobū-gawa* when the lines that divided the blades of grass were phased out to create solid, fingernail-shaped blocks, the various patterns of which are collectively referred to as *tsume-gata*, or 'nail shaped'.

Smoked leather versions of *koberi-gawa* referred to as *fusebe-gawa* were also utilized. These were generally yellow or brown in colour depending on how long the material was exposed to the smoking process. Patterns were created by attaching cut pieces of waste paper with a light paste made from rice to the surface of a hide before it was smoked. The applied paper patterns prevented the areas under them from being discoloured by the staining effects of the smoke that was created by fires stoked with pine needles. When the paper patterns were washed off, the areas that had been covered would still be the original off-white colour of the hide and contrast against the yellowish brown tones of the hide that had

A close-up of the *muna-ita* portion of a cuirass that shows the details of numerous different components. The *fukurin* edge trim moulding is cleary visible. This has been etched with a scrolling foliage motif. This same artistic design has also been used to decorate the large *kohaze* toggle that is suspended from the end the leather-sheathed *takahimo* cord. Note the *koberi-gawa* edge trim that surrounds the inner panel of *e-gawa* that faces the *muna-ita*. Also note the silk thread *fusegumi* piping that physical secures these two sections of leather together. Some of the individual threads of the *fusegumi* stitching are visible. Note the raised *mizu-hiki* ridge along the lower edge of the central *e-gawa* panel that help it to protrude outward toward the *sane-gashira*. This subtle ridge, which helped to transition the height difference between the *sane-gashira* and the facing surface of the *muna-ita*, was commonly formed by placing rolled lengths of waste paper under the leather before it was adhered to the *muna-ita*.

been exposed during the smoking process.

Indigo-dyed examples of *shobū-gawa* were generally made by tightly wrapping the leather around long cylindrical wooden tubes which had the desired pattern either carved directly onto the surface of the drum or affixed to it so the pattern was raised in relief. The leather would then be dipped in dye, which would not permeate the doe-skin in the areas where the hide was pressed against the raised-in-relief designs on the cylinder, which prevented the dye from coming into contact with the material.

Both the inner panel of *e-gawa* and the outer-edge *koberi-gawa* pieces of stencilled leather would be glued to the surface of the piece of armour that they were facing. The seam between the two materials where they butted up against each other was then painstakingly sewn together, using three different colours of thread on early-period armours and up to five different colours on items of armour produced in later periods. The threads were carefully stitched in accordance with an arranged pattern that created a repetitive, multicoloured, herringbone-like, decorative braid-like stitch that is referred to as *fusegumi*.

While strong, effective and aesthetically beautiful, *fusegumi* stitching was an immensely labour-intensive process. For this reason it became common in the Edo period to substitute two multicoloured lengths of braided cord in place of hand-stitched *fusegumi* to cover the seams between adjoining sections of leather. One length of cord would be braided with a counter-clockwise S-twist while the other would be made using a clockwise Z-twist. When the two lengths of cords were laid side-by-side and tacked together, the opposite spiral of their braids produced a chevron-like pattern that somewhat resembled *fusegumi*. Unlike the latter, however, the braided *jabara-ito* or 'serpent's belly', as these cords came to be referred to, did not actually bind the seams of the adjoining materials together in the way that *fusegumi* stitching did. Instead the primary purpose of *jabara-ito* was to conceal the seam which was tacked together when the *jabara-ito* was stitched in place.

Whenever the solid-plate portions of an item of armour were faced, and as was generally the rule also backed by sections of leather (stencilled, smoked or otherwise), the outer edges of the solid metal-plate pieces were always capped with a metal moulding called a *fukurin*. Generally made from copper that had been gilded, the *fukurin* was primarily added to help prevent the exterior edges of applied leather facing and backing materials from being peeled back along the outer edges of the plate. The inverted U-shaped *fukurin* mouldings were made slightly wider than the thickness of the plate they were to cap so they could be slid over the leather-faced plates without peeling the leather coverings away. The moulding was then gently but firmly crimped, which caused the trim to pinch down on and anchor itself to the edge of the plate. Tiny rivets were used to secure the ends of the *fukurin* in place whenever the moulding was cut or terminated. As they were generally made to fit, the ends of the mouldings often feature small round tabs that were pre-drilled to accommodate the anchoring rivets. And while the primary purpose of the *fukurin* was to secure the leather coverings, they also helped to give the *muna-ita*, *oshitsuke-no-ita* and other solid-plate pieces a smooth-finished appearance around their outer edges.

Six ornate chrysanthemum-shaped domed rivets called *hassō-no-byō* rivets were used to secure both the *muna-ita* and upper-back *oshitsuke-no-ita* plates to the lower lames of the *yoroi*. The rivets were usually arranged in closely spaced pairs of two that were positioned near the left, centre and right-hand edges of the horizontal joint. Through trial and error in the centuries before the *yoroi* was introduced, armour makers had learned that rivets anchored directly through *kozane* quickly damaged the scales, which were unable to stand up to the long-term wear and tear and

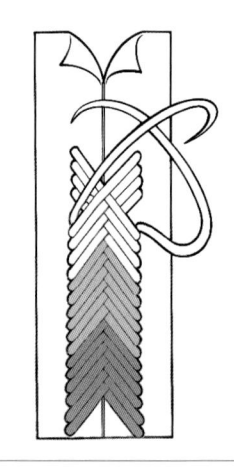

An illustration that shows how the threads of the *fusegumi* secure two pieces of *e-gawa* together along a seam. Also note how the threads were strung to create the decorative herringbone pattern indicative of this ornate style of piping.

Braided multi-coloured cords were commonly used during the Edo period as an alternative to *fusegumi*. When two lengths of cord with the braid running in opposite directions were set side by side and tacked together so as to cover a seam between adjacent pieces of leather the cords, called *jabara-ito*, closely resembled hand-stitched *fusegumi*.

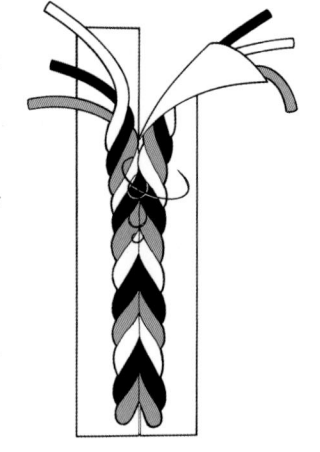

EARLY FORMS OF SAMURAI ARMOUR

As Japan is poor in natural resources, the Japanese armour makers made great efforts to maximize the usefulness of the materials available. Recycled *washi* paper, every inch of which had been written on, was commonly used. Waste paper was rolled into cords that were used a filler for the *mizu-hiki* strips on a cuirass.

strain of the weight loads that were anchored to them. They overcame this problem by placing a long narrow splint of wood over the *sane-gashira* on the exterior face of the lame that was being secured to a solid upper-plate portion of armour. Anchoring the rivets through the wood helped to remove the localized strain on individual *kozane* and their surrounds. It also helped to clamp the entire length of the lame to the stepped lower portion of the solid upper plate *muna-ita*, with the

A view of the *oshitsuke-no-ita* and *wadagami* of a *yoroi*. These have been faced with *e-gawa* and trimmed with *koberi-gawa* with *fusegumi* piping. As this cuirass was produced after the 16th century the *wadagami* have been riveted to the *oshitsuke-no-ita*, as can be noted by the presence of two pairs of small domed rivets on either side of the back-plate. The *koberi-gawa-*wrapped *keshō-no-ita* is also clearly visible. Note the ornate open metalwork *iri-hassō* fixtures that help to pin this leather-covered strip of wood in place over top of the *sane-gashira* of the uppermost *sane-ita*. Decorative filler white and orange silk-wrapped *mizu-hiki* strips are visible along the lower edge of the *keshō-no-ita*.

split shanks of the *hassō-no-byō* passing through the wood and lame before they were folded down and flat against the reverse of the lower stepped portion of the rawhide chest plate.

To improve the aesthetic appearance of these strips of wood or bamboo, they were generally covered with a length of *koberi* or *shobū-gawa*. The *keshō-no-ita*, or 'cosmetic board', as the leather-sheath-covered strip was referred to, was further augmented by the addition of two narrow strips of twill-covered piping called *mizu-hiki*, which were tightly butted up to the lower edge of the *keshō-no-ita*. The *mizu-hiki* strip immediately below the *keshō-no-ita* was generally covered in red *aya* while the lower strip of piping was almost always sheathed in white twill. The fabric was usually folded over a rolled paper core, though narrow splints of wood and dried plant stems were also utilized to fill out the piping, which further enhanced the visual presentation of these decorative edge trims. The folded-back edges of the twill coverings were tucked behind and glued to the back side of the *keshō-no-ita*.

The *sane-gashira* of the uppermost lame of the *nagakawa* along the left-hand side between the *mae-tateage* and *ushiro-tateage* of the *yoroi* was capped with a protective trim that was aesthetically identical in appearance to the *keshō-no-ita* and accompanying *mizu-hiki* strips that were fitted to the front and back of the cuirass. Unlike a conventional *keshō-no-ita*, however, the edge trim was devoid of the rigid wooden core. The leather covering was also cut much wider, which allowed it to be drawn up and over the heads of the scales along that portion of the lamellar board and be pinned to the interior face of the cuirass. Covering the *sane-gashira* in this manner prevented the scales from pinching the wearer and helped to prevent clothing and other items from snagging on and damaging the armour.

The *oshitsuke-no-ita* was attached to the uppermost lame of the *ushiro-tateage*, or the *ichi-no-ita*. The *oshitsuke-no-ita*, like the *muna-ita* on early-period examples of armour such as

143

the *yoroi* and most other forms of cuirass made prior to the 16th century, were generally made from rawhide. Unlike the *muna-ita*, the lower edge of the *oshitsuke-no-ita* was not stepped inward as this would have created an uncomfortable horizontal ridge across the upper back on the interior of the cuirass. This resulted in the *keshō-no-ita* sitting out from the surface of the *oshitsuke-no-ita*. The height difference along the lower edge of the *keshō-no-ita* was not particularly noticeable due to the fact that the *saka-ita* also stood out some from the back of the cuirass. However, it stood about 1–1.5 cm from the rear surface of the cuirass along its upper edge. To hide this fact and help transition the height difference between the rear surface of the *oshitsuke-no-ita* and the *keshō-no-ita*, armour makers placed a strip of wood with a rounded triangular cross-section called an *ichimonji* under the *e-gawa* that covered the back plate, the upper face of which was slightly rounded.

The squared-off U-shaped cut of horse rawhide used to create the *oshitsuke-no-ita* would be moistened and fitted to a wooden mould to create the arched curvature of the shoulder straps. Four or five additional layers of shaped rawhide were bound and glued to the underside surfaces of the *wadagami* to reinforce the shoulder straps and give them form. A layer of padding made from various materials including paper, straw or bulrush cotton would also be applied to the underside of the *wadagami*. The padding was held in place by a cover of brown leather that was glued around the edges and then tightly tucked between the upper strap portion of the

---

Top: An example of a *shoji-no-ita* that has been fitted to the central apex of a *wadagami*. Note the braided cord-like design of edge moulding, referred to as *nawame-fukurin*. Also note the *fusegumi*.

Middle: A *takahimo* cord protruding from the forward end of a *wadagami*. As the cuirass shown here was produced after the 16th century, the upper *takahimo* have been strung with the *seme-kohaze*. On a cuirass produced prior to the 16th century, the upper *takahimo* would feature *kohaze*, while the lower *takahimo* would be strung with the *seme-kohaze*.

Bottom: A detailed view of the *takahimo* cords. The arrangement is again that of a post-16th century cuirass. After the *kohaze*-strung *takahimo* have been inserted through the open loop ends of the corresponding opposite pair of *takahimo*, the *seme-kohaze* on the latter could be slid tight up against the *kohaze*. This would cinch the looped end of the *takahimo* closed, effectively trapping the *kohaze* in place. Note the grommet-fitted apertures and the *sode-tsuke-no-gumi-wa*.

wadagami and the first supporting piece of rawhide applied to its underside. This gave the shoulder straps a flat, keel-like shape in cross-section 1.5–2 cm deep that helped the *wadagami* to better conform to the natural indentation between the inner shoulder and the side of the neck, which in turn made the cuirass more comfortable to wear. The *wadagami* generally measured about 26 cm in overall length from the centre of the inner space between the two shoulder straps. The *wadagami* tended to taper from about 5.5 cm in the middle of the shoulder strap to about 4 cm in width near their forward edge.

Surmounting the *wadagami* were the *shoji-no-ita*. Early examples of *shoji-no-ita* were generally low half-oval-shaped metal plates with flat bases or tabs along their lower edges that were bent at right angles to the main face of the plate. These allowed the *shoji-no-ita* to be riveted to the central upper surface of the *wadagami* near the arched apex of the shoulder straps so that the plates could stand erect like reversed dorsal fins. The *shoji-no-ita* were added to protect the warrior's neck from the upper edges of the large shoulder guards that were attached to the *wadagami*, which had a tendency to be driven inward toward the neck when the arms were raised. They also helped to protect the neck from missiles and sword cuts.

The shape of the *shoji-no-ita* gradually took on a low shark-fin-like shape over the centuries, with the rounded upper peak of the plate pointing towards the front of the armour and tapering off downwards towards the rear. Both sides of the *shoji-no-ita* were usually covered with a small panel of *e-gawa* that would be framed by a *fusegumi*-piped band of *koberi-gawa* and capped with a *fukurin* moulding in the same manner as the other solid-plate portions of the *yoroi* and accompanying parts of the armour grouping, the solid metal-plate pieces of which are also, as already noted, collectively referred to as the *kanagu mawari*, or 'metal all around' parts. On a *yoroi* complete with its other pieces the *kanagu mawari* includes the solid metal-plate portion of the *waidate*, called the *tsubo-ita*, and the upper plate portions of the *kyūbi-no-ita* and *sendan-no-ita*. It also includes the *kanmuri-no-ita* of the shoulder guards and *mabizashi* visor portion of the *kabuto*. On later-period versions of cuirass, where the *muna-ita* and *oshitsuke-no-ita* were made of metal they are also considered to be part of the *kanagu mawari*, as are metal-plate *waki-ita* or armpit plates when they started to be incorporated into the construction of most makes of cuirass.

The *wadagami* and *oshitsuke-no-ita* were faced with an inner *e-gawa* band with a *fusegumi*-stitched *koberi-gawa* trim. Unlike other solid-plate pieces where a *fukurin* moulding was applied, the thickness of the *wadagami* made the use of a *fukurin* impossible. As such the *koberi-gawa* leather was cut wider so that it could be wrapped around the outside edge of the shoulder strap, glued and then tucked between the upper layer of the *wadagami* and the attached piece of *nerigawa* immediately below it.

CORDING AND TOGGLES: *MARU-HIMO* AND *KOHAZE*

Protruding from the upper outside-edge surface of the *wadagami* near the forward edge of the *shoji-no-ita* and around the middle of the erect plate were two closed loops of cord called the *sode-tsuke-no-gumi-wa*. These closed loops were threaded with short oblong metal fixtures called *sode-tsuke-no-kuda*. The *sode-tsuke-no-gumi-wa* were anchoring points that allowed the large *ō-sode* shoulder guards to be secured to the shoulder straps. The *sode-tsuke-no-kuda,* which are also sometimes referred to as the *gumi-kanamono,* were threaded over the *sode-tsuke-no-gumi-wa* to help protect the latter from the wearing effects of the shoulder-guard cords. The *sode-tsuke-no-kuda* were initially just plain metal tubes about 1.5–2 cm in length but over time they gradually became more ornate and were often etched with decorative patterns matching whatever designs were being incorporated into other elements of the armour, such as the *fukurin* mouldings.

Suspended from the forward ends of the *wadagami* were the upper portions of the *takahimo* cords. The *takahimo* were a set of four closed loops of thick cord, the upper set of which hung from the forward ends of the *wadagami* while the lower, vertically aligned set protruded upward from the left- and right-hand sides of the *muna-ita*. The upper, male pair of *takahimo* cords were threaded with flat, lozenge-shaped toggles or frogs, called *kohaze*. These were usually about 4.5–5 cm in length and were generally made from copper with a gilt finish. Like the *sode-tsuke-no-kuda*, the *kohaze* were traditionally quite plain, but over time it became common to decorate them with engraved designs.

The lower, female pair of *takahimo* cords were strung with a small, generally oval-shaped metal bead-like fixture called a *seme-kohaze*. The *seme-kohaze* was drilled with a pair of aligned holes that allowed it to slide up and down over the parallel lengths of cord that formed the closed loop of the lower *takahimo*. The combination of *takahimo* cords was what secured the front of the cuirass to the back of the cuirass and allowed it to be worn suspended over the shoulders.

Securing the upper male and lower female *takahimo* together was achieved by inserting the *kohaze* of the upper fastening cord through the closed loop end on the top end of the corresponding vertically aligned lower female *takahimo* cord. The *seme-kohaze* on the female *takahimo* was then slid upwards to trap the toggled end of the male *takahimo*, which made it impossible to withdraw the toggle back through the small, tightened end loop of the female *takahimo*.

A *sode-tsuke-no-gumi-wa* on a *wadagami*. Numerous details are visible. Note the *koberi-gawa* edge trim and *fusegumi* piping. Also note the leather-sheathed cord and the etched floral design on the tubular *kuda*.

Exactly what material was used to make the *takahimo* cords on most late classical and early medieval-period cuirasses is not entirely clear due to a lack of extant examples. Surviving examples from the latter part of the Kamakura period were primarily made from lengths of braided cord that were sheathed in red *go-sei-aka-gawa* or other varieties of *koberi-gawa*. Over time *takahimo* made from unsheathed lengths of braided hemp, cotton, and silk cord were also introduced, with solid or multicoloured varieties of silk braid *maru-himo*, or 'round cord', eventually becoming one of the most common materials utilized for this purpose. To help the cords bear the heavy weight of the cuirass, they were generally braided around an inner core of sturdy fibres, which helped prevent the braided cord from stretching under the weight of the cuirass.

To help protect the *takahimo*, *sode-tsuke-no-gumi-wa* and other lengths of cord that protruded from the surfaces of the *yoroi* from wear, armour makers gradually started to line the openings that the cords exited through with gilded copper grommets called *shidome*. These helped protect the cords from the edges of the solid-plate surfaces, which over time could cause the cords to fray as they were drawn back and forth across them in a saw-like manner due to the swaying movements of the armour pieces that were suspended from them.

THE 'BOWSTRING RUNNING LEATHER': *TSURUBASHIRI-GAWA*

One of the most visible and attractive features of cuirass made in the *yoroi* style was the *tsurubashiri-gawa*, 'bowstring running leather'. This was a large panel of generally ornately stencilled *e-gawa* that was fitted over the front face of a *yoroi* to prevent the bowstring of the warrior's *yumi* (bow) catching and damaging the *sane-gashira* when an arrow was released. Likewise, the *tsurubashiri-gawa* also prevented the lamellar board from fouling the bowstring and interfering when the bow was being drawn. The need for the *tsurubashiri-gawa* was amplified by the fact that the only practical way to fire a bow while mounted was to release the arrow directly across the front of the body. Furthermore, the large helmets worn by the samurai made it difficult to draw the bowstring up to and parallel with the general area of the mouth in the usual manner. For this reason, warriors learned to draw and release their bows closer to the base of the neck, which in turn brought the bowstring into close proximity to the upper chest area.

The *tsurubashiri-gawa* was always made from the same pattern or design of *e-gawa* covering that was used to face the *kanagu mawari* and other solid-plate portions of the set of armour. In some cases another piece of more durable leather was used to back the *e-gawa* front panel. The actual cut of the *tsurubashiri-gawa* was

---

Above: A rare view of a *yoroi* with the *tsurubashiri-gawa* pulled back. The *tsurubashiri-gawa* was fitted over the façade of the cuirass to prevent the bowstring of a *yumi* from snagging on the *sane-gashira* of the scales.

Left: A close-up of the *tsurubashiri* panel fitted to façade of a *yoroi*. The panel is made from two layers of thick leather. The surface layer features a theme of mythical *shishi* gambolling against a background of foliage interspersed with red peonies. Note the *koberi-gawa* edge trim and *fusegumi* piping. The *tsurubashiri-gawa* is secured in place by cords that have been strung through eyelets in the corners of the protective panel. Note that the *waidate* should not cap the right side of the cuirass, but should be worn inside it, with the outer edge of the *yoroi* closing over it.

SAMURAI ARMOUR

almost square in shape with a vertical rectangular portion cut from the upper right-hand corner. This was because the *tsurubashiri-gawa* not only covered the front of the cuirass but also wrapped about one-third to half-way around the left-hand side of the *yoroi* to accommodate the full potential of the warrior's arc of fire while mounted with a bow.

The left- and right-hand sides and bottom edge of the *tsurubashiri-gawa* were trimmed with *fusegumi* and *koberi-gawa*. The upper horizontal edge was rolled back, pressed flat and stitched on the reverse to create a crisp, straight line so that the *tsurubashiri-gawa* butted tight up against the underside of the *mizu-hiki* below the *keshō-no-ita*. The same was done with the upper horizontal edge of the *tsurubashiri-gawa* where it wrapped around the left-hand side of the cuirass. Small gilded copper split-shank rivets called *sanshō-no-byō*, or 'pepper corn rivets', were used to tack the *tsurubashiri-gawa* to the façade of the *yoroi* to ensure that it was drawn taut across the front of the cuirass.

AUXILIARY UPPER TORSO ARMOUR: *KYŪBI-NO-ITA* AND *SENDAN-NO-ITA*

While technically not part of the *yoroi*, two additional component pieces of armour that were suspended from the *wadagami* should be mentioned here. These were the *kyūbi-no-ita* and the *sendan-no-ita*, which were hung from the ends of the *wadagami* to protect the vulnerable *takahimo* cords. They also provided an additional degree of protection for the armpit areas of a warrior, particularly when the arms were raised to use a bow, for the angle of

NOMENCLATURE OF THE *KYŪBI-NO-ITA* AND *SENDAN-NO-ITA*

Terms marked with * can be applied to multiple pieces

Sendan-no-ita labels: Kanmuri-no-ita, Mizu-hiki, Ichi-no-ita, Ni-no-ita, Kedate*, Uname*, Hishinui-no-ita, Hishinui*, Tsuke-o*, Fukurin*, Koberi-gawa*, Suemon*, Fusegumi*, E-gawa*, Keshō-no-ita, Hassō-no-byō, Kozane*

Kyūbi-no-ita labels: Fukurin*, Koberi-gawa*, Fusegumi*, Suemon*, E-gawa*, Tsuke-o*, Hikae-no-o, Byō*

Early Forms of Samurai Armour

the shoulders during such movements tended to push the tops of these suspended pieces of armour downward and away from the centre, which in turn caused their lower ends to pivot out and upward so they covered some of the exposed areas of the armpits. While it is unlikely that the *kyūbi-no-ita* or the *sendan-no-ita* were designed to do anything but protect the *takahimo*, armour makers appear gradually to have recognized how certain body movements affected the positioning of these suspended pieces and so they revised their designs to capitalize on this unanticipated benefit.

The *sendan-no-ita* was suspended from the right-hand *wadagami*. It consisted of a solid metal upper plate called the *kanmuri-no-ita* and a number of attached suspended lamellar sections. The majority of the *kanmuri-no-ita* were shaped like a wide tombstone with outer edges that briefly flared upward before dropping back down. As a solid metal plate, the *kanmuri-no-ita* of the *sendan-no-ita* was finished in the same manner as the other *kanagu mawari* pieces of the armour grouping, being faced with an *e-gawa* centre panel that was trimmed with *fusegumi*-piped *koberi-gawa* and capped with a gilt *fukurin*. It was common for most early medieval examples of *sendan-no-ita* to be decorated with a large gilded copper chrysanthemum-shaped fixture called a *suemon*, which would be mounted in the centre of the *kanmuri-no-ita*. The back side of the plate was sometimes finished with the same *e-gawa* as was used to face the *kanmuri-no-ita*, though it was not uncommon for the same material as was employed to finish the undersides of the *wadagami* to be utilized. A closed metal ring protruded from the middle of the back face of the plate. Two additional rings were set into the left- and right-hand sides of the *kanmuri-no-ita* along its lower edge just below the notched step on the back of the plate behind the *keshō-no-ita*.

Affixed to the inward stepped lower edge of the *kanmuri-no-ita* were the suspended *sane-ita*, which were assembled and laced in an identical manner to the *yoroi*. A *keshō-no-ita* was applied to secure the two portions of the *sendan-no-ita* together. Two or sometimes four *hassō-no-byō* were used to anchor the suspended *sane-ita* to the *kanmuri-no-ita* via the cosmetic board with the rivets being arranged in two horizontally aligned pairs when four *hassō-no-byō* were utilized. The three suspended lames were referred to in descending order as the *ichi-no-ita*, *ni-no-ita* and the

When mounted, the warrior's arc of fire with the *yumi* was restricted. This was in part due to the long length of the bows, which prevented them from easily being moved to the right side of the horse's back. It was also because warriors were taught use their right arms to draw, seat and release arrows, which were therefore directed to the left.

lowermost *sane-ita* as the *hishinui-no-ita*. The lamellar construction of the *sendan-no-ita* was important as it allowed the suspended pendant-like section of armour to collapse onto itself so that it did not interfere with the movements of the warrior's right arm as he wielded his bow or sword.

The *tsuke-o* cord that was used to attach the *sendan-no-ita* to the *wadagami* was strung through the lower two rings on the back of the *kanmuri-no-ita* first and was then drawn up and through the upper ring, with each end of the cord passing through in the opposite direction, which created a triangle of cord between the three eyelets. The loose ends were then tied around the *takahimo* or through a closed loop of cord threaded with *sode-tsuke-no-kuda* hung from the end of the *wadagami* to secure the *sendan-no-ita* if one was included in the construction of the *yoroi*.

The *kyūbi-no-ita* differed from the *sendan-no-ita* in that it comprised a single long, subtly arched rectangular metal plate that was generally cut so that the plate tapered in width from top to bottom. Though narrower, the upper portion of the *kyūbi-no-ita* was always the same shape as the *kanmuri-no-ita* of the *sendan-no-ita*. It was also finished in the same manner as the *kanmuri-no-ita* of the *sendan-no-ita* with the exception that as a single solid plate the stencilled leather coverings, piping and *fukurin* encompassed the entire façade of the *kyūbi-no-ita*. A decorative *suemon* was commonly fitted to the upper half portion of the *kyūbi-no-ita*, generally being offset somewhere between the middle and the top half of the plate.

Scholars believe that the earliest examples of *kyūbi-no-ita* were more than likely assembled from lamellar pieces like the *sendan-no-ita*. Two factors seem to have influenced the transition to a solid plate, both of which stemmed from the use of the bow as the warrior's primary weapon. When the *kyūbi-no-ita* was made in lamellar fashion, the lower *sane-ita* flopped around due to the fact that they were secured together by lacing. The irregular and uncontrolled movements of a lamellar *kyūbi-no-ita* more than likely interfered with the draw and release of the bowstring. Constructing the *kyūbi-no-ita* as a solid plate resolved this issue. Fashioning it from metal also greatly enhanced the protective abilities of the *kyūbi-no-ita*, which was important as the upper left armpit area of the torso was one of the most exposed areas of the body of a warrior when he was sighting his bow. Thus warriors welcomed the extra coverage and protection offered by the *kyūbi-no-ita*.

The reverse was generally finished in the same manner as the *kanmuri-no-ita* of the *sendan-no-ita*. A gilded copper eyelet was mounted centrally behind where the *suemon* fixture was mounted on the facing side of the plate. This was strung with a cord, or *tsuke-o*, that was knotted in place with a decorative lark's head knot so that the *kyūbi-no-ita* could be secured to the *takahimo* or *wadagami* in the same manner as the *sendan-no-ita*.

Some *kyūbi-no-ita* also featured an additional long closed loop of cord called a *hikae-no-o* secured to the lower right-hand edge of the plate. The *hikae-no-o* could be looped around the *takahimo* to anchor the bottom end of the *kyūbi-no-ita* in place to prevent it from

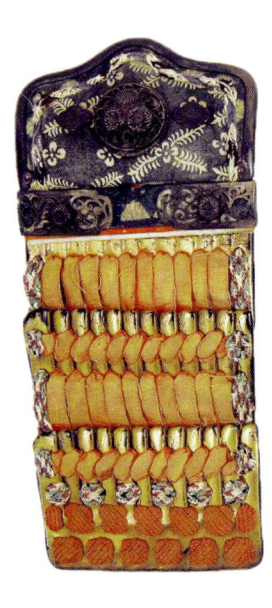

The *kyūbi-no-ita* and *sendan-no-ita* from an *ō-yoroi*. The *kyūbi-no-ita* was assembled from laced-together *sane-ita* that allowed it to flex. This prevented it from interfering with the movements of the warrior's right arm as he set and released arrows. The smooth, rigid design of the *sendan-no-ita* help to prevent bowstrings from catching on it. It also reduced movement of this piece that could interfere with the use of a bow.

EARLY FORMS OF SAMURAI ARMOUR

swinging. This may have been something that warriors preferred when they were not engaged in battle to help stop the *kyūbi-no-ita* from scarring the stencilled design on the *tsurubashiri-gawa*. Some examples of *sendan-no-ita* were also fitted with *hikae-no-o*.

THIGH ARMOUR: *KUSAZURI*

From the base of the *yoroi* were suspended three trapezoid *kusazuri*. The *mae-no-kusazuri* and *hitsushiki-no-kusazuri* on the oldest examples of *yoroi* were assembled from four *sane-ita*, each lame of which was slightly longer than the next in descending order. These were referred to in descending order as *ichi-no-ita* (first board), *ni-no-ita* (second board), *san-no-ita* (third board) and the lowermost section as the *hishinui-no-ita*.

The left-hand side section of hip armour, or *imuke-no-kusazuri*, was however assembled from five lamellar pieces, as was the *kusazuri* on the right side which was attached to the separate *waidate* plate, which is discussed further below. The addition of a fifth piece meant that the fourth *sane-ita* from the top was referred to as the *yon-no-ita* (fourth board) while the lowest one continued to be referred to as the *hishinui-no-ita*.

Other than for the fact that each of the suspended *sane-ita* that formed the *mae-no-kusazuri* and *hitsushiki-no-kusazuri* were horizontally longer than the *sane-ita* that they were suspended from, the *kusazuri* were fundamentally a continuation of the cuirass. The left-hand side portion of hip armour, however, was different in that it was attached to the *dō* by an intermediate band of *e-gawa*-faced leather called a *kōmori-tsuke*. The term *kōmori-tsuke*, which literally means 'bat leather', more than likely originated in a later century when upper chest protectors called *nodowa* were introduced. Most examples of *nodowa* featured a lower plate suspended from the main neck ring by an intermediate band of leather the cut of which somewhat resembles the outstretched wings of a bat in flight.

The visible portion of the *kōmori-tsuke* was about the same width as a *sane-ita*. While the *imuke-no-kusazuri* could have been laced directly to the cuirass, armour makers added the *kōmori-tsuke* to prevent the sword, *tanto* dagger and bowstring holder that were secured by belts and cords to the left side of the body from rubbing on and damaging the connective lacing along the left side of the cuirass. This was done as it was much easier to replace a worn panel of leather than it was to replace worn sections of lacing. Because the *kōmori-tsuke* was structural and expected to be subject to wear it was backed by another piece of leather. The panels were trimmed with *koberi-gawa* and *fusegumi* piping along the left and

A view of the rear of a *yoroi*. The trapezoid shape of the *kusazuri* is clearly visible in this image. Note the externally overlapping *saka-ita*, which was reverse-laced into the middle of the *ushiro-tateage*. This arrangement allowed the *oshitsuke-no-ita* and attached *wadagami* to be bent backwards, making the cuirass more comfortable to wear and easier to put on. Note the sturdy *agemaki-no-kan* that has been fitted to the middle of the *saka-ita*. Also note how the *nagakawa* continues past the *ushiro-tateage* on the right side of the *yoroi*. This allowed it to overlap the *waidate* side panel, which helped to ensure that no gaps were visible between these two pieces of armour.

right vertical edges, while the upper and lower edges were rolled back, tucked under and stitched closed to make a smooth edge. The *kōmori-tsuke* was laced to the lowest lame of the *nagakawa* using the same *odoshi-ge* as was utilized to lace the rest of the *yoroi*. The lacing itself was strung through the apertures in the lamellar board for the *nawame-garami* portions of the connective lacing. When the *kōmori-tsuke* was laced to the base of the cuirass the leather panel was turned upside down and laid so that its outer surface rested against the façade of the cuirass. After the panel had been secured in place it would be folded backwards over itself to reveal the *e-gawa* façade of the *kōmori-tsuke* as it hung from the arched-over panel.

The *ichi-no-ita* or uppermost lamellar board of the *imuke-no-kusazuri* was then laid over the lower-edge surface of the *kōmori-tsuke* and laced to the latter through the holes for the *nawame-garami*. Six split-shank *hassō-no-byō* arranged in pairs were also used to help anchor the uppermost *sane-ita* of the *kusazuri* to the *kōmori-tsuke*. In some cases a rawhide-strip-lined *keshō-no-ita* with accompanying *mizu-hiki* was fitted across the joint.

As the *imuke-no-kusazuri* was composed of the same number of sections as the front and back pendants of hip armour, the presence of the *kōmori-tsuke* caused it to hang several centimetres lower. This, however, was not considered unsightly by the Japanese, despite their strong penchant for symmetry. It was

WAIDATE NOMENCLATURE

Terms marked with * can be applied to multiple pieces

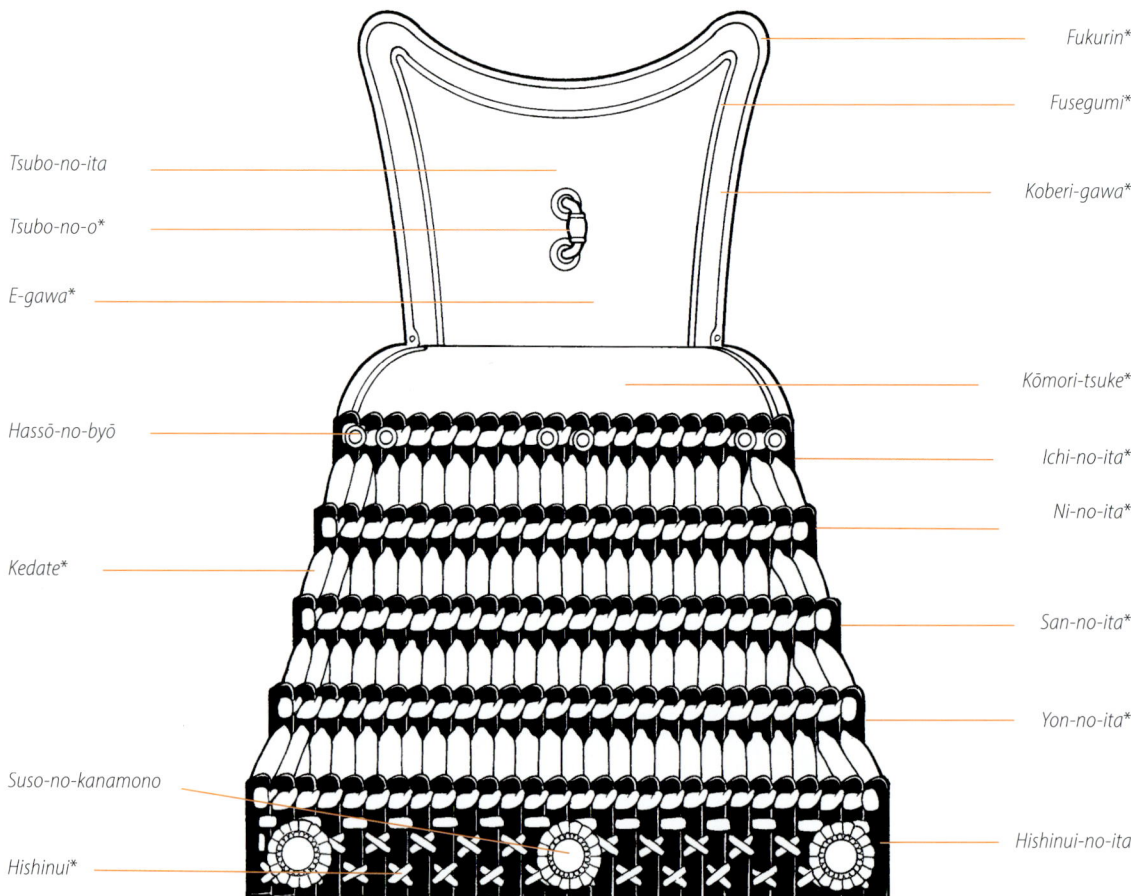

Tsubo-no-ita
Tsubo-no-o*
E-gawa*

Hassō-no-byō

Kedate*

Suso-no-kanamono

Hishinui*

Fukurin*
Fusegumi*
Koberi-gawa*

Kōmori-tsuke*

Ichi-no-ita*
Ni-no-ita*
San-no-ita*
Yon-no-ita*

Hishinui-no-ita

EARLY FORMS OF SAMURAI ARMOUR

instead considered beneficial, as the lower hang of the *kusazuri* on the side of the body meant that an even greater percentage of the thigh was protected, especially when the warrior was mounted. For when seated the thighs were drawn up higher and thus an even greater area of the upper leg was covered by the *kusazuri*. Likewise, the shorter back and front *kusazuri* made them somewhat less inconvenient and less likely to swing underneath the warrior when he attempted to seat himself in his saddle. By the 12th century, armour makers started to include a fifth board in the construction of the *mae-no-kusazuri* and *hitsushiki-no-kusazuri* so that all four hip-armour pendants hung evenly. *Katchū-shi* also began to divide the *hishinui-no-ita* on the front and back *kusazuri* into two equal-length pieces to better facilitate the movement of the legs, particularly when walking while wearing the cuirass. While this was not a universal feature it was fairly common. Other than for the physical separation between the two portions of the *hishinui-no-ita* the only visible difference between a single continuous *hishinui-no-ita* and the divided style was that the two short vertical lengths of *mimi-ito* were strung from the inside edges of the two *hishinui-no-ita* up to the *yon-no-ita*, which created an inverted V-shaped portion of *mimi-ito* lacing in the middle of the *kedate* lacing of the *yon-no-ita*.

AUXILIARY TORSO ARMOUR: *WAIDATE*

The *waidate* was a piece of secondary armour that filled the gap on the right side of the torso left exposed by the C-shaped design of the *yoroi*. Unlike the cuirass, only the suspended *kusazuri* portion of the *waidate* was of lamellar construction. The upper-body segment, called the *tsubo-no-ita* due to its resemblance to the shape of a form of narrow-mouthed Japanese jug, was made from a large shaped metal plate that was generally constructed of between two and four small metal plates riveted together, though occasionally a single solid plate was also utilized.

The earliest examples of *tsubo-no-ita* were generally rectangular plates that were taller than they were wide. The

A rare view of the open right side of a *yoroi*. The opening on the right side of the cuirass reflects the centuries-long challenge that had faced armour makers: how to fully protect the torso without making the armour difficult both to make and wear. Producing the main body of the *yoroi* as a single C-shaped piece limited potential vulnerable points. The decision to place the opening on the right most likely reflected the fact that the right flank was most commonly the target for attack, due to the manner in which mounted archers fought. Thus as the right side required extra protection it was deemed easier to produce the armour as a separate piece instead of incorporating a section of heavier armour into a single continuous design of cuirass.

upper edge of the plate was shaped with a concave indentation to accommodate the underside of the arm while the entire plate was rolled to give it a subtle horizontal curvature that allowed it to better contour to the side of the torso. Over time the shape of the *tsubo-no-ita* changed so that it tapered from top to bottom with a subtle inward curve. The bottom edge of the plate was also arched up and outward so that the *tsubo-no-ita* sat more comfortably on the hip.

As one of the major pieces amongst the *kanagu mawari*, the *tsubo-no-ita* portion of the *waidate* was finished in the usual manner, with the façade of the plate being covered with a panel of *e-gawa* that would be edged with a *fusegumi*-piped *koberi-gawa*. The back would also be faced with leather and the plate capped with a gilt copper *fukurin*. At least five *shidome*-fitted apertures would be drilled through the *tsubo-no-ita*. Two of these were generally set somewhere along the upper half of the vertical middle line of the plate while a third was often set off to the left-hand front edge of the plate about mid-height between the two apertures. It was common for a closed loop of cord, called the *tsubo-no-o*, to protrude from the two central *shidome*-fitted apertures on the *tsubo-no-ita*. Likewise, another smaller closed loop of cord, often threaded with a *kuda*, generally hung from the third aperture.

The purpose of the three cord-strung apertures was to provide anchoring points to secure the *kata-o*, or the 'shoulder cord', which was worn diagonally across the body like a shoulder strap to help keep the *waidate* from sliding downward and out of position. While there were several alternative ways of fastening the *kata-o*, it was generally fastened around the *tsubo-no-o*, commonly with a lark's head knot. The ends of the cord were then passed behind the body up to the left shoulder where it was looped around the neck. From there they were drawn downward across the chest and secured to the *sode-tsuke-no-kuda*-threaded closed loop of cord hanging from the forward upper edge of

Front and back views of a *waidate*. The separate *tsubo-no-ita* side plate of the *waidate* is clearly visible in the second image. The folded-over method of securing the *komori-no-tsuke* intermediary panel of the leather is also evident. Note the use of two different patterns of *e-gawa* to cover the front and back faces of these plates. Also note the extended interior length of the *tsubo-no-o* that is used to fasten the *waidate* over the shoulder and to the side of the body.

the *tsubo-no-ita*. If the *tsubo-no-ita* was designed without the loop of cord, as was sometimes the case, then the cord of the *kata-o* was simply secured through or to the *tsubo-no-o*.

The other two grommet-fitted apertures were located near the lower left- and right-hand edges of the *tsubo-no-ita*. Closed loops of cord threaded with *sode-tsuke-no-kuda* generally protruded from these openings as well. These provided anchoring points to secure a cord, called a *koshi-o*, or 'waist cord', around the hips, which helped to keep the *waidate* securely seated in position at the side of the torso over the warrior's right hip.

It was quite common for warriors to wear the *waidate* and some of the other items of armour for the extremities while they were waiting to go into action, to save time when it came to donning the *yoroi*. When worn in this way these items were referred to as the *ko-gusoku*. The combination of items that were included in the *ko-gusoku* evolved over time from just the *waidate* and *suneate* shin guards to include also a *kote* armoured sleeve and *nodowa* upper chest protector by the latter part of the 14th century.

It should be noted that the *waidate* had to be secured in place using the *kata-o* and *koshi-o* cords before the *yoroi* itself could be worn. The *koshi-o* is shown secured around the exterior of the *yoroi* in many reference sources, possibly necessitated by the fact that when such items are displayed there is no internal structure to tie the *koshi-o* cords around. This, however, was not how the *waidate* were designed to be worn. Furthermore, this was unnecessary, particularly on later-period examples of cuirasses made in the *yoroi* style, which incorporated sturdy closed loops of leather-sheathed cords called *kurijime-no-o-no-wana*, or 'pull cord tight loop'. These were often anchored to one or both of the lower right-hand corners of the cuirass to provide anchor points to secure a sturdy cord, referred to as a *dō-jime*, which could be cinched tight and tied to draw the cuirass closed around the waist, which in turn helped to further secure the *waidate* in position. Prior to the introduction of the *kurijime-no-o-no-wana*, the *dō-jime* was simply lark's-head-looped through itself and drawn tight around the waist and tied to secure the cuirass in position.

It should also be noted that *yoroi* featured cords affixed to both edges on the right side of the cuirass called *hikiawase-no-o*, or 'draw-

A warrior wearing the *ko-gusoku*, which comprised the *waidate*, a *kote*, the *suneate* and in some cases a *nodowa* upper chest protector. These items were worn when action was deemed imminent in order to speed up the process of donning the complex *yoroi* style of cuirass. (Image © and courtesy of the Kyōto Costume Museum)

together cords'. After the *yoroi* was put on, these too were tied together over the middle of the *tsubo-no-ita* portion of the *waidate* to help ensure there was no exposed gap down the right of the torso between the cuirass and *waidate*. Thus the *hikiawase-no-o* only added further to the number of bindings that helped to keep the *waidate* firmly in seated position on the right side of the torso.

The *kusazuri* suspended from the *tsubo-no-ita* was secured to the side plate in the same manner as the hip armour was attached to the left side of the cuirass. The upper edge of the intermediate *kōmori-tsuke* leather band was laced to the face of the *tsubo-no-ita* several centimetres above its lower edge through a series of pre-drilled holes. When the *kōmori-tsuke* was folded backwards over itself and the *kusazuri*, the closed loops of cord that were used to tie the side plate in place at the waist were hidden underneath the connective leather band.

The seam between the *kōmori-tsuke* and the suspended lamellar section of the *kusazuri* was likewise secured in the same manner as was used to join the *imuke-no-kusazuri* to the intermediate leather band on the left side of the cuirass. If a *keshō-no-ita* and decorative *mizu-hiki* strips were fitted across the connective seam on the left side of the *yoroi*, then these same fixtures would also be applied to the seam between the *kōmori-tsuke* and suspended lamellar portion of the *waidate*.

THE *YOROI* IN PRACTICAL USE

The average suspended length of a complete *yoroi* during the Heian period, when measured from the upper edge of the *shoji-no-ita* to the lower skirt of the *kusazuri*, was generally 80–90 cm, which meant that the hip armour terminated just above the knees of most warriors, whose average height during that time period was around 155 cm according to the Tōkyō University Professor Hiramoto Yoshisuke. By the Kamakura period the overall length of the *yoroi* had been shortened by about 10 cm due to the trend that had occurred over the centuries towards the production of *kozane* of smaller proportions.[10]

While the weight varied from cuirass to cuirass, based on the ratio of materials that were used to assemble the *yoroi*, such as the mixture of *tetsu-zane* to *kawa-zane*, the average *yoroi* style of cuirass, accompanied by a *waidate*, *kyūbi-no-ita* and *sendan-no-ita*, was generally about 16–18 kg. The helmet, shoulder guards and other equipment could increase this load to 26–30 kg, which was quite substantial considering that the average weight of a Japanese male would have been around 55 kg.[11]

The weight, while considerable, was bearable as long as a warrior was mounted and was not required to wear the *yoroi* for a prolonged period. For the vast majority of the weight of the *yoroi* was, by the nature of its design, borne upon the shoulders. This was due to the fact that the *yoroi* was intentionally made to be larger than the proportions of the warrior it encapsulated so that the space between the interior surface of the cuirass and the body of the individual within would create a buffer zone that kept the protruding tips of arrows that were stopped by, but lodged in, the armour away from the wearer's body. While there were obvious benefits to this design, it prevented the weight load of the cuirass from being distributed over or borne by other areas of the upper body.

This was not really an issue prior to the latter part of the 12th century as most engagements were relatively short in duration and were primarily fought on horseback. This allowed the cuirass to rest on the upper thighs and the back of the saddle for periods of time, which would provide relief to the shoulders, prolonging the warrior's ability to wear the armour. When the warrior was dismounted, however, the rigid,

Yoroi made prior to the later part of the 15th century were unable to sit erect like this late-Edo period cuirass, which has had the *sane-ita* secured together by lengths of leather thongs called *tomegawa*. Prior to the introduction of the structural ties, lamellar cuirasses like the *yoroi* would have collapsed telescope-like on themselves.

pill-box-like qualities of the *yoroi* that made it so effective for mounted archers made it impractical for warriors fighting on foot, who were weighed down and hobbled by the heavy and inflexible construction of the cuirass, the large dimensions of which made it unbalanced and awkward to move in.

Other factors also began to undermine the dominance of the *yoroi*, including the fact that it often took the better part of three-quarters of a year to produce one with its full complement of accompanying armour pieces. And while the weather could prolong production, limiting as it did when certain types of work could be done, such as the cutting of *nerigawa* and the application of *urushi*, the overall complexity and the sheer number of various parts and pieces that went into the construction of a *yoroi* and its additional pieces required a huge amount of time and man-hours to prepare and assemble.

For part and parcel with the production of the *yoroi* by the 12th century was a *kabuto*, a pair of *ō-sode*, a *waidate*, a *kyūbi-no-ita* and a *sendan-no-ita*, a single *kote* armoured sleeve (until the 13th century) and a pair of *suneate* shin guards, the entire ensemble of which created what was referred to as an *ō-yoroi*, or 'great armour'. In later centuries a *nodowa* upper chest protector and rudimentary form of facial armour called a *happuri* (described in detail in Volume II) were also commonly worn with the *ō-yoroi*, though the *happuri* was considered to be a separate accessory and not part of the standard ensemble of an *ō-yoroi*.[*]

---

[*] It should be noted that the 'ō' in the term ō-yoroi is sometimes referred to as being an honorific, or *bikago*, which is a form of beautifying prefix that the Japanese commonly add to nouns to demonstrate a respectful deference towards a person, place or thing. This, however, is not the case. The honorific is written using a single hiragana character 'o' that, alone, has no meaning. The compound word *ō-yoroi*, however, is written using two kanji characters, the first one of which is the character 'ō' for 'big' or 'great'.

SAMURAI ARMOUR

While the production time was of concern, then as now, time equals money, which meant that an *ō-yoroi* was anything but cheap. In *Samurai, Warfare and the State in Early Medieval Japan*, Karl Friday references 'one document from 1107' that records a set of *ō-yoroi* costing eighty *hiki* (rolls of silk), which Friday records as equal to the 'cost of eight short swords (uchi-gatana), and to several months' wages for an ordinary worker of the period'. Eighty *hiki* had the same overall monetary value as eighty *koku*, with a single *koku* being valued at 150 kg of rice (180 litres), which was considered to be the amount of rice that one man would consume in one year. One *koku* was valued at approximately

Left: An excellent representation of a warrior from the 11th century wearing the *ō-yoroi*. Note the position of the *kyūbi* and *sendan-no-ita*. (Image © and courtesy of the Kyōto Costume Museum)

Right: Right-side view: the fact that the *waidate* is a separate piece of armour is not noticeable once the armour has been securely tied in place. The protective benefits offered by the *sendan-no-ita* are also visible from this angle. When mounted, very little of the warrior's body was exposed to an opponent. Even the unprotected portions of the lower thighs were largely covered by the suspended *kusazuri* when the warrior was seated in the saddle. (Image © and courtesy of the Kyōto Costume Museum)

EARLY FORMS OF SAMURAI ARMOUR

one *ryō*, or 16.5 g of gold in the late 16th century, which came in the form of a large flat coin. As monetary values were said to have been relatively consistent from the 10th through 16th centuries in Japan, this would mean that an average set of *ō-yoroi* during that time would have cost the equivalent of around $55,000 USD to produce in 2015 gold prices. While this figure may be mathematically correct, efforts by various museums in Japan in recent decades to accurately reconstruct sets of *ō-yoroi* using historically correct construction techniques have commonly taken two to three years to complete and cost several times more to produce than the above estimate.

Left: Left-side view. The need to protect the exposed bow arm, which initially led to the introduction of a single *kote* some time in the 11th century, is better appreciated when a warrior is viewed from this angle. The benefit of using a *kōmori-no-tsuke* to secure the *imuke-no-kusazuri* is apparent when the cuirass is seen with the various items of equipment that were worn with the *yoroi* all securely tied in positon. It is easy to appreciate how silk lacing would quickly be damaged by the *tantō*, *tachi* and spare bowstring holder that were secured to the left side of the *yoroi*. (Image © and courtesy of the Kyōto Costume Museum)

Right: A rear view of the same warrior. Note the complex arrangement of cords that were used to secure the massive *ō-sode* shoulder guards. (Image © and courtesy of the Kyōto Costume Museum)

The various campaigns of the Genpei War during the latter part of the 12th century appear to have been something of a turning point for many warriors. For though the *yoroi* was considered the only suitable form of armour for a warrior of rank, its many drawbacks became increasingly apparent as warriors trained to fight on horseback frequently found themselves fighting on foot and even at sea in their burdensome *yoroi*, such as during the famous naval battle of Dan-no-Ura in the Shimonoseki Strait in 1185.

THE RISE OF THE *HARAMAKI*

Had the *yoroi* been the only form of armour fielded at that time, the obvious limitations of its design for warriors when fighting in a dismounted role may not have been so immediately apparent. This, however, was not the case. For another, far more practical design of cuirass called the *haramaki*, or 'belly wrap', had existed alongside the *yoroi* since its introduction in the early 10th century. In fact, the *haramaki*, which was fundamentally the equivalent of a 9th century *migi-hikiawase* (right side pulled close) *keikō* from the proto-historical period had been one of the evolutionary predecessors of the *yoroi*. And though the *haramaki* design was historically older than the *yoroi*, those produced after the introduction of the *yoroi* were assembled using the same basic construction techniques as the *yoroi* and were therefore not as archaic as the antiquity of their design would tend to suggest.

The *haramaki* had been retained for use by low-ranking, foot-borne retainers, whose primary duties revolved around supporting the mounted samurai. This often required the retainers to run alongside their mounted lords to support them during engagements, which they did by carrying additional quivers loaded with arrows and pole-arms to dispatch enemy riders who had been felled by their lord. A *yoroi* would have severely hampered the ability of a retainer to perform such tasks, even if its cost of production had not already precluded its use by these lower ranks.

The *haramaki* was almost everything the *yoroi* was not, both by design and by intent. It was simple, relatively form-fitting, easy to wear, fairly light and most importantly well suited to the needs of a foot-borne warrior. This was in part due to the fact that its shape allowed the cuirass to be secured at the waist, which meant that some of its weight rested on the hips. This allowed retainers to support the weight of the cuirass for a longer period of time. It also allowed them to run, as the *haramaki* did not ride up and down on the body and hammer down on the shoulders of the wearer, since it was secured fairly tightly around the waist by an independent length of cord.

As the *haramaki* was made for retainers, its construction was intentionally kept simple, without the decorative details and fixtures that were standard to even the most rudimentary examples of *yoroi*. This helped reduce the weight of the cuirass, as did the fact that they were often fabricated without, or with only a limited number of, expensive *tetsu-zane*. The hip armour was also made from a larger number of narrow *kusazuri*, which greatly enhanced the ability of the wearer to walk or run unhindered.

While the *haramaki* is known to have existed both before the *yoroi* and alongside the latter after its introduction, it does not appear in any historical Japanese records until the later part of the 12th century, with the first visual representation being found in the *Ban Dainagon Ekotoba,* or the 'Tale of the Courtier Ban Dainagon', scrolls. The oldest extant examples, which are housed in the prestigious Ōyamazumi Jinja Museum collection, also date to this same period. The fact that the *haramaki* was fundamentally ignored for most of its early history alongside the *yoroi* was most likely a reflection of its association with low-ranking retainers, like the hooded and black-clad assistants of Japanese *bunraku* puppet masters, who are meant to be ignored so as to not take away from the performance of the master they support, who, dressed in formal attire and without a hood, is meant to be highly visible to the audience.

The *haramaki* only began to receive recognition when it shifted from being an item of armour worn exclusively by low-ranking retainers to one that was also used by mounted, high-ranking warriors, by which time the *haramaki* had begun to be constructed with some of the same decorative trappings that were typical of the prestigious *yoroi*. Only then, when the *haramaki* of a samurai could be clearly differentiated from the simple *haramaki* of a retainer, did such pieces start to be included in the items that were offered at shrines and temples across Japan, whose alcoves and *kura* storehouses would ultimately house some of the oldest and only surviving examples of classical and early-period forms of Japanese armour.

The Genpei War appears to have been the event that brought the humble *haramaki* to the attention of many high-ranking samurai, who, unaccustomed and unprepared to fight dismounted, suddenly found their impressive *yoroi* highly cumbersome and impractical outside of the formal mounted archery duels they had been used to. Struggling forward on foot surrounded by their obviously far less fatigued retainers must have been a painful eye-opener for many samurai, especially when they realized that the *haramaki* design worn by their servants was actually a far more practical form of cuirass for fighting on foot.

The *haramaki* of the 10th, 11th and much of the 12th centuries generally had a *nagakawa* assembled from four long, generally oval *sane-ita*, though some early-period examples utilized only three *sane-ita*. These sections were constructed so as to be long enough to encompass the entire torso with sufficient additional length to create an overlap on the right side of the body, removing the need for a separate *waidate*. The overlap was arranged so that the back section of the cuirass extended further forward than the front part extended toward the back. The back vertical edge of the cuirass was always arranged so that it overlapped the front edge when the cuirass was closed around the torso. This was done to deny enemies a point where they could grab the cuirass in close-quarter fighting. For the back-over-front overlap meant that hands or weapons trying to snag the side of the armour would slip off, unable to find an edge to grasp. Naturally, this did not work from behind, but as most engagements were expected to be face-to-face against an opponent this was

A superb example of a mid-Edo period *dō-maru*. Originally referred to as a *haramaki*, this make of cuirass was later renamed the *dō-maru*. Other than for the *kanamono* fitted to the *hishinui-no-ita* of the *kusazuri*, this cuirass is a highly accurate representation of a high-quality example of 14th century *dō-maru*. Note the convex shape of the *kusazuri*. Also note the smoked *fusebe-gawa* that has been used to line the *wadagami* and *oshitsuke-no-ita*.

Samurai Armour

NOMENCLATURE OF THE *HARAMAKI* (10TH–14TH CENTURIES) AND *DŌ-MARU* (14TH–19TH CENTURIES)

Terms marked with * can be applied to multiple pieces

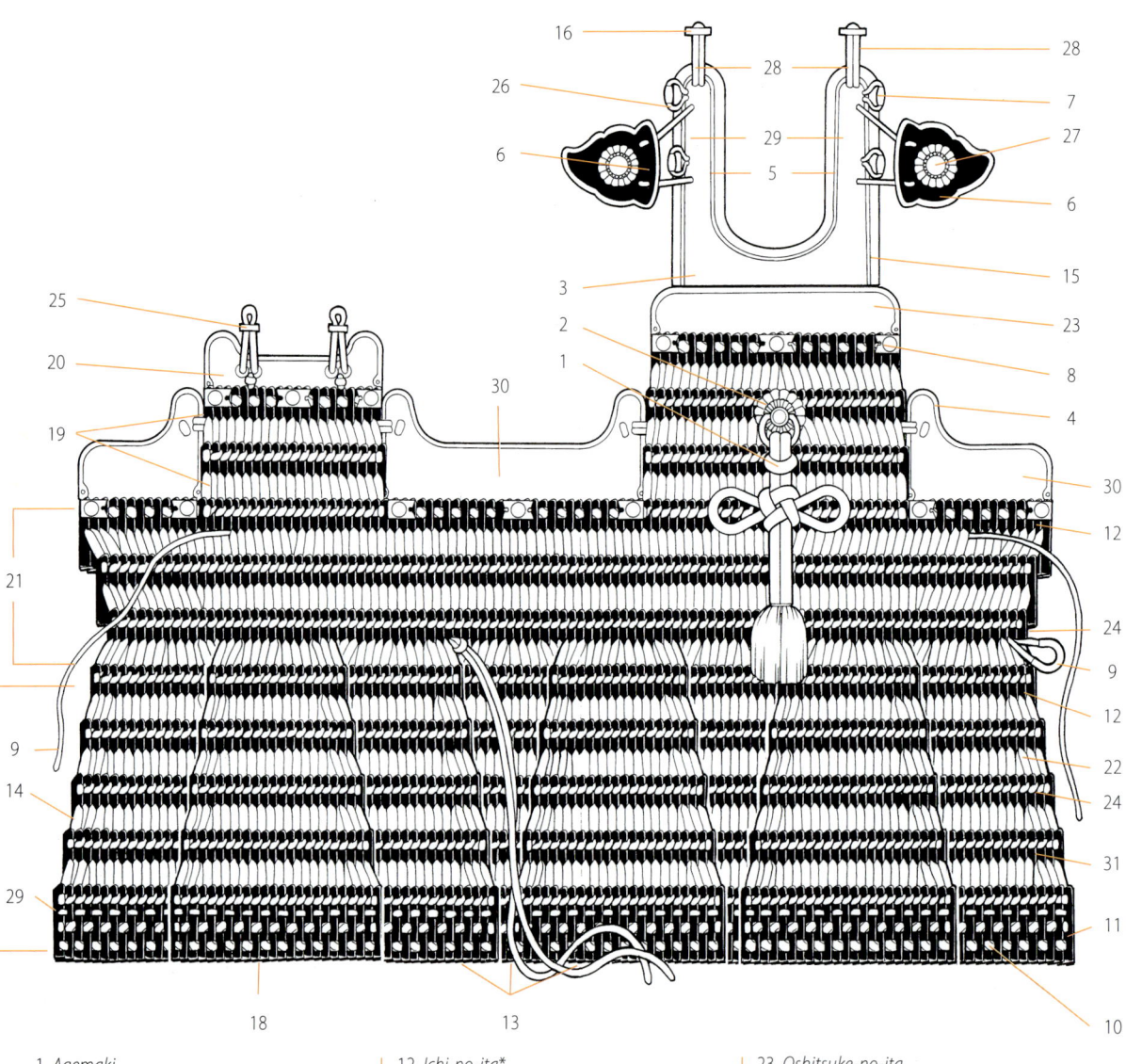

1. *Agemaki*
2. *Agemaki-no-kan*
3. *E-gawa**
4. *Fukurin**
5. *Fusegumi**
6. *Gyōyō**
7. *Gumi kanamono**
8. *Hassō-no-byō**
9. *Hikiawase-no-o**
10. *Hishinui**
11. *Hishinui-no-ita**
12. *Ichi-no-ita**
13. *Imuke-no-kusazuri*
14. *Kedate**
15. *Koberi-gawa**
16. *Kohaze**
17. *Kusazuri**
18. *Mae-no-kusazuri*
19. *Mae-tateage*
20. *Muna-ita*
21. *Nagakawa*
22. *Ni-no-ita**
23. *Oshitsuke-no-ita*
24. *San-no-ita**
25. *Seme-kohaze**
26. *Sode-tsuke-no-gumi-wa**
27. *Suemon*
28. *Takahimo**
29. *Wadagami**
30. *Waki-ita**
31. *Yon-no-ita**

considered to be the best arrangement. The success of this arrangement was borne out by the test of time, for it became common practice until the end of the Japanese feudal period in all cuirasses that had overlapping side panels for the rear sections always to overlap the front pieces. This was true for cuirasses that were designed with overlaps on the left side of the torso as well.

Unlike the *yoroi* of the late classical and early medieval periods where all four *sane-ita* of the *nagakawa* were generally of the same overall length or even increased slightly in length in descending order, the lamellar sections used to construct the *nagakawa* of a *haramaki* decreased in length from top to bottom. For example, the famous *murasaki-kawa odoshi dō-maru* in the Ōyamazumi Jinja Museum collection features an *ichi-no-ita* assembled from ninety *sane*. The lower *ni-no-ita* was constructed using ninety-eight *sane*. The *san-no-ita* was made from ninety-seven *kozane*, while the bottom section of the *nagakawa* was assembled using ninety-six *sane*. While subtle, the decreasing number of scales used to construct each descending section of the *nagakawa* after the *ichi-no-ita* helped to make the *haramaki* a more form-fitting design of cuirass.

Why the scale count of sections that formed the *nagakawa* of a *dō-maru* is used as a reference to explain the construction of the *nagakawa* of a *haramaki* requires some explanation. It is because the *haramaki* as described above was renamed the *dō-maru* in the early 14th century. Further compounding this confusion was the fact that the *haramaki* name was reassigned to yet another new form of cuirass that appeared sometime during the later part of the Kamakura period.

While it is easier to start simply by referring to the *haramaki* as the *dō-maru*, this would be historically incorrect. Thus it is important to understand that examples of *dō-maru* made prior to the early part of the 14th century were technically *haramaki*, and this text will therefore continue to use the term *haramaki* in reference to lamellar *migi-hikiawase ichi-mai-dō* until the late Kamakura version of *haramaki* is introduced later in this chapter.

The *mae-tateage* of the *haramaki* was composed of two short lengths of *sane-ita* while the *ushiro-tateage* was assembled from three sections. Initially the *muna-ita* and *oshitsuke-no-ita* were fundamentally the same in overall form as those on a *yoroi*, with *fukurin*-capped smoked leather or *e-gawa* facings, the latter of which were, however, devoid of *koberi-gawa* and *fusegumi* piping. One of the key differences with the *muna-ita* was that the lower pair of *takahimo* cords exited through apertures in the upper outside corners of the chest plate rather than

A *haramaki* (*dō-maru*) laid out flat to show the continuous *ichi-mai-dō* construction of this form of lamellar cuirass. The *kanagu mawari* are clearly visible in this image as all of the associated components are arranged around the base of the *nagakawa*. The two *kusazuri* on the outside edges of the cuirass are referred to as the *mete-no-kusazuri*, or right hip tassets, as they come together on the right side of the torso when the cuirass is closed around the body. The second tasset from the left is referred to as the *mae-no-kusazuri*, while the middle two are referred to as the *imuke-no-kusazuri* as they hang on the left side of the torso. The second and third from the right are referred to as the *ushiro-no-kusazuri*.

from below it as was the case with the *yoroi*. In some cases the *takahimo* cords were also strung so that they rose up behind the smoked-leather-faced *muna-ita*, which helped to protect them, as the early retainer-quality version of the *haramaki* was devoid of additional accoutrements such as a *kyūbi-no-ita* and a *sendan-no-ita*.

The *muna-ita* was constructed with a flat lower edge because, unlike the *yoroi*, the chest plate was laced directly to the upper lame of the *mae-tateage* via the holes in the *sane-ita* that were usually strung with the *nawame-garami* portions of the connective lacing. To ensure that the *muna-ita* was securely laced to the *ichi-no-ita* of the *mae-tateage* the lacing was strung in the cross-knots called *hishi-toji*, which should not be confused with *hishinui*; the latter term only applies to cross-knots strung along the lower edge of a *sane-ita*.

As the *haramaki* was initially designed to be worn by retainers, the face of the cuirass was not covered with a *tsurubashiri-gawa*; this would be unnecessary as the bow was a weapon reserved for warriors of rank.

The *oshitsuke-no-ita* was attached in the same manner as the *muna-ita*, using *hishi-toji* cross-knots to lace it directly to the *ichi-no-ita* of the *ushiro-tateage*. The joint was devoid of a *keshō-no-ita* and the accompanying *mizu-hiki* strips that were common to the *yoroi*. To protect the exposed *sane-gashira* along the joint, a long, rolled tube of paper was placed under the leather facing material just above the point where the upper edge of the *sane-ita* terminated to create a raised ridge called an *omeri* that helped to cap the *sane-gashira*. The *ushiro-tateage* was also made up of three regular *sane-ita* laced together in the conventional manner without the reverse-laced *agemaki-no-kan*-mounted *saka-ita* found on the *yoroi*.

As with the *yoroi*, the exposed upper edge of the *ichi-no-ita* of the *nagakawa* in the areas between the *mae-tateage* and the *ushiro-tateage* on both sides of the cuirass were capped with sections of leather that were pinned in place with small rivets to protect the *sane-gashira*.

The *wadagami* were devoid of *sode-tsuke-no-gumi-wa* as retainers were not provided with the large, static shield-like shoulder guards that were suspended from the shoulder straps of the *yoroi*.

Early examples of *haramaki* appear to have featured an arrangement of five hip-armour

A retainer wearing the *dō-maru* form of cuirass. Note the *gyōyō* resting on top of the warrior's shoulders. This was the original position for these fixtures, which eventually shifted forward to replace the *kyūbi* and *sendan-no-ita* on some later-period cuirasses. Also note the *happuri*, the oldest form of facial armour used by the samurai. (Image © and courtesy of the Kyōto Costume Museum)

A close-up view of the mae-tateage, muna-ita and waki-ita of a hon kozane dō-maru. Note the gilt fukurin that caps the kanagu mawari plates. Five colours of silk thread have been used to stitch the connective fusegumi piping that secures the koberi-gawa with the central panels of e-gawa. Also note the iri-hassō plates that help anchor the kanagu mawari to the lamellar sections of the cuirass. Note the small kohaze that secure the vertical edges of the waki-ita.

pendants referred to as *goken-no-kusazuri*. The front, left and back hip-armour pendants were attached in the same manner as on the *yoroi*. The *kusazuri* on the right-hand side of the cuirass, however, was by necessity divided down the middle to accommodate the vertical opening down the right side of the torso.

As the *haramaki* increasingly became associated with retainers and dismounted warriors, smiths started to divide the *kusazuri* further to better facilitate the movements of the legs while wearing the armour. Initially this encompassed splitting the front, back and rear hip-armour pendants in half from the *ni-no-ita* downward, which retained the *goken-no-kusazuri* format around the lower edge of the cuirass. This practice was soon abandoned, however, in favour of dividing the hip armour into eight independent *kusazuri*. This number was eventually reduced to seven as the design of the *haramaki* was refined further over the course of the 11th and 12th centuries and the armour makers veered away from the squared-off shape of the *yoroi* in favour of creating a *nagakawa* for the *haramaki* that was generally oval in horizontal cross-section.

The two *kusazuri* that hung down the right side of the torso came to be known as the *mete-saki* or *mete-no-kusazuri*, which literally means 'horse hand hip armour', due to the fact that the Japanese generally held the reins in the right hand. Thus *mete* was sometimes used to described the right side of something. The rear two tassets were called the *ushiro-kusazuri*, while the term *imuke-no-kusazuri*, which had originally been applied to the single large left hand tasset on the *yoroi*, was applied to the left rear, left side and front left side *kusazuri* collectively. The front central tasset continued to be called the *mae-no-kusazuri*.

One additional feature of the *haramaki* was a pair of apricot-shaped shoulder guards called *gyōyō*. While technically not part of the *haramaki*, the *gyōyō*, like the *kyūbi-no-ita* and *sendan-no-ita* of the *yoroi*, were a fundamental and intrinsic aspect of the retainer's *haramaki*. When *gyōyō* were first introduced is unclear, though it was more than likely sometime during the latter part of the 11th century, for they were apparently quite common by the end of the Heian period, based on images of retainers documented in historical scrolls such as the *Nenjū Gyōji Emaki* or the 'Annual Observance Scroll' and the *Heike no Monogatari* or 'Tale of the Heike'.

The *gyōyō* were originally quite large, generally triangular leaf-shaped metal plates with a subtle side-to-side convex arch. The wide upper end of each *gyōyō* was secured by means of cords or toggles to the outside edges of the left and right *wadagami* of the *haramaki* so that the *gyōyō* rested on top of the shoulders like spaulders, ostensibly to provide a degree of protection for the latter.

The willingness of more practical-minded samurai of rank to wear this style of cuirass irrespective of social stereotypes that reserved it exclusively for low-ranking retainers was another milestone in the evolution of Japanese armour. For it not only signified that the manner in which warfare was being conducted in Japan had changed, it also demonstrated a willingness on the part of some samurai to brush aside established social norms to achieve a goal. In other words, if a warrior could fight more effectively in what was perceived to be a less dignified form of armour, then that was the armour they were prepared to wear.

This is not to say that the majority of high-ranking samurai were prepared to don the simple *haramaki* of their retainers, for they were not. They were, however, prepared to utilize examples of *haramaki* that, like the *yoroi*, displayed all the visible indicators that had come to signify the owner's status as a warrior of rank.

This started a relatively short-lived trend around the end of the 12th century and into the early 13th century where a hybrid form of *haramaki* with *yoroi*-like features was created, called the *dō-maru yoroi*. In reality, however, the *dō-maru yoroi* was fundamentally nothing more than a squared-off *haramaki* with a *tsurubashiri-gawa* fitted across the face of the cuirass and a *saka-ita* inserted into the construction of the *ushiro-tateage*. It was, however, liberally decorated with the array of aesthetic details that were virtually universal to the *yoroi*, including *keshō-no-ita*, *mizu-hiki* and *agemaki-no-kan*. The *kanagu mawari* were faced with *e-gawa* and trimmed with *koberi-gawa* with *fusegumi* piping and capped with *fukurin*. *Kyūbi-no-ita* and *sendan-no-ita* were suspended from the *wadagami*, which were fitted with *shoji-no-ita* and *sode-tsuke-no-gumi-wa* from which the large *ō-sode*-style shoulder guards were suspended.

The effort to make the *haramaki* more palatable by dressing it up as a *yoroi*, however, nullified some of the advantages that had originally attracted some samurai to the *haramaki* design. Key amongst these was the squaring of the cuirass, which took away its ability to rest on the hips, since this had helped to take some of the load off the warrior's shoulders. Its unencumbered simplicity was also destroyed as it was festooned with fixtures such as the *kyūbi-no-ita* and *sendan-no-ita* that many warriors had come to see as being more of a hindrance in battle than a help. Thus the *dō-maru yoroi* faded out in favour of heavily

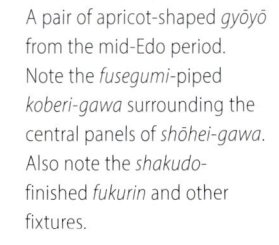

A pair of apricot-shaped *gyōyō* from the mid-Edo period. Note the *fusegumi*-piped *koberi-gawa* surrounding the central panels of *shōhei-gawa*. Also note the *shakudo*-finished *fukurin* and other fixtures.

A late 19th century photograph by Ogawa Kazumasa that depicts a retainer from the 13th century. Note the truncated *hara-ate* style of cuirass that was indicative of low-ranking warriors. Typically for most retainers, the warrior is without other items of armour except for a rudimentary pair of *kote* armour sleeves.

upgraded examples of cuirass made in the correct form of a *haramaki*, that like the *yoroi* were constructed from *ichi-mai-maze*-assembled lames.

To accommodate the massive shoulder guards, *sode-tsuke-no-gumi-wa* were added to the *wadagami* and an *agemaki-no-kan* was affixed to the middle of one of the lames of the *ushiro-tateage* to provide an anchor point for the various stabilizing cords of the *ō-sode*. In some instances *shoji-no-ita* were also fitted though their presence was not universal.

The front of the cuirass was not covered with a *tsurubashiri-gawa,* which was seen as unnecessary, and the cumbersome *kyūbi-no-ita* and *sendan-no-ita* were discarded. In their place a smaller design of *gyōyō* was suspended from the forward ends of the *wadagami* to cover the *takahimo*.

Around the middle of the 13th century a new feature called *waki-ita*, or armpit plates, was introduced to the construction of both the *haramaki* and *yoroi*. The *waki-ita* were solid plates, generally made from metal, that were designed to fill some of the void that existed above the *nagakawa* in the underarm area on a cuirass between the *mae-tateage* and *ushiro-tateage*. Modelled on the upper edge of the *waidate*, the *waki-ita* were shaped to conform to the horizontal curvature of the torso along

NOMENCLATURE OF THE *HARA-ATE*

Terms marked with * can be applied to multiple pieces

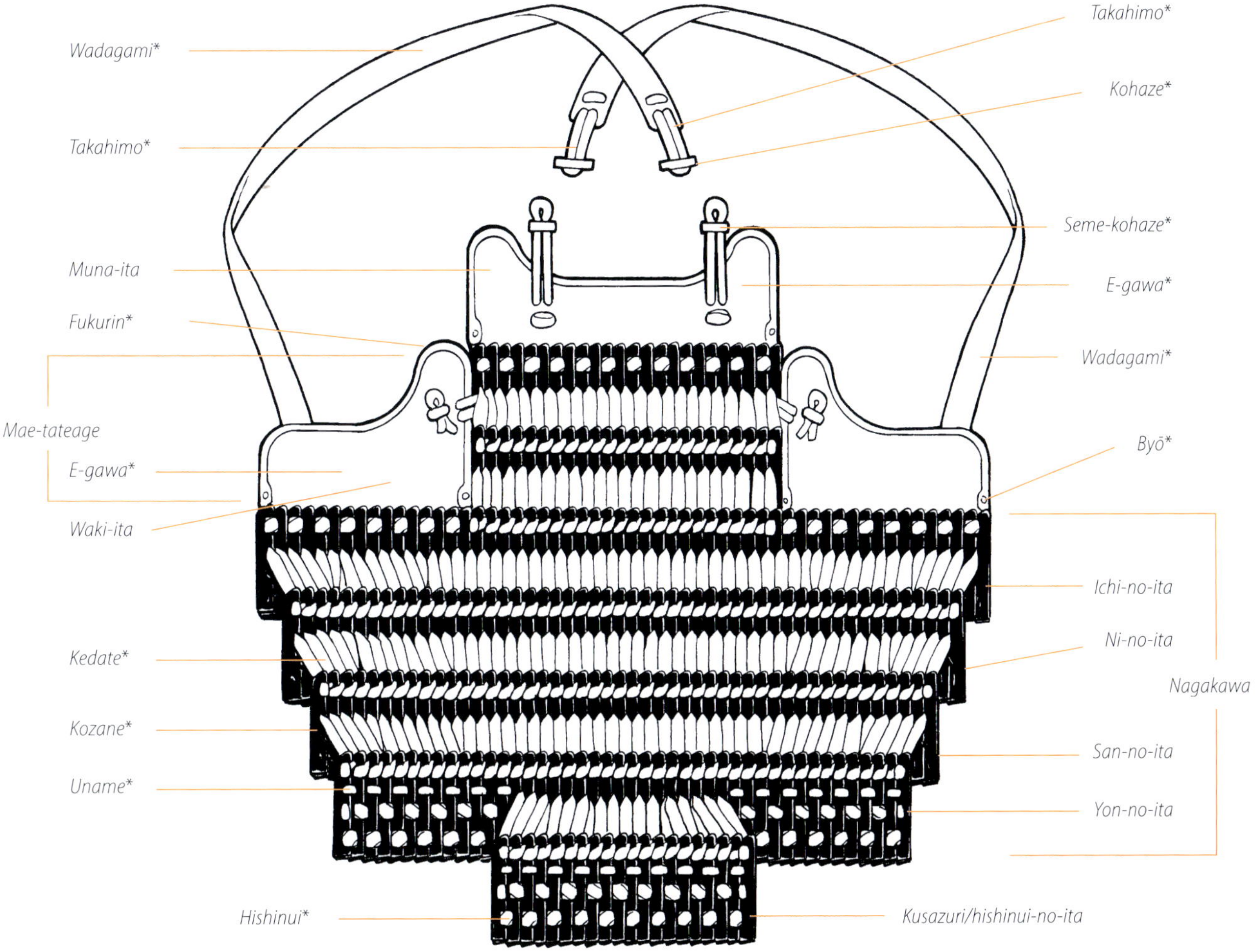

Takahimo*
Wadagami*
Kohaze*
Takahimo*
Seme-kohaze*
Muna-ita
E-gawa*
Fukurin*
Wadagami*
Mae-tateage
Byō*
E-gawa*
Waki-ita
Ichi-no-ita
Ni-no-ita
Kedate*
Nagakawa
Kozane*
San-no-ita
Uname*
Yon-no-ita
Hishinui*
Kusazuri/hishinui-no-ita

the side of the body without impeding the arm's freedom of movement. This was achieved by shaping the upper edge of the *waki-ita* like a wide, compressed U, which allowed the plate to reach up and cover the torso to the front and back of the arm while dipping down in the middle to accommodate the limb's freedom of movement, with the visible portion of the *waki-ita* generally being about the same height as one of the *sane-ita* of the *nagakawa* at its shallowest point. To accommodate the design of the *haramaki*, which closed together on the right of the torso, the *waki-ita* on the right side of the cuirass was split into two identical, though mirrored opposite plates.

As solid plates, the *waki-ita* joined the ranks of the *kanagu mawari* and as such were finished in the same manner as the other solid-plate pieces of the armour to which they were fitted.

The horizontal edges of the *waki-ita* were secured to the upper edges of the *ichi-no-ita* of the *nagakawa* in the same manner as the *muna-ita* or *oshitsuke-no-ita* were secured to the latter, which in the case of a *yoroi* often involved a *keshō-no-ita*, while on a *haramaki* the plates were generally *hishi-toji*-knotted in place.

Small *kohaze*- and *seme-kohaze*-threaded loops of cord strung between the upper outside edges of the *waki-ita* and the outside edge of the neighbouring *sane-ita* of the *mae-tateage* or corresponding portion of the *ushiro-tateage* were used to secure the otherwise free-floating upper portions of the armpit plates in position. Though simple, this method of attachment was effective. It also allowed the plates to move to a degree which more comfortably accommodated the movements of the arms and upper body.

Gilded copper plates called *hassō-no-kanamono*, generally rectangular in shape and with etched designs, began to be fitted under the *hassō-no-byō*. Fundamentally an elaborate form of washer, the *hassō-no-kanamono*, which are also sometimes referred to as *aida-no-kanamono*, were designed to protect the *kozane* from damage in areas where the scales had been drilled and had rivets inserted through them to connect two sections of the armour together, such as along the joint between the *muna-ita* and *ichi-no-ita* of the *mae-tateage* on a cuirass. When joints were anchored by *hassō-no-byō* alone, the flexing of the pieces caused the heads of the rivets to wear the lacquer finishes of the scales, which over time would eventually compromise the structural integrity of the scales that were affected. By placing the *hassō-no-kanamono* under the rivets before they were anchored in place, the stress on the lamellar section was dispersed across a wider surface area. And as the *hassō-no-kanamono* were flat they helped to limit how much the *sane-gashira* flexed, which like a *keshō-no-ita* helped to reduce the strain and damaging effects that rivets could have on the *kozane* in the area of the connective joints if used by themselves.

When *hassō-no-kanamono* were utilized they were generally applied in sets of three, reflecting the paired application of sets of *hassō-no-byō*. Of the three plates in a set, two had the ends of the plates squared off so they could be fitted to the

An 18th century example of a *hara-ate* assembled using the *Mōgami* method of construction. Unlike the *haramaki* worn by retainers prior to the late 15th century, this example has been made from solid horizontal plates rather than *sane-ita*. It has also been laced in the open *sugake odoshi* style, which was not introduced until the late 15th century. As can be noted by this example, the *hara-ate* only provided protection for the front and sides of the torso. Note the crossed leather shoulder straps that held the cuirass in place. These were affixed by *kohaze* toggles. More basic examples of *hara-ate* were commonly fabricated without the full complement of plates in the *kusazuri*, which were often reduced to just one or two plates per tasset.

One of the most famous scenes from the famous *Mōko Shūrai Ekotoba* scrolls that the samurai Suenaga Takezaki commissioned to document his service during the Mongol invasion of 1274. The two scrolls, which were completed in 1293, were used by Suenaga to petition the Shōgunate for compensation for his service during the first Mongol Invasion. In the above scene, Suenaga, who was a relatively low-ranking warrior, is depicted braving a barrage of arrows fired at him by Mongol auxiliaries, one of which pierced his helmet. The scene is also famous for the fact that it records the first known use of explosive devices in Japan, in the form of fire-bombs that the Mongols flung with catapults at the Japanese. Suenaga, who had been impoverished by his contribution to repelling the invasion, sold his horse and saddle to finance a trip to the capital in Kamakura. There he skilfully presented himself before the Shōgunate, and eventually earned an audience with the Shōgun. Suenaga's martial exploits and subsequent efforts resulted in him being granted a fiefdom in the present-day prefecture of Kumamoto in Kyūshū. (Wikimedia Commons/Public Domain)

outside edges of a *sane-ita*, while the third plate, which would be mounted in the middle of a joint, was made to have the same shape on both ends. If the *hassō-no-kanamono* featured incised edges, they were referred to as *iri-hassō*. If the ends of the fixture bulged outward to give the plate a lozenge-like shape, then it was referred to as a *de-hassō*. In later centuries it became common, particularly on high-quality sets of armour, for custom-made *hassō-no-byō* to be utilized that were crafted so that the head of the rivet depicted the warrior's family crest, or *kamon*. While less necessary on joints where *keshō-no-ita* were applied, it became common practice to apply *hassō-no-kanamono* to the façade of the cosmetic boards as well, primarily due to how they further enhanced the aesthetic appearance of the latter.

Another version of cuirass also began to appear around the same time that the *haramaki* worn by retainers began to transition into a cuirass that was also worn by samurai of rank. Called a *hara-ate*, or 'applied belly', it was fundamentally an abbreviated version of the *haramaki* that, as its name suggests, was designed to cover only the front and side portions of the torso. The *hara-ate*, sometimes also referred to as the *shita haramaki*, or 'under belly wrap', had evolved from the use of the *haramaki* as a form of protective armour that could be worn with, or under, everyday clothing by guards and officials due to the increased need for vigilance that had arisen out of the turbulent times of the late Heian period.

While a standard *haramaki* could function in this role, it was clearly more than was required most of the time and so armour makers began to abbreviate the design, which ultimately led to the *nagakawa* terminating under the left arm with no coverage being provided for the back of the torso. The *nagakawa* generally comprised only three crescent-shaped lames, while the number of *sane-ita* in the *mae-tateage* ranged between one and three, though two was by far the most common. Three full-length *kusazuri* were originally retained along the lower edge of the *nagakawa*, though these too were soon abbreviated, until the two outside *kusazuri* eventually comprised a single *hishinui*-finished section while the middle one consisted of two.

As the *hara-ate* was devoid of *wadagami*, straps fitted with *kohaze* were secured to the upper outside corners of the *ichi-no-ita* of the *nagakawa*. These were crossed behind the back and passed up and over the shoulders where the *kohaze* were inserted through the *seme-kohaze*-threaded *takahimo* cords strung through the *muna-ita*. When *waki-ita* were introduced they were attached to the *nagakawa* and *mae-tateage* in the usual manner, with the lower ends of the shoulder straps being secured to their upper rear edges of the armpit plates.

INNOVATIONS IN ARMOUR ARISING FROM THE MONGOL INVASIONS

The increasingly simplified and rudimentary design of the *haramaki* made it an ideal candidate for issuing to retainers, for it was relatively cheap and easy to produce. This was important as the number of retainers that were required to keep a warrior of rank in the field grew over the centuries, as the campaigns they engaged in became increasingly complex and prolonged.

A prime example of this was the two Mongol invasions of Japan that occurred during the latter part of the 13th century. Samurai from across the country were called to arms to resist the invaders. And while the first invasion in 1274 had been limited to a few relatively minor engagements before the invading fleet was devastated by a powerful and highly fortuitous typhoon, the Japanese were well aware that it had been a close-run thing. They were more than conscious of the fact that had it not been for the *kamikaze*, or 'divine wind', as the Japanese referred to the storm that miraculously saved them, they might have been conquered. And for this reason they also understood that the Mongols would be back. So they set about building defensive walls along the coast of Hakata Bay in north-western Kyūshū where the Mongols had made their landings in 1274, which they garrisoned with thousands of samurai.

A second, much larger invasion came several years later in 1281. This time the samurai found themselves pitted against the Mongols and their Korean and Chinese auxiliaries on numerous occasions over a period of a couple of months as the invaders struggled to establish a beachhead in the face of fierce samurai resistance. Even so, ultimate victory again appeared to have been heaven sent as another *kamikaze* materialized to scatter and smash the massed invasion fleets, once more saving the Japanese from the possibility of defeat and occupation.

Centuries of isolation had left the Japanese unprepared to fight a foe who did not observe the formalized styles of combat that had become an integral part of the samurai ethos. Their armour, however, had served them well overall. It had been more than capable of standing up to the weaponry employed by the Mongols. What these engagements had highlighted, though, was what many samurai had already come to understand: the *ō-yoroi*, while an excellent form of armour for a mounted archer, was poorly suited to the needs of a warrior fighting outside the limited scope of that role, as had been the case in many of the engagements during the second invasion. For the samurai had frequently found themselves fighting on foot and even from the decks of small boats.

Production of cuirasses made in the *yoroi* style declined dramatically in the decades following the failed Mongol invasions, with the majority of samurai preferring to wear the far more practical, battle-proven *haramaki* over the *yoroi*. And yet, the *yoroi*, irrespective of its many failings and limitations, was retained.

Like a revered war hero from a previous generation, the *ō-yoroi* was highly respected by the samurai, for it had been an integral part of the identity of the rising warrior class almost since their inception. Thus like the famous old warrior who was no longer fit to serve, the *ō-yoroi* was elevated in status but largely removed from active service. In other words, it continued to be worn primarily by the elite of the warrior class, who by the nature of their positions were unlikely to be deeply involved in most engagements and who were therefore not particularly concerned that their armour might compromise their ability to fight. This gradually redefined what the *ō-yoroi* symbolized. Its ownership was no longer simply synonymous with membership of the rising warrior class, but had evolved to signify that a warrior wearing a *yoroi* was a member of the elite within that society.

Not surprisingly this gradually undermined the viability of the *ō-yoroi* even further as an effective form of armour, because the sets became increasingly ornate. An extreme, though telling example of this transition is the famous 14th century *aka-ito odoshi take ni susume tora kanamono yoroi* (red laced with sparrows in bamboo with tigers *yoroi*) that Minamoto Yoshitsune was said to have dedicated to the Kasuga Shrine. This renowned masterpiece is so encumbered with rich, decorative fixtures that it would have been all but useless in combat. And while it was almost certainly never intended to be worn anywhere near a battlefield, it attests to the passing of the *yoroi* in the eyes of the samurai from being an effective form of armour to a design of cuirass that was better suited to ceremonial purposes.

The *aka-ito odoshi take ni susume tora kanamono yoroi* was a milestone in another respect. It attested to just how talented the various artisans whose labours were required to create a set of armour had become since the start of the first millennium. And while this *yoroi* was clearly intended to be exceptional, it was largely extraordinary due to the level of ornamentation as opposed to the quality of the workmanship. For most armour sets had, as Bottomley and Hopson wrote, increasingly become 'more of a vehicle for applied ornamentation and decoration' throughout the 14th century.[12]

Few extant armours from that period, however, can compare to the *ō-yoroi* in the Kasuga Shrine for ostentatious beauty. For virtually all of the armour's *kanagu mawari* and other flat surfaces, including the *mabizashi* and *fukigaeshi* flanges of the helmet and the *hishinui-no-ita* of the *kusazuri*, *sode* and *shikoro* neck guard, were fitted with highly ornate

The famous 14th century *aka-ito odoshi take ni suzume tora kanamono no yoroi*. This phenomenal *ō-yoroi*, which is now one of Japan's National Treasures, is said to have been dedicated to the Kasuga Shrine, where it is still resides, by Minamoto Yoshitsune. Considered to be one the most beautiful examples of an *ō-yoroi* ever produced, this armour attests to the incredible talent of the Japanese artisans of the late Kamakura period. While an aesthetic masterpiece, the armour was clearly never meant to be utilized. (Image © and courtesy of the Kasuga Shrine, Aomori Japan) open metalwork, gilt-finished *kanamono* of phenomenal detail. These featured a theme of sparrows flying amongst a thick bamboo grove, with tigers sitting idly nearby observing them. Yet while all of the *kanamono* are spectacular, it is the fixtures fitted to the façades of the massive *ō-sode* of the set that are the most eye-catching. For each shoulder guard is faced with a huge yet delicate *kanamono* shaped in the form of a pair of tall, thickly leaved bamboo stocks that overhang a separate fixture that depicts a seated tiger. That the delicate bamboo-stock *kanamono* fixtures extend over the better part of six of the seven lames of the shoulder guards, preventing them from being able to flex or telescope past each other without damaging the fixture, attests to the purely ceremonial purpose of this beautiful *ō-yoroi*, which is one of Japan's great national treasures.

During the Mongol invasions many samurai had discarded their bows in favour of the *naginata*, a pole-arm with a short sword-like blade affixed to the end. Traditionally a weapon carried by retainers to protect the mounted warriors, the samurai had found the *naginata* to be a highly effective weapon in close-quarter combat when dismounted. This experience led to an increased reliance on edged weaponry throughout the 14th century and saw the gradual demise of the bow as the warrior's primary weapon.

As Japanese armour had primarily been designed to protect against missiles, namely arrows, changes had to be made to account for the new forms of edged weaponry that warriors were encountering on the battlefield. This brought about a number of key innovations in how the *kozane* used to construct *sane-ita* were made and finished, which as an unintended consequence improved their overall appearance.

To help prevent the possibility of large lamellar sections being severed from one another by a blow from an edged weapon, armour makers decided to increase the number of connective lengths of *kedate* between adjoined sections of *sane-ita*. To achieve this, they reduced the size of the *kozane* used to assemble the armour pieces. This meant that more *kozane* were required to assemble a lame, which in turn increased the number of connective bindings between *sane-ita*. It also reduced the overall area of flat surfaces across the frontage of a lamellar section. This was not only because the scales were narrower, but also because the visible right-hand edge of each scale was embossed, which gave the *kozane* a subtle 'S'-like shape when viewed in cross-section. While the roof-tile-like appearance of this form of scale, known as *kara kozane*, helped to increase the overall strength of each scale, the primary purpose behind the embossing of the *kozane* was to help protect the connective *odoshi-ge*. For the lacing stood above the surface of lames assembled from conventional *kozane* due to the relatively flat form of the latter. Arching the *kozane* helped to nullify this difference in height, which in turn helped to reduce the number of individual lengths of *odoshi-ge* that could be damaged by a single blow from an edged weapon.

While both effective and aesthetically attractive in appearance, pieces assembled from *kara kozane* were costly and time-consuming to produce. This was in part because each scale had to be individually moulded or shaped. It was also a reflection of the fact that the smaller size of the scales meant that more *kozane* were required to produce a single set of armour. In fact, it was not uncommon for as many as 3,000 *kozane* to be used to construct a set of armour made in the *haramaki* style in the 14th century, which was nearly 1,000 more scales than had been required to produce a similar set of armour in the 13th century.

The complexity of producing *kara kozane* quickly led armour makers to come up with an innovative alternative method of creating a shaped form of scale, which they did by giving a curved shape to a flat scale through the skilful application of lacquer. This was done by binding flat *kozane* together to create a *sane-ita*. Thick applications of coarse lacquer were then applied to the exposed right-hand edge of each scale to

EARLY FORMS OF SAMURAI ARMOUR

The minimal overlap between *iyozane* scales is depicted in the above illustration.
1) A standard *iyozane* scale.
2) An example of the *yahazu-gashira* style of *iyozane*.
3) A group of *iyozane* scales arranged to create a section of *sane-ita*. Note the small degree of overlap between neighbouring scales.
4) A comparative group of conventional *kozane* arranged as they would be to make a section of armour. The considerable saving in both material and time that the production of armour assembled from *iyozane* scales made possible is evident when the two groups of scales are compared.

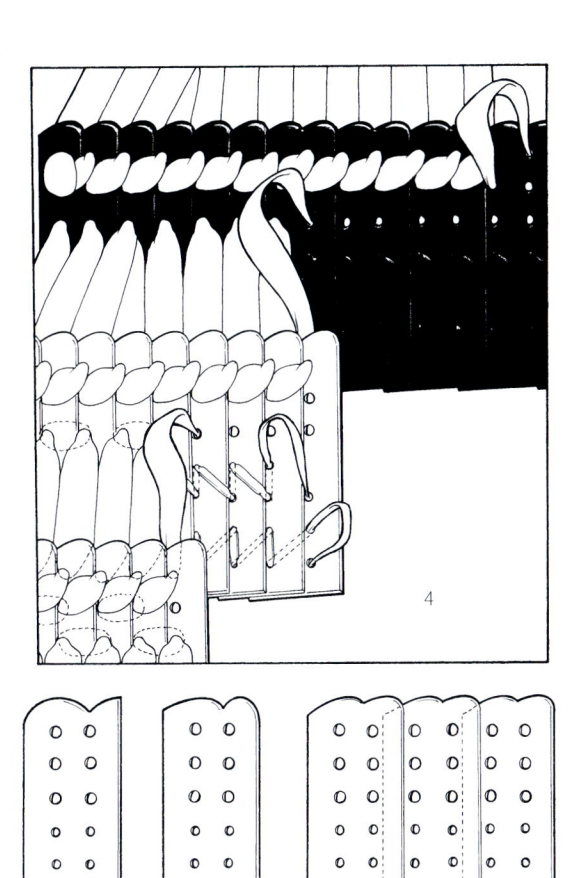

create a long, narrow, vertical mound that replicated the convex ridge of an embossed *kara kozane* scale. This process, appropriately referred to as *moriage*, or 'built up', could be quickly and consistently repeated by a talented *katchū-shi* dozens of times in just a few minutes compared with the hours of work required to physically form an equal number of individual scales.

Though the *kozane* were bound into lames before the lacquered edges were applied, the individual scales were originally referred to as *moriage kozane*. Over time, however, the term *moriage* was dropped as virtually all *kozane* were made in the *moriage* style.

Within a fairly short period, *katchū-shi* took the *moriage* concept of using lacquer to give a scale three-dimensional form one step further when they introduced the *iyozane* style of *kozane* during the later part of the Kamakura period. While ostensibly a new form of scale, named after the region in which it is said to have first appeared, the *iyozane* was actually a throwback to the style of scales and methods of lacing that had been used during the Nara and Heian periods. Unlike conventional *kozane* that generally overlapped the scale to the immediate right by half, *iyozane* were arranged so they only partially overlapped the outer edge of the neighbouring scale to the right. To achieve this, the number of holes in the left-hand column of apertures on the scale was increased to seven, with the addition of one more *karami-no-ana* so that the number and arrangement of holes was identical to those on the right. Binding the scales together in this manner, with a minimal degree of overlap, allowed a single *iyozane* scale to cover the same amount of space as two conventional 14th-century *kozane*. This greatly reduced the number of scales that were required to create a set of armour, which in turn significantly reduced the overall weight of the items of armour assembled using *iyozane*. The fact that only a single scale was being used to cover an area that had hitherto been covered by two scales was hidden through the skilful application of lacquer, which could make the façade of one scale look like as though it was actually two separate scales. This illusion was heightened by cutting a small indentation in the wide *sane-gashira* of the *iyozane* which made the top scale look as though two *kozane* were occupying that space.

One of the factors that made the *iyozane* possible was the need to create armour that could provide protection from a wider range of weaponry, even though arrows still inflicted approximately 73 per cent of all wounds, according to Thomas Conlan, who studied over 1,300 period documents that referred to such matters. Such studies seem to undermine the growing importance of edged weaponry on the battlefields of 14th century Japan, but they may fail to capture the fact that while arrows still caused the majority of casualties, it may have been edged weapons that carried the day. For it is well documented that while very few men were killed by bayonets during the Napoleonic Wars in comparison with those who were killed by firearms, it was 'fear of the bayonet, rather than the bayonet itself' which often forced one side or the other to relinquish the battlefield.[13] This assertion is further supported by numerous examples of casualty figures and statistics that were collected by Napoleonic period doctors, such as Dominique Jean Larrey, a surgeon in the French Grand Armée, following major battles in which bayonet wounds were consistently found to be the least common of all injuries.

To compensate for the limited overlap between *iyozane*, which accounted for a considerable degree of the overall structural strength and integrity of conventional lengths of *sane-ita*, armour makers introduced the *kawa-shiki*. This was a narrow strip of rawhide that was applied to the rear face of a section of armour to help it keep its form. The *kawa-shiki* was positioned so that it was bound in place by the *hishi-toji* bindings of the *shita-garami* when the lame was being assembled.

The Mongol invasions may also have led to the eventual abandonment of the use of horse hide to create *oshitsuke-no-ita* with integral *wadagami*. This may have come about due to the number of engagements that took place near or on the ocean, during which the moulded shoulder guards were soaked with water, which would have caused them to lose their form and distort over time. Whatever the influence was, by the early 14th century, it was common for the *wadagami* and *oshitsuke-no-ita* to be fabricated independently of each other and to be made from metal. In fact, some Japanese scholars believe that this transition may have given rise to the term *oshitsuke*, which can be translated as 'press and attach'. For the iron *wadagami* were shaped, or 'pressed', over wooden moulds before they were riveted to the back face of the generally rectangular back plate. Padding was then fitted and the pieces finished in the usual manner, with one of the few outwardly visible differences being the fitting of a *fukurin* around the *oshitsuke-no-ita*.

As late as the 1330s, the after-effects of the Mongol invasions were still being felt. This was in part due to the fact that the samurai had traditionally been reimbursed and awarded for their service by being presented with a percentage of the spoils taken as a result of a campaign. More often than not this came in the form of land. But as the campaigns against the Mongols had been fought to protect Japanese territories, there were no spoils for the Kamakura Shōgunate to divide up to reward the numerous samurai families who had fought to defend the country, many of whom had expended considerable personal wealth for this cause. For the samurai had been forced to garrison the coast for years between the first and second invasions, and for a number of years after that, for the Japanese had not dismissed the possibility of a third invasion attempt. These issues and others culminated in a seismic rift that led to a five-decade-long series of conflicts that are collectively referred to as the Nanbokuchō, or 'Southern and Northern Courts', period.

Considering the intensity and duration of the conflicts during the latter half of the 14th century it is surprising to note that relatively few advances were made in cuirass construction techniques or designs. Numerous other armour-related developments, however, did occur, including the introduction of mail, or *kusari*, as well as a number of items of armour for the extremities. These included the wearing of armoured sleeves, or *kote*, on both arms, improved designs of *suneate* shin guards and the appearance of a rudimentary form of facial armour referred to as a *hanbo*, or half mask, all of which are discussed in Volume II of this text.

Largely due to the smaller sizes of *kozane* that were being utilized, which averaged about 6.2 cm in height and 1.9 cm in width, the overall length of the *haramaki* and *yoroi* had been shortened even further to 60–70 cm. This prompted the introduction of another item of armour for the extremities, the first rudimentary examples of *haidate*, or armour protection for the lower thighs.

Early Forms of Samurai Armour

Three rear views of a *haramaki* with an accompanying *sei-ita*. Though the *haramaki* was originally designed to be worn without a *sei-ita*, by the late 14th century it had become common for warriors to wear this additional back-plate, which is visible affixed in place in the first image. In the second image, the *sei-ita* has been loosened on one side to expose the opening down the center of the back that is indicative of the *haramaki* design of cuirass. The same cuirass is seen in the last image with the *sei-ita* completely removed.

The number of warriors who wore the *yoroi* continued to decline throughout this period as the changing nature of warfare increasingly highlighted the archaic nature of its design. This was further compounded by the appearance of an alternative design of *haramaki* that appeared around the beginning of the 14th century. The new version of *haramaki* was unique amongst the various forms of cuirass previously in use by the Japanese in that it opened down the middle of the back of the armour. For reasons unknown the name *haramaki*, which had been used for centuries to refer to the existing design of *migi-hikiawase ichi-mai-dō*, was reassigned to this new form of cuirass, while the original examples of *haramaki* were rebranded as being *dō-maru*, which literally translates as 'body around'.

While there are no known extant examples of transitional designs of *hara-ate* or *dō-maru* to conclusively say which design of cuirass was the more influential in helping to bring about this new version of the *haramaki*, both designs clearly contributed to the development of the new *haramaki*. That said, the overall method of assembly and construction of a *haramaki* fundamentally differed little from that of a *dō-maru* with the obvious exception of where the opening was located on the *nagakawa*, which required that the *ushiro-tateage* and *oshitsuke-no-ita* be divided into equal left- and right-hand side sections. Unlike the *dō-maru*, however, where the *sane-ita* of the *nagakawa* were intentionally made longer to allow the edges of the cuirass to overlap to ensure that there was no gap in the protective covering of the torso, the rear edges of the *haramaki* were not designed to overlap and cover the gap that existed down the middle of the back.

The gap down the middle of the back of the *haramaki* made it an extremely practical design.

175

SAMURAI ARMOUR

Technically it allowed a single cuirass to fit a large range of persons of various builds, for it could be drawn closer together for a person with a thin build or be spread further apart for someone who was heavier set. The resulting gap was not considered to be of significant concern since the prevailing logic was that the majority of dangers facing a warrior would be to his front and sides as he engaged a foe, and in theory there was no situation in which a warrior's back would ever be exposed to an enemy, although reality might suggest otherwise. Yet the majority of samurai appear to have used the *haramaki* as it was for the better part of two centuries with the middle of the back left exposed.

That said, at some point during the latter part of the 14th century a separate piece of armour called a *sei-ita*, which literally means 'back plate', was introduced. The earliest examples of *sei-ita* were quite large and covered almost the entire back of the cuirass, though over time they would narrow considerably. Constructed in the same manner as the cuirass itself, including sections of *e-gawa*, *koberi*, *fusegumi* and other details, the generally hourglass-shaped *sei-ita* was assembled from the same number of lames as it took to match the combined count of the *sane-ita* that were in the *oshitsuke-no-ita*, *ushiro-tateage*, *nagakawa* and *kusazuri* of the cuirass.

Seme-kohaze-threaded lengths of cords called *sei-ita-tsuke-no-seme-kohaze* hung from the rear of the two *wadagami* to attach the *sei-ita* that was suspended by *kohaze*-threaded cords protruding from the *oshitsuke-no-ita* portion of the back plate. The *dō-saki-no-o* used to secure the cuirass at the waist helped keep the *sei-ita* in place around the lower back of the armour.

In later centuries, the *sei-ita* was sometimes referred to as the *okubyō-no-ita*, or 'coward's plate', suggesting that it was only utilized by a warrior who was concerned about his fate. This, however, was not the case. While it was easy for the unbloodied and largely inexperienced armchair-general-like samurai of the Edo era to have bought into such fables, raised in the unrealistic and overdramatized ideals of their time period that determined what a true warrior was supposed to be, the reality surrounding the actual purpose of the *sei-ita* was quite different. Its primary purpose was to simplify how the various cords of the large *ō-sode* shoulder guards were secured to the cuirass. For without a *sei-ita* the centrally mounted *agemaki-no-kan* that was fitted to the backs of cuirasses made in the *yoroi* and *dō-maru* styles could not be mounted.

On *haramaki* without a *sei-ita*, additional fastening points were added to the *wadagami* and to the two halves of the *oshitsuke-no-ita* to secure the shoulder guards. And while functional, the arrangement of cords without an *agemaki-no-kan* was not as aesthetically

A high-quality Edo period example of a haramaki. The central opening down the middle of the back of the cuirass is clearly visible. The river barge hull-like shape of the wadagami is visible in this image. This shape was created by adhering multiple layers of nerigawa together to create an inverted and truncated pyramid section, which was then sheathed in e-gawa. Note the iri-hassō fixtures that help to secure the kanagu mawari to the sane-ita. The undulating appearance of the scales along the sane-ita is typical of lamellar boards, and due to the fact that, while each scale is similar, they are never identical, which causes subtle irregularities in the sane-ita.

Early Forms of Samurai Armour

attractive as it was with this fixture. Thus for the most part, the majority of *haramaki* were not fitted with *sei-ita* until well into the 15th century, when they gradually started to be seen as something of a separate yet integral feature of *haramaki*. Prior to that, however, the *sei-ita* was largely seen as indicative of high-quality sets of armour and therefore as something that was predominately associated with samurai of wealth and status.

14TH–19TH CENTURY *HARAMAKI* NOMENCLATURE

Terms marked with * can be applied to multiple pieces

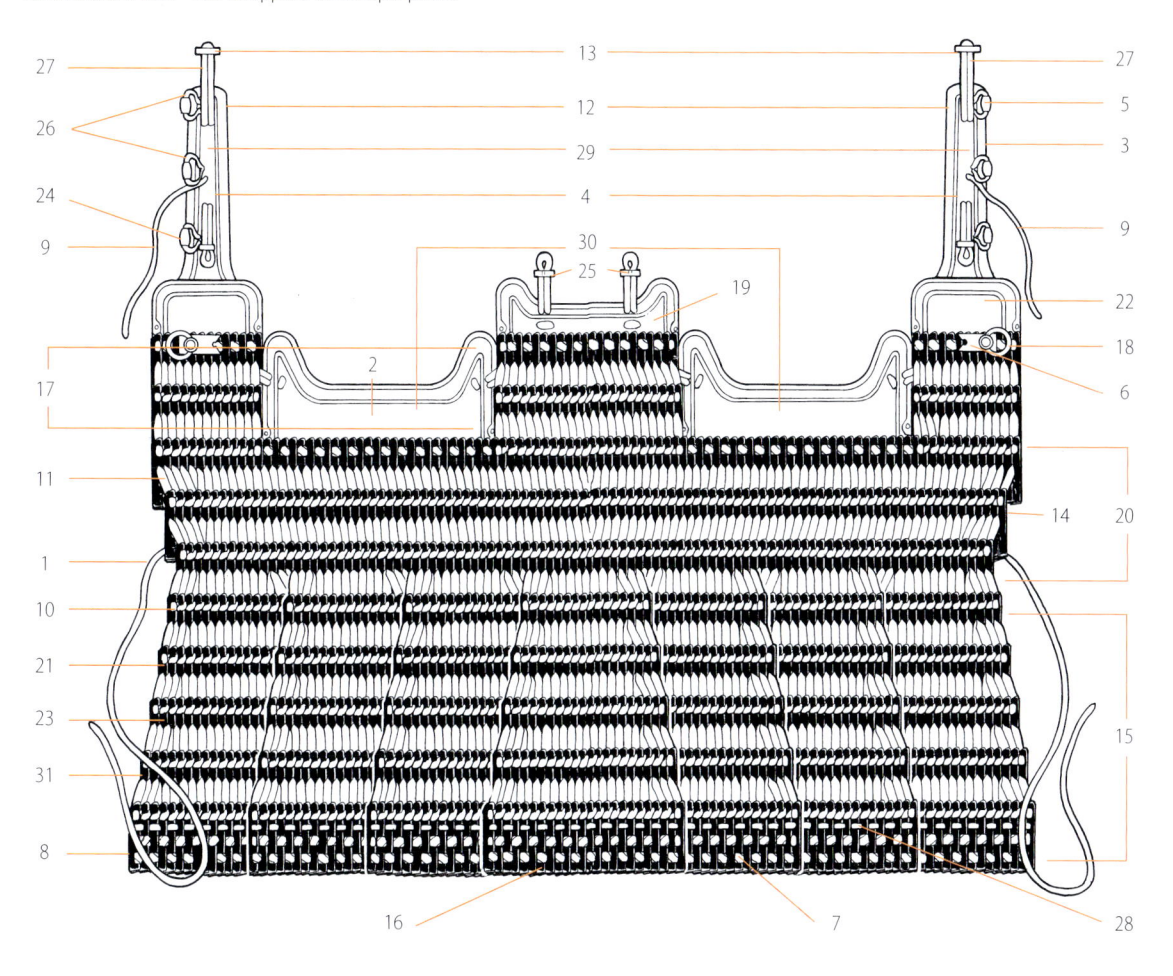

1. Dō-saki-no-o*
2. E-gawa*
3. Fukurin*
4. Fusegumi*
5. Gumi kanamono*
6. Hassō-no-za*
7. Hishinui
8. Hishinui-no-ita*
9. Hikiawase-no-o*
10. Ichi-no-ita*
11. Kedate*
12. Koberi-gawa*
13. Kohaze*
14. Kozane*
15. Kusazuri*
16. Mae-no-kusazuri
17. Mae-tateage
18. Mizunomi-no-o-tsuke-kan
19. Muna-ita
20. Nagakawa
21. Ni-no-ita*
22. Oshitsuke-no-ita
23. San-no-ita*
24. Sei-ita-tsuke-no-gumi-wa
25. Seme-kohaze*
26. Sode-tsuke-no-gumi-wa*
27. Takahimo*
28. Uname*
29. Wadagami*
30. Waki-ita*
31. Yon-no-ita*

Samurai Armour

SEI-ITA NOMENCLATURE

Terms marked with * can be applied to multiple pieces

- Fukurin*
- Takahimo*
- Fusegumi*
- Koberi-gawa*
- Kohaze*
- E-gawa*
- Oshitsuke-no-ita
- Ushiro-tateage*
- Agemaki-no-kan
- Ichi-no-ita*
- Nagakawa
- Ni-no-ita*
- San-no-ita*
- Yon-no-ita*
- Agemaki
- Ichi-no-ita*
- Kozane*
- Ni-no-ita*
- Kusazuri*
- San-no-ita*
- Kedate*
- Yon-no-ita*
- Uname*
- Hishinui
- Hishinui-no-ita*

Front and back views of a *sei-ita*. In overall construction the *sei-ita* was generally identical to the main cuirass. As such it would not only be made with the same materials, it would also be assembled from the same number of *sane-ita* as were used in the *nagakawa* and *kusazuri* of the 'parent' armour. The *sei-ita* also provided a convenient place to the secure the *agemaki-no-kan* and accompanying *agemaki*, which were still required to secure and control the *sode* on most examples of *haramaki*.

LEATHER WRAPPING: *KAWA-TSUZUMI*

An unusual alternative method of constructing cuirasses made in the *dō-maru* and *haramaki* styles also appeared during the latter part of the 14th century. Referred to as *kawa-tsuzumi*, or literally 'leather-wrapped', this method used sheets of smoked-leather *fusube-gawa* applied to the exterior surface of items of lamellar armour to connect the *sane-ita* together. This was presumably done to eliminate the need for the vulnerable intermediate *kedate* lengths of *odoshi-ge* that the conventional manner of assembly made universal to all items of lamellar armour.

This was achieved by placing the facing surface of a lamellar section against the back surface of a panel of *fusube-gawa*. An *odoshi-ge* was then strung from the back of the armour section via the *kedate* and the lower of the two right-hand side *karami-no-ana* holes in the individual *kozane*. It was passed through the lamellar piece and holes punched in the *fusube-gawa* and pulled through to the facing surface of the smoked-leather panel. It was then passed diagonally over the surface of the *fusube-gawa* in the required direction before it was inserted into another hole so that it could be drawn out through the back face. This effectively suspended the *sane-ita* from the back of the *fusube-gawa* sheet via the series of *hishi-toji* cross-knots and removed the need for the connective lengths of *kedate*. The uppermost row of *karami-no-ana* used for the *nawame-garami* portion of the bindings was left void except along the lames that formed *hishinui-no-ita*, where they were strung with lacing in the *uname* style.

While the *fusube-gawa* façade did make it far more difficult to cut away a lamellar section with an edged weapon, in many ways the concept appears to have been rather short-sighted, for a damaged section of leather could also be quite troublesome and time-consuming to replace. And when they were replaced it was extremely hard to get the new panels of *fusebe-gawa* to match the older leather, weather-faded pieces already fitted to the cuirass, which gave repaired armour something of a patchwork-like appearance. This was an undesirable characteristic for a cuirass that was already by the nature of its fabrication quite plain in comparison with the elaborate colours and patterns of lacing that commonly appeared on most makes of cuirass assembled in a conventional manner.

Aesthetics aside, the cuirasses assembled in the *kawa-tsuzumi* style were also more susceptible to the negative effects of inclement weather than conventionally assembled types. For heavily saturated leather was prone to tearing, while leather that dried improperly could shrink, distort or even harden, severely impacting the performance and serviceability of a cuirass. This may be why the *kawa-tsuzumi* method of fabrication appears to have been a rather short-lived trend that was largely discontinued by the early part of the 15th century, as the relatively few surviving examples of *kawa-tsuzumi dō-maru* and *haramaki* appear to attest. However, two changes to how cuirasses were made that did find acceptance during the latter part of the 14th century were the continued trend towards cuirasses with increasingly tapered waistlines and rounded *kusazuri*.

While the *nagakawa* of cuirasses had gradually grown smaller over the centuries, armour makers started to add an obvious inward taper to the lower bands of the *nagakawa* as this

A rare example of a *fusebe-gawa-tsuzumi haramaki*. While it was faster to secure the *sane-ita* together by binding them to sheets of leather than it was to lace them together with *odoshi-ge* to make a cuirass, there were many drawbacks to cuirasses assembled in this manner. While the large sheet of leather did help to prevent pieces of the armour from being cut away by edged weapons, as sometimes occurred when *odoshi-ge* was severed, it was nonetheless difficult to repair and replace the large panels of leather when they were damaged. And when repairs were made it was also difficult to match the colour of replacement panels with the existing panels. This created a patchwork look that further undermined the rather sombre appearance of cuirasses made in this style. (Image courtesy of Thomas Del Mar Ltd.)

SAMURAI ARMOUR

A 15th century *haramaki* that was gifted to the New York Metropolitan Museum in 1914 by Bashford Dean. While the *haramaki* was one of the most advanced and practical forms of lamellar armour, like all examples of scale-made armour, it was extremely labour intensive and as such, costly to produce. The changing nature of warfare and the forms of weaponry that were in use by the late 15th century began to highlight some of the drawbacks and weaknesses that were largely universal to lamellar armour: they were difficult to repair and prone to mildew when worn on prolonged campaigns. Such problems ultimately led to the development of new, more practical forms of armour. Note the convex curvature of the *kusazuri*. This was done to help it better conform to the shape of the upper legs. (New York Metropolitan Museum of Art/CC0 1.0)

Detail of how *sane-ita* were attached to panels of leather when a cuirass or section of armour was finished in the *fusebe-gawa-tsuzumi* style, in comparison with traditional lacing. In general, lengths of leather thong cross-knotted in the *hishi-toji* style were used to bind the *sane-ita* to the leather coverings. The *hishi-toji* were narrower and appeared closer together on *sane-ita* made using *kozane*, while they were wider apart and larger on *sane-ita* assembled from *iyozane*. The unused *karami-no-ana* were also sometimes threaded with leather thong.

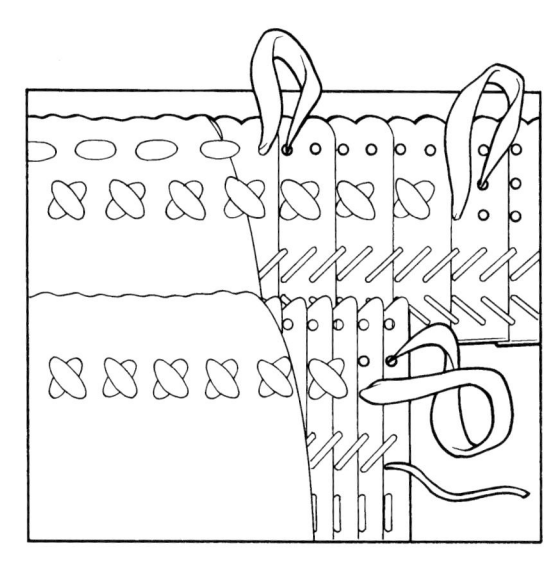

helped to transfer an even greater percentage of a cuirass's weight load from the shoulders of a warrior to his hips, which made the cuirass easier to wear while dismounted. The lames of the *kusazuri* meanwhile were shaped to give them an obvious horizontally convex form that helped them better conform to the natural curvature of the thighs and buttocks. This was achieved by replacing the *kawa-shiki* strips that were sometimes fitted to the backs of lamellar sections with narrow pre-shaped iron bands called *shiki-gane*, which were anchored in place under the *shita-garami* bindings before the *sane-ita* were lacquered, to create strong, arching lames.

While a relatively minor evolutionary development, rounded *kusazuri* were indicative of the Japanese armour makers' ongoing efforts to constantly improve upon existing armour designs, a process that saw the awkward, box-like *yoroi* slowly metamorphose over the centuries into the highly functional, form-fitting *dō-maru* and *haramaki* styles of cuirass. These changes had been driven by the need to keep up with and counter the changing nature of the way warfare was conducted and the weaponry that warriors were encountering on the battlefield.

Though the changes that had occurred in armour designs had largely been reactive in nature, armour makers had always been able to tweak the design or method of construction of lamellar armour sufficiently to overcome the problems faced by their clientele. This changed, however, during the latter half of the 15th century, when a number of conflicts simultaneously erupted across Japan, for the scale of these conflicts was unlike anything that had been seen before, with multiple massive armies simultaneously taking to the field.

This placed immense pressure on the *katchū-shi*, who were overwhelmed with commissions for armour. Unlike the dilemmas of past centuries, however, when the problems that armour makers had faced had been how to change lamellar armour designs to meet the needs of their clients, they were suddenly confronted by a need to quickly produce a large amount of armour in as little time as possible to satisfy the desperate needs of their clientele and benefactors, which was something that no amount of subtle tweaking was going to change.

A unique *gusoku* featuring a *kawa-tsuzumi* finished example of cuirass made in the *Mōgami* style from the late 16th century that was used by the Tachibana Muneshige, the first Lord of the Yanagawa clan. (Tachibana Museum)

CHAPTER 5

PRE-MODERN *DŌ* DESIGNS

The *Mōgami, nuinobe* and *tatami* methods, late 15th–16th centuries

The Northern Court's victory over the Southern branch of the imperial line brought the Nanbokuchō Wars to an end in 1392 after fifty-six years of bitter conflict. Ostensibly the wars were fought over a legitimacy dispute between the two main branches of the imperial line. In reality, however, the two courts were largely fronts, for neither could achieve ascendancy over the state without the military backing of Japan's most powerful warrior families. This pitted the puppet emperors of the Northern Court, who were controlled by the Ashikaga shōguns, against the so-called 'loyalist' armies of the Southern Court, who in theory wished to see control over the state revert to the Emperor, as it did for a brief period during the short-lived three-year reign of Emperor Go-Daigo from 1333 to 1336.

The actual trigger for these events, however, was the Mongol invasions, or specifically, the huge financial cost that the Shōgunate had incurred defending Japan. For while the campaigns had been costly, it was the ongoing costs of subsidizing the garrisoning of troops on the defensive walls along the coast of western Kyūshū during the post-invasion years that had bled the state's finances almost dry.

With near-empty coffers and no booty to divide, the Shōgunate was unable to properly compensate and reward the samurai and powerful warrior families, many of whom had at their own expense made substantial contributions in both men and material to the nation's defence. Not surprisingly this created discontent among the samurai class, whose faith in the central government suffered as a result. This was particularly true of the large, land-owning warrior families away from the centres of government control, who increasingly began to run their domains like almost independent states.

In a bid to regain dominance over the state, the victorious Ashikaga Shōgunate enacted an edict that allowed these already powerful regional magnates to utilize 50 per cent of their regional tax base to develop their military forces. While this had been done to develop the forces loyal to the Shōgunate to ensure that the puppet Northern Court was victorious, it simultaneously set in motion a number of factors that would ultimately rip Japan apart in the following century. For while the *hanzei* or 'half tax' policy helped to create strong, short-term allies for the Shōgunate, it had the unintended long-term effect of weakening the latter's control over the state, as it helped to develop the military capabilities of the increasingly independent regional land owners.

The extent to which this policy backfired on the Shōgunate was made abundantly clear in 1467, when another legitimacy dispute, this time over who the next Ashikaga Shōgun would be, brought rival warrior clans into the capital to help influence their preferred candidate's ascendancy. The size of these forces surpassed anything ever before seen in Japan, with one faction alone fielding 20,000 troops. The ten-year-long conflict known as the Ōnin War that ultimately erupted over this impasse obliterated most of the capital of Kyōto, and along with it any last remnants of central government authority over the state. For though the Shōgunate survived, by the end of the conflict its authority had been thoroughly undermined. This was largely due to the shocking degree of distracted indifference that the serving Ashikaga Shōgun displayed towards the conflict that was being waged on his behalf. As a result, real power slowly ebbed from the Shōgunate into the hands of the powerful Hosokawa clan until the Shōguns, like the Emperors, were little more than puppet figureheads.

By the time the conflict came to its rather anticlimactic end in 1477, Kyōto was virtually unrecognizable. The destruction of the capital's numerous stately palaces, majestic temples, shrines and prosperous business-lined boulevards foreshadowed the fate that was about to befall the entire country. For nothing had been spared, including the existing social

A depiction of Yoshisada Nitta in his final moments of life during the siege of the Kuromaru fortress 1338. While not shown here, Nitta's left leg was supposedly trapped under his fallen mount. Unable to extract himself, some sources say that Nitta chose to cut his own throat in order to avoid capture. Nitta is depicted wearing a yoroi, *as would have been typical of a warrior of his rank in the mid 14th century. While Nitta is presented wielding his swords, the bow and arrow was still the mounted warrior's primary weapon during Nitta's lifetime and is more than likely what actually killed him.*

A depiction of Maeda Toshiie, who became one of Nobunaga Oda's most capable generals, returning from battle with the severed heads of enemies he personally dispatched during the battle of Okehazama in 1560. While Toshiie is depicted carrying four heads, historical records show that he actually reported taking just three heads at Okehazama. Note the long *yari*: his nickname was 'Yari-no-Mataza', or 'Mataza the Spear', due to his preference for wielding a massive 6.3 metre-long *yari* in battle. The evolution in the forms of equipment and the weaponry that were utilized by the samurai between the mid-14th and mid-16th centuries are evident in this image.

order, which like the capital had been laid waste. Too many of the various protagonists had seen how easily the reins of political power, which had traditionally only been held by men of esteemed lineage, had fallen into the hands of supposedly lesser men who had the ability to project military power.

This reversal of the existing hierarchical top-down social order, referred to as *gekokujō* in Japanese, was 'the lower rules the higher', or 'the low overcomes the high', as this term is often translated. It aptly characterizes the socio-economic environment that prevailed in Japan for most of the following century, which would eventually come to be known to history as the 'Country at War' period, or the Sengoku Jidai.

When considering the 'Country at War' period it is important to understand that the word 'country' in this context technically refers to some 260 small independent provinces or feudal domains that the modern-day nation of Japan was at that time divided into, each of which was viewed as being a separate *kuni*, or 'country'.

The spark that ignited the Sengoku Jidai was the Ōnin War, and though the Ōnin War ended in a fairly inconclusive manner with neither of the original protagonists having achieved their original objectives, the conflict inadvertently triggered a number of truly momentous socio-economic changes. Key amongst these was the significantly watered-down status of the Shōgunate, which had been instrumental in keeping the various regional magnates and military families across Japan in check over the centuries. With the Shōgunate largely nullified, neighbouring domains began to fall upon each other all across the country as they saw an opportunity to gain land and status. In other cases, clan leaders returned from the Ōnin War to find that their domains had been usurped by those they had left behind to govern their territories in their absence.

Many of these conflicts, particularly the internal ones, were so bitter that they caused the local populations to rise up in revolt in an effort to save themselves from the dangerous and debilitating burden of their overseers. The success of many of these provincial revolts may in part have been due to the Ōnin War as well. For the Ōnin War was one of the first major conflicts since the rise of the warrior class in which the samurai did not make up the bulk of the fighting force. Instead, Ōnin War period armies often found themselves taking to the field with over 50 per cent of their force being made up of quasi-auxiliary troops called *ashigaru*, or literally 'light-feet'.

Unpaid and unequipped, the vast majority of men who became *ashigaru* were generally desperately poor peasant farmers, hooligans and the others who made up the socially undesirable riff-raff of feudal-era Japanese society. The early bodies of *ashigaru* were primarily little more than mercenaries who attached themselves to armies irrespective of the goals of the force they had joined, in the hope that they might be able to improve their lot in life by partaking in the very real possibility of any post-battle plundering.

The first recorded reference to the *ashigaru* appears in the *Taiheiki*, which refers to a force of 800 'light archers' being employed to support a 1200-strong contingent of samurai at the battle of Shijo Nawate in 1348. In fact, it may have been the Mongols who introduced the Japanese to the concept of utilizing minimally skilled troops of auxiliary warriors to complement the more professional units in the field. For the Mongols had employed hordes of men during their invasion whose only duty was to suppress the samurai with vast volleys of arrows, which ran counter to the traditional samurai method of using the bow in skilled one-to-one engagements of precision shooting.

Thirteen days after leading a revolt against his lord, Oda Nobunaga, in 1582, General Akechi Mitsuhide's reign as Shōgun abruptly ended when he was killed by Nakamura Chōbei, a peasant bandit. The Japanese term for such an event is *gekokujō*, which means 'the low overcomes the high'. *Gekokujō* defines the Sengoku period and the level of social upheaval that gripped most of the 260 small kingdoms across the archipelago throughout that turbulent era.

Pre-Modern *Dō* Designs

While the full potential of the *ashigaru* to complement the actions of professional bodies of troops was never fully realized during the Ōnin War, the seed had been planted. No army would take to the field again in feudal-era Japan without utilizing such forces, which more astute commanders began to mould slowly into quasi-professional semi-permanent auxiliary forces that were gradually incorporated into the military hierarchy of their personal armies over the course of the late 15th and early 16th centuries.

While the *ashigaru* were changing the nature of warfare in Japan they were also changing the social order. For many ultimately had become fairly skilled fighters by the time that they began to drift away from the capital as the Ōnin War gradually drew to a close. Of these, many no doubt established themselves in rural areas as *ji-zamurai*, or farmer samurai, while others continued to survive as mercenaries, hiring themselves out to communities as enforcers to protect them from the numerous gangs of bandits that thrived in the post-war instability, the majority of whom were also more than likely former *ashigaru*.

This development was significant, for the large infusion of moderately skilled, armed fighting men into the countryside almost certainly helped to contribute to the success of a number of large-scale peasant uprisings in the provinces around Kyōto. In one early and highly influential rising in the province of Yamashiro, the regional military families were expelled from the province after they were defeated by an *ikki*, or communal army composed primarily of *ji-zamurai*, peasants and monks. *Ikki*, which can roughly be translated to mean both a 'communal league' and 'uprising', was the ideal name for these forces, which began to spread to other parts of Japan. By far the most successful of these groups was the followers of the militant Buddhist Jōdo Shinshū (True Pure Land) sect, known as the *Ikko-ikki*, which seized control of the province of Kaga in 1488 and held it for nearly a century.

Surprisingly, armour designs and construction techniques appear to have advanced little during the Ōnin War. If anything, the conflict seems to have rolled back the level of artistic decoration and detailing that had become almost commonplace by the end of the Nanbokuchō Wars at the end of the 14th century.

A 12th century warrior monk. The monk is wearing a *hara-ate* under his surplice-like outer garments. When worn in this manner the *hara-ate* was sometimes referred to as a *shita-haramaki*, literally 'under belly wrap'. Warrior monks dressed in this manner were common until the late 16th century. (Image © and courtesy of the Kyōto Costume Museum)

DEVELOPMENTS IN ARMOUR ASSEMBLY: THE *SUGAKE ODOSHI* METHOD OF LACING

This was most likely a result of the huge surge in demand that armour makers found themselves facing, which almost certainly forced many of them to reduce the degree of ornate detailing that had been typical of many pre-war armours in order simply to keep up with the pace of demand. This trend may also have reflected the substantial reduction in the number of supporting artisans who had previously assisted with such work, large numbers of whom may have lost their businesses or fled during the fighting that took place within the capital.

The one significant change that appears to have come about as a direct result of the massive demand for armour that occurred during the conflict was a new method of lacing armour that over time came to be referred to as *sugake odoshi*, or 'simple hang'. *Sugake odoshi*, which was originally referred to as *arame odoshi* or literally 'rough eye', was, in the words of Anthony Bryant, the 'hurried armourer's best friend', for it substantially reduced the amount of time that was required to lace a set of armour by reducing the volume of *odoshi-ge* that was utilized, which in turn also helped to reduce the overall cost of production.[1]

The *sugake odoshi* method of lacing differed from the traditional *kebiki odoshi* style in two key ways. Visually, the more obvious of the two ways was that the tightly arranged vertical bands of *odoshi-ge* that connected two vertically adjacent pieces of armour together along their entire horizontal length was reduced to a series of regularly spaced vertical pairs of laces. This one change significantly altered the aesthetics of how the existing conventional forms of armour appeared when complete. For a substantial portion of their aesthetic effect was derived from the large amount of visible lacing that adorned the façades of these forms of cuirass.

The second significant, though visually less obvious difference between the *sugake* and *kebiki odoshi* methods of lacing was that unlike *kebiki odoshi*, where the lacing was strung back and forth between two vertically adjacent pieces of armour to secure them together along their horizontal length, *sugake odoshi* was strung horizontally so that each length of lacing connected together all of the individual components of a single segment of armour, irrespective of the number of pieces. In other words, while *kebiki* was laced from left to right between two parts, *sugake odoshi* was strung from top to bottom so as to connect multiple parts simultaneously.

This was achieved by inserting both end points of a single long length of *odoshi-ge* through from the back face of the top *karami-no-ana* of two adjacent scales, generally beginning with the scales at the extreme left- or right-hand edge of the topmost *sane-ita* in a vertically arranged series of lames. The two ends were pulled through to the front of the scales where they were crossed, with the left-hand lace

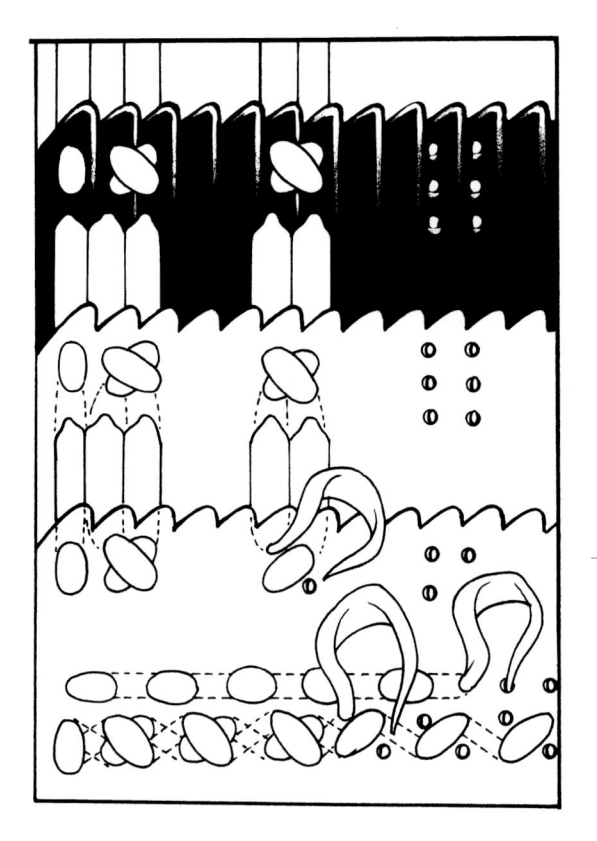

An illustration that shows the 'simple hang' or *sugake odoshi* method of lacing which was limited to regularly spaced pairs of laces vertically strung between *sane-ita*. Note the separate *mimi-odoshi*, *uname* and decorative *hishinui*.

Pre-Modern Dō Designs

being drawn downward diagonally to the right, where it was inserted through the second *karami-no-ana* of the adjacent scale and drawn out towards the back of the *sane-ita*. The length of lacing that originated on the right was then passed over the top of the left lace and pulled diagonally downward and to the left, where it too was inserted into the second *karami-no-ana* of the scale to the left of the one it originated from. This created an 'X'-like cross-knot pattern that was fundamentally the same as a *hishinui* in appearance on the visible façade of the *sane-ita*. That said, it is important to note that a *hishinui* was generally strung from left to right, thus the knots are technically not the same thing.

The two ends of lacing were then pulled straight downward and inserted outward through the *kedate-no-ana* on their respective scales. The ends were drawn through to the front of the scales and then pulled downward over the face of the *sane-ita*, creating the *kedate* portions of the lacing. The process was then repeated as the ends were inserted from behind through the top *karami-no-ana* of the *sane-ita* that was being suspended from the section of armour where the lacing had originated, in the descending order of that particular portion of armour and so on, until all the component pieces in a particular section were connected together top to bottom by a continuous row of paired vertical bands of lacing. The lacing process was unchanged by the reintroduction of solid-plate *ita-mono* to construct armour, which appears to have occurred within less than a decade of the end of the Ōnin War.

Sugake odoshi could also be strung by feeding just one end of a single lace from top to bottom through a series of vertical lames, following the downward side-to-side crossover pattern described above. The lace was then reversed at the bottom and run upwards in the reverse order to create the second of the two vertical bands of laces.

One unique, though not universal, characteristic of lacing strung in the *sugake odoshi* style was the use of small, thin triangular pieces of soft leather to anchor the laces once they had been drawn through an aperture. This was ostensibly done to prevent the suspended *ita-mono* from slipping out of horizontal alignment if a strong force pulled the plates up or down on the continuous vertical bands of *odoshi-ge*. It also helped prevent a space showing in the aperture above the lace of the latter when it was under load, which was often the case with lacing strung in the *sugake odoshi* style due to the reduced number of laces that were used to connect the individual sections of armour.

This was done by inserting the small plugs of leather or in some cases rolled ends of paper, narrow tip forward, as the *odoshi-ge* was being drawn through an aperture from the rear to the front. The plug was drawn along with the lacing until it was trapped in place by the increasing thickness of its tapered shape. The *odoshi-ge* was then drawn taut, which locked it in place due to the combined thickness of the plug and lacing.

It should be noted that towards the end of the 16th century a variation of the *sugake odoshi* style lacing was introduced. Referred to variously as

A late Edo period example of a *dō-maru* made in the *nuinobe* style utilizing *sane-ita* assembled from *iyozane*. The *sane-ita* are secured together by pairs of laces strung in the *sugake odoshi* style. The cuirass is an example of a *tachi-dō* because it is able to hold itself erect due to the use of internal leather thongs, called *tomegawa*, that bind the overlapping vertically stacked lamellar together. The *tomegawa* bindings are visible on the interior of the cuirass. Note the *ita-mono kusazuri*.

SAMURAI ARMOUR

chikara odoshi, *midokoro gake odoshi*, *mitsu suji gaki* or *shikime-me-nui*, this method of lacing was strung in the same general manner as *sugake odoshi* with the exception that a third set of holes was introduced to accommodate an independent third length of *odoshi-ge*, which was strung vertically, straight up between the two outside bands. As the two outside laces were overlapped by the third or central lace, the cross-knot had an asterisk-like appearance, which is one of the distinguishing features of this method of lacing.

Another Edo period variation of the *sugake odoshi* method of lacing was to string the paired laces together in tight groups consisting of three, four or five sets of laces. These were separated from the next vertical groups of laces by an equally large unlaced area of armour.

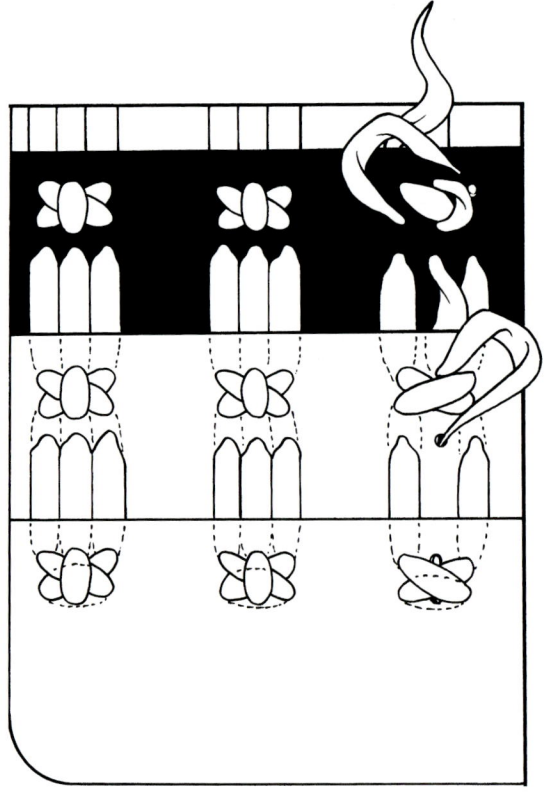

A rare alternative form of lacing referred to as *shikime-me-nui*, or literally 'cover eye sewing'. Also sometimes referred to as *chikiri odoshi*, this style of lacing required an alternative arrangement of apertures punched in the *sane* or *ita-mono* to be strung in this manner.

While many were quick to appreciate the economic and practical advantages of lacing armour in the *sugake odoshi* style, its popularity was initially rather limited, as conventional scale armour laced in the *sugake odoshi* style was aesthetically unappealing. This was due to the fact that the existing forms of armour construction techniques and designs had evolved over the centuries to be both structurally, and to a larger degree, aesthetically reliant on the presence of large horizontal bands of *odoshi-ge*. For the lacing hid a considerable portion of the visible details associated with scale construction techniques. It also helped to soften the appearance of armour while simultaneously ennobling it with colour.

Irrespective of this, *sugake odoshi* was a harbinger of things to come. That aesthetic considerations were beginning to take a back seat to other factors when it came to the design and construction of armour attested to the rapidly changing nature of the political and hence military landscape across Japan. For as the conflicts that erupted throughout the archipelago grew in number and size, the ability of armour makers to produce armour at a pace in keeping with the demand was

A late 16th century example of a *ni-mai-dō* made with a *nuinobe*-like façade. Note the unique appearance of the paired vertical rows of regularly spaced laces that is indicative of the *sugake odoshi* style of lacing. The obvious saving in both time and material that this method of lacing made possible is immediately evident when compared with the *iro-iro kebiki odoshi*-laced *kiritsuke kozane* hip armour tassets.

190

Pre-Modern Dō Designs

increasingly stretched to the limit. And while *sugake odoshi* had helped to improve the overall cost and time of production for a set of armour, it did not address the fundamental problem of the time and labour required to produce the scales.

While the solution to this impasse was far from immediate, the pressing nature of the demand for armour gradually led to the development of three alternative methods of armour construction over the course of the last few decades of the 15th century.

The first of these to appear was the *nuinobe* method of fabrication and assembly, which focused on reducing the number of scales that were required to assemble lamellar armour and the problems that were associated with that process.

An 18th century example of a folding cuirass, or *tatami-dō*, made from a series of card-like solid plates called *karuta* fastened together by intermediary bands of lacquered mail, or *kusari*.

The second technique, which was no doubt inspired in part by the concepts being developed around the *nuinobe* method of construction, made a huge evolutionary step forward by discontinuing the use of *sane-ita* altogether in favour of assembling armour from solid plates of leather or metal. This method of construction came to be known as the *Mōgami* style.

The third and final innovation came about through trial and error as armour makers sought a practical method of assembling *ita-mono* to create a cuirass that was form-fitting and easy to wear. The solution to this problem was to anchor the armoured plates to a fabric bodice. As pieces assembled in this manner are able to fold, this method of construction is referred to as *tatami*, after the Japanese verb for folding, *tatamu*.

What is important to note about the *nuinobe*, *Mōgami* and *tatami* styles of armour construction is that they did not represent new styles of cuirass, but only alternative ways of fabricating and assembling the forms of armour that already existed before the beginning of the 16th century, namely the *dō-maru*, *haramaki* and *hara-ate*, the *yoroi* having become virtually obsolete by that time.

It is also important to note that while each of these alternative methods of armour construction was to some degree influenced by aspects of the variation that had preceded it, it was ultimately the combination of all three methods of construction that led to the development of the *tosei-gusoku*, or so-called 'modern armour' forms of cuirass, the forerunners of which began to appear in the decades just prior to the middle of the 16th century.

NUINOBE

The almost eight-decade-long process that saw armour designs and construction techniques metamorphose from the classic forms to the 'modern' *tosei* styles began with the introduction of *sugake odoshi*. And though the classic forms of armour were generally unattractive when laced in this style, *sugake odoshi* prevailed for the simple reason that it saved the *katchū-shi* and their clientele a significant amount of both time and money by reducing the quantity of material and labour that was required to lace an armour. As such, it was not going away once it was discovered. Instead it proved to be the catalyst that inspired armour makers to find additional ways of simplifying the method by which armour was constructed.

One early answer to this problem was to discontinue the use of *kozane* in favour of *sane-ita* fabricated from the large *iyozane* style of scale, which reduced the number of scales used to assemble a section of *sane-ita*. *Iyozane* also looked better than *kozane*-laced lengths of *sane-ita* when laced in the *sugake odoshi* style.

While a step in the right direction, overall it made little difference. For the time-consuming and labour-intensive process of constructing armour from lames assembled from dozens of individual scales continued to be the only conceivable way to make armour as far as the Japanese armour makers of that period were concerned. Their inability to think outside the box in regards to this immensely restricting factor severely limited their options for change.

Even so, an alternative was eventually found in the method of construction called *nuinobe*, which means 'sewn spread'. This derived its name from how the *iyozane*-made lames that were universal to this style were assembled. The *nobe* or 'spread' portion of this name referred to the fact that the overlap between adjacent *iyozane* scales was reduced to a mere 2 mm. This maximized the visible frontage of each *iyozane* as they were 'spread out' along the length of the lame and thus reduced the number of scales that were required overall.

Changing the amount of overlap between scales, however, substantially altered the structural integrity of *sane-ita*. This in turn forced the *katchū-shi* to make additional changes in how they assembled the scales, including how the *shita-garami* were *nui* or 'sewn'. The

An Edo period example of a *hara-ate* assembled using the hinged, solid-plate and *sugake odoshi*-laced *Mōgami* method of armour fabrication.

widened spread of the scales increased the length of the bindings between scales when the *shita-garami* were bound in the conventional manner, and this created a greater degree of both horizontal and vertical play between the bound *iyozane* which undermined the overall strength and rigidity of the lame.

The new *nuinobe* method of binding the *shita-garami* created a distinctive pattern of two parallel columns of horizontal dashes across the lower façade of the *sane-ita*. This band was offset by an upper row of bindings that appeared as a series of left-to-right angled upward leaning dashes.

In the case of the latter this was achieved by stringing the *shita-garami* from the front to the

Pre-Modern *Dō* Designs

A close-up view of a cuirass that was constructed using *sane-ita* assembled using the *nuinobe* method. The small amount of overlap between adjacent scales indicative of this method of construction is clearly visible. Unseen, however, is the unique method of binding the *shita-garami* which compensated for the reduced overlap between the *shiki-gane*-reinforced lengths of *sane-ita* assembled from *iyozane*. Thin sheets of dog hide were used to sheath the *sane-ita* to help further offset the reduced amount of overlap between scales. Note the parallel pairs of lacing strung in the *sugake odoshi* style.

A view of the back side of *gessan* assembled from *iyozane* scales. The minimal amount of overlap between scales is clearly evident, as is the significantly reduced number of scales required to construct a *sane-ita* when *iyozane* are utilized. Note the *shiki-gane* that have been bound to the back of the *sane-ita* by the *shita-garami* bindings. Though only partial visible on the leftmost *gessan*, decorative bear fur trims were applied to the lower façades of the *suso-no-ita*. Because the fur was embedded in wet lacquer to adhere it to the *sane-ita* it is referred to as *ue-kuma-ge*, or literally 'planted bear fur'.

back through the uppermost *shita-garami-no-ana* of the left-hand row of holes in the *iyozane* at the left edge of the arranged row of scales. The binding was drawn through, leaving a short end piece protruding from the face of the scale that could be trapped and locked under a returning portion of the binding. The *shita-garami* hanging at the back of the scale was pulled straight down and pushed out to the front of the same scale through the third-from-the-bottom *shita-garami-no-ana*. It was drawn taut and then laced diagonally upward to the right, overlapping the end piece to anchor the latter, before it was inserted into the upper, right-hand-most *shita-garami-no-ana* of the original scale. The binding was pushed through to the rear of the scale and then pulled horizontally across to the right, bridging the overlap between the original scale and the *iyozane* to the immediate right. The *shita-garami* was then inserted into the uppermost *shita-garami-no-ana* of the right-hand scale from the back and drawn out to the front. From here it was pulled downward and to the left where it was inserted into the third *shita-garami-no-ana* in the right-hand row of apertures in the original scale. The binding was then inserted outward through the back of the scale and pulled to the right, where it was inserted into the third *shita-garami-no-ana* from the bottom of the right-hand scale and drawn back out to the front of the scale. From here the diagonal process of binding repeated itself across the length of the lame.

A sturdy, and generally iron, *shiki-gane* was carefully positioned and secured under the loops of the above-mentioned *shita-garami* as it was threaded along the length of the lame to help improve the structural integrity of the *sane-ita*.

The lower binding was bound in the reverse mirrored order of the upper band of *shita-garami*, with the diagonal band portions of binding running diagonally downward from left to right on the back side face of the *sane-ita*. This resulted in two vertically aligned continuous rows of horizontal dashes of binding appearing on the face of the armour at the point where each scale overlapped.

Even with the changed method of binding the *shita-garami*, *sane-ita* assembled from the *iyozane* that were spread out in the *nuinobe* style were still not as resilient as a conventional section of *sane-ita* assembled from *kozane*. For this reason, smiths began to wrap, and in some cases simply face, the individual *sane-ita* in thin sheets of leather in the *kawa-tsuzumi*, literally 'leather-wrapped', style, to help make them more resilient. Though horse hide was utilized, dog hides, or *inu-gawa*, were preferred for this purpose because they were more supple and thinner.

While this added an additional step to the method of assembly, it also helped to significantly reduce the overall time required to finish a lame due to the fact that the applied lacquer finishes were now hidden under the *inu-gawa*. This meant that the final layers of lacquer did not have to be applied and polished, which saved a considerable amount of time and effort.

The leather was attached with glue and smoothed into place to reveal the *kedate* and *nawame-garami* apertures, which were pushed through with a tool to open them. The leather covering was then itself lacquered over, which considerably strengthened the lame.

While not hinted at in the *nuinobe* name, wrapping the *iyozane*-assembled lames in leather was, along with *sugake odoshi*, one of the defining features of a cuirass constructed in the *nuinobe* style. However, the *kawa-tsuzumi* step of this process faded out as alternative methods of armour construction were introduced during the latter half of the 16th century. By that time, however, *dō* made in the *nuinobe* style had become so common that even after the original method of fabrication that characterized this form of construction had largely been discontinued, any cuirass that featured an *iyozane*, *sugake odoshi*-laced façade was still deemed to be an example of a *nuinobe*-made cuirass. This is discussed further in Chapter 6.

It appears that most *nuinobe*-made examples of cuirass were *dō-maru*, though *haramaki-* and *hara-ate*-made examples were also produced. The assembly of cuirasses made in the *nuinobe* form was identical to those made in the traditional manner, including the number of lames that were used to construct the *nagakawa*, *mae-tateage* and *ushiro-tateage*. The one key difference was that the individual lames were secured together horizontally by a series of leather ties made from dog hide called *tomegawa*, which literally translates as 'stopping leathers'. The *tomegawa* were threaded through the uppermost *karami-no-ana* of every second row of *sugake odoshi* before the lacing was strung, which allowed them to be hidden under the cross-knot of the lacing when the latter was tied. The ends of the *tomegawa* ties were pulled through two corresponding apertures that were punched in the lower edge of the plate immediately above and behind the one from where the cord originated, where they were tied off. This meant that each lame of the *nagakawa* was generally attached to the one immediately above or below it by only around fifteen of these delicate ties, which represented a serious weakness in the design of cuirasses assembled in the *nuinobe* style. Further compounding the strain that the *tomegawa* were under was the fact that their knotted ends were exposed around

A close-up view of *sane-ita* that have been fabricated in the *nuinobe* style that clearly shows the use of thin sheets of dog-leather, or *inu-gawa* to wrap the *iyozane*-assembled *sane-ita*, which was an integral part of the original *nuinobe* method of the construction. Just visible in the gaps between the *sane-ita* are the leather *tomegawa* bindings that were used to secure the bands together, which helped to make the cuirass more rigid and to hold it erect. For this reason *dō* assembled in this manner are sometimes referred to as 'standing cuirasses', or *tachi-dō*. Note the *gattari* bracket affixed to the middle of the *oshitsuke-no-ita*.

A rare view of the interior of a *dō-maru* assembled using the *nuinobe* method of construction. The individually leather-wrapped lengths of *iyozane*-constructed *sane-ita* can be noted, as can the *shiki-gane* strips that were bound to the rear of the *sane-ita* by the *shita-garami*. The multitude of *tomegawa* ties that bind the overlapping *sane-ita* together can be noted. The inherent weakness associated with this method of securing the bands together is immediately evident, with the exposed ties constantly being subject to wear-and-tear when the *dō* was worn. Note how the lowest *sane-ita* of the *nagakawa* arches upwards to contour to the hips along the sides of the torso.

An excellent study of a cuirass that has been constructed in the *nuinobe* style. In keeping with the fact that *nuinobe* refers to a method of construction and not a unique form of cuirass, the armour itself is a *dō-maru* as can be noted by its continuous one-piece wraparound, *ichi-mai-dō* form. The *iyozane*-assembled *sane-ita*, including those used for the *gessan* and the solid plates of the *kanagu mawari* have all been sheathed in leather and laced together in the open *sugake odoshi* style. The only features on this cuirass that would not have been typical of a late 15th century *nuinobe*-made *dō* are the *gattari* and the padded *eri-dai* shoulder yoke with its integral brigandine collar and *kobire*.

the interior surface of the cuirass. This meant they were subject to the additional wear and tear of the body movements of the warrior, which often caused them to come undone.

Securing the *sane-ita* together in this manner not only held them in position but also caused the *dō* to stand erect, as the bindings limited how far the cuirass could collapse vertically. *Dō* made with this initially unusual feature were referred to as *tachi-dō*, or literally 'standing cuirass', differentiating them from conventional forms of lamellar *dō*, which devoid of the internal *tomegawa* bindings tended to collapse, or telescope inward upon themselves. The *tomegawa* bindings between the *sane-ita* were generally hidden under the cross-knot portions of every second column of *sugake odoshi* lacing, being tied before the lacing was strung.

MŌGAMI-DŌ

While some armour makers experimented with refining the *nuinobe* method of fabrication, others were beginning to develop another far more revolutionary form of armour construction and assembly technique that would come to be known as the *Mōgami* style. And though it is impossible to say for sure, there is a strong probability that the *Mōgami* method of armour making was developed by the hordes of recently elevated *ji-zamurai* and rag-tag armies of men who made up the various *ikki* around Japan. For many of these groups had started to produce armour for themselves in an effort to arm the large numbers of men amongst their ranks who were for the most part without equipment. Their hand was somewhat forced in this regard by the fact that their risings had in many cases severed their access to armour and the artisans who generally contributed to its fabrication and who lived outside the boundaries of their domains.

Not surprisingly the items of armour that were created in these regions broke with the status quo, out of necessity but also due to the fact that they were produced by and for men who were predominately pragmatist. The humble means of these men, both craftsmen and clientele alike, was reflected in the end product. For it is likely that much of the armour produced was created by blacksmiths who had turned to armour making, which is why most of the locally produced items of armour were generally rather crude, simple in overall form and free of all but the most rudimentary forms of decoration. Locally produced items of armour of this kind are well documented as there are numerous surviving pieces that were made in the province of Kii by the local Saiga-ikki smiths, whose works, particularly the *kabuto*, are covered in greater detail in the companion book, Volume II, of this text.

Pressed for time, short of resources and lacking experience in armour making, it is easy to see why the next great evolutionary leap, of a return to making armour from sections of solid plate, most likely took place amongst the isolated low-level echelons of relatively inexperienced rural armour makers and their clientele.

Supporting this theory is the fact that the first known extant examples of post-10th century items of armour assembled entirely from sections of solid plate are said to have originated in the *Mōgami* area of what is now the present-day Yamagata Prefecture. And while there is no hard evidence to prove that the first examples of cuirass assembled in this revolutionary new manner originated in *Mōgami*, the fact that cuirasses assembled in this style were common throughout the Tōhoku or northern region of Honshū by the first half of the 16th century tends to support the rural northern origins of this method of construction.

Though we cannot be sure of exactly how the *Mōgami* method of construction came about, it can be surmised that armour makers, perhaps more knowledgeable in the production of tools and other implements, began to craft items of armour made from solid plates. Being

This unusual *isei-dō* captures the simplicity that was at the core of the *Mōgami* method of armour construction: easily fabricated solid metal plate sections joined together by hinges and laced in the conservative *sugake odoshi* style. Note the use of *kawa-odoshi*. The *saihai-no-kan* swivel ring affixed to the *muna-ita* is clearly a later and, most likely, modern addition. It should be fitted to the *mae-tateage* and not be anchored through the *karami-no-ana* used for the lacing as it is in the example.

Pre-Modern *Dō* Designs

better versed in the making of articles from flat metal plates they began to try to create cuirasses based on the two main existing forms of *dō*. As with the *nuinobe* method of armour construction, this tends to suggest that it was not the objective of the armour makers who came up with this technique to create new forms of *dō*, but rather to simplify the production of the already existing makes of cuirass.

That they chose a radical new approach by utilizing plate, or *ita-mono*, instead of scales may have initially been less an ingenious act of foresight than a reflection on the general inability of the relatively inexperienced *katchū-shi* in these regions to create armour using more complex processes. Supporting this theory is the fact that the *Mōgami* method of construction existed for two or three decades before such armour began to be worn by the samurai, who initially viewed it as a form of cuirass that was only suitable for use by lower-ranking warriors, such as the *ji-zamurai* and the few *ashigaru* who could privately acquire such items. This contradicts the commonly accepted premise that the established *katchū-shi*, hard pressed to produce scale armour in sufficient quantities, suddenly came upon the idea of creating armour from sections of solid plate, which they made more palatable to the samurai they sold them to by covering the *ita-mono* with a façade of false scales shaped out in lacquer. They would indeed do this, but such practices did not occur until much later in the evolutionary development of such pieces.

Instead it seems far more plausible that the full potential of this revolutionary armour-construction technique was not fully appreciated until the samurai began to witness a growing number of low-ranking troops wearing examples of *dō* made in *Mōgami* style on campaign, where the functional practicality of these simple yet resilient makes of cuirass was amply demonstrated.

It was most likely the samurai who, having been impressed, brought the idea of assembling armour from *ita-mono* into vogue with the mainstream armour makers. This is not to say that the latter were unaware of the *Mōgami* method of construction by this period, but that they had largely continued to produce armour in accordance with what their market wanted rather than what the market needed. Once this bridge was crossed, however, they were quick both to capitalize on the advantages of constructing armour from plate and to improve upon the existing design and method of construction. In time these changes and developments began to include methods that allowed armour makers to dress up the façades

A *haramaki* made using the *Mōgami* method. The simple, battleworthy and practical nature of this construction method is immediately evident when compared with the complex methods of scale construction that had been utilized until the later part of the 15th century. Note the padded *wadagami* and the *kohaze*-threaded cords that help to secure the *waki-ita* in place.

197

Samurai Armour

of the *ita-mono* in a way that made them look as though they were *sane-ita*. This allowed the *katchū-shi* to market plate-made armour to the more conservative elements amongst the samurai class who continued to prefer the traditional forms of armour and for those samurai to benefit from the practical and cost-saving advantages of armour assembled from *ita-mono*. Such innovations, however, appeared many decades after the first examples of cuirasses constructed in the *Mōgami* style had started to appear, and as such are further discussed later on in this chapter.

Understanding the *Mōgami* method of armour design and construction is essential, for its introduction was the proverbial missing link between the classic forms of armour assembled from scale and the so-called 'modern armour', or *tosei-gusoku*, that ultimately superseded them as the primary forms of armour by the middle of the 16th century.

Beyond knowing they were made from *ita-mono* and laced in the *sugake odoshi* style, we can only surmise how the earliest examples of *Mōgami*-made versions of *dō-maru* or *haramaki* were actually assembled. For the main stumbling block in making these two forms of *dō* from plate was the same problem that had confronted *katchū-shi* for centuries: how to make a cuirass from solid metal plates that properly conformed

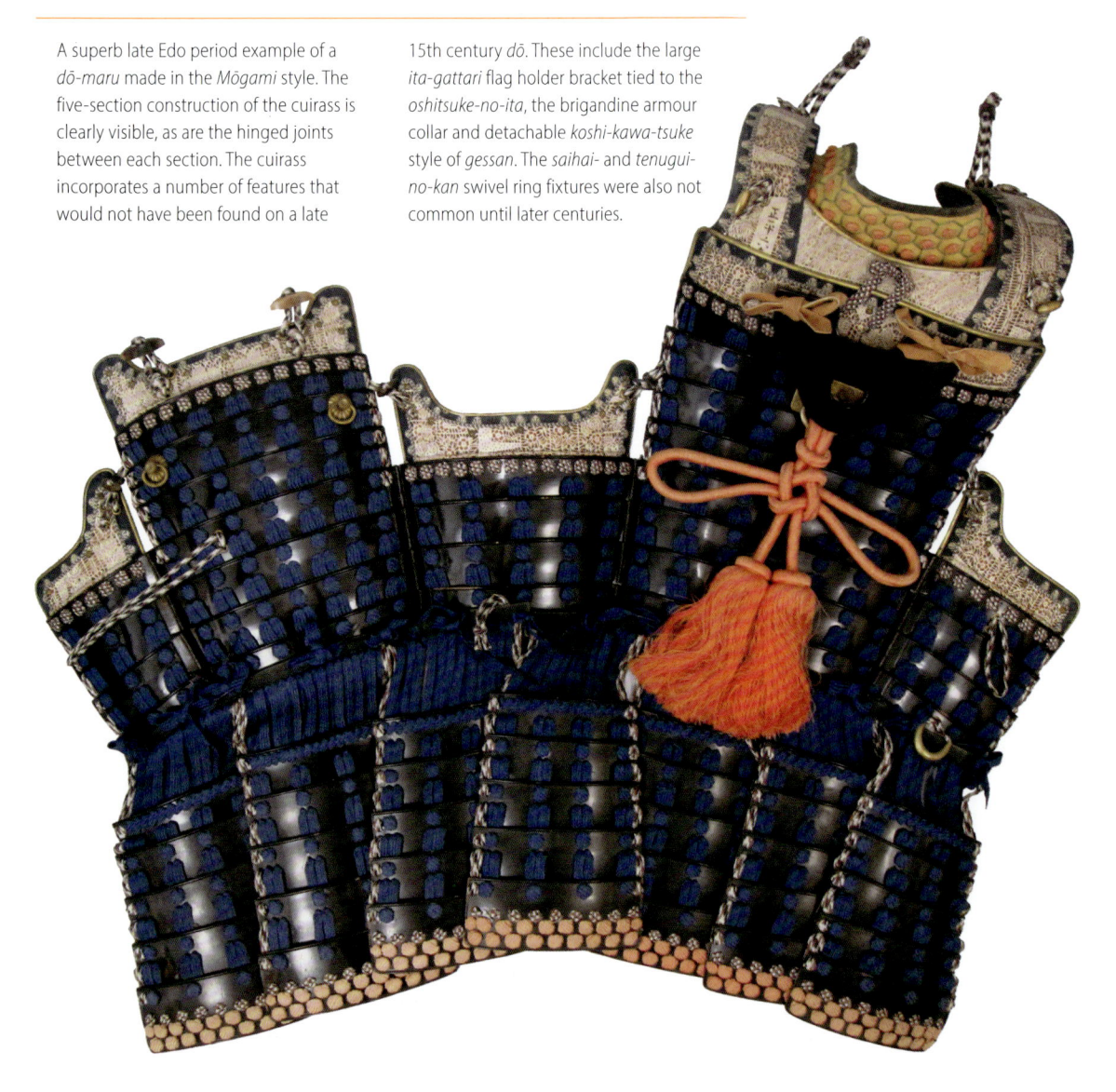

A superb late Edo period example of a *dō-maru* made in the *Mōgami* style. The five-section construction of the cuirass is clearly visible, as are the hinged joints between each section. The cuirass incorporates a number of features that would not have been found on a late 15th century *dō*. These include the large *ita-gattari* flag holder bracket tied to the *oshitsuke-no-ita*, the brigandine armour collar and detachable *koshi-kawa-tsuke* style of *gessan*. The *saihai-* and *tenugui-no-kan* swivel ring fixtures were also not common until later centuries.

to the curvatures of the torso and that was still easy to wear? The answer to this dilemma when it came was as straightforward as it was brilliant: assemble each of the individual horizontal bands of the *nagakawa* from five separate but conjoined plates that could articulate in a way that allowed the cuirass literally to fold around the body.

Constructing the *nagakawa* in this manner, from a series of subtly curved plates, greatly simplified the production of a cuirass and therefore also reduced the amount of time required. This was not only a result of the fact that *ita-mono* were used in lieu of *sane-ita*, but was also due to the articulating nature of the *Mōgami* method of construction, which removed the need to forge plates with complex curvatures. While this saved on time, it also meant that even moderately skilled smiths could produce *ita-mono* in the shapes required, which enabled more men to produce a greater amount of armour in a shorter period of time.

For a *dō-maru* constructed in the *Mōgami* style, the bands of the *nagakawa* were assembled in a manner beginning on the front, right-hand side of the torso, which would be protected by several short plates, or *ita-mono*, about 6.5 cm in height, that extended horizontally just over half-way back along the right side of the body. Long *ita-mono* that extended across the front of the body were hinged to the forward edge of each of the right side plates. In turn, each of the long torso-covering *ita-mono* would likewise have another horizontal plate hinged to their left-hand edges. These would extend from the front left of the torso back to the rear left-hand side of the body. Long *ita-mono* to cover the back of the torso would then be secured to the rear vertical edges of each of the left side plates. The fifth and final column of narrow, horizontally arranged *ita-mono* was attached to the rear, right-hand edges of each of the back plates. Being hinged in the same manner as the rest of the armour, these plates could be articulated to fold forward so as to cover the rear right-hand side of the body, thus fully enclosing the torso within the protective covering of the cuirass.

Haramaki-style cuirasses made in the *Mōgami* style featured long chest plates, with full-sized side plates that reached to the back of the torso affixed to either side of them. Short lengths that could be folded inward were attached to the rear edges of the side plates to cover the left and right sides of the back of the torso in the usual style of a 15th century *haramaki*. As with conventional *haramaki*,

A view of the rear of a *Mōgami dō-maru*. The cuirass has been fitted with an auxiliary *sei-ita* of matching construction. Note how an arrangement of *kohaze-* and *seme-kohaze-* strung cords has been used to secure the *sei-ita* to the *dō*. The sturdy *dō-jime* cords anchored to the bottom of the *nagakawa* are also used hold the *sei-ita* in position.

some examples of *Mōgami haramaki* were fitted with *sei-ita* which were to have the same number of rows of solid plates in their assembly as were used to construct the cuirass, inclusive of its suspended *kusazuri*.

How the individual segments of the *nagakawa* were joined together on the earliest examples is unknown, but it appears that several variations of rudimentary hinge were utilized. One of the earliest versions may have employed small lamellar sections to connect the neighbouring lengths of solid plates, like one example of *Mōgami haramaki* that is housed in the Shimizu Shrine collection. These were assembled from short lengths of *kozane* that were devoid of the reinforcing *shiki-gane* strips, which allowed them to flex. While functional, the small sections of *kozane* were in many ways an overly complex method of hinging independent pieces of armour plating together. And while it was probably not a matter of concern, the combination of solid plate overlaid in places by small panels of scale tended to make cuirasses made in this manner look as though they had been assembled from parts scavenged from other *dō*, which may in fact have been the case.

Alternative methods of joining the *nagakawa* plates saw use of thick bands of leather, which like the sections of *kozane* were laced to the ends of adjoined plates. While practical, the narrow band of leather that was exposed at the joint between the plating represented an obvious weak point in the armour. Experiments in this regard, however, may have inadvertently led to the development of an entirely new variety of armour that came to be known as *tatami yoroi*, or folding armour, which is addressed later in this chapter.

The solution to this problem was to join the individual plates of the *nagakawa* together using metal hinges. This both nullified the weak points at the joints and generally simplified the manner of production, with the hinges being riveted in place. Exactly when metal hinges became the norm is difficult to say, though they appear to have been virtually universal by the

A close-up view of the small knuckled style of *chotsugai* that were used to join sections of *ita-mono* together on cuirasses made in the *Mōgami* style. The small size of the hinges meant they were rather delicate for the job they had to perform.

A view of the interior of the same *dō*. The knuckled hinges between adjacent *ita-mono* are clearly visible. Note the tied bows of *tomegawa* behind every second column of *sugake odoshi*. Also note the small plugs of leather that helped to prevent the lacing from being pulled back through the apertures in the plate after it was strung.

end of the 15th century. Their introduction may have represented innovations introduced by some of the old-school armour makers as they began to learn about and experiment with making armour using the *Mōgami* method of construction.

The *kusazuri* too were typically made from *ita-mono* laced in the *sugake odoshi* style. In some cases, however, *sugake*-laced *sane-ita* were also utilized. In some cases it may simply have represented the cannibalization and recycling of useable materials from older cuirasses that were beyond repair, while in others it was done as a way of reducing the overall weight of a cuirass assembled from metal plates.

It was common for the upper and side edges of each plate to be rolled slightly forward to create a subtle though important flange. This feature, which may have come about through trial and error, helped to prevent the upper edge of the plates from wearing on the connective *kedate* portions of the *sugake odoshi*. It may also have helped to stop the vertically telescoping arrangement of plates from slipping out of place and hanging up on top of each other.

The plates were generally finished in lacquer, with the rolled edges being applied so as to create a soft rolled bead-like lip. In most cases the lengths of leather were glued to the roughly lacquered backs of the plates, which were secured together vertically by a series of *tomegawa* ties in the same manner that cuirasses constructed in the *nuinobe* style were assembled, and this meant that *Mōgami*-made cuirasses were subject to the same structural weaknesses.

Even so, the *Mōgami* method of construction continued to grow in popularity as the level and intensity of the various conflicts across Japan escalated in size and number. For these conflicts had begun to highlight additional issues with lamellar armour constructed in the traditional manner that even the scale of the Ōnin War had not brought to light. This was largely because the majority of the fighting

A view of the open central channel down the rear of a *haramaki* made in the *Mōgami* style. Note the ability of the cuirass to sit erect without support due to the *tomegawa* bindings visible on the interior of the *dō*. The presence of *shiki-gane* on the interior faces of the *ita-mono* indicates that the *dō* has been made from *nerigawa*.

SAMURAI ARMOUR

during the Ōnin War had taken place within an urban environment. The conflicts that erupted after the Ōnin War, however, were largely fought along the rural frontiers between neighbouring domains. They also tended to be long, drawn-out affairs that kept opposing forces in the field for substantially longer periods than had been common during the conflicts of earlier times.

This situation wreaked havoc on the traditional *kebiki odoshi*-laced forms of armour. As Sakakibara notes in his definitive thesis on armour, *The Manufacture of Armour and Helmets in Sixteenth Century Japan* (*Chūko Katchū Seisakuben*), the 'large quantity of lacing is a disadvantage', for 'when soaked with water it becomes very heavy and cannot be quickly dried.' This, he observes, made it oppressive in summer and liable to freeze in winter. Sakakibara also noted that 'no amount of washing will completely free the lacing from any mud that may have penetrated it.' This caused the lacing to become 'evil smelling and overrun by ants and lice, with consequent ill effects on the health of the wearer'.[2]

Sakakibara goes on to note how the increased usage of edged weaponry such as spears also easily damaged the lacing strung in the *kebiki odoshi* style, for the tightly spaced laces tended to 'retain a spear instead of letting it glide off harmlessly'. Aside from the damage caused to the lacing, such situations also greatly increased the likelihood of the wearer being killed or severely injured. In fact, Sakikibara's statement is given ample credence by a statistical study by Thomas Conlan of battle wounds between 1467 and 1600, charting a growing use of polearms, which by 1600 accounted for an astonishing 98% of all the non-projectile wounds received in battle.[3]

For samurai already in possession of *kebiki odoshi*-laced sets of lamellar armour, the solution to this problem was to have them re-laced in the *sugake odoshi* style and to have the unused holes in *kozane* filled in with lacquer. For samurai acquiring new sets of armour, however, the decision was an increasingly obvious one; by the early part of the 16th century even higher-ranking members of the warrior class also came to prefer sets that were constructed in the *Mōgami* style, which is probably why almost two centuries later Sakakibara Kōzan mistakenly concluded that the *Mōgami* style of cuirass 'probably dates from the Taiyei Era (1521–28)'.[4]

A warrior from the late 15th century wearing a *haramaki* made in the *Mōgami* style. Note the *gyōyō* suspended from the ends of the *wadagami* and the smaller *ita-mono sode* shoulder guards. The warrior is depicted wearing a rigid style of *eboshi* cap and *suneate*. *Haidate* thigh armour was still relatively uncommon during this period. (Image © and courtesy of the Kyōto Costume Museum)

Pre-Modern *Dō* Designs

An example of tassets made in the *kiritsuke kozane* style. The façade of replicated small scales applied to the *ita-mono* is highly convincing and almost impossible to differentiate from armour made from scales except upon close inspection. Gilt *kaze-domari kanamono* have been affixed to the *suso-no-ita*. Note how the split shanks of these fixtures have been covered with leather patches on the back of the lames. Also note the sparing use of *shu urushi*, which was more costly and toxic to use than conventional black lacquer.

Naturally the quality of the cuirasses produced in the *Mōgami* style improved as acceptance of this method of construction spread. This in turn gradually saw the return of many of the features that the earliest examples of *Mōgami*-made *dō* had been devoid of, such as *e-gawa*-faced *muna-*, *oshitsuke-*, and *waki-no-ita* plates. Changes such as these were primarily driven by the wealthier members of the warrior class, who demanded armour more in keeping with their refined aesthetic sensibilities and desire to differentiate themselves from the rank-and-file samurai.

This ultimately resulted in a hybrid *kebiki odoshi*-laced *ita-mono* version of the cuirass made in the *Mōgami* style being introduced during the first few decades of the 16th century. While this produced a *dō* that was aesthetically similar in overall appearance to a conventional *sane-ita*-assembled cuirass, the large number of perforations that were required to lace the *ita-mono* in this manner considerably undermined much of the structural integrity of the plates. This drawback, however, was offset somewhat by the fact that the *kebiki odoshi* helped to improve the physical structure of the cuirass by taking a substantial amount of the connective burden of the internal leather ties.

The two-steps forward, one-step back aspect of incorporating *kebiki odoshi* into the *Mōgami* method of construction reflected the infatuation that many samurai continued to have with the appearance of *dō* made in the classical styles. While many could appreciate the 'eminently practical' aspects of the *Mōgami* style, they were put off by the visual simplicity of its finished form, which was an integral part of its design and assembly.[5]

The solution when it came in the decades leading up to the middle of the 16th century was an innovative one. Armour makers learned to make *ita-mono* resemble *sane-ita* by clipping small, inverted right-angle triangular indentations along the entire upper length of a plate to create a saw-blade-like edge, with each 'tooth' being cut to correspond to the width of a single *kozane*. This allowed *katchū-shi* to 'imitate a scale armour while maintaining much of the utility of one made of plate'.[6]

This novel idea was quickly improved upon by moulding the surface of the *ita-mono* into vertical ribs, formed using *kokuso*.[7] These were then lacquered over and finished in such a way as to accurately replicate the façade of a section of armour assembled from individual *kozane*. The effect can be highly realistic when the work is done properly, so much so that when viewed face on, true scale and replicated scale boards are often virtually indistinguishable from each other without very close inspection. *Ita-mono* finished in this manner are aptly referred to as *kiritsuke kozane*, or literally 'cut and applied scales'.

Gradually smiths began to replicate other forms of *sane-ita* using this process, which they slowly expanded upon to further enhance the realism of the visual illusion they were creating, examples of which are further discussed in the next chapter. This new technique, however, could not be practically applied to *nuinobe*-made cuirasses, for the simple reason that as with the *tankō* of the first millennium, the utilization of

Left: A close-up view of the highly realistic *kiritsuke kozane* façade that has been applied to the *suso-no-ita* of a *gessan*. Note how the lower *shita-garami* was threaded through the board to further enhance the illusion that the lame was assembled from scale.

Right: The reverse of the same *gessan*. The presence of *shiki-gane* confirm that the *ita-mono* have been fabricated from *nerigawa*. The *shiki-gane* helped the lames maintain their subtle curvature. The lower, decorative *shita-garami* is visible under the *urushi*.

solid plates to construct a continuous one-piece cuirass made it exceptionally difficult to access the *dō* to wear it. Likewise, the repetitive practice of springing the cuirass apart to open it slowly but progressively damaged and weakened the *ita-mono* around the continuous left flank of the body.

The multitude of changes and innovations that can ultimately be traced back to the introduction of the *Mōgami* method of *dō* construction are part of the reason why Japanese armour experts are unable to agree on what constitutes a cuirass made in the *Mōgami* style. For some, a *dō* must be assembled from *ita-mono* and be laced in the *sugake odoshi* style to be considered an example of the *Mōgami* method of construction. Others, however, are of the opinion that cuirasses assembled from *kebiki odoshi*-laced *ita-mono* can also be considered to be made in the *Mōgami* style.

Both arguments are somewhat incidental, however, considering that the true defining feature of a *Mōgami*-made cuirass is a *dō* that features a *nagakawa* assembled from independent bands, each of which is composed of five separate plates that are connected horizontally by some form of articulating joint in four locations. As such, a *ni-mai-dō* cannot be considered to be an example of a cuirass made in the *Mōgami* style even if it is assembled from *ita-mono* that have been laced in the *sugake odoshi* style.

Having said this, it is important to differentiate *dō* made in the *Mōgami* style from the *go-mai-dō* of later periods that are discussed in detail in Chapter 9, and which were clearly inspired by the *Mōgami* method of construction. Even though the construction techniques of both were based on a *nagakawa* divided into five sections, the bands of the *nagakawa* on *go-mai-dō* are joined together to form vertical sections of armour, each of which can be separated from its neighbour by the removal of a shared hinge pin. The bands of the *nagakawa* of a *Mōgami*-made cuirass, however, are independent of each other vertically, with only the lacing and internal ties holding them together. And though the bands of the *nagakawa* are hinged, the latter are fixed in place. As such the *nagakawa* is one continuous piece, which means that both *Mōgami dō-maru* and *Mōgami haramaki* are examples of *ichi-mai-dō* irrespective of the fact that the *nagakawa* of these cuirasses articulate.

TATAMI-DŌ

This was also true of cuirasses that were made using the *tatami* method of armour construction, which was originally no more than an experimental offshoot of the *Mōgami* style. Unlike its parent form, however, the *tatami* method of stitching *ita-mono* to cloth bodices to create armour met with relatively little success during the latter part of the 15th and the early 16th centuries.

PRE-MODERN *DŌ* DESIGNS

was, however, clearly not the case. For there are no known extant examples of mass-produced items of *tatami* made from the late 15th or early 16th centuries.

The general scarcity of *tatami*-made items of armour is reflected in the fact that they do not appear on any of the famous Japanese screens with painted battle scenes, which, even though most of them were painted decades after the events that they depict, remain among the best sources for what was happening in the Sengoku period. While it could be argued that *tatami* items do not appear because Japanese artists

A high-quality late Edo period *tatami-dō* made from lacquered *nerigawa* card-like plates called *karuta* sewn to a cloth bodice. The earliest examples of folding armour were more than likely fabricated in a manner similar to this cuirass.

A high-quality 18th century example of *tatami-dō* that has been fabricated using long, vertically arranged solid plates, or *tatehagi-ita*, secured together by intermediary bands of lacquered *kusari*. While folding armour appears to have been invented in the late 15th century, cuirasses made in this manner were rare until well into the 17th century.

Why this was the case is unclear, considering that this construction technique went on to become quite common in later centuries. This phenomenon may, however, be explained by the fact that *ita-mono* sewn to fabric lacked rigidity and therefore gave inadequate protection against the force of a blow.[8]

That the *tatami* method of construction was not abandoned altogether was largely due to the fact that this method of fabrication produced armour that, while structurally weak, was exceptionally easy to store and transport. This aspect of *tatami*-made items of armour would gradually come to be seen as one of its most valuable characteristics in later centuries as the dynamics of the feudal-period Japanese armies changed. This stands in contrast with how *tatami*-made items of armour have generally been presented, which is that they were produced in bulk for low-ranking warriors during the 16th century; this

simply chose to neglect them in favour of showing more impressive and presentable forms of armour, this is unlikely. For though the artists of earlier periods had often intentionally failed to include the presence of the samurai's low retainers on the battlefield, the illustrations of the 16th and 17th centuries regularly depicted the *ashigaru* and as such had no reason to hide or alter the appearance of their armour and equipment. Evidence of this is clearly apparent in the famous *Zōhyō Monogatari* scrolls, commonly referred to as the 'Tales of the Ashigaru', that are believed to have been made around 1637–38. This amazing document records in minute detail numerous aspects of the duties, equipment, and lifestyle of an *ashigaru* of the early Edo period. And though there is ample evidence to support the existence of the many hundreds of other items that are shown being used by the *ashigaru* in the scroll, nowhere is an *ashigaru* ever depicted wearing a form of *tatami*-made cuirass.

While this is not to say that some forms of *tatami*-made cuirass were not in existence and utilized during the 16th century, such examples were clearly a rarity in that period.[9] That said, there is documentary evidence of a senior member of the Hosokawa clan owning a set of armour made in the *tatami* style dating from 1636, according to the Japanese armour authorities Yamagishi Yasuo and Miyazaki Masumi in their book *Nihon Katchū no Kiso Chishiki Shinsōban* (Basic Knowledge of Japanese Armour, New Edition).

Further undermining the idea that the *tatami*-made version of the cuirass was commonly issued to low-ranking warriors during the 16th century is the fact that, contrary to what is often suggested, items of *tatami*-made armour are not easy to make. They can be just as complex or even more complex and time-consuming to make than a very basic conventional example of *tosei ni-mai-dō*. For it would appear to be much easier to fabricate the *nagakawa* of a cuirass from several long strips than to do so using a

A low-ranking *ashigaru* warrior wearing an *okashi* (lent) *tatami gusoku*. Modern imagery commonly depicts the *ashigaru* of the Sengoku period wearing this form of armour irrespective of the fact that there are no known period sources or illustrations of *ashigaru* equipped in this manner. (Image © and courtesy of the Kyōto Costume Museum)

multitude of small rectangular plates. This is especially true when one considers that the latter were also usually connected by intermediary bands of *kusari*, all of which had to be sewn to a fabric or leather bodice, which itself also had to be made. Yet the so-called simplicity of the *tatami*-made examples of cuirass is often cited as the reason why they were the go-to form of armour for issuing to the growing and gradually regimented ranks of *ashigaru* warriors. While this was partly true in later centuries for different reasons, during the 16th century *tatami*-made cuirasses were clearly not the ideal choice when it came to equipping the legions of *ashigaru* that every feudal Japanese army was cultivating around its elite core of samurai.

In fact, as both extant examples and historical images document, the *ashigaru* and low-ranking soldiers wore extremely rudimentary versions of *okegawa-dō* accompanied by *jingasa*. It is for this reason that the various *tatami* makes of *dō* are discussed further in the following chapters, as cuirasses made in this form primarily came into their own during the latter half of the Edo period.

A beautiful 18th century example of a *tetsu-sabiji hatomune byō-toji tsure-yamamichi ni-mai-dō gusoku*. (New York Metropolitan Museum of Art/CC0 1.0)

CHAPTER 6

TOSEI-DŌ MODERN CUIRASS DESIGNS, PART I

Yokohagi-okegawa and related styles of *dō*, 16th century onward

By the second or third decade of the 16th century, the vast majority of cuirasses were being made in accordance with either the *Mōgami* or *nuinobe* method of construction, both of which were highly refined by this time. Of the two, however, cuirasses made in the *Mōgami* style enjoyed a greater degree of popularity, most likely due to the fact that their *ita-mono* construction could now be finished to look like *sane-ita*, which allowed smiths to create a number of finished-form variations of cuirasses assembled in this style. Yet other than for its ability to be created with a greater number of aesthetically different façades, the *Mōgami* style of construction, like the *nuinobe* method, had reached its zenith.

Although the *katchū-shi* of that period were almost certainly unaware of it, they had already invented most of the key elements of the construction techniques that would propel Japanese armour out of the classical period and into the modern age. All they were missing, quite literally, was the means to put it all together. Then, rather suddenly, in the decade leading up to the middle of the 16th century, Japanese armour makers had their eureka moment, when they struck upon the idea of riveting the various pieces of a cuirass together instead of assembling them using bindings and lace.

Why this most obvious of solutions had eluded the Japanese for so long is hard to understand, especially in light of the fact that in previous centuries they had produced *dō* from sections of solid plate riveted together. How they missed this blatantly obvious alternative is even harder to fathom in light of the fact that for several centuries they had been using rivets to construct helmet bowls from a complex arrangement of multiple independent curved metal plates.

That they had missed the obvious for so long tends to suggest that the idea might not have been their own when it did come, and there is strong evidence to support this theory. For in 1542 or 1543, the exact year being uncertain, a Chinese junk with three Portuguese travellers on board drifted ashore on the island of Tanegashima off the coast of the island of Kyūshū. These Portuguese were the first recorded Westerners to set foot on Japanese soil.

This monumental moment in history would in just a few short years have huge ramifications for how the Japanese would make armour and how they would fight wars. For on board the wrecked Chinese junk were examples of a highly advanced Portuguese firearm: the matchlock arquebus.

Many sources mark 1542/43 as the point in history when the Japanese were first introduced to firearms. This, however, is not true, for the Japanese had knowledge of both explosives and firearms stretching back at least to the time of the Mongol invasions, when the latter had utilized a grenade-like form of explosive canister against the samurai.

In fact, it appears that the Japanese may have been introduced to a primitive form of Chinese-made iron cannon known as a *teppō* in the years just prior to the Mongol invasions. There is also documentary evidence, according to the Japanese historian Uezato Takashi, of an Okinawan embassy from the then still independent archipelago of Ryūkyū to Kyōto in 1466, when the Okinawans honoured the Shōgun with a celebratory fusillade from another form of Chinese-made firearm.[1]

There is also historical evidence that indicates that an example of an Ottoman-made arquebus found its way to Ōsaka in 1510, possibly through the hands of Japanese pirates. This weapon is believed to have come from a large arsenal of firearms that the Portuguese had captured in Goa that same year.

Portuguese trade galleons such as this played a vital role in the economy of late 16th century Japan. The iron ingots, brocades, pressed leathers, silks, and wool cloth they carried quickly became essential materials in the production of samurai armour. (16th–17th century Japanese screen, Kobe Museum)

Why the Japanese had failed to capitalize on their earlier encounters with this technology is unclear, but the version of arquebus that the Portuguese brought with them in 1542/43 was a significant improvement on the firearm that the Japanese had studied in 1510. For under the direction of the Portuguese, the arsenal in Goa had started to produce a substantially upgraded version of matchlock arquebus that utilized a much more reliable form of European-designed forward falling lock and trigger mechanism. They had also introduced a better, more resilient form of sighted barrel and other features such as a pistol-grip-like stock, all of which made these firearms both easier to use and far more reliable.

The Japanese were apparently far more impressed with the capabilities of this upgraded version of arquebus. For they had supposedly produced over 300,000 of their own improved copies of these firearms by 1556, according to the book now commonly referred to as *The Travels of Mendes Pinto*, which was posthumously published in 1614 based on the manuscript of the Portuguese adventurer Fernão Mendes

A 19th century version of a Japanese *tanegashima* matchlock. While the Japanese had knowledge of firearms prior to the arrival of the first European traders in 1542/43, they had been unimpressed by this form of weaponry until they were introduced to the Portuguese arquebus. Within a few decades the Japanese were mass producing their own superior version of arquebus with specially trained bodies of warriors firing them in volleys on the battlefield. (Image courtesy of Tennants Auctions Ltd. UK)

Tosei-Dō Modern Cuirass Designs, Part I

Pinto. Pinto, who claimed to have been one of the first three Westerners that reached Japan in 1542/43, had continued dealings with Japan in various roles for well over a decade.

While Pinto's estimate was almost certainly highly exaggerated, it is clear that by the middle of the 16th century the Japanese were aggressively producing their own further improved version of Portuguese arquebus, which they commonly referred to as *tanegashima*, *teppō* or *hinawajū*, which means 'fuse gun'.

That the Portuguese had come ashore at Tanegashima was probably less to do with chance than intent. For though they were wrecked on the coast, Tanegashima was almost certainly an objective of theirs, as it was a well established trade centre at that time. That it was also significant as a centre of sword production was probably irrelevant to them. For the Japanese, however, that the Westerners came ashore at Tanegashima was a highly auspicious bit of luck, for, according to James Tracy, 'it was relatively easy for sword-smiths to turn out musket barrels instead, ready for the merchants to distribute.'[2] This situation no doubt greatly helped to expedite the rapid spread of firearms throughout Japan within just a few years of their 'reintroduction', with the samurai using them for the first time in battle during the siege of Kajiki in 1549.

As the use of firearms exponentially gained pace over the following decades, the nature of warfare in Japan was drastically altered, and along with it the manner in which the Japanese made and assembled armour. While the introduction of the arquebus clearly influenced some of the rapid changes that occurred during those years, there is strong evidence to suggest that the catalyst for the most significant transformation in Japanese armour designs and construction techniques to have occurred in Japan since the end of the first millennium was brought about as a result of contact with the West. For within a year of the first Portuguese coming ashore in Tanegashima, others had followed, bringing with them further examples of European knowledge and technology, including examples of the most modern versions of Western-made cuirasses.

The enormous influence that these European-made items of armour had on Japanese armour makers is undeniable, for it was in around 1550 that a revolution took place in Japanese armour making.[3] That this seismic shift in the way the Japanese made and assembled their armour came almost immediately in the aftermath of contact with the Portuguese has led many Japanese armour historians to speculate that one led to the other, advancing the theory that Japanese armourers emulated the solid Western cuirass style by making their own armour solid, and subsequently reproducing the pigeon-breasted European cuirasses exactly.

In *Samurai 1550–1600*, however, Anthony Bryant observes that solid *dō* were the 'next logical development' in the evolutionary trajectory of Japanese armour designs and construction techniques and that thus it was highly probable that they would have eventually

A German-made example of the peascod style of breastplate dating from between 1550 and 1560. European cuirasses such as this directly influenced the development of the Japanese *tosei-dō* or modern cuirass, which began to appear shortly after the first Portuguese traders began arriving in Japan during the first half of the 1540s. (Image courtesy of Wade Allan Antiques)

SAMURAI ARMOUR

discovered ways to produce armour in a similar manner without any Western influence.[4]

The form of armour that appears to have most impressed the Japanese was the extremely popular peascod style of cuirass, which featured a prominent medial ridge down the centre of the breastplate. As well as being aesthetically attractive, the raised ridge also significantly improved the ability of the peascod to deflect blows from edged weapons and missiles, including arquebus shots. Ironically, this feature had originally been incorporated into the design of the peascod simply to mimic the tapered pouter pigeon-like fronts that were in fashion and common to the doublets worn by most European men in the 16th century.

A *tetsu kuro urushi nuri yokohagi-okegawa go-mai-dō*. Note the impact dents from matchlock ball strikes on four of the five panels of this cuirass. Referred to as *tameshi*, these were shots intentionally fired at the armour to prove that it was shot-proof. Persons unfamiliar with the practice of *tameshi* often assume that the damage was incurred during battle.

OKEGAWA-DŌ

With just a few examples of European-made cuirasses in hand, Japanese armour makers were able to catapult domestic armour-making techniques forward several decades in the span of just a few short years. For they discovered in these foreign-made pieces concepts that had for some strange reason eluded them for centuries. The most obvious of these revolutionary new ideas

TOSEI-DŌ NOMENCLATURE

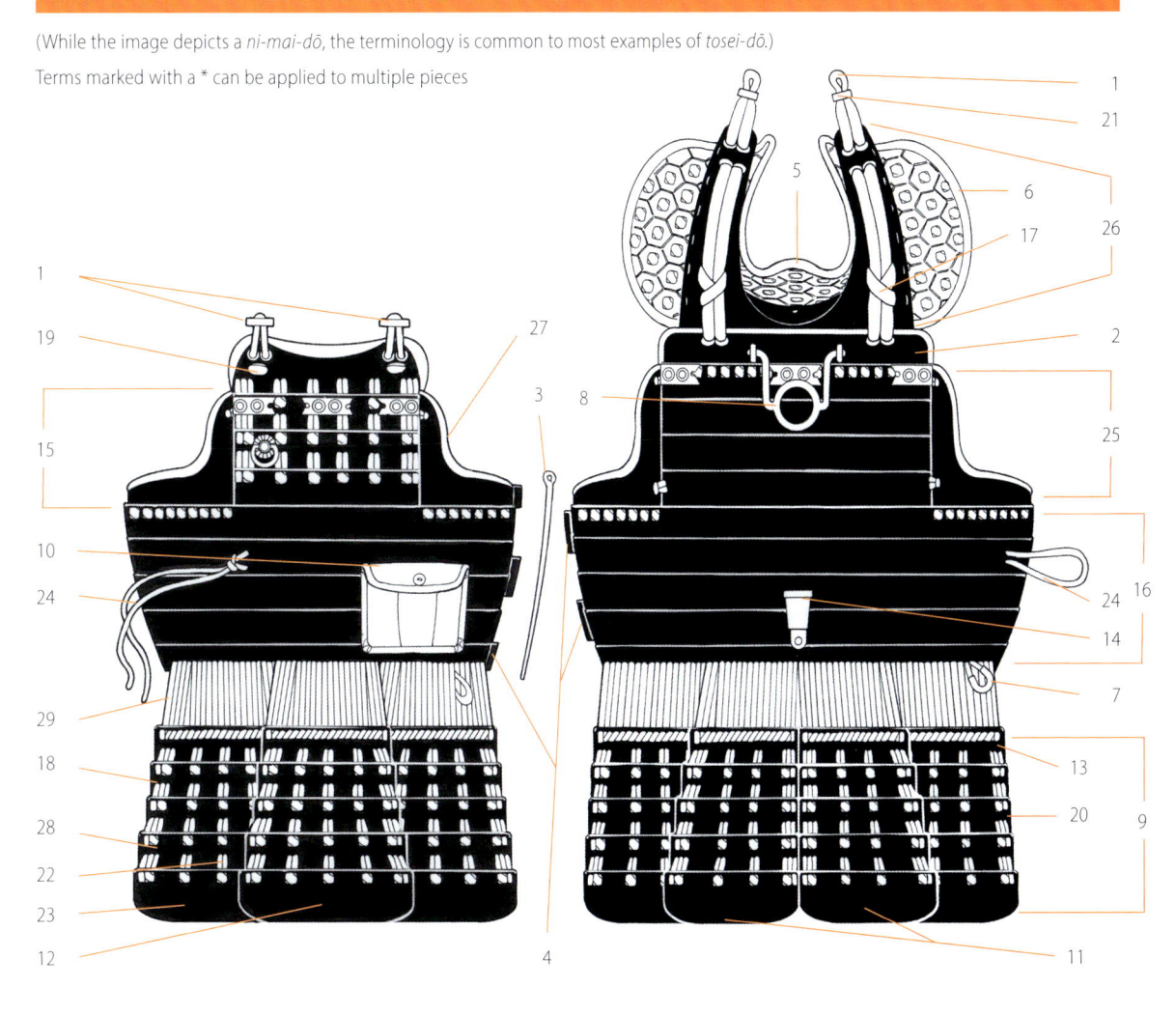

(While the image depicts a *ni-mai-dō*, the terminology is common to most examples of *tosei-dō*.)
Terms marked with a * can be applied to multiple pieces

1. *Aibiki-no-o*
2. *Bokō-no-ita*
3. *Chotsugai-kugi*
4. *Chotsugai*
5. *Eri-mawashi*
6. *Kobire*
7. *Kurijime-no-o-kan*
8. *Gattari*
9. *Gessan**
10. *Hanakami-bukuro*
11. *Hishiki-gessan**
12. *Kintama kakushi*
13. *Ichi-no-ita*
14. *Machi-uke*
15. *Mae-tateage*
16. *Nagakawa*
17. *Ninawa-musubi**
18. *Ni-no-ita*
19. *Onidamari-no-ita*
20. *San-no-ita*
21. *Seme-kohaze**
22. *Sugake odoshi*
23. *Suso-no-ita**
24. *Takahimo**
25. *Ushiro-tateage*
26. *Wadagami**
27. *Waki-ita**
28. *Yon-no-ita*
29. *Yurugi-no-ita**

was to utilize rivets to assemble a series of solid-plate pieces together to form a rigid cuirass.

Japanese *katchū-shi* were also able to benefit from the many decades of practical experience that European armour makers had already had in dealing with the effects of firearms on armour. As such the Japanese were able to produce some highly effective shot-proof makes of cuirass within a very short period of time. In fact, the famous *daimyō* and later Shōgun Tokugawa Ieyasu is said to have removed an example of this new make of Japanese-made cuirass at the end of one battle only to see a handful of bullets fall out. It appears the bullets had penetrated the armour, but so much of their force had been absorbed that Ieyasu was unharmed and had been unaware he had even been shot.

The validity of stories such as this have been borne out by tests, such as those that were conducted by the renowned *gendai* (present era) Japanese armour maker Miura Shigetoshi in conjunction with a major Japanese TV broadcasting company. During his experiments, Miura found that a medial-ridge example of Japanese *dō* constructed from armour plate only 3 mm in thickness was more than capable of stopping and deflecting a ball fired from a *tanegashima*-type firearm at a distance of just 15 metres.[5] The protective abilities of such cuirasses, however, were not entirely due to their design, for the Japanese *katchū-shi* had also made significant advances in the art of producing metal plate from a layered combination of iron and steel by this time, as was noted in the Introduction.

Such considerations were still in the future, however, during the latter half of the 1540s, as Japanese armour makers experimented with ways of merging European armour-making techniques with the existing domestic methods of construction and cuirass designs. These efforts ultimately resulted in the creation of the revolutionary clam-shell-like form of two-section cuirass that came to be known as the *okegawa ni-mai-dō*, and which shall be referred to as *okegawa-dō* from here on unless the actual number of sectional pieces is being discussed, due to the fact that not all *okegawa-dō* are *ni-mai-dō*.

The *okegawa-dō*, which, according to Sakakibara, originated in Owari province, was the first true example of a cuirass that would now be referred to as a *tosei-dō*, or 'modern cuirass'. It is important to keep in mind, however, that while the *okegawa-dō* and every other new form of cuirass that was created after its introduction are now collectively referred to as *tosei-dō*, or 'modern cuirasses', the same was also technically once true of the *haramaki* or an early example of cuirass made in the *Mōgami* style. Irrespective of this, the term *tosei* should be understood to refer to items of armour that were produced from the late 1540s onward.

In its original form, the *okegawa-dō* consisted of independent front and back plate sections of armour that were constructed from several overlapping solid metal plate *ita-mono*. Each plate had the *ita-mono* above it in the vertical assembly of the cuirass riveted to its inside face along its upper edge using countersunk *byō* in a style that came to be referred to as *yokohagi-ita*. The fixed nature of this method of assembly also made the *okegawa-dō* a variety of *tachi-dō*.

The separate front and back pieces could be secured together to create a full cuirass by means of what Sakakibara described as a *maki* or 'spiral' type of hinge. Sakakibara's description referred to a conventional form of tubular hinge that consists of two sections. Both halves of the cuirass would have one leaf of the alternately knuckled hinge fitted to the left-hand edge of the *dō*. When the two segments and the hinge leaves were aligned, a removable pin could be inserted to lock the front *mae-dō* and back *ushiro-dō* portions of the armour together to create a full cuirass. The *hikiawase* fastening cords strung through the right-hand sides of the two sections of the *dō* allowed the cuirass to be tied closed around the torso, with the *ushiro-dō* overlapping the *mae-dō* section in the usual manner. It should be noted that for some reason the *katchū-shi* abandoned the use of the term *hikiawase* around his time and began referring to the fastening cords anchored to the side of a cuirass as the *takahimo*, with the component parts that had hitherto been referred to by that name also being renamed, as will be discussed in the following paragraphs.

The *okegawa-dō*, as Dr Yoshihiko Sasama notes in *Nihon no Katchū Bugu Jiten*, derived its name from the fact that its round and riveted vertical metal-plate construction bore a resemblance to a bucket, which in Japanese is referred to as *oke*, while *gawa* means 'sides'. Some other names for this style of cuirass also existed, such as *jabara-dō*, or 'snake belly', which was derived from the visual similarity of the *yokohagi-ita* construction of this make of cuirass to the underbelly of a snake.

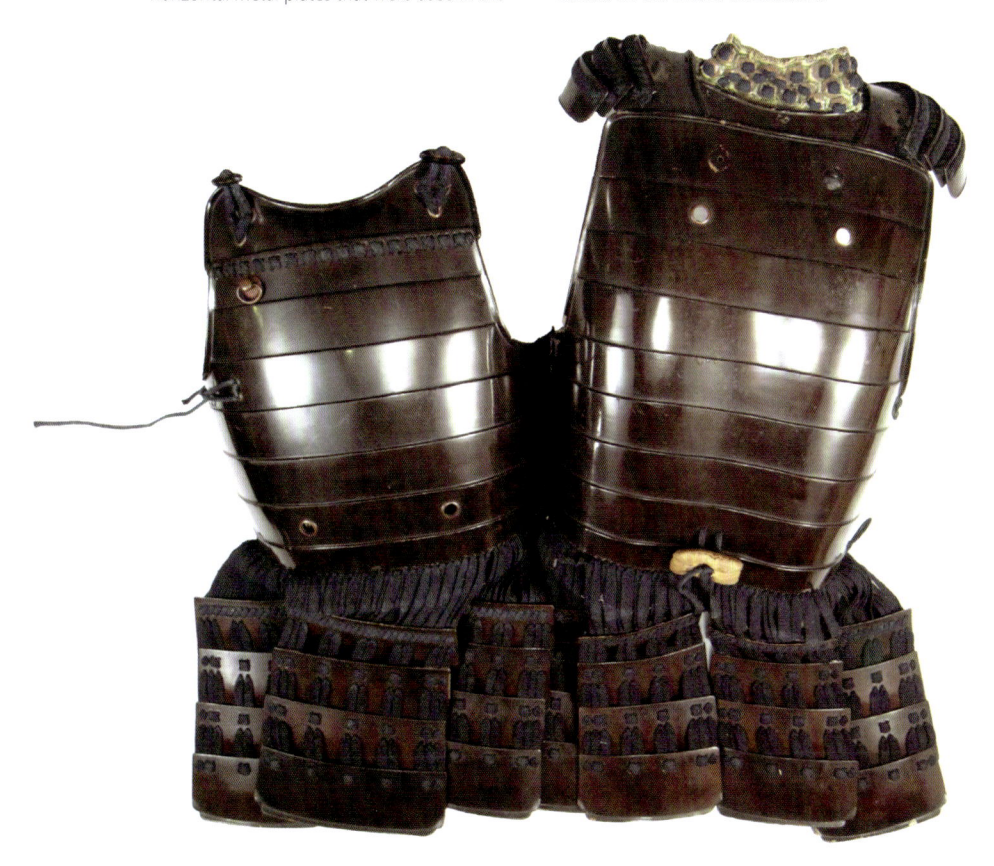

While the *Mōgami* method of hinging *ita-mono* together was clearly incorporated into the *okegawa-dō* design, in its finished form the *okegawa-dō* resembled a *nuinobe*-made version of cuirass as it contoured more closely to the curvatures of the torso. Dr Sasama also suggests that the *tatami* method of construction helped to influence the design and form of the *okegawa-dō*. How it did so, however, is hard to ascertain. And as Dr Sasama never documented his reasoning in this regard it remains unclear exactly how the *tatami* method of construction influenced development of the *okegawa-dō* other than by having been one of the links in the evolutionary process that ultimately led to its creation. That said, it is important to keep in mind the fact that the *tatami* method of construction did lead to a number of evolutionary adaptions of the *tosei-dō* in the latter part of the 16th century and continued to do so throughout the remainder of the Japanese feudal period, as will be discussed later on.

The revolutionary design of the *okegawa-dō* included a number of other significant changes to how cuirasses were constructed. Paramount amongst these were changes to the number of vertical sections of armour that were used to form the *nagakawa*, *mae-tateage* and *ushiro-tateage*. This included one additional vertical band of armour in the *mae-tateage*, which increased it to three *yokohagi-ita* and *muna-ita*, while the *ushiro-tateage* was also increased by one plate to a total of four horizontally arranged plates capped by the *oshitsuke-no-ita*. This was also true of the *nagakawa*, which was increased in the *mae* and *ushiro-dō* by one *yokohagi-ita* to a total of five plates each.

The addition of the extra plates helped to extend the *nagakawa* so that it covered more of the lower torso, particularly in the area of the lower abdomen, which again may have been influenced by the triangulated shape of the lower edge of the peascod. In the case of the *okegawa-dō*, however, this also allowed the cuirass to rest on the wearer's hips, which in turn transferred a significant portion of the weight of

A *tetsu kuro urushi nuri yokohagi-okegawa renjaku ni-mai-dō*. Though a late Edo period example, the revolutionary *okegawa* design and method of construction is clearly visible. It is easy to visualize how the independent horizontal metal plates that were used in the *Mōgami* method of fabrication were riveted together to create a rigid *tachi-dō*. Cords similar to braces were strung through the grommet-fitted *renjaku-no-ana* holes in the cuirass and helped to take some of the weight of the cuirass off the wearer's shoulders.

the *dō* off the wearer's shoulders and onto his lower torso. This made the *okegawa-dō* far more comfortable to wear than the pre-existing forms of cuirass had been, which in turn enabled warriors to wear armour for longer periods of time. For the form-fitting, hip-riding design of the *tosei-dō* made the wearing of armour a far less physically demanding experience.

To achieve this the lower plates of the *nagakawa* were arched subtly upwards along the sides of the *dō*, which helped it to better contour the shape of the body. This not only ensured that the cuirass would sit on top of the *obi*-padded hips but also prevented the bottom of the armour from interfering with the movements of the upper legs.

The extra plates in the *mae-tateage* and *ushiro-tateage* also played an essential part in helping to elevate the cuirass off the shoulders. They also raised the overall height of the *muna-ita* and *boko-no-ita* in relationship to the upper torso, which helped reduce some of the vulnerable areas around the base and back of the neck that were common to most examples of pre-*tosei* cuirass.

For reasons unknown, armour makers began to utilize a number of new terms during this time period to refer to many of the pre-existing parts of a *dō*. Included amongst these were the *muna-ita*, which became the *oni-damari*, or 'devil stopper', and the *oshitsuke-no-ita*, which was renamed the *boko-no-ita*.

The *oni-damari* name hints at one of the other new features that was incorporated into the design of the *okegawa-dō*, which Bottomley and Hopson refer to as a 'stop-rib' in *Arms and Armour of the Samurai*. These were outward-rolled rims along the upper leading edges of the *oni-damari*, *waki-ita* and *boko-no-ita* plates, the most pronounced of which was along the frontage of the *oni-damari*. They were designed to catch and redirect weapons that had been stopped or deflected by the armour off to the sides of the body and away from the vulnerable openings along the upper edges of the cuirass. This feature was almost certainly added to counter the increased use of straight-bladed spears, which were highly effective at piercing armour assembled from *sane-ita*.[6]

The *oni-damari* and *boko-no-ita* on the earliest examples of *okegawa-dō* were generally riveted to the upper edges of the *mae-* and *ushiro-tateage*. This practice, however, slowly reverted over time to include the option of lacing the two pieces in place. *Fukurin* were also commonly fitted to the leading edges of these plates, including the *waki-ita* on most examples of *okegawa* and *tosei-dō*. This, however, was generally not the case on the most rudimentary cuirasses, particularly those that were produced for low-ranking warriors.

The *waki-ita* for the most part remained largely unchanged in overall form, though they were extended slightly to increase their height

A view of the interior of a *tetsu yokohagi-okegawa ni-mai-dō*. The curved shape of the lower *yokohagi-ita* plates that allowed the cuirass to sit comfortably on the hips without interfering with the movements of the legs, while simultaneously covering as much of the lower abdomen as possible, can clearly be noted in this image. The *yokohagi-ita* construction is visible through the taut leather liner. Note the brigandine collar and padded shoulder yoke assembly.

TOSEI-DŌ MODERN CUIRASS DESIGNS, PART I

Right: The outward-rolled edge along the top of the *oni-damari* is clearly visible in this image. This feature was designed to catch edged weapons that had been blocked by the armour, preventing them from skidding off into an unprotected area of the upper torso. This prominent outward-curving flange was typically applied to the upper edges of all of the *kanagu mawari* plates. Note the *chotsugai* hinge on the side of the cuirass and removable hinge pin.

Below: A view of the brigandine-like *eri-mawashi* collar and the *kobire* upper shoulder guards. Note the *keshi* frill around the upper edge of the collar. The *keshi* was inspired by the elaborate lace collars that were worn by the first Europeans to arrive in Japan in the mid-16th century. Also note the *kamon* crest-decorated *gyōyō* pendant that has been secured by a hinge to the forward edge of the *wadagami*.

in conjunction with the increased height of the *mae-* and *ushiro-tateage* portions of the cuirass. Unlike the other parts of the *dō*, the *waki-ita* continued to be laced in place in most cases. This was done by *kebiki odoshi*-lacing the lower edge of each armpit plate to the upper edge of the *ichi-no-ita*, or uppermost bands of the *nagakawa* of the *mae-dō* and *ushiro-dō*. The erect vertical flanges of the *waki-ita* were anchored to the *mae-tageage*, *ushiro-tateage*, *oni-damari* and *boko-no-ita* by one or two short, knotted lengths of *odoshi-ge*. This arrangement allowed the *waki-ita* to flex in position slightly, which helped to better accommodate the movements of the arms.

Over a few decades, the shape of the *waki-ita* would slowly begin to metamorphose to include a raised convex arch in the area immediately under the armpit. This was done again to increase the overall area of the torso that was protected by the cuirass, with the vulnerable armpit area being one of the spots that warriors commonly targeted in battle. The left-hand *waki-ita* plate featured a single fully formed mound along its upper central edge, while the divided right-hand side *waki-ita* plates each featured a slightly elongated half-portion of the raised mound. These were offset towards the outside vertical edges of the plates so that when the two armpit-plate pieces of the *mae-dō* and *ushiro-dō* were overlapped, when the cuirass was closed on the right side of the body, they would generally form the outline of a single convex mound under the right armpit. This unique feature, while common, was not universal to all cuirasses made during the latter half of the 16th and early part of the 17th centuries. It was, however, virtually unique to *dō* from that period and is an excellent visual indicator of the overall age of a *tosei-dō*.

The *wadagami* remained unchanged for the most part, though the practice of fitting *shoji-no-ita* to them was largely discontinued due to the new style of *shikoro* neck guards that were being fitted to the *kabuto* of that time, which were designed to hang lower and fit more closely to the contours of the upper shoulders. Details of these

SAMURAI ARMOUR

are discussed further in the companion book, Volume II. Protection for the neck was now divided between the *shikoro* and a form of erect brigandine armoured collar called an *eri-mawashi* that was most likely inspired by the European gorget form of neck protector. In fact, many examples of *eri-mawashi* attached to high-quality sets of armour often also featured a form of folded crepe-silk frill along the upper edge of the collar called a *keshi* that was inspired by the elaborate lace ruffs worn by the Europeans of that period.

An example of a *hidari waki-ita* from a variety of *go-mai-dō* referred to as a *Yukinoshita-dō*. The convex form of the mid-section along the upper edge of the armpit plate is clearly visible in this image. This feature was common on cuirasses produced during the latter half of the 16th century and is generally a good indicator as to the actual age of a cuirass. Note the external hinges and decorative *maki-e*.

ACCESSORIES AND INDEPENDENT ARMOUR PIECES

It is highly probable that the earliest examples of *okegawa-dō* and other forms of *tosei-dō* were not originally made with *eri-mawashi* and many of the other features that will be described in the following paragraphs. Instead these items were most likely independent accessories that were worn separately along with the cuirass to cover some of the exposed areas of the upper body. Such pieces are best exemplified by the *manchira*, which was a form of brigandine vest that could be worn under a cuirass.

While there are a large number of alternative forms of *manchira* (the name for which comes from the Portuguese word *mantilla*), the most complex versions of these vest-like brigandine garments provided additional protection for the neck, outer shoulders, upper chest and back and for the exposed areas immediately under the arms, all of which were not generally covered by the design of most conventional makes of pre-*tosei* or *tosei* styles of cuirass.

Producing the *manchira* as a separate complementary item of armour was an extremely logical idea. For it made the *manchira* a sort of quasi-disposable accessory that could be easily repaired or changed out as needed without requiring the entire cuirass to be withdrawn from service if it became damaged or worn, as would be the case if it were made as an integral part of the cuirass. Thus it is plausible to assume that many *dō* made during the latter half of the 16th and early part of the 17th centuries were never fitted with an integral *eri-mawashi* and other such related features. In later periods, however, the majority of cuirasses were more than likely retroactively fitted with these features as they were undergoing maintenance-related repairs and upgrades during a time when it had become common to construct *dō* with these items attached directly to them.

An alternative view of an *eri-mawashi* and *kobire*. The shape of the internal *kikkō* are clearly defined by the outline stitching, which was generally applied using thread that contrasted with the fabric used to cover the brigandine. The *kobire* have been laced to the outer edge of the *wadagami*. The *eri-mawashi* is removable, as can be noted by observing the *odoshi-ge* that is used to secure it in place protruding from the back of the cuirass just below the collar. Note the metal *gattari* bracket hinged in place on the rear of the cuirass.

Tosei-Dō Modern Cuirass Designs, Part I

A high-quality example of a *manchira*. Hidden beneath the rich silk brocade facing material are internal panels of lacquered *kusari*. The *manchira* features a *kikkō* brigandine *eri-mawashi*. Note how the vest-like garment has been tailored to cover the shoulders so as provide an additional degree of padding under the *wadagami* as well as protection for the outer shoulders in the form of integral *kobire*. (New York Metropolitan Museum of Art/CC0 1.0)

This is not to say that such features were never attached directly to the earliest examples of *tosei-dō*, but rather that this practice almost certainly became more common over time. For as the long period of peace that followed the Sengoku period took hold, many of the realities of warfare quickly faded from the collective memory of the samurai class. As a result, attaching the *eri-mawashi* and other features directly to the cuirass would have been seen as a far more practical design by many over having to put on an additional item of armour. It would also have made items of armour that spent a considerable amount of time sitting on display look far more presentable.

When a *manchira* was not used, the *eri-mawashi* was usually an integral part of an *eri-dai* (sometimes spelled *yeri-dai*), which was a form of large, cushion-like shoulder yoke that was generally secured to the *boko-no-ita* and inner edges of the *wadagami* by either lacing or thread. In most cases the *eri-mawashi* was assembled from a series of small, generally slightly convex, coin-sized hexagonal pieces fashioned from *tetsu* or *nerigawa* and called *kikkō-gane* or simply *kikkō*, which means 'tortoiseshell', due to its resemblance to the hexagonal pattern of the shell of a tortoise or turtle. These were perforated in the middle with four holes that allowed them to be laced between layers of fabric. Most *eri-mawashi* were constructed from three horizontally arranged rows of *kikkō*, with each *kikkō* sitting in the angle between two adjacent ones, which allowed neighbouring *kikkō* to sit almost flush against each other along the flat surfaces of the brigandine. This required that every other row of *kikkō* be offset when they were arranged in rows, as was generally the case. The small gaps that resulted at the ends of the offset rows were filled by a piece of *kikkō* that was cut in half.

Exactly how the Japanese came to utilize *kikkō* is unclear, as is its origin, for there is almost no evidence of this form of protective armour having been used in Japan prior to the middle of the 16th century. In fact, the only reported example of *kikkō* that is said to pre-date this period is a shirt of *kikkō*-like brigandine on display in a small private museum in north-western Kyūshū, which is said to have been worn by a Mongol warrior during one of the 13th century invasions of Japan. While similar, it is hard to see how such an item could have been responsible for the sudden, large-scale appearance and use of *kikkō* across Japan during the latter part of the Muromachi period.

This being the case, it seems highly likely that *kikkō* was another of the innovative ideas that were introduced into Japan after contact with the Europeans during the 1540s. The use of brigandine was well documented in the West by this time period, as it had been on the Asian mainland for several centuries. That *kikkō* bears

SAMURAI ARMOUR

Most examples of brigandine that were fabricated using *kikko* were assembled from three layers of fabric. The *kikko* were anchored in placed using *odoshi-ge* and outline stitching. Rolled lengths of paper were commonly used to to anchor the outline stitching to prevent it from being pulled through the coarsely woven internal layer of fabric. Note the convex shape of the *kikko*.

a great similarity to some of the existing Asian forms of brigandine suggests that it may have been inspired by items of Asian-made armour that were introduced to the Japanese via European traders, who in their travels acquired such items for personal use or trade prior to arriving in Japan.

While there were more than likely a few ways to construct sections of Japanese brigandine, the most common method was to pinch a *kikkō* between a layer of coarse-weave hemp cloth, or *asa*, and another layer of thin leather or high-quality fabric that would form the exterior of the section of brigandine when it was complete. A variety of imported European woollen cloth, referred to as *rasha* by the Japanese, quickly became one of the most popular materials for this purpose, though this was often influenced by the budget of the warrior commissioning the piece.

The *katchū-shi* would begin by threading a single long length of *odoshi-ge* with a knotted end through hemp cloth backing material from behind. As they did so they would ensure that it went through the lower left-hand corner of the four holes punched in the centre of the *kikkō*, which would be laid on the hemp cloth so that its convex face bowed away from the backing material. The *odoshi-ge* would then be pushed through holes pierced in the facing material and drawn out to the front of the panel of brigandine. It would then be pulled upward and to the right over the cloth before it was inserted back through the *rasha* and threaded through the upper right-hand corner hole of the same *kikkō* and out to the back of the *asa* liner. At this point

The facing material and liner have both worn away on the *eri-mawashi* seen here, exposing the iron *kikkō* and braided thread outline stitching. The rolled lengths of paper that the outline stitching was anchored around when it was sewn can be seen on the interior face of the collar. Note how the *odoshi-ge* was strung.

220

A view of the underside of the internal layer of fabric of an *eri-mawashi* and the various threads and cords that secured the *kikko* to the facing surface of that layer of fabric. Note the employment of used sheets of *washi* paper to line and further stiffen the fabric collar.

the *odoshi-ge* would be drawn across to the left and threaded back through the hemp via the top left-hand hole in the *kikkō* and out to the facing surface of the *rasha*. It would then be pulled downward to the right, crossing over the small diagonal dash that had been created on the surface of the woollen cloth where it had previously been threaded. The lacing was finally inserted back through the *rasha* via the lower right-hand corner hole in the *kikkō* and out to the back side of the hemp fabric. This created a small *hishinui*-like cross-knot on the façade of the fabric that effectively locked the *kikkō* in position. The next *kikkō* was then positioned 2–3 mm to the right of the first one. The original length of *odoshi-ge* would then be drawn horizontally across the back face of the hemp and inserted through the lower left-hand hole of the second *kikkō*, at which point the lacing process described above would be repeated as many times as was required to form a single horizontal row of brigandine.

The *kikkō* were then outline-stitched using thick thread. This was done to help sandwich the brigandine between the facing cloth and hemp liner so as to prevent the edges of the *kikkō* wearing on the fabrics through too much free play. It was common for the outline-stitching to be double threaded and for it to be of a colour that made it stand out in contrast against the colour of the face material. This created an attractive hexagonal pattern around the *kikkō* that significantly improved the aesthetic appearance of the brigandine.

To outline-stitch the *kikkō*, smiths would roll waste pieces of *washi* paper into long, narrow tubes. These would be aligned on the back face of the hemp liner with the top and bottom of each row of *kikkō*. The knotted double length of thread would be pushed through the back of the hemp liner to the facing side beginning at the bottom corner of the first *kikkō*. It would then be pulled upward and to the left over the surface of the facing material parallel to the lower diagonal edge of the *kikkō*. At the first corner of the *kikkō* it would be pulled back through the facing material and out to the rear of the *asa* liner. Here it would be looped over the rolled paper tube, which provided a cheap, lightweight internal anchoring point, before the thread was inserted back out to the face of the panel of brigandine. Careful attention was paid to ensure that the threads exited from almost the same point in the material where they had been inserted. The double thread was then pulled upward to the next corner of the *kikkō* where it was again inserted through and out to the back side of the hemp liner. It would then be looped over the paper roll along the upper-edge row of *kikkō* and again threaded back out to the facing surface of the panel. This process was repeated around the entire edge of each *kikkō* so that every piece in a length of arranged brigandine was fully outlined.

When complete, the panel of *kikkō* was covered on the reverse by a layer of finer-weave durable cloth to hide the internal construction of the section of brigandine. It was common for layers of *washi* paper to be laid over the stitched and knotted back face of the hemp cloth to help create a smoother finished surface for the lined reverse of the panel. The three layers would be tacked together around the edges of the panel

SAMURAI ARMOUR

before a stencilled leather or woven cloth edge trim called *sasaheri* was applied. This was a plain weave fabric with additional rows of floating threads that produced a ridged pattern in the material. The end result was a reasonably flexible form of fairly resilient armour that was also rather decorative in appearance. This could be further enhanced with the addition of a *keshi*, or frill, along the upper edge of the collar. *Keshi*, which were inspired by the elaborate lace collars that were worn by Europeans of that time period, were generally made from two or three rows of box-pleated crepe silk, or *chirimen*. Panels of brigandine made from *kikkō* were commonly incorporated into the design of some of the other components of most examples of *tosei-gusoku* and into a number of other accessory items that many warriors acquired to further augment their personal protection.

If the *eri-mawashi* was attached to an *eri-dai*, as was generally the case, the material used to line the inside face of the collar would also be used to fabricate the shoulder yoke. In cases where a high-quality fabric was used to line the collar, it would generally terminate at the base of the collar where it was sewn to the *eri-dai*, and the latter would be constructed from a more durable form of material, with a fine-weave hemp cloth being common for this purpose. In some cases, the back-side face of the shoulder yoke where it rested against the inside face of the cuirass was made from leather to further add to its overall durability. Most examples of *eri-dai* were pillow-like, being filled with layers of cotton wadding. The yokes would generally conform to the width and depth of the *boko-no-ita* in most cases and would usually feature integral extensions that protruded forward under the length of the *wadagami* to provide padding for the top of the shoulders.

Another new feature that began to appear on *okegawa-dō* were the *kobire*, or 'little fins'. These were small, generally half-oval-shaped plates or panels of brigandine that protruded from or were attached directly to the outside edges of the *wadagami* to protect the top of the outer shoulder.

Top: A removable *eri-mawashi* with an integral cotton-stuffed padded *eri-dai*. Note the lengths of *odoshi-ge* that are used to secure the shoulder yoke and collar to the the *wadagami* of a cuirass. Also note how a better quality fabric has been used to face the more exposed forward ends of the harness, while a more durable and more than likely less expensive material was used to tailor the areas of the harness that would not be visible.

Bottom: An excellent view of an *eri-mawashi* with an integral *eri-dai*. The padded shoulder yoke was tailored to contour to the shape of the *boko-no-ita* and *wadagami*. A rich brocade cloth has been used to face the visible façade of the *eri-dai* and brigandine collar. Note the *kebiki odoshi*-laced *ita-mono kobire* and how these would provide ample protection to the outer shoulders. Also note the protruding *sode-tsuke-no-o* protected under the *kobire*.

Tosei-Dō Modern Cuirass Designs, Part 1

The *kobire*, like the *eri-mawashi*, were also more than likely inspired by the Western gorget. They were, however, another of the changing features on Japanese armour that more than likely would eventually have evolved on their own. For two major changes occurred with armour designs during the first half of the 16th century to require the development and introduction of a new protective feature like the *kobire*.

First amongst these was the fact that the wide *shikoro* neck guards that in previous centuries had protected most of the upper shoulder from downward blows were starting to grow steadily narrower in circumference and steeper in profile. This situation was compounded by the fact that samurai were starting to discard the massive *ō-sode* style of shoulder guards that had been utilized for centuries in favour of smaller, more moderate forms of shoulder guards by the time the Portuguese arrived in the early 1540s. This trend continued to intensify over the first few decades after the middle of the 16th century until it became common for armour to be worn without *sode*. As such there was a strong need for an additional or alternative form of armour to help protect this vulnerable part of the upper body.

Originally it was common for the *kobire* to be fabricated from panels of *kikkō*. These would be laced to the outer edges of the *wadagami* or in some cases be a physical extension of the *eri-dai*. In such cases the area of the shoulder harness where it passed under the *wadagami* would be devoid of *kikkō*. As the decades passed, and the *sode* became increasingly smaller or were dispensed with altogether, it became common to fabricate the *kobire* out of solid plates. In some cases *kebiki* or *sugake odoshi* would be used to lace two or three *ita-mono* together. Other designs featured large, rounded shark-fin-shaped plates that would be hinged to the outside edges of the *wadagami*. *Kusari* was also sometimes used either to face the *kobire* or in lieu of the internal layer of *kikkō* brigandine.

As the *okegawa-dō* was not designed to be fitted with *ō-sode*, the *katchū-shi* discontinued the practice of stringing the *wadagami* with the *sode-tsuke-no-gumi-wa*. In their place an alternative version of attaching cord referred to as a *sode-tsuke-ne-o* was strung that featured a *kasa-kohaze* in place of the large *sode-tsuke-no-kuda* previously utilized. It also became common practice to lace the *sode-tsuke-ne-o* so they were protected under the *kobire*. This involved either stringing the cords for the *sode-tsuke-ne-o* through from the top of the *wadagami*, with their bulbous ends hidden under the lengths of *odoshi-ge* that were used to secure the *kobire* or *eri-dai* to the shoulder straps, or, if the *wadagami* were made from layers of *nerigawa*, horizontally through the latter before the leather covers were fully applied.

The method of attaching the cords at the front of the cuirass that joined the *wadagami* with *oni-damari* also changed, as did the terminology that was used to refer to them. The old term *takahimo* was discontinued for use in this context with the connective cords being

A single-plate example of a *kobire* indicative of the styles of outer shoulder guards that were generally fitted to cuirasses made in the Yukinoshita or so-called Sendai-dō styles.

The *sode-tsuke-no-o* were most likely later additions, for *wadagami* fitted with *kobire* were not as a rule designed to have *sode* suspended from them.

Samurai Armour

renamed as the *aibiki-no-o*. In regards to the *aibiki-no-o* cords that extended upwards from the *oni-damari* to meet the portions of *aibiki-no-o* that extended downwards from the ends of the *wadagami*, relatively little changed, except that the cut ends of the cords were hidden on the inside face of the breastplate where they were anchored behind the holes in the chest plate by turning the cut ends inward on themselves to create a bulb shape.

The manner in which the *aibiki-no-o* were strung on the *wadagami*, however, changed substantially, with the cords being lengthened significantly so that they extended from the front of the *wadagami* all the way to the top of the *boko-no-ita* at the rear of the cuirass. While there is no definitive answer as to why this is done, the most logical reason for this arrangement is that the extended lengths of the *aibiki-no-o* were intended to act as a form of emergency shoulder strap in the event that the *wadagami* failed or was broken. This seems plausible since the cords were firmly anchored through two vertically aligned pairs of holes pierced in the upper outside edges of the *boko-no-ita*. Thus as long as the *seme-kohaze*-threaded front-end length of the *aibiki-no-o* continued to lock the *kohaze* at the top end of the portion of *aibiki-no-o* that extended upwards from the *oni-damari* on the front of the cuirass, it is highly likely that the *aibiki-no-o* cords could have supported the *dō* over the shoulder. Why this was deemed likely to happen, however, is hard to understand.

Another peculiar characteristic of the *aibiki-no-o* cords stretched over the *wadagami* was that they were generally tied in a knot in the area of the mid-upper arching curve of the shoulder strap. The knot is named after the manner in which it is tied, *ninawa-musubi*, which is an extremely straightforward knot that simply involved looping the double length of cord through itself. The purpose of the *ninawa-musubi* knot was most likely to prevent the long, parallel lengths of the *aibiki-no-o* from easily becoming snagged on items.

Top: A view of a *sugake odoshi*-laced *ita-mono kobire*. Note the *gyōyō* pendant hinged to the forward edge of the *wadagami*, which is itself affixed to the cuirass by means of a *chotsugai*. Also note the arrangement of the heavy *aibiki-no-o* cords tied with a *ninawa-musubi* knot.

Bottom: The *aibiki-no-o* tied with a *ninawa-musubi* knot can be seen here traversing the *wadagami*. Originating from holes drilled in the *boko-no-ita*, these cords extended over the shoulders to the point where their ends, strung with *seme-kohaze*, could be secured to the corresponding cords fitted with *kohaze* protruding upward from the *onidamari-no-ita*. While the exact purpose of the *aibiki-no-o* arrangement of cords is unclear, many scholars believe that they were intended to act as form of auxiliary shoulder strap should the *wadagami* break or otherwise fail while the cuirass was being worn.

224

Tosei-Dō Modern Cuirass Designs, Part I

In some cases *gyōyō* were still hung from the ends of the *wadagami* to protect the *aibiki-no-o*. However, use of the independent leaf-like style of *gyōyō* largely faded out during the late 16th and early 17th centuries in favour of a solid-plate form of *gyōyō* that was hinged directly to the forward leading edge of the *wadagami*. This form of often integral, though sometimes removable style of hinged *gyōyō* was generally fabricated to be the same width as the forward edge of the *wadagami* so that it looked like an extension of the latter. In some cases, hinged *gyōyō* were even attached to the leading edges of the *kobire* as was the case with the *shu-urushi nuri okegawa go-mai-dō* that was used by the Momoyama-Aizuchi-period *daimyō* of the renowned Soma clan. It should be noted though, that while practical, attached plate-like *gyōyō* were not a universal feature of the *okegawa-dō* design or most other makes of *tosei-dō*.

A number of changes also occurred around the bottom of the cuirass, with the length of the suspensory lacing and number of *kusazuri* changing, along with the name used for the upper thigh guards, which on *tosei-dō* are referred to as the *gessan*. Initially the number of *gessan* was standardized to three pendants suspended from the *mae-dō* portion of the cuirass and four from the *ushiro-dō*. While this count would vary as other modern styles of cuirass were introduced, the vast majority of *tosei-dō* will feature an arrangement of seven *gessan*, each one of which will generally comprise five suspended plates.

The middle of the three *gessan* suspended from the *mae-dō* is individually referred to as

Most conventional examples of *tosei-dō* feature seven *gessan*. In the case of a *ni-mai-dō*, the hip armour was commonly arranged with three *gessan* suspended from the *mae-dō* and four from the *ushiro-dō*. Note the *uke-zutsu*, which transitions in shape from round to square, and how it is secured by the *gattari* and lower *machi-uke*.

kintama-kakushi, which literally translates as 'golden ball hiding'. While aptly named, it is unclear why armour makers chose to name this specific *gessan*. The same is also true of the middle two *gessan* suspended from the *ushiro-dō*, which can both be referred to as *hishiki gessan*, which roughly translates as 'pull sit on', possibly in reference to the fact that these *gessan* commonly needed to be pulled aside to prevent them from being sat upon.

Due to the fact that, like the cuirass itself, the *dan* (plates, literally 'levels') for the *gessan* were also primarily fabricated from solid plate, there was no longer a need for the connective and decorative *hishinui* bindings that had over the centuries come to be one of the distinguishing features of the lowest *dan* of the hip armour tassets. As such, the term *suso-no-ita,* which translates as 'hem plate', was revived. And while, technically, *suso-no-ita* should be used to refer to the lowermost *dan* on all cuirasses after the mid 16th century, irrespective of whether the *dan* features *hishinui* or not, it is quite common for the pre-mid-16th century term *hishinui-no-ita* to be used when referring to the lowermost *dan* on a suspended section of armour on *tosei-dō* when the armour features *hishinui* bindings.

It should also be noted that the *suso-no-ita* on cuirasses produced during the latter half of the 16th and early 17th century were commonly fabricated with a rounded lower edge that curved subtly upwards toward the outside bottom corners of the plates. This feature faded out in the Edo period, when the majority of *gessan* lames were generally quite rectangular in overall form.

In most cases the *gessan* were constructed to match the finished appearance of the *dō*, including the manner in which the latter was laced. Thus if the cuirass was a black-lacquered *okegawa-dō* that was made with *nuinobe*-like features from *ita-mono* that were shaped to look like individual *iyozane*, then the *gessan* would in most cases also be fabricated to look like they had been assembled from *iyozane* scales that were laced together in the *sugake odoshi* style.

The *koshi-kawa-tsuke gessan* for the *mae-dō* of a *ni-mai-dō*. The detachable *gessan* are shown in conjunction with an auxiliary item of armour called a *koshi kusari*, which in this case is a mail-faced panel of fabric. This could be suspended behind the vulnerable *yurugi-ito* to help protect the exposed lower torso area.

Tosei-Dō Modern Cuirass Designs, Part I

Irrespective of whether the cuirass itself was constructed from real scale or *ita-mono* with a replicated façade, which will be discussed more in the following paragraphs, the *gessan* were quite often made from *ita-mono* fabricated from pieces of *nerigawa*. This was done to help reduce the overall weight of the cuirass due to the fact that almost all early examples of *tosei-dō* were made entirely from *tetsu ita-mono*. During the Edo period, as armour was worn less frequently, it was common for the *gessan* to also be fabricated from iron. The *katchū-shi* strapped iron *shiki-gane* to the back of the *ita-mono* made from *nerigawa* before the lames were lacquered to help the *nerigawa* plates maintain the curved shape that was virtually universal to all *gessan* by this time.

Having said this, it is important to keep in mind the fact that there are always exceptions when it comes to Japanese armour. This is especially true of the *tosei-dō*. As such it is important to be able to properly identify the number, style and construction of the *gessan* when describing a *dō*, for unlike the vast majority of pre-*tosei-dō*, the factors mentioned above can vary considerably on modern cuirass. As such the first thing to identify when describing the *gessan* is to find out how many are suspended from the cuirass, with each individual pendant being referred to as a *ken*. The number of *dan* that each *ken* is assembled from should then be counted. Thus a conventional *tosei-dō* should feature *gessan* armour assembly that would be described as *nana-ken go-dan gessan* (seven thigh guard pendants of five plates each). If the finished style of the *gessan* plates is included in the description, as it should be, then such details are always mentioned along with the style of lacing used to assemble the *gessan*. Therefore, a conventional *tosei-dō* with red-lacquered thigh-guard pendants made out of *sane-ita* assembled from *iyozane* scales and laced in the open *sugake odoshi* style will be described as being *shu-urushi nuri hon-iyozane sugake odoshi nana-ken go-dan gessan*.

The connective *yurugi-ito* strands of lacing were almost double in overall length on *tosei-dō*, with the laces measuring about 10 cm from the base of the cuirass to the top of the *ichi-no-ita* of the *gessan*. This was done for two reasons, the most of important of which was to allow a long cloth *obi* to be wrapped tightly around the base of the cuirass to cinch it tight in order to ensure that the *dō* stayed firmly seated on top of the hips during vigorous movements. The long *yurugi-ito* also allowed the *gessan* to move more freely, which in turn ensured they would not restrict the movements of the legs.

In the vast majority of cases, the *yurugi-ito* was strung in the *kebiki odoshi* style, irrespective of the style of lacing that was used to lace the cuirass. The only time that *sugake odoshi* was used to lace the *gessan* to a *dō* was in the case of what Anthony Bryant calls 'the cheapest or most deliberately understated armours'.[7] Bryant was referring to cuirasses that were produced for low-ranking warriors, particularly the extremely rudimentary versions of *tosei-dō* that were starting to be mass-produced to equip the growing number of *ashigaru* that many *daimyō*

A *ni-mai-dō* with its detachable *kawa-koshi-tsuke gessan* belt removed. The lengths of *odoshi-ge* used to secure the hip armour are visible.

227

SAMURAI ARMOUR

were recruiting to serve as permanent bodies of auxiliary troops in their armies. In such cases the *yurigi-ito* was usually reduced to about four pairs of laces per *gessan*, with the individual lames being laced together by the same number of cords.

Additionally, the extended length of the *yurigi-ito*, while necessary, also left a large area of the lower torso undefended. To compensate for this, many samurai augmented their armour with panels of brigandine or mail that were attached by various means to the lower edge of the *dō* behind the *yurigi-ito*. As these items were often acquired separately, it was quite common for them to be fabricated from material that did not match the cuirass or other items of the armour. Matched or not, this form of additional protection most commonly took the form of several small, partially overlapping rectangular panels of fabric suspended from a sturdy cloth belt. These would usually be about the same size as or slightly longer than the width of the *yurigi-ito*. Lacquer mail was often sewn to the faces of these panels, in which case the panels were referred to as *koshi-gusari*, or 'waist mail'.

By the latter part of the 16th century it was not uncommon for *dō* to be constructed with removable *gessan*, which would be suspended from leather belts that could be tied, buttoned, or toggled to the base of the cuirass. This style of thigh-guard armour is referred to as *koshi-kawa-tsuke gessan*, which literally translates as 'waist leather applied'. While *koshi-kawa-tsuke gessan* were not unique to any one form of *tosei-dō*, they are most often applied to varieties of cuirass that appeared in the decades following the introduction of the *okegawa-dō* and as such are discussed further in Chapter 7.

Another feature that was common, though not universal, to many early examples of *tosei-dō* was a small cloth pocket called a *hanakami-bukuro*, or 'nose tissue bag'. These were often riveted or laced to the lower left-hand side of the *nagakawa* of the *mae-dō* area of a cuirass or to the reverse face of the *kintama-kakushi gessan* pendant. They could likewise be attached to the reverse of

some of the other *gessan*, with some cuirasses featuring two or even three *hanakami-bukuro* fitted to each of the three front *gessan*. While the name suggests that these handy little pockets were used exclusively for carrying a handkerchief or paper tissue, in reality any small item that was deemed a necessity could be carried.

This is reflected in the fact that these pockets were sometimes also referred to as *kusuri-ire*, or 'medicine holders'. *Hanakami-bukuro* fitted to the façade of a *dō* were also sometimes referred to as *mae-bukuro*, or 'front bag', for obvious reasons.

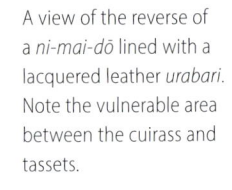

A view of the reverse of a *ni-mai-dō* lined with a lacquered leather *urabari*. Note the vulnerable area between the cuirass and tassets.

Rotating metal toggles along the lower edge of a *hon kozane*-constructed cuirass that were used to secure the *kawa-koshi-tsuke gessan* belt to the base. The belt of the detachable hip armour was fabricated with apertures fitted with grommets which corresponded with the protruding toggles.

Tosei-Dō Modern Cuirass Designs, Part I

A *hanakami-bukuro* fitted to the reverse of a *gessan*. While there was no rule as to which *gessan* the *hanakami-bukuro* was fitted to, or even how many *gessan* might have pouches secured to them, most *dō* featured a single *hanakami-bukuro* attached to the reverse of the *kintama kakushi gessan*. These pouches were generally made from the same materials as were used to make other fabric-based components of the armour, such as the *eri-mawashi*.

To prevent the contents from spilling out, the *hanakami-bukuro* were invariably fabricated with a flap or cover that could be buttoned down over the mouth of the pocket to keep it closed. When the *hanakami-bukuro* was fitted to the *gessan* the flap was usually located near the top of the thigh-guard panel. In some cases, however, it was positioned on the side of the pocket or even at the bottom, which made it easier to access the pouch when the *gessan* was being held. All manner of material was used to fabricate the *hanakami-bukuro*, such as leather, hemp, *rasha* and other fabrics. When present, however, they were commonly constructed from fabrics that had been used to make some of the other component parts of the armour and as such generally shared some form of visual relationship with the other parts of the armour.

Some scholars believe that armour makers fitted the *hanakami-bukuro* to the lower left-hand side of the cuirass in an effort to help protect the front of the *dō* from the damaging effects that the fixtures on the warrior's swords, such as the *tsuba* (hilt), had on the lacquered surfaces of the cuirass when they rubbed against the armour. *Hanakami-bukuro* fitted here were thus also sometimes referred to as *tsuba-ate*, or 'hilt touch'. Supporting this theory is the fact that it was not uncommon for many late-16th century examples of *tosei-dō* to have panels of edged leather riveted or laced to the lower left-hand sides for this very purpose. Perhaps the best-known example of this practice was the armour worn by members of the Uesugi *han* of modern-day Yamagata Prefecture.

ACCESSORIES FOR JAPANESE HERALDRY

With the development of disciplined units of specially trained fighting men such as the various cohorts of what Stephen Turnbull calls 'long service ashigaru', the feudal-period Japanese armies became not only larger but much better organized. An essential part of maintaining and coordinating these large forces in the field was the use of heraldry, which, alongside signals from drums and conch-shell trumpeters, became one of the main methods by which tactical control over an army was maintained and executed.[8]

This development manifested itself in the addition of several new and largely universal features to the exterior façade of most examples of *tosei-dō*. From the standpoint of heraldry, the *gattari*, *uke-zutsu* and *machi-uke* were by far the most important as these three fixtures enabled a warrior to affix a short flagpole and unit- or individual-specific identifying banner called a *sashimono* directly to the back of his armour. This was achieved by inserting the flagpole portion of the *sashimono* into a special tubular holder called the *uke-zutsu*, which literally means 'receiving tube'. Most examples of *uke-zutsu* were either long cylindrical tubes or square hollow shafts about 3.5 cm in diameter and 60 cm in overall length that slightly tapered in width from top to bottom. These were often made from two pieces of bamboo or wood that would be glued together and then bound in fabric before a smooth lacquer finish was applied. Most examples of *uke-zutsu* had gilded copper metal end caps called *kuchi-gane*, or 'mouth metal', fitted to the top end of the shaft that helped to prevent the holder from splitting. Metal rims protruded from the upper edges of the *kuchi-gane* that allowed the shafts to sit within a special metal bracket fitted to the rear of a cuirass, called a *gattari*, without falling through.

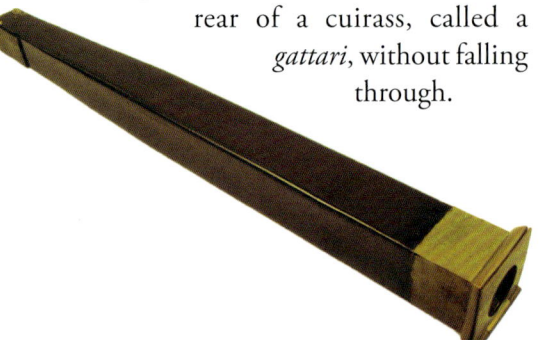

A *tetsu kuro urushi nuri nuinobe ni-mai-dō*. The cuirass features a large thick panel of *fusebe-gawa* affixed to the lower left of the *mae-dō*. This feature, which was commonly found on many *dō* worn by samurai associated with the Uesugi *han*, was applied to help protect the lacquer finish and lacing from the wearing effect of the warrior's swords.

An *uke-zutsu* mount used to secure the flag pole of a warrior's heraldic *sashimono*. Note the sprung metal clip at the base of the holder and the flared rim around the end cap. Also note the flat plate hinged to the face of the cap plate that helped to hold the flagpole in the *uke-zutsu*.

Tosei-Dō Modern Cuirass Designs, Part I

A sturdy lacquered iron *gattari* bracket suspended from open-eyelet swivel rings anchored in the *ichi-no-ita* of the *ushiro-tateage*. Note the decorative *maki-e* cherry blossom motif. Also note the knot of *odoshi-ge* that secures the *eri-mawashi* collar to the *boko-no-ita*.

The lower end of many examples of *uke-zutsu* was often fitted with a V-shaped sprung metal clip applied point-down to one face of the shaft. The outward pushing tension of this clip helped to hold the *uke-zutsu* in place when its lower end was inserted into a special receiving cup, called a *machi-uke*, that was fitted to the lower back of a *dō* in vertical alignment with the middle of the upper *gattari* bracket. In other cases, the bottom of the *uke-zutsu* would have a pair of horizontally aligned holes drilled through it. In such cases a special padded cushion would be fitted to the base of the *dō* with cords protruding from it that could be threaded through the apertures in the *uke-zutsu* to tie the latter down and anchor it to the base of the cuirass.

While most *uke-zutsu* were generally fairly similar in overall form, they could be finished in a number of different ways. In general, however, they were lacquered the same colour as the cuirass they were meant to accompany. Better-quality examples might feature applied *maki-e*

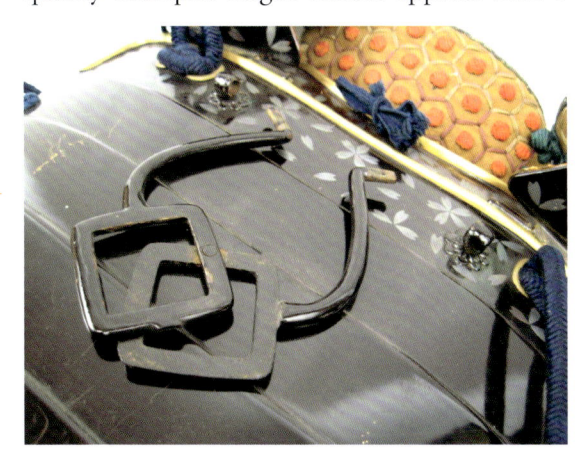

This *gattari* pivots on a central hinge that allows the arms to scissor inward. This enables the bracket to be removed. When the *uke-zutsu* was seated, the *gattari* would be unable to fold, which would lock it in place.

designs on them, or other decorative detailing. This was also true of *kuchi-gane* which might feature *kebori*, or literally 'hair engraving' on high-quality pieces, or flat metal plates hinged to their upper surface that acted as a form of lock for the flagpole assembly. This simple system utilized the changing angle between the perforated top plate and the main opening of the *kuchi-gane* to bind the flagpole in position. For as the flagpole moved upward in the holder the hinged top plate would move with it until the changing angle of the top plate caused it to bind on the flagpole, the tension of which was sufficient to prevent the flagpole from sliding further upward in the holder.

Additional accessories could also be inserted into or fitted to conventional *uke-zutsu* that allowed the holder to support a number of smaller flags at different angles or other fixtures.

The most common form of *gattari* bracket was a wide U-shaped metal band that had a round or square metal ring set in the middle of, or attached to the bottom inside edge of, the flat lower portion of the U. If the central fixture is round in shape the holder is called a *maru-gattari*. If it is square, then it is referred to as *shikaku-gattari*. The upper ends of the bracket were usually bent outward at right angles. This allowed them to be inserted through protruding eyelets that were anchored by split shanks to the lower middle of the *boko-no-ita* of a cuirass, which allowed the *gattari* to pivot in position, so the bracket could lie flat against the back of the cuirass when not in use or be raised upright to receive an *uke-zutsu* when required. Some brackets like the *hajikami-gattari* hinged in the middle, which allowed them to be removed from the cuirass when not required. In the case of the *hajikami-gattari* this was achieved by joining two mirrored half-pieces of a bracket together with a pin inset into one of the outside corners of the central receptacle for the *uke-zutsu*, which allowed the *gattari* to scissor on itself. When an *uke-zutsu* was inserted through the central aperture, however, the presence of the flag holder prevented the bracket from

SAMURAI ARMOUR

pivoting and as such ensured that the *gattari* remained firmly locked into the receiving eyelets on the back of the cuirass while in use.

Another common form of bracket was the *ita-gattari*, which as may be surmised from the name was fundamentally a flat board-like panel with an open central aperture cut in to receive the *uke-zutsu*. *Ita-gattari* were commonly laced to the back of the cuirass using narrow strips of leather that were tied through holes in the bracket for this purpose. This arrangement allowed the *gattari* to pivot and made it easy to remove. *Nerigawa* and wood were both commonly used to make *ita-gattari*, which would generally be wrapped in a coarse weave of linen and then be lacquered to match the cuirass that it was meant to accompany.

The *machi-uke* cups were small, rectangular metal receptacles that were generally fitted vertically to the lower middle of the *nagakawa* of a *dō*. The top of the *machi-uke* was usually riveted to the cuirass, while the bottom end of the cup was quite often laced in place. A small, cotton-stuffed cushion or section of rolled leather called a *koshi-makura*, or 'lower back pillow', was often positioned behind the bottom portion of the *machi-uke*, where it would be held in place by the lacing that was strung through both the base of the *dō* and the *koshi-makura*, where it was tied off. These padded cushions were presumably added to help protect the bottom rear of the *dō* from the pressure inward that would be placed on the *machi-uke* from the backward drag of a *sashimono*, which would be transmitted downward through the *uke-zutsu* and into the base of the receiving cup and from there into the lower back of the cuirass.

The cups usually tapered in width from top to bottom and often had a small opening on one or more sides. These were important as they allowed a warrior to depress the retention-spring clip at the base of an *uke-zutsu* when one had been inserted in order to remove it from the holder. Most *machi-uke* were also pierced centrally with a small hole in the bottom of the cup called a *tsuyu-otoshi-no-ana* that allowed

A *hon kozane ginpaku oshi* (silver foil applied) *kuro urushi nuri ni-mai-dō* (*maru-dō*). The *gattari* and the *machi-uke* cup affixed to the lower back of the *ushiro-dō* are clearly visible. Note the three-piece collapsible *eri-mawashi* collar which buttons together, and the *aibiki-no-o* knotted with a *ninawa-musubi* traversing the *wadagami*.

water trapped in the holder to drain. It was also quite common for *machi-uke* to be fabricated with a small metal tail that arched forward and upward from the lower base of the cup. The actual purpose of this appendage is unclear, though it may have been intended to help prevent the *dō-jime* and other cords that fastened around the waist from riding up and past the *machi-uke* and dislodging the *uke-zutsu*. Alternatively, it may have been a guide to help

A shock-absorbing *koshi-makura* cotton-stuffed leather pillow secured by a leather thong between the lower end of a *machi-uke* and the base of the cuirass.

An example of a machi-uke receiving cup. Note the open window that allowed a finger to depress a spring-loaded retaining clip fitted to the base of the uke-zutsu. Also note the rolled leather koshi-makura between the lower end of the cup and the rear surface of the cuirass.

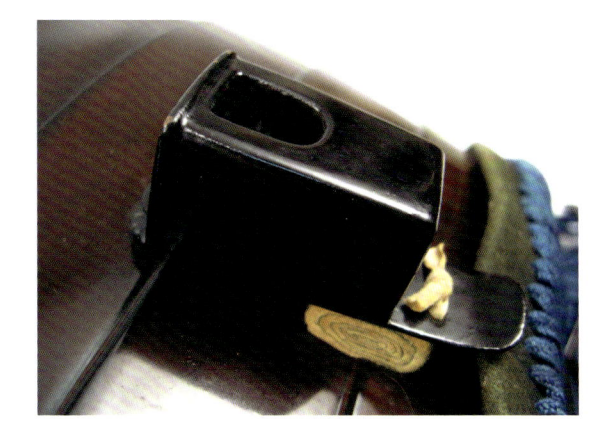

keep the *dō-jime* in place around the rear of the cuirass, with the cords being held in the hollow of the appendage under the cup.

The one other feature that began to appear on generally better-quality examples of *okegawa-dō* and that needs to be mentioned was a small swivel-ring that was sometimes fitted to the upper right-hand breast area of the *ni-no-ita* of the *mae-tateage* in the area of the right nipple. Though there are a multitude of terms used to refer to this fixture it is most commonly known as the *saihai-no-kan* or *saihai tsuke-no-kan*. Though decorative in appearance, the *saihai-no-kan* was initially applied to serve a functional role and was largely limited to the armours of higher-ranking samurai who carried a form of tasselled command-baton called a *saihai*. The *saihai* was used as a form of signalling device that could be waved to give visual commands on the battlefield. As such the *saihai* was also symbolic of a person of rank.

The *saihai-no-kan* allowed commanders to hang the baton from their armour when they were not using it or otherwise to free up their hands. This was done by looping the tasselled double cord on the end of the *saihai* through the *kan* and then dropping the *saihai* between the cords. Attaching the baton to the armour in this way also prevented it from becoming lost during battle.

The *kan* ring is generally mounted upon a single or arranged layer of floral or scallop-edged base washers that will generally be gilded or feature other ornate alloy finishes such as red copper or *shakudō*, an alloy of copper and gold that produces a purplish-black colouration. The layers of the base washer will often be a combination of more than one of these varied finishes to add to the overall aesthetic appeal of the *kan*. The head of the *kan* will generally be etched in a grid-like pattern to resemble a chrysanthemum, though in later periods it was also common for them to be made in the shape of a heraldic *kamon* crest device.

By the mid-Edo period, however, *saihai-no-kan* were common to most armours and were little more than a form of decorative accoutrement, often being hung with decorative *ko-busa* tassels. Attesting to the growing decorative nature of this fixture was the fact that much later Edo-period armour also featured an identical *kan*, often referred to as a *tenugui-no-kan* or *dansen-osame-no-kan*, fitted to the left breast of the *dō*. This additional fixture was added for purely aesthetic reasons in order to balance out the appearance of the cuirass. Some sources say it was used it to hang a towel that allowed the samurai to wipe the sweat from their faces during battle. This,

A high-quality mid-Edo-period cuirass fitted with a saihai tsuke-no-kan swivel ring fixture (left) and matching tenugui-no-kan (right). Originally only found on the cuirasses of commanders, saihai tsuke-no-kan were designed to hang the warrior's command baton from to free his hands.

Samurai Armour

though, is rather unlikely, for few samurai ever saw anything close to battle by the time this additional ring-fixture came into vogue. Nor were they likely to be inclined to want to hang a grubby towel from the front of their armour, which by that time period had become increasingly ornate in appearance.

It is important to note that many cuirasses that were never originally fitted with a *saihai-no-kan* or the later *tenugui-no-kan* often had these *kanamono* mounted on them retroactively in later periods, when it became fashionable to have such accoutrements decorate the *dō*. One of the key differences with early-period *kanamono* of this kind and those from later periods was the swivel ring. On early-period examples the ring was generally of a consistent diameter around its entire circumference. On later-period pieces, however, the ring generally gained in overall thickness and diameter towards the suspended bottom of the closed loop.

The split shanks and rivets that held the *saihai-no-kan* and other fixtures like the *gattari* and *machi-uke* in place were hidden under the leather *urabari* panels that were glued to the interior surfaces of the cuirass, as was discussed in the opening chapter. These not only helped to hide the riveted construction of a *dō*, but also saved smiths a considerable degree of time and effort in having to forge, file and finish the back sides of the *ita-mono* for a somewhat presentable appearance.

DESIGN VARIATIONS

Understanding the vast number of features that have been described in the preceding pages is essential, as most of them were largely universal to the vast majority of alternative varieties of *tosei-dō* that sprang up in quick succession after the introduction of the *okegawa-dō*.

An ornate example of a *yokohagi-okegawa ni-mai-dō*. Note the superfluous *tsurubashiri-gawa*.

As the skilfully lacquered façade of these *kiritsuke kozane ita-mono* show, even on close inspection, it can often be quite difficult to differentiate between real scales and replicated ones. Note the iron *shiki-gane* applied to the back of the *nerigawa ita-mono*.

Another similarity shared by most early examples of *okegawa-dō* and other early alternative forms of *tosei-dō* was their overall weight. In *The Samurai 1550–1600* Anthony Bryant records that a conventional *okegawa-dō* with *kusazuri* [*gessan*] weighed 7.7–9.5 kg, and some 18.8 kg of iron was ultimately required to produce a single 5.7 kg cuirass (devoid of *gessan*) assembled from iron plate of just 2 mm thickness.[9] Much of the original weight of the iron was lost through the forging process as the iron was heated, hammered flat, folded and reheated again multiple times until the iron was almost pure and remarkably strong.

The thickness of the *ita-mono* or the amount of steel that was incorporated into the production of the plate armour could, however, easily increase the overall weight of the cuirass by a few kilograms. Thus it was not uncommon for two cuirasses of almost identical construction and size to differ notably in weight.

The sheer simplicity of the *okegawa-dō* was its greatest attribute. For armour makers could produce four or more *okegawa-dō* for what Bryant estimates is the same cost in time and materials needed for a single cuirass produced in the *Mōgami* style. This factor alone was obviously a game changer. But beyond that, it was the chameleon-like qualities of the *okegawa-dō* that made it the single most common and popular form of cuirass ever to be produced in Japan. This was due to the fact that without having to deviate significantly from the base form of construction, the *katchū-shi* were capable of producing a vast array of seemingly different forms of cuirass, each example of which could then be finished in any number of different ways to make those *dō* also appear to be unique pieces. As a result, it could be dressed up to be a cuirass worthy of a *daimyō* or be dressed down to its barebones basics for general issue to lowly *ashigaru*-grade retainers.

This unique quality of the *okegawa-dō* method of construction and design more than likely initially went unrecognized when this make of cuirass first appeared, being hidden in plain view by the then still revolutionary nature of its appearance in comparison to anything that had hitherto existed in the collective memory of the samurai. As such many warriors were more than happy to wear the *okegawa-dō* even in its most basic early form.

Within a very short period, however, armour makers saw how to incorporate the popular appearance of the cuirasses made in the *nuinobe* style with the *okegawa-dō* concept. For the hinged *ni-mai-dō* construction of the *okegawa-dō* was the liberating factor when it came to furthering the *nuinobe* style, as smiths were finally able to utilize *ita-mono* to construct cuirasses with a *nuinobe*-like façade. This they did with an incredible degree of realism, using the *kiritsuke* method of cutting the upper edges of the *ita-mono* to look like the *sane-gashira* of overlapping *iyozane*, the shapes of which were formed through thick applications of lacquer. In some cases, the *katchū-shi*, according to Bottomley and Hopson, even went as far as fitting *kawashiki*, held in place by imitation lacing fastened through two rows of holes drilled along the centre line of the plate. When lacquered the sewing and ridge formed by the *kawashiki* on the inside added considerably to the realism; only the rigidity of the solid plate betrayed the true method of construction. Such situations were, however, primarily limited to the *gessan*, where the underside of the plates were more likely to be seen.

Thus for the first time, armour makers were able to produce armour from solid plates that on all but the closest of examinations looked and fitted like a cuirass that had been assembled from *sane-ita*. With this achievement the dam had been breached. Over the course of the next three decades, from roughly 1545 onward, new versions and variations of *tosei-dō* began to appear at a bewildering pace as armour makers experimented with the seemingly limitless number of different versions of cuirass that could be produced as result of this new approach to armour construction.

In short order, *tatehagi-ita*-constructed examples of *okegawa-dō* began to appear alongside the original *yokohagi-ita* version of this form of cuirass. These were quickly followed by *ichi-mai-ita*-assembled examples of *ni-mai-dō* as Japanese armour makers attempted to physically replicate the Western forms of cuirass that they were encountering. Within a few decades there were *san-mai-dō*, *yon-mai-dō*, *go-mai-dō*, *roku-mai-dō* and potentially even *isei-dō* versions of the *okegawa-dō* being assembled from one of the three different arrangements of *ita-mono* or even *sane-ita*. When such varying characteristics as the number of sectional pieces a cuirass was to be constructed from was combined with the huge multitude of possible façades, alternative methods of assembly and other varied aesthetic details that could substantially transform the appearance of a *dō*, it is easy to forget that every make of cuirass that appeared in Japan from the mid-1540s onward can trace its origin back to the 'family tree of the *okegawa-dō*'.[10]

Unlike the *kebiki odoshi*-laced version of *Mōgami*-made *dō-maru* or *haramaki* that smiths had produced a few decades earlier in an effort to replicate the look of a cuirass assembled from *sane-ita*, the false façades that were applied to some of the new alternative examples of *okegawa-dō* were so convincing that for the first time in the history of Japanese armour it was often impossible to determine exactly how a cuirass had been constructed based solely on a visual examination of its exterior surfaces. As a result, it became increasingly common for cuirasses to be identified by the physical characteristics of their façade rather than their actual method of assembly.

A prime example of this is the *tosei-dō* version of cuirass that is constructed with *nuinobe*-like features, commonly referred to as a *nuinobe-dō*. As already noted, *nuinobe* is a method of construction and not a style, thus technically it

A *shu urushi*-finished *nuinobe ni-mai-dō*. Unlike a real *nuinobe*-made *dō*, this cuirass is really a *yokohagi-okegawa dō* with a replicated *iyozane* façade with *sugake odoshi* lacing.

Tosei-Dō Modern Cuirass Designs, Part I

A cha *(brown)* urushi nuri nuinobe ni-mai-dō. There are several features to note on this classic Sengoku period style of cuirass. Note the sturdy *nerigawa* ita-mono *style of* gattari *that is laced to the back of the* dō *and the large* machi-uke *and accompanying* koshi-makura. *Also note the* rasha *cloth* hanakami-bukuro *fitted to the lower left side of the* mae-dō.

were nullified. For the *iyozane* could be replaced by *ita-mono*, which in turn voided the need for the distinctive 'sewn spread' *shita-garami* and leather covering to reinforce the *sane-ita*. In fact, even the characteristic *sugake odoshi* was reduced to being nothing more than a decorative embellishment. That the replicated version can differ so significantly from the original and still be referred to using the same term is confusing, as is the fact that conventional examples of modern *dō* made to look like an authentic *nuinobe*-assembled cuirass can also be described as being *kawa-tsuzumi* (leather-wrapped) *kiritsuke-iyozane sugake odoshi okegawa ni-mai-dō*, for in fact that is what it is. Which is right and which is wrong is, according to Dr Sasama, a 'very difficult question' and still very much a matter of debate amongst Japanese armour experts.[11] While technically the latter, lengthier term is correct, established convention leans towards the practice of referring to cuirasses that look as though they were made in the *nuinobe* style as *nuinobe-dō*. This is most likely due to the convenience of being able to identify several commonly associated aesthetic features using just one word. This practice of using the façade to describe the type of cuirass is so well established at this point in time that it is difficult to suggest doing otherwise.

Unlike their pre-*tosei* predecessors, modern examples of *nuinobe-dō* can be both *ita-mono* and *sane-ita* in construction. As such it is important to differentiate between the two whenever possible, with cuirasses assembled from actual lengths of *sane-ita* being referred to as *hon iyozane*, or literally 'real *iyozane*', while those made from replicated boards are referred to as *kiritsuke iyozane nuinobe-dō*. As the lamellar boards should be wrapped in leather, this can often be difficult to determine. When a leather covering is absent, though, the vast majority of examples will be *kiritsuke* in construction.

The *tosei* version of *nuinobe-dō* almost certainly led to the development of the next few alternative forms of *okegawa-dō*, with the *hishi-toji okegawa-dō* most likely being the first one to

is not possible to have *nuinobe-dō*, only an example of a certain form of cuirass constructed in the *nuinobe* style. The *okegawa-dō* method of assembling a cuirass from *ita-mono* joined together vertically by rivets essentially made the *nuinobe* method of construction obsolete. That said, *nuinobe*-assembled cuirasses were both common and highly popular by the time of the first examples of *tosei-dō*, largely due to the aesthetically attractive appearance this method produced. The eminently practical and generally superior design of the *okegawa-dō*, in contrast, was extremely dull, even in comparison to the significantly subdued standards of cuirasses made using the *nuinobe* method. Thus it is not surprising that efforts began almost immediately to incorporate the *nuinobe* look with the newly developed *okegawa-dō* method of construction.

In doing so, however, many of the characteristics that made the *nuinobe* what it was appear. The *hishi-toji* or 'cross-knot' version of the modern cuirass in some ways represented a step backwards in armour design, for it reverted to utilizing lengths of *tomegawa* instead of rivets to bind the individual *yokohagi-ita* together. Why this approach would have been favoured over rivets is hard to understand. The fashion may have originated with older *nuinobe*-made versions of cuirass that were being refurbished, with armour makers deciding to dispense with the largely superfluous vertical lengths of *sugake odoshi*, possibly in an effort to create a cuirass that was closer in appearance to the new and popular look of the smooth, clean façade of a conventional *okegawa-dō*.

With the *sugake odoshi* removed, the connective cross-knots of the *tomegawa* that had previously been hidden under the lacing became visible on the exterior of the cuirass. As these were regularly spaced they created a very rudimentary, though attractive pattern across the surface of the cuirass not unlike the façades of the *fusebe-gawa kawa-tsuzumi* version of cuirass that had been produced in the early centuries.

To improve the appearance of the cross-knots, which had hitherto been purely functional, wider, more regulated widths of *inu-gawa* were used to bind the plates together. This was also done to offset the fact that the connective *sugake odoshi* lacing between *ita-mono* had been done away with. The manner in which the cross-knots were tied also became much more regimented, ensuring that every knot crossed in the same manner and maintained a uniform overall appearance. The *katchū-shi* were quick to realize that the cross-knot façade looked even better if they offset every second row of *hishi-toji* in the vertical assembly of the cuirass so that they staggered back and forth up the face of the *dō*.

While the *hishi-toji* style most likely began with cuirasses made from *sane-ita*, it was also used to construct *dō* assembled from *ita-mono*. When leather ties were used, the exposed cross-knot portion of the tie on the exterior of the cuirass was usually covered over in *urushi* to help protect and preserve it. In most cases they were lacquered over using the same *urushi* that was applied to the rest of the cuirass, but in some cases their outline was picked out in a lacquer of contrasting colour to highlight the knots and enhance their overall aesthetic appearance.

Silk *odoshi-ge* also began to be utilized as it greatly enhanced the visual presentation of the knots. When silk was used, however, it was not uncommon for the *ita-mono* to be riveted together as the silk was far more prone to damage and wear than leather ties. While the *hishi-toji* still traversed between the overlapping plates in such cases, they were little more than decorative in nature with no real influence on the structural integrity of the *dō*.

The *hishi-toji okegawa-dō* method of assembling a cuirass quickly gave rise to another laced-together form of *tosei-dō* that came to be known as the *uname-toji okegawa-dō*. As the name suggests, cuirasses constructed in this style had the *ita-mono* or *sane-ita* that they were assembled from bound together using lengths of leather thong that were strung horizontally through the *kedate-no-ana*, which created a dash-like pattern similar to *uname* across the

A fine example of a *cha urushi nuri hishitoji iyozane ni-mai-dō*. Note how the leather *hishi-toji* cross-knot bindings have been picked out in black lacquer. A large *gattari* bracket is hinged to a rather shallow *boko-no-ita*. Also note the *machi-uke* and the *maru-himo* cords used to secure the detachable *koshi-kawa-tsuke gessan* belt.

Tosei-Dō Modern Cuirass Designs, Part I

façade of the armour. This style is relatively rare and seldom encountered outside of the 'Sansai-ryū', or 'Sansai style' version of this make of *dō* that was favoured by the warriors of the Hosokawa clan. The so-called *Sansai-ryū* is said to have been developed by the famous lord of that clan, Hosokawa Sansai (1563–1648), who showed a strong personal interest in the design and construction of armour. Sansai's version of *uname-toji*-made cuirass was constructed from *sane-ita* assembled using a unique form of flat-headed or rectangular *iyozane* that are referred to as *ichimonji gashira*. As the *sane-ita* were wrapped in leather they are classified as being a variety of lamellar board made in the *nuinobe* style. Unlike in a conventional *nuinobe*-made cuirass, however, the *sane-ita* are laced together horizontally with leather bindings strung in the

A superb Sengoku period example of *tetsu kuro urushi nuri hishi-toji ni-mai-dō*. The cuirass features large externally mounted auxiliary armour *waki-biki* to protect the armpit areas. It was also designed to have a *koshi-kusari* panel suspended around the exterior of the *dō* to cover the *yurugi-no-ito*. Note the bear fur trims applied the façades of the *gessan suso-no-ita*.

An example of an *uname-toji ichi-mai-dō*. The cuirass has been assembled from rectangular *ichimonji kozane* horizontally laced together with lengths of leather thong. Note the applied leather façade. Also note the convex shape of the *waki-ita*. This feature was commonly seen on cuirasses that were made during the latter half of the 16th and early part of the 17th centuries.

uname style. As such the proper name for this make of *tosei-dō* is *ichimonji gashira nuinobe uname-toji ni-mai-dō*, though it is not uncommon for this version of cuirass to be referred to as a Hosokawa, Sansai or simply *uname-dō*. It should be noted that a large number of the Hosokawa type of *ichimonji gashira nuinobe uname-toji*-made cuirasses are *dō-maru* in form. Their *sane-ita*, *ichi-mai-dō* construction often results in them being confused for a pre-*tosei* cuirass.

It is extremely rare for the *uname-toji* method of assembly to be used to construct cuirasses made from *ita-mono*, especially solid metal plates. In such cases, the *uname-toji* is almost always purely decorative in nature, with countersunk rivets being used to secure *tetsu ita-mono* together in the manner of a conventional *okegawa-dō*.

While aesthetically attractive, the inherent weakness in binding the *ita-mono* together in the *hishi-toji* style almost certainly led to the development of the *byō-toji*, or 'rivet closed' form of *tosei-dō*. Cuirasses made in this manner had the *ita-mono* riveted together in the manner of a conventional *okegawa-dō*. Additional rivets with prominent heads were then mounted to the exterior façade of the cuirass to replicate the *hishi-toji* cross-knots. In fact, the earliest examples of *byō-toji-dō*, as cuirasses made in this manner came to be known, most likely featured rivets that were fabricated to look like *hishinui* cross-knots. This practice was relatively short-lived, however, as smiths realized the huge number of different aesthetic possibilities that could be achieved by simply changing the appearance of the external rivets. As such, in short order, rivets made in the shape of cherry blossom, family crests and various snowflake-like geometric shapes began to appear. In general, however, domed rivets, often gilded for contrast, were the most common. It was not uncommon for these to be seated upon scallop-edged base washers for additional aesthetic effect.

At some point smiths began to assemble *okegawa-dō* using *ita-mono* that were cut to feature an undulating wave-like shape along their upper edges. This concept was clearly borrowed from the *kiritsuke* method of replicating *sane-ita* by cutting the form of the scales into the upper edge of the *ita-mono*. As there was no intent to replicate a scale façade, however, the *katchū-shi* were free to experiment with a number of different designs, the vast majority of which tended to revolve around a repetitive

A fine example of a *tetsu-sabiji byō-toji hira-yamamichi ni-mai-dō*. The use of external rivets resulted in cuirasses that were structurally stronger and more resilient that similar makes of *dō* assembled using *hishi-toji*. Note the *e-gawa*-faced *kanagu mawari* and rich patina of the russet-iron-finished plates of the *nagakawa* and the *mae-* and *ushiro-tateage*. Also note the *gattari*, *machi-uke* and the unusual leather-wrapped *fukurin*.

A classic Sengoku period *tetsu cha urushi nuri byō-toji kiritsuke iyozane ni-mai-dō*. Note the *maki-e* design of *kamon* crests set amongst scrolling foliage that have been applied to the façades of the *kanagu mawari*. Also note the *eri-dai*, *kiritsuke kozane ita-mono kobire* and the arrangement of seven gold lacquer-finished *gessan*.

A late 16th century example of a *cha urushi nuri* finish *uma gawa* (horse leather) *tsutsu-mi hotoko-dō*. The smooth leather façades applied to cuirasses finished in this style often hides the actual method of construction. A small hole in the leather cover of the *ushiro-dō* of this cuirass reveals that the armour was assembled from what appears to be an *ichi-mai-maze* mix of *nerigawa* and *tetsu iyozane*. Note the large lacquered *nerigawa* board-like *gattari*, the *saihai-tsuke-no-kan* and the ivory-buttoned *rasha* cloth *hanakami-bukuro*.

wave-like pattern. And though the form of these patterns had no connection to *sane*, the term *gashira* continued to be used to refer to the patterns, though in this case it would be more accurate to translate it as meaning 'leading edge' than 'head'. The Japanese apparently saw the rolling outline of distant mountains in the various examples of *gashira* they produced, for the vast majority of them are named after their perceived association with a specific mountain vista, the most commonly seen example of which is known as *tsure-yamamichi gashira*, meaning 'mountain paths coming together leading edge'. Other variations include *hira-yamamichi gashira*, or 'even mountain path leading edge', and *hanare-yamamichi gashira*, or 'separated mountain paths leading edge'.

The spaces between, on, or under the peaks and valleys of the undulating upper edges of these plates were ideally suited to the positioning of decorative rivets. In such cases, which are quite common, the form of the undulating edge of the plate is introduced before the *byō* are mentioned in the formal title of a cuirass, which in the case of many examples of *tosei-dō* could become extremely complex. For example, a russet-iron-finished horizontal plate *okegawa ni-mai-dō* that was assembled using *ita-mono* featuring the *tsure-yamamichi* style of finished upper edge line and prominent external rivets would be referred in Japanese as a *tetsu-sabiji tsure-yamamichi gashira byō-toji yokohagi-okegawa ni-mai-dō*.

In stark contrast to this cuirass were examples of *okegawa-dō* that had their characteristic ribbed construction concealed by the lacquering to produce a smooth surface. Cuirasses made in this style are referred to as *hotoke-dō* and were a Japanese variety of the European globose breastplate. The term *hotoke* alludes to the Buddha, but in the case of the *hotoke-dō* the term is generic and derived from the visual similarity in appearance of the façade of cuirass finished in this manner with the smooth, round bellies of Buddhist statues. To achieve this effect, armourerers glued a layer of fabric or thin leather over the armour and applied layers of lacquer until the surface of the cuirass was completely smooth.

The bold, smooth and rounded finish of the *hotoke* version of *okegawa-dō* was an immediate sensation, for it was, yet again, a complete break with anything that had been seen before. It also capitalized on the status-symbol aspects of owning an actual *nanban-dō*, or an imported Western-made 'southern barbarian cuirass', which were extremely scarce in Japan during the latter half of the 16th century. As such their ownership was generally limited to the wealthiest of high-ranking warriors, as is discussed further in Chapter 7. Even so, the *hotoke-dō* was not viewed as a poor man's stand-in for a *nanban-dō*. Attesting to this fact is the famous *hotoke*-style cuirass and armour set that was worn by Tokugawa Ieyasu, which had the entire façade

SAMURAI ARMOUR

of the armour covered in gold dust that was sprinkled over a clear lacquer, or *tomoe urushi*, before the lacquer dried. The formal title of this stunning yet simple armour, which is now housed in the Tōsho-gu Shrine in Nikkō, Japan, is *kintame-nuri hotoke muna-tori ni-mai-dō gusoku*.

Sakakibara Kōzan stated that the *hotoke-dō* was 'the precursor of the one-piece *dō*'.[12] By this he was referring to *ni-mai-dō* made from two separate half-sections, each of which was forged from a single solid plate. He was probably correct in this regard as it appears to have taken the Japanese a while to learn how to fabricate and forge metal sheets that were large enough to produce a single half-section of a cuirass. Efforts in this regard almost certainly led to the development of the *tatehagi* method of construction, where the *okegawa-dō* were assembled from a number of wide, vertically arranged *ita-mono*. *Tatehagi-okegawa-dō* are discussed further in the next chapter. It is therefore important to remember that *hotoke-dō* can be either *yokohagi* or *tatehagi* in construction. However, as the applied façade generally makes it impossible to determine which method of construction was used to make the cuirass, it is not necessary to include this information in the formal title of a *hotoke-dō*.

While unique for the barren simplicity of its appearance, it did not take armour makers long before they began to view the smooth, finished surface of the *hotoke-dō* as a blank canvas awaiting artistic expression. Examples of *hotoke-dō* with decorative rows of staggered *hishi-toji* or prominent *byō-toji* dotted across their façade are common. It was also common for two different colours of *urushi* to be used to finish the cuirass, with, for example, the *nagakawa* being *kuro urushi nuri* while all the upper-body sections were lacquered in red *shu urushi*, or vice versa. These two-tone lacquer façades could divide a cuirass diagonally, vertically or into patchwork-like sections, or band it like the abdomen of a hornet. Heraldic emblems and other often highly detailed decorative designs could also be applied to the lacquered or *kawa-tsuzumi* leather-covered exteriors of a cuirass. These could vary in the extreme, with one well-known example of late 16th century *hotoke-dō* worn by a samurai of the Sanada *han*, now housed in the Sanada Treasure House in Nagano, Japan, featuring little more than the diagonal ladder-like crest across the face of the cuirass, while another *dō* from the same general period, now housed in the

A modern reproduction of one of the famous gold leaf-finished *hotoke ni-mai-dō* that was owned by Tokugawa Ieyasu. Note the *muna-tori* lacing. While a decent reproduction, it is not entirely accurate. The original armour, for example, featured panels of black felt-covered fabric in lieu of *yurugi-ito*. The protective coverings of each tight apron panel on the *haidate*, or thigh armour, were also different, in that each panel of the original was covered by four rows of eight gold leaf-faced lacquered leather plates.

Tosei-Dō Modern Cuirass Designs, Part I

Ōsaka Castle Museum collection, features a scene applied in gold *maki-e* of a monkey reaching for the moon. It should be noted, however, that such scenes were generally very subtle on early examples of *hotoke-dō*, while those from the later Edo period are often large and highly ornate.

It is of course possible for a *hotoke-dō* to simultaneously present several of the aforementioned features, which can often make it hard to identify the base form of the cuirass. That said, if the plate construction of a cuirass cannot be observed and the façade is smooth other than for applied decorations, then the item is a *hotoke-dō*.

An interesting alternative example of *hotoke-dō* that demonstrates this point is the famous *kuma-ge ue hotoke ni-mai-dō gusoku* (bear fur planted *hotoke* two-section cuirass armour) now housed in the Tokugawa Museum in Nagoya, Japan. This armour, which had bear fur adhered to all of its exterior surfaces, was apparently commissioned by Tokugawa Ieyasu in jest, responding to a joking comment made to him by Oda Nobunaga about Ieyasu becoming the 'cow of the Kantō', after Nobunaga awarded Ieyasu the still extremely rural Kantō territories for his actions during the siege of Odawara in 1590.

One of the most striking versions of *hotoke-dō* to be developed replicated the naked torso of the human body through the skilful application of lacquer. So unusual were cuirasses finished in this manner that they quickly began to be recognized as a unique subset of *okegawa-dō*, which are commonly referred to as *Niō-dō*. This style of cuirass derives its name from its similarity with the barechested *Niō* statues that are often found standing guard on either side of the entrances to Buddhist temples. These fierce-looking, wrath-filled guardian deities are placed at the temple gates to ward off demons and other evil spirits as well as to deter thieves and ne'er-do-wells.

While the *Niō* statues are profoundly muscular, the vast majority of *Niō-dō* tend to resemble an emaciated torso like that of a starving monk or old man. How the features of the torso are depicted ultimately led to several subcategorizations of *Niō-dō*, the most basic example of which will depict some aspects of the ribs, breast area and navel on the façade of the cuirass. The pectoral muscle area of the chest will usually be depicted as being withered, sagging and wrinkled. The navel will also commonly be draped by wrinkles.

Cuirasses fabricated with a façade of extremely pronounced ribs are referred to as *abara-dō*, literally 'ribbed cuirass'. Some examples of *abara-dō* will even depict the bones of the ribs, shoulder blades and spine on the rear section of the cuirass as well. When the upper chest is withered and boney and the lower belly area is swollen, the style is referred to as *gakibara-dō*. This style is said to be based on the *gaki*, a grotesque form of ghost from Japanese folklore.

The large, rounded belly of the cuirass made in the *hotei-dō*, or 'Buddha cuirass', style can look somewhat similar to the swollen abdomens on *gakibara-dō*. Unlike the latter, however,

A classic example of a *Niō-dō gusoku*. A variation of the *hotoke* style, the *Niō-dō* was made with a façade that replicated the emaciated torso of a starved or elderly man. Note the cuirass was made to be worn without *sode*. (Image © and courtesy of the Tōkyō National Museum)

SAMURAI ARMOUR

hotei-dō are meant to depict the well-fed rolling belly of a happy Buddhist deity. As such the upper chest pectoral muscles will be rounded and breast-like, which clearly differentiates a *hotei-dō* from the skeletal, as though starving, *gakibara-dō* style of *Niō-dō*.

The shocking appearance of cuirasses made in these styles, which were almost certainly intended to be both visually and psychologically intimidating, were often further enhanced through the use of flesh-coloured lacquer tones. In the case of *gakibara-dō*, pale, almost white tones of *urushi* were applied.

A scene from a 12th century scroll housed in the Kyōto National Museum that depicts *gaki*, or 'hungry ghosts'. These grotesque creatures were the reincarnated souls of selfish, greedy and otherwise immoral persons. As ghosts they were cursed with insatiable appetites, often for repugnant things such as human faeces and rotten corpses. Aside from the obvious psychological impression that such a cuirass would have on an opponent, the *gaki*-like appearance may have been meant to intimidate, as *gaki* were often persons who had killed and murdered in their previous life. (Tōkyō National Museum/Wikimedia Commons/Public Domain)

Tosei-Dō Modern Cuirass Designs, Part I

A classic example of a *dangae-dō*. The transition from *kiritsuke kozane kebiki odoshi*-laced *ita-mono* to *sugake odoshi*-laced *kiritsuke iyozane ita-mono* is clearly visible. It is important to note that a *dangae-dō* can be any form of cuirass where the scales and style of lacing change from the top to the bottom half of the *dō*. Thus if the cuirass seen here had a *kiritsuke-iyozane sugake odoshi*-laced *mae-tateage* and *kiritsuke kozane kebiki odoshi*-strung *nagakawa*, the armour would still be considered a *dangae-dō*. Note the *kebiki odoshi*-laced *kiritsuke iyozane gessan*.

One other unique form of cuirass to evolve out of the *Niō-dō* style was the *katahada nugi-dō*, or 'bared shoulder cuirass'. As the name suggests, the façade of the cuirass was finished to show only half of a bared upper body, generally the right side. The clothed, covered-over left side of the *dō* would be constructed to look like a conventional cuirass, featuring, for example, a *kiritsuke kozane kebiki odoshi*-laced façade. The scales and lacing, which were separated from the bared-chest portion of the cuirass by a piece of thick cord, would be arranged to drape off the upper left shoulder and down across the torso to make it look like clothing hanging from the shoulder. The inspiration for this style is taken from the practice of Japanese warriors of withdrawing their right arm from the sleeve of their kimono when using a bow. Allowing the garment and sleeve to hang loose down the right side of the body helped to ensure that it could not foul the bowstring. One of the most well-known examples of late 16th century cuirass made in this style is the *katahada nugi ni-mai-dō gusoku* said to have been worn by the famous warlord Katō Kiyomasa, which is now housed in the Tōkyō National Museum in Ueno.

As the *kiritsuke kozane* façade of the *katahada nugi-dō* denotes, by the latter part of the 16th century, Japanese armour makers had become highly proficient at producing examples of *okegawa-dō* that were virtually indistinguishable from the true-scale forms of cuirass of the previous century. In fact, well before the end of the 16th century *hon kozane* examples of *ni-mai-dō* were being produced. The first tentative steps towards such pieces

A well-made modern reproduction of a *katahada nugi-dō*, or 'bared shoulder cuirass'. A variation of *Niō-dō*, this style of cuirass features a façade of which one side resembles the emaciated chest of an old priest, while the other side is finished with *kiritsuke kozane* to give the impression of a garment hanging down over one side of the torso. Note the *maru-himo* used to divide the two halves of the cuirass and the colourful *iro-iro* style of *kebiki odoshi* lacing.

A superb example of a *tetsu kuro urushi nuri yokohagi-okegawa koshi-muna-tori ni-mai-dō*. The *koshi-muna-tori* feature is clearly visible on this *dō*, with the *mae-tateage* and the *san* and *yon-no-ita* of the *nagakawa* being *kebiki odoshi*-laced *kiritsuke kozane* finished *ita-mono*. Note the textured gold-coloured lacquer finish of the *kanagu mawari* plates. Made for a samurai of considerable wealth and girth, note that the *mae-dō* features four *gessan*, while five are suspended from the *ushiro-dō*. Note the *hanakami-bukuro* and the *agemaki* suspended from the *agemaki-no-kan*.

began with the first hybrid examples of *nuinobe*-made versions of *okegawa-dō*.

While some armour makers worked to develop the *hishi-toji*, *byō-toji* version of cuirass from the *nuinobe-dō*, others working independently were experimenting at the same time with alternative ways of enhancing the aesthetic appearance of the *nuinobe-dō*. At some point an armour maker came up with the idea of highlighting the *nuinobe*-like upper portion of the armour by finishing the lowermost bands of the *nagakawa* to look like *kebiki odoshi*-laced bands of *kozane*, a practice that came to be referred to as *koshi-tori*, or 'waist around'. Surprisingly, the two contrasting methods of construction complemented each other and significantly enhanced the overall aesthetic appeal of cuirasses finished in this manner. As the type of scales used abruptly transitioned from *kozane* to *iyozane* and the lacing from *kebiki* to *sugake*, *tosei-dō* finished in this manner came to be referred to as *dangae-dō*, which literally means 'step changing cuirass'.

The *dangae-dō* was an immediate success when it first appeared, so much so that it quickly gave rise to two alternative variations, the first of which saw the original pattern reversed, with *kebiki odoshi*-laced *kozane* sections being used in the upper-chest *mae-tateage* area of the cuirass. As such, this arrangement came to be referred to as *muna-tori*, or 'chest around'. The other new design, called *muna-koshi-tori*, or 'chest waist around', featured bands of *kebiki odoshi*-laced *kozane* scales around both the upper *mae-tateage* and lower bands of the *nagakawa*.

While it was easy to identify the original *koshi-tori* versions of modern cuirasses as being *dangae-dō*, this became increasing difficult to do over time as more and more variations of

The mae-dō portion of a superb tetsu kuro urushi nuri byō-toji yokohagi-okegawa muna-tori ryō-hikiawase roku-mai-dō made for a senior member of the powerful Hosokawa han. This armour illustrates how katchū-shi combined new designs and methods of construction as they were introduced throughout the latter half of the 16th century. Note the use of kanamono made with the kamon crest of the Hosokawa and the removable gessan belt.

muna-koshi-tori were introduced. This was largely due to the fact that other than for the bands of *kebiki*-laced scales, there were no other consistent features to define this make of cuirass. Even the number of bands of *kebiki*-laced scales could vary, which is why the *dangae-dō* is a mix of styles rather than a style in its own right. This is why the *dangae* features on other prominent forms of *tosei-dō* are generally observed by their physical placement on the cuirass and are secondary to the primary style of cuirass. For example, a two-section cuirass with prominent external rivets and with *kebiki*-laced scale bands around both its upper and lower edges would be referred to as being a *byō-toji koshi-muna-tori ni-mai-dō* and not as a *byō-toji dangae ni-mai-dō*.

One innovation that may have evolved out of the *muna-tori* version of *dangae-dō* was a return to the practice of lacing the *oni-damari-ita* to the *mae-tateage*. This not only helped to make a set of armour more comfortable to wear, but also helped to slightly increase the potential range of upper-body movements. This practice was also sometimes replicated along the base of the *nagakawa*, with the *koshi-tori* bands actually being laced to the cuirass and not simply fabricated to look like independent *sane-ita*. And while it undermined many of the goals that the original *tosei-dō* concept embodied, in some cases armour makers actually began to utilize real *sane-ita* to construct the *dangae* portions of some cuirasses.

In fact, within a few decades of the development of the *okegawa-dō*, some armour makers were producing hybrid versions of *dō-maru* that were *hon kozane kebiki odoshi*-laced *ni-mai-dō*. While visually similar, cuirasses made in this style are referred to as *maru-dō* to differentiate them from actual *dō-maru*-made cuirasses, which continued to be produced, albeit in relatively small numbers. Two excellent examples of early 17th century *dō-maru* are the two famous *hon kozane kebiki odoshi dō-maru* that Tokugawa Ieyasu sent as gifts to King James I of England, which are now housed in the Royal Armoury in Leeds. These sets show how, in a time when all of the forms of *yokohagi-okegawa-dō* discussed in this chapter would already have been present in a huge number of highly unique variations, the samurai class maintained its infatuation with the classical forms of lamellar armour.

A striking example of a *ryō-hikiawase go-mai-dō gusoku* from the mid-18th century. This armour was made for the seventh Lord of Yanagawa, Tachibana Akinao. (Tachibana Museum)

CHAPTER 7

TOSEI-DŌ MODERN CUIRASS DESIGNS, PART II

Tatehagi-okegawa and related styles of *dō*, 16th century onward

Within a decade of their introduction to firearms, the Japanese were not only mass-producing a superior domestic version of matchlock, they were also developing tactics for its deployment, including the highly disciplined manoeuvre of volley fire. This tactic was used for the very first time in history in 1575 by Oda Nobunaga at the battle of Nagashino to devastating effect against the powerful forces of the Takeda clan. Nobunaga, having drilled his men to fire in volleys to keep up continuous fire, deployed 3,000 of them to devastating effect against the cavalry charges of the Takeda clan, annihilating them. Although the Takeda clan had been most famous for their use of cavalry, ironically they had been at the forefront of gun adoption. It would be almost another twenty years before similar tactics were used in Europe for the first time in 1592, with the Dutch apparently developing their own volley-fire drills independently of any knowledge of the methods that were by then common practice in Japan.

In fact, there is some evidence to suggest that Nobunaga had employed volley-fire-like tactics as early as 1554 during the siege of Muraki a mere decade after the Japanese had started producing their own firearms. And within twenty years of their introduction, firearms were becoming an increasingly common and effective weapon on the battlefield, with many feudal armies fielding entire units of specially trained *teppō-tai* musketeers. Had Tokugawa Ieyasu not been a high-ranking lord equipped with a cuirass and armour made from metal plates of the very highest quality, there is a strong probability that he would not have survived the several hits he sustained during the second battle of Azukizaka in 1564. The rarity of cuirasses of that calibre, however, was reflected in the prohibitively high cost of their production, which made them virtually unobtainable for all but the highest ranking and wealthiest of warriors. This meant that the average samurai was far less likely to survive the sort of front-line encounter that Ieyasu braved while fighting the Ikko-ikki at Azukizaka. Which is why in 1567 Takeda Shingen, the famous *daimyō* of the Takeda clan that Nobunaga's troops would literally shoot to pieces a decade later, is reported to have said 'Hereafter, the guns will be the most important arms. Therefore, decrease the number of spears per unit, and have your most capable men carry guns.' Ironically, Shingen was said to have been killed by a bullet himself six years later.[1]

Not surprisingly there was a direct correlation between the increased presence and effectiveness of firearms and the growing demand for shot-proof armour, the finest and most effective early examples of which were imported European-made cuirasses. This was due to the simple fact that Western armour makers were already well versed in countering the effects of firearms on armour, for they had being dealing with this problem for several decades prior to the arrival of the first Portuguese traders in Japan.

The Japanese were of course, as is often pointed out, drawn to Western-made cuirasses, such as the peascod, for other reasons, including the unique aesthetic appearance of this design from the Japanese perspective. There was also a great deal of prestige in being able to own any form of imported European-made item, for it clearly stated that the owner was a man of considerable wealth and power to be able to possess such an extraordinarily rare item. What is often overlooked in many texts on this subject matter, however, is just how effective Western-made cuirasses were, particularly at providing protection from firearms, and how this characteristic almost certainly helped attract many warriors to these items.

A full peascod, circa 1580, made in the shape of the popular doublet style of jacket worn during that time in Europe. The medial ridge down the middle of the front of the 26 lb cuirass was decorated with a series brass-capped iron rivets to replicate buttons. (Image courtesy of Wade Allen of Allen Antiques, UK)

The prevailing thought on Western armour is that it began to slowly trickle into Japan shortly after the arrival of the first Portuguese traders and that such items slowly began to be incorporated into sets of Japanese armour with a few necessary modifications, such as the addition of *gessan*, which the Japanese considered to be essential components in any make of cuirass. The scarcity and therefore prohibitively high cost of acquiring a *nanban-dō*, or 'southern barbarian cuirass' as the Japanese began to refer to European-made examples of cuirass, is often cited as the reason why Japanese armour makers started to make copies of Western cuirasses that came to be known as *wasei nanban-dō*, or 'Japanese-made southern barbarian cuirass'. While there is clearly no doubt that this was the situation, it appears that actual *nanban-dō* were far scarcer than prevailing theories would tend to suggest. In fact, evidence, or rather the lack of evidence, of extant examples of European cuirasses in Japan prior to the last few decades

Tosei-Dō Modern Cuirass Designs, Part II

of the 16th century suggest that the Japanese had almost no alternative but to produce their own *wasei* copies of Western cuirasses based on just a handful of pieces that they were able to study or possibly acquire.

Supporting this opinion is the fact that Toyotomi Hideyoshi did not own a *nanban-dō* until he received a few as diplomatic gifts from King Philip II of Spain in the 1590s. Tokugawa Ieyasu too would not own a Western-made cuirass until the beginning of the 16th century and may only have acquired his from some of the items that were seized from the *Liefde*, which was the first Dutch ship to reach Japan in 1600. That two of the most powerful warlords in Japan during the latter half of the 16th century did not own such items until half a century after first contact with the West indicates that actual *nanban-dō* were almost impossible to acquire.

It also suggests the *nanban-jin*, or 'southern barbarian people', a term which quickly became synonymous with all Westerners and who, from the Japanese perspective, arrived in Japan sailing north out of the southern Pacific Ocean, were less than eager to provide the Japanese with armour, based on the number of known extant pieces. In fact, most of the examples of *nanban-dō gusoku* that are known to exist appear to have been created after the arrival of the *Liefde*, which Miura Shigetoshi estimates carried about ten or so cuirasses on board for the officers amongst the crew.[2] Supporting Shigetoshi's estimates are inventories that were taken at the time by Jesuit missionaries on behalf of the Japanese of the items found on board the *Liefde*, and which recorded that there were three cases which contained 'brestplates and cuirasses'.[3] Of the ten, Miura notes that at least one was definitely incorporated into the *nanban-dō gusoku* that Tokugawa Ieyasu commissioned for himself and which he is said to have had with him at the battle of Sekigahara, though there is no evidence to suggest that he actually wore it during the battle. And while rumours persist that Tokugawa may have owned as many as five different *nanban-dō gusoku*, there is no evidence to substantiate such claims, which may be based on the fact that he is known to have gifted a number of *nanban-dō gusoku* in the years immediately following the taking of the *Liefde* to favoured members of his immediate family and to some of his closest retainers, that were presumably constructed around the *nanban-dō* were confiscated from the *Liefde*.

One of these cuirasses may have been incorporated into the *nanban-dō gusoku* that was given to Sakakibara Yasumasu by Tokugawa just before the battle of Sekigahara that is now housed in the Tōkyō National Museum. Yet another appears to have gone to Watanabe Moritsuna, while five others seem to have been stored in the Ōsaka Castle warehouse where they were discovered in 1691 during an

The *nanban-dō gusoku* of Tokugawa Ieyasu's tenth son, Yorinobu. The cuirass is pitted in ten places with the *tameshi* dents from the impact of matchlock balls fired at the armour to prove its shot-proof qualities. Note the massive European fauld-like design of articulated *gessan*. (Image courtesy of the Wakayama Prefectural Museum)

SAMURAI ARMOUR

inventory, which accredited them as having been gifted to the Tokugawa by a Korean named Miura Anjin. Miura Anjin was in fact William Adams, the first Englishman to reach Japan in 1600 on board the *Liefde*, and was the real life inspiration for the fictional character John Blackthorne in the famous novel *Shōgun* by James Clavell. It is also possible that a *nanban-dō gusoku* used by Tokugawa Ieyasu's tenth son Yorinobu, which is now housed in the Wakayama Prefectural Museum, also came from among the cuirasses that were seized from the *Liefde*. Though sometimes described as a *nanban-dō*, the cuirass that was said to have been worn by the senior Tokugawa retainer Honda Tadamasa at the siege of Ōsaka Castle in 1615 was more than likely a Japanese reproduction of a *nanban-dō*. Thus, as the preceding paragraphs show, there is almost no evidence to suggest that any examples of *nanban-dō* actually existed in Japan until almost the end of the 16th century and possibly no *nanban-dō gusoku* until the very beginning of the 17th century.

Having said this, it is obvious that soon after the arrival of the first Portuguese traders, a few Japanese armour makers did have access to some examples of Western-made cuirasses. Whether they were able to acquire a few pieces or simply study them is impossible to say. Regardless of how they gained their understanding of Western armour design and methods of construction, the *katchū-shi* who studied these items clearly understood them. For as extant examples of *wasei nanban-dō gusoku* can attest, the Japanese were producing highly accurate reproductions of European-style cuirasses within a decade of the Portuguese traders' arrival, or possibly even earlier. A final example of such a set is the *wasei nanban-dō gusoku* that is said to have been worn by Sekiguchi Gyōbu, who committed suicide after the battle of Okehazama in 1560. A similar though possibly slightly later-period example is the armour believed to have been used by Akechi Sama no Suke Mitsutoshi, who died in 1582, which is now housed in the Tōkyō National Museum.

Why so few Western-made cuirasses reached Japan in the five and half decades of trade that occurred between the arrival of the first Europeans in the 1540s and the start of the 17th century is hard to understand. The generic answers such as the prohibitively high cost of these items, while true early on, fail to justify this situation, for surely the price would have dropped substantially had these items being imported en masse. Nor can the commonly referenced belief that Western armour simply did not fit the average Japanese explain why so few European cuirasses reached Japan.[4] For as

The famous *nanban-dō gusoku* that Tokugawa Ieyasu is said to have worn at the battle of Sekigahara. According to research conducted by the renowned *gendai katchū-shi* Miura Shigetoshi, the European cuirass at the centre of this *gusoku* was more than likely originally one of the dozen or so peascods that Tokugawa Ieyasu seized from the Dutch trade ship, the *Liefde*. The vast majority of *nanban-dō*-based *gusoku* appear to have come into existence in the wake of the arrival of the *Liefde* in 1600. (Image © and courtesy of the Tōshō-gū Shrine, Nikkō)

Tosei-Dō Modern Cuirass Designs, Part II

the example of the *Liefde* demonstrated, at least five of the ten assorted cuirasses that were on board the ship, none of which were intended to be used by anyone but the officers of the ship's European crew, appear to have been incorporated into sets of Japanese armour without issue. This example also undermines the idea that Western traders made efforts to place large orders for smaller-sized examples of European cuirass, but that this process took too long, by which time Japanese demand had dried up with the introduction of the cheaper examples of domestically made *wasei nanban-dō* that were fundamentally identical, if not superior, to the Western-made pieces that they were based on. For, as demonstrated, whenever European armour could be obtained it was always highly prized.

Thus the question arises: did the Portuguese, Spanish and Dutch traders make a deliberate decision not to market Western-made items of armour to the Japanese? This possibility seems unlikely considering that the Europeans had no issue selling weapons, including cannons, to the Japanese. Thus the absence of real *nanban-dō* may simply have been a reflection of business-based decisions, with the traders choosing their cargo according to which items could ensure the greatest profit margins based on their weight and the amount of space that they took up in the ship's hold, a calculation that clearly favoured items like rolls of silk cloth over piles of armour.

The sudden appearance of a number of *nanban-dō gusoku* amongst the elite retainers and family members of the all-powerful Tokugawa clan during the opening decade of the 17th century might have triggered a serious trade in Western armour as other samurai followed their lead, had it not been for the fact that trouble between the Japanese and Europeans was beginning to escalate by the time that the then-Shōgun, Tokugawa Ieyasu, died in 1616. One of the main sources of contention was the growing strength and influence of the Christian faith in Japan, which some scholars believe may have exceeded over 300,000 practitioners by the 1630s. The devotion of these Japanese Christians to their faith and hence also to the Pope in Rome represented a serious challenge to the hierarchical social structure that was being established in Japan under the samurai, who had officially become a distinct hereditary class at the top of society under an edict issued by Hideyoshi in 1591.

Other issues also fanned the flames until the Spanish were ultimately expelled from the country in 1624. This was followed by the execution of many thousands of Christian

A tetsu-sabiji nanban-dō gusoku housed in the Tōkyō National Museum. This armour was originally commissioned by Tokugawa Ieyasu. Ieyasu is said to have bestowed it upon Sakakibara Yasumasa, one of his talented generals, on the eve of the battle of Sekigahara in 1600. Though commonly referred to as a *nanban-dō*, there is evidence to suggest that this cuirass may have been produced in Japan and that it is in fact a *wasei nanban-dō*. (Image: TNM Image Archives)

converts in 1629 and finally by the introduction of the so-called Sakoku, or 'Closed Country' Edict in 1635 issued by the third Tokugawa Shōgun, Iemitsu, which prohibited on pain of death any foreigner from entering Japan or any Japanese person from leaving its shores, or, if they did, from ever returning. Iemitsu, perhaps noting the huge impact that this law was having on the availability of imported wool, silk and several other materials that were by then essential in the production of many of the items of clothing and equipment that were used by the samurai class, including armour, relented somewhat in 1636, when he agreed to allow the Dutch to continue their trade operations with Japan. The Dutch, however, and their activities were restricted to the small artificial island of Dejima in Nagasaki Bay, which allowed the Shōgunate to save face by saying the foreigners were not on actual Japanese territory. These changes, along with the fact that a large number of the estimated 37,000 rebels that were killed by the Shōgunate during the brutal suppression of the Shimabara Rebellion in 1637–38 were devoted Japanese Christian converts, truly sullied the image of anything Western in the eyes of the Japanese of that period. This is probably the reason why so few *nanban-dō*-based *gusoku* seem to have been made after the second decade of the 17th century and why there was a fairly rapid return to makes of armour with more of a traditional Japanese aesthetic.

Irrespective of the fact that actual *nanban-dō* were virtually unobtainable in Japan until late in the 16th century, it is necessary to describe these items first, since the handful of pieces that the Japanese did observe or possibly obtained early on after contact with the West formed the basis upon which they fabricated their own *wasei nanban-dō*.

The majority of the pieces that reached Japan were peascod cuirasses of Italian or Flemish

Two views of the Western-style cuirass at the centre of the *nanban-dō gusoku* associated with Sakakibara Yasumasa. Note the unique tapering two-piece construction of the uppermost boards of the *kintama-kakushi gessan* that help the latter conform with the prominent V-shaped lower edge of the cuirass. (Image: TNM Image Archives)

A superb *tetsu-sabiji nanban-dō* that is said to have belonged to Akechi Mitsuhide. One of Oda Nobunaga's generals, Akechi led a short-lived rebellion that resulted in the death of Nobunaga in 1582, before he too was killed by the loyal Oda forces commanded by Toyotomi Hideyoshi. The kanji character *ten* or 'heaven' has been embossed into the upper chest of the converted European-made cuirass. Though not visible in this image, the back of the cuirass was decorated with an embossed image of Mt Fuji. (Image: TNM Image Archives)

manufacture with medial ridges down the centre front of the breastplate. In accordance with the styles of that period, as Miura Shigetoshi writes in *Katchū Nishi to Higashi* (Armour West and East), most examples of peascod cuirasses were generally slightly elongated and narrow in shape. The lower edge of the breastplate was also fashioned to taper to a soft point below the medial ridge above the groin area. Many peascod cuirasses, particularly the ones that were mass-produced by the Dutch for Spanish officers, featured a polished façade that was etched with a series of vertical lines. These were generally arranged to fan slightly outward to the sides of the cuirass from the central ridge as they rose up from the base of the armour. In some cases the field between alternating rows of the lines would be darkened with linseed oil and etched with additional scrolling, floral patterns, as was the case with the *nanban-dō* that is said to have belonged to Tokugawa Yorinobu and which is now housed in the Wakayama Prefectural Museum.

The Japanese generally dulled the polished surfaces of imported cuirasses with controlled applications of rust blooms to produce a subdued *tetsu-sabiji* russet iron patina. Alternatively, they would cover the façade of the armour with lacquer or, in the case of some later-period examples, encase the cuirass in leather. *Gessan* would invariably be fitted to the lower edges of the *dō* to make the armour more compatible with domestic design and needs. This sometimes required the shape and number of individual plates used in the *gessan* to be altered to accommodate the downward tapering form of the *mae-dō*. This was particularly true of the *kintama-kakushi* tasset, which was often assembled using one fewer *ita-mono*. In other cases, the uppermost *ichi-no-ita* of the *kintama-kakushi* was divided into two pieces to help it better conform to the lower-central-point shape of the cuirass. In the case of Yorinobu's cuirass, two massive multi-plate *gessan* resembling European tassets were suspended from the front of the armour. Each tasset was assembled from nine rows of three *sugake odoshi*-laced *kuro urushi nuri ita-mono* hinged together, with three more single *ita-mono* plates fitted between each *gessan* and the bottom edge of the cuirass.

While the *gessan* fitted to the *nanban-dō* worn by Yorinobu were clearly inspired by Western designs, it was rare for the Japanese to utilize other forms of Western-made items of armour with the *nanban-dō* that they incorporated into *gusoku*, with the exception of some varieties of imported European helmets, which are discussed further in Volume II. One of the few *nanban-dō gusoku* that deviated from this practice was the set made for Tokugawa Ieyasu that is now housed in the Tōsho-gu Shrine in Nikkō. This armour, which was built around an Italian-made peascod from the 1580s, also incorporated a Western-made gorget neck guard into its finished design, which was capped off by a European cabasset helmet.

The first examples of European cuirass studied or acquired by the Japanese clearly incorporated most of the aforementioned features, for most of them were reproduced in the oldest known extant example of *wasei nanban-dō gusoku*, which is said to have been worn by Sekiguchi Gyōbu. This is also true of the *wasei nanban-dō gusoku* that is said to have belonged to Akechi Sama no Suke Mitsutoshi, who died in 1582, and which is now housed in the Tōkyō National Museum.

That so few *wasei nanban-dō gusoku* are known to exist suggests that only a handful of *katchū-shi* really understood what Western armour looked like and how it was made. Even so, clearly enough information was available about certain characteristics of European-made cuirasses for Japanese armour makers who had never seen these items to have understood them well enough to incorporate *nanban-dō*-like features such as the smooth *hotoke* façade into the construction and design techniques of domestically made *dō*. The *hatomune* medial ridge also began to appear on some of the various forms of *okegawa-dō* that were being produced. Whether this was done because the Japanese were quick to grasp how this feature improved the protective quality of a cuirass or if it was at first included primarily for aesthetic reasons is unclear.

Over time, however, the Japanese clearly gleaned many valuable lessons from their studies of Western-made armour, including the true benefit of forging a metal plate with a medial ridge, as will be discussed in the following paragraphs. What they also appear to have learned is that while they were more than capable of producing highly accurate reproductions of Western-type cuirasses, which were extremely effective at stopping matchlock ball shots even at surprisingly close ranges, producing *wasei nanban-dō* entailed considerable effort. This was primarily because one of the great strengths of Western-made cuirasses was that the front and back plates were each forged from a single large piece of metal plate. This was something that was very difficult for Japanese armour makers to do, largely due to the restrictive nature of the traditional form of Japanese forges that made it extremely difficult to work with large pieces of metal. This is why most *ita-mono*-assembled items of armour produced by the Japanese were constructed from a series of relatively narrow metal plates about 6–7 cm in height including the portion allotted for the required amount of overlap.

Yet the *katchū-shi* who were working to reproduce cuirasses based on Western designs prevailed, and through trial and error learned to forge the sectional halves of a cuirass from single pieces of metal. Their efforts in this regard more than likely led to the introduction of the *uchidashi*, or the 'hammering into form' metalworking technique, into Japanese armour making. While this technique had been practised in other metalworking disciplines in Japan for centuries, traditional armour-making had not required smiths to emboss and form metal in the ways that were necessary to accurately reproduce Western styles of cuirass.

An unusual 17th century example of a *tetsu-sabiji wasei nanban-dō gusoku*. The European influence that gave rise to this form of cuirass is almost indiscernible on this *dō*, which is almost kettle-like in form. (Image: TNM Image Archives)

Tosei-Dō Modern Cuirass Designs, Part II

Having mastered the form, the *katchū-shi* must have been quick to realize that it was not simply the shape of a *nanban-dō* that made them often virtually impregnable to the effects of firearms, but also the quality and strength of the metal that was used to construct the cuirass, which in the case of a shot-proof armour required the use of steel. And while the Japanese were capable of producing high-quality steel, once again they struggled to overcome the lack of domestically available high-quality ore as well as the limitations of traditional smelting techniques. This issue was partially alleviated by the import of steel billets as trade between Japan and the West grew over the course of the latter half of the 16th century.

While access to steel was one problem, working with it to make plates for armour was another. It is clear from studied examples that *katchū-shi* understood that, after a steel billet had been folded, welded and forged into a flat plate with the welds parallel to the surface, the plate was apt to flake when it was struck. They appear also to have understood that if the billet was hammered out so that the weld planes were at right angles to the surface of the plate, the welds were as likely to split when struck. To prevent these problems, *katchū-shi* first prepared the steel billet in the latter manner then cut it into two halves which they welded together with the grains running at right-angles to one another. This complex process, which Sakakibara Kōzan discussed in considerable detail in his book *Chūko Katchū Seisakuben*, is referred to as *jumonji kitae*, or cross-pattern forging, and was essential in producing a *tetsu ita-mono* that was capable of stopping a shot from a matchlock.[5]

However, as Sakakibara noted, a shot-proof armour was not simply a cuirass made from steel but was instead assembled from plate that was a hybrid laminate combination of a hard steel façade backed by a layer of soft iron. The steel facing layer of the plate meant that the armour would withstand an arrow or bullet while the iron backing would deaden the force of an impact. An *ita-mono* made entirely of steel would be too brittle, and would simply shatter when struck, while one made of softer iron would be dented and pierced. For this reason, a combination of the two materials was required to prevent either of these things occurring, while creating the most resilient type of *tetsu ita-mono*.

The costs associated with the huge amount of additional forge work that was required just to produce armour plate of this quality ensured that very few samurai ever owned a cuirass constructed of *tetsu-ita-mono* of this calibre.

The highly unique *wasei nanban-dō gusoku* that Honda Tadamasa, one of Tokugawa Ieyasu's senior retainers, is said to have worn at the siege of Ōsaka Castle in 1615. Note how the red-lacquered *kanagu mawari*-like portions of the cuirass have been fashioned to look like they have been constructed from *kozane*-like scales. Also note the decorative use of open metalwork floral *kiri-tetsu* fixtures. (Image: TNM Image Archives)

Add in the expense of creating the large single-plate pieces that were required to reproduce accurate copies of Western-made cuirass and the price of such items was simply so far beyond the financial means of most samurai that it is easy to understand why so few examples of *wasei nanban-dō* appear to have been produced.

Most of those that were made, however, tended to follow the European models in regards to their overall shape and appearance. But, just like the actual *nanban-dō* that the Japanese acquired, the *wasei nanban-dō* versions incorporated features that the Japanese had come to view as being an integral part of the construction and design of a cuirass, including the practice of hinging the *mae-dō* and *ushiro-dō* portions of the cuirass together along the left side of the armour in the usual style of a *tosei ni-mai-dō*.

One typical peascod cuirass feature that was commonly eliminated from the design of many examples of *wasei nanban-dō* was the triangular downward-pointing taper along the lower front edge of the breastplate. This was in part because this feature simply did not appeal to the aesthetic tastes of the Japanese. That said, the fact that it interfered with how the *gessan* were suspended from the base of the *dō* is what actually led Japanese armour makers to do away with it. Because of this, the lower edge around many *wasei nanban-dō* is generally fairly consistent with that of most other conventional examples of *tosei-dō*, with a standard number of *gessan* suspended in the usual manner.

Other differences included the addition of *wadagami* to the *ushiro-dō*. These were commonly forged as an integral part of the *ushiro-dō*, though they were sometimes fabricated separately and riveted in place. In most cases the *wadagami* were fitted with some form of *kobire* and often featured integral *gyōyō* to protect the various cords of the *aibiki-no-o*. It was also common for the rear inside edges of the *wadagami* and the upper back edge of the *ushiro-dō* to be raised to create a low, integral form of protective collar known as a *nanban eri*. The exterior edges of the plates were generally rolled over to create a smooth trim called a *makikomi fukurin*. It was not uncommon for a continuous spiral-like pattern to be carved into the surfaces of rolled edges, which gave them a rope-like appearance referred to as *nawame-kizami*.

The medial ridge that ran vertically down the middle of the *mae-dō* was universal to almost all *wasei nanban-dō*, though it was more pronounced in some examples than others. This feature, which came to be referred to as a *hatomune*, or literally 'pigeon chest', by the Japanese was not only one of the most visually impressive characteristics of the *wasei nanban-dō*, it was also one of its most important. For while the angled frontage helped make weapons slide off on impact, it also had the effect of increasing the thickness of the armour when exposed to a missile, such as a matchlock ball. The angled frontage meant that any impact other than one that hit at a perfect right-angle to the surface of the *dō* was resisted by the angled thickness of the armour plate. Thus a 3 mm thick plate hit at an angle could potentially have the same resistive qualities as metal plate 4–5 mm thick, which made it significantly harder for a missile to defeat and penetrate the armour.

While incredibly strong and stylish, *wasei nanban-dō* was a highly impractical design of cuirass due to the complexity of production and the cost and time required, which ensured that this form of *dō* would never be more than a novelty as a style of cuirass, irrespective of its positive aspects. The development of the *wasei nanban-dō*, however, appears to have made significant contributions to the evolution of other forms of the *tosei-dō* and may even have led to the creation of the *tatehagi* method of horizontally arranged *ita-mono* plate construction.

Prior to this development, though, it is clear that many of the advances associated with the evolution of the *wasei nanban-dō* were finding their way into the designs of some of the various forms of *okegawa-dō*, such as the *hatomune*. *Hotoke-dō*, which, as already noted, were inspired by the appearance of *nanban-dō* and

A tetsu-sabiji nanban-dō. (Courtesy of the Miyakonojo Shimazu Lore Museum, Miyakonojo, Japan)

other makes of *okegawa-dō*, also began to be constructed using hybrid combinations of steel and iron plate to strengthen them against the effects of firearms. And though the riveted plate construction of such cuirasses meant that they were not as strong as a solid-plate *wasei nanban-dō*, they were substantially easier to produce and still quite effective. And as firearms had played a relatively minor role in most engagements prior to the years leading up to the middle of the 1560s, conventional designs of cuirass that were fabricated using steel were likely considered to be more than sufficient when it came to providing protection from firearms, as it was still relatively rare for warriors to be killed in this way. This factor no doubt played a large part in limiting the need for the much more resilient *wasei nanban-dō* makes of cuirass.

Tokugawa Ieyasu's experience of being hit several times by matchlock balls at Azukizaka in 1564 foretold the changes that were taking place in warfare across Japan. For the number of firearms being used in battle had started to increase exponentially with each passing year. Compounding this were the increasingly sophisticated tactics that were being developed for the deployment of firearms, which greatly increased the lethality of these weapons, as Oda Nobunaga demonstrated so effectively at Nagashino in 1575.

The slaughter of the flower of Takeda cavalry units at Nagashino, the vast majority of whom were shot from their horses well before they had any hope of engaging the Oda forces, sent a shock wave through the warrior class across Japan, for it was abundantly clear to all concerned that firearms were now the pre-eminent weapon on the battlefield. That they were primarily wielded by the vast hordes of riff-raff that made up the rank and file of the *ashigaru* troubled the samurai. For the *tanegashima* or *teppō* had become the 'great equalizer'. Bottomley records that the *tanegashima* was 'relatively cheap to produce, effective under the right weather conditions and could, with minimal training, turn the rawest recruits into a valuable adjunct to other forces', making them just as effective on the battlefield as the 'finest of samurai, without the long arduous training' in various martial arts that was the cornerstone of the samurai's world.[6] This detestable situation, backed by the horrendous number of casualties amongst the Takeda samurai, reinvigorated the demand for shot-proof designs of armour, which 'consequently became the subject of earnest investigation' all across Japan.[7]

One of the first monumental steps towards resolving this dilemma appears to have taken place during the later part of the 1570s with the introduction of the brilliantly conceived *Yukinoshita-dō*. These unique shot-proof cuirasses, 'elegant in their lack of pretension', as Bryant descibes them on the *Sengoku Daimyō* website, are said to have been named after the small rural hamlet of Yukinoshita, which means 'below the snow', located near Kamakura, in the present-day prefecture of Kanagawa, where this style of *dō* is believed to have first been produced.

Attesting to the importance of the *Yukinoshita-dō* design of cuirass is the fact that its creation is commonly accredited to the renowned Myōchin School of *katchū-shi*, whose genealogical records claim that the first recognizable prototype of *Yukinoshita-dō* was made by Myōchin Kunihisa (who also used the working name Narikuni) around the middle of the 16th century in Kami-no-Kuni, in what is now part of present-day Gunma Prefecture. Myōchin records indicate that while Kunihisa was instrumental in establishing many of the basic features associated with what would become known as the *Yukinoshita-dō*, the honour of its creation ultimately went to two other Myōchin smiths, Hisaie and his son Masaie of Yukinoshita, who independently improved on Kunihisa's early designs to create the first true example of *Yukinoshita-dō*. The Myōchin genealogy goes on to claim that Date Masamune, one of the most renowned warlords of the late Sengoku period, ultimately invited Myōchin Masaie to his domain of Ōshū to produce *Yukinoshita-dō* for himself and his retainers after he became acquainted with the many excellent battleworthy qualities of this unique make of cuirass.

This commonly referenced story is, however, almost certainly untrue, as are most of those that were documented in the genealogical record created by the Myōchin in the early 1700s to establish their school's lineage. In fact, there is no historical evidence to substantiate any Myōchin claim that they were involved in the creation of the *Yukinoshita-dō*, including the presence of Hisaiye and his son Masaie in the town of Yukinoshita, which did and continues to exist in Kanegawa Prefecture, and from which this form of cuirass is said to have derived its name. Instead it appears that the Myōchin, who were masters at promoting their products, laid claim to the creation of the *Yukinoshita-dō* as they did with virtually all popular or well-made items of armour by fabricating bogus pedigrees that interjected and connected themselves with the evolution of those items. These connections were almost always established long after the fact and as such were difficult to dispute, particularly after the early 1700s, by which time the Myōchin had already firmly established themselves in the minds of the majority of the samurai class as being the oldest and most prestigious school of armour makers in Japan. Thus Masaie, who did exist, was by default retroactively proclaimed to have been a member of the Myōchin School of armour makers.

So successful were the Myōchin in their efforts to establish their pre-eminence that by the middle of the 18th century, many people actively conspired to have their items of armour

Date Masamune (1567–1636). A talented warlord, Masamune, who had lost his right eye to illness as a youth, was referred to as the *dokuganryū*, or 'one-eyed dragon'. (Wikimedia Commons/Public Domain)

Tosei-Dō Modern Cuirass Designs, Part II

A statue of the famous daimyō Date Masamune in Sendai, Miyagi Prefecture, which was once part of the Date clan's feudal domain. Masamune is depicted wearing a Yukinoshita-dō, the design of which so impressed him that he had his entire army equipped with dō that were based on this very basic, yet battleworthy form of cuirass. (Photo by Wikimedia Commons/ CC-BY-SA-3.0)

associated with the Myōchin School due to the potential for monetary gain, which was one of the more alluring attributes of association with such a prestigious name. Thus it was not uncommon for even unrelated smiths to claim a Myōchin lineage or for samurai to accredit the items of armour that they owned to a smith from the Myōchin School, even when the school had not done so itself.

The actual origin of the *Yukinoshita-dō* appears to have started with a family of bridle makers named Yukinoshita who had been employed by the fifteenth Ashikaga Shōgun, Yoshiaki. When Yoshiaki was deposed by Oda Nobunaga in 1568, the Yukinoshita family was forced to relocate to Aizu, where they began to produce armour for the powerful Ashina clan. In 1566 Date Masamune was born in the neighbouring fiefdom of Mutsu, in the castle town of Yonezawa. Though Date's father, himself a powerful warlord, had maintained cordial relations with the kingdoms neighbouring his domain, Masamune developed a strong adversarial position towards the Ashina clan, which boiled over into open conflict in 1584 when he became head of the Date *han*, and again in 1589, when he crushed the Ashina at the battle of Suriagehara.

Some historical records suggest that at some point during the campaign of 1589 the Yukinoshita armour makers were captured by Date samurai and forced to relocate to Ōshū to produce armour for the Date clan. This is difficult to prove, however. It is equally plausible to assume that Masamune simply invited the Yukinoshita *katchū-shi* to relocate to his capital of Sendai, in Ōshū (present-day Miyagi Prefecture) to produce armour for his retainers and himself after having witnessed the impressive protective qualities of the items of armour that were being worn by many of his former Ashina opponents. Such an offer would more than likely have appealed to the conquered and newly unemployed Yukinoshita armour makers.

Vague as the historical record may be, there is ample evidence to show that the *katchū-shi* employed by Date Masamune suddenly began to focus almost exclusively on the production of cuirasses made in the *Yukinoshita-dō* style right around the end of the 1580s. That Masamune himself, a hardened warlord with considerable battlefield experience, chose to wear a *Yukinoshita-dō* spoke volumes about the battleworthy qualities that he saw in this make of cuirass, as did the fact that he chose to outfit all of his retainers in *Yukinoshita-dō* or cuirasses based on the *Yukinoshita-dō* design, a precedent that the samurai of the Date *han* would continue to observe until the very end of the Japanese feudal period almost three centuries later.

While it is impossible to say exactly what attributes attracted Masamune to this revolutionary new design of cuirass, it is clear that he recognized that the *Yukinoshita-dō* represented another huge evolutionary step forward in armour designs. That it would be one of the last, however, he could not have known.

Having said this, it is important to note that while a considerable number of the extant examples of *Yukinoshita-dō* were produced for the samurai of the Date *han*, other clans and samurai owned and continued to acquire and make use of cuirasses made in the *Yukinoshita-dō* style as well, either originals commissioned through Yukinoshita smiths or copies produced by other groups of *katchū-shi*. Of the latter, smiths from the Myōchin School seem to have been the largest producers of *Yukinoshita-dō* from the mid-17th century onward, which is probably why they were able market themselves as having been the inventors of this make of cuirass.

Like the *Mōgami* method of *dō* fabrication from the latter half of the 15th century, the *Yukinoshita-dō* was assembled from sections of armour plating that were hinged together in a manner that allowed the cuirass to articulate so it could be wrapped around the torso. Unlike the cuirasses made in the *Mōgami* style, however, with their 'multiplicity of small hinges and rather delicate internal ties', which Bottomley and Hopson describe as 'serious weaknesses',[8] the *nagakawa* of the sectional pieces of a *Yukinoshita-dō* were each made from a single large piece of heavy metal plate. This was also true of the *kanagu mawari*, each of which was also forged from a single piece of armoured plate that was riveted directly to its corresponding portion of the *nagakawa*. This one difference alone meant that the *Yukinoshita-dō* was structurally much stronger than a cuirass made in the *Mōgami* style upon which the *Yukinoshita-dō* design was based. As both methods of construction were founded on the principle of creating a simple, easy-to-produce, form-fitting style of armour assembled from metal plate, the *Yukinoshita-dō* design was fundamentally the *Mōgami* method of construction taken to the next level after a further century of advances in armour designs and construction techniques and, most importantly from the standpoint of the *Yukinoshita-dō*, the introduction of firearms.

Though it is impossible to know for sure, it seems highly likely that the goal of the creator of the *Yukinoshita-dō* was to produce a shot-proof cuirass similar to the *nanban* or *wasei nanban-dō*, both of which were well recognized for their protective qualities. That they were both also virtually unattainable for the numerous reasons already discussed only heightened the need for an alternative form of shot-proof armour. Recognizing that a significant portion of the resistive strength of a *nanban* or *wasei nanban-dō* to the impact of firearms came from the fact that they were constructed from large, solid-plate sectional pieces, the creator of the *Yukinoshita-dō* was most likely attempting to retain this characteristic in the make of cuirass that he was designing. He also appears, however, to have been cognizant of the fact that the forge work that was required to create form-fitting front and back plate sections of armour from a single piece of metal was, in the case of *wasei nanban-dō* at least, its Achilles' heel.

An example of a *tetsu-sabiji Yukinoshita-dō*. The simple, battlefield practicality of the *Yukinoshita-dō* design is evident here. The smooth, unembellished façade allowed spears and other edged weapons to slide off the surface. Damaged segments could easily be removed to be repaired or replaced. The cuirass could also be quickly disassembled, allowing for easy transport and storage. Note the hinged *wadagami*, with plate-like *gyōyō* and the *ita-mono kobire*. Also note the *sugake odoshi*-laced *tetsu kuro urushi nuri koshi-kawa-tsuke gessan*.

Tosei-Dō Modern Cuirass Designs, Part II

A *nerigawa* example of a *Yukinoshita-dō* laid out flat to show each of the five segments of the cuirass. Note how each segment is a single *ichi-mai-ita* with the corresponding *kanagu mawari* plate riveted to its upper edge, with the exception of the *ushiro-dō*, which is a single continuous plate. Note the erect flanges behind the *aibiki-no-o* on the outer edges of the *onidamari-no-ita* and *gyōyō* hinged to the ends of the *wadagami*, which would cover the *aibiki-no-o* when the cuirass was worn.

The right-hand *mete* or *migi-waki-dō* plates from a *Yukinoshita-dō*. These two plates were fundamentally mirrored copies of each other that were designed to come together like a pair of overlapping saloon doors on the right side of the torso. Note the sturdy *chotsugai-kugi* hinge pins and the convex upper edge of the *waki-ita*.

allowed smiths of even moderate skill levels to contribute to the production of the individual component parts.

The *Yukinoshita-dō* was most likely the first true example of a *go-mai-dō*. For unlike the sectional design of cuirasses made in the *Mōgami* style, a *Yukinoshita-dō* could actually be disassembled into five independent sectional pieces. These included the *mae-dō*, *ushiro-dō*, a single *hidari waki-dō* or 'left side armpit plate' and two narrower right-hand side *migi waki-dō* plates. These are differentiated from each other based on whether they are designed to secure to the right-hand edge of *mae-dō* or *ushiro-dō*, with the right-hand side plate that fits to the *mae-dō* being referred to as the *mae migi waki-dō* and the rear one as the *ushiro migi waki-dō*. All five plates were forged to subtly increase in width toward the upper edge of the piece, so they were wider across the top of the plate than they were along their base. This difference was usually most pronounced on the *ushiro-dō*, which generally had a very distinct inverted trapezium-like shape to it, with a narrow lower width and then widening towards the plate's upper edge. The lower edges of these plates were originally cut straight across in the *ichimonji* style, but over time smiths began slightly to curve the lower edges of the side plates to help the *dō* sit more comfortably on the wearer's hips.

This complex, costly and time-consuming process could, however, be greatly reduced by constructing the cuirass from a series of a solid-plate section pieces that ensured that the most exposed areas of the torso continued to be covered by large, solid sections of armoured plate. This process could be taken even further by significantly reducing the rounded form-fitting nature of the individual plates, which, like the old *Mōgami* method of construction,

Because the plates were hammered and worked to have a smooth façade, which was generally treated to produce a *tetsu-sabiji* finish, *Yukinoshita-dō* are sometimes referred to as being *hotoke go-mai-dō*. This is a practice that should be avoided, though, due to the fact that the *Yukinoshita-dō* is a truly unique form of cuirass, with a well-defined set of distinctive characteristic features that are an integral part of its design and method of construction. This was not the case with cuirasses made in the *hotoke* style, however, which, as already noted, is actually a façade and not a method of construction. For unlike a *Yukinoshita-dō*, which can only be made one way, a *hotoke go-mai-dō*, for example, could be assembled using *tatehagi*, *yokohagi* or *ichi-mai-*

ita, with the façade being created through the application of lacquer or leather depending on the method of construction.

With the exception of the *mae* and *ushiro migi waki-dō* plates, all of the other segments of the cuirass featured an alternating arrangement of hinge knuckles, or *chotsugai*, fitted to both vertical edges of the *nagakawa* portion of the plate armour. These were absent on the outside edges of the two right-hand side plates as the *dō* was tied closed across the overlap between the two plates in the usual manner. The edges in these areas, as with the other areas of the cuirass that were not fitted with *chotsugai*, were rolled over in the *makikomi fukurin* style.

To help maintain the shot-proof integrity of the armour in the area of the hinged joints, the *chotsugai* were riveted to the exterior surface of the plating. This allowed the vertical edges of separate pieces of the cuirass to butt directly up against each other, eliminating any gaps.

It also placed the *chotsugai* over the gaps. As the knuckles were generally made from metal that was the same thickness as the main armour plating, this more than doubled the thickness of the armour over the gaps; the knuckles were circular in cross-section and actually the roll-back extensions of the sturdy metal base plate that they sat on. The sturdy *chotsugai kugi*, or hinge pins, were commonly forged with a closed loop on the upper end of the pin. This allowed cord that protruded through a small hole in the plate armour to be tied to the *chotsugai kugi* to help prevent it from being lost.

The *wadagami* were also fabricated as independent pieces that attached to the *boko-no-ita* by *chotsugai*. *Gyōyō* were also commonly hinged to the forward edge of the shoulder straps, to protect the *aibiki-no-o*, which, it should be noted, protruded upward through a distinctive three-hole arrangement pierced in either side of the *oni-damari-no-ita* to accommodate these cords, which was originally unique to the *Yukinoshita* design.

The *gyōyō*, unlike most of the other component parts of the cuirass, usually had the protruding ends of the *chotsugai kugi* that secured them in place hammered over, to prevent the latter from being lost, and as such they were commonly not removable. Almost all examples of *Yukinoshita-dō* feature large detachable solid-plate, half-moon-shaped independent *kobire* that were affixed by *chotsugai* to the outside edges of the *wadagami*. The substantial portions of the convex, arched *kobire* often jutted out from the shoulder boards, extending over the points of the shoulder by several centimetres. This appears to have nullified the need for *sode* in the eyes of many samurai, an increasing number of whom appear to have already adopted the practice of wearing their armour without *sode* by the time the *Yukinoshita-dō* was developed, and begun to further promote this trend, which continued to

The right-hand *mete* or *migi-waki-dō* plates from a *Yukinoshita-dō*. These two plates were fundamentally mirrored copies of each other that were designed to come together like a pair of overlapping saloon doors on the right side of the torso. Note the sturdy *chotsugai-kugi* hinge pins and the convex upper edge of the *waki-ita*.

Tosei-Dō Modern Cuirass Designs, Part II

grow in popularity throughout the latter part of the Momoyama-Aizuchi period. That many of the extant *gusoku* that are formed around early-period examples of *Yukinoshita-dō* feature *sode* is generally the result of the attachments to support shoulder guards having been retroactively fitted to the *wadagami* in later centuries when an armour without *sode* was deemed to look incomplete. In such cases the *kobire* often needed to be removed or to stand erect for it to be possible to attach the shoulder guards to the *sode-tsuke-no-o* on the *wadagami*.

Like most examples of *tosei-dō* made during the last few decades of the 16th century, *Yukinoshita-dō* were generally fitted with the usual arrangement of additional features and fixtures that were found on cuirass from that period, such as *eri-mawashi*, *gattari* and *machi-uke*. Most early examples also tended to feature *waki-ita* fabricated with a convex half-moon shaped *tsukigata* upper edge line along the top edge of the plate. In some cases, the *oni-damari* was also forged with a *tsukigata* mounting slightly upwards in the centre of the plate's upper edge line.

Unlike most conventional *tosei-dō*, however, the *Yukinoshita-dō* featured eight *gessan* instead of the usual seven, with each section of the cuirass having two tassets suspended from it, except for the two *migi waki-dō* plates, each of which supported a single *gessan*. Because the cuirass itself could be disassembled, it was common for the upper thigh-guard tassets to be the removable variety of *koshi-kawa-tsuke gessan*.

While armour makers may have understood how the sectional construction and design of *Yukinoshita-dō* would simplify efforts to store and transport the cuirass, they may not have foreseen how it would also greatly simplify the process of repairs. For unlike a conventional cuirass when damaged, where the entire piece would have to be taken out of service to fix a problem, with a *Yukinoshita-dō* only the damaged section needed to be sent for repair, and if the warrior was lucky, he could possibly even substitute the damaged segment with another similar sectional piece of armour while the work was taking place, thus ensuring that he could continue to utilize the cuirass if required.

Like all shot-proof armours, the *Yukinoshita-dō* was extremely heavy. One feature called *renjaku* seems to have been introduced around the same time that *Yukinoshita-dō* began to appear. *Renjaku* could be either a single continuous length of cord or cloth or two separate lengths of material that were tied between two sets of holes in a cuirass to create a simple form of internal brace-like suspension. This helped prevent the weight of the armour from being driven downward onto the shoulders and hips of a warrior during vigorous movement, like jumping or riding. To accommodate the *renjaku* a pair of horizontally aligned, grommet-fitted apertures were generally punched several centimetres apart in the *boko-no-ita* just above the general area of the shoulder blades. A second

A *tetsu kuro urushi nuri yokohagi-okegawa go-mai-dō*. Note the *koshi-kawa-tsuke gessan* and hinged *wadagami* and *ita-mono kobire*.

pair of similarly spaced, centrally positioned holes would usually be pierced in the lower area of the *nagakawa* of the *mae-dō*. A cord or cords could then be strung between the two sets of holes to create shoulder-strap-like braces, with the ends of the cords being knotted together on the exterior surface of the cuirass. The cords or cloth were almost certainly braided or arranged in a way that prevented them from cutting into the wearer's shoulder whenever the weight of the cuirass bore down on the *renjaku*.

This feature quickly began to be incorporated into other, generally heavy, shot-proof forms of *tosei-dō*. As such it is not uncommon for various makes of cuirass with the open apertures for *renjaku* to be referred to as *renjaku-dō*. This practice should be avoided, for *renjaku* are really little more than an accessory feature. Their presence is at best supplementary to the actual design and method of construction of a cuirass and thus should not be used to identify the style of a *dō*, even though this is commonly done.

The other, far more important innovation that appears to have been brought about by the introduction of the *Yukinoshita-dō* was the *tatehagi* method of construction. In fact, the earliest examples of vertically arranged plate construction would have been the portions of *ita-mono* that were used to fabricate the *nagakawa* of the *hidari* and *migi waki-dō* sections of the *Yukinoshita-dō*. And while these were basically *ichi-mai-ita*, their long, narrow, vertical shape almost certainly led to the development of the *tatehagi-ita*, which appears to have begun in Sendai as Masaie started to introduce changes to the design and method of construction of the *Yukinoshita-dō* that culminated in the fully evolved form of the armour.

This development appears to have been inspired by Date Masamune's desire to have all of his troops equipped with *Yukinoshita-dō*-like cuirasses. While the additional cost in time and money that went hand-in-hand with fabricating the *mae-dō* and *ushiro-dō* portions of the cuirass from large solid-plate sections could be justified when it came to producing armour for the high-ranking Date retainers and other samurai, most of whom were responsible for financing the cost of their own armour, it was simply not feasible to do so when it came to fabricating cuirasses for the hordes of lower-ranking warriors in Masamune's service.

The initial solution to this dilemma was to use three trapezoid *tatehagi-ita* to construct the generally less-exposed *ushiro-dō* portion of the cuirass. These were arranged with the middle plate being overlapped along both vertical edges by the two outside plates, which were riveted in place. This created a shallow step up the middle of the *ushiro-dō* that generally corresponded with the natural hollow up the middle of the back.

This new method of construction allowed the Sendai armour makers to mass-produce a *Yukinoshita-dō*-like version of cuirass, commonly

A *tetsu cha urushi nuri yokohagi-okegawa go-mai-dō*. Note the auxiliary *nodowa*-like throat protector toggled to the *oni-damari-no-ita*. Note also that the *yon-no-ita* of the individual sections of the *nagakawa* is laced to the bottom of the *dō*. Also note the hinged *gyōyō*.

referred to as *Sendai-dō*, for the rank-and-file members of Masamune's army. The *Sendai-dō* differed from the original *Yukinoshita-dō* design in that the *mae-dō* was also assembled from three trapezoid *tatehagi-ita*, which greatly reduced the time and cost of production for cuirasses made in this style. Further savings were made in the quality of the metal used, which varied considerably depending on whom the *dō* was being made for.

The examples produced for the lowest-ranking *ashigaru*-grade retainers were accordingly very rudimentary. The number of *gessan* was often reduced on these to seven, with each tasset being made up of just four *ita-mono*. Typical of low-grade *okashi*, or 'lent' items of armour, the *gessan* were generally secured to the cuirass by only three widely spaced lengths of coarse-weave *yurugi-ito* that continued as *sugake odoshi*. This can be contrasted with some higher-quality, later-period examples of *Sendai-dō* that in some cases had nine *gessan* of five or six plates each, or eleven *gessan* of six plates each.

Unlike *Yukinoshita-dō*, the *oni-damari* could be laced to the upper edge of the *nagakawa* on a *Sendai-dō*. The *hidari waki-dō* was also sometimes assembled from two *tatehagi-ita*. Another key difference was that *Sendai-dō* differed from *Yukinoshita-dō* in that they almost always featured a *kuro urushi nuri* finish. Both makes of cuirass were often finished on their interior surfaces with linen that was adhered in place and then covered in lacquer. Better-quality examples, particularly of the later Edo period, often featured rich *byakudan*-finished leather *urabari*, where clear lacquer, or *tome urushi*, was brushed over gold leaf that was applied to the interior of the cuirass, though such examples were the exception and not the rule.

Sendai-dō are also sometimes referred to as *Ōshū-dō* after the area of northern Japan that was controlled by the Date *han*. However, not all *tatehagi-okegawa-dō* are by default *Sendai-* or *Ōshū-dō*, for similar cuirasses were also produced in other parts of Japan, including the Kantō region where the *Yukinoshita-dō* first appeared.

For this reason, it is not uncommon for some reference sources also to refer to *tatehagi-okegawa-dō* as *Kantō-dō*.

Titles aside, all of these cuirasses were based on the newly developed *tatehagi* method of construction that was introduced through the evolution of the *Yukinoshita-dō*, and which was quickly adopted by armour makers across Japan. Within a few short years, makes of cuirass that had hitherto only existed as variations of *yokohagi-okegawa-dō* were also being constructed as *tatehagi-okegawa-dō*, which massively increased the number of visually unique forms of cuirass that could be produced once all the other sub-variations and different aesthetic details that were possible were incorporated. Likewise, armour makers also began to assemble *go-mai-dō* using the *yokohagi* method of construction. That said, *tatehagi-okegawa-dō* are far less common than *yokohagi-okegawa-dō*-made versions of cuirass. This is probably due to the relatively late arrival of this method of construction, which did not really start to become common until the last couple of decades of the 16th century, as is attested by the lack of documented examples of *tatehagi-okegawa-dō* in historical images prior to that time. This fact is supported by the absence of any known example of *tatehagi*-constructed *dō* having been worn by any of the well-known Sengoku-period *daimyō* until Masamune began wearing his own customized version of the *Yukinoshita-dō*.

The relative imbalance between extant examples of *tatehagi-okegawa-dō* and *yokohagi-okegawa-dō* can also be traced back to the fact that most *tatehagi-okegawa-dō* were, by the nature of their design and construction, generally rather sober in appearance, which naturally limited their appeal. This situation was compounded even further by the growing trend towards ever more ornate forms of armour that started only a few decades into the 17th century and which continued until the end of the Japanese feudal period.

One of the by-products of the trend towards ornamentation was the so-called *uchidashi-dō*.

SAMURAI ARMOUR

Two beautiful examples of the *tetsu-sabiji uchidashi mae-dō* plates from a *go-mai-dō*. The large flat façade of the *mae-dō* portion of most examples of *go-mai-dō* and *Yukinoshita-dō*-like cuirasses made them an excellent and popular medium for smiths to demonstrate their talents in the art of *uchidashi*. While aesthetically beautiful, embossing greatly undermined the structural resilience of the protective iron plate. The embossed motifs also nullified the benefit of the smooth façades of these makes of *dō* that helped to ensure that edged weaponry would slide off the surface. The example on the right is attributed to Myōchin Muneie (1573–1623). The left example embossed with the image of Fudo Myō-ō is credited with having been made by Katsusada Miyata (1653–1727). (The Walters Art Museum/CC0)

These were primarily *hotoke-* or *Yukinoshita-dō* that had some form of decorative design created in *repoussé* on the broad, unadorned frontage of the *mae-dō*. This was achieved by embossing the flat metal surfaces of the cuirass from the reverse to create images in low relief on the façade. Coiling dragons, kanji characters, and Buddhist deities were common, though the embossed themes could vary considerably, as is attested by the numerous extant examples of cuirass that feature *uchidashi* motifs such as *shishi*, *oni* (demon) masks, or chrysanthemums.

Kanji characters that imparted religious or moral virtues were particularly popular, with the most commonly reproduced kanji being characters such as 'ten' (天, heaven) and 'tenchi' (天地, heaven and earth). Others included 'yashiro' (社, shrine), 'gi' (義, righteousness) and 'sei' (精, purity). 'Dō' (道), which is now commonly associated with the teachings of *bushi-dō*, was common, though during the feudal period its actual interpretation was most likely a reference to moral teachings. The character 'cho' (長, leader) was also a popular theme for an embossed motif.

Sakakibara Kōzan wrote that the practice of embossing cuirasses did not begin until the time of Kunimichi, the twenty-first Myōchin Master, who produced armour between 1624 and 1643. Sakakibara is probably correct in this estimate, though it is again debatable if this practice originated with the Myōchin.

A unique example of a *tetsu kuro urushi nuri hishi-toji san-mai-dō*. The cuirass is fundamentally a *ni-mai-dō* with a separate *mete* or *migi-ita* hinged to the rear edge of the *ushiro-dō*, presumably added to make it easier to put the armour on. Note the *nerigawa kiritsuke iyozane sugake odoshi*-laced *gessan*.

Having said this, it is only reasonable to assume that less elaborate examples of *uchidashi* had preceded and slowly set the stage for the highly detailed works of *repoussé* that Sakakibara discussed. For armour makers had clearly started to employ embossing techniques even before the development of the *Yukinoshita-dō*, which they used to form the characteristics that defined some of the other styles of cuirasses that existed, such as the nipples, sagging pectoral muscles and outlining wrinkles on the façades of *abara-dō* that were constructed using *ichi-mai-ita*. The *nanban-dō* worn by Akechi Mitsutoshi had the kanji character 'ten' embossed into the upper chest area of the *mae-dō* and the silhouette of a snow-capped Mt Fuji on the back of the cuirass. By the middle of the Edo period, however, embossed iron cuirasses had become a speciality and a great source of pride to the Myōchin School of armour makers, a number of whose *katchū-shi* were renowned for producing cuirasses with stunning *repoussé* designs.

The phenomenal metalworking skills of many of Japan's most talented *katchū-shi* are embodied in the numerous surviving examples of cuirass and other items of armour from the mid-to-late Edo period that feature decorative *uchidashi* motifs. And while aesthetically attractive, embossing of the smooth surfaces of a cuirass significantly weakened the structural integrity of the metal and effectively destroyed the shot-proof qualities of the armour. The raised-in-relief designs also had 'a way of retaining arrows and spears instead of letting them glide off harmlessly', as Sakakibara noted, which in his words made such cuirasses 'mere toys, meant to tickle the fancy of art connoisseurs'.[9]

One factor that is rarely discussed when it comes to *uchidashi-dō* is that a considerable percentage of embossed motifs found on cuirasses were actually applied during the Meiji period to cater to the tourist market. In the vast majority of cases it is relatively easy to distinguish an authentic feudal-period example of *uchidashi-dō* from a cuirass that was retroactively decorated

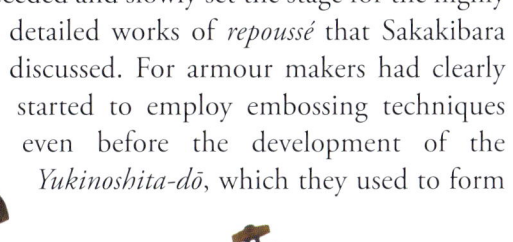

A Kaga *han*-made example of a *tetsu-sabiji ryō-hikiawase roku-mai-dō*. Note the hinged *boko-no-ita* and affixed metalwork lion motif.

A *nerigawa shu urushi nuri ryō-hikiawase roku-mai-dō* made in the general form of a *Yukinoshita-dō*. Note the unique staggered *kebiki odoshi* style of lacing used to secure the *ita-mono* of the *gessan* together.

with a *repoussé* design in the post-feudal period, due to the unnecessarily elaborate and crude quality of both the design and embossing. The poor quality of these items is often explained away by claims that the embossing is a rare early example of Japanese *repoussé*. Another common excuse is that the lacquer finish that originally covered the embossing chipped away over time, exposing the tool marks of the *uchidashi* process. This is an extremely poor excuse, however, as the vast majority of authentic examples of *uchidashi* were intentionally applied to surfaces finished in *tetsu-sabiji* that allowed connoisseurs of such work to observe the smith's workmanship in minute detail.

The five-section design of the *Yukinoshita-dō* seems also to have inspired Japanese armour makers to experiment with other combinations of sectional construction, which prior to the development of the *Yukinoshita-dō* had been limited to *ichi-mai-* and *ni-mai-dō* varieties of cuirass. The *roku-mai-dō*, or six-section cuirass, was probably the next form of *dō* to be developed since it was essentially 'a *go-mai-dō* that had the *hidari-waki-ita* divided into two separate plates' in the same manner as the *migi-waki-ita* on a conventional *go-mai-dō*.[10] In some cases, the *hidari-waki-ita* were hinged together but more often than not the cuirass was divided into two separate three-section halves, with a frontal portion comprising single

A superb *tetsu kawa-tsuzumi byō-toji tsure-yamamichi muna-koshi-tori rurisai ni-mai-dō*. If the lower two *ita-mono* of the *nagakawa* were part of the side panels, the cuirass would be a *yon-mai-dō*. Note the *kinkara-gawa*-faced *kanagu mawari* and the unusual arrangement of five *gessan* hung from the *mae-dō* and four from the *ushiro-dō*.

A view of the hinged access panel incorporated into a *tetsu kuro urushi nuri hotoko rurisai ni-mai-dō*. The saloon door-like panels are held closed by the *takahimo* cords that cinch the cuirass together across right side of the torso.

Why the protective integrity of a cuirass was deemed secondary to the apparent need for a warrior to be able to access the interior of his *dō* while it was being worn is difficult to comprehend.

hidari and *migi-waki-ita* hinged to either side of the *mae-dō*, and with a back portion of similar assembly but with an *ushiro-dō* section fitted with the appropriate side plates. In such cases the vertical edges of the *hidari-waki-ita* plates under the armpit were made to be devoid of *chotsugai*, which allowed the two plates to be overlapped in the same back-over-front manner as the *migi-waki-ita* plates when the cuirass was tied closed around the torso. *Roku-mai-dō* that were tied closed on both sides of the torso are referred to as *ryō-hikiawase roku-mai-dō*, which literally means 'pulled together on both sides six-section cuirass'. A set of armour in the possession of the Date clan that is said to have been worn by Uesugi Kenshi was made in this manner. If this was the case it must have been one of the last armours owned by Uesugi Kenshi, who died in 1578.

One of the supposed advantages of the *roku-mai-dō* design is that it allowed a warrior to wear only the *mae-dō* portion of the armour like a *hara-ate* in a situation when full armour was deemed unnecessary. While this may have indeed been the case with low-quality munitions-grade *okashi gusoku*, the somewhat dubious advantages of this feature were offset by a number of actual disadvantages, one of which was the tendency for the front and back halves of the cuirass to slip out of alignment with each other during vigorous activity. Another reason why not many armours in this style were made may have been difficulties in tying and putting on this style of cuirass.[11]

The *katchū-shi* also experimented with making cuirasses assembled from three or four individual sectional pieces. That both *san-mai-* and *yon-mai-dō* are extraordinarily scarce attest to the relatively poor results they obtained producing functional forms of cuirass of this construction: most examples of *san-mai-* and *yon-mai-dō* are fundamentally conventional *ni-mai-dō* with either a single or two separate *migi-waki-ita* fitted to the right side of the cuirass. The apparent lack of any obvious advantages that went with producing cuirasses in this manner clearly limited the success of such designs.

Other than for sectional combinations as described above, or *san-mai* examples of *hara-ate*, one of the only practical examples of *san-mai-dō* that I have ever seen was a cuirass formerly in my collection. This highly unusual *dō* featured a single-piece *tetsu-sabiji byō-toji yokohagi-ita*-constructed *ushiro-dō* that had a *tetsu-sabiji byō-toji tatehagi-ita*-constructed *mae-dō* hinged by a removable *chotsugai kugi* to the vertical right-hand edge of the *ushiro-dō* with another matched construction *tetsu-sabiji byō-toji yokohagi-ita*-assembled *mae-dō* hinged to the left-hand side of the *ushiro-dō*. The *tatehagi byō-toji mae-dō* portion of the cuirass was designed to be able to close over the front of the torso and then have the *byō-toji yokohagi mae-dō* close over the top of itself. The idea behind this double-layer *mae-dō* design was presumably to create a cuirass that

An extremely interesting example of a *san-mai-dō*. The armour features a single *ushiro-dō* with two *mae-dō* sections, one attached to the left and one to the right side of the back plate. Note how the outer *mae-dō* section has been assembled from *yokohagi ita-mono* while the inner *mae-dō* panel is made using *tatehagi ita-mono*. The contrasting arrangement of the overlay between the *ita-mono* of the separate panels would significantly add to the overall resilience of the *dō*. Also note how the outer *mae-dō* is designed to be suspended from the *gyōyō*, nullifying the need for *aibiki-no-o*.

was shot-proof from the front. This may in part explain why both the *tatehagi* and *yokohagi* methods of construction were utilized, with the opposite layering of the plates adding to the overall structural resilience of the frontal armour. The inner *mae-dō* portion was hinged in place, which allowed it to be removed when not required to reduce the overall weight of the cuirass.

Around the middle of the Edo period some examples of cuirasses began to be produced with small independent panels of armour plating within a larger subsection of a cuirass, such as the *mae-dō*, that were either hinged in place or quite often fully removable. Cuirasses made with this bizarre option are referred to as *Rurisai-dō* after Rurisai Gen'emon, the armour maker who is supposed to have invented this feature around the third and fourth decades of the 17th century. That no examples of this type of armour made in that period survive tends to undermine the theory that Rurisai was responsible for introducing this idea.

The supposed purpose of these removable or hinged panels was to allow a samurai to access the interior of his armour while he was wearing it, ostensibly to insert or withdraw important or necessary items. Why this would be the case, however, is hard to comprehend, since items could be better stored in the *hanakami-bukuro*. For articles stored between the body and interior of the cuirass were sure to be a source of discomfort and irritation if they were anything other than a folded document or something else flat and thin; and even paper, unless in a lacquered leather sheath, would quickly become saturated with sweat. Regardless of this fact, it raises the question of why armour makers found it easier to fabricate a separate sectional area of armour than riveting or lacing a cloth *hanakami-bukuro* to the façade of a *dō* or the reverse of a *gessan*. While several rather 'far-fetched theories', in the words of Dr Sasama, exist to justify the usefulness of this feature, none of them justify how this undermined the structural strength of a *dō*.[12]

This was particularly true of examples that were made with removable plates in the area of the *oni-damari*, which slid into position tongue-and-groove-style and were often held there by little more than gravity and the snugness of the

A view of the rich *kinpaku oshi*-faced leather *urabari* panels and gold dust-coloured lacquered finishes applied to the reverse of the *tetsu kawa-tsuzumi tsure-yamamichi byō-toji muna-koshi-tori rurisai ni-mai-dō* seen in the preceding images. Note how the lowest two bands of the *nagakawa* have been laced to the base of the cuirass. While this allowed the armour to articulate when a warrior was bending, making the cuirass more comfortable to wear in the short term, it would have made the cuirass more taxing to wear for longer periods of time. For the laced lower *ita-mono* prevented the weight of the cuirass from being carried on the hips as was possible with a rigidly constructed *tachi-dō*. Note the two hinged side panels and the two *hanakami-bukuro* affixed to the reverse of the *gessan*. The presence of *shiki-gane* attests to the fact that the tassets have been fabricated from *nerigawa*.

fit. If plates were dislodged during vigorous or violent movements, however, a vital area of the body was exposed. The hinged door-like panel examples of *Rurisai-dō* invariably include some method of securing the panel closed. This could be as simple as cords protruding through the façade of the cuirass for this purpose or a toggle that locked the panel closed when rotated.

Differentiating between a cuirass that is multisectional in construction and *Rurisai-dō* with a hinged panel can be difficult in some situations. If the hinged portion is window-like and surrounded by a larger section of the armour, then cuirass would be identified as a *Rurisai-dō*. If a portion of a panel forms part of the outside vertical or horizontal edges of a larger sectional piece of the armour, then the cuirass would still be considered to be *Rurisai-dō*. When the entire vertical edge segment of a cuirass articulates as an independent piece, however, then that portion is counted as a *mai*. Thus a cuirass constructed from two half-sections, which had two shorter panels hinged to the right-hand side leading edges of both the *mae* and *ushiro-dō* and that did not extend the entire vertical length of the right-hand edges of the two segments, would be a *Rurisai ni-mai-dō* and not a *yon-mai-dō*.

A stunning example of a mid-17th century *tatami-dō gusoku* said to have belonged to Tachibana Akitora, the third Lord of the Yanagawa clan. (Tachibana Museum)

CHAPTER 8

TOSEI-DŌ MODERN CUIRASS DESIGNS, PART III

Ashigaru, tatami and variations

By the end of the Ōnin War in 1477, the ability of the *ashigaru* to complement and support the military operations of a warlord's main body of samurai troops was well understood. As a fighting force, though, the *ashigaru* were a fairly unreliable mob, composed as they were of *ji-zamurai*, mercenaries and generally less-than-enthusiastic conscript peasantry. It was the famous *daimyō* Takeda Shingen who made the first serious efforts in 1547 towards developing the *ashigaru* into a semi-professional auxiliary fighting force in order to better harness the full military potential of this body of manpower. He did this by abolishing the existing practice in his domain of relying on levies that obligated men to serve when they were needed in favour of a system that selectively recruited sturdy young men for more or less permanent duty. These men were fed and housed at the clan's expense, and this helped to strengthen the bond between the *ashigaru* and their lord, whose success was now intrinsically linked with theirs.

Freed from many of the domestic concerns that undermined the reliability of the traditional free-agent style of *ashigaru*, Takeda's *ashigaru* units could be coached in military tactics, albeit at a very basic level. It also gave them the time they needed to become proficient in the use of the weapons that they were assigned. Such training, along with the fact that the men were formed into small-unit groups who lived together, established a certain degree of *esprit de corps*. This was elevated further by the issuing of cheap cuirasses, generally emblazoned with the lord's personal heraldic device, a conical *jingasa* and a few other mass-produced pieces of armour for the extremities in some cases, which created a sort of rudimentary uniform that helped to further bind these men together in the service of their *daimyō*. And while the issuing of armour may have been partly self-serving, as a step taken by the *daimyō* simply to protect his investment, it also paid huge dividends when it came to strengthening the cohesiveness and morale of the troops in the warlord's army.

Along with their growing importance and the integration of the *ashigaru* into the structural hierarchy of the mid-16th century feudal-period armies, there came a limited and perhaps even reluctant degree of recognition that entitled these low-ranking warriors to promotion and reward if they distinguished themselves in battle or otherwise brought themselves to the attention of their superiors through some form of meritorious action. Toyotomi Hideyoshi is perhaps the most famous example of just how far up the martial social ladder a man could climb if the fortunes of war smiled on him, as they did under this system of rewards. For in less than two decades Hideyoshi rose from being one of Oda Nobunaga's *ashigaru* sandal-bearers to being one his most trusted generals and successor after Nobunaga was assassinated in 1587 at Honnō-ji Temple in Kyōto.

Takeda's innovative ideas could not have come at a more auspicious time, for the matchlock, which been introduced only a few years earlier into Japan, was used almost exclusively by infantry. This was largely due to the size and the considerable recoil of the *teppō*, as well as to the fact that both hands had to be utilized to reload the weapon, which made the matchlock a rather impractical weapon for mounted warriors. The inconvenient aspects of the *teppō* were, however, more than offset by the fact that within a short period even the most unskilled of *ashigaru* could be trained to effectively utilize a matchlock once they had been taught how to load, prime, aim and fire the weapon, for there was little more to the skill than the four basic steps. Thus the powerful potential of firearms was entrusted to the *ashigaru*, who thanks to Takeda's far-sighted initiatives were already starting to function as well-disciplined small-unit entities in the armies of the majority of *daimyō*, who had been quick to adopt Takeda's innovative ideas.

A classic example of an *ashigaru okashi gusoku*, or 'lent armour set'. Like almost all cuirasses issued to the *ashigaru*, the armour is a very rudimentary black-lacquered *yokohagi-okegawa ni-mai-dō*. Note the matched crest emblazoned on the ten-plate iron *jingasa*.

That such units were exactly what was required to successfully utilize firearms was most likely the chance intersection of two separately evolving historical paths and not something that Takeda had envisioned when he began thinking about how to restructure the *ashigaru* into a more effective force. Ironically, however, it was just such a force that ultimately destroyed the powerful army that Takeda Shingen had built and bequeathed to his son.

The *yokohagi-okegawa-dō*, which was inspired by Western-made cuirasses that had reached Japan around the same time as the first *teppō*, also proved to be instrumental in the development of the *ashigaru* as integral units within feudal-period armies. For prior to the development of the

Tosei-Dō Modern Cuirass Designs, Part III

yokohagi-okegawa-dō there had simply been no way to produce a large amount of armour in a short time for a reasonable price. Without the uniformity and *esprit de corps* that was created with the issuing of a universal form of equipment for the *ashigaru* in the service of a lord, it could be argued that these units might not have performed nearly as well as they did.

A study of period images including *byōbu* (decorated folding screens) and illustrated documents like the *Tales of the Ashigaru* scrolls and the numerous extant examples of the items of armour that were issued to *ashigaru*-grade warriors from the mid-16th century onwards clearly show that there was a remarkable degree of consistency in both the design and quality of the items that were produced for these low-ranking warriors.

Almost without exception, excluding the *tatehagi-okegawa go-mai-dō* that were produced for the *ashigaru* who served the Date *han*, all armies tended to equip their *ashigaru* with very rudimentary examples of *yokohagi-okegawa ni-mai-dō* that were usually of one generic size. The construction of these could vary, with some examples featuring a *nagakawa* consisting of five *yokohagi-ita* while others used only four. The number of *ita-mono* used to construct the

An image of two *teppō-tai* (matchlock troop) *ashigaru* from the early 17th century *Zōhyō Monogatari* (Tales of the Ashigaru) scrolls. The warrior with the *teppō* is a low-ranking member of the unit. To his right stands the *teppō-tai ko-gashira*, or matchlock unit leader, who carries a marked *ma-shaku* range-finding pole. He also carries several spare slow-burning matches for his gunners wrapped around his left arm. Note how the unit leader is distinguished from his men by the gold lacquer finishes to the *shino* plates of the *kote* he wears and to the façades of the *gessan* suspended from his black-lacquered *hotoke ni-mai-dō*. (Image: TNM Image Archives)

Samurai Armour

mae-tateage was sometimes reduced to just one plate, which would be capped by the *oni-damari-ita*, while other cuirasses were more conventional in construction.

Many designs dispensed with the use of independent *waki-ita*. In lieu of these the uppermost *yokohagi-ita* of the *mae-* and *ushiro-dō* portion of the *nagakawa* was forged to arch downward along their upper rear edges in the area immediately under the armpits at both ends of the plate. The *oni-damari-ita* and *boko-no-ita* were almost always riveted directly to the upper edge of the *mae-* or *ushiro-tateage*. The *wadagami* were almost always separate plates that were riveted to the upper outside edge of the *boko-no-ita*. In the case of some better-quality examples of cuirass, *kobire* and even rudimentary *eri-mawashi* were fitted to the *wadagami*. As the hexagonal *kikkō* scales were generally cut from *nerigawa*, the brigandine was only outline-stitched in place and devoid of the usual arrangement of anchoring cross-knots.

The cords of the *aibiki* were generally fairly universal in their arrangement, as were the *kohaze* and *seme-kohaze* that they supported, though both toggles and cords were generally quite coarse and poorly finished in comparison to those seen on cuirasses worn by samurai.

Almost all *okashi-dō*, or 'lent cuirasses', as these munitions-grade armours were described owing their being issued equipment, were finished on both surfaces with applications of lacquer. In the case of better-quality examples, the exterior of the cuirass was often finished smoothly in the *hotoke* style. In many cases, the heraldic crest, or *kamon* device, of the lord who owned and issued the armour was applied using lacquer to the façade of the *mae-dō*.

In some cases the crest was also applied to the rear of the cuirass. In lieu of a *kamon*, unit-specific designs were also sometimes applied to the façades of cuirasses. Such markings could be as basic as one or two horizontal bands of *shu urushi* around *dō* that made it easier to distinguish between otherwise identically equipped units.

The quality and finish of an *okashi-dō* could also vary depending on the *ashigaru* manner of employment. Those who worked in close proximity to a senior-grade warrior as retainers were provided with aesthetically better-looking

A *byakudan nuri*-finished *hotoke yokohagi-okegawa ni-mai-dō*. The added expense of applying gold leaf to a munitions-grade cuirass suggests that *okashi-dō* such as this were limited in their issuance to elite units or only worn on special occasions. Note the matching *byakudan*-finished *jingasa* and *shino-gote* sleeves. Aside from their rich façades, the *dō* and other items are all low-quality pieces of armour.

and often superior items of equipment. This was done to ensure that the retainers complemented and enhance the public presence of the samurai whom they served. Thus it is not uncommon to find rather low-quality examples of *yokohagi-okegawa ni-mai-dō* with *kinpaku* or *byakudan*-finished façades.

In fact, *okashi-dō* were not strictly limited to the simple outfits worn by the majority of *ashigaru*. Lent armour could include full sets of matched armour, referred to as *okashi gusoku*. While most *okashi gusoku* were generally rather basic in overall design, they were the same as those worn by the samurai. It was quite common for men serving in special heavy-calibre *teppō-tai*, or matchlock units, to be issued *okashi gusoku*. This was also true of the leaders of *ashigaru* units called *ashigaru ko-gashira*, who were themselves promoted *ashigaru*. *Ashigaru* serving in regular *teppō-tai* units were often also issued simple helmets along with *jingasa*.

The interior surfaces of the lent armour were sometimes lined with a thin layer of lacquered-over linen or hemp cloth that helped to hide the generally coarse nature of the finished workmanship. The layer of applied fabric also helped to protect the garments of the wearer from the rough, hammered-down ends of the rivets that were used to fasten the individual *yokohagi-ita* together. Numbers and other identifying characters were commonly applied in a contrasting colour of *urushi* to the interior surfaces of *okashi-dō* to help track and record

Above: The *sangu*, or extremities armour items for an *okashi gusoku*. Though difficult to make out in the image, each piece of armour bears a red lacquer arsenal number that shows that these pieces were *okashi* items.

Right: An example of an *okashi gusoku* issued to a messenger. Lent armour such as this was fundamentally identical in overall appearance to that worn by the samurai. The quality of the finished workmanship, though, was generally quite poor, as were the materials used to fabricate the armour. The bold *kinpaku oshi* markings helped to identify a messenger so he was not constantly impeded in his duties. Note the unmatched *sode* included with this armour. This reflects the modern view that an armour without *sode* is incomplete, when in fact many armours were never meant to be worn with *sode*.

SAMURAI ARMOUR

the issuing of the armour. This was also true of other issued items of equipment, like the *jingasa*, *kote* and *suneate*. These markings sometimes matched *mae-* and *ushiro-dō* sections together or recorded where the cuirass was to be stored and its number in the arsenal's inventory. If an

Three identical *okashi-dō*. Note the *shu urushi* kanji characters used to identify each cuirass. These arsenal markings not only helped to keep track of which items of equipment had been issued or were secured away in the storehouse, they also helped ensure that the *mae-dō* was married up with the corresponding *ushiro-dō*. Note the thinly padded stencilled hemp cloth *eri-dai* with integral collars and *kobire*.

Tosei-Dō Modern Cuirass Designs, Part III

item was specifically assigned to a warrior, his name might also be applied to the interior of the cuirass to ensure the same armour was received by that man each time it was required.

Almost all examples of *okashi-dō*, with the exception of the *tatehagi-okegawa go-mai-dō* version of cuirass that was worn by the *ashigaru* of the Date *han*, feature an arrangement of *roku-ken yon-dan gessan*, or six four-plate *sugake odoshi*-laced upper-thigh-guard tassets, with three *gessan* being suspended from both the *mae-* and *ushiro-dō*. The *yurugi-ita* was generally reduced to no more than the three or four paired strands of coarse-weave lacing that would continue on as the same number of strands that were required to lace the *ita-mono* of the *gessan* together in the *sugake odoshi* style. One alternative, though fairly rare, method of connecting the *gessan* together and to the cuirass was to stitch the individual *ita-mono* to a panel of sturdy cloth that was itself then laced to the base of the cuirass. *Okashi-dō* were almost never fitted with any form of decorative *kanamono* or other fixtures, including *gattari* and *machi-uke*,

with *sashimono* simply being tied in place by lengths of cord if they were required.

Hara-ate examples of *okashi-dō* were also produced. Other than for the arrangement of cords that held the cuirass in place over the shoulder and across the back, such pieces generally differed very little from the *mae-dō* portions of conventional *ni-mai-dō* examples of lent cuirass.

As the other items of equipment that were commonly issued as part of an *okashi gusoku* to an *ashigaru*-grade warrior, such as the *jingasa*, *kote* and *suneate*, were generally rather universal in overall construction and design, it is best to introduce those items in conjunction with a discussion of *okashi-dō*.

All *ashigaru* were issued with some form of *jingasa*, the vast majority of which were generally of low conical shape in overall form. Most issued examples of *jingasa* were either made from several triangular pieces of iron plate riveted together or were made from panels of *nerigawa*. In the case of *jingasa* made from *nerigawa*, the joined vertical edges would be

An unusual example of *gessan* of which each pendant or *ken* was constructed from a two-layer panel of sturdy fabric woven from hemp. The individual *ita-mono* were then sewn to the fabric panels. Note how the cord is threaded through pre-punched holes along the upper edges of each *ita-mono*. Also note the thin, unrefined surface of the lacquer that has been applied to the *tetsu ita-mono*. The poor quality of the workmanship attests to its low-budget, mass-produced status which defined the vast majority of examples of munitions-grade items of armour.

SAMURAI ARMOUR

laced together with a rawhide thong. To help the hat keep its circular form a ring, generally made from bamboo, was laced in place around the lower edge of the *jingasa*.

Irrespective of what the *jingasa* was made from, which also included both layered and woven lengths of rolled paper in the later Edo period, lacquer was applied to both surfaces to weatherproof the hat. In the case of *jingasa* made from iron plates, strips of fabric were often lacquered to the underside surface of the hat as well, to help conceal the unfinished quality of the metal plates and to cover the sharp hammered-over stems of the connective rivets. It was common, particularly in the Edo period, to lacquer the underside surfaces of *jingasa* with red *shu urushi*, though this practice was not always universally followed when it came to *okashi* items. Heraldic crests were commonly applied in lacquer, or in some cases gold leaf, to the upper surfaces of most issued examples of *jingasa*.

Four small closed loops of metal or leather, depending on what the *jingasa* was constructed from, were anchored to the upper inside surface of most *jingasa*. These allowed a small *makura*, or pillow, stuffed with straw, barley husks or cotton to be secured to the underside of the *jingasa* to create a rudimentary form of padded liner. Fabric or woven rice-reed cords used to secure the *jingasa* to the head were also tied to these anchor points. These generally consisted of two long closed-loop rings with two cross-straps. One cross-strap was positioned so that it would lie horizontally behind the back of the head just at the base of the skull when the *jingasa* was being worn. The other, which was left loose on one end, was positioned so that would rest in the hollow just below the lower lip when it was tied closed across the chin.

Almost all examples of munitions-grade *kote* issued to *ashigaru* were made in the *shino-gote* style. This form of *kote* consisted of a number of long, narrow, roughly lacquered iron splints stitched to the lower forearm *tesaki* portion of the tubular cloth *kote-bukuro* or 'sleeve bag'. In

A view of the underside of a *jingasa* made from a single piece of rawhide. The rawhide is folded over and sewn around a narrow bamboo strip that helps to give the *jingasa* its circular form. Note the leather fobs in the crown of the hat that provide anchoring points for securing a liner.

A pair of above-average-quality *okashi-gote* made in the *shino-gote* style that features a series of long, narrow iron splints to protect the forearm. A large floral pattern has been stencilled on the hemp cloth facing material used to make the *kote-bukuro*. Note the rudimentary *tekkō* and intermediary connective sections of mail.

Tosei-Dō Modern Cuirass Designs, Part III

Arsenal markings applied in red lacquer to the *kanmuri-no-ita* plates along the upper edge of the *okashi shino-gote* seen below. Note the *byakudan* finishes applied to the *ko-shino* splints that are stitched to the sleeve bodice. Also note the lacquer bands of single-link *so-gusari* and the indigo-dyed hemp cloth *kote-bukuro*.

A pair of *byakudan*-finished *okashi-gote*. The use of gold leaf to finish these armoured sleeves, which have been made in the *shino-gote* style, suggest they were issued for wear on special occasions. They may also have been reserved for senior *ashigaru* as an indicator of the man's rank and position or for use by an elite body of *ashigaru*-grade retainers. Note that the sleeves are devoid of hand coverings, as was common for *kote* issued to the *ashigaru*.

most cases the edges of the *kote-bukuro* were sewn together down the inside face of the sleeve where it would rest against the sides of the torso, though in some cases they were laced together using lengths of cord in a manner which is discussed further in Volume II, and which allowed the circumference of the sleeves to be adjusted as required.

Some examples of munitions-grade *kote* feature *tekkō*, or plates that covered the back of the hands, and in those cases the *kote-bukuro* was tailored to accommodate them. In many cases, however, *okashi-gote* were devoid of *tekkō*, with the sleeve terminating at the wrist, or *tekubi*. While this was done in part as a matter of economy, it was also a pragmatic approach to the fact that the *ashigaru* performed a considerable amount of labour-intensive physical chores and therefore needed their hands to be free and unencumbered. And while it is difficult to say for sure, it is likely that examples of *okashi-gote* with *tekkō* were either items made for more elite units or those performing special duties as already described. Likewise, they may also represent later Edo-period items when armour was primarily worn for guard duty and other formal activities by the *ashigaru* and not for prolonged periods of time in the field when the presence of *tekkō* would have proved to be more of a hindrance.

Most examples of *kote-bukuro* were generally made from two layers of indigo-dyed, coarse-weave hemp cloth. A rough fabric trim was commonly used to edge the sleeves, though in some cases leather was also used for the *sasaheri*. Due to the fact that munitions-grade *kote* were generally devoid of the third layer of fabric that lined the interior of the sleeves, or *kote-ura*, as was universal to the *kote* that were used by the samurai, the stitching that tacked the protective plates to the *kote-bukuro* was usually visible on the interior of the sleeve bag. This was also true of the knotted ends of the coarse lengths of braided-cord *maru-himo* that were used to form the *makidome*, or 'wrap hold' wrist ties and other fastenings that connected the *kote* to the wadagami of the *dō*. In some cases, the cords at the top of the sleeves were made quite long, which allowed the two *kote-bukuro* to be tied together across the body.

The bottom end of each *shino* was usually linked by mail to a narrow band of *kusari* that was tacked in place with stitching across the facing surface of the *tekubi*. If the *kote* featured *tekkō*, the band of *kusari* would be wider and would be connected to the upper edge of the hand-guard plate. *Kusari* was also used to connect the upper ends of the *shino* and to cover the mid-arm portion of the *kote*. The mail in this area was commonly arranged in an open grid-like pattern, *kōshi-gusari*, also sometimes referred to as *jūji-gusari*, that allowed the arm to flex without the mail binding onto itself or bulking up on the inside of the elbow.

The upper-arm *kata* portion of most examples of *okashi-gote* was generally covered by an arrangement of small, slightly convex rectangular iron plates referred to as *ko-shino*. These were usually arranged in three to four separate columns, each one of which usually comprised four to six *ko-shino*. Horizontal bands of *kusari* linked the upper and lower edges of the *ko-shino* to each other as well as to the narrow *kanmuri-no-ita* plate that generally capped the horizontal upper edge of most examples of *kote*.

Some sets of *ashigaru*-grade *okashi gusoku* also came with a matched pair of *suneate* shin guards. If present, the *suneate*, like the *kote*, were also made in the *shino-suneate* style, generally from five long, narrow and slightly convex vertically arranged iron splints that were spaced about 3–4 cm apart. The splints were commonly connected together by three or four narrow horizontal bands of *kusari*. These were positioned near the top, middle and bottom edges of the

A pair of *okashi-zuneate* made in the *shino-zuneate* style. The rudimentary construction of these simple splint shin guards is immediately evident. Note the rough metal finishes and the coarse application of low-grade lacquer. The coarse hemp backings have been edged with green cloth *sasaheri*. Also note the long hemp straps.

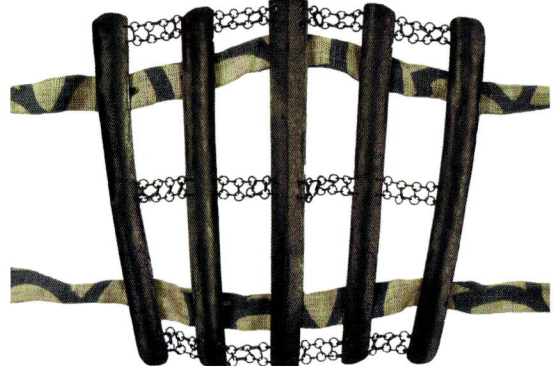

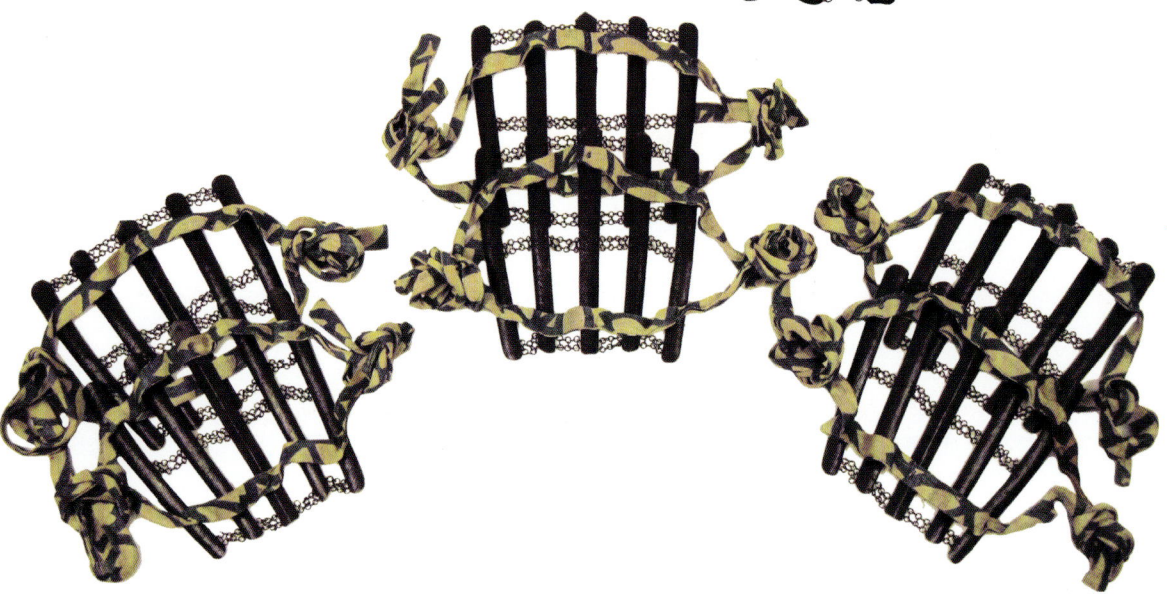

Three identical pairs of *okashi shino-zuneate*. It was common for *okashi*-grade items of armour such as *suneate* to be fabricated without cloth backings. Note the long hemp cloth ties and how these have been affixed to the rear faces of the *suneate*, as was typical when the shin guards were devoid of a cloth backing.

shino. The *shino* were sometimes sewn to *ieji*, or cloth, bodices that would be fundamentally identical in overall construction to how most of the *kote-bukuro* were fabricated, other than for the obvious difference in sizes and so forth. That said, *okashi-zuneate* were also quite often fabricated without *ieji* backings. In such cases the splints were stitched to the two long lengths of doubled-over fabric that were used to secure the shin guards around the lower legs and that are commonly referred to as the *ue-no-o*, or 'upper cord', and *shita-no-o*, or 'lower cord'. These were tacked to the facing surfaces of the splints when the *shino* were sewn to the cloth bodices. When the *suneate* were made without cloth backings, however, the *shino* were laid on top of the cords and tacked in place. This arrangement required warriors to wear separate cloth coverings over the lower legs, called *habaki*, before they fastened the *suneate* in place.

In general, the design, calibre and quality of most of the *okashi* items of armour that were made for and issued to the *ashigaru* changed very little between the mid-16th century and the end of the feudal period. In fact, the only notable change in regards to the equipment

An *ashigaru* putting on a cuirass. Note how the *aibiki-no-o* are secured together over the left shoulder before the *dō* is put on. The warrior wears *momohiki* trousers with separate *habaki* gaiters. Note the *uchikai-bukuro* provision bag. Rations were divided into separate balls of rice that were tied into a length of cloth which itself was tied and worn over the shoulder. Each ball represents one meal. (Image: TNM Image Archives)

issued to the *ashigaru* was the gradual introduction of *tatami*-made examples of cuirasses and headgear to the list of equipment that was held in the arsenals of many *daimyō* by the latter part of the 17th century.

The main catalyst for this change appears to have been a decree by the Tokugawa Shōgunate, known as *sankin-kōtai*, that by 1642 required all *daimyō* to alternate their residence for periods of a year at a time between their fiefs and the capital Edo. The *sankin-kōtai* was in part intended to strain the finances of the *daimyō* in order to help keep them in check. For it forced the warlords to shoulder the cost of moving themselves and possibly hundreds of retainers back and forth between their domains and the capital, which they had to do in a manner that was commensurate with their rank and social status. It also required them to maintain fully staffed official residences worthy of their rank in Edo, where their wives and family were obliged to remain as the Shōgun's unofficial hostages.

While dedicated roadways and stop-over points developed over the centuries to accommodate these highly formalized processions of warlords, known as *daimyō gyō-ritsu*, that snaked their way to and from Edo, nothing could be left to chance. Thus a considerable amount of equipment and household goods needed to be carried on these marches, including armour. And while armour was rarely ever utilized other than for ceremonial purposes as the columns passed over boundaries or through major towns and cities, no column moved without such items.

Initially the samurai and *ashigaru* would have brought conventional items of armour with them on these journeys. This practice gradually fell into decline, however, as Japan comfortably slipped further into the prolonged period of peace that was to be synonymous with most of the Edo era. The growing sense of security and waning memory of warfare amongst the samurai class motivated many to discontinue the practice of having traditional

Three *okashi-gusoku* sets of armour for *ashigaru*. These extremely well preserved items of armour clearly demonstrate that such items were produced in bulk in a generic manner that allowed pieces to be issued as and when required, without having to match certain items with a specific set of armour. While above average in quality for *okashi* items, the fabrics utilized and overall level of construction is rather rudimentary compared with the items of armour worn by most samurai. Each item is individually marked with a red lacquer arsenal number.

items of armour brought along in favour of items of *tatami*-made armour. For these were not only lighter and much easier to wear than conventional armour, they were by the nature of their design also easy to store and transport, which in itself was an important factor, considering the logistical aspects of these journeys that could in some cases take many weeks to complete. That this transition had become commonplace by the beginning of the 18th century is attested to by the fact that the eighth Tokugawa Shōgun Yoshimune, who came to power in 1716, always took light armour such as *tatami-gusoku* or *hara-ate* with him when he travelled.

It should be noted that the *ashigaru* in effect did not exist after 1591, when Toyotomi Hideyoshi implemented the Separation Edict,

Tosei-Dō Modern Cuirass Designs, Part III

which prohibited movement between the classes, such as samurai becoming farmers or vice versa. Thus after 1591 the *ashigaru* were basically low-ranking samurai retainers. However, as all samurai were fundamentally retainers, for the sake of clarity it is easier to continue to use the *ashigaru* moniker to identify these low-ranking warriors who, irrespective of their changed post-1591 status, continued to be issued with relatively poor-quality munitions-grade items of armour and equipment.

While the *sankin-kōtai* may have been instrumental in creating a demand for *tatami*-made items of armour amongst the warrior class, who had hitherto shown relatively little interest in items constructed in this manner, it may have been the two invasions of the Korean peninsula launched by Hideyoshi in the late 1590s that reignited an interest amongst the Japanese in plate armour sewn to fabric. For both the Korean and Chinese troops that the samurai fought made considerable use of a number of different forms of brigandine and armour constructed from metal and leather plates sewn to fabric bodices. And while the Japanese may not have initially adopted these ideas, they almost certainly brought back examples and information about these forms of armour. Attesting to this fact are several new alternative forms of helmet bowl that were introduced in Japan in the wake of these campaigns and that were clearly inspired by those worn by the Koreans and their Chinese allies. That many of the high-quality examples of *tatami-dō* that started to be produced in Japan around the mid-17th century featured an external layer of ornate brocade cloth over the armour plating, as was often done with many Korean- and Chinese-made items, suggests that the Japanese borrowed some ideas from styles of armour worn by their former mainland foes.

These were commonly covered on the exterior surfaces with rich silk brocade cloth.

A high-quality example of a *tatami-dō* that features a rich silk cloth covering over *karuta* plates. Note the silk lacing *hishi-toji* cross-knots.

Most of these were either *ichi-mai* or *ni-mai-dō* assembled from lacquered rectangular plates of iron, called *karuta-gane* or simply *karuta*, that were joined together by intermediate bands of lacquered *kusari*. Such cuirasses were referred to as *karuta-gane kusari ichi-mai-dō* or, if they were made in two independent half-section pieces, *ryō-hikiawase ni-mai-dō*. *Chotsugai* were commonly used to secure most examples of *ni-mai-dō* together, though cords, and even rotating toggles, were also sometimes employed. More elaborate designs sometimes utilized large hexagonal iron plates and as such were referred to as *kikkō-gane kusari dō*. The plates, which could also be made from *nerigawa* and *kusari*, were stitched to fabric bodices that often featured integral *gessan* of identical construction. It was not uncommon for better-quality examples of *tatami-dō* to be fabricated with detachable *koshi-kawa-tsuke gessan* belts, which allowed the armour for the torso to be worn under even relatively close-fitting garments if a warrior felt the need for protection but did not want to advertise his concerns.

The cloth bodices were generally made from three layers of fabric. Hemp, or *asa*, was commonly employed because of its durability, though silk and other fine-weave fabrics were also used. Most examples featured an internal or *naka-no-ieji* layer of coarse-weave hemp cloth referred to as *saimi*. *Saimi* was often soaked in *shibu*, a juice made from unripened persimmon, which was said to help repel insects and waterproof the fabric. Alternatively a concoction made from the root of the *ōbaku* tree (*ptreocarpus flavus*) was utilized on the *saimi*, which, according to Sakakibara, helped to render the padding worm-proof. A glue-like paste was also applied that stiffen the *saimi*, which helped the fabric bodices that were tailored over the *saimi* to retain their form. The material used for the *ura-ieji*, or liner, could vary from hemp to finer weaves of fabric depending on the overall quality of the item. Leather was commonly used to edge *tatami*-made items of armour, though fabric *sasaheri* were also utilized. It was not uncommon for high-quality examples of *tatami-dō* to have the protective plating and mail covered by an external layer of cloth or *e-gawa* in some cases. The fabric would be tacked down and the stitching hidden under silk piping that would outline the exterior edges of the internal plates.

Most of the features found on a conventional *tosei-dō* such as *kobire*, *eri-mawashi*, *gattari* and *machi-uke* were also incorporated into the construction of many better-quality examples of *tatami-dō*. As the upper ranks of the warrior class began to appreciate the benefits of *tatami*-made items of armour, it seems likely that many *daimyō* chose to have similar items issued to their *ashigaru*-grade retainers. These items may have been produced in limited numbers specifically for use on the *sankin-kōtai* as it is highly unlikely that any *daimyō* would have dispensed with his existing stock of *okashi yokohagi-okegawa-dō* simply because *tatami-dō* took up less room in his arsenal. This explanation

A conventional example of *tatami-dō* assembled from iron *karuta* plates joined by lacquered bands of mail.

A high-quality example of a *kuro urushi nuri karuta-gane tatami-dō*. The folding cuirass features a rich silk facing material visible under the protective plating. It also includes a *kikkō* *eri-mawashi* with matching brigandine *kobire*. Note the decorative *hishi-nui* on the *suso-no-ita*, *koshi-makura*, and *saihan-no-kan*. Also note the cloth *dō-jime* belt.

A high-quality *tatami-dō gusoku* complete with a collapsible *chōchin kabuto* and facial armour.

A relatively modest *tatami-dō gusoku*. The facial armour is most likely a later unrelated addition.

may in part account for why the image of the *tatami-dō* is so intrinsically entwined with that of the *ashigaru*. For while they were not the most common form of cuirass in an arsenal it was clearly the form of armour that the *ashigaru* were most commonly seen wearing in the various *daimyō gyō-ritsu* that trudged back and forth across Japan to and from the capital from the mid-Edo period onward.

Amongst the samurai the wearing of traditional armour continued to decline through the 18th century until it was rarely worn outside of periodic ceremonial situations. Conventional armour was also poorly suited to the few duties that many samurai had when some form of protection was actually required. In fact, the single most dangerous duty that samurai were likely to face from the mid-17th century onward in the pursuit of which they might be risking their lives was while helping to lead fire-fighting efforts, which was one of the many new duties that were assigned to the samurai during the Edo era. Armour was of course useless in such situations and reduced to little more than a form of lightweight fire helmet called a *kaji-kabuto*. Ironically the majority of these items were made from *papier mâché* with applied lacquer finishes that were also sometimes overlaid with thin silver- or gilt-finished copper plates. Ornamentation reflective of the features found on many conventional examples of *kabuto* often decorated the façades of these helmets. These commonly included columns of prominent gilded copper rivets, applied *suji* and *shinodare* flanges. The apex of the helmet was normally mounted with an ornate multistage tiered *tehen-no-kanamono* fixture, the individual sections of which featured contrasting alloy finishes, such as *shakudō* and gilt.

An erect and commonly ornately decorated *mabizashi* visor would protrude from the front of the helmet bowl which would be framed by large *fukigaeshi* flanges. These latter were commonly faced with thin plates of gilded copper that were themselves surmounted with ornate *suemon* devices. A removable *maedate* crest was commonly mounted in the centre above the *mabizashi* via the *tsunamoto* prong. A long, often detachable, thick fabric cape called a *tarenuno*, or literally 'hanging fabric', was secured around the sides and rear of the helmet to protect the face and neck from flying embers during fires. This *tarenuno* was tailored with indentations near the upper outside edges of the left- and right-hand sides of the cap that allowed the cap to closely frame the face when the bottom portions of the panels were folded over each other and buttoned closed across the front of the body.

The only other official duty where a samurai faced any serious likelihood of being injured or possibly killed was if he were assigned to 'patrol duties', which, as Ikegami Eiko writes, resembled those of 'a modern police officer'.[1] While such work periodically required the warrior to don protective attire, other than for some of the items of armour that were made for the extremities, such as the *kote* and *suneate*, conventional armour was poorly suited to such work and as such not utilized. A *tatami-dō*, however, particularly one with detachable *gessan*, was much better suited to this kind of activity, for as already noted it could be worn under the officer's regular garments.

One of the factors helping to push warriors towards *tatami-* and *kusari-*made items of armour, particularly those on official duties such as policing, was that they were rarely confronted by anything other than edged weaponry, since bows and spears had been restricted to the military class along with swords since Hideyoshi's famous 'Sword Hunt' decree of 1588, whereby farmers were forbidden from owning weapons, and all the weapons in the possession of peasants were confiscated. This was also true of firearms, the ownership of which had been even further restricted by decrees implemented by Tokugawa Ieyasu in 1607.

Thus the official duties of many samurai, including for some the participation in *sankin-kōtai*, actually helped to undermine demand for

小磯笑雪玉女

conventional sets of armour. And as the acquisition of armour often represented a serious strain on the finances of most samurai that could be equated to the pressure of a modern-day mortgage on the wages of an average blue-collar worker, it is not surprising that more and more samurai chose to acquire *tatami-gusoku* over more traditional forms of armour. For in doing so they could justify the expense in knowing it was one of the few forms of armour that they might actually be able to make use of, which of course was a consideration that the privileged upper ranks of the warrior class did not have to trouble themselves with.

Attesting to this transition was the famous Forty-Seven Rōnin incident of 1703, when a group of former retainers seeking revenge for the death of their lord and the subsequent disbanding of their clan raided the mansion of Kira Yoshihisa (commonly referred to as Yoshinaka), a high-ranking Shōgunate official whom they blamed for their troubles, and beheaded him. That all forty-seven attackers in this well-documented incident are said to have worn some form of *tatami-* or *kusari-*made armour demonstrates just how common these items had become by this time period.

As the Forty-Seven Rōnin incident demonstrates, the traditional *gusoku* seems to have slowly evolved over the latter half of the 17th century into something equivalent to a dress uniform. The trend towards ever more elaborate, richly decorated *gusoku* that had started early in the 17th century had clearly contributed to this situation as those who had armour grew increasingly reluctant to wear their *gusoku* for anything but ceremonial occasions. It also pushed many lower-ranking samurai out of the market. For the level of armour these men could afford often equated to little more than a public pronouncement of their strained financial situation.

As the *tatami-gusoku* became increasingly common, armour makers started to experiment more with this style of armour, which resulted in a huge degree of alternative designs and methods of construction being introduced. Large plate *tatehagi-ita* and *yokohagi-ita* versions were produced, as were a number of hybrid designs that combined large, single-section, quasi-conventional sections of armour with portions assembled using the *tatami* method of construction. These experiments also led to the construction of *tatami* armour assembled from protective plating of various shapes and sizes, sometimes simultaneously, which led in turn to a greater reliance on the usage of *kusari* to fill in the voids that were left between combinations of differently shaped plates.

The Japanese were probably introduced to mail as far back as the Kofun period via the Korean peninsula. They appear not to have made use of this imported technology, however, until the latter part of the Heian period when they began to cover the inner arm and wrist areas of the *kote* that were being introduced with mail in the areas that needed to articulate.

While mail may have been an introduced technology, the Japanese ultimately produced a number of distinctive variations of *kusari* that were unique to Japan. Most of these were assembled from a combination of lacquered circular rings and lozenge-shaped intermediate links arranged in geometric-like patterns. The round rings, called *naka-gusari*, or 'middle mail', were fabricated from loops of a sturdy wire coil that would have the severed ends of each ring aligned and butted together in the *hamiawase* style, which relied on the strength of the metal to ensure that the loops maintained their shape and that the ends did not shift once aligned. The *naka-gusari* rings were arranged to lie parallel to whatever surface they were being applied to, while the connective links, known as

---

Opposite: An *ukiyo-e* entitled *Jūichidanme*, or 'Act Eleven' from a series of prints that depict the key events of the Forty-Seven Rōnin story. The print is of interest in that it appears to show that at least some of the *rōnin* wore *kusari-katabira* or other mail-covered items of protection under their garments. Protective headgear appears largely to have been limited to papier-mâché *kaji-kabuto* fire helmets. This scene is indicative of the fact that most low-ranking samurai were no longer able to afford conventional armour by the mid-18th century, and thus primarily relied upon items such as *kusari-katabira* when protective attire was required. (Image courtesy of the US Library of Congress)

kake-gusari, which were fabricated from a lighter gauge of wire, were only visible in profile.

The *naka-gusari* were made by tightly wrapping steel wire around a metal baton with a groove running the length of the baton. A chisel was hammered into the groove to cut the wire and form the links. In general, four *kake-gusari* links would be looped around each *naka-gusari* ring at the 12, 3, 6 and 9 o'clock positions, from which they would each connect to a neighbouring *naka-gusari* ring that when repeated created a grid-like form of mail referred to as *so-gusari*. Different geometric patterns could be created depending on the arrangement and number of rings and links that were used. One combination that used *naka-gusari* looped with three or four *kake-gusari*, depending on the positioning of the latter, produced a hexagonal pattern of mail referred to as *kikkō-gusari*, or in some cases as *kameko-gusari*. An alternative four-link arrangement produced a diamond-like pattern known as *kagome-gusari*, while a six-link version produced a tight, grid form of *kusari* that is referred to as *asa-no-ha gusari*, or 'hemp leaf mail'.

In most cases, particularly on lower-grade quality items of armour, the *kake-gusari* were a single *hamiawase* loop, which is why *so-gusari* is sometimes also referred to as *hamiawase gusari*, or *hitoe-gusari*, which means 'one turn mail'. Better-quality items of armour often used mail that featured *kake-gusari* made from twice the usual length of wire. This allowed the link to be folded back on itself so as to double its thickness where it looped around the *naka-gusari*. Mail assembled in this manner is commonly referred to as *futae-gusari*, or 'double turn mail'. This style is also sometimes referred to as *shime-kaeshi gusari*, which means 'turned back closed mail', after the manner of individual *kake-gusari* links, which can be referred to as *shime-gusari* when made in this way. A much less common though even stronger variation of mail referred to as *seirō gusari* featured *kake-gusari* made from with three visible turns of wire. Mail made from a very tightly linked mesh of thin gauge wire is referred to as *chirimengusari*.

The Japanese also developed some alternative styles of mail of their own design during the Edo period, all of which were extremely complex and labour-intensive to produce. One variety, known as *nawame-gusari*, was made from two lengths of steel wire that were twisted together to form a braid. The braided wire was then wrapped around a mandrel and cut into rings in the usual manner, with the cut ends being welded together. Another very uncommon form of alternative mail is referred to as *chigiri-gusari* and appears to have been made from two short lengths of steel wire with looped ends. The looped ends were pointed away from each other and the wire ends spliced together before a third wire was wrapped tightly around them. There appear to have been other ways of creating the links used in this extremely rare form of mail, which was usually arranged in a honeycomb or repetitive triangular pattern.

The arrival of Europeans in the mid-16th century introduced the Japanese to the 'four-in-one' style of linking mail which had been common throughout Europe and the Asian subcontinent since the early part of the first millennium. This new form of mail was referred to by the Japanese as *nanban-gusari*. It appears, however, that very little imported Western-made mail was used by the Japanese, thus almost all examples seen are in fact actually *wasei nanban-gusari*. Irrespective of

A unique example of a *tatami-dō* that has been fabricated using iron *karuta* connected by lacquered mail positioned around a large hexagonal chest-plate. An image of two circling fox-like creatures has been applied in gold lacquer to the face of the chest-plate. Note the leather *sasaheri* around the cuirass.

Tosei-Dō Modern Cuirass Designs, Part III

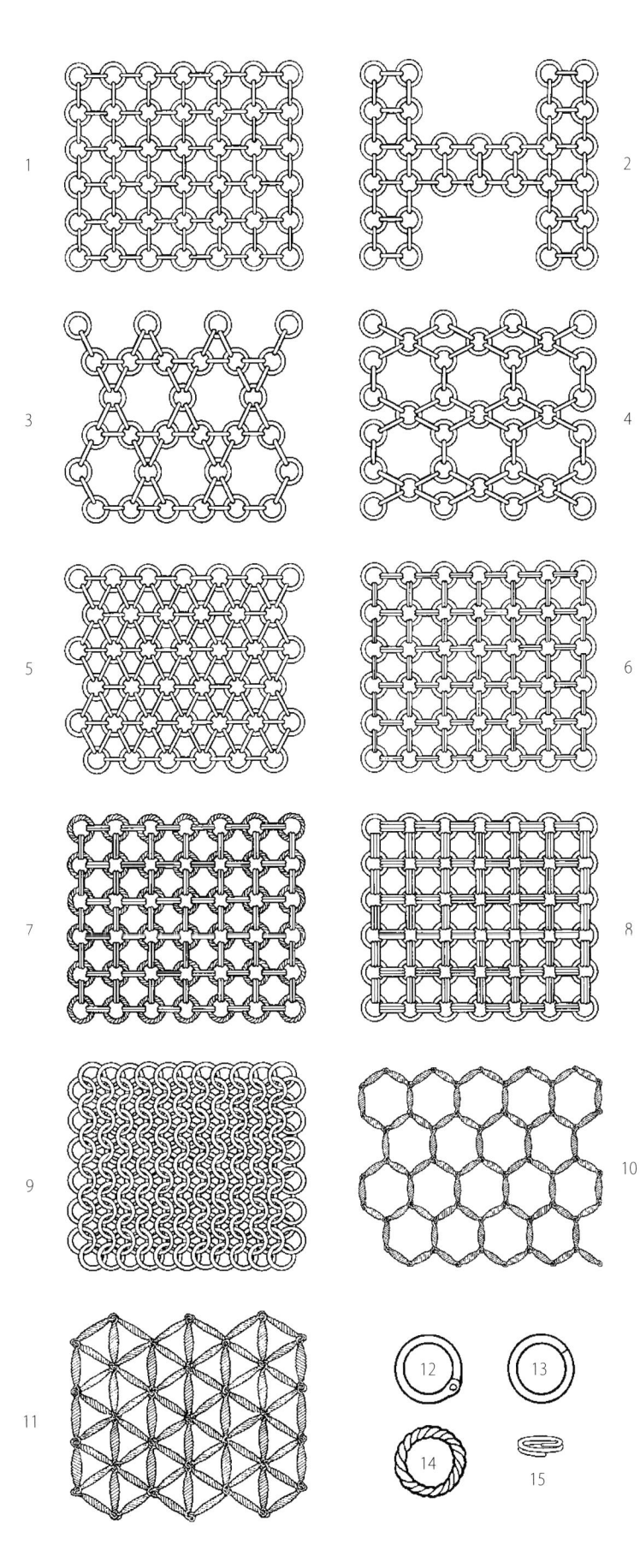

this, foreign-made mail introduced the Japanese to four major innovations beginning with the four-in-one method of linking the mail, which produced a much tighter mesh than any of the existing forms of Japanese *kusari*. The four-in-one method of linking rings also allowed the mail to expand laterally, a feature that would become increasingly important as the Japanese began to place a greater reliance on *kusari* to create protective garments. *Nanban-gusari* also appears to have introduced the Japanese to the idea of using brass to make mail and to the practice of riveting the cut ends of the individual links closed, as well as to the process of galvanization, none of which, however, were ever widely utilized.

Of these four innovations, the last two raise some serious questions about the actual origin of the items of mail that the Japanese were introduced to. For unlike European-made mail that utilized wedges cut from flattened wire to rivet the individual links of mail together, Japanese riveted mail, referred to as *karakuri-gusari*, was riveted using round pins with domed heads that resembled the type used in India. Why the Japanese decided to reproduce European-like mail but to disregard this one particular key detail is hard to understand, especially in light of the fact that they were extremely good at accurately reproducing the foreign-made items of armour that they were introduced to. And while this could be chalked up to the Japanese choosing to improve on the designs they studied, it is interesting to note that Western Europeans never galvanized the mail they produced.

However, extant examples of Indo-Persian-made mail confirm that the galvanizing process was known and used in the Asian subcontinent possibly as far back as the early part of the 16th century. That the Japanese learned of this process and utilized it somewhat is confirmed by Sakakibara, who wrote that some examples of Japanese-made *nanban-gusari* were heavy because the links are 'tinned', which refers to the colouration of the steel links after they had been treated with a protective application of zinc.

Different arrangements of Japanese mail: 1) *So-gusari*; 2) *So-gusari* in the *kōshi-gusari* grid-like arrangement; 3) *Kagome-gusari*; 4) *Kikkō-gusari*; 5) *Asa-no-ha-gusari*; 6) *Seirō-gusari*; 7) *Nawame-gusari*; 8) *Futae-gusari*; 9) *Nanban-gusari*; 10) *Chigiri-gusari*; 11) An alternative make of *chigiri-gusari*; 12) *Karakuri naka-gusari*; 13) *Hamiawase naka-gusari*; 14) *Nawame naka-gusari*; 15) *Kake-gusari/futae-gusari*.

Sakakibara also recorded that some examples of galvanized mail were sharp-edged, having been punched from iron plate. This again tends to suggest an Indo-Persian influence, as some examples of mail made on the Asian subcontinent are thought to have been assembled from punched links. That said, there is also evidence to suggest that some European- and Eastern European-made mail was also assembled from punched links. Thus it is hard to say if there was a specific cultural or foreign influence in this regard, or if the Japanese independently experimented with various methods of producing *kusari* using punched links.

It is, however, worth noting that the wearing of mail for protection had already fallen off sharply by the mid-16th century in Europe, though it continued to be worn in Eastern Europe, the Middle East and throughout the Asian subcontinent, specifically India and Persia, well into the 19th century. Thus it seems logical to conclude that while *nanban-gusari* was clearly introduced to Japan via European traders, the mail that the Japanese actually saw may not have been European in manufacture. Instead it may have been produced in the Asian subcontinent and acquired in modest quantities at one of the major ports-of-call that the European traders visited on their way to Japan, such as Goa. Supporting this theory is the well-documented fact that the Japanese acquired a huge variety of items from the Asian subcontinent via European traders, including everything from exotic animals and their hides to fabrics and medicines.

This being the case, it is equally probable that the Japanese were at least in part also influenced by the designs of the items of mail and plate armour that they were being introduced to by or acquiring from the European traders. For it is highly unlikely that they were simply shown small examples of mail that were not part of complete pieces of armour. And if this was the case, then it is also reasonable to assume that Japanese armour makers were also in part influenced by the designs and forms of the Indo-Persian-made armour that they were able to study. That the latter often made extensive use of mail in combination with small, strategically inset solid-plate pieces of armour is also significant, for a considerable degree of similarity exists between the mail-based items of armour the Japanese began to produce from the latter part of the 17th century onward and many Indo-Persian-made examples of this type of armour from the same period.

That said, there is no doubt that the evolutionary trend within Japan by that period was already heading towards a greater reliance on non-conventional items of armour that incorporated a greater amount of mail in their construction. As such the Japanese more than

An example of *karakuri* (riveted) *wasei nanban gusari* made in the Western 'four-in-one' style. Riveted mail of any kind, where the ends of each individual *naka-gusari* ring have been physically secured together with a small wedge-shaped pin cut from wire, was rare in Japan.

An Indo-Persian *zirah baktar* (left) and a Japanese *karuta-katabira* (right). The use of mail to make protective garments did not develop in Japan until after the contact with European traders. Examples of Western and Indo-Persian-made items of mail and plate armour may have influenced the Japanese in the development of the *katabira*.

Tosei-Dō Modern Cuirass Designs, Part III

likely would have created some form of lightweight armour better suited to the evolving needs of the warrior class, with or without foreign influences, which would only have helped to accelerate an inevitable transition that was driven by a greater need for ever more practical forms of armour that could comfortably and less obviously be worn under clothing if required, and that were also easy to store and transport. And while *tatami*-made items performed this job well, their mostly plate-armour construction was best suited to providing protection from missiles such as arrows, and direct thrusts from weapons such as spears, threats that were rarely ever encountered by the samurai in the performance of their regular duties during the Edo period. The main threat throughout most of this period was clearly from edged weaponry, and more specifically swords and daggers.

This situation was reflected in the development of a number of different varieties of garment-like *tatami*-made items of armour that collectively came to be known as *yoroi katabira*. Unlike conventional examples of *tatami-dō*, for example, that both looked like a conventional cuirass in overall form and were worn like one, *yoroi katabira* resembled short, overcoat-like garments that were worn closed across the chest. *Yoroi katabira* either had protective materials such as *karuta*, *kusari* or *kikkō*, or combinations of the latter sewn onto the surface or layered within the internal construction of the coat. These items were identified and categorized based on which one of the forms of protective covering was the most prominent. As such there are *karuta*, *kikkō* and *kusari katabira* that were fabricated using *nerigawa* and *tetsu* or combinations of both. Examples which are difficult to categorize, either because they utilize a relatively balanced amount of the conventional forms of protective covering or that utilize pieces not commonly incorporated into this type of armour, such as *shino* splints, are generally referred to by the default title of *yoroi katabira*.

While specific details about the origin of the *yoroi katabira* are unknown, it is fairly apparent that these items were fundamentally a hybrid of the garment-like brigandine

---

Top: A *kusari-katabira*. The garment has been covered with a screen of thick lacquered rawhide squares that have been interconnected by bands of *kusari*.

Middle: A *kusari-katabira*. A heavy screen of lacquered *kusari* has been stitched to the façade of the coat-like garment.

Bottom: A *karuta-katabira*. The protective covering is formed by a staggered arrangement of gold lacquer-finished iron *karuta* plates. These are connected and augmented by sections of *kusari*.

SAMURAI ARMOUR

qualities of the *manchira* and the more resilient, protective qualities of the full torso-covering design of the *tatami-dō*.

These generally featured integral sleeves that terminated around the middle of the lower arm. Many examples were designed to allow matching gauntlets covered in mail or fabricated with an internal layer of *kikkō* brigandine to be buttoned to the sleeve cuff.

Interestingly, the introduction of *kusari katabira* corresponds with the same general period when sources such as Sakakibara suggest that mail made in the *karakuri-gusari* style first began to be utilized by the Japanese, which was not until the late 17th century. While known, dateable examples support this, it is unlikely that the Japanese actually waited more than a century before they began to produce their own versions of riveted mail, considering that they were introduced to the four-in-one style of riveted mail during the Sengoku period.[2] Thus it is far more probable that *karakuri-gusari* was made and used in Japan as far back as the mid- to late 16th century, albeit on a very limited scale. Support for this argument can also be found in the fact that Sakakibara noted that Kunitaka Fukushima, the late Sengoku period armourer and pupil of Ujifusa Hojo, was commonly credited with the invention of *karakuri-gusari*.

One of the primary reasons why historians such as Russell suggested that riveted mail was not utilized in Japan until well into the Edo period is that the vast majority of known examples of this form of *kusari* were produced by the renowned mid-Edo period Myōchin smith Ryōei. Ryōei incorporated *karakuri-gusari* into the fabrication of many of the items of armour that he produced to the point that Ryōei's preference for the production of *kusari* made in this style resulted in this form of mail being referred to as *Ryōei karakuri-gusari*.[3] That this was the case attests to just how uncommon this style of mail must have had been prior to Ryōei having utilized it in his works. The relative scarcity of even post-17th century examples of *karakuri-gusari* can in part probably be explained by the fact that *kusari* was traditionally viewed as a form of auxiliary armour by the Japanese that was primarily used to cover and connect areas that needed to articulate, like the inner arm or other spaces that were not easily covered by conventional portions of scale- or plate-made armour. As such they may have found it hard to justify the additional cost in time and labour that was required to produce riveted mail. Likewise, the domestic varieties of mail they produced were by the nature of their designs generally easier to work with as a

A *manchira*. An auxiliary item of armour that was worn in conjunction with conventional armour. Worn under the cuirass, the *manchira* commonly provided flexible protection, commonly in the form of mail or brigandine, for the areas of the torso that rigid armour simply could not cover without impeding the warrior's movements. Worn vest-like, this *manchira* protects the upper shoulders and armpit areas. It also features an integral *eri-mawashi* collar.

connective material than would have been the case with riveted mail.

Thus, while we know from a handful of documented extant examples and historical records, such as the writings of Sakakibara, that the Japanese did make items of armour using *karakuri-gusari*, this form of mail never caught on in Japan. That it failed to do so during a period when the traditional forms of armour were rapidly being replaced for all but ceremonial purposes by *kusari-* and *tatami*-made items of armour suggests that riveted mail in the eyes of the Japanese was never more than a novelty.

The massive proliferation of *yoroi katabira* resulted in a huge number of variations of these items being produced, from extremely rudimentary pieces to very complex and ornate examples, the latter of which often featured an external shell of rich fabric over the mail, plate or brigandine covering. *Yoroi katabira* tended be constructed in two ways, the first of which was in the style of a conventional coat that buttoned or toggled closed with an overlap across the front of the body or vertically up the middle of the chest. They were also sometimes made from a large poncho-like garment divided down the centre front and with extensions to protect the arms. This variety was constructed by lacing the two front panels to the larger single-section back panel down the sides of the body using cords. The lacing was continued along the undersides of the arms to create tubular sleeves. The primary benefit of this rather complex method of construction mostly likely was that such coats could be unlaced and folded quite flat, which made for easy storage and transport in a manner that could not be achieved with jacket-like forms of *yoroi katabira*. Many examples were made to hang quite low, which removed the need to wear a separate *haidate* to protect the upper thigh area. It was common for examples of *yoroi katabira* to feature some form of brigandine protective collar, most of which were fabricated using *kikkō* made from *nerigawa*. A wide range of *karuta-*, *kikkō-* and *kusari-* covered accessory items of armour that could be worn in conjunction with a *yoroi katabira* were also produced, such as gauntlets, footwear, hoods and even trousers. When these articles were worn in combination they formed a *yoroi katabira gusoku*. While many matched sets were produced, most of those seen on the market today are usually composed of various similar though unrelated component pieces.

This situation is likely to change, though, in coming decades, thanks in large part to the huge advances in photographic equipment that have occurred and the ability to disseminate information widely via the Internet. For prior to cheap, easy-to-reproduce high-quality digital photography, very few items of *yoroi katabira* warranted documentation. And as most of the existing literature on samurai armour for more than a century has primarily focused on the much more spectacular and visually interesting forms of conventional armour that were used by the samurai, items like *yoroi katabira* have largely been overlooked.

In the last decade alone, however, more images and examples of *yoroi katabira* and related items of armour have been documented than ever before. This situation should have many armour historians and students of Japanese armour seriously reconsidering their understanding of Japanese armour during the latter half of the Edo period. For as this growing body of evidence attests, the *yoroi katabira* in its various forms represented the final development in the evolutionary history of Japanese armour, and as this fact is better understood and documented, even more items will likely begin to surface as collectors and dealers alike begin to better appreciate the actual historical value and rarity of these last forms of samurai armour.

Sadly, the exclusion of these items from most post-feudal-period records of Japanese armour has almost certainly resulted in the loss or destruction of a great number of these extremely interesting items. In fact, as this author can personally attest, for many decades Japanese antiques dealers have tried to add market value to these generally hard-to-sell items by pitching them as 'ninja *yoroi*'. While this absurd concept was able to capitalize to a certain degree on the popularity of the highly fictionalized post-war pop culture and movie industry depiction of the ninja, these items for the most part remain extremely undervalued, even in comparison to poor-quality contemporary items of conventional Japanese armour.

As the samurai grew more reliant on auxiliary forms of armour like *tatami-dō* and *yoroi katabira*, contemporary plate and scale armour designs became increasingly ornate and in many cases *avant-garde* as armour makers, no longer restrained by the need to produce battleworthy armour, pushed the boundaries of artistic license with the full blessing of their clientele, most of

A late Edo or early Meiji period photograph of four samurai taken by Felice Beato. The image is of interest for the fact that, with the exception of the presumed leader, who is wearing a conventional set of armour, the remaining samurai are all wearing *kusari-katabira* in conjunction with *hitai-ate* chainmail hoods. While staged pictures were common, there is evidence to suggest that by the late Edo period, conventional armour was seldom worn other than for ceremonial purposes, having largely been replaced by items like the *kusari-katabira* when a samurai need to wear protective attire. (Digital image courtesy of the Getty's Open Content Program)

Tosei-Dō Modern Cuirass Designs, Part III

whom were the third- or fourth-generation descendants of samurai who had never seen battle. The result was a huge number of bizarre, one-off forms of cuirass that are referred to in Japanese as *isei-gusoku*, or 'armours of uncommon make'. These items, particularly the cuirass, are often hybrids of several different styles and construction techniques, which make them extremely difficult to categorize. A prime example of an *isei-dō*, formerly owned by the author, featured a smooth black lacquered *nerigawa mae-dō* with a *hatomune* medial ridge and *muna-tori* lacing. Independent *hidari-dō* and *migi-dō* segments of matched construction were hinged to either side of the *mae-dō*. The latter both had large panels of *kikkō* laced to their rear vertical edges that allowed the cuirass to be closed like a *haramaki* together down the centre of the back. In lieu of *wadagami* and *kobire* the cuirass utilized large *kikkō ire* panels fabricated with an integral, though divided, *eri-mawashi*. The shoulder panels were made long enough to hang down over the back to cover the area occupied by the *boko-no-ita* on a conventional cuirass, where they could be buttoned to the panels of brigandine fitted to the side panels to completely enclose the back of the torso.

How is a cuirass assembled in this manner to be categorized? Is it a *haramaki*, a *san-mai-dō* or *go-mai-dō*? Or should it be referred to as a combination of one or the other key features? As it is often difficult to reach a consensus on such pieces, they are generally grouped into the default category of *isei-dō*. It should be noted that while

Above and right: A highly unconventional late Edo period cuirass. The mixed nature of the design and construction of this *dō* make it difficult to categorize for the armour shares characteristics with a number of different forms of cuirass. Bizarre, hybrid combinations of various construction techniques and cuirass styles were common during the late Edo period.

most *isei-dō* or *gusoku* are from the mid-to-late Edo period, a few pieces dating back as far as the Momoyama period are known to exist.

While many highly unique forms of *isei-dō* have been documented, the vast majority have not. Of these it is highly likely that a great many have already been lost to history, while many more remain unrecognized and undocumented. The reason for this in many cases boils down to the fact that as anomalies, most *isei-dō* fail to appeal to collectors who have been schooled for more than a century on literature focusing on the most well-known and generally more elaborate forms of conventional *tosei-gusoku*. Items of armour that have failed to correspond with those relatively narrow parameters have for the most part been passed over in favour of more conventional items. The unfortunate consequence is that many *isei* items have been rather poorly cared for over the last 150 or more years, with the true historical value of these items being misunderstood in the shadow of more conventional items of armour. Sadly, this has almost certainly resulted in the further destruction of many surviving examples, as Japanese antique dealers tend to view such items as commodities and so have no qualms about parting with such items or altering them if it helps to increase their marketability.

One of the few well-documented forms of *isei-gusoku* are items made from large, fish-scale-shaped plates referred to as *uroko-zane*. Generally U-shaped in form, most examples of *uroko-zane* are made from *nerigawa* with the usual protective applications of *urushi*. The scales are generally sewn onto single-piece *ichi-mai-dō* cloth-bodice backings with the rounded bottom ends of the scales hanging downward.

Three examples of the unconventional late Edo period *gusoku*. While visually unique, the *uroko-zane isei-gusoku* in the first image is the most conventional of the three. The second and third *gusoku* illustrate the growing usage of *kusari* as the primary protective material. Note the *kusari*-covered *kabuto*, *sode* and *gessan* on the last set of armour.

The scales are usually arranged to overlap each other from the top downward, with each row being offset so that the rounded base of a scale from an upper row always covers the point where two neighbouring scales in a lower row butt up against each other. As the *uroko-zane* are usually sewn only along the flat upper edge of the scale to anchor them to the *ieji* backing, it is possible to lift the bottom of the scale. This feature is said to have allowed the scales to 'straighten up in water to create a certain degree of buoyancy'[4], which may in fact have been the case, though only for a brief period of time. How relevant this particular characteristic was once a warrior had donned his entire ensemble of armour and equipment, however, is debatable. Irrespective of this, it appears that samurai who worked near boats or on the water on a regular basis did have a preference for items of armour made from *uroko-zane*, which are also commonly referred to as *funate-gusoku,* or literally 'boat hand armour set'.

Another unusual form of *isei-gusoku* that apparently existed in enough numbers to be relatively well documented are items made from *uma-yoroi-zane*, another unusual, alternative form of scale. *Uma-yoroi-zane* are unique in that they are square in shape, generally measuring about 2–3 cm on a side. Most examples feature a round convex dome in the middle of the scale with a thick, raised exterior rim. Holes were punched in the sunken inside corners of each scale that allowed them to be stitched to a fabric bodice. *Uma-yoroi-zane*, which literally means 'horse armour scale', were, as the name suggests, originally utilized to make protective panels of armour for horses, or bardings. While the Japanese had produced armour for horses as far back as the 8th century, such equipment was never particularly common. Even in the late 16th century when *uma-yoroi* enjoyed something of a revival amongst the elite of the samurai class, with renowned warlords like Hideyoshi and others owning such items, actual *uma-yoroi* remained relatively rare. Dr Sasama records that items of armour made for humans from *uma-yoroi-zane* were constructed as far back as the later part of the mid-16th century, but this is difficult to prove for lack of extant examples or other reliable evidence. What is certain, however, is that armour for horses made from *uma-yoroi-zane* did not exist in the 11th century as Bashford Dean errantly claimed in his 1903 *Catalogue of the Loan Collection of Japanese Armour*.

Because only wealthy samurai could afford the extravagance of bardings for their horses, it was common for the lacquered façades of *uma-yoroi-zane* to be covered with gold leaf. That this is also usually the case with many of the extant examples of *uma-yoroi-dō* or *gusoku*, which are themselves relatively simplistic items of armour based on their overall construction and design, suggests that in some cases at least, such armours were constructed utilizing recycled sections of actual *uma-yoroi*.

Because *uma-yoroi-zane* cannot be overlapped, they are invariably sewn directly onto the façades of fabric bodices, with the scales almost always being arranged in regimented, horizontally and vertically aligned parallel rows. Like *uroko-dō*, most examples of *uma-yoroi-zane-dō* are *ichi-mai-* or *ryō-hikiawase ni-mai-dō*. The *gessan* on most such examples were generally also constructed using *uma-yoroi-zane*.

According to Dr Sasama, items of armour assembled from *sane* fashioned from ivory or tortoiseshell may also have been made. But while not impossible, the author is unaware of any surviving examples of *dō* made using such materials, which would lack the resilience needed to be an effective protective material, despite their aesthetic appeal. By contrast, however, exotic materials like shark skin (*same-gawa*) were sometimes used in armour construction, though *same-gawa* was utilized as a covering for armour plating and not as the primary protective material.

As the example of shark skin demonstrates, unusual characteristics should not be misinterpreted, for while they may be unique, the feature itself may not override the identifiable base form in which the cuirass has been

SAMURAI ARMOUR

A leather Edo period panel of barding, or *uma-yoroi*.

constructed. For example, the author once owned a cuirass that was made from large, corrugated-iron-like plates. While extremely unusual in overall form and construction, the cuirass was still clearly identifiable as a variation of *yokohagi-okegawa ni-mai-dō*. Likewise, the author previously owned a *yokohagi-okegawa ni-mai-dō* that was rather bizarrely constructed with a reverse overlap that had the *ita-mono* overlapping each other from the top down. Irrespective of this, the cuirass would still be considered an example of *yokohagi-okegawa ni-mai-dō*.

One final variety of *tosei-gusoku* that requires discussion is the unique armour that was produced by the extremely talented Haruta School of smiths working in the Kaga domain, who were employed by the powerful Maeda *han daimyō* of Kaga. The clan had decided to produce armour for resale as one of two major projects that were designed to help offset the tremendous costs of the public works that the

Shōgunate foisted on all the powerful clans, including the Maeda, as a way to keep them in check by undermining their financial stability.[5] The first Haruta smiths arrived in 1623 and within a short period of time began to produce a considerable quantity of quality armour. The

A close-up of the small, square embossed-leather *uma-yoroi-zane*. These unique scales were sometimes used to fabricate *dō* and other items of armour in the late Edo period.

302

Tosei-Dō Modern Cuirass Designs, Part III

volume of armour produced was in large part due to the fact that a large number of low-ranking Maeda *han* retainers had been assigned to work in the armour shops as labourers. This allowed the Haruta *katchū-shi*, whose ranks swelled throughout the 1630s and 1640s as other smiths from their school moved to Kaga, to supervise the base-level operation while they focused their attentions on the more skilled parts of the work.

While the Haruta *katchū-shi* of Kaga did not introduce any new forms of cuirass, the manner in which they fabricated and decorated the items they made was unique to this group of smiths. Their work often incorporated exotic imported materials like ivory and velvet, and showed influences from beyond Japanese shores. This was almost certainly the result of the Maeda clan's privileged connections with the important *machidoshiyori* administrative offices that oversaw the import of foreign products into Japan. This gave the Maeda a significant market advantage when it came to some of the various commercial dealings that occurred with the Chinese and Dutch traders at Dejima in Nagasaki.

While the Maeda *han katchū-shi* fabricated cuirasses in most of the conventional forms of *tosei-dō*, they tended to favour producing *ryō-hikiawase* examples of *roku-mai-dō*. These were commonly assembled from several rather large plates finished in the *hotoke* style with a distinctive style of *muna-koshi tori*. If the

A unique example of a *ryō-hikiawase roku-mai-dō* produced in the Kaga region by *katchū-shi* employed by the Maeda *han*. Note the use of *kinkara-gawa* to face the *kanagu mawari* sections and the images of Buddhist deities applied to the front and back half-sections of the cuirass. Note the undulating lames and staggered *hishinui* of the *gessan*.

SAMURAI ARMOUR

lower plates of the cuirass were independent *yokohagi-ita*, the upper edges of the plates were generally finished in the undulating *hira-* or *tsure-yamamichi* style and either *sugake* or *kebiki odoshi*-laced in the bottom of the main portion of the *nagakawa*. If the lower portion of the *nagakawa* was continuous, however, it was usually decorated with an overlaid plate shaped in the form of a stylized cloud or undulating wave-like motif. If the façade of the cuirass featured a *tetsu-sabiji* finish, as was quite common, the decorative designs around the lower edge of the *dō* would be formed through overlaid, cut metal plates. If the cuirass was faced with leather, typically of the wrinkled 'Chinese' variety as was also commonly done, then the overlaid portion would generally be cut from thin sheets of *nerigawa* that would be attached to the surface of the cuirass before the leather façade was applied. When the overlaid portion was covered in leather it was commonly lacquered

A close-up view of a panel of *kinkara-gawa* applied to the *muna-ita* of a cuirass. Note that the *muna-ita* overlaps the *mae-tateage*. Also note the raised rim that is designed to prevent edged weapons from sliding off the armour into the body.

Three different examples of Maeda *han*-produced *gusoku*. Some of the many distinctive characteristics of the armours produced by *katchū-shi* working in Kaga are immediately apparent. Note the absence of shoulder guards and the generous use of gold lacquer. All three examples of cuirass are of the *ryō-hikiawase* style. The use of fabric panels, or *fuhaku*, in lieu of *odoshi-ge* to connect the *gessan* was also a common feature, as was the fact the hip armour was almost always of the removable *koshi-kawa-tsuke gessan* variety. Note that the *muna-ita* have been laced to *mae-dō* sections of the cuirass, the latter of which feature integral *mae-tateage*.

in a contrasting colour to the main surface of the cuirass or finished with *kinpaku*. In many cases these undulating patterns were further decorated with short, staggered rows of different coloured blocks of *hishinui* cross-knots. Blue, green, orange and white *odoshi-ge* were commonly used for this purpose.

The *oni-damari-ita* on Kaga-made cuirasses were almost always laced to the *nagakawa*. This plate was commonly finished in a reddish-coloured lacquer or, in the case of better-quality cuirasses, gold lacquer or even *kinpaku*. Alternatively, the *oni-damari-ita* on many high-quality cuirasses were faced with a panel of imported Dutch *kinkara-gawa*, which was a form of embossed leather with a gilt finish. Contrary to popular belief, however, the rich gold-coloured finish of *kinkara-gawa* was not produced through the use of gold leaf. Instead silver leaf was utilized to gild the surfaces of the leather. The gold colour was the result of a varnish that was brushed over the gilding to prevent the silver foil from oxidizing.

If *kinkara-gawa* was applied to the *oni-damari-ita* it was also generally applied to the *waki-ita* and *boko-no-ita*. Having said this, many examples of Kaga-made cuirasses were fabricated without independent *waki-ita*. In such cases the arched form of the *waki-ita* was incorporated directly into the design of the *mae-* and *ushiro-tateage*. It was also common for the *mae-* and *ushiro-dō* segments of many examples of *Kaga-dō* to be made from large, single-plate pieces that merged the *nagakawa* with the *mae-tateage* or *ushiro-tateage*. When independent *waki-ita* were present they were quite often fabricated in a half-horseshoe-like shape that corresponded to the outer edge shape of the *nagakawa* or *mae-tateage* and *ushiro-tateage*.

The façade of the *mae-dō* was commonly decorated with ornate metal fixtures that were usually splashed with a molten silver alloy called *sawari*. The random droplets of *sawari* were intended to replicate the dew or rain on the surfaces of the plates and were one of the trademark characteristics of items produced in Kaga. While the iron fixtures took many forms, Buddhist themes were popular, as were coiling dragons and stylized cloud motifs. Alternatively, designs created through raised lacquer *maki-e* were also applied. While *kuro urushi* finishes were common for the main surfaces, the Maeda *katchū-shi* also often made use of flat green and subdued rust-coloured lacquer tones that were rarely ever used on items of armour not produced in Kaga.

The *wadagami* were quite often hinged to the *boko-no-ita* on better-quality cuirasses. In other cases, the *wadagami* were affixed directly to the *boko-no-ita* in the conventional manner, while the *boko-no-ita* was itself hinged to the top of the *ushiro-tateage*. The edges of the shoulder straps were usually rolled erect like the *suji* flanges on *kabuto-bachi* helmet bowls. This helped to significantly increase the overall strength of the *wadagami*, which was particularly relevant in the case of cuirasses made from *nerigawa*, as was commonly the case with *Kaga-*

The *mae-dō* section of a *ryō-hikiawase roku-mai-dō*. A large Sanskrit character finished in *sawari*, a molten silver alloy, has been applied to the face of the cuirass. Note the textured leather facings on the *kanagu mawari* and the laced-in-place *muna-ita*. Also note the distinctive four-lobed *kohaze* and the unique *saihai-no-kan* which is also finished with *sawari*.

SAMURAI ARMOUR

dō. In some cases, the raised inner edges along the *wadagami* were increased in height in conjunction with the upper edge of the *boko-no-ita* in the area of the back of the neck to create a form of integral protective collar referred to as a *nanban-eri*. Very few Kaga-made cuirasses were fitted with a *kikkō-ire eri-mawashi* or *kobire*, the latter of which would be replaced by the wearing of a brigandine or mail-covered *manchira*.

Another feature that was indicative of, though not entirely universal to, the items of armour that were produced in Kaga was the use of *kohaze* with a distinctively four-lobed shape. The same was done with the *seme-kohaze*, which featured an incised midsection that gave the sliders a figure-of-eight-like shape.

The Kaga preferred irregular and often three-dimensional forms of *kanamono* for fixtures such as the *saihai-no-kan*, the base washers of which were quite often rather realistic in form. In some cases, the individual petals of a floral washer of a *saihai-no-kan*, for example, would curl upwards, peeling up and away from the surface of the cuirass. And while highly artistic, the potential for fixtures like this to get caught up on other items attests to the dwindling concern that armour makers had for practical battlefield considerations. Having said that, the considerable number of sets of armour that were produced by the *katchū-shi* in Kaga between the mid-17th century and 1725, when the Maeda *han* eventually discontinued their armour-making operations, were for their period some of the more functional, potentially battleworthy forms of armour that were produced, next only perhaps to those made in Ōshū under the Date.

The *gessan* were typical of the usual arrangement of seven tassets, each of which was composed of five *ita-mono*. It was, however, common for panels of fabric, or *fuhaku*, to be used to connect the *gessan* in lieu of lengths of *odoshi-ge* for the *yurugi-ito*. The *gessan* themselves were generally laced together in the *sugake odoshi* style, with white, light blue and light green coloured silk lacing being typical of Kaga-made items of armour. The four uppermost lames were often fabricated with undulating upper edges, while both the top and bottom edges of the lowermost *ita-mono* would be undulating. In many cases the outside corners of the lowermost *gessan ita-mono* were decorated with heart-shaped apertures called *inome*.

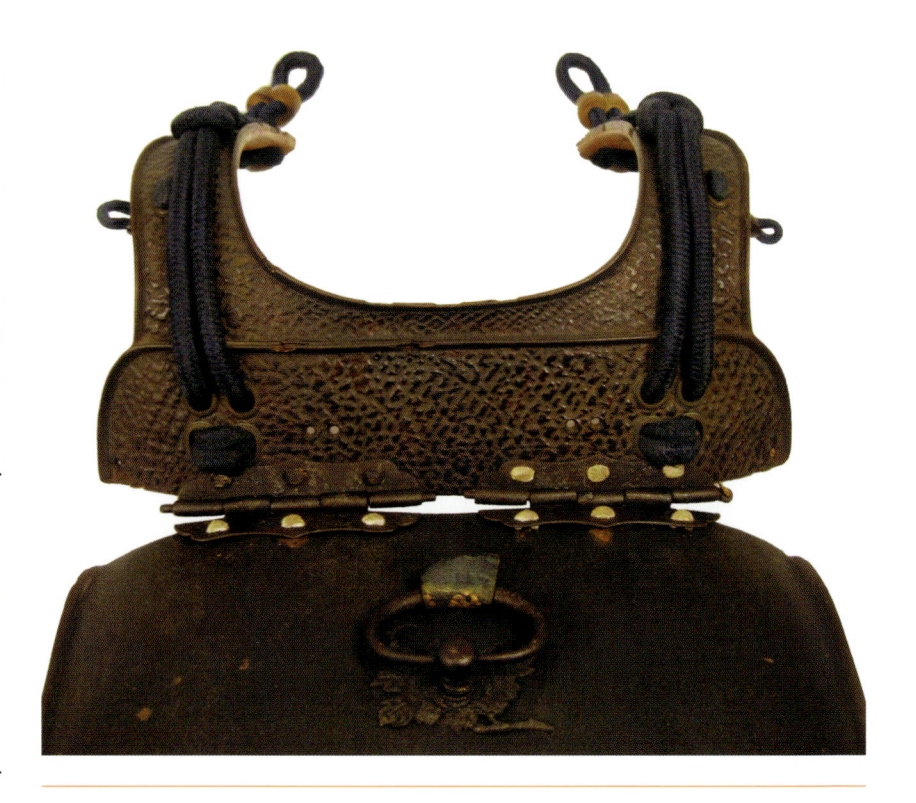

Amongst the many distinctive features of Kaga-made cuirasses were *boko-no-ita* and *wadagami* hinged to the *ushiro-tateage*. Note that the hinges have been laced to the cuirass. Also note the *ninawa-musubi*-knotted *aibiki-no-o* cords stretched over the *wadagami*. A large *sawari*-speckled *agemaki-no-kan* in the form of leafy stem has been fitted to the *ushiro-dō*.

A unique leafy stem-like design has been used to create the base washer portion of this ornate *saihai-no-kan*. The Kaga *katchū-shi* tended to prefer unusually shaped fixtures such as this over mass-produced, generic forms of *kanamono*. Note how the *kan* thickens towards the lower part of the ring fixture.

306

The façade of the lowest *dan* of each *gessan* was almost always finished with gold leaf or a gold-lacquer finish, irrespective of whether the lames were faced in leather or lacquered, except on relatively low-grade cuirasses in which case a reddish colour of lacquer was often used.

When the lowest lame was lacquered, the *urushi* was generally worked to have some form of textured finish. This commonly took the form of wavy lines dragged through the *urushi*, or a dimple finish that Bottomley describes as giving a 'hammered' appearance. The rippled

The *mae-dō* section of this stunning *ryō-hikiawase roku-mai-dō* has been surmounted with masterfully executed embossed mythical *shishi*. Note the laced-in-place leather-faced lower plates of the *nagakawa*.

tataki-nuri style of lacquer finish was also commonly utilized. The rippled texture indicative of this style of lacquer finish was created by lightly dabbing the still-tacky surface of the *urushi*, which would create an irregular pattern of subtle ridges in the lacquer once the *urushi* dried. In some cases, short staggered rows of *hishinui* laced in alternating colours of *odoshi-ge* were also used to decorate the façade of the lowermost *dan*. The interior surfaces on the majority of better-quality cuirasses produced in Kaga were finished with gold leaf or gold lacquer. This was often applied over a very fine, open-weave mesh-like fabric that was attached to the base layers of *urushi*.

Large-scale production of the original Haruta style of Kaga-made armour came to an end around 1725 when the thirteenth Maeda *daimyō* withdrew the clan's sponsored backing and the assigned labour force of retainers from their armour-making duties. Why they made this choice is unclear, but it may have been due in part to a decline in the demand for armour, which would have been consistent with the trends that were sweeping across Japan during this same general period.

The majority of the various Haruta smiths in the region appear to have stayed on, manufacturing high-end sets of armour for wealthy samurai, who represented one of the few groups who continued to acquire armour. Attracted by the considerable wealth of the Maeda *han*, other armour makers such as the Myōchin and Iwai eventually began to establish themselves in the region towards the end of the 18th century.

A unique example of a Kaga *katchū-shi*-made *ni-mai-dō gusoku*. Leather *hishi-toji* decorate the large, stylized scale-like bands that have been created through the application of gold lacquer. Note the unusual *kusari*-lined protective covering of rings on the *kote*. Also note the combination of *hishinui* and *uname* on the red *rasha* cloth-faced *suso-no-ita*. While not described as being a partial composite *gusoku* when it was displayed at the Ishikawa Prefectural History Museum, it is evident that the *menpo* and *suneate* are not original to the armour.

Tosei-Dō Modern Cuirass Designs, Part III

A view of the reverse of a *ryō-hikiawase roku-mai-dō*. The six-section construction of the main body of the cuirass and the hinged *boko-no-ita* and *wadagami* are all clearly visible. The leather binding along the bottom of the *nagakawa* shows where decorative plates have been bound to the façade of the *dō*. A fine mesh has been adhered to the interior of the cuirass and covered with gold lacquer. Note the *koshi-kawa-tsuke gessan* which make use of *fuhaku*, or fabric panels, in lieu of lacing to fasten the individual lames of the *gessan* together and the tassets themselves to the *dō*.

By the time the Myōchin and later Iwai schools began to produce armour in Kaga, many of the unique characteristics that had originally defined the production of armour in the region under the Haruta had already been discontinued. As such, most of the armour made from the mid-18th century onwards in Kaga became increasingly conventional in overall form and design, until ultimately very few of the original Haruta characteristics were visible in the items of armour that were produced by any of the major schools of armour makers working in Kaga.

A *gusoku* from the 18th century that is believed to have belonged to a lord from the powerful Maeda clan of Kaga. (New York Metropolitan Museum of Art/CC0 1.0)

CHAPTER 9

COMING FULL CIRCLE

The revival of ancient armour styles, 17th–19th centuries

The fall of Ōsaka Castle in 1615 to the forces of the Tokugawa Shōgunate was a decisive event in Japanese history, for it marked the end of nearly 150 years of continuous civil war. Unbeknownst to the samurai, it was also to mark the beginning of almost two and a half centuries of uninterrupted peace and stability in Japan, neither of which were beneficial developments from the standpoint of the warrior whose stock-in-trade was war. For the samurai had traditionally relied on conflict to create opportunities for advancement. Without war, many samurai found themselves being ordered to assume the responsibilities of low-level bureaucrats, which offered them little hope of improving their lot in life.

Even so, within a few generations, these petty administrative roles quickly became highly desirable, for few samurai could support themselves without the additional income that such work ensured. Prudent warrior families thus began to reduce the amount of time that their sons spent in studying the martial arts in favour of more scholastic endeavours. It became clear that the best hope of advancement and success lay with those who could more effectively wield a brush as administrators, as Tokugawa Japan ultimately became one of the most organized, and in turn bureaucratic, societies in the world.

By the end of the 17th century, most samurai were little more than administrative paper-pushers dressed in military garb. Though technically the dominant social class, the majority of samurai had become increasingly disillusioned and detached from their warrior pedigrees as they observed with envy the dramatic rise of the socially lower classes of artisans and merchants, who prospered in the long decades of unaccustomed peace, while the warriors found it increasingly difficult to make ends meet. For a prosperous society leads to luxury and excess, and the age-old game of keeping up appearances for sake of one's neighbours was a social reality that the self-conscious samurai were particularly susceptible to, if not obligated to maintain. This burden was made even heavier with the evolving martial etiquette of that period that required

SAMURAI ARMOUR

aspiring warriors to acquire multiple forms of increasingly more elaborate attire for each of their various duties.

Overwhelmed with the ever-expanding burden of their bureaucratic obligations, few samurai found the time or felt the need or inclination to maintain their former martial ways. This mindset was exacerbated further with each new generation, until it reached almost epidemic levels in the late 17th century that were so evident that the Shōgunate ultimately deemed it necessary to issue decrees that forced warriors to maintain their weapons and armour or face punishment under the law. These decrees were followed in 1694 by additional laws that also compelled warriors to practise the martial arts. The flagging *esprit de corps* of the warrior class thus became a subject of major concern to the state, whose authority derived from and rested upon the shoulders of the samurai. The samurai had to be stabilized and given a sense of purpose to solidify them and prevent them from wilting away for lack of an identity.

Salvation came in the form of a number of important publications and theses that not only ennobled and glorified the warrior, but also spelled out in minute detail the exact characteristics, acts and deeds that defined precisely how a true samurai was to live and die. An example of the creational doctrine that was being produced as part of this movement is the 1,300 commentaries that were written by a samurai named Yamamoto Tsunatomo in the years leading up to 1716, which are now collectively referred to as the *Hagakure Kikigaki*, or the 'Hidden Leaves'.

A superb 18th century example of *kuro urushi nuri hon-kozane kebiki odoshi dōmaru-dō gusoku*. The growing trend towards 'revivalist' styles of armour is evident in the construction of this masterfully produced set of armour, which draws heavily on the forms of armour that were popular in the 14th century, including the *Yoshitsune-gote* style of *kote* armoured sleeves. These have been liberally embellished with highly detailed raised-in-relief floral designs created in lacquer. Note the skilfully executed, though impractical, *somen* full face mask.

A hand-painted scroll that identifies the key components of a *yoroi*-like style of cuirass. The early 18th century *Honchō Gunkikō* scrolls featured images and diagrams similar to those seen here. Such images significantly influenced armour design throughout most of the later half of the Edo period, as the nostalgic samurai, eager to be worthy of their heroic forefathers, increasingly chose to acquire and wear *gusoku* that that mimicked the styles of armour in use prior to the mid-16th century.

The *Hagakure Kikigaki* did not promote new ideas, but instead documented existing concepts and practices that had until then not been recorded in print. The fact that the commentaries dealt primarily with the moral and social duties of the average, low-ranking samurai retainer is what made the works unique, for they were effectively outlining what would later become known as the core principles of *bushidō*, or the 'way of the warrior'. That said, it is important to note that the *Hagakure Kikigaki* was largely unknown outside of the small fief of Saga where Yamamoto had served as a third retainer to Nabeshima Mitsushige until well after the end of the Japanese feudal period, and as such they cannot be credited with having played a central role in evolving the samurai ethos that developed amongst Yamamoto's warrior contemporaries. Instead the *Hagakure Kikigaki* represents just one of a multitude of publications and teachings that came about at the start of the 17th century and that helped to formalize a belief system and doctrine amongst the warrior class.

Most of what we now consider to be the quintessential characteristics of the samurai would likely have been alien concepts to the majority of warriors before the 18th century and even long after that. However, the foundations of a unique central identity were created, which did help to shore up and stabilize the edifice that had been crumbling around the warrior class. This, though, was largely done for the benefit of the state. For while the samurai were strengthened through a formalized identity, they were also being stifled by the restrictive nature of the martial and moral obligations that they were expected to uphold and live by, which should not be confused with the much-vaunted concept of the code of *bushidō*. For *bushidō* was still only a vague ideal in the early 1700s and in fact did not really even exist in the form that it is now spoken of until Nitobe Inazō published his famous book, *Bushi-dō: The Soul of Japan*, in 1899.

From the standpoint of the evolutionary development of Japanese armour, the creation of a formalized identity for the samurai class would turn out to be a devastating event. For a considerable portion of the teachings that were being expounded in the early 18th century focused on the actions and deeds of the samurai who had lived during the times of the Genpei War, the Mongol invasions and the Nanbokuchō War. In their conscious or subconscious efforts to create an identifying ethos for the samurai class, 18th century Japanese historians and scholars drew heavily on the historical past to establish and sanctify the developing ideal of the quintessential samurai, who gradually emerged to be a hybrid version of the warriors who had existed between the 12th and 16th centuries. As a result, many samurai, particularly the elite, who had the time, wealth and need to emulate the new principles that were being formalized, started to develop an interest in the items of armour that were used by their ancient forbears.

This prompted one of the era's great scholars and statesman, Arai Hakuseki, who was an advisor to the sixth and seventh Tokugawa Shōguns, to publish a twelve-volume work in 1722 called the *Honchō Gunkikō*, which described the forms of armour that were known to have been used in Japan between the 10th and early 16th centuries. Appearing when it did, at the height of a massive push to define and revive the identity of the samurai class, the *Honchō Gunkikō* quickly became a hugely influential publication. For many samurai, who had already eagerly latched on to the doctrine that stated they should emulate the virtuous warriors from the 12th through 14th centuries, were for the first time seeing representations of the items of armour that their much-idolized patriarchs had once used. In their nostalgic desire to prove themselves the equals of their forefathers, a revivalist trend towards the ancient styles of armour was born.

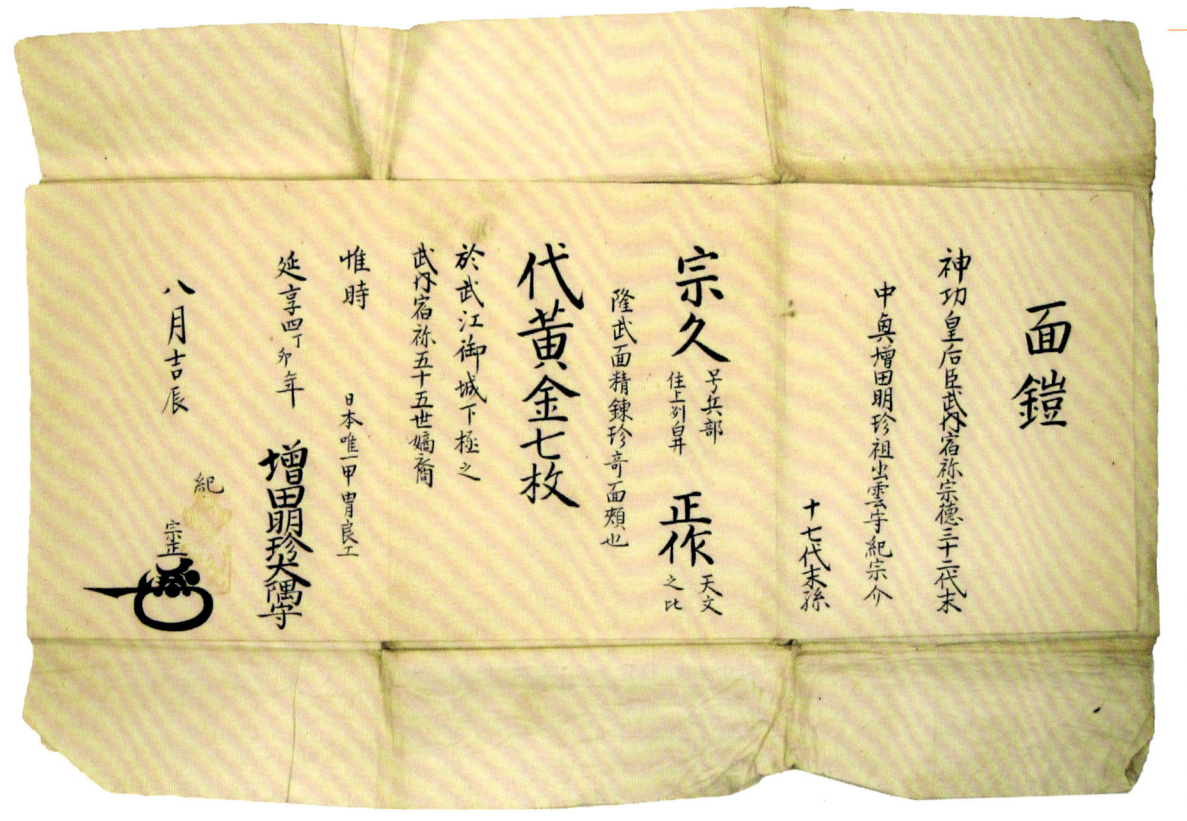

A *kiwame fuda*, or appraisal document issued and signed by Myōchin Munemasa, son of the proclaimed twenty-fourth Myōchin master smith Munesuke. The document accredits a *mengu* (face mask) as having been made by the mid-16th century *katchū-shi*, Munehisa, who was absorbed into the largely mythical Myōchin family genealogy that was created by Munesuke and his father Kunimichi in the late 17th century. The *kiwame fuda* values the face mask at 7 gold *ōban*. An *ōban* was the equivalent of ten *ryō*, which had a nominal value of one *koku* of rice. One *koku* was the amount of rice required to feed one person for one year. Thus the mask was valued as equal to the amount of food required to sustain 70 people for one year.

COMING FULL CIRCLE

Unlike the *Hagakure Kirigaki*, however, the *Honchō Gunkikō* had not been written with the intent of influencing the beliefs of the samurai class. It had simply been produced to accommodate the growing interest in the subject matter of the ancient forms of armour. Irrespective of this fact, Japanese armour designs began to regress backwards in time due to the publication of the *Honchō Gunkikō* and other works, such as the seven-volume *Gun Yo Ki* (Military Matters), produced by samurai scholar Ise Sadatake in the mid-1700s, which further expounded on the aesthetic beauty of the ancient styles of armour.

The first tentative devolutionary developments had in fact already taken place prior to the appearance of the *Honchō Gunkikō*. These were extremely minor in nature, however, compared to the changes that would ultimately occur between the late 1720s and mid-1800s. For the most part, the items of armour that were produced during the first half of the 17th century were fundamentally the same sleek, battleworthy and Spartan-looking designs of armour that had been utilized at the end of the 16th century. By the latter half of the 16th century, however, the armour had already started to become increasingly ornate as the realities of battle began to fade from memory.

The first real change came within a few decades of the last great battles with the gradual reintroduction of the small *ko-sode* varieties of shoulder guards that had largely been abandoned towards the end of the 16th century. Even so, most *kote* continued to be fabricated with *kote-bukuro* (sleeve bodices) that were heavily armoured along the upper portion of the sleeve, which allowed the armour to be worn without *sode* if desired. This practice, however, gradually faded out during the 17th century, as *sode* once again came to be seen as an integral part of a full *gusoku*.

A superb Edo period *tetsu-sabiji go-mai dō* that has had the *mae-dō* embossed. Note the *uchidashi tsutsu-gote* and *tsutsu-suneate*. While aesthetically attractive, metal plate was significantly weakened when it was embossed.

315

As the trend to wear *sode* again took hold, sets of armour that had originally been constructed to be worn without *sode* began to be retroactively fitted with shoulder guards. This was often done even when the need for *sode* had been nullified by the presence of alternative forms of upper-arm and shoulder protection, such as *kote* that had the upper body of the sleeve covered with some sturdy protective covering, or prominent *kobire*, like those fitted to most conventional examples of *Yukinoshita-dō*. The result of these unintended additions is often obvious. For the *sode* are often forced to hang far out, off the sides of the shoulders, by the protruding *kobire*. In other cases, the *kobire* have to stand erect to allow the shoulder guards to be secured to the *wadagami*, which undermines the protective value of the *kobire* that then look awkward and out of place when worn with *sode*. The move away from the extensive use of *odoshi-ge* was also gradually reversed as the aesthetically simplistic, smooth-finished *hotoke* designs of *dō* declined in popularity in favour of cuirasses that utilized *odoshi-ge* as an aesthetic feature in the method of fabrication, which in turn led to an increase in the number of cuirasses assembled from *kiritsuke kozane ita* laced in the *kebiki odoshi* style.

No longer pressed to produce volumes of armour, for the first time in centuries the *katchū-shi* were able to focus their efforts on perfecting their techniques and workmanship, which reached new levels of excellence throughout the 17th century. Styles were defined as the different schools of armour makers began to brand their products in a manner not previously practised.

Foremost amongst these was the renowned Myōchin School, who under the auspices of Myōchin Munesuke and his grandfather Kunimichi fabricated the elaborate family genealogy that allowed the Myōchin to take credit for many of the best unsigned and ancient pieces of armour that existed throughout the Japanese archipelago. They did this by following the example of the Honnami clan, who had established themselves as the pre-eminent authority in the appraisal of swords. Unlike the Honnami, however, the *kiwame fuda* or appraisals certificates that Munesuke provided accredited the production of any item of obvious excellence and antiquity to one of his family's numerous bogus historical forefathers. Munesuke was able to carry out this ruse in part due to the obvious

A detailed view of the *uchidashi tetsu-sabiji go-mai dō* seen in the previous image. The image embossed onto the main panel of the *mae-dō* of the cuirass is of 'Ah', a mythical Chinese *shishi*, or guardian lion-like creature. While *uchidashi* work such as this is visually impressive and a testament to the immense talent of the *katchū-shi* who produced this cuirass, embossing on this scale significantly undermined the structural resilience of the armour plating. The raised features were also likely to catch, rather than deflect, strikes from edged weaponry.

COMING FULL CIRCLE

excellence of the huge number of well-documented pieces that the Myōchin family had been producing since the early 16th century. Supporting these claims further was the fact that Munesuke himself was also an exceptionally talented smith, whose skill in the embossing of metal was virtually unrivalled.

The pieces Munesuke produced, however, though artistically superb, were perhaps the first examples of armour that were no longer functional as a result of the aesthetic detailing, though this may not have been appreciated at the time. For by embossing the metal plates of items such as the *mae-dō* of a *Yukinoshita-dō*, which was one of his favourite canvasses, Munesuke weakened the metal through the process of pounding it outward into the ornate designs he created. Likewise, decorative embossing on the face of a cuirass was prone to trapping the tips of stabbing weapons such as *yari* (spears), which was one reason why the *Yukinoshita-dō* was originally designed to be devoid of surface decoration. Unaware, or more likely unconcerned, the samurai class's infatuation with embossed items of armour drove the demand for ever more elaborate examples of *uchidashi* throughout the latter half of the 18th and into the early part of the 19th century, when it reached its zenith, with sets of armour that featured areas of *uchidashi* on all of the components of the *gusoku*, including the helmet bowl.

Such sets were, however, still the extreme and were largely limited in their use to the elite of the warrior class, while the vast majority of middle- and lower-rank warriors made do with more conventional examples of armour. These middle- to lower-rank sets, however, were generally superior to anything that had come before as

A fine example of late Edo period *nerigawa muna-koshi-tori kawa-tsuzumi kiritsuke iyozane ni-mai-dō gusoku*. Well-made examples of armour fabricated from rawhide such as this are virtually impossible to visually differentiate from sets of armour made from metal. Contrary to popular belief, rawhide was not considered to be a poor man's material for making armour. Many wealthy, high-ranking samurai preferred the lightweight convenience of well-made set of *nerigawa* armour.

SAMURAI ARMOUR

they were not only meticulously crafted, but also decorated with an ever greater degree of ornately finished fixtures, features and fabrics that had not been commonly attainable in previous centuries. By the end of the 17th century, however, such items and materials had become quite common due to the huge advances that artisans and craftsmen had made after several decades of uninterrupted peace. It is for this reason that the items of armour produced around the time of the Genroku regnal period (*c.* 1688–1704) are perhaps some of the finest examples of Japanese armour that are still battleworthy.

Included amongst these were a growing number of superbly crafted *nerigawa gusoku* that were virtually impossible to distinguish from items of armour that were made of iron or steel without testing the item's weight. The excellent quality of many of these sets, particularly those produced by the Iwai, was attested by the Tokugawa Shōguns' continued patronage of this talented school of armour makers. *Nerigawa*-made *gusoku*, however, were not limited to the elite of the samurai class, but were also commonly favoured by the older warriors who found this lighter-weight armour much less taxing to wear when they were obligated to so for some official duty.

Within a few short years of the appearance of the *Honchō Gunkikō*, however, Japanese armour designs had begun to change drastically as more and more samurai began to commission sets of armour that incorporated some of the most

---

A stunning mid-Edo period example of a *tetsu cha urushi nuri hon kozane kebiki-odoshi ni-mai-(maru-)dō gusoku*. The immense talent of the armour makers of this time is evident in every aspect of this outstanding *gusoku*. This armour also embodies many of the features indicative of the early revivalist movement in Japanese armour designs, which increasingly saw many obsolete features that had been common to items of armour between the 10th and 15th centuries being merged with post-16th century armour designs and fabrication techniques. Note the alternative *kai-sode*, or 'changing shoulder guards' displayed next to the *suneate* shin guards. Many well-made high quality armours came with *kai-sode* that could be worn in lieu of the massive and largely ceremonial *ō-sode* design of shoulder guards, which had fallen out of common use amongst the samurai in the later part of the 15th century.

COMING FULL CIRCLE

obvious aesthetic features from the forms of armour that they saw the heroic warriors of earlier centuries wearing in various illustrated depictions, such as those that were published in the *Honchō Gunkikō*. One of the first of these features to reappear was the reintroduction of the long obsolete *ō-sode* style of shoulder guards. These were primarily intended to be worn for ceremonial purposes, such as the many *gyō-ritsu* parades that were commonly associated with the *sankin kōtai*. In many cases a more practical pair of matched-construction *kai-sode*, or literally 'changing shoulder guards', was provided. These were invariably fabricated in a smaller, more practical size that allowed them to be utilized for more conventional purposes, such as training exercises.

The return of the *ō-sode* presented armour makers with a number of problems, the first of which was that most of them had never seen or produced armour with *ō-sode*. Thus most of them were unsure of how the *ō-sode* were to be attached. And though such matters were ultimately overcome, the solutions were in themselves often problematic. For rather than remove features, such as the *kobire*, that had come about since the *ō-sode* had fallen out of favour in the 15th century, the *katchū-shi* chose to merge the various old and new features together in hybrid combinations that often hampered the effectiveness of both the existing features and those that they were trying to reintroduce.

The *sashimono*-holding *uke-zutsu*, *gattari* and *machi-uke* are excellent examples of features that were affected by the drive to merge old features with new ones. For the *gattari* occupied the same general area where the *agemaki-no-kan* had once been mounted. Armours that were made with *ō-sode* required this fixture to support the complex array of cords that both secured the large shoulder guards and kept them in position. Both features were now in competition for the same space. In some cases, this bulging knot of the *agemaki* prevented the *uke-zutsu* from being seated in the *machi-uke*. This forced warriors to insert the holder through the *agemaki* in some cases, which prevented the knot from moving as it was designed to do, which in turn affected how the shoulder guards moved and thus protected the upper body.

Sode-tsuke-no-gumi had to be reintroduced to the *wadagami* to provide anchoring points to secure the *ō-sode*. *Shoji-no-ita* also reappeared, even though the latter in many ways duplicated the role of the *eri-mawashi*. Even the wearing of *ō-sode* became an issue, for, as they had been obsolete for so long, very few samurai knew how they were to be secured. This resulted in the publication of a number of illustrated manuals that showed warriors how the *ō-sode* and their accompanying cords were to be worn and how the various cords were to be tied and secured.

The *shikoro* neck guards on *kabuto* also began to widen, to mimic those on the helmets of early centuries. This, however, often resulted in them

A superb *kinpaku oshi hon kozane kebiki odoshi ni-mai-dō gusoku* from the late Edo period. The hybrid combination of *tosei* and pre-*tosei gusoku* features seen on this set are indicative of the revivalist styles of armour that were produced throughout the later half of the Edo period. The massive umbrella-like *shikoro* neck guard on the *kabuto*, *kuwagata* appendages, *kyūbi* and *sendan-no-ita*, the large *ō-sode* shoulder guards and the rigid *ō-tateage* style of shin guards are all features that had largely become obsolete or been replaced by more practical by the mid-16th century. While aesthetically beautifully, the profusion of unnecessary and obsolete parts made many such *gusoku* useless as fighting armour.

SAMURAI ARMOUR

pushing against the shaft of the pole that held the *sashimono* when the head was tilted back. Unable to give, the pole would often force the helmet forward and down over the warrior's brow. The *fukigaeshi* flanges on the sides of the *kabuto* likewise also began to increase their proportion irrespective of the historical factors that had resulted in them substantially shrinking between the late 15th and mid-16th centuries.

The removable forms of *maedate* lightweight helmet crests that had become popular in the 16th century likewise began to fall out of favour, giving way to the ancient styles of permanently affixed *kuwagata-dai* holders and simulated horn-like *kuwagata* appendages. While these added weight to the helmets, these fixtures were rigid accoutrements that would not give or easily break away if they were caught up on something or were grabbed in a close-quarter engagement. This transition again demonstrated the slow demise of items and designs that had come about as a result of experiences gained on the hard-fought battlefields of the 15th and 16th centuries.

Gyōyō, *kyūbi-no-ita*, *sendan-no-ita* and *nodowa* neck-guard rings were also reintroduced, with the latter often being worn in conjunction with an item of *mengu* facial armour, even though *tare*, or neck guards, which were an integral part of almost all *mengu*, effectively eliminated the need for a *nodowa*. The protective apron-like *haidate* thigh-guard panels also began to widen, while the massive *ō-tateage* styles of rigid *suneate* shin guards like those worn in the 13th and 14th centuries also began to reappear.

In short, within a matter of just two or three generations, the battlefield worthiness of most examples of Japanese armour had been significantly

---

A bold *kinpaku oshi nerigawa hon iyozane ni-mai-dō gusoku* from the late Edo period. While this armour shows signs of post-19th century restoration, it still accurately reflects many of the characteristics of a revivalist movement style of armour. The massive *fukigaeshi* side flanges and sweeping *shikoro* neck guard on the *kabuto* are particularly evident, as are the 14th century style of *Yoshitsune-gote* armoured sleeves. The use of sturdy iron *shikigane* visible laced to the interior of the lamellar bands of the *shikoro* is a telltale sign that this armour is made from *nerigawa*.

Coming Full Circle

A somewhat unusal example of a Kaga *han katchū-shi*-made *tetsu cha urushi nuri hatomune yokohagi-okegawa ni-mai-dō gusoku*. As well as being aesthetically attractive, Kaga-made *gusoku* such as this generally continued to be fairly functional, battleworthy sets of armour. This characteristic is easily discerned in this *gusoku*, which in form is far more indicative of a set of armour from the late 16th century than of one from the early 18th century.

impaired. Even so, the vast majority of these armours were still relatively practical in comparison to the sets that started to be produced from the mid-18th century onward. For the factors that had initially derailed the evolutionary train of Japanese armour, namely the growing fascination with and idolization of the 12th through 14th century concept of the quintessential warrior, had grown to such an extent amongst the warrior class that it ultimately drove the train right off the tracks and over the embankment into de-evolutionary absurdity. For as the fabricated concept of the warrior took root amongst the samurai class, it had the effect of pushing them further down the road into nostalgic idolization of their largely mythical ancient forefathers, spurred on as they were by the enforced practice and study of the martial arts, which only added fuel to the fire. For outside the practice dojo, there were few real avenues to display one's martial skills and knowledge. The armour they commissioned, however, could be utilized as a visual statement of their mastery of the warrior precept.

From a modern perspective, this movement ultimately resulted in some of the most beautiful and spectacular examples of armour ever made in Japan, most of which were, however, simultaneously some of the most impractical and useless items of armour ever produced. For the further down the rabbit hole into historical obscurity the samurai went in the effort to reconnect with their historical forefathers, the more detached they became from the realities of warfare and the actual role of the warrior. For contrary to popular belief, the firearm had never been discarded in favour of the sword. Nor was Japan a society in absolute isolation from and ignorance of the outside world, as is commonly believed to have been the case. Thus, it is a testament to their need for an identity that the warrior class so wilfully bought into their own propaganda when it came explaining who they were and what they represented.

The overwhelming popularity of the revivalist movement may also have helped contribute to the demise of the highly practical yet artistic Kaga style of *tosei-gusoku* around the middle of the 18th century, which had hitherto been one of the more sought-after forms of armour produced in Japan since the middle of the 17th century.

The motives of the samurai's *katchū-shi* co-conspirators in this devolutionary process are much easier to understand: money. They were willing to accommodate the needs of their clientele irrespective of the absurdity of the items that they were being asked to produce. And as artists, which is what many armour makers had become, the revivalist-style armours that they were being asked to produce almost certainly represented exciting creative challenges. For again, very few *katchū-shi* had ever seen the items they were being asked to construct, which resulted in a great many of the early examples of revivalist styles of armour being substantially inferior to the ancient items of armour that they were meant to replicate.

The trend continued rapidly backwards in time to revisit the *haramaki*, *dō-maru* and ultimately even the *yoroi* styles of cuirass. Initially many of these revivalist styles of *dō* were bizarre, hybrid versions that combined aspects of these ancient cuirass styles with those of the modern *tosei* varieties of *dō*. In time, however, the accuracy and quality of these reproduced items improved, until many *katchū-shi* were able precisely to recreate near-perfect copies of even the long-obsolete *yoroi*. This was largely due to the efforts of the elite of the warrior class, who commissioned agents to scour the *kura* and temples across Japan in search of authentic examples of ancient forms of armour for them to buy. The pieces that were discovered were

A fabulous *tetsu kuro urushi nuri sugake odoshi Mōgami go-mai-dō gusoku* from the late Edo era. While ornate, a significant reversal can be noted in the design of this armour compared to some of the various examples of revivalist styles of armour seen in the preceding images. While the *Mōgami* style of cuirass was still inferior to the various rigid forms of *tosei-dō* that were developed during the later half of the 16th century, it was still a far more realistic design than the various reproductions of pre-15th century cuirasses that many samurai had incorporated into the sets of armour they commissioned.

then usually refurbished by *katchū-shi* for incorporation into new sets of armour for these wealthy patrons. This was especially true of ancient examples of *kabuto bachi* (helmet bowls), though *dō* and other items such as *ō-sode* were also merged with new or existing sets of armour after being refurbished. In general, however, the latter were usually reserved for display in the homes of the elite.

The end result of these self-aggrandizing efforts was twofold. Firstly, they allowed armour makers to study in detail how the early medieval forms of armour had been made and what they really looked like. This in turn allowed them to accurately reproduce these items. Secondly, these actions most likely helped to preserve a great many ancient armour sets from destruction, for, being made from organic materials, they would naturally deteriorate with age after hundreds of years of storage.

The astute Myōchin further capitalized on the revivalist trend by promoting and specializing in the construction of the ancient styles of massive external rivet *ō-boshi suji bachi* forms of helmet bowls, which they finished with a deep *sabiji*, or russet iron patina, to help give the helmets a more authentic and aged appearance. Many of the *kabuto* produced were fitted with massive umbrella-like *kasa-jikoroiye* neck guards reminiscent of those that had been popular at the height of the 14th century during the Nanbokuchō period.

So prolific had the revivalist trend become that it was not uncommon to find simple *yokohagi-okegawa ni-mai dō* made with *waidate*, or for panels of stencilled *e-gawa* to be riveted to the façade of the *nagakawa* of the *mae-dō* in an attempt to replicate the *tsurubashiri-gawa* of the early medieval period *yoroi*-style of cuirass.

At what point the absurdity of the revivalist movement became apparent to some amongst the samurai class is impossible to say. In fact, it may have been apparent to a core group all along, but it was not until Sakakibara Kōzan published *Chuko Katchū Seisakuban* in 1800 that some amongst the warrior class began to reconsider the logic behind the glorification of the early medieval forms of armour that led to the physical revival of many long-obsolete forms. This led to a second, though smaller and less well-known revivalist movement, where armour makers began to produce *gusoku* reminiscent of those that were built around cuirasses made in the *Mōgami* style that had been fabricated during the latter part of the Muromachi period.

This reversal in ideology however, came too slowly and too late to save the samurai from themselves. This fact must have been painfully evident to the warriors who lined the coastline of Uraga Bay near Edo in 1853 in their archaic and impractical armour, as they watched the explosive Paixhans shells fired from the gun decks of Commodore Perry's small fleet of 'black' steamships bombard buildings in the harbour as a demonstration of his intent to use force to open negotiations with the Shōgunate. For even the most obtuse amongst them must have recognized the technological superiority of the first serious foreign encroachment upon Japanese lands since the Mongol invasions seven centuries earlier. And while the enemy was new and mysterious to the vast majority of rank-and-file warriors and Japanese, the samurai themselves prepared to do battle in virtually the same equipment that their much-idolized forefathers had worn when they faced Kublai Khan's invading hordes in the 13th century. This time, however, no *shinpū*, or *kamikaze* as it is now commonly referred to, materialized to save the samurai from their folly.

An impressive *ō-yoroi*-like *gusoku* from the early 19th century. With the exception of the butterfly-like *maedate* helmet crest, *hanbo* facial mask and the *haidate* thigh guard armour, this *gusoku* is a fairly accurate representation of the forms of armour that were commonly utilized in the 14th century. Though difficult to perceive in this photograph, note the use of patterned *kawa-odoshi* as lacing material. Though heavily faded, the *tsurubashiri-gawa* was originally emblazoned with an image of the sword-carrying Buddhist deity Fudo Myō-ō and his two loyal attendants standing on small islands surrounded by flames

An absolutely stunning 18th century example of a hybrid armour made for the eighth Lord of Yanagawa, Tachibana Akihisa. While the cuirass looks like a *yoroi*, it is actually a *dō-maru* constructed in the *Mōgami* style with a *tsurubashiri* secured to the front of the *dō*. (Tachibana Museum)

CHAPTER 10

THE WESTERNIZATION OF JAPANESE ARMOUR

Post-feudal era armour, 19th–early 20th centuries

The Treaty of Kanagawa in 1854, between the Government of the United States of America and the Tokugawa Shōgunate, is often presented as the event that opened Japan up to the outside world after almost two and a half centuries of self-imposed isolation. This perception, however, is only partially correct. For Japan was never totally isolated from the outside world. In fact, the Tokugawa Shōgunate maintained trading relationships with several countries, kingdoms and peoples throughout the entire Sakoku, or so-called 'island-in-chains' period. In fact, the term *sakoku* did not even exist in the Japanese language prior to 1801, when it was created by the famous Japanese astronomer Shizuki Tadao in an effort to translate the writings of the 17th century German traveller and renowned physician, Engelbert Kaempfer, who had rather ironically travelled extensively in Japan between 1689 and 1692.

The Japanese interpretation of *sakoku* was not one of self-imposed isolation, but rather a means of controlling their trade balances with other nations, which was extremely important to a resource-poor country such as Japan. It was, however, also a means of limiting outside cultural influences, particularly the spread of Christianity, which many among the elite of the warrior class saw as an up-and-coming rival to their hegemony. The impact of this measure can still be noted today, with less than 1 per cent of Japanese proclaiming themselves to be Christian. This contrasts sharply with countries such as the Philippines, where over 90 per cent of the population is Christian following centuries of Spanish and then American control.

Trade, however, was conducted through four gateway domains, or *han*, under the control of feudal lords with close ties of loyalty to the Shōgunate. The most well-known of these entry ports was the man-made island of Dejima in Nagasaki harbour where the Dutch East India Company had conducted operations since 1639, after moving there from the port of Hirado where they had first established themselves in 1609. Trade with China was also conducted through Nagasaki, while trade with

Korea was conducted via the Fuchū *han* of Tsushima. Trade goods also entered Japan through the Ryūkyū Kingdom that occupied the present-day islands of Okinawa via the Shimazu *han* of Satsuma in southern Kyūshū, while commerce in the north was dominated by the Matsumae *han* who traded with the Ainu peoples on the southern tip of Ezo, or modern-day Hokkaidō.

Thus from a historical perspective, it would be more accurate to say that Perry opened Japan up to trade with the United States, rather than that he opened up an isolated country to the world. Ironically Perry is not often credited with his greatest achievement, which was to make the Japanese bend to the will of a foreign power, for at no time in their history prior to that time period had they ever done so. Even during their ancient association and interaction with the kingdoms on the Korean peninsula, the Japanese or Yayoi peoples appear to have willingly entered into those relationships.

Perry, however, forced the Japanese to accept terms, conditions and realities that they neither wanted nor were prepared to deal with, a situation for which the Japanese themselves were solely to blame. For as has already been noted, the Shōgunate was far from ignorant of world events. It knew of many of the incredible scientific and technological advances that had occurred in Europe and North America since the early 17th century, for the Tokugawa Shōguns regularly received missions to Edo from the countries that they traded with, including the Dutch. It was common for these emissaries to offer a generous array of presents during their audiences with the Shōguns, a considerable portion of which included examples of the latest in Western technologies and scientific literature.

This is the reason why the Shōgunate chose to negotiate with Commodore Perry when he returned to Japan in 1854 to see what the Japanese had decided to do in regards to his 1853 ultimatum to negotiate landing and trading rights with the United States. For many amongst the elite of the warrior class were aware of the military superiority of the Western nations, and they knew that Japan would be defeated if it attempted to resist these Westerners in open battle. At least, this was the situation in 1854 as far as they were concerned. Given time to prepare and perhaps to modernize themselves, so they could fight on a more even playing field, then it would be possible to expel the impetuous 'southern barbarians'.

While many of the elite within the Shōgunate may have understood this situation, the rank-and-file samurai, steeped as they were in the increasingly artificial and self-aggrandizing doctrine of the

A late 19th century painting attributed to Osai depicting the 'black ships' of the US Navy's East India Squadron, which, under the command of Commodore Matthew C. Perry, sailed into Uraga Bay within sight of Edo in 1854, to force the Japanese into negotiations aimed at opening their ports to American trade. (Courtesy of the Yale Collection of Western Americana, Beinecke Rare Book and Manuscript Library, Yale University, New Haven, Connecticut/Wikimedia Commons/Public Domain)

A less than flattering Japanese image of Perry from the 1854 Japanese 'Black Ship' scrolls. Perry has intentionally been made to look like a mythical goblin-like Japanese *tengu* creature. He is also depicted with a beard, even though he was clean-shaven throughout the expedition, in keeping with the Japanese stereotype that Westerners were 'hairy barbarians'. (Honolulu Museum of Art/Wikimedia Commons/Public Domain)

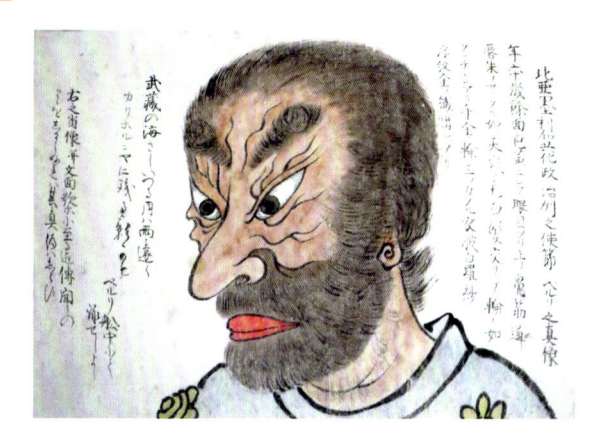

warrior class, were largely ignorant of the abilities of these unwelcome foreign intruders. They simply could not conceive or comprehend the technological advantages and massive destructive potential that the armed forces of a modern, industrial nation was capable of bringing to bear upon them.

Ignorant or not of these realities, many amongst the samurai saw this as their chance to finally prove themselves as warriors. It was their opportunity to live up to the hyper-inflated and largely mythical ideal of their much-admired forefathers. The uninvited intrusion of a truly alien foreign power was the ultimate *raison d'être* for the existence of a warrior class within Japan; which is why most warriors were flabbergasted when they learned that the Shōgun himself, the mightiest warrior in the land, had acquiesced to the treaty terms presented by Perry.

For the samurai, the Treaty of Kanagawa was the equivalent of the iceberg that tore the gaping gash in the hull of the unsinkable *Titanic*. It was a traumatic event, yet it was one that most of them felt could be overcome and eventually rectified. Very few amongst them could have guessed that the treaty was in fact their death knell. Likewise, it would have been impossible for the samurai to fathom the fact that they themselves, and not the foreign powers, would be the group who would ultimately end up destroying their class's centuries-old grip on power and with it their elite and privileged status within Japanese society.

This was because most samurai failed to realize that the Shōgunate's willingness to sign the treaty had in fact been something of a ploy. For the Shōgunate, like most of its vassals, wanted to resist the incursions of these foreign powers. How and when this was to be done was the question that needed to be answered. In signing the treaty, the Shōgunate was simply hoping to buy time until a consensus on how to deal with this conundrum could be reached. The question was not what to do but how to do it. For while some camps wanted to resist immediately, others realized that they would lose and in turn be occupied if they tried to challenge the foreigners as things stood. These groups were in favour of buying time for themselves by initially agreeing to work with the Western powers until they could level the playing field. The more astute amongst them realized that this would take a considerable amount of time, for they would need to master the technologies and reproduce the weaponry of their foreign foes before they could hope to challenge them. Only then would they be in a position to offer serious resistance, at which point they believed that they would again be able to secure Japan away from the world in a state of controlled isolation.

This highly controversial point of contention was exacerbated further when the Emperor Kōmei, who had originally felt that trade should be allowed, reversed his stance on the matter and issued an order to 'expel the barbarians'. Many *han*, particularly those that had held a 250-year-long grudge against the Shōgunate for having been reduced in status and size after being on the losing side in the battle of Sekigahara, were quick to echo this new battle-cry. For while most of them agreed with this policy, it also provided them with a much-longed-for opportunity to attack and undermine the authority of the Tokugawa Shōguns. This set the stage for a civil war that would ultimately see the samurai fight each other, with some clans supporting the Shōgunate while others allied themselves to the side of the Emperor, who had called for the immediate expulsion of all foreigners. And while the ultimate objectives of both sides were the same, they could not agree on how and when this was to be achieved.

The effect on Japanese armour was immediate. For a large number of samurai, particularly those amongst the lower ranks, suddenly found themselves scrambling to acquire armour, due to the fact that generations of samurai, as already noted in the preceding chapters, had often gone without conventional armour. This was largely through their inability to afford and maintain such items as well as the fact that armour was seldom if ever utilized outside of ceremonial purposes in the centuries leading up to the arrival of the Perry and his black ships. When they had needed it, most warriors had been able either to borrow or lease armour for the short periods of time that it was required.

Armour makers suddenly found themselves swamped with orders for cheap and battleworthy sets of armour, neither of which demands they were particularly adept at meeting by the mid-19th century, as the multitude of kingdoms across the archipelago began to drift towards civil war. This resulted in the production of a considerable amount of rather poor-quality, though relatively battleworthy sets of armour in the late 1850s and 1860s that in overall form were reminiscent of the types of armour that had been used during the latter part of the 16th century. Many samurai, however, unable to afford or to wait for a traditional set of armour to be produced, chose to utilize the *kusari-* and *tatami-*made items of armour that the majority of them did own and use for their various official duties.

As the intensity of the internal conflicts gradually rose throughout the first half of the 1860s, many samurai also began to carry firearms, which they found to be a fast and effective way to eliminate their opponents. Even the master swordsman and gun-runner Sakamoto Ryōma had taken to carrying an 1863 pattern Smith & Wesson US Army model .32 calibre revolver, which he kept tucked into the waistband of his *hakama*.

Thus the revival of Sengoku-period *tosei-gusoku* was extremely short-lived. For within less than a decade the majority of samurai on both sides of the political debate were once again carrying and utilizing firearms. This time, however, they were making use of some of the most advanced modern firearms that could be acquired through the same 'barbarians' that they were fighting each other ultimately to expel from their country. As a result, the wearing of

Commodore Matthew C. Perry, Commander of the US Navy East India Squadron. This photograph was taken by M. Brady after the successful completion of Perry's 1854 diplomatic trade mission to Japan. (Library of Congress, Prints & Photographs Division, LC-USZC4-7502)

Emperor Kōmei broke with long-standing tradition when he publicly voiced his strong anti-foreigner sentiments in 1863 and issued his 'expel the barbarians' order, which greatly undermined the Shōgunate and its centuries-old hegemony over state power. (*Taiyō* magazine/Wikimedia Commons/Public Domain)

most forms of armour quickly fell by the wayside, with the exception of some largely ceremonial and cosmetic items, such as the simple metal-plate *hitai-ate* headband-like forehead protectors.

The unofficial state of civil war that had existed in Japan since the mid-1850s finally came to a head with the abdication of the last Shōgun, Tokugawa Yoshinobu, in 1867, which saw him cede authority over the state back to the imperial family in Kyōto, and the young Emperor Meiji.

This event was followed almost immediately by the outbreak of the climactic Boshin War of 1868–69, which saw the Western-armed governmental troops loyal to the Tokugawa, backed by French military advisors, squaring off against heavily armed pro-Imperial forces, who were equipped with British-made weaponry acquired through the Satsuma *han*. Thus, the last great samurai battles were not fought by sword-wielding, armour-clad samurai, but were instead waged by warriors wielding Western-made firearms who fought each other using European military tactics.

In short, the Japanese had inadvertently Westernized themselves in an effort to stave off Westernization. For once they had started down that road, they found it much more difficult than they had anticipated to revert to the sort of society that they had originally set out to preserve. For as they discovered, to protect Japan from foreign encroachment they would not only require a modern army, but they would also need a modern navy. To achieve these, they required industry. To operate their industries, they would require abundant natural resources such as coal and iron, which they did not have. This in turn drove them towards colonization, which they had observed was how the small island nation of Great Britain achieved and maintained her industries as well as her immense naval strength.

So successful were the Japanese in their efforts to Westernize for their own protection that they conquered and colonized Formosa (modern-day Taiwan) and much of the Korean peninsula before the end of the 19th century with their modern Westernized army and navy. While these had been important stepping stones, the ultimate test came at the start of the 20th century when the Japanese army and navy separately defeated two of the greatest Western forces in the world at that time, the massive Russian Army and mighty Russian Navy during the Russo-Japanese War of 1904–5.

While the Japanese had finally achieved their five-decade-old goal of being able to wage a modern industrial war on a scale that would allow them to resist colonizing Western powers and influences, the success of their defence through an ideology of adaptation had come at a cost. For to achieve the degree of Westernization that was required to resist the West, the Japanese had been force to significantly restructure their society. Many of the various imperial decrees and edicts that were implemented between the late 1860s and mid-1870s gradually began to undermine the elite position of the samurai within Japanese society. And while many of the nails in their collective coffin had already been driven in, the last four came in quick succession between 1871 and 1876, beginning with the *Danpatsurei* Edict of 1871, which ordered the samurai to cut off their distinctive top-knots and to adopt Western hair styles. This was followed in 1873 by the creation of an Imperial Army and universal conscription, which effectively severed the samurai class from its hereditary monopoly over all military matters. This devastating change was followed in short order by an equally destructive blow when the government abolished the stipend, the payment system by which all samurai in the service of a lord had survived for more than a millennium. The final nail was driven home in 1876 when the samurai were prohibited from wearing their swords, which had been a symbol of their elite position in Japanese society for centuries.

Fundamentally obsolete even before their former owners, the items of armour that the samurai had worn with pride for close to a millennium began to fill the curio shops across Japan as the toppled warrior class started to pawn off their possessions in an effort to make ends meet while they struggled to re-establish themselves in the new social order of post-feudal, Meiji period Japan.

That the samurai sold their possessions to survive is understandable. What is harder to fathom, however, is just how quickly the majority of them managed to disassociate themselves from the trappings of their former identity and the general indifference with which many of them seemed to have made the transition from being supposedly elite warriors at the top of the

Left: Sakamoto Ryōma, the famous anti-Shōgunate Tosa samurai who envisioned a modern, democratic Japan in the mid-1860s. Though a skilled swordsman, in keeping with his beliefs, Ryōma made it known that he carried a US military issue revolver and that he was prepared to use it.

Right: A Meiji period oil painting by Kinji Tamaki of the fifteenth and last Tokugawa Shōgun, Yoshinobu, in formal court attire in 1867. Yoshinobu resigned as Shōgun and returned power to the Emperor in November of the same year. (Kinji Tamaki/Wikimedia Commons/Public Domain)

social order to being soldiers in the new Imperial Army or policemen walking a beat.

No doubt this transition was made easier by the fact that, in reality, being a hereditary warrior had been a hard and unrewarding existence for many samurai for centuries, a large number of whom had lived most of their lives in semi-poverty, irrespective of their supposed elite status in society. The end of their kind was clearly a release for many of them who found hope and opportunity in the modernizing events that were occurring in Japan.

Whatever the reason, the fact remains that within a few short years a huge number of former samurai had discarded their arms and armour for the little bit of money they could get for them, which was almost certainly no more than the modern Western equivalent of pennies on the dollar. For few Japanese, other than the curio shop dealers, had any interest in acquiring the discarded husks of their former overseers, which most Japanese viewed as being archaic and utterly useless items. This was especially true at a time when anyone who was anyone amongst the new and up-and-coming social elite within post-feudal Japan was wearing frock coats and top hats in the European style.

There was one group, however, who had an almost insatiable appetite for anything to do with Japan and the recently defunct samurai

Shōgunate troops during the Boshin War. Note the astonishing metamorphosis of the samurai, who fifteen years after the arrival of Perry's 'black ships' in 1853 wear a strange combination of Western and Japanese attire and equipment, including carrying swords along with modern muskets.

class: the ultra-wealthy elite from Europe and the United States, who had started to flood into the country as tourists shortly after Japan had begun to open up her ports. For they were eager to see this mysterious island nation that the Western world was told had been locked away in time. This idea greatly appealed to the romantic Western mindset of the 19th century, and it was especially true of the social elite, who had both the means and time to idealize over the utopian ideal of what they thought was a purer form of pre-industrial society.

The preconceived ideas with which many foreign tourists came to Japan were heavily influenced by a flood of well-publicized photographs that naturally focused on images emphasizing views of Japan that added to the unique cultural mystique of that country and its people. Naturally, the samurai were a favourite theme for many of these early photographers, who had no qualms about paying peasants to dress up in discarded items of armour to achieve photographs of 'real samurai'.

The idea of the noble samurai warrior greatly appealed to Westerners, for it fitted well with their own view of the social order. For most European states were dominated by royal families and their interconnected social elites, the majority of whom dressed in military attire in keeping with the age-old practice of the officer class being filled with junior members of the nobility.

Thus the idea of a noble samurai warrior greatly appealed to most Westerners, who tended mistakenly to equate the samurai with the chivalrous European knights of old. Thus a considerable portion of the image surrounding the samurai that developed in the West was skewed from the start. For while Westerners tended to want to view the samurai in a way that better conformed to their own beliefs, many in Japan were just as happy to promote this ideal if it helped to keep these wealthy Western tourists coming.

Westerners who were keen to learn about the samurai were generally educated with answers that relied heavily on the mythology that had been popular through the latter half of the Edo period. For not only were such answers attractive, the Japanese themselves generally had nothing better to offer. Not surprisingly, these answers became the foundation upon which much of the Western image of the samurai and his armour evolved. As some of the oldest reference material on this subject matter, this information has been revisited for several generations now, to the point that despite much of it having been based on incorrect information, it has been referenced and quoted so many times over the past century and half that it is now a challenge to refute and deconstruct certain myths and misconceptions that continue to surround this subject matter.

In keeping with Western practices of this time, these early tourists loaded up on trophies as proof of their travels, which they shipped home to decorate their mansions. And Japanese armour was one of the items that few Westerners could leave Japan without, for the flamboyant and ancient-looking sets of samurai armour were for many of them the quintessential souvenir of the former feudal society.

An 1888 woodblock print by Inoue Tankei from his 'Famous Places in Tōkyō' series. The scene depicts a crowd gathered at the new, and very Western-style, Azuma bridge watching a torpedo being successfully tested in the Sumida River. Note the extremely Westernized appearance of the populace, which includes a number of soldiers and sailors. Many of the men are depicted wearing suits with bowler hats while the women are portrayed wearing skirts draped over prominent bustles. While this print almost certainly exaggerates the extent of Western fashion adoption amongst the majority of the populace, it depicts how the Japanese wanted themselves to be seen during the late 19th century.

The Westernization of Japanese Armour

An illustration by Kasai Torajirō depicting the capitulation of Russian troops to the Japanese at the battle of Teh-li-sz in June 1904, during the Russo-Japanese War. In defeating the huge Russian Army and powerful naval forces, Japan had achieved the goal it set for itself at the end of the Edo period. By mastering Western technologies and practices, the Japanese had levelled the playing field and were finally confident in their ability to resist the colonizing aspirations of the West. (Library of Congress, Prints & Photographs Division/ LC-DIG-jpd-02529)

Tokugawa Yoshinobu in the uniform of a French general of the empire of Napoleon III only a few years after he resigned as Shōgun. Yoshinobu's striking visual metamorphosis from supreme samurai warlord (see page 330) to Western-style military commander epitomises the phenomenal transformation that took place in Japan during the latter part of the 19th century as it raced to rapidly transition from feudal society into modern industrial state. (Image courtesy of Kazue Takamori, http://k-takamori.com/)

This fact was not lost upon the Japanese curio and pawn shop owners, whose stores lined the streets wherever foreign tourists were likely to be found. These shops were packed with 'fine collections of ancient armour' that could be 'purchased at a price that was really less than the value of the material', according the English clergyman, Biblical scholar and ornithologist, Henry Baker Tristram, who visited Japan in the early 1880s.[1]

As with astute businessmen anywhere, the Japanese curio shop dealers began to notice that their Western clientele favoured certain styles of armour over others, the least popular of which were not surprisingly the older, more simplistic looking and practical battleworthy sets. Thus they began to modify their merchandise to suit the tastes of their foreign clientele.

They did this by hiring retired and unemployed armour makers to refurbish sets in a way that made them more attractive to Westerners, who seemed to have had a penchant for items that were emblazoned with dragons and other rather clichéd east Asian symbols. Depending on the style of the *dō*, decorative additions such as this could be affixed, embossed or painted on the façade of a cuirass. If an armour was excessively plain in appearance, it was often disassembled and rebuilt. Bold colours of *odoshi-ge* were utilized and numerous decorative *kanamono* and bows fitted to the armour to help make it more appealing to the aesthetic tastes of these foreign tourists.

333

Samurai Armour

Thus after a period of time the armour began to cycle West and was no longer really an accurate reflection of what Japanese armour had been. Instead these items gradually metamorphosed

Left: A photograph of 'A General of the Fujiwara Epoch' from Ogawa Kazumasa's highly accurate 1893 publication *Military Costumes in Old Japan*. Note the warrior wears only a single *kote* armour sleeve to protect his bow arm as was correct prior to the 13th century. Also note the correct absence of *haidate* thigh armour. The warrior wears a cloth *eboshi* cap that would be worn under a helmet as additional padding.

Below: An image by the Meiji period photographer Felice Beato of a Japanese curio shop. The rapid fall of the samurai both socially and economically is represented by the large number of swords, firearms and items of armour included amongst the vendor's merchandise, all of which had once been synonymous with the elevated status of the hereditary warrior class. Note the use of wooden mannequins to display the sets of armour being offered for sale. The vendor's knowledge of armour was apparently limited to its monetary value for re-sale to foreign tourists, for he has the *sode* on back-to-front on one of the two displayed *gusoku*. (Image courtesy of The Phillips Museum of Art, Franklin & Marshall College)

The Westernization of Japanese Armour

into the idealized Western representation of what Japanese armour was expected to be, which in turn only further reinforced the stereotyped Western conception of these items.

One example of the kind of post-feudal-period items of samurai armour that the Japanese produced to satisfy foreign tastes are the *ryū uchidashi tetsu-sabiji jingasa*, or russet iron *jingasa* with embossed dragon motifs, which are still highly popular amongst collectors. Machine pressed, these attractive *jingasa* conical hats were then finished by hand to create the illusion that the embossing work had also been done by hand. Elaborate fixtures, such as ornate *tehen-no-kanamono*, were fitted to the central apex. Surrounding the *tehen-no-kanamono* across the upper surface of the *jingasa* were raised-in-relief designs of dragons coiling amongst stylized clouds. Not surprisingly, these *jingasa* were immensely popular with Western tourists, for they embodied many of the clichéd characteristics that most foreigners expected to find when it came to items associated with the samurai.

As the stocks of armour began to be depleted over the decades, Japanese antique dealers increasingly found themselves needing to refurbish items due to the fact that many sets of armour had begun to deteriorate from decades of storage and disuse. The more they restored or altered items, however, the more the finished products took on something of a generic appearance. This may have been due in part to a decline in the number of craftsman who were capable of doing such work, which meant that most of these items were produced by a relatively small number of individuals. Other factors more than likely also contributed to the growing degree of aesthetic similarity

Three different examples of Meiji period *uchidashi jingasa*. Note the striking similarities between all three pieces. The position of the dragon design is identical and has simply been placed in different positions around the *jingasa* after the swirling cloud-like motif had first been stamped. Gilt finishes and a different-shaped *kanamono* give each *jingasa* a unique appearance, even though they are fundamentally identical.

that had gradually crept in, including the relatively limited supply of parts and other materials that were available to restore these items. That said, the production of these items was still largely market-driven, and as such the items that were created must have reflected the desires of the clientele, most of whom continued to be Westerners well into the first few decades of the 20th century.

The vast majority of the armours that were created for this market were resurrected as red or orange *odoshi-ge*-laced examples of gold-lacquer finished *kiritsuke kozane ni-mai-dō gusoku* with *ō-sode*. These sets typically featured a ribbed *suji* or large external-rivet *hoshi-bachi* helmet that was fitted with the *kasa-jikoro* style of neck guard. The erect, stylized horn-like *kuwagata* flanges were almost always seated in a special holder, called a *kuwagata-dai*, that would be fitted to the front of the *kabuto* just above the visor. In many cases a large, *maedate* helmet crest in the form of a dragon would be affixed centrally between the *kuwagata*.

Ironically, as the political undertones in Japan moved that nation towards nationalism in the late 1920s and early 1930s, this style of armour, which had evolved to reflect Western tastes, began to become the poster-child of Japan's growing martial spirit even amongst the Japanese, the vast majority of whom, by the early part of the 20th century, were just as ignorant about the realities of Japanese armour as most Westerners were. Thus not only had the Westernizing of Japanese armour skewed the understanding of what samurai armour was to people outside Japan, it had gone on for so long that it had ultimately come full circle to the point where it also distorted the Japanese understanding of what samurai armour had once been. This is a fact that can still be seen in most reproductions of samurai armour that are produced in Japan to the present day.

By the early 1930s the once despised and archaic image of the samurai was itself being dusted off and refurbished by the increasingly nationalistic governments that ruled Japan, who were keen to tap into the largely mythical self-sacrificing martial nature of these warriors from their nation's recent past, whom they held up as exemplars of the sort of moral and spiritual fortitude that the state desired to kindle amongst its populace.

This created something of a revivalist movement amongst the Japanese, who for the first time since the end of their feudal period began to show a renewed degree of domestic interest in all things samurai, including their

Another posed Meiji period studio photograph by Baron Raimund von Stillfried. Only the man on the far left is for the most part correctly wearing what appears to be a largely complete set of full armour. The man second from the right is wearing *haidate* as shin coverings, while the man on the right is wearing his shin guards on the wrong leg, with the the left guard on the right leg and the right one on the left. Note that about half of the armour items being worn are either folding or collapsible designs of armour.

highly symbolic items of armour. While this trend may have caused few Japanese to acquire antique armours, families or individuals who still possessed such items began to display them with pride. For a considerable degree of prestige was associated with being able to connect one's family with the nation's martial heritage and the former warrior class, whose much-idealized images were used to promote everything from household products to the government's domestic and international agendas.

One of the positive by-products of the resurgent domestic interest in the samurai was the publication of some of the first in-depth Japanese texts on the subject of samurai armour, just as Arai Hakuseki's scrolls on armour had been produced in response to the early 18th century samurai's growing interest in the armour styles of their ancient forefathers. Paramount amongst these works were those published by Yamagami Hachirō and Suenaga Masao, the latter of whom produced a number of excellent reproductions of the proto-historical-period *keikō* and *tankō* forms of armour in an effort to understand how they had been constructed.

For samurai armour, the timing was excellent. As the majority of items that had not been sold abroad had, in most cases, lingered for close to 60 years or longer in storage, many items were now of an age or approaching an age when general maintenance-related restoration was going to be necessary to ensure their long-term preservation, a fact that most Japanese were more than likely unaware of by this time. For by the 1930s there were very few people still alive in Japan with any serious knowledge about samurai armour. In fact, by the 1930s few Japanese even knew how samurai armour was to be worn, though there was a considerable number of members of the former samurai class still alive. This was due to the fact that many of them had never owned armour or had an opportunity to wear a *gusoku* during the closing decades of the Tokugawa Shōgunate. And as the rest of the population had been strictly excluded from such knowledge and were for the most part indifferent to such matters, it is not surprising that several centuries' worth of practical knowledge of the wearing of armour had been virtually erased from the collective memory of the Japanese within less than three generations.

This trend was already evident in many of the posed photographs of 'samurai' from the early Meiji period. For many of the so-called 'noble warriors' in these images were clearly just models who had no idea how samurai armour was supposed to be worn, even though the images had been taken within as little as a decade or two of the end of the feudal period. This fact is attested to by the large number of images where 'samurai' are shown wearing items of armour incorrectly, backwards, or without some of the other various component pieces that were virtually universal to all *gusoku* by the latter part of the Edo period.

A prime example of just how little the average Japanese person knew about samurai armour by the late 1920s is recorded in an image that appeared in major newspapers and magazines all across Japan in 1928 in articles that covered the exploits of a certain Lieutenant Kanamura Koaki of the imperial Japanese Army. Kanamura, who was serving with the Manchuria-based Imperial Japanese Kwantung Army, became something of a national celebrity when he wore an Edo-era *dō* and *kabuto* into battle in Jinan, China, while fighting in one of the Kwantung Army's many unauthorized engagements during that era against Chiang Kai-shek's Chinese National Forces. In a much publicized press release Lieutenant Kanamura is seen posed in uniform holding a *zunari kabuto* and wearing what appears to be a *hotoke koshi-tori ni-mai-dō*. The cuirass, however, is clearly on backwards. This glaring error is made all the more obvious by the fact that the *gattari* is visible hanging suspended in the area of Kanamura's upper chest.

That Kanamura, who clearly took great pride in his martial heritage, seemed to be unaware of the fact that he was wearing the cuirass backwards is somewhat surprising, as

A picture of Lieutenant Kanamura of the imperial Japanese Army that was widely circulated in the Japanese press in 1928. While Kanamura was celebrated in Japan for his martial spirit for having worn samurai armour into battle while serving in Manchuria, his knowledge of armour was lacking. For as this photograph shows, he has the *dō* on backwards.

SAMURAI ARMOUR

the form of the *dō* itself should have made the front–back orientation of the cuirass more than obvious to even the most casual of observers. That he was able to wear it backwards around his fellow officers and soldiers, however, without any of them apparently noticing the incorrect orientation of the cuirass is likewise hard to believe. What is most surprising, however, is the fact that the photograph of Kanamura, wearing his armour backwards, made it into newspapers and magazines all across Japan. Thus it demonstrates just how little the Japanese in general knew about samurai armour by the late 1920s. For Japan was already well into its slide towards militaristic nationalism when this image was released, which therefore meant that even the military censors, liaison personnel and senior officers who approved the press release were by this time just as ignorant about armour as everyone else involved, from the photographer through to the people working for the press.

There is no better evidence of just how little the average person in Japan knew in the late 1920s about the samurai and the armour that they had worn than this image of Lieutenant Kanamura. For even the Japanese military, which had eagerly embraced the ideas of *bushidō*, had failed to notice this almost inconceivable error, and that at a time when the military in Japan were consciously and publicly pushing the idea that they were the inheritors of the noble traditions of the samurai and upholders of the way of the warrior. That this oversight occurred clearly demonstrates just how quickly a millennium's worth of historical tradition and knowledge relating to samurai armour had been flushed from the collective memory of the Japanese.

Ironically, Kanamura's well-documented exploits in samurai armour, which he apparently continued to wear backwards, were ultimately used against him as evidence of his militant nature during his war-crime trial in China after Japan's crushing defeat in 1945, which had resulted in the deaths of almost 5 per cent of the Japanese population and the destruction of most of the country's urban centres.

Aside from the immense and tragic loss in human life was the wide-scale destruction of a huge array of irreplaceable cultural and historical items that included a countless number of items of armour, the vast majority being destroyed by the devastating aerial fire-bombing campaign that the US Air Force conducted over Japan between 1944 and 1945, which on average gutted 40 per cent of the urban areas of sixty-six of Japan's largest cities.

Post-war Japan turned its back on militarism with the same speed and motivated forgetfulness

This well-known studio portrait of a 'samurai' published by Stillfried & Anderson in 1877 is clearly staged using a model. Like the photographer, the model did not understand how samurai armour was worn. It is clear that the model is not wearing thigh armour or proper under-armour attire. Furthermore the *sode* are on the wrong way around, with the right *sode* being worn on the left and the left *sode* on the right. This can be noted by the fact that narrow *kōgai-kanamono* plates fitted to the middle of the shoulder guards are facing forwards. These reinforcing fixtures should always point towards the rear of the wearer. (Library of Congress, Prints & Photographs Division/LC-USZC4-14302)

that it had on its feudal past at the end of the Tokugawa era. Samurai armour, with its obvious symbolic ties to the nation's failed, nationalistic militant policies, once again came to be seen by many as being archaic and superfluous items from a bygone age that was best forgotten. As such, many Japanese did what their grandparents had done almost exactly sixty years earlier; they began selling off the items of armour they owned for a fraction of what they were worth in order to make ends meet in Japan's devastated post-war economy.

The majority of these items once again found their way into the hands of the owners of the local curio and pawn shops, who were able to tap into an old and reliable market for these items: foreigners, who this time found themselves in Japan as part of the various Allied armies' post-war occupation forces.

Thanks in part to the pre-war Japanese military's efforts to merge its image with the ideal of the samurai, many troops amongst the occupying forces saw Japanese swords and items of antique samurai armour as the ultimate symbolic trophies of their defeated foe, and so once again these items poured out of Japan and into the curio cabinets of collectors across Europe and North America.

Samurai armour remained an item for export to foreign tourists well into the early 1960s, when Japan's incredible post-war economic recovery began to take hold. While the US had originally intended for Japan to revert into an agrarian society, it abruptly reversed this policy shortly after the outbreak of the Korean War, when it suddenly came to see Japan as an unsinkable offshore arsenal in its fight against communist expansion in Asia. Thus the Japanese, rather ironically, began producing military goods and other items for the United States, the same nation whose gunboat diplomacy had initially driven them to industrialize in a forlorn effort to stave off subjugation at the hands of the Americans.

The Korean War, Cold War and Vietnam War all greatly benefitted Japanese industry. And with the increasing prosperity that came with economic success the Japanese once again began to regain some of their national self-confidence. With this resurgence in national pride came a return to popularity of many of the nation's most iconic symbols, including samurai armour. For by the late 1970s, the

A famous 1942 propaganda poster produced by the Italian artist Boccasile Viaggiata to commemorate the Axis alliance and Japan's surprise attack on Pearl Harbour. This image was widely circulated in Japan irrespective of its highly inaccurate depiction of samurai armour. (Courtesy of MyMilitaria, Milan, Italy)

Japanese themselves were seeking ways to explain to the world how they had overcome their terrible defeat in 1945 to rise to become one of the world's leading industrial nations. Not surprisingly perhaps, they found the answer to this question in their samurai lineage. For it was the disciplined, loyal and determined nature of the descendants of a society infused with the traditions of the samurai that the Japanese said had allowed them to achieve such spectacular results, under such trying conditions, in such a short period of time.

As such, by the early 1980s, the ownership and display of a set of samurai armour was almost a prerequisite for any serious businessman or entrepreneur in Japan. Irrespective of a number of important external and internal factors, the incredible climb and success of the Japanese economy was increasingly linked not only to the unique characteristics and social structure of the Japanese people, but also to the long-ingrained martial traditions of *bushidō*. The Japanese businessman began to be compared to the noble, self-sacrificing and loyal samurai of old. Their incredible success in the hard-fought arenas of international business and finance was accredited to their adherence to and respect for their samurai heritage. They were 'samurai in suits', irrespective of the fact that only a small percentage of the Japanese population could claim to be the descendants of actual samurai.

Irrespective of the truth behind these self-aggrandizing illusions, which were widely then believed both domestically and abroad, from the perspective of samurai armour, Japan's post-war economic boom could not have occurred at a better time, for many of the surviving authentic items were beginning to show the first serious signs of natural deterioration from the effects of age by the 1970s. Thus the domestic revival that occurred in regards to the samurai and by association their items of armour almost certainly helped to ensure the long-term preservation of a huge number of items that might otherwise have been lost to history without the regular

The spirit of *bushidō*, or the 'way of the warrior' is often cited as having played an instrumental part in Japan's incredible post-war economic recovery and success. While the concept of *bushidō* as it is now understood actually came about in the early 20th century, long after the demise of the warrior class to whom it is attributed, this quasi-samurai-based ideology clearly did play a significant role in the operational mindset of many of Japan's post-war corporations and industries. The amalgamation of the 'warrior's code' and big business is more than evident in this 1973 photograph of models dressed in authentic sets of samurai armour being used to help promote a new line of Toyota vehicles at a London car show. (Photo by Keystone-France/Gamma-Rapho via Getty Images)

The Japanese 'salaryman' is commonly portrayed as the modern-day equivalent of the determined and self-sacrificing samurai. This concept first began to appear in the late 1920s as the Japanese state became progressively more militant and nationalistic in its domestic and international policies. (YOSHIKAZU TSUNO/AFP/Getty Images)

maintenance-related restoration work that is required to sustain them. Had the Japanese lacked either an interest in samurai armour or the disposable incomes that were available to many during this time, much of the important restorative work that took place during the latter half of the 20th century, during Japan's economic miracle, would more than likely never have taken place on the scale that it did.

The sharp rise in the domestic consumption of these items had other effects on the market for antique samurai armour as well. Firstly, it drove the price of these items dramatically higher. This in turn drastically shrank the export market to a mere trickle as Japanese dealers began to benefit from the convenience of doing business with a swelling number of domestic clientele who had deep pockets and a seemingly insatiable appetite for antique items of samurai armour. This situation ultimately led to a substantial number of items of armour that had been sold abroad being repatriated as Japanese dealers and collectors began to feel their way into the international market in their ongoing search to possess these items.

The higher price and increased demand for samurai armour also helped to draw many of the sets that had been stored away and largely forgotten in the corners and *kura* of Japanese homes for generations out and into circulation. This too was important as it helped to prevent many of these items from simply rotting away in storage to the point that they were no longer salvageable, as did unfortunately occur in a great number of cases due to Japan's generally hot and extremely humid climate.

As the price of antique armour surged, the use of old items of armour as movie props, which had been quite common in many of the samurai-related films produced up until the mid-1960s, suddenly dropped off, as this kind of use was no longer justified by their monetary value. This situation, along with the general degree of public interest in samurai armour, helped to give rise to a number of companies that began to produce the first 100 per cent reproduction items of samurai

The famous Japanese 'samurai' actor Mifune Toshirō, in a scene from the classic Kurosawa Akira film, *The Seven Samurai*. Until well into the early 1960s authentic items of samurai armour were commonly used in films with samurai themes. (AFP/AFP/Getty Images))

SAMURAI ARMOUR

armour. Many of these reproduction items were initially of excellent quality and were often astonishingly accurate in their overall method of construction and levels of aesthetic detailing.

The historical accuracy of some of the early sets of reproduction armour was most likely made possible by the fact that wages were still relatively low in Japan throughout the 1970s, while the monetary value of armour was by domestic standards quite high. As such, it was financially feasible to make high-quality reproductions, even with their painstakingly minute attention to detail, much of which was clearly copied from original period pieces.

Having said this, these items were reproductions. And while their façades were quite convincing, the actual methods of construction used often bore little resemblance to how authentic items of armour had been constructed. For example it was quite common for 'lamellar' sections to actually be solid resin boards that were made from moulds taken from lengths of actual *sane-ita*. As such, the creation of these items did not lead to a substantial revival in the understanding of how armour had traditionally been made. For the goals of the companies who produced such items was not to replicate how armour was made, but rather simply to replicate how it looked.

Much has changed in the Japanese antiques market in regards to items of samurai armour since the dizzying days of the country's rapidly expanding bubble economy, which ultimately burst in 1991. What happened to this market and how it operates today are discussed in detail in Volume II of this text along with a number of other important related topics, such as how the antique armour market was

A superbly crafted *yokohagi-okegawa ni-mai-dō gusoku* with an outstanding *naga-eboshi kabuto* made by the extremely talented *gendai katchū-shi* Fukube Ichirō. Numerous examples of this talented late-20th century smith's works can be found in well-known collections around the world where they are commonly incorrectly identified as being authentic period pieces of samurai armour.

flooded with a huge number of extremely well-made and high-quality modern reproductions and fakes during the closing decades of the 20th century. So well made were many of these items that today a surprising number of them can be found in important collections, both private and public, around the world.

Aside from covering the other components of Japanese armour that are not reviewed in this text, Volume II also takes an in-depth look at how samurai armour is appraised in Japan, and what is legally required to export these items abroad. Volume II also includes a buyer's guide, which covers in minute detail the sort of things that presumptive collectors should be checking for before they invest their hard-earned cash in antique items of samurai armour if they are not already extremely well acquainted with these items.

Part and parcel with buying these items is knowing how to properly set up and correctly display an antique set of samurai armour. Pre-display preparations, such as the form of display stand that should be used and some of the many environmental factors that need to be considered when choosing a suitable location for displaying these items, are therefore also discussed in Volume II. Accompanying this information is a step-by-step guide, supported by an in-depth array of photographs, that demonstrates how to erect a full set of Japanese armour for display in order to help ensure the long-term preservation of these fantastic historical items. Numerous line drawings and images that demonstrate how to properly tie the various cords and belts that commonly accompany these items are included to help ensure the historical accuracy of these presentations.

NOTES

Preface

1 Ikegami Eiko, *Bonds of Civility: Aesthetic Networks and the Political Origins of Japanese Culture* (New York, NY: Cambridge University Press, 2005), p. 7

Chapter 1

1 George A. De Vos and Hiroshi Wagatsuma, *Japan's Invisible Race: Caste in Culture and Personality* (Berkeley and Los Angeles: University of California Press, 1966), p. 15
2 Anthony Bryant, *Early Samurai AD 200–1500* (Oxford: Osprey, 1991), p. 7
3 Peter Duus, *Feudalism in Japan* (New York: Alfred A. Knopf, 1969), p. 21
4 George B. Sansom, *Japan: A Short Cultural History* (Stanford, CA: Stanford University Press, 1931), p. 199
5 Ibid., p. 102

Chapter 2

1 Stephen Turnbull, *Samurai: World of the Warrior* (Oxford: Osprey, 2003), p. 14
2 Ian Bottomley, *Japanese Armor: The Galeno Collection* (Berkeley, CA: Stone Bridge Press, 1998), p. 9
3 Ibid., p. 12
4 Ibid., p. 15

Chapter 3

1 Joseph Ryan and Gina Barnes, 'Armor in Japan and Korea' in Helaine Selin (ed.) *Encyclopaedia of the History of Science, Technology, and Medicine in Non-Western Cultures*, (Springer Netherlands, 2015)
2 Ian Bottomley and Jock Hopson, *Arms and Armour of the Samurai* (London: Bison Books, 1988), p. 9
3 Hashimoto Tatsuya, 'Kofun/Sangoku Jidai no Ita-yoroi no Keifu' [Development of plate armor in the Kofun and Three Kingdoms periods] in Okauchi Mitsuzane (ed.), *Gijutsu to Kōryū no Kōkogaku* (Tōkyō: Dōseisha, 2013), pp. 336–47
4 Dr Sasama Yoshihiko, *Nihon Dai Katchū Zu-Kan* [Large Illustrated Book of Japanese Armour] (Tōkyō: Kashiwa Shobō, 1988)
5 Hashimoto, 'Kofun/Sangoku Jidai no Ita-yoroi no Keifu'
6 Bottomley and Hopson, *Arms and Armour of the Samurai*, p. 13
7 Nakanishi, Ritta, *A History of Japanese Armour, Volume I: From the Yayoi Period to Muromachi Period* (Tōkyō: Dai Nippon Kaiga, 2009) p. 21
8 Bryant, *Early Samurai AD 200–1500*, p. 46
9 Ibid., p. 57

Chapter 4

1 Described by Thomas Conlan, 'Instruments of Change' in John A. Ferejohn and Frances McCall Rosenbluth (eds), *War and State Building in Medieval Japan* (Stanford: Stanford University Press, 2010), p. 131
2 Bottomley and Hopson, *Arms and Armour of the Samurai*, p. 31
3 Ibid., p. 32
4 Jacqui Carey, *Samurai Undressed* (Torquay: Devonshire Press, 1995), p. 60
5 Bryant, *Early Samurai AD 200–1500*, p. 48
6 Thomas Conlan, 'The Nature of Warfare in Fourteenth-Century Japan: The Record of Nomoto Tomoyuki', *Journal of Japanese Studies* vol 25, no. 2 (1999), p. 317
7 Ibid., p. 318
8 Ibid., p. 317
9 Bottomley and Hopson, *Arms and Armour of the Samurai*, p. 33
10 Hiramoto Yoshisuke, 'Joumon Jidai kara Gendai ni Itaru Kantouchihoujin Shinchou no Jidaiteki Henka' [Variation in Height over Time of the People of the Kantō Region from the Jōmon Period to the Present],

Journal of the Anthropological Society of Nippon, Vol. 80 (1972) No. 3, p. 221–36

11 Ibid.

12 Bottomley and Hopson, *Arms and Armour of the Samurai,* p. 54

13 Philip Haythornthwaite, *Weapons and Equipment of the Napoleonic Wars* (Poole: Blandford Press, 1979), p. 27

Chapter 5

1 www.sengokudaimyo.com/katchu/katchu.ch05.html

2 Sakakibara Kōzan, *The Manufacture of Armour and Helmets in Sixteenth Century Japan*, trans. T. Wakameda, ed. H. Russell Robinson (London: Holland Press, 1962) (originally published in Japanese as *Chūko Katchū Seisakuben*, Tōkyō, 1800), p. 93

3 Thomas Conlan, 'Instruments of Change' in John A. Ferejohn and Frances McCall Rosenbluth (eds), *War and State Building in Medieval Japan* (Stanford: Stanford University Press, 2010), p. 135

4 Sakakibara, *Manufacture of Armour and Helmets in Sixteenth Century Japan*, p. 95

5 Bottomley, *Japanese Armor: The Galeno Collection*, p. 14

6 Ibid., p. 15

7 Bottomley and Hopson, *Arms and Armour of the Samurai*, p. 105

8 Ibid., p. 92

9 For further discussion of this topic, see http://samuraiantiqueworld.proboards.com/thread/231/tatami-armor-used-pre-period

Chapter 6

1 Uezato Takashi, *Ryūkyū Sengoku Retsuden* [Ryūkyū Islands Warring States Series of Biographies] (Naha: Border Ink Publishing, 2015), p. 27

2 James D. Tracy (ed.), *The Political Economy of Merchant Empires: State Power and World Trade, 1350–1750* (Studies in Comparative Early Modern History), (Cambridge: Cambridge University Press, 1991) p. 188

3 Anthony Bryant, *The Samurai* (Oxford: Osprey, 1989), p. 51

4 Anthony Bryant, *Samurai 1550–1600* (Oxford: Osprey, 1994), p. 30

5 Itabashi Kuritsu Kyōdo Shiryōkan, *Katchū Nishi to Higashi* [Armour West and East] (Itabashi Kuritsu Kyōdo Shiryōkan, 2009)

6 Bottomley and Hopson, *Arms and Armour of the Samurai*, p. 106

7 Anthony Bryant, *Sengokyu Daimyo* website

8 Stephen Turnbull, *Samurai Heraldry* (Oxford: Osprey, 2002)

9 Bryant, *Samurai 1550–1600* (Oxford: Osprey, 1994), p. 46

10 Ibid., p. 31

11 Dr Sasama Yoshihiko, *Nihon Dai Katchū Zu-Kan* [Large Illustrated Book of Japanese Armour], p. 279

12 Sakakibara Kōzan, *Manufacture of Armour and Helmets in Sixteenth Century Japan*, p. 96

Chapter 7

1 Gwynne Dyer, *War* (London: Bodley Head, 1986), p. 57

2 Itabashi Kuritsu Kyōdo Shiryōkan, *Katchū Nishi to Higashi*

3 Dr Dirk J. Barreveld, *The Dutch Discovery of Japan, The True Story Behind James Clavell's Famous Novel Shogun*, (Lincoln, NE: Writers Club Press, 2001), p. 2008

4 Dr Sasama Yoshihiko, *Nihon Dai Katchū Zu-Kan* [Large Illustrated Book of Japanese Armour]

5 Sakakibara, *The Manufacture of Armour and Helmets in Sixteenth Century Japan*, p. 25

6 Bottomley and Hopson, *Arms and Armour of the Samurai*, p. 126

7 Sakakibara, *Manufacture of Armour and Helmets in Sixteenth Century Japan*, p. 98

8 Bottomley and Hopson, *Arms and Armour of the Samurai*, p. 92

9 Sakakibara, *Manufacture of Armour and Helmets in Sixteenth Century Japan*, p. 99

10 Dr Sasama Yoshihiko, *Nihon Dai Katchū Zu-Kan* [Large Illustrated Book of Japanese Armour], p. 232

11 Ibid., p. 232

12 Ibid., p. 233

Chapter 8

1 Ikegami Eiko, *Bonds of Civility*, p. 307.

2 Yamagami Hachirō, *Nihon katchū no shin kenkyū* [New Study of Japanese Armour] (Tōkyō: Yoyohatamachi Tōkyōfu, 1928)

3 Ibid., p. 1153

4 Dr Sasama Yoshihiko, *Zuroku Nihon no Katchū Bugu Jiten* [An Illustrated Encyclopaedia of Japanese Arms and Armour] (Tōkyō: Kashiwa Shobō, 1981), p. 234

5 Bottomley and Hopson, *Arms and Armour of the Samurai*

Chapter 10

1 Henry Baker Tristram, *Rambles in Japan: Land of the Rising Sun* (New York: F. H. Revell, 1895), p. 58

BIBLIOGRAPHY

Absolon, Trevor, *Toraba Collection, Gusoku Series, Volume 1: A Detailed Study of Tokugawa Clan & Bakufu Daimyō Samurai Armour Sets* (Victoria, BC: Digital Direct Printing, 2001)

——, *Watanabe Art Museum Samurai Amour Collection, Volume I: Kabuto and Mengu* (Victoria, BC: Digital Direct Printing, 2001)

Anderson, L.J., *Japanese Armour: An Illustrated Guide to the Works of Myōchin and Saotome Families from the Fifteenth to the Twentieth Century* (London: Arms and Armour Press, 1968)

Arai, Hakuseki, *Honchō Gunkikō* [General History of Military Discipline] (London: Charles E. Tuttle, 1964) (originally published 1722)

Barreveld, Dr Dirk J., *The Dutch Discovery of Japan, The True Story Behind James Clavell's Famous Novel Shogun*, (Lincoln, NE: Writers Club Press, 2001)

Bottomley, Ian, *Japanese Armor: The Galeno Collection* (Berkeley: Stone Bridge Press, 1998)

——, *An Introduction to Japanese Armour* (Leeds: Trustees of the Royal Armouries, 2002)

Bottomley, Ian and Hopson, Jock, *Arms and Armour of the Samurai* (London: Bison Books, 1988)

Bryant, Anthony, *The Samurai* (Oxford: Osprey, 1989)

——, *Early Samurai AD 200–1500* (Oxford: Osprey, 1991)

——, *Samurai 1550–1600* (Oxford: Osprey, 1994)

Carey, Jacqui, *Samurai Undressed* (Torquay: Devonshire Press, 1995)

Kei Kaneda Chappelear, *Japanese Armour Makers for the Samurai* (Tōkyō: Miyoshi, 1987)

Conlan, Thomas, 'The Nature of Warfare in Fourteenth-Century Japan: The Record of Nomoto Tomoyuki', *Journal of Japanese Studies* vol 25, no. 2 (1999), pp. 299–330

Conlan, Thomas, 'Instruments of Change' in John A. Ferejohn and Frances McCall Rosenbluth (eds), *War and State Building in Medieval Japan* (Stanford: Stanford University Press, 2010)

Dean, Bashford, *Catalogue of the Loan Collection of Japanese Armor* (New York: Metropolitan Museum of Art, 1903)

Duus, Peter, *Feudalism in Japan* (New York: Alfred A. Knopf, 1969)

Dyer, Gwynne, *War* (London: Bodley Head, 1986)

Hashimoto, Tatsuya, 'Kofun/Sangoku Jidai no Ita-yoroi no Keifu' [Development of Plate Armour in the Kofun and Three Kingdoms Periods] in Okauchi Mitsuzane (ed.), *Gijutsu to Kōryū no Kōkogaku* (Tōkyō: Dōseisha, 2013)

Haythornthwaite, Philip, *Weapons and Equipment of the Napoleonic Wars* (Poole: Blandford Press, 1979)

Hiramoto, Yoshisuke, 'Jōmon Jidai kara Gendai ni Itaru Kantouchihoujin Shinchou no Jidaiteki Henka' ['Variation in Height over Time of the People of the Kantō Region from the Jōmon Period to the Present'], *Journal of the Anthropological Society of Nippon*, vol. 80, no. 3 (1972), pp. 221–36

Ikegami, Eiko, *Bonds of Civility: Aesthetic Networks and the Political Origins of Japanese Culture* (New York, NY: Cambridge University Press, 2005)

Itabashi Kuritsu Kyōdo Shiryōkan, *Katchū Nishi to Higashi* [Armour West and East] (Itabashi Kuritsu Kyōdo Shiryōkan, 2009)

Kure, Mitsuo, *Samurai, An Illustrated History* (Tuttle: Tōkyō, 2001)

Miyazaki, Masumi and Yamagishi, Motō, *Nihon no Katchū Kiso Chishiki Shinsōban* [Japanese Armour Basic Knowledge New Edition] (Tōkyō: Yūzankaku, 2006)

Nakanishi, Ritta, *A History of Japanese Armour, Volume I: From the Yayoi Period to Muromachi Period* (Tōkyō: Dai Nippon Kaiga, 2009)

——, *A History of Japanese Armour, Volume II: From the Warring State Period to Edo Period* (Tōkyō: Dai Nippon Kaiga, 2009)

Robinson, H. Russell, *Japanese Arms and Armor* (New York: Crown, 1969)

Ryan, Joseph and Barnes, Gina, 'Armor in Japan and Korea' in Selin, Helaine (ed.) *Encyclopaedia of the History of Science, Technology, and Medicine in Non-Western Cultures*, (Springer Netherlands, 2015), pp. 1–16

Sakakibara, Kōzan, *The Manufacture of Armour and Helmets in Sixteenth Century Japan*, trans. T. Wakameda, ed. H. Russell Robinson (London: Holland Press, 1962) (originally published in Japanese as *Chūko Katchū Seisakuben*, Tōkyō, 1800)

Sansom, George B., *Japan: A Short Cultural History* (Stanford, CA: Stanford University Press, 1931)

——, *A History of Japan to 1334* (Stanford, CA: Stanford University Press, 1963)

——, *A History of Japan 1334–1615* (Stanford, CA: Stanford University Press, 1961)

——, *A History of Japan 1615–1867* (Stanford, CA: Stanford University Press, 1963)

Sasama, Dr Yoshihiko, *Nihon no Mei Kabuto* [Famous Japanese Helmets], 3 volumes (Tōkyō: Yūzankaku, 1972)

——, *Zuroku Nihon no Katchū Bugu Jiten* [An Illustrated Encyclopaedia of Japanese Arms and Armour] (Tōkyō: Kashiwa Shobō, 1981)

——, *Nihon Dai Katchū Zu-Kan* [Large Illustrated Book of Japanese Armour] (Tōkyō: Kashiwa Shobō, 1988)

Starley, D., *The Metallurgy of Japanese Plate Armour* (R. A. AM1973) (Leeds: Royal Armouries Museum, 2006)

Stone, George Cameron, *A Glossary of the Construction, Decoration and Use of Arms and Armor in all Countries in all Times* (New York: Jack Brussel, 1961) (originally published Portland, ME by the Southworth Press, 1934)

Suenaga, Masao, *Nihon Jōdai no Katchū* [Ancient Period Japanese Armour] (Ōsaka: Somotosha, 1944)

Suzuki, Masaya, *Teppō to Nihonjin* [Guns and the Japanese] (Tōkyō: Chikumashobō, 2000)

——, *Katana to Kubitori: Sengoku Kassen Isetsu* [Sword and Neck Taking: Sengoku Battle Episodes] (Tōkyō: Shinso, 2000)

Tracy, James D. (ed.), *The Political Economy of Merchant Empires: State Power and World Trade, 1350–1750* (Studies in Comparative Early Modern History), (Cambridge: Cambridge University Press, 1991)

Tristram, Henry Baker, *Rambles in Japan: Land of the Rising Sun* (New York: F. H. Revell, 1895)

Turnbull, Stephen, *The Book of Samurai, The Warrior Class of Japan* (London: PRC, 1982)

——, *Samurai Heraldry* (Oxford: Osprey, 2002)

Uezato, Takashi, *Ryūkyū Sengoku Retsuden* [Ryūkyū Islands Warring States Series of Biographies] (Naha: Border Ink Publishing, 2015)

De Vos, George A. and Wagatsuma, Hiroshi, *Japan's Invisible Race: Caste in Culture and Personality* (Berkeley and Los Angeles: University of California Press, 1966)

Yamagami, Hachirō, *Nihon Katchū no Shin Kenkyū* [New Study of Japanese Armour] (Tōkyō: Yoyohatamachi Tōkyōfu, 1928)

Websites

Bryant, Anthony, *Sengoku Daimyō* http://www.sengokudaimyo.com/

The Samurai Armour Forum http://thesamuraiarmourforum.com/

The Samurai Archives http://www.samurai-archives.com/

Samurai Archives Japanese History Podcast http://www.samuraipodcast.com/

IMAGE SOURCES

The following sources have provided images for use in this publication:

Allen Antiques
www.allenantiques.com

The Beinecke Rare Book & Manuscript Library
beinecke.library.yale.edu/

Kyōto Costume Museum
www.iz2.or.jp

Gunma Prefectural Museum of History
grekisi.pref.gunma.jp

Historiographical Institute of the University of Tōkyō
www.hi.u-tokyo.ac.jp/index.html

Hokkaidō University Northern Studies Collection
www2.lib.hokudai.ac.jp/hoppodb/ [pending]

The J. Paul Getty Museum
www.getty.edu/art/collection/

Kansai University Museum
www.kansai-u.ac.jp/Museum/index.html

Kasugataisha Shrine
www.kasugataisha.or.jp

Katchushi Armour Studio
www.katchushi.com

The Lavenberg Collection of Japanese Prints
www.myjapanesehanga.com

Library of Congress
www.loc.gov/collections/

The Metropolitan Art Museum
www.metmuseum.org/art/collection

Miyakonojō Shimazu Residence
www.city.miyakonojo.miyazaki.jp/shimazu/

Nikkō Tōshōgū Shrine
www.toshogu.jp/english/shrine

Ōme Municipal Museum of Provincial History
www.ome-tky.ed.jp/shakai/kyodo/

Ōsaka University Department of Archaeology
www.let.osaka-u.ac.jp/kouko/

Tachibana Museum
www.tachibana-museum.jp/

Tōkyō National Museum
www.tnm.jp/?lang=en

The Tom Burnett Collection
www.tomburnettcollection.com

The Walters Art Museum
art.thewalters.org/browse/

Yamanashi Prefectural Museum
www.museum.pref.yamanashi.jp

GLOSSARY

abara-dō — Literally 'ribbed cuirass'. A grotesque form of cuirass shaped to replicate the appearance of ribs on the human torso, either by embossing or through the application of lacquer.

aida-no-kanamono — See *hassō-no-kanamono*.

agemaki — A large bow suspended from an *agemaki-no-kan* fitted to the rear of a *dō*. The cords used to control the movements of the *sode* were tied to the *agemaki*. Primarily an accoutrement on *tosei-dō*.

agemaki-no-kan — A swivel-ring form of *kanamono* providing an anchoring point to fasten cords, commonly fitted to the rear of a *dō*.

aibiki-no-o — A set of four *kohaze-* or *seme-kohaze-*strung cords that make up the shoulder strap fastening on a *tosei dō*.

akabe-yoroi — A form of gorget that was often worn in conjunction with the *tankō* and *keikō* forms of cuirass.

asa — Hemp.

ashigaru — Literally 'light feet'. Low-ranking samurai foot soldiers.

aya — Twill.

aya odoshi-ge — Lacing made from twill or a twill sheath wrapped around an inner core of an alternative fabric.

boko-no-ita — The uppermost solid horizontal plate piece across the rear of a cuirass to which the *wadagami* are attached on a *tosei-dō*.

bushi-haniwa — Terracotta statues of warriors made in Japan between the 3rd and 6th century AD.

byakudan — Clear lacquer applied over a gold leaf, producing a rich golden-yellow coloured finish.

byō-dome — Literally 'rivet-stopped'. Items of armour fastened together using rivets. This term is predominantly associated with pre-10th century forms of cuirass such as the *tankō*.

byō-toji — Literally 'rivet-closed'. A *tosei-dō* term that describes a cuirass assembled from *ita-mono* secured together by rivets.

byō-toji-dō — A variety of *tosei-dō* assembled using rivets where the rivet heads are large and feature prominently in the finished appearance of the cuirass.

chidori — The Japanese term for a pattern that resembles a plover.

chirimen — Crepe silk. A unique Japanese silk weave that produces subtle wrinkles in the fabric.

chotsugai — Knuckled hinge.

chotsugai kugi — Hinge pin.

daimyō — A feudal samurai warlord and ruler of an independent *kuni* or 'country', who was beholden only to the Shōgun. A *daimyō*'s *kuni* was often a hereditary domain.

dangae — Literally 'step changing cuirass'. A style in which the method of lacing abruptly changes from one style to

	another between the top and bottom half of the armour piece.
dangae-dō	A *dō* the lacing of which changes between the top and bottom half of the cuirass (e.g. from *sugake odoshi* to *kebiki odoshi*).
dan odoshi	A lacing pattern in which two different colours of *odoshi-ge* are strung in a repetitive pattern of alternating horizontal bands.
dansen-osame-no-kan	See *tenugui-no-kan*.
de-hassō	A term that can be used to refer to any generally rectangular *kanamono* fixture of which the horizontal ends protrude outward in soft arrow-head-shaped points.
dō	A cuirass.
dō-jime	A length of sturdy cord that would be anchored around the *kurijime-no-o-no-wana* to tie a cuirass closed around the waist.
dō-maru	A late 14th-century term used to refer to a scale armour that wrapped around the torso and closed vertically down the right-hand side of the torso. Prior to the late 14th century the *dō-maru* was referred to as the *haramaki*.
dō-maru yoroi	A short-lived hybrid version of the *haramaki* (later *dō-maru*) cuirass produced in the late 12th to early 13th centuries, which resembled the *yoroi* in appearance, with square sides and a *tsurubashiri* fitted to the frontage of the cuirass.
e-gawa	Leather featuring a printed or stencilled decorative pattern or design on one surface.
Emishi	A term used to refer to the primarily non-Japanese descendants of the early indigenous peoples which inhabited the northern areas of the Japanese island of Honshū from around the 8th century to the 14th century AD.
eri-dai	A padded shoulder yoke. *Eri-dai* were commonly fabricated with an integral *eri-mawashi* brigandine collar and in some cases *kobire*.
eri-mawashi	A form of brigandine armour collar, commonly comprising outline-stitched *kikkō* or *kusari* sandwiched between layers of fabric.
fudo-no-e-gawa	A distinctive variety of *e-gawa* depicting the warlike Buddhist diety Fudo Myō-ō and his attendants.
fukigaeshi	Erect flanges that are either extensions of, or additions to, one or more of the upper bands of a *shikoro* that stand upright along either side of the visor of a *kabuto*.
fukurin	A form of decorative edge trim moulding made of leather or metal, commonly applied to items of armour. It is common for metal *fukurin* to be gilded and to feature etched designs.
fusebe-gawa	A yellow or brown variety of smoked leather sometimes featuring decorative patterns.
fusegumi	An ornate and complex form of decorative silk thread piping used to stitch together and cover the seam where a section of *kobire-gawa* butts up against a section of *e-gawa*.
gakibara-dō	A grotesque style of *tosei-dō* which replicates the bloated and bony torso of a traditional form of Japanese ghost called a *gaki*, either by embossing or the application of lacquer.
gattari	A bracket, commonly mounted between the shoulder blades on the back of a cuirass, that is used to secure the upper end of the holder that allows a *sashimono* battle flag to be affixed to a *dō*.
gessan	A term used after the mid-16th century to refer to the protective hip armour tassets suspended from the lower edge of a *tosei-dō*.

goken-no-kusazuri	A term used to refer to a unique arrangement of five *kusazuri* suspended from a *haramaki*.	*hara-ate*	An abbreviated form of cuirass that only covered the front and side of the torso.
go-mai-dō	A cuirass formed from five independent though conjoined vertical sectional pieces of armour.	*haramaki*	A late Heian and Kamakura period form of *dō* primarily worn by retainers, which wrapped around the body and closed down the right-hand side of the torso. From the 14th century onward the term *haramaki* refers to a cuirass that wraps around the body and that closes down the middle of the back.
gumi-kanamono	See *sode-tsuke-no-kuda*.		
gusoku	A complete set of armour. This term primarily refers to armour from after the mid-16th century.		
gyōyō	Small protective plates, commonly leaf-shaped, originally designed to protect the upper shoulders. They were suspended from the *wadagami* of non-*yoroi* makes of *dō* from the 13th century onward to protect the shoulder strap cords.		
		Haruta	A renowned school of Japanese armour makers. One of the oldest documented working guilds of *katchū-shi* and one of the first groups to sign the pieces they produced.
haidate	A bifurcated, or split, apron-like form of thigh guard amour.	*hassō-no-byō*	A large split-shank domed rivet. The head of the rivet is commonly made in the form of a chrysanthemum. Originally used to anchor sections of *sane-ita* to the *kanagu mawari*.
hajikami-gattari	A unique form of two-piece *gattari* that could scissor or pivot on itself, allowing for the bracket to be removed when it was not being used to hold an *uke-zutsu*.		
		hassō-no-kanamono	A form of rectangular and often ornately decorated washer used in conjunction with the *hassō-no-byō*. Sometimes also referred to as *aida-no-kanamono*.
hamiawase	A method of assembling *kusari* in which the severed ends of the individual rings are aligned and butted together.		
han	A domain. A term associated with the territories and membership of a feudal dynastic warrior clan.	*hatomune*	A cuirass that features a prominent medial ridge down the centre of the *mae-dō*.
hanakami-bukuro	Literally 'nose tissue bag'. Small pockets affixed to either façade of a *dō* or to the reverse of one or more *gessan*. Alternatively sometimes also referred to as *mae-bukuro* (front bag), *kusuri-ire* (medicine holder) or *tsuba-ate* (hilt touch).	*hidari-dō-no-ita*	An independent sectional piece of armour made to cover the the left-hand side of the torso.
		hidari-waki-dō	Left-hand side armpit plate. Part of the *kanagu mawari*.
		hikae-no-o	A cord on the lower right-hand edge of a *kyūbi-no-ita* used to prevent the plate from swinging.
hanare-yamamichi-gashira	Literally 'separated mountain paths leading edge'. A romanticized name used to describe a specific pattern of undulating edge cut along the upper horizontal length of a section of *ita-mono*.	*hikiawase-no-o*	Literally 'draw-together cord'. Cords attached to both sides of a cuirass, used to pulled the *dō* closed where the two edges come together.
		hinawajū	See *tanegashima*.
hanbō	A 'half mask'. An early form of *mengu* that only covered and protected the chin and cheeks.	*hira-yamamichi-gashira*	Literally 'even mountain path leading edge'. A romanticized name used to describe a specific pattern of

	undulating edge cut along the upper horizontal length of a section of *ita-mono*.
hishinui	A cross-knot. A structural binding on scale armour and an aesthetic detail on plate armour.
hishinui-no-ita	The lowest suspended *sane-ita* on a scale armour. Will feature *hishinui*.
hishi-toji	Structural cross-knot bindings anywhere on an item of armour other than the *hishinui-no-ita*, which are used to secure sections of plate or scale armour together.
hishiki gessan	The two rearmost *gessan* on a *tosei-dō*.
hitsushiki-no-kusazuri	The two rearmost *kusazuri* on pre-*tosei-dō* designs of cuirass. Refers to a single *kusazuri* on a *yoroi*.
hōkei-ita	A generally rectangular plate used to construct *tankō*.
hotei-dō	Literally 'Buddha cuirass'. A variety of *tosei-dō* that is embossed or finished to create a façade that resembles the smooth naked torso of an overweight male, or more specifically a Buddhist diety. While similar to a *gakibara-dō* in appearance, *hotei-dō* are devoid of exposed or protruding ribs.
hotoke	An aesthetic style in which a *tosei-dō* is fabricated or finished to have a smooth façade.
hotoke-dō	A *tosei-dō* fabricated or finished with a smooth external façade.
ichi-mai-dō	Any form of cuirass that is assembled as one continuous piece, such as a *haramaki*.
ichi-mai-maze	A method of assembling *sane-ita* whereby leather and iron scales are used in an alternating pattern in a one-to-one ratio.
ichimonji-gashira	*Kozane* that are generally rectangular in shape with a flat upper edge line.
ichimonji	A rounded, triangular in cross-section strip of *e-gawa*-sheathed wood fitted to the rear of a scale armour to help disguise the height difference between the *oshitsuke-no-ita* and *kesho-no-ita* where the two plates are laced together.
imuke-no-kusazuri	The left-hand *kusazuri* on a *yoroi*. Can also be applied to two or more *kusazuri* suspended from the left-hand side of any other form of pre-*tosei* design of cuirass.
inu-gawa	Literally 'dog hide'.
iri-hassō	A term that can be used to refer to any generally rectangular *kanamono* fixture where the horizontal ends of the piece are incised inwards with soft arrow-head-shaped indentations.
isei-dō	Any form of *tosei-dō* that does not conform in its method of construction with any of the other major identified styles of cuirass, e.g. a cuirass assembled from eight conjoined sectional pieces.
isei-gusoku	Any full set of armour that is assembled around an unconventional *isei-dō* style of cuirass.
ita-mono	A flat board-like section of armour made from a solid plate of metal or leather.
ito-bishi	Literally 'cord diamonds'. A term used to refer to *hishinui* that have been formed using woven cotton, hemp or silk *odoshi-ge*. Commonly translated to mean 'laced diamonds'.
ito odoshi-ge	Literally 'cord lacing hair'. Woven lacing made from materials such as cotton and hemp.
ieji	Cloth.
iyozane	A broad form of scale arranged so as to have minimal overlap between neighbouring scales. *Iyozane* can feature several different styles of *sane-gashira*.
jabara-ito	Literally 'serpent's belly'. Multi-coloured braided cords used as

GLOSSARY

	piping, commonly used during the Edo period as a substitute for *fusegumi*.
jikabari	Literally 'directly applied'. This term is used when leather or fabric is adhered directly to the interior surface of the cuirass to form a liner.
jingasa	A form of shallow hat, generally conical in shape.
Jōmon	A period in early Japanese history, from around 14,500 BC to AD 300. This term can also be used to collectively refer to the first recognizable communities of indigenous peoples who lived in Japan.
jūji-gusari	Literally 'cross mail'. See *kōshi-gusari*.
kabuto	A helmet inclusive of the *shikoro* neck guard.
Kaga-dō	A *tosei-dō* produced in the Kaga region of Japan between the mid-17th and mid-18th centuries by armour makers employed by the Maeda *han*.
kaji-kabuto	A unique form of lightweight fire-helmet fitted with a protective cloth face- and neck-guard cape, worn by samurai while employed in fire-fighting efforts during the Edo period.
kaki-bishi	Literally 'brushed diamond'. Refers to *hishinui* that have red lacquer applied over them to highlight their presence when otherwise obscured under *urushi*.
kami-zane	Literally 'paper scale'. *Sane* that are fabricated from multiple layers of waste paper glued together.
kamon	A heraldic Japanese family crest.
kan	A swivel-ring.
kanagu mawari	Literally 'metal pieces all around'. A generic term for all of the solid upper body plate portions of a cuirass. Originally always fabricated from metal, the *kanagu mawari* on a pre-*tosei* cuirass can include the *muna-ita*, *oshitsuke-no-ita*, all *waki-ita* if present, and the *wadagami*. On a *tosei-dō* the *kanagu mawari* are represented by the *oni-damari-no-ita*, *boko-no-ita*, all *waki-ita* and the *wadagami*.
kanamono	A generic term that can be applied to any metal fixture affixed to an item of armour. *Kanamono* are used for both practical and structural purposes as well as for aesthetic reasons.
kanmuri-no-ita	The uppermost solid plate on a *sendan-no-ita*, *kyūbi-no-ita*, or *sode*.
Kantō-dō	An alternative name for a distinctive variety of *go-mai-dō* originally produced and commonly favoured in the northern Tōhoku region of Japan. Also referred to as Ōshū-dō and Sendai-dō.
kara aya odoshi	A form of *odoshi-ge* that features an inner band of fabric covered by an external sheath of imported Chinese twill.
karage	Horizontal or lateral bindings used on pre-*yoroi* makes of armour to bind individual *sane* together to form rows.
kara kozane	A *kozane* scale moulded so as to have a subtle S-like cross-section, giving the scale a roof-tile-like appearance.
karakuri-gusari	A form of kusari where the cut ends of the individual rings of mail are closed together using small round rivets.
karami-no-ana	The uppermost holes in a *kozane* through which the connective *kedate* portions of lacing are strung and drawn upwards towards the next lamellar section. The top hole in the left-hand column of apertures and the top two holes on the right-hand column of holes in a conventional *kozane* are all collectively referred to as *karami-no-ana*. The one additional hole in the upper left-hand column

	of apertures on an *iyozane* scale is also referred to as *karami-no-ana*.
katahada-nugi dō	Literally 'bare-shoulder cuirass'. A unique variety of *niō-dō* that is fabricated to have a façade that looks as though one shoulder has been bared in the manner typical of practitioners of Japanese *kyūdō* (traditional archery).
katchū	Literally 'armour and helmet', this is a generic term for Japanese armour. Derived from the Sino-Japanese reading for the kanji characters for the words *yoroi* and *kabuto*.
karuta-gane	A rectangular protective plate of armour. *Karuta-gane* can vary, but generally are card-like in size. The name is derived from the Portuguese word *carta* meaning playing card, which were introduced to Japan in the 16th century.
karuta katabira	A coat-like protective garment that features either an internal or external layer of card-shaped *karuta-gane* protective plates, which were commonly fastened together by intermediate bands of *kusari*.
kasa-jikoro	A wide and often almost horizontal umbrella-like design of *shikoro* neck guard affixed to a *kabuto* helmet.
kata-o	Literally 'shoulder cord'. A cord anchored to the *tsubo-no-o* that was worn over the shoulder and diagonally across the body to help keep a *waidate* in position against the right side of the torso.
kata-tsumadori odoshi	A lacing pattern in which an upward-pointing wedge, created through the use of one or more contrasting colours of *odoshi-ge*, is created down the edge of a laced section of armour.
katchū-shi	A Japanese armour maker or armourer.
kawa-bishi	A term used to describe *hishinui* that have been bound using dyed lengths of leather.
kawa-fukurin	A narrow band of leather that has been laced, stitched or otherwise adhered to and around the exterior edge of an item of armour.
kawa-shiki	A reinforcing leather strip.
kawa-toji	Leather thongs used to bind sectional pieces or armour plating together.
kawa-tsuzumi	Literally 'leather-wrapped'. A section of plate or scale armour of which the façade is covered with a panel of smoked or dyed leather.
kawa-zane	A scale made from *nerigawa*.
kawa odoshi-ge	Literally 'leather lacing hair'. A narrow strip of dyed, smoked or stencilled leather approximately 1 cm in width, used for lacing.
kebiki odoshi	Literally 'hair spread all over'. Commonly referred to as 'full lacing', *kebiki odoshi* is a closely spaced method of lacing used with scale and replicated scale makes of armour.
kebori	Literally 'hair engraving'. Fine engraved-line designs commonly etched into the façades of the various *kanamono* fitted to a set of armour.
kedate-no-ana	The holes in a *kozane* through which the connective *odoshi-ge* from a lower length of *sane-ita* are threaded. On a *kozane* scale the *kedate-no-ana* are the second hole from the top in the left-hand column of apertures and the third hole from the top in the right-hand column. On an *iyozane* scale the *kedate-no-ana* are the third hole from the top of the scale in both columns of apertures.
keikō	A 5th century form of lamellar armour.
keshō-no-ita	A leather-covered strip of wood that clamps down and covers the *sane-gashira* of a length of *sane-ita* where it is affixed to a solid plate.
kikkō	Literally 'tortoiseshell'. A type of brigandine made in the form of small

	hexagonal leather or iron plates, generally laced to an internal layer of fabric that is covered and backed before being outline-stitched. Also sometimes referred to as *kikkō-gane* if the brigandine is made of metal.
kikkō katabira	A coat-like protective garment that is either covered with or features an internal quilted layer of *kikkō*.
kinkara-gawa	Imported Dutch leather with gilt finishes and embossed designs.
kinpaku	Literally 'gold pressed'. The term refers to gold leaf, which is sometimes adhered to armour surfaces with lacquer.
kintama-kakushi	Literally 'golden ball hiding'. An apt name for the middle *gessan* suspended from the *mae-dō* portion of a *tosei-dō* that covers the groin area.
kinu	Silk.
kinu-ito odoshi-ge	Literally 'silk cord lacing hair'. Lacing woven using silk. As silk lacing was extremely common, the term *odoshi-ge* is fundamentally synonymous with the concept of lacing made from silk.
kiritsuke kozane	A solid plate with an applied lacquer finish that is intentionally crafted to make the *ita-mono* look as though it is a length of *sane-ita* assembled from individual scales.
kiwame fuda	Armour appraisal certificates, first issued in the early 18th century by Myōchin Munesuke and his grandfather Kunimichi. While valuable in themselves, the historical accuracy of these appraisal certificates is highly dubious.
kobire	Small subtly convex and generally half-oval plates or sections of quilted brigandine affixed to the outside edges of the *wadagami* on *tosei-dō* to protect the upper shoulders.
kobusa	A small, specially tied knotted bow in the shape of a crucifix. Originally suspended from swivel rings affixed to the rear of helmet bowls, but also commonly suspended from fixtures such as the *saihai-no-kan* on Edo period *gusoku*.
ko-gusoku	A term used to refer to the items of armour that were put on during a preparatory stage before donning a *yoroi*. Initially the *ko-gusoku* consisted of the *waidate* and *suneate* only, but by the late 14th century it also included the wearing of a single *kote* on the left arm and a *nodowa*.
kokusa	A special thick mix of *urushi*, often mixed with fibres, that was used to build up thick base layers on *kozane*.
kōmori-tsuke	An intermediate band of reinforced leather used to connect one section of armour to another.
kon	Indigo blue.
koshi-gusari	Small panels of fabric that either feature mail-covered façades or internal layers of *kusari*, and which are suspended by a belt or toggles from the base of a cuirass to provide additional protection for the exposed areas of the lower torso behind the *yurugi-ito*.
kōshi-gusari	Mail arranged in an open grid-like pattern. Commonly used on the inner arm of *kote* as this arrangement allowed the arm to flex without the mail binding onto itself or bulking up on the inside of the elbow. Sometimes referred to as *jūji-gusari*.
koshi-kawa-tsuke gessan	Literally 'waist leather applied hip armour'. Removable *gessan* that are attached by means of toggles or cords to the base of a cuirass. Can be in the form of one continuous belt of *gessan* or several independently attached *gessan* pendants.
koshi-makura	Literally 'lower back pillow'. A small stuffed pillow of fabric or leather placed behind the base of a *machi-uke* to absorb some of the reflexive strain placed on the holder.

koshi-o	A length of cord fastened to a *waidate* that is used to anchor it around the waist. This term is also used to refer to the belt-like straps used to tie a *haidate* around the waist.
koshi-tori	Literally 'waist around'. An aesthetic feature where the lower bands of the nagakawa of a *sugake odoshi*-laced cuirass with an *iyozane* façade are fabricated from *kozane* or with *kiritsuke kozane* façades and laced in *kebiki odoshi*.
koshi-zane	Literally 'waist scale'. Long, specialized scales used to connect the upper half of a lamellar *keikō* with the lower skirt of the cuirass.
kote	An armoured sleeve.
kote-bukuro	The fabric sleeve bodice portion of a *kote*.
kote-ura	The inner liner fabric layer of a *kote-bukuro*.
kōtetsu	Steel.
kozakura-gawa	Literally 'small cherry blossom leather'. A variety of *e-gawa* that features a pattern of small cherry blossom offset against a background field of a contrasting colour, such as white on blue, or green on yellow.
kozane	Literally 'small scale'. A common variety of scale. Can be rawhide or metal.
kuchi-gane	Literally 'mouth metal'. A metal end cap fitted to the upper end of an *uke-zutsu*.
kuda	A small tubular metal bead threaded over a closed loop of cord to protect it from wear. See *sode-tsuke-no-kuda*.
kumihimo	Long lengths of leather applied vertically to the façade of a lamellar armour. The heads of the *sane* in each row of scales were individually laced to the connective *kumihimo*.
kurijime-no-o-no-wana	Literally 'pull cord tight loop'. A closed loop of cord secured to the base of a *dō* that provides an anchor point to attach a *dō-jime* for cinching a cuirass tightly closed around the waist.
kurijime-no-kan	A curved metal tube slid over a *kurijime-no-o-no-wana* to protect the cord from wear when a *dō-jime* cord is looped around it.
kusari	Mail.
kusari katabira	A coat-like protective garment that is either covered with or features an internal quilted layer of *kusari*.
kusazuri	The protective hip armour pendants suspended from the base of pre-mid-16th century forms of cuirass.
kusuri-ire	See *hanakami-bukuro*.
kuwagata	A pair of decorative stylized horn-like appendages that are worn fitted to a *kabuto*.
kyūbi-no-ita	A long, narrow protective plate that was suspended from the left-hand *wadagami* of a cuirass, designed to help protect the left armpit area of the torso.
mabizashi	The visor-like portion of a *kabuto*.
mae-bukuro	See *hanakami-bukuro*.
mae-dō	The area of a cuirass, such as the front section of a *ni-mai-dō,* that protects the front half of the torso. When the *mae-dō* is an independent solid piece of armour that protects the front of the torso, such as in the case of a *go-mai-dō*, it is referred to as *mae-dō-no-ita*.
mae-dō-no-ita	An independent solid piece of armour that protects the front of the torso.
mae-migi-dō-no-ita	An independent sectional piece of armour made to cover the front right-hand side of the torso. Universal to *go-mai-dō*. May also be found utilized on the *san-mai, yon-mai* and *roku-mai-dō*.
mae-no-kusazuri	The front *kusazuri* on a *yoroi* or the middle *kusazuri* suspended from a *mae-dō* or frontal portion of a pre-*tosei* design of cuirass.

mae-tateage	The protective areas of armour between the top of the *nagakawa* and the base of the *muna-ita* on pre-*tosei-dō* forms of cuirass or the *oni-damari-no-ita* of a *tosei-dō*.
maki-dome	Literally 'wrap tied'. Long cords secured to the cuff of a *kote-bukuro* that are wrapped around the cuff of the sleeve and tied when the latter is being worn.
maki-e	Decorative designs applied to lacquered finishes that are created through the skilful application of sprinkled granules or small individually positioned flecks of gold, silver and other alloy metals on wet lacquered surfaces.
makikomi fukurin	A rounded edge trim created by rolling the upper edges of solid metal plates over upon themselves.
manchira	A form of brigandine vest that is designed to be worn under a cuirass as auxiliary armour.
maru-gattari	A *gattari* bracket of which the central holder is made circular in shape to receive a round *uke-zutsu*.
maruhimo	Literally 'round cord'.
mei-mi-no-ana	A small opening intentionally tailored or crafted in a liner to allow the viewing of engraved signature of a *katchu-shi*. Commonly found in the liners of helmet bowls and cuirasses.
mengu	Literally 'face equipment'. A generic term commonly used to refer to any form of protective facial armour.
men'ōchū	Literally 'cotton coat'. A still largely unknown form of brigandine or jazerant-like protective overcoat-like garment utilized in Japan between the late 6th and 9th centuries AD.
mete-no-kusazuri	Literally means 'horse hand hip armour'. The term refers to the two *kusazuri* suspended from the right side of pre-*tosei* designs of cuirass, but not the *kusazuri* portion of a *waidate*. Sometimes also referred to as the *mete-saki*.
mete-no-gessan	The *gessan* suspended from the right-hand side of a *tosei-dō*.
mete-saki	See *mete-no-kusazuri*.
migi-waki-dō	The armpit plate(s) on the right-hand side of a cuirass.
mimi-ito	Literally 'ear cord'. Long vertically strung strands of a slightly wider weave of connective *odoshi-ge* generally used to lace the exterior edges of items of armour. Commonly features a peppered pattern in the weave and is generally of a contrasting colour to the primary *odoshi-ge*.
mimi-zane	Literally 'ear-scale'. A special *kozane* made in the form of the right half of a conventional *kozane*. *Mimi-zane* are applied to the outer edges of a *sane-ita* in order to keep the thickness of the board consistent right up the outer edges.
mitsume-zane	Literally 'three-eyed scale'. A special *kozane* a third wider than the standard, which permitted three layers of overlap. These scales have an addition of a third column of apertures.
mitsumono	Literally 'three things'. A term used to describe the three items that comprised a full set of early classical period armour: a *kabuto*, a *yoroi* and a pair of *ō-sode*.
mizuhiki	Long decorative silk twill-covered wooden splints or tubular plant stems anchored under the *keshō-no-ita* for aesthetic effect.
Mōgami	A method of cuirass construction whereby each layer of the *dō* is assembled from a series of permanently joined hinged protective plates, secured together vertically by lengths of *sugake odoshi*.
mokusei-katchū	Literally 'wood-made armour'. Armour that utilizes wood as the primary protective material.

mongara odoshi	A style of lacing in which a simple design or shape is created through the use of contrasting colours of *odoshi-ge*.	*naka-gusari*	Literally 'middle mail'. Round metal *hamiawase* rings used in forms of Japanese mail that lie parallel to the surface they are covering and that are secured together by intermediary bands of lighter-gauge wire called *kake-gusari*.
moriage	Literally 'built up'. A term used the describe the thick application of lacquer applied to the visible façade of a scale to replicate the appearance of a scale made in the *kara kozane* style.		
		naka-no-ieji	A term for an internal layer of fabric sandwiched between other layers of material. Hemp cloth was commonly used for the *naka-no-ieji* portions of items of armour.
muna-koshi-tori	Literally 'chest waist around'. An aesthetic finish in which a *tosei-dō* features bands of *kebiki odoshi*-laced *kozane* or *kiritsuke kozane* scales around both the upper *mae-tateage* and lower bands of the *nagakawa*, while the upper bands of the *nagakawa* are finished in an alternative manner.	Nanbokuchō	Literally 'Southern and Northern Courts'. A period in Japanese history of considerable turmoil and military activity that occurred at the start of the Muromachi era, between around 1336 and 1392 AD.
		nanban-dō	Literally 'southern barbarian cuirass'. A Western or European-made cuirass.
muna-ita	The uppermost solid plate section of armour on the *mae-dō* portion of a pre-16th century *tosei-dō*. Part of the *kanagu mawari*.	*nanban-gusari*	Literally 'southern barbarian mail'. While technically referring to Western-made mail, this term is commonly used to describe Japanese-made mail that is made in the Western 'four-in-one' method of ring linking, which produces a tighter mesh than most conventional makes of Japanese mail.
muna-tori	Literally 'chest around'. An aesthetic finish in which a *tosei-dō* features a band or bands of *kebiki odoshi*-laced *kozane* or *kiritsuke kozane* scales across the *mae-tateage* portion of the cuirass, which contrast with the finished faced of the applied to the rest of the *dō*.		
		nawame-garami	A single visible 'stitch' in the *nawame-odoshi* band of connective lacing.
		nawame odoshi	Literally 'wave eye lacing'. A method of lacing where the *nawame* portions of *odoshi-ge* are strung diagonally upward and to the right between adjacent scales.
Myōchin	A renowned school of *katchū-shi*, founded by the master smith Myōchin Nobuie in the early 16th century. The largest and most prolific group of armour makers in Japan from the mid-16th century onward.		
		ni-mai-dō	A two-section cuirass. Commonly composed of a front and back section hinged together on the left side of the torso.
nagakawa	The portion of a cuirass that extends from roughly below the base of the sternum to a line about 1.5 cm below the navel. It commonly comprises between four and five horizontal bands of *sane-ita* or protective plating.	*nerigawa*	Rawhide.
		ninawa-musubi	The name used for the knot that is tied in the middle of the doubled lengths of thick *maruhimo* that run

GLOSSARY

	parallel with and over the surface of the *wadagami* on some examples of *tosei-dō*.
Niō-dō	A variety of *tosei-dō* that is fabricated to resemble the naked form of a male torso.
nioi odoshi	A term used to describe a pattern of lacing where the *odoshi-ge* is strung so that it transitions through the use of different shades of a certain colour from dark to light in the descending order of the suspended section of armour.
nodowa	Literally 'throat ring'. A generally U-shaped plate of armour with a suspended pendant-like section designed to provide protection for the neck and upper chest.
nuinobe	Literally 'sewn spread'. A distinctive armour fabrication technique introduced in the late 15th century that utilized *iyozane* scales that were bound and laced together in a unique manner.
nurigata-zane	Literally 'lacquer-stiffened scale'. A length of bound-together *kozane* that have been lacquered after being assembled to create a rigid board.
nurigome	Thick applications of *urushi*.
nurigome-hotoke	A *tosei-dō* of the *hotoke* variety where the smooth façade of the cuirass has been created through a thick application of lacquer.
ō-arame-zane	Literally 'big rough scale'. An extremely wide variety of *sane*.
odoshi-ge	Literally 'lacing hair'. Any form of connective lacing material that is used to assemble items of armour. Generally refers to woven forms of lacing and is most commonly associated with lacing woven from silk.
odoshi-ito	Lacing made from a woven material.
okashi-dō	Literally 'lent cuirass'. A *dō* that is lent to a retainer in the service of a higher-ranking samurai or warlord, from the arsenal of the latter.
okashi-gote	Literally 'lent armoured sleeve'. A pair of *kote* that are lent to a retainer in the service of a higher-ranking samurai or warlord, from the arsenal of the latter.
okashi-zuneate	Literally 'lent shin guards'. A pair of *suneate* that are lent to a retainer in the service of a higher-ranking samurai or warlord, from the arsenal of the latter.
okegawa-dō	Literally 'bucket sides cuirass'. A distinctive form of ribbed or ringed *tosei-dō* initially assembled from horizontally and later vertically arranged plates fastened together with countersunk rivets.
omodaka odoshi	A pyramid-shaped pattern created using lacing of a contrasting colour within a large laced section of armour.
oni-damari	Literally 'devil-stopping'. The uppermost solid-plate piece of armour on the *mae-dō* portion of a cuirass immediately above the *mae-tateage*. Part of the *kanagu mawari*.
oshitsuke-no-ita	The uppermost solid-plate piece of armour across the top of the *ushiro-dō* portion of a pre-*tosei-dō*, to which the *wadagami* are attached.
ō-sode	A large rectangular shield-like design of shoulder guard. Commonly worn in conjunction with the *yoroi* and other pre-*tosei* designs of cuirass.
Ōshū-dō	See *Sendai-dō*.
ō-tateage	A style of *suneate* with a prominent form of erect brigandine panel or protective plate covering for the knee.
ō-yoroi	A complete armour grouping assembled around a cuirass made in the *yoroi* style. In its simplest form an *ō-yoroi* should include the cuirass, a *kabuto* and a pair of *ō-sode*.
ō-zane	An alternative name for an *ō-arame-zane*.

Paekche	One of the three major kingdoms on the Korean peninsula during the first half of the first millennium, which lasted from around 18 BC to AD 660.	*saimi*	A course hemp fabric commonly used as a lining material.
rasha	Imported European woollen cloth.	*saka-ita*	A *sane-ita* laced in the reverse to the *san-no-ita* of the *ushiro-tateage* of a cuirass, that allowed the *oshitsuke-no-ita* and *wadagami* to be swung backwards.
renjaku	An internal suspensory system fitted to some examples of *tosei-dō*, designed to lift some of the weight of an armour off the wearer's shoulders.		
		sane-gashira	The upper portion or head of a scale.
		sane-ita	A section of armour assembled from *sane*.
renjaku-dō	Any make of *tosei-dō* fabricated with the necessary apertures to allow for the attaching of *renjaku*.	*sangu*	A term used to refer to the three items of armour for the extremities that were common to most examples of *tosei gusoku*. A conventional *sangu* set should include a pair of *kote*, a *haidate* and a pair of *suneate*.
roku-mai-dō	A *tosei-dō* where the protective covering for the torso is formed by six independent though conjoined pieces of armour. Many examples are also *ryō-hikiawase*.		
		sankaku-ita	Literally 'triangle board'. A triangular piece of solid-plate armour.
rōketetsu-zome	A method of resist-dyeing used to create decorative patterns on cloth or leather surfaces, in which wax is applied to prevent dyes from adhering in certain areas.	*san-mai-dō*	A cuirass that is composed of and requires three independent sectional pieces of conjoined armour to cover the torso. A rather uncommon form of cuirass.
Rurisai-dō	Makes of *tosei-dō* that are fabricated with small, often hinged door-like openings in the front or side of the cuirass that allow access to the interior of the armour while it is being worn.	*Sansai-ryū*	A manner of armour making partially developed and promoted by the Hosokawa clan. Sometimes referred to as the Sansai style.
		sanshō-no-byō	Literally 'peppercorn rivets'. A term used for the small, generally flat-headed rivets that were often used to anchor the *tsurubashiri-gawa* to the face of a cuirass.
ryō-hikiawase	Literally 'both sides pull together'. A term used to describe any variety of cuirass that is made with two separate half sections that need to be brought together and secured by cords on either side of the torso. Common to many examples of *ni-mai-dō* and *roku-mai-dō*.	*sasaheri*	Leather strips or woven materials used to edge the fabric areas of an armour and its accompanying *sangu* items.
		sashimono	A heraldic device or flag flown from a pole secured in mounts affixed to the rear of an armour.
sabitsuke	An alternative name for *kokusa*.		
saihai-no-kan	A swivel-ring form of *kanamono* commonly found fitted to the right breast of many examples of *tosei-dō*. Originally used to hang a commander's *saihai* baton from when the hands needed to be free.	*sei-ita*	A narrow auxiliary item of armour often worn with cuirasses made in the post-14th-century *haramaki* style to cover the exposed gap down the middle of the back, a common problem with this type of *dō*.
saihai-tsuke-no-kan	An alternative name for the *saihai-no-kan*.	*Sendai-dō*	An alternative name for a distinctive regional variety of *go-mai-dō*

	originally produced in the northern Tōhoku region of Japan and favoured by the samurai of the Date *han*. Also referred to as *Ōshū-dō* and outside the Tōhoku area as *Kantō-dō*.
sendan-no-ita	A narrow pendant-like section of generally lamellar armour suspended from the right *wadagami* of a cuirass to protect the right armpit area.
seme-kohaze	A double-holed bead threaded on a closed loop of cord that can be slid along the cord and cinched tight around a *kohaze* to join or close a section of an item of armour.
seshime urushi	An inferior grade of *urushi* commonly used for the base layer, which helped other applications of lacquer adhere to a surface.
shakudō	An alloy of copper and gold that has a purplish-black colouration.
shibu	Juice from unripened persimmon fruit used to insect- and waterproof fabrics.
shidome	A grommet, commonly made from copper and gilded.
shikaku-gattari	A *gattari* bracket the central holder of which is made square to receive a square in cross-section *uke-zutsu*.
shiki-gane	A narrow strip of iron secured to the rear of a *nerigawa* plate by the *shita-garami* binding that helped the plate maintain its form.
shikka-gawa	Deer hide, generally that of a domestic species of spotted Japanese deer.
shikoro	The telescoping neck guard portion of a *kabuto*.
shino-gote	A style of a *kote* in which the protective armour covering for the forearm is formed by a number of long narrow splints usually secured together by sections of *kusari*.
shino-suneate	A style of a *suneate* in which the protective armour covering for the shin is formed by a number of long narrow splints usually secured together by sections of *kusari*.
shishi	A mythical Chinese dog-like lion creature. Images of *shishi* were commonly used in decorative designs, particularly in various patterns of *e-gawa*.
shishi-no-sakura-gawa	A highly popular pattern of *e-gawa* that features *shishi* set on a background field of leaves and peony blossoms.
shita-garami	Horizontally strung lengths of leather thongs that are used to bind *sane* together to create sections of *sane-ita*.
shita-garami-no-ana	The bottom four holes in a single column of apertures pierced in a conventional *kozane* that are used to string the *shita-garami* bindings through.
shita-haramaki	Literally 'under belly wrap'. An alternative name for a *hara-ate*.
shobū-gawa	Indigo-dyed leathers that feature a repetitive pattern of vertically and horizontally aligned off-white irises flanked by blades of grass or leaves. The details of the designs can vary and in some cases be extremely vague, to the point that the key elements of the design merge into a single geometric tombstone-like block.
shōen	A non-taxed private landholding. Fundamentally autonomous states that proved to be instrumental in development of the samurai class.
Shōgun	Literally 'barbarian-quelling general'. An 8th century AD title. Formally *Jeisetsu Sei I Shōgun*, which roughly equated to the rank of commander-in-chief of an expeditionary force. The term became synonymous with a hereditary military dictator from the 12th century onward.
Shōgunate	A feudal Japanese form of government that was a hereditary military dictatorship.

shōhei-gawa	A highly popular pattern of *e-gawa* first introduced in the 14th century AD, featuring *shishi* set among foliage and floral blooms, with a small framed area of kanji characters that record a commemorative date in 1352.		of a certain colour from light to dark, from top to bottom of the section of armour.
shōji-no-ita	A generally oval plate that is affixed to the *wadagami* so that it stands erect.	*suso-no-kanamono*	Large gilded copper domed chrysanthemum-shaped split-shank rivets. Primarily decorative, they are usually mounted in regularly spaced sets of three on the *hishinui-no-ita* portions of an armour, such as on the *kusazuri* of the cuirass and *sode*.
shu	A deep red colouration. Commonly derived from cinnabar.		
shu urushi	A deep red lacquer.	*suso-no-ita*	Literally 'hem-plate'. The lowermost plate in a suspended section of armour. This term is used for items of armour both before the 10th century and after the mid-16th century.
sode	A shoulder guard.		
sode-tsuke-no-kuda	A short metal tube threaded over the *sode-tsuke-no-gumi-wa* to help protect the closed loop of cord from wear. Sometimes referred to as *gumi kanamono*.		
		tachi-dō	Literally 'standing cuirass'. A term used to refer to a cuirass that, through the use of internal bindings or based on its manner of fabrication is able to stand erect without support.
sode tsuke-no-o	*Kasa-kohaze*-strung cords protruding from the *wadagami* on a *tosei-dō*, used to fasten the *sode* to the cuirass.		
		takahimo	The shoulder strap fastening cords on pre-16th century forms of cuirass, anchored to the flanks or open vertical edges of a *tosei-dō* and which are used to pull and tie the cuirass closed around the torso.
sode-tsuke-no-gumi-wa	Closed loops of cord, generally threaded with a *sode-tsuke-no-kuda*, which protrude from the *wadagami* to provide anchoring points to secure the *sode* to a cuirass. Primarily associated with pre-*tosei-dō* forms of armour.		
		takanoha-uchi	Literally 'hawk feather braid'. A popular pattern of *mimi-ito* that features a chevron-like design in the weave.
suemon	Large gilded copper domed chrysanthemum-shaped split-shank rivets. Often used for decorative purposes. Also referred to as *suemon-no-kanamono*.		
		takuboku-uchi	Literally 'woodpecker braid'. A popular multi-coloured weave of *mimi-ito* that features a speckled pattern produced through a combination of dark blue, green, purple and white threads.
suneate	Shin guards.		
sugake odoshi	Literally 'simple hang'. A lacing technique whereby pairs of regularly spaced laces are strung vertically upwards and cross-knotted on each plate within a section of armour. *Sugake odoshi* was introduced in the late 15th century to both speed up the production and lighten the weight of a cuirass.		
		tanegashima	A Japanese-made matchlock. Also commonly referred to as *hinawajū* and *teppō*.
		tankō	An early form of plate armour produced between the 4th and 6th centuries.
susogu odoshi	A term used to describe a pattern of lacing whereby the *odoshi-ge* transitions through different shades	*tarenuno*	Literally 'hanging fabric'. A protective cloth cape suspended from the underside of the brim of a *kaji-kabuto*.

tataki-nuri	An *urushi* finish applied so as to create a rippled texture.		*shōhei-gawa* pattern, it features a bogus commemorative year stamp of 740 AD.
tatami-dō	Literally 'folding cuirass'. A form of cuirass assembled from small, generally rectangular plates sewn to a fabric backing, allowing the *dō* to be folded for easy storage or transport. The protective plates are generally connected by bands of *kusari*.	*tenugui-no-kan*	Literally 'hand wring towel swivel ring'. A swivel-ring type of *kanamono* that is sometimes found fitted to the left breast of a cuirass. A *dō* should only feature a *tenugui-no-kan* if it also has a *saihai-no-kan*, which it should usually be an identical copy of. Sometimes referred to as *dansen-osame-no-kan*.
tatami yoroi	Items of armour that can be collapsed and folded for easy storage and transport.	*teppō*	See *tanegashima*.
tate	A small section of lacing or binding visible on the façade of a *sane-ita* where the material appears as a short vertical band between the two *karami-no-ana* on the right side of a scale.	*tetsu*	Iron. It should be noted that *tetsu* is commonly used as a generic term for all ferrous metals when discussing items of armour.
tateawe odoshi	A method of lacing in which two or more different colours of *odoshi-ge* are strung side by side in undulating rows down the length of a section of armour.	*tetsu-sabiji*	A russet-iron patina.
		tetsu-zane	A scale made from iron.
		tomegawa	Literally 'stopping leather'. Lengths of leather thong that were used to horizontally bind plates or sections of lamellar board together to make a cuirass more rigid vertically.
tatedori	Short vertical lengths of visible *odoshi-ge* strung between the two *karami-no-ana* on the right side of a scale. Primarily associated with the *tate odoshi* method of lacing.	*tome urushi*	Clear lacquer. Commonly applied over *kinpaku* or when producing *maki-e* designs.
tatehagi-okegawa	A method of assembling the cuirass from a series of conjoined vertically arranged plates.	*tosei*	Literally 'modern'. Is most commonly associated with the items of armour that were produced after the mid-16th century.
tate odoshi	An early method of lacing lamellar amour in which the *odoshi-ge* was strung straight up and down between *sane-ita*. Largely discontinued by the start of the 11th century AD.	*tosei-dō*	Any new form of cuirass that was developed and introduced from around the 1540s onwards.
		tosei-gusoku	A complete grouping of armour, inclusive of armour for the extremities, or *sangu*, compiled around a *tosei-dō*.
tatehagi-ita	A solid plate specifically shaped to be used vertically in the assembly of armour.	*tsuba-ate*	See *hanakami-bukuro*.
		tsubo-no-ita	A large inverted trapezoid plate designed to protect the right side of the torso. Part of the *waidate* and worn with a *yoroi*.
tatehagi okegawa	A method of assembling a cuirass from a series of conjoined vertically arranged plates.		
tekubi	The wrist portion of a sleeve.		
tenpyō-gawa	A pattern of *e-gawa* introduced in the 16th century. Designed to mimic and compete with the popular	*tsubo-no-o*	A small closed loop of cord often threaded with a *kuda* that protrudes from the façade of a *waidate* to

	provide an anchoring point for the shoulder strap-like *tsubo-no-o* cord.
tsukigata	Literally 'moon-shaped'. A term used to describe the shape of any object of which at least one half is round or oval.
tsumadori odoshi	A lacing pattern in which two or more contrasting colours of *odoshi-ge* are used to create a wedge shape extending out from the vertical edge of the armour piece.
tsure-yamamichi-gashira	Literally 'mountain paths coming together leading edge'. A romanticized name used to describe a specific pattern of undulating edge cut along the upper edge of a section of *ita-mono*.
tsurubashiri-gawa	A large, generally square panel of reinforced *e-gawa* fastened by cord or rivets over the front face of a lamellar cuirass, which prevented the heads of the scales in the *sane-ita* from fouling or snagging a warrior's bow-string. Primarily associated with the *yoroi*.
tsuyu-otoshi-no-ana	A small hole in the base of a *machi-uke* that allowed water trapped in the holder to drain.
uchidashi-dō	A variety of *tosei-dō* featuring embossed designs.
uchikake-keikō	Literally 'long garment hanging shell'. An early poncho-like form of lamellar armour worn with independent side plates that covered the flanks of the torso.
uke-zutsu	A long, hollow baton-like shaft designed to receive the bottom of the flagpole of a *sashimono* or other pole-mounted heraldic device, enabling it to be affixed to a set of armour by means of additional mounts and brackets.
uma-gawa	Horse leather.
uma-yoroi-zane	Small embossed squares of moulded leather scales, commonly employed to produce protective panel coverings for horses. Periodically used to produce cuirasses and other items, the majority of which can be classified as being varieties of *tatami-dō*.
uname	See *uname-garami*.
uname-garami	Literally 'path between rice fields'. The band lacing or leather thong strung horizontally across the façade of a *hishinui-no-ita* immediately above the *hishinui* bindings.
uname-toji	A method of assembling *sane-ita* that uses leather thongs strung through the *kedate-no-ana* horizontally across the length of a section. Commonly used in the construction of cuirasses made in accordance with the *Sansai-ryū* methods favoured by the Hosokawa.
uroko-zane	Large inverted U-shaped *kozane* that resemble a fish scale in overall form. Generally fashioned from *nerigawa*.
urabari	Literally 'back applied'. A fabric or leather liner stretched across the interior surface of a cuirass.
urushi	Lacquer.
ushiro-dō	The area of a cuirass that corresponds with the back half of the torso, such as the rear half section of a *ni-mai-dō*. When the *ushiro-dō* is an independent solid sectional piece of armour which corresponds to the very back of the torso, such as in the case of a *go-mai-dō*, it is referred to as the *ushiro-dō-no-ita*.
ushiro-dō-no-ita	An independent solid sectional piece of armour that corresponds to the back area of the torso.
ushiro-migi-dō-no-ita	An independent sectional piece of armour made to cover the rear right-hand side of the torso. Universal to *go-mai-dō*. May also be found utilized on *san-mai*, *yon-mai* and *roku-mai-dō*.
ushiro-tateage	The protective areas of armour between the top of the *nagakawa* and the base of the *oshitsuke-no-ita*

	on pre-*tosei-dō* forms of cuirass, or the *boko-no-ita* of a *tosei-dō*.	*yon-mai-dō*	A cuirass that is composed of four independent conjoined pieces of sectional armour to cover the torso. A rather uncommon form of cuirass.
waki-biki	Auxiliary panels of protective brigandine, *sane-ita* or plate that are worn to protect the armpit areas.		
waki-ita	Armpit plates. Part of the *kanagu mawari*.	*yoroi*	A box-like form of lamellar armour, C-shaped in cross section, first introduced in the 10th century. The *yoroi* was worn with a separate auxiliary piece of armour called a *waidate* which covered the right side of the torso that was not protected by the *yoroi*. Is also used as a generic term for armour.
wadagami	Literally 'shoulder above'. The shoulder strap portions of a cuirass. Commonly also written as *watagami*. Sometimes translated as 'cotton chew' depending on the kanji character combination used.		
wasei nanban-dō	Literally 'Japanese-made southern barbarian cuirass'. A Japanese-made *dō* that is made to replicate the style and form of a Western or European-made cuirass.	*yoroi katabira*	A form of brigandine armoured coat. Particularly common during the later half of the Edo period.
		Yukinoshita-dō	A distinctive design of *go-mai-dō* with prominent external hinges.
Yamato	The first centralized governmental state in Japan, established in Nara and continuing from around AD 250 to 710.	*yumi*	A Japanese bow.
		yurugi-ito	The connective lengths of lacing that secure the hip armour tassets to the base of a cuirass. Significantly longer on examples of *tosei-dō*.
yokohagi-ita	A solid plate shaped to be used horizontally in the assembly of armour.		
yokohagi-okegawa	A method of assembling the cuirass from a series of conjoined horizontally arranged plates.	*yurugi-zane*	A length of *sane-ita* the scales of which have been individually lacquered before being bound together.

INDEX

References to images are in **bold**.

A

Adams, William 252
aesthetics 19–20, 27, 53–54, 63, 64, 67
agriculture 34, 35, 48
aibiki-no-o (cords) 224–25
Ainu people **43**
Akechi Mitsuhide **186**
Akechi Sama no Mitsutoshi 252, 256, 269
Amaterasu 40
Arai Hakuseki 119, 122, 314
archaeology 34, 35, 87–88
archers 43–44
armour makers *see katchū-shi*
armour *see dō; gusoku*
armpit plates *see waki-ita*
artisans 13, 20, 188
ashigaru ('light-feet') troops 186–87, 197, 206–207, 227–28
and armour 276–86, 289
and firearms 259
and Separation Edict 286–87
and Shingen 275–76
Ashikaga Shōgunate 183–84
Ashina clan 261
Asuka period 38
aya-odoshi-ge (silk lacing) 126–27
Azukizaka, battle of (1564) 250, 259

B

badges *see jirushi; kamon*
bamboo 28–29
blacksmiths 196, 256–57
Boshin War (1868–69) 329, **331**
Buddhism 36, 38, 40, **73**, 98, 104–105
and statues 241, 243–44
burial mounds 36–37, 94, 98
bushi-haniwa (terracotta statues) 83, 85, 92, 93, **94**
bushidō (way of the warrior) 313–14, 340
byō (rivets) 64, 81–82, 142–43, 168–69, 209–10, 241

C

China 35, 112, 325–26; *see also* Tang Dynasty
Christianity 253–54, 325
colour 121, 122–23, 127–29, 130–34, 141–42
conscript army 43, 44–46, 47, 48, 96
costs 158–59, 258
craftsmen 13, 20

cuirasses *see dō*
curios **14**, 15, 330, 333–36, 339
custom-made armour 82–83

D

Dan-no-Ura, battle of (1185) 160
dangae style 67–68, 246–47
Date clan 13, 261
Date Masamune 260, 261, 266
dating 57–58, 59–60
Dean, Dr Bashford **15**
decoration 137–45, 267–70
deer hide 119–20
dies 81, **83**, 108

dō (cuirass) 13, **22**, 23, 26–27, 30, **32**, 77–79
and armour protection 69–71
and design 58–61, **62–63**
and evolution 54–56, 57–58, 99–100, 211–12
and history 53
and identification 64–69
and lining 71–73, 74–75
and markings 73–74
and subcategories **59**, 61, 63, 64
see also haramaki; *isei-dō*; *keikō*; *Mōgami-dō*; *nanban-dō*; *nuinobe*; *tankō*; *tatami-dō*; *tosei-dō*; *yoroi dō*; *Yukinoshita-dō*
dō-maru **161**, 163, 166, 175, **189**
Dutch, the 251, 254

E

e-gawa (picture leather) 137–42
East India Company 325
Edo period **22**, 56, 286

Emishi (barbarians) 44, 45–47, 48–49, 50, 99
equestrianism 38, 40, 42–44, 86–87, 88

eri-mawashi (collar) 218, 219, 222
Europeans *see* Westerners

F

fables 19, 33
fabric 96–97
feudalism 16
floral motifs 137–39, 141

Forty-Seven Rōnin incident (1703) **290**, 291
Fudo Myō-ō 139
Fujiwara clan 42, 103, 128

fukurin (metal moulding) 142
Fukushima Kunitaka 296
fusegumi (braid) 142–45

E

gaki (hungry ghosts) **244**
gattari (holder) 230, 231–32
Genpei War (1180–85) 54, 105, 160, 161
Genroku period 318
gessan (hip armour) 70–71, 225–28, 255
Go-Daigo, Emperor 183

go-mai-dō ('five section' cuirass) 58–59, 60, 63, 64, **65, 66**, 263–64
and *Yukinoshita-dō* 68–69
gold leaf 57, 73, **86**, 305
Gosannen Kassen ('Late Three Years War') (1083–89) 105
Goyuryo 38

Gun Yo Ki (Sadatake) 315
gusari see kusari
gusoku (set of armour) **22**, 23, 27–28, **52**, 53
and development 291
and nomenclature **24**
gyōyō (shoulder guards) **164**, 165, **166**, 225

H

Hagakure Kikigaki ('Hidden Leaves') (Tsunatomo) 312–13
haidate (apron panel) 23, 174
Hakusukinoe, battle of (663) 39
hanakami-bukuro (pockets) 228–30
hanbo (half mask) 174
hara-ate ('under belly wrap') 167, **168**, 169–70, **192**
haramaki ('belly wrap') 160–70, 175–81
and *Mōgami* 199–200, **201**, **202**
helmets *see kabuto*
heraldry 230–33
Himiko of Yamatai-koku, Queen 36, 103
hinges 200–201
hip armour *see gessan*; *kusazuri*
hishi-toji (cross knots) 238–39, 240
hishinui ('diamond lacing') 116–19
Honchō Gunkikō (Hakuseki) **313**, 314–15, 318–19
Honda Tadamasa 252
Honnami clan 316
horses 42–43; *see also* equestrianism
Hosokawa clan 184, 239–40
Hosokawa Sansai 239–40
hotoke-dō 241–43, 258–59

I

Ikegami Eiko 19
ikki (communal army) 187, 196
Imperial Army 330, 331
indigo 127, 128
iron *see tetsu*
isei-gusoku ('armour of uncommon make') 299–301
Ise Sadatake 315
ita-mono (plate) 197–201, 203–204
and *okegawa-dō* 214, 227, 240–41
ito-odoshi-ge (silk lacing) 127
iyozane (scales) 173, 174, 192–94

J

Japan 20–21, 34, **35**, 51
and imperial court 40–42, 44–45, 47–49, 50, 103–104
and Mongol invasions 170
and revivalism 336–38, 339–41
and social order 183–87
and Westernization 329–30
Japanese language 23–26
ji-zamurai (peasant samurai) 187, 196, 197, 275
Jimmu, Emperor 40
jingasa (hat) 281–82, 335
Jingū, Empress Regent **37**, 100
jirushi (marks) 129
Jōdo Shinshū sect 187
Jōmon period 34–35, 36, 42–44

K

kabuto (helmet) 23, 27, 147, 289, 319–20
Kaga-dō 302–309
Kajiki, siege of (1549) 211
Kamakura Shōgunate 50–51, 105
kamon (family crests) 129
Kanagawa, Treaty of (1854) 325, 327
Kanai Higashiura site 87–88
Kanamura Koaki, Lt 337–38
Kanmu, Emperor 98, 103
Kantō plain 40, 46
karage (thong) 92, 93
katchū-shi (armour makers) 13–14, 30, 72, 181, 192, 322–23
and European armour 214,

256–58
and Haruta School 302–309
and lacing 116, 117, 118, **123**, 124, 125–26
and Myōchin School 260–61, 262, 268–69, 316–17
and *okegawa-dō* 235–36, 245–46
and plate 197–98, 203
and signatures 73, 74
kawa-zane (rawhide scales) 107–108, 110
Kaya 38
kebiki odoshi ('hair spread over lacing') 124–25
keikō (early lamellar armour) **76**, 88–94; *see also uchikake-keikō*
kikkō (hexagonal pieces) 219–22
Ki no Kosami, Shōgun 46, 47
kinpaku (gold leaf) **57**, 73, **86**, 305
kiwame fuda (appraisal) certificates **314**, 316–17
Kiyohara clan 105
kobire ('little fins') 222–23, 316
Kofun period 36–37, 98
kohaze (toggles) 146
Kojiki (Records of Ancient Matters) 37, 40
Kōmei, Emperor 327–28, **329**
kon (indigo blue) 127, 128
Korean peninsula **35**, 37–38, 39, 43, 87
and armour design 78, 79, 81
and invasions 287
and trade 325–26
koshi-zane (waist scales) 90–1, 92, 100
kote (sleeves) 23, 174, 282–84
kōtetsu (steel) 29–31, 257–59
Kōtoku, Emperor 38
kozane (scales) 66, 113–14, 115–19, 168, 172–73
and *yoroi* 107–112, 134, 136
kuro urushi (black lacquer) 28
kusari (mail) 28, 56–57, 174, 228, 291–95, 296–97
kusazuri (hip armour) 70, 71, 83, 85–86, **87**, **89**, **118**
and *haramaki* 165, 181
and *keikō* 90–92, 93
and *Mōgami* 201
and *yoroi* 110, 151–53
Kyōto 184–85

L

lacing **27**, 28, 63, 66–67, 202
 and colour 128–29
 and *keikō* 93–94
 and *okegawa-dō* 217, 227–28
 and patterns 130–34
 and *sugake odoshi* 188–92
 and *tomegawa* 194–95
 and *tosei-dō* 238–39, 240
 and vertical 69
and *yoroi* 108–109, **110**, 115–28
lacquer work *see urushi*
lamellar construction 30, 55, 80, 86, 87–88, 98–99; *see also keikō*
land 41, 48, 51
leather 20, 28, 91–92, 147–48
 and decorative 137–42
and lacing 119–20
and shoulder straps 82, **85**, 90
and thongs 78, 79, 81
see also nerigawa
Liefde (ship) 251, 252, 253
Lyman, Benjamin 26

M

machi-uke (cup for *uke-zutsu*) 230, 231, 232–33
Maeda clan 74, 302–309
Maeda Toshiie **185**
mail *see kusari*
manchira (vest) 218–19
martial arts 312
materials 28–31
Meiji, Emperor 329
Meiji period 16, 269–70
mengu (facial armour) 23
men'ōchū (cotton coat) 96–98, 99
merchants 14, 15
metal 20, 28, 29–31, 35, 55–56, 61
and embossing 268–70
mimi-ito ('ear cord' lacing) 122–24
Minamoto clan 50, 103, 105
Minamoto Tatetomo 112
Minamoto Yoshiie 105
Minamoto Yoshitsune 126, 171

mitsume-zane ('three-eyed scales') 110–12
Miura Shigetoshi 214
Mōgami-dō **182**, 191, 195–204, 209
mokusei katchū (wooden armour) 77–78, **79**
Mongols 51, 170, 174, 183, 186
muna-ita 136, **141**, 163–64
Myōchin Kunihisa 260
Myōchin Munesuke 316–17

N

nagakawa (cuirass portion) 58, 61, 179, 181
and *haramaki* 161, 163, 164, 169
and *keikō* 89, 90
and *Mōgami* 199–200, 204
and *okegawa-dō* 215–16
and *yoroi* 134, 136
Nagashino, battle of (1575) 249, 259
nanban-dō 250–53, 254–59
Nanbokuchō period 174, 183
nawame-odoshi ('wave eye lacing') 125
nerigawa (rawhide) 28, 29–30, 79, 96
and *dō* 61, 65, 69
and scales 107–108
Nihon Shoki (Chronicles of Japan) 37, 40
Niō-dō 243–44
Northern Court 183, 184
nuinobe construction 191–95, 235, 236–38, 246

O

Oda Nobunaga 51, 249
ō-yoroi **102**, **104**, 157–58, 170–72
odoshi-ge (silk lacing) 118–19, 120–22, 124–29
odoshi no moyō (lacing patterns) 130–34
okashi-dō ('lent armour') **276**, 278–86
okegawa-dō 214–30, 235–37, 240–42
Ōnin War (1467–77) 184, 185, 186, 187, 201–202
Ōsaka Castle, siege of (1615) 252, 311

P

Paekche 38–40, 46, 95–96
pattern 122–23, 130–34; *see also* decoration
peascod cuirass **211**, 212, 250, 254–55, 258
Perry, Commodore Matthew 323, 326, 327, **328**
Philip II of Spain, King 251
Pinto, Fernão Mendes 210–11
plate *see* ita-mono
Portuguese, the 210–11, 250
pronunciation 23–26

R

rawhide *see* nerigawa
recycling 60
rendaku (morphophonology) 25–26
renjaku (cord suspension) 265–66
retainers 160, 161, 164, 165, **166**, 170
rivets *see* byō
roku-mai-dō (six-section cuirass) 270–71, 303–305
Rurisai-dō 272–73
Russo-Japanese War (1904–5) 329, **333**
Ryōei 296

S

saihai-no-kan (swivel ring) 233–34
Sakamoto Ryōma 328, **330**
Sakanoue no Tamuramaro, Shōgun 48, 49
Sakoku ('Closed Country') Edict (1635) 254
samurai 18–19, 31, 54, 161, 165–66
 and civil war 327–29
 and colours 128–29
 and creation 103, 104, 105
 and duties 289, 291, 311–14
 and *hanzei* ('half tax') 183–84
 and history 34, 37, 40, 48–51
 and Mongols 170, 174
 and revivalism 321–23, 336–37, 339–43
 and Westernization 329–32
san-mai-dō 271–72
sane (scales) 30, 66, 89–90, 91–94, 106–108

sane-ita 58, 192–94
sangu ('set of three') 23, 28
sankin-kōtai decree (1642) 286, 287
scales *see iyozane; koshi-zane; sane*
sei-ita (back plate) 176, 177–79
Sekigahara, battle of (1600) 51
Sekiguchi Gyōbu 252, 256
Sendai-dō 266–67
sendan-no-ita 148–51
Sengoku Jidai period 51, 185
sericulture 120, **121**
Seven Samurai, The (film) **341**
Shimabara Rebellion (1637–38) 254
shin guards *see suneate*
Shintō 40
shishi (mythical lions) 138, 139–40
shita-garami ('lower stitches) 115–16, 192–94
shōen (private landholdings) 41, 42, 45, 46–48, 50, 99

shoulder guards *see sode*
shoulder straps *see wadagami*
silk (*odoshi-ge*) lacing 118–19, 120–22, 124–29
Silla 38, 39, 40
sleeves *see kote*
sode (shoulder guards) 23, 145–46, 223, 264–65, 315–16, 319
sōhei (monk armies) 104–105
Soma Michitane **17**
Soma Noma-oi Festival 16–18
Soma Yoritane **17**
Southern Court 183
steel *see kōtetsu*
stencils 137–38
Subuse, battle of (789) 45–46
Suenaga Masao, Dr 92, 93, 124, 337
sugake odoshi ('simple hang') lacing 188–92, 202, 238
suneate (shin guards) 23, 174, 284–85
Susanoo no Mikoto **41**

T

Tachibana Akinao **248**
Taihō Code 40, 45, 96
Taika Reforms 38–39
Taira clan 50, 103–104, 105, 128
Taira no Masakado 16, 17, **47**, 103–104
takahimo (looped cord) 146, 163–64
Takeda clan 249, 250, 259
Takeda Shingen 250, 275, 276
Tang Dynasty 38–39, 40, 41, 49, 96, 98–99
tankō ('short shell') **55**, 79, 80–83, **84**, 85–88, **89**
tatami-dō 191, 204–207,

286–89, 291
tatehagi-kawa-toji (iron armour) 79, **80**
tatehagi method 267, 272
tetsu (iron) 29–30, 65, 69, 79, 96, 109–10
Tokugawa Iemitsu 254
Tokugawa Ieyasu 51, 214, 241–42, 247
 and Azukizaka 249–50, 259
 and Western armour 251, 252, 255
Tokugawa Shōgunate 51, 56, 286
Tokugawa Yorinobu 255
Tokugawa Yoshimune 286

Tokugawa Yoshinobu 329, **330**, 333
tosei-dō (modern cuirass) 55–56, 63–65, 66, 72, 213, 234–35; *see also hotoke-dō; Kaga-dō; okashi-dō; okegawa-dō; Sendai-dō; tatami-dō; Yukinoshita-dō*
Toshirō Mifune **341**
Toyotomi Hideyoshi 51, 251, 276, 286–87
trade 325–26
tsurubashiri-gawa (bowstring running leather) 147–48

U

uchidashi technique 256–57, 267–70
uchikake-keikō 94–95, 99–101, 124
Uesugi Kenshi 271
uke-zutsu (tube holder) 230–32

ultraviolet rays 127
uma-yoroi-zane (scales) 301, **302**
United States of America (USA) 323, 326, 327, 339
urabari (liner) 71–73, 74
urushi (lacquer) 20, 27, 28, **111**, 112–14, 118, 242
and *dō* 64, 65
and lacing 125–26
and *okashi-dō* 282
and scales 173

V

'varnish tree' (*Rhus vernicifera*) **111**, 113

W

wadagami (shoulder straps) 90, 100–101, 145–46, 148–49, 174, 223–25, 258
waidate 152, 153–56
waki-ita (armpit plates) 167–68, 170, 216–17
warriors *see* samurai
weaponry 96, 172, 173–74, 289
  arquebus 210–11
  arrows 53
  bows (*yumi*) 44, 100, 101, 110, 111, 147, **149**
  firearms 30, 214, 249–50, 259, 328–29
  matchlock 210, 214, 276, **277**
  polearms 202
  swords 30
weight 82, 109, 111–12
  and *haramaki* 160
  and *okegawa-dō* 215–16
  and *tosei-dō* 235
and *yoroi* 156–57
and *Yukinoshita-dō* 265–66
Westerners 14–16, 210–12, 219–20
  and armour 250–53, 254–59
  and Christianity 253–54
  and mail 293, 294
  and tourism 332–36, 339
wood 28, 77–78, 81, **83**
World War II (1939–45) 337, 338, **339**

Y

Yamagami Hachirō 337
Yamamoto Tsunatomo 312–13
Yamato period 36–41, 43, 80, 81, 96
Yayoi period **34**, 35–36, 37, 44, 112
yokohagi-okegawa-dō 276–80
yoroi dō 26, 53–54, **60, 151**, 153, 156–60
  and decline 170–71, 175
  and decoration 137–45
  and design 106–112
  and lacing 115–28
  and lacquer 114
  and *nagakawa* 134, 136
  and nomenclature **135**
yoroi katabira ('overcoat') 295–98
Yoshisada Nitta **184**
Yukinoshita-dō 68–69, 259–60, 261–67